The Evolution of Central Banking and Monetary Policy in the Asia-Pacific

For

My former teachers and colleagues who extended their helping hands when I needed them most:

Late Mofizuddin Ahmad,
Amin Muhammad Ali,
Amirul Islam Chowdhury,
Donal J. Donovan,
Late Mirza Md. Mozammel Hoque,
D. Barry Hughes,
Mohsin S. Khan,
Jerome R. La Pittus and
Khandaker Mustahidur Rahman.

The Evolution of Central Banking and Monetary Policy in the Asia-Pacific

Akhand Akhtar Hossain

Associate Professor of Economics, The University of Newcastle, Australia

Edward Elgar
PUBLISHING

Cheltenham, UK • Northampton, MA, USA

Published by
Edward Elgar Publishing Limited
The Lypiatts
15 Lansdown Road
Cheltenham
Glos GL50 2JA
UK

Edward Elgar Publishing, Inc.
William Pratt House
9 Dewey Court
Northampton
Massachusetts 01060
USA

A catalogue record for this book
is available from the British Library

Library of Congress Control Number: 2015935880

This book is available electronically in the **Elgar**online
Economics subject collection
DOI 10.4337/9780857937810

MIX
Paper from responsible sources
FSC® C013056
FSC www.fsc.org

ISBN 978 0 85793 780 3 (cased)
ISBN 978 0 85793 781 0 (eBook)

Typeset by Servis Filmsetting Ltd, Stockport, Cheshire
Printed and bound in Great Britain by T.J. International Ltd, Padstow

Contents

Preface

This volume of case studies is intended to be used as a supplementary companion book to my reference text *Central Banking and Monetary Policy in the Asia-Pacific* (Hossain, 2009). The 2009 text surveyed the major theories, models and approaches to inflation and monetary policy with a focus on selected developing countries of the Asia-Pacific, highlighting contemporary issues in monetary policy for price stability using the benchmark definition of 'price stability' in monetary policy practice as 'low and stable inflation'. Given space constraints, in 2009 only a preliminary discussion could be undertaken of country-specific issues in inflation and monetary policy for some selected countries in an historical context. The contents of the earlier text fall into what has emerged as a central sub-discipline of economics – monetary macroeconomics (Friedman and Woodford, 2011). Monetary macroeconomics, while looking to theoretical developments for the latest analytical tools and directions, is essentially events-driven and policy-oriented in an operational context, revolving around such topics as inflation, monetary policy, capital flows, the behaviour of interest rates and exchange rates in the midst of structural rigidities; and policy restrictions and controls.

Major recent developments in monetary theory and policy have refined and extended key conventional theories, models and approaches to inflation and monetary policy that have been shown historically to be practised, persisted and evolved over centuries (Hossain, 2009). Modern econometric techniques allow empirical validation and interpretive reconciliation of those theories with real-world events and experiences. Major events, such as the East-Southeast Asian financial crisis of 1997–98 and the US-global financial crisis[1] of 2007–09, have brought fiscal and monetary policy issues to the research frontier and shaped contemporary policy debate on the efficacy of monetary and fiscal policies in economic stabilization under a rational expectations paradigm (Taylor, 2009, 2011). The debate began primarily focused on the design and conduct of monetary policy in the United States and its encompassing implications for macroeconomic imbalances and management across the globe. From an even earlier date, the present sustained disinflation-stagnation in Japan that began in the early 1990s raised the fundamental question of whether discretionary monetary policy could be effective for economic stabilization, as doubted by new classical economists operating under rational expectations theory, or would create a boom-bust cycle as predicted by Monetarist-New Classical theory.

The consequences of financial crises and the mechanics of transmission of monetary or real shocks to the economy remain instrumental to improved understanding of the fundamental principles of monetary macroeconomics. This allows policymakers to draw the implications of monetary, fiscal and exchange rate policies for economic stability in general and price stability in particular. Developing countries, having underdeveloped political and economic institutions, remain vulnerable to global events and shocks, irrespective of their origins and dynamics. One way to minimize, if not insulate, these economies from global shocks is to conduct rule-based monetary and fiscal policies to achieve well-defined policy objectives.

The monetary literature of the 1950s and 1960s is replete with case studies of developing countries, especially in Latin America, that underwent macroeconomic crises arising from populist expansionary fiscal and monetary policies. Partly as a response to that unfortunate experience, developing countries of the Asia-Pacific generally had by the mid 2000s moved away from macroeconomic populism. Consequently, their policy responses to the US-global financial crisis differed fundamentally from the policy expansionism of the United States and some other developed countries. To varying degrees, these countries largely avoided contracting sustained, major economic damage from that crisis. After relatively small, brief slowdowns, they have recovered rapid economic growth with or without some fiscal-monetary stimulus.

It is hoped that the case studies presented in this book will be received favourably as a modest contribution to monetary macroeconomics. It reviews and analyses, in an historical context, country-specific experience and issues in inflation and monetary policy. In doing so, key ideas and views on the sources and dynamics of inflation and monetary policy behaviour are investigated after taking into account those institutional arrangements that impinge upon the formulation and conduct of fiscal and monetary policies in each country considered. The book includes case studies for 12 judiciously selected countries, all at different stages of development and operating under different monetary policy frameworks.[2] It also includes an expanded discussion on generalized core issues in inflation and monetary policy. These core issues form the theme of the case studies.

Monetary policy frameworks in the selected countries include exchange rate pegging, monetary targeting and inflation targeting under varied restrictions on capital flows. The core issue upon which the book attempts to shed some light is the question of how the selected countries, with their diverse institutional arrangements, have conducted monetary policy since at least the 1960s, with the varying macroeconomic outcomes observed.

The selected countries have varied characteristics along several dimensions, including the strategy of development adopted and the level achieved, economic openness, inflation history and the monetary policy strategy response. The focus, therefore, is not on a narrow set of analytical themes but rather to highlight some core issues in inflation and monetary policy for investigation under different monetary policy arrangements. Furthermore, the book is not strongly prescriptive in tone and substance. The aim is to highlight key policy issues and investigate some of these econometrically, in a limited form, to draw policy implications.

It is important for the reader to be aware that the major theories of inflation and monetary policy have been devised within the environment and context of robust developed-country society, culture, politics and institutional frameworks and dynamics. These theories have only later been adapted to developing country contexts. Therefore, to set the background of the present analytical exercise, four developed countries are selected for detailed discussion of their inflation histories and consequent experience in the conduct of monetary policy. Policy lessons are drawn, together with some general implications for the macroeconomic management of developing countries. The contemporary monetary literature indicates that concepts and principles in monetary theory and policy, and the econometric techniques deployed for monetary analysis, remain relevant to all countries irrespective of their levels of development and institutional arrangements for conducting monetary policy. Moreover, some developing countries in the sample are rapidly moving towards gaining developed-country status and have already established economic and political institutions for achieving and sustaining monetary and fiscal discipline within an integrated, outward-oriented, market-driven development strategy.

The case studies in the book are not organized following a pre-set format or theme, except that the countries selected are presented in alphabetical order. The case analysis for each country is organized to reflect the evolution of inflationary trends and movements and to discuss the framework of monetary policy targeting stated objectives – usually price stability and economic growth. Each country chapter analyses the available data to yield dynamic information on several key macroeconomic variables, and reports empirical findings on some key monetary relations that have implications for monetary and exchange rate policies. However, the empirical analysis is suggestive and exploratory, not exhaustive given the limited scope of this study. The overall analysis is concise and informed by received economic theory, policy issues and some lessons of experience that the countries may draw. Importantly, these include institutional issues with respect to the design and conduct of rule-based monetary policy, especially the closely related phenomena of exchange rate arrangements, interest rate controls, credit allocation policy and capital-flow policy.

For econometric analysis, the data are drawn from domestic and international publications. The main source of data is the International Monetary Fund's (IMF) *International Financial Statistics*. Depending on the context of analysis, the historical data are reported in a summary form for individual countries and for the time periods for which data have been collected and are available. To streamline the analysis, econometric techniques are applied to investigate some aspects of inflation, together with the underlying relations in monetary theory and policy determining inflation.

While the econometric analysis is undertaken to provide evidentiary and illustrative findings,[3] the book is in no way an applied-econometric treatise. Econometric analysis is secondary to, and supportive of, analytical discussion on policy issues that are all-encompassing in a macroeconomic sense. However, to avoid repetitive discussion for each country, either on analytical issues in monetary policy or on econometric models and techniques deployed for empirical analysis, some topics are selected for brief review and then presented in the form of appendices.

The titles of the appendices provide some indication of their content. They are arranged as follows:

- Appendix 1: Money growth, output growth and inflation
- Appendix 2: Inflation persistence: a brief literature review
- Appendix 3: Non-linearity in inflation and the KSS (Kapetanios, Shin and Snell) test for unit root
- Appendix 4: The Taylor curve
- Appendix 5: Inflation volatility and money demand
- Appendix 6: Inflation, real interest rate, real exchange rate and real output
- Appendix 7: Controls over interest and exchange rates and inflation volatility
- Appendix 8: Money, output and prices
- Appendix 9: A SVAR (structural vector autoregression) model for money, output and prices
- Appendix 10: Money-growth rule and related issues.

Together with their extant sister reference text, the case studies in this book provide materials for at least two separate single-semester advanced undergraduate courses on monetary theory and policy focused on countries of the Asia-Pacific region. Moreover, they can be adopted as complementary texts for courses on money, banking and finance, including Islamic banking and finance. Although the literature on monetary macroeconomics in general and inflation and monetary policy in particular has expanded rapidly in both quantity and sophistication since the early 1970s, the present book, together with its extant sister reference text, covers the concepts and principles in a moderately rigorous, but not 'too mathematical', form needed for expositional purposes.[4] To make the work accessible to non-specialist readers with some interest in monetary policy issues, the book, like its companion before it, is written in a precise and matter-of-fact style with empirical orientation and policy focus. Most policy issues are analysed and illustrated with real-world events and examples. Readers requiring more in-depth analysis are referred to specialized readings such as journal articles that cover analytical issues or contain advanced empirical analysis.[5]

In writing this book of case studies and the earlier reference text, I have benefited from constructive and useful comments on issues in inflation and monetary policy from many students and colleagues at the University of Newcastle, Australia, and in other places where I taught, worked and visited. I have fulfilled my original intention in writing the 2009 book by adopting it as the prescribed text for my popular course 'ECON3004 Money and Banking' at the University of Newcastle, Australia. This has given me an opportunity to interact with advanced undergraduate students, many from countries in the East and Southeast Asian regions and having diverse academic backgrounds. From them I have received generous feedback on aspects of the text from pedagogical and policy viewpoints. This text is used in various courses at universities and institutes across the region. To enable wider use in courses at Indonesian universities, it has been translated into the Indonesian language.

Complimentary comments on the text from students and colleagues encouraged me to accept an invitation from the managing director of Edward Elgar Publishing to prepare this book of case studies of monetary policy. In my 2009 text I hinted that such case studies are essential for improved understanding of monetary relations and policy issues, especially in the rapidly growing economies of the Asia-Pacific region. I remain grateful to Edward Elgar and the production team of Edward Elgar Publishing for their support throughout the completion of this project.

In preparing the manuscript, I have benefited from the support of several institutions and persons. I am grateful to the Faculty of Business and Law at the University of Newcastle for awarding me two research grants to fund part-time employment of a research assistant during 2011–12. I used other research funds to employ a research assistant in 2013–14. I thank my colleague Gregory Bauer for his excellent work since the inception of this project as research assistant. He has been a reader, commentator and critic of earlier drafts of the book and assisted me in preparing the figures, tables and data compilation. In addition, he identified errors, omissions and weaknesses in the texts and provided suggestions for raising both the quality of analysis and presentation of materials in a reader-friendly form.

I conducted some research for the book while visiting at the University of Melbourne and the University of Malaya for about five months in 2012 as part of my 'outside studies programme' (sabbatical leave). I am grateful to Professor Robert Dixon of Melbourne University and Professor Eu Chye Tan of the University of Malaya for inviting me to work at the economics departments of these reputed universities. I am grateful to the authorities of these universities for providing me with the facilities needed to undertake research and other professional activities.

Time has passed so fast since I joined the academic profession that this is a perfect opportunity to acknowledge my substantive intellectual debt to some of my former teachers and colleagues and to a few professional economists with whom I had the opportunity to work in a challenging environment at both the IMF-Singapore Regional Training Institute (IMF-STI) and the Bangladesh Bank (central bank of Bangladesh) as World Bank Resident Economic Advisor.

Although somewhat autobiographical, I would like to indulge a little to make my debt public as part of an intellectual journey that began in Bangladesh at a difficult time in its recent turbulent history. I completed my BSc (Hons) and MSc degrees in Economics at Jahangirnagar University, Dhaka, Bangladesh during 1975–82. After my graduation and a brief period of teaching, I left Jahangirnagar to undertake higher studies in Australia and later settled in this beautiful country to work and raise a family. Nevertheless, I still cherish the quiet, picturesque campus life of Jahangirnagar University located, as it is, in a spacious, rugged-bushy area on the outskirts of Dhaka. Student life in the Al-Beruni Residential Hall at Jahangirnagar University where I resided was 'slow and monotonous' but 'beautiful and meaningful' for poets, philosophers and those who have romantic disposition. I was not one of them, at least overtly. Hence, it was fine for me to learn 'dry' economics as much as possible in a highly competitive academic environment. I remember fondly five professors, including the late Professor Mirza Md. Mozammel Hoque and the late Professor Mofizuddin Ahmad. Together with Professor Amirul Islam Chowdhury, Professor Khandaker Mustahidur Rahman and Professor Amin Muhammad Ali, they taught me economics – 'fundamentals of economics' – and a lot of it: passionately and quantitatively and with a sense of purpose. Professor Hoque and Professor Ahmad have passed away but left a sweet memory for me. Without any formal arrangement, they became my natural de facto mentors and played a role in my smooth navigation through the university phase of my life without any major scratch, mental or physical.

Professor D. Barry Hughes brought me to the University of Newcastle in 1989 as a new recruit from Melbourne, where I had completed my post-graduate degrees at the University of Melbourne and La Trobe University. Although Barry left the University of Newcastle after a few years for full-time professional work at Credit Suisse First Boston investment banking, I remained in touch with him for many years, only occasionally lately. I have found him a kind-hearted person and conscientious colleague and a valuable mentor at an early stage of my career. I cherish his friendship, empathy and words of wisdom.

Having moved from the university ivory tower to work at an international organization of repute, the International Monetary Fund, I found myself somewhat short of being fully prepared to comprehend the intensity and enormity of the day-to-day tasks of the IMF, dealing with macroeconomic problems and issues, mostly practical in nature; and this, despite already having been strongly influenced by policy-oriented writings of such economists as Rudiger Dornbusch, Stanley Fischer, Victor Corbo, Sebastian Edwards and others. Mohsin Khan's writings in particular were influential in my PhD research on macroeconomic and monetary policy issues in developing countries. Later – within the last few years, in fact – from Khan's writings, some with Professor Abbas Mirakhor and others, I developed some interest in monetary theory and policy in the context of a newly emerged sub-discipline of economics: Islamic banking and finance. Finally, I mention the names of two of my colleagues at the IMF-STI with whom I worked closely during 1999–2002. They are Dr Donal J. Donovan and Dr Jerome R. La Pittus. I enjoyed their friendship and support, which made my work experience at the Institute productive, rewarding and memorable. They taught me how to conceptualize, analyse and empirically investigate both monetary policy and exchange rate policy issues in developing countries within the framework of IMF's flagship *Financial Programming and Policies*. This framework is broad enough to design stabilization and structural adjustment policies for developing countries facing macroeconomic crises. During the first half of 2004, I worked at the Bangladesh Bank as World Bank Resident Economic Advisor. This gave me an opportunity to work with the top management, including Dr Fakhruddin Ahmed, Governor, to establish a unit for conducting research in monetary policy and also providing intensive training to 22 selected staff members for undertaking research on contemporary issues in monetary policy and central banking.

In general, my work experience at both the IMF-STI and the Bangladesh

Bank were, and remain, both germane and useful to my later and current research on policy-oriented issues in Bangladesh and Indonesia, in particular and, more generally, developing countries of the Asia-Pacific. For me, the East-Southeast Asian financial crisis of 1997–98 was a real-world laboratory case study for understanding the interrelations among fiscal, monetary and exchange rate policies in an open and deregulated financial environment. Moreover, for understanding the practical issues of macroeconomic management in developing countries, I benefited from discussions with many high officials from central banks and different economics ministries of about 30 countries of the Asia-Pacific, who either attended various professional courses at the IMF-STI over three years or whom I met with later in other forums and occasions. Therefore, this book of case studies in central banking and monetary policy can be considered an outcome of my research interest that was generated when I worked for the IMF-STI in Singapore at a challenging time not too long after the East-Southeast Asian financial crisis.

At a personal level, I take this opportunity to thank my wife, Nilufar, and our children, Andaleeb, Ayeeda, Afeeya and Azleena, for their support and understanding of my academic research and professional works. They have grown up 'rather quickly' and are able to appreciate the burden and responsibility of academic research. Of course, my wife was not amused by one excuse or other that I provided for avoiding household chores and many family and social events. Special thanks go to Ayeeda and Afeeya, undergraduate students at the Australian National University, who read some parts of the book and made valuable suggestions to make the materials more useful to undergraduates, especially to give a greater focus on the historical evolution of monetary policy in a changing economic environment.

Finally, I will feel amply rewarded if students, policymakers, central bankers and researchers working in and on the Asia-Pacific in particular find the book, together with the 2009 text, useful to improve their understanding of inflation and its dynamics and to design and implement appropriate monetary policy strategy to achieve and sustain low and stable inflation in a rapidly changing economic environment.

Any remaining errors and shortcomings of this book are my sole responsibility. Productive comments and suggestions are welcome from readers for updating the book, if any opportunity arises, and for my future research on related topics and policy issues in the Asia-Pacific.

NOTES

1. The financial crisis originated in the United States in 2007 and then spread across the globe, including the Eurozone economies.
2. The selected countries include the inflation and monetary policy experience of four developed countries, namely, Australia, Japan, New Zealand and the United States. The remaining eight developing 'countries' are China (Mainland), Hong Kong, SAR (Special Administrative Region) of China, India, South Korea, the Philippines, Singapore, Sri Lanka and Thailand. Hong Kong, SAR of China is not a country but its macroeconomy is useful as a separate economic entity since its unique currency board exchange rate system carries major policy implications. I have written a book of case studies, *Central Banking and Monetary Policy of Muslim-Majority Countries* (Hossain, 2015), which examines the inflation and monetary policy experience of nine Muslim-majority countries, namely, Bahrain, Bangladesh, Egypt, Indonesia, Iran, Malaysia, Pakistan, Saudi Arabia and Turkey.
3. The conventional econometric techniques deployed include the multiple regression analysis, unit root tests, ARCH-GARCH (autoregressive conditional heteroskedasticity-generalized autoregressive conditional heteroskedasticity) modelling and VAR/VECM/SVAR (vector autoregression/vector error correction model/structural vector autoregression) modelling. The key references are Hill et al. (2011) and Stock and Watson (2012). To supplement discussion on the commonly used ADF (augmented Dickey-Fuller) and KPSS (Kwiatkowski, Phillips, Schmidt and Shin) tests, Appendix 3 provides an outline of the KSS test conducted, if needed, within a nonlinear framework.
4. The mathematical symbols used in this book are not standardized but are chapter- or model-specific. They are defined as frequently as needed for exposition at the risk of repetition. This allows the reader to navigate through the text without any risk of distraction by having to refer back to the symbols and their meanings defined earlier.
5. In drafting the text I have drawn and synthesized materials from a wide range of published sources, including specialist texts, journal articles and other publications, such as working papers and raw drafts. While I have given references for materials drawn from sources that can be identified and attributed to certain authors, I have avoided providing detailed references, given the space constraint, on themes and ideas that are generic and have been developed by many scholars in different contexts over time. Any specific material drawn from any identifiable source without appropriate acknowledgement or citation is an entirely unintentional oversight.

REFERENCES

Friedman, B.M. and M. Woodford (eds) (2011), *Handbook of Monetary Economics*, Vols 3A and 3B, Amsterdam: Elsevier Science.

Hill, R.C., W.E. Griffiths and G.C. Lim (2011), *Principles of Econometrics*, New York: John Wiley and Sons.

Hossain, A. (2009), *Central Banking and Monetary Policy in the Asia-Pacific*, Cheltenham, UK and Northampton, MA, USA: Edward Elgar.

Hossain, A. (2015), *Central Banking and Monetary Policy in Muslim-Majority Countries*, Cheltenham, UK and Northampton, MA, USA: Edward Elgar.

IMF (International Monetary Fund) (various years), *Financial Programming and Policies*, Washington, DC: IMF.

IMF (International Monetary Fund) (various years), *International Financial Statistics*, Washington, DC: IMF.

Stock, J.H. and M.W. Watson (2012), *Introduction to Econometrics*, New York: Pearson Education.

Taylor, J.B. (2009), 'The lack of empirical rationale for a revival of discretionary fiscal policy', *American Economic Review* (*Papers and Proceedings*), **99**(2), 550–5.

Taylor, J.B. (2011), 'An empirical analysis of the revival of fiscal activism in the 2000s', *Journal of Economic Literature*, **49**, 686–702.

Abbreviations and acronyms

ACTU	Australian Council of Trade Unions
ADF	augmented Dickey-Fuller
A$	Australian dollar
AIC	Akaike Information Criterion
ALP	Australian Labor Party
APRA	Australian Prudential Regulatory Authority
AR	autoregression
ARCH	autoregressive conditional heteroskedasticity
ARDL	autoregressive distributed lag
ASEAN	Association of Southeast Asian Nations
BBC	basket-band-crawl
BIS	Bank for International Settlements
BM	broad money (representing M2 or a broader monetary aggregate)
BMGR	broad money growth rate
BOJ	Bank of Japan
BOK	Bank of Korea
BOT	Bank of Thailand
BSP	Bangko Sentral ng Pilipinas
CBA	Commonwealth Bank of Australia
CBP	Central Bank of the Philippines
CBSL	Central Bank of Sri Lanka
CDs	Certificates of Deposits
CIs	Certificates of Indebtedness
CPI	consumer price index
CUSUM	cumulative sum (of residuals)
CUSUMSQ	cumulative sum of squared (residuals)
DBS	Development Bank of Singapore
DOLS	dynamic ordinary least squares
EFAC	Exchange Fund Advisory Committee
ESA	Exchange Settlement Account
FIR	foreign interest rate (for example, US Treasury bill rate or US Federal funds rate)
FOMC	Federal Open Market Committee

FRB	Federal Reserve Bank
FRS	Federal Reserve System (or simply the Fed)
GARCH	generalized autoregressive conditional heteroskedasticity
GDP	gross domestic product
GMM	Generalized Method of Moments
HKD/HK$	Hong Kong dollar
HKMA	Hong Kong Monetary Authority
HSBC	Hong Kong and Shanghai Banking Corporation
IMF	International Monetary Fund
IMF-STI	IMF-Singapore Regional Training Institute
IS	IS (curve)
KFH	Kuwait Finance House
KPSS	Kwiatkowski, Phillips, Schmidt and Shin
KSS	Kapetanios, Shin and Snell
LAF	Liquidity Adjustment Facility
LM	LM (curve)
MAS	Monetary Authority of Singapore
MLA	Monetary Law Act
MPC	Monetary Policy Committee
M1	narrow money (currency plus demand deposits)
M2	broad money (currency plus demand and time deposits)
M3	a money stock that is somewhat broader than M2 and may include short- and long-term deposits held in non-banking financial institutions including saving deposits in post offices
NEER	nominal effective exchange rate (index)
NER	nominal exchange rate between two currencies (or bilateral exchange rate)
NERI	nominal exchange rate index
NIR	nominal interest rate
NM	narrow money (representing M1)
NMGR	narrow money growth rate
NTUC	National Trades Union Congress
NZ	New Zealand
NZD/NZ$	New Zealand dollar
OCBC	Overseas Chinese Banking Corporation
OECD	Organisation for Economic Co-operation and Development
OLIR	optimal level of the inflation rate
OLS	ordinary least squares
OPEC	Organization of the Petroleum Exporting Countries
PBC	People's Bank of China

PPP	purchasing power parity
PRC	People's Republic of China
PTA	Policy Targets Agreement
RA	Republic Act
RBA	Reserve Bank of Australia
RBI	Reserve Bank of India
RBNZ	Reserve Bank of New Zealand
REER	real effective exchange rate (index)
RER	real exchange rate between two currencies (or bilateral real exchange rate)
RGDP	real gross domestic product or GDP at constant prices
RIR	real interest rate (or nominal interest rate adjusted for inflation)
RMB	renminbi
SAR	Special Administrative Region (of China)
SBC	Schwarz Bayesian Criterion
SOE	state-owned enterprises
S$	Singapore dollar
SVAR	structural vector autoregression
TWI	trade weighted index
UK£	UK pound
US$	US dollar
USFFR	US Federal funds rate
USTBR	US Treasury bill rate
VAR	vector autoregression
VECM	vector error-correction model

1. Introduction

MONEY, OUTPUT AND PRICES

The question of what effects money exerts upon economic activity and the price level, together with the magnitude of those effects, remains the central issue in monetary economics. Classical monetary theory suggests that monetary expansion, at a rate exceeding the rate of increase of demand for it, first stimulates output and then, over a considerable time lag of unpredictable duration, lowers output and raises the price level and ensures neutrality of money in the long run (Hume, 1752 [1970]; Marquis, 1996; Appendix 8). Modern monetary economists suggest that prices and wages have rigidities and therefore adjust slowly, conferring 'transitory' impact of monetary expansion on output – the non-neutrality theory of money.[1] There is substantial debate whether discretionary monetary expansion to achieve temporary economic gains is a sound strategy. The central hypothesis under investigation is that unanticipated monetary expansions create output fluctuations, inflation uncertainty and, over time, higher unemployment.[2] Modern monetary macroeconomics includes a growing body of literature on monetary theory and policy concerning this and related issues.[3] The following discussion reviews the historical debate and suggests its relevance to the design and conduct of monetary policy in the present context.

The Great Depression of the 1930s and the subsequent emergence of Keynesian economics reduced the role of money in economic activity until Milton Friedman and others[4] in the 1960s were successful in rehabilitating the role of money in income determination.[5] Friedman and Schwartz (1963a) in particular demonstrated the importance of money in economic activity in their classic *A Monetary History of the United States, 1867–1960*. They posited the relations among money, output and prices and provided empirical evidence, which is consistent with Classical monetary theory, by studying the turning points in money and output.

Having maintained the proposition of long-run neutrality of money, they suggested reasons behind a short-run causality running from money to economic activity. The New Classical School that invokes the rational expectations hypothesis and became prominent in the 1970s, however, does not share this view. It suggests that only unanticipated monetary expansion affects output[6] and only in the short run. Unanticipated monetary expansion, however, does not improve economic welfare, except in the case when the monetary authority possesses more and better information than the public.[7] Like Monetarists, they suggest that monetary expansion does not raise output in the long run and that a rule-based monetary policy should be deployed to maintain price stability, meaning very low, if not zero, inflation.

Friedman (1960, 1968) provided a monetary framework to justify price stability as the objective of monetary policy. He argued that monetary policy should not be deployed to achieve real objectives, since money does not exert significant long-run impact on real variables, such as output, employment, real interest rates and real exchange rates. This does not, however, prevent monetary policy from playing a catalytic role in economic growth. Monetary policy can create a stable monetary climate that could be 'favorable to the effective operation of those basic forces of enterprise, ingenuity, invention, hard work, and thrift that are the true springs of economic growth' (Friedman, 1968, p. 17).

One central issue in short-run macroeconomics is whether monetary policy should be deployed to minimize the business cycle, which is considered a common phenomenon in a capitalist economy. Monetarists rely on the market mechanisms for restoring economic imbalances that are created by random shocks and do not see any need for activist monetary policy to stabilize the economy. Poole and Wheelock (2008, pp. 6–7) put emphasis on price stability as the objective of monetary policy that promotes economic growth and stability:

> Price stability is the most powerful tool the central bank has to promote economic growth, high employment and financial stability. Price stability also enables monetary authorities to pursue secondary objectives, including the reduction of fluctuations in real economic activity and the management of financial and/or liquidity crises. These are referred to as secondary goals because a central bank is unlikely to succeed at limiting fluctuations in economic activity or containing financial crises unless the price level is stable.

Therefore, one major theme has emerged that there is a well-defined objective of monetary policy (that is, price stability) and that monetary policy should be conducted in a transparent and predictable way to avoid creating policy uncertainty. Friedman (1960) maintained the view that to sustain price stability, monetary policy should be conducted by following a constant money supply growth rule. He thought this was more efficient than the other available methods of keeping a lid on inflation so as to maintain the nominal interest rate as low as possible. A very low rate of the nominal interest rate, preferably at a zero level, would increase the holding of real money balances needed for maximizing efficiency of transactions in a monetary economy (Woodford, 1990). Other strategies of monetary policy include pegging the nominal interest rate, or the exchange rate, or leaving the conduct of monetary policy at the discretion of the monetary authority.[8] All these strategies of monetary policy are likely to generate inflation volatility and consequently destabilize the economy (Friedman, 1968).

Friedman (1956a) relied heavily on the modern interpretation of the *Quantity Theory of Money* as a theory of money demand and then derived a monetary model of inflation for empirical validation with data across countries and over historical periods. Friedman and other monetary economists at the University of Chicago put emphasis on the universal applicability of the monetary model of inflation.[9] The key message that came through from their studies on money demand and inflation for different countries over different sample periods of time was the presence of a stable money-demand function and a linkage between money supply growth and inflation, with causality running predominantly from money growth to inflation.[10]

Therefore, the major contributions of Friedman and his collaborators in the 1960s were the establishment of two monetary propositions on inflation and business cycles (Nelson and Schwartz, 2008). Besides the monetary interpretation of inflation, Friedman and Schwartz (1963a, 1963b) provided a monetary interpretation of the business cycles. Later, Friedman (1973, p. 28) elaborated the monetary view of inflation in the context of developing countries as follows: 'inflation is always and everywhere a monetary phenomenon in the sense that it is and can be produced only by a more rapid increase in the quantity of money than in output'. This was in direct contrast with the view that money growth is the effect, not the cause of inflation in developing countries that suffer from myriad structural rigidities. Within Friedman's monetary framework, inflation represents a steady and sustained rise in prices while suggesting that 'the reason for the rapid increase in the quantity of money may be different under different circumstances' (p. 28). Barro (1993) has provided an interpretation of Friedman's monetary view of inflation by incorporating factors that bring changes in money demand and then become a potential or secondary source of inflation. The inclusion of both the demand and supply sides of the money market in an inflation model has allowed monetary economists to explain high and hyperinflations where there is a feedback relation between money supply growth and inflation (Hossain, 2009).

Many studies since the 1960s have validated the monetary interpretation of inflation while acknowledging that non-monetary factors may have some impact on inflation in the short run (McCallum, 1990). Earlier, Friedman (1983) acknowledged the importance of supply shocks and other non-monetary factors in affecting inflation in the short run while maintaining that inflation cannot be sustained over the long run without monetary accommodation. Monetary accommodation in turn represents a policy decision of the monetary authority that intends to eliminate the short-run impacts of supply shocks on output and employment before completion of adjustment of the economy through the market forces. There is considerable evidence that monetary accommodation led the surge of inflation in many countries following the Organization of the Petroleum Exporting Countries (OPEC) oil price shocks in the 1970s (Cline and Weintraub, 1981).

Stability of the Money-demand Function and Money Growth-inflation Relationship

The modern debate on the importance of money as a source of inflation can be understood from two underlying monetary relations. The first is the testable proposition that the demand for money is a stable function of a small number of arguments, such as real income, the interest rate and the expected rate of inflation.[11] The second is the stable relation between money base, which is controlled by the monetary authority, and a broader monetary aggregate that is linked to economic activity, prices and exchange rates. This second relation is debated on the issue of controllability of the money supply and its links with other nominal variables. At an analytical level, the debate is on the proposition that the velocity of money is stably related to the determinants of money holding in a way that produces a causal relationship between money supply growth and inflation.[12]

Economists of the Keynesian persuasion argue that the velocity of money is unstable and therefore no stable relation exists between money and prices. In contrast, Monetarists emphasize that the velocity of money is a stable function of such variables as income, the interest rate and the expected rate of inflation. Any rising or falling trend of the velocity of money does not represent instability of the velocity of money; instead, it reflects a lower or greater than one income elasticity of demand for money and the rising or falling interest rate or the expected rate of inflation.

Statistically, the velocity of money is stationary or trend-stationary while real money balances and real income are, or are most likely to be, non-stationary with a dominant stochastic trend and hence they remain eligible to establish a cointegral relation. An implication is that although the velocity of money is not constant, it remains predictable given the constant unconditional long-run mean and variance of a stationary series. The short-run volatility of the velocity of money in effect reflects the volatility of the interest rate or the expected rate of inflation, which could be due to discretionary monetary policy that the monetary authorities undertake to achieve some real objectives such as raising economic growth or lowering the rate of unemployment. Provided that the monetary authorities deploy a rule-based monetary policy such as a constant money-growth rule, the velocity of money would exhibit stability in a statistical sense; that is, the time-varying volatility of the velocity of money would be predictable although the forecasting error is likely to be larger during periods of high volatility.

The Role of Interest Rate in the Money-demand Function

The early debate on the causal linkage between money and prices focused on the question of whether the nominal interest rate, along with real income or wealth or both, is a determinant of money demand and whether flexibility, not necessarily volatility, of the interest rate makes the velocity of money unpredictable. Friedman (1956a, 1959) downplayed the role of the interest rate in the money-demand function although acknowledging it to be statistically significant. He argued that even when the interest rate is statistically significant, its coefficient value is generally 'very small' (roughly within the range −0.5 to −1.0), not infinite, and that this finding does not alter his conclusion on the role and conduct of monetary policy for price stability (Friedman, 1969). It follows that a very high, if not infinite, interest elasticity of demand for money is inconsistent with the *Quantity Theory of Money* that suggests a zero-degree homogeneity of real money balances with respect to all nominal variables, except the expected rate of inflation, and a causal linkage between money and prices. To maintain the long-run dichotomy between real and nominal variables, Friedman (1992) relied on the Classical view that real income is ultimately determined by real factors on the supply side of the economy and that the price level is the only variable that alters in the long run in the event of monetary expansion adjusted for any increase in output. Equilibrium in the money market requires equality between money demand and money supply and an increase in the money supply does not affect real income or the interest rate, implying that it does not have any impact on long-run money demand.

The empirical findings across countries with data until the 1970s were consistent with Friedman's proposition that the money-demand function is stable and that the key source of inflation is excess money supply (Friedman, 1991; Laidler, 1993). The nominal interest rate is found not to have an impact on money demand or the velocity of money in a way that invalidates the relationship between money supply growth and inflation.

Since the 1970s, questions have been raised over the stability of the money-demand function and whether the linkage between money supply growth and inflation has been weakened due to financial deregulation and innovation. Some evidence was provided to suggest that the money-demand function became unstable in developed countries contemporarily with financial deregulation and reform during the 1980s (Goldfeld and Sichel, 1990).[13]

Monetarists argue that any weak linkage between money supply growth and inflation in some countries during the 1980s and 1990s was primarily due to high and volatile money growth and that raised the interest rate and made it volatile. This was the outcome of discretionary monetary policy that aimed at achieving multiple objectives in the midst of financial deregulation. Money-growth instability led to inflation instability, which in turn affected money demand and inflation itself. In the late 1990s, however, following completion of the deregulatory and reform transition, the money-demand function regained stability in developed countries. It was a different story in the developing world, which also implemented economic reforms in the 1980s and 1990s, mainly in the transition from inward-oriented to outward-oriented development strategy. Money-demand functions in developing countries have remained stable throughout. This was one of the suggested reasons for continuation of a stable linkage between money supply growth and inflation in these countries (Hossain, 2009).

Another dimension of the modern monetary literature suggests that the stability of the money-demand relationship is not at all necessary for establishing a link between money supply growth and inflation. Lucas (1980) in particular rejected any dependence of a money growth-inflation linkage on stability of the money-demand function. McCallum and Nelson (2011) have illustrated this view as follows. For example, although a unit root in the error term of the money-demand function, which represents a money-demand shock, violates dynamic stability in the money-demand function, it still implies a first-difference causal link between money supply growth and inflation that exists in most countries across the globe. Likewise, there can be a weak relation between money supply growth and inflation even when the money-demand function remains stable.

McCallum and Nelson (2011) note that one of the factors that can be attributed to the weakening link between money supply growth and inflation in the United States is the non-zero average value for the change in the interest rate over the sample period of study beginning from the 1970s. While such interpretation of weak mapping between the stability of money demand and the closeness of the money growth-inflation relationship could be useful in some respect, it does not diminish the importance of the stability of the money-demand function in a broad macroeconomic context. The presence of a stable money-demand relation provides a theoretical foundation for the establishment of a long-run relation among money, output, prices and exchange rates that Classical monetary theory postulates. Modern econometric techniques can establish such structural relations within a cointegration and error-correction modelling framework. Monetary macroeconomics has therefore become empirical-oriented, concerning real-world events and policy issues in maintaining macroeconomic stability in general and price stability in particular.

Monetary Policy: With or Without Money?

While the debate continues on the causal linkage between money supply growth and inflation, a body of literature has emerged since the early 2000s that claims that monetary policy does not require the deployment of monetary aggregates to achieve price stability. This theme has emerged in the literature more prominently since the introduction of inflation targeting in some developed countries in the early 1990s. Issing (2013) has been critical of the demise of money in 'monetary models' of inflation and business cycles. He writes:

> How long will we have to wait until the neglect of money and credit in monetary (!) theory and policy will be understood as the major source of macro policy mistakes? Is it not strange, to say the least, that in a world in which money, credit and financial markets play a fundamental role, models which give these variables hardly any active role are still dominant . . . Considering the developments that have taken place over the decades, one would expect that the time of 'monetary' macroeconomics and monetary policy without 'money and credit' will come to an end. (p. 284)

Under inflation targeting, a short-term interest rate is generally used to conduct monetary policy to maintain inflation at a target level, on average. The issue is whether the interest rate has any link with monetary aggregates. A widely held view is that the interest rate and monetary aggregate are two sides of the same coin in so far as monetary management is concerned. Changes in the nominal interest rate are associated with changes in monetary aggregates, due to a change in the monetary base or the money multiplier or both. A short-run negative relation indeed exists between the interest rate and money supply growth while this relation could be positive in the long run (Mishkin, 2013). Whether or not the interest rate or monetary aggregate to be used as an instrument of monetary policy is a tactical issue, it does not necessarily make money redundant in the inflation process. Alvarez et al. (2001) have shown how the use of the interest rate as a monetary policy instrument is consistent with the linkage between money supply growth and inflation.

In the monetary literature, the interest rate is determined in the credit market by the interaction of credit demand and credit supply. A central bank can influence the interest rate because of the central bank's ability and willingness to take part as a major supplier (or potential supplier) of credit for settlements in interbank markets. The nominal interest rate can be considered a monetary variable because of its 'one-for-one' positive relation with the expected rate of inflation. Within a monetary modelling framework, the expected rate of inflation equals the predicted growth of the money supply adjusted for expected economic growth. However, the real component of the nominal interest rate is determined in the long run by real factors, namely the productivity of capital, population growth, the rate of depreciation of capital and the rate of saving (Sorensen and Whitta-Jacobsen, 2005). Changes in the real interest rate affect saving, investment and economic growth. Money growth or inflation does not affect the real interest rate at the steady state unless it leads to a change in wealth or real income.

Whether to use money or credit or the interest rate for the conduct of monetary policy depends on the institutional arrangement within which monetary policy operates and the structural characteristics of the economy. Money and credit, although conceptually different, are highly correlated and both appear with equal prominence in monetary policy analysis. Poole (1970) has demonstrated that whether money or the interest rate is best suited as an instrument of monetary policy to stabilize an economy depends on the economy's exposure to real shocks or monetary shocks or both.

Therefore, the increasing preference for the interest rate as an instrument of monetary policy can be viewed as tactical; it does not necessarily invalidate the monetary interpretation of inflation or make money unimportant as a source of inflation. Given short-run price rigidities, any change in the nominal interest rate represents a change in the real interest rate. It is the real interest rate that affects both consumption and investment spending. When the nominal interest rate adjusts fully and quickly to the expected rate of inflation, the real interest rate may not change much. A change in the nominal interest rate leads to a change in the real interest rate only when the nominal interest rate does not adjust completely to the expected rate of inflation. The Taylor rule explains how a very short-term nominal interest rate is changed by the central bank in response to changes in the inflation gap and output gap (Taylor, 1993). According to the Taylor principle, a central bank is required to raise the real interest rate to lower the rate of inflation. It indicates that to become effective as a demand management instrument, the nominal interest rate must rise more than proportionately to the expected rise in the rate of inflation.

In the midst of such debate on the relevance of money in monetary policy, there has been a revival of interest in the deployment of monetary aggregates for the conduct of monetary policy. McCallum and Nelson (2011) have provided evidence of a stable causal linkage between money supply growth and inflation. They argue that a causality exists between money supply growth and inflation irrespective of the exchange rate regime and whether that regime makes the money stock exogenous or endogenous and whether there exists a stable money-demand function. They do not see the need for averaging data to extract the relationship between money supply growth and inflation. In their analysis, they have argued for using non-averaged time-series data while allowing for lags explicitly instead of implicitly for tracking the money growth-inflation relationship with historical data.

Given the robust linkage between money supply growth and inflation, a monetary aggregate remains a natural instrument for the conduct of monetary policy within a longer time horizon. Earlier, Friedman (1991) considered a properly defined monetary aggregate suitable to be the intermediate target of monetary policy.[14] Contemporary preference for the interest rate over a monetary aggregate does not indicate the demise of Friedman's interpretation of inflation as a monetary phenomenon. However, the deployment of the interest rate as an instrument of monetary policy is not innocuous. It has the potential to destabilize the money-demand function, with money-growth volatility leading to inflation volatility, in turn affecting, both positively and negatively, money demand and hence inflation itself. This explains why inflation volatility can be a determinant of money demand, especially in countries that do not follow a binding monetary policy rule to maintain price stability, meaning 'low and stable' inflation, not 'low and unstable' inflation. Even countries that operate under monetary targeting do not follow a money-growth rule strictly. Consequently, inflation remains high and volatile in most countries, which lowers economic efficiency and growth by making both the real interest rate and real exchange rate excessively volatile. This is one of the major issues under investigation in the present study.

Role of Monetary Policy in Economic Stabilization

Whether or not the interest rate or a monetary aggregate is used as an instrument of monetary policy, most central banks accept price stability as the main, if not the sole, objective of monetary policy. This reflects the emerging consensus on four basic propositions: (1) monetary expansion has a lasting effect only on the price level, not on output or employment; (2) inflation is costly in resource misallocation (efficiency costs), or in reduced long-term output growth (breakdown of super-neutrality of money), or in both types of opportunity cost; (3) monetary policy has transitory effects on several real variables, but there is imperfect understanding of the nature and the size of such effects; and (4) monetary policy affects inflation with lags of uncertain duration and with variable strength, thereby undermining the central bank's ability to control inflation on a period-by-period basis (Hossain, 2009). The debate remains whether monetary policy should be used to stimulate economic activity in the short run – emerging consensus item (1) suggests that it has no effect in the long run.

Monetarism suggests that the stimulatory impact of monetary expansion is transitory and has costly destabilizing influence, so that policymakers should avoid the temptation to exploit it (Meltzer, 1998, 2012). New Classicism goes one step further. It asserts that Monetarists are too generous in subscribing to the view that monetary policy is effective in generating economic stimulus. Under the rational expectations hypothesis, monetary policy actions that are anticipated cannot change output even in the short run.[15] Like Monetarists, New Classical economists favour a money supply growth rule over discretionary monetary policy to keep inflation low and stable.

While Monetarists put emphasis on the difficulties in conducting discretionary monetary policy due to, firstly, uncertainty in both the magnitude and the lag-length of monetary policy impacts and, secondly, policymakers' inefficiency and overreaction that create economic uncertainty, New Classical economists believe that the private sector is efficient and takes countervailing steps to neutralize any impact of systematic monetary policy on economic activity. Consequently, it is not inefficiency of policymakers but efficiency of the private sector that makes monetary policy ineffective in changing real output. In the New Classical view, a further disadvantage of discretionary monetary policy is that it increases output volatility, defined as the variance of output around its natural level.[16]

Contrary to a discretionary monetary policy, a constant money supply growth rule is considered superior because it minimizes the variance of output although this rule may not necessarily be optimal under general conditions. Sargent and Wallace (1975) show that a pegging of the interest rate upholds the policy-ineffectiveness proposition under the rational expectations hypothesis. The price level, however, becomes indeterminate under an interest rate rule. When a country operates under flexible inflation targeting, the deployment of the interest rate as an instrument may keep inflation closer to its target level on average. Under this environment, inflation may, however, become more volatile if the economy experiences shocks, a common feature of developing economies (Frankel, 2011). Inflation also becomes volatile in countries where the monetary authorities attempt to stabilize output under flexible inflation targeting. Policymakers operate under the belief that a tradeoff exists between inflation volatility and output volatility. Appendix 4 reviews this relationship, known as the Taylor curve relationship. Whether such a tradeoff exists under general conditions remains a debatable issue.

Political Economy of Economic Stabilization

The early debate on monetary policy activism raised the issues of whether there is the need for economic stabilization interventions in a market economy with flexible wages, prices and exchange rates and, if needed, how effective government intervention could be. If the prices, interest rates and exchange rates are determined by market forces and there are no rigidities in wage determination, both demand and supply shocks would dissipate quickly without government interventions. Monetarists oppose activist monetary policy to neutralize economic shocks, even while acknowledging some rigidity in wages and prices. They put emphasis on the uncertain magnitude and lag-length effects of monetary policy responses to shocks, which may make the economy more volatile.

Some micro studies of price changes have raised doubt about the assumed price-stickiness in the Keynesian models of monetary non-neutrality (Bils and Klenow, 2004; Klenow and Malin, 2011). Moreover, the real business cycle theory considers economic fluctuations as the outcomes of real shocks, as distinct from monetary shocks (Kydland and Prescott, 1982; Prescott, 1986). The effects of such real shocks do not dissipate but sustain while the effects of monetary shocks dissipate within a short period of time as they are temporary in nature. Consequently, the real business cycle theory does not see any need for monetary policy actions for stabilizing the economy.

One further contentious issue is whether monetary policy 'surprises' aimed at raising economic activity or neutralizing shocks are politically motivated. In the literature, there is the suggestion that a linkage exists between fiscal and monetary policies, especially in developing countries (Frankel, 2011). In a competitive political system, politicians make myopic economic decisions to secure voter patronage (Alesina and Stella, 2011). Due to presumed voter aversion to increased taxes, this myopia leads to a policy preference for government borrowing, rather than taxing, to finance increased spending.[17] In developing countries, expansionary fiscal policy generally represents excess borrowing from the banking system, especially from central banks, implying a monetization of budget deficits. Consequently, these countries experience high and volatile inflation, originating from fiscal measures that are funded by money creation. This indicates that, in the ultimate power politics, the fiscal authority dominates the monetary authority and hence the monetary authority does not have control over inflation. Further, political polarization, political uncertainty and limited commitment and credibility of the monetary authority lead to high and volatile inflation (Cukierman and Webb, 1995; Cukierman et al., 1992). While this analysis suggests that the monetary authority does not often have control over inflation, it does not mean that it cannot prevent inflation if it desires and is allowed to do so (McCallum, 1990).

High and volatile inflation raises economic uncertainty and retards economic efficiency and growth. Once inflation reaches a high level, policy measures to lower inflation, which is inertial, incur huge explicit and implicit costs. Inflation control is difficult without the benefit of a strong and determined government which puts emphasis on steady economic growth in a low-inflationary environment. Central bank credibility, along with the government's commitment and determination, is considered critical for maintaining low and steady inflation. When society is not prepared to bear the efficiency costs of central bank adoption of accommodative monetary policy to achieve political objectives, costs that are paid in damagingly volatile output, employment and inflation, the central bank can be made operationally independent for the conduct of monetary policy for price stability. Provided that the central bank's accountability to the public is ensured, its operational independence would improve monetary policy effectiveness by raising policy transparency and credibility. In reality, in most countries, central banks do not have autonomy in conducting monetary policy for price stability. Inflation control therefore remains a costly and time-consuming exercise (Alesina and Stella, 2011; Williamson, 2008). This is reflected in high inflation persistence, irrespective of monetary policy strategy deployed to maintain low inflation on average (Appendix 2).

Assimilation of the rational expectations proposition into mainstream macroeconomics leads the New Classical economists to argue that raised credibility of anti-inflationary monetary policy can lower inflation at little or no cost to output or employment. In contrast, low monetary policy credibility of central banks makes it difficult to lower inflationary expectations. Contractionary measures to control inflation then run the risk of tipping an economy into recession and its subsequent slow recovery. A rise in credibility of monetary policy is therefore expected to lower the degree of inflation persistence. Central banks' problem is that monetary policy credibility is difficult to achieve. It is subject to technological, administrative (political) and strategic constraints.[18] One path towards gaining credibility is as follows. When low monetary policy credibility originates in dynamic inconsistency of monetary policy within a game-theoretic framework, the granting of central banks' independence may raise monetary policy credibility provided that they commit to apply a non-discretionary, binding policy rule to determine monetary policy for price stability.[19]

In contrast, any short-run deployment of monetary policy to achieve real objectives carries the danger that it would create policy uncertainty and the very dynamic, time-inconsistency problem that the monetary policy rule attempts to eliminate. Nevertheless, Keynesian economists continue to prescribe the use of monetary policy to generate real effects in the short run if the economy moves towards recession due to shocks or coordination failure in the private sector.[20] Essentially, the Keynesian prescription is for ongoing policy change in response to disruption in the real sector, compromising its efficiency through continuous volatility of output, employment and inflation. The main concern is that the 2007–09 US-global financial crisis has apparently diminished the independence of central banks across the globe. In an environment of expansionary fiscal measures, central banks have been induced to introduce expansionary, not contractionary, monetary measures to prevent the economies from entering into a deep recession. Therefore, to maintain low and stable inflation over the long run, there is the suggestion for strengthening monetary and fiscal institutions to withstand political pressures and sustain policy rules (Taylor, 2012, 2013). In a relatively low-inflationary environment, policymakers are not inclined to accept this prescription.

The main theme of this book and Hossain (2015) is that central banks should maintain low and stable inflation. Low volatility of inflation would keep the real interest and exchange rates stable and hence avoid boom-bust cycles. Another theme of this book and Hossain (2015) is the recommendation for the adoption of freely floating exchange rates that can absorb economic shocks better in an open economy. A freely floating exchange rate generally would exhibit high variability. A high variability of the exchange rate, however, does not necessarily lead to such high volatility that it may affect trade flows, investment and economic growth. Unexpected large capital flows, however, can raise the volatility of the exchange rate. Highly volatile real interest rate and real exchange rate may also trigger large capital flows. Therefore, some market-based capital control measures may be useful to maintain exchange rate stability for countries where financial stability comes under pressure from large-scale capital movements for both economic and non-economic reasons (Ball, 2011; Frankel, 2011).

MONETARY POLICY IN DEVELOPING COUNTRIES

Historically, the role of monetary policy in developed countries has been associated with taming business cycles, while in developing countries monetary policy has been targeted at promoting economic growth. The dichotomy in the role of monetary policy reflects the differential economic issues and priorities facing the respective policymakers. While the principal preoccupation in developing countries has been rapid economic growth through technical progress-based structural change in the economy, this preoccupation remains closely linked to the concern for price stability and external balances. For example, the experiences of Latin American countries during the 1960s and 1970s suggest that if the inflationary pressure emergent from the development process is ignored, any consequential rapid inflation rises may lead to an inefficient allocation of productive resources. In turn, resource misallocation feeds back counterproductively into impeded economic growth and structural distortion (less efficient structural change). Latin American development experiences also suggest that higher inflation rates in these countries vis-à-vis their trading partners caused their trade uncompetitiveness and worsening balance-of-payments problems. Exchange rate crisis that emanates from deteriorating balance-of-payments triggers capital flight, adversely affecting investment and economic growth (Corbo and de Melo, 1987; Dornbusch, 1993).

In contrast to Latin America, one lesson from the experiences of East Asian industrializing economies (Hong Kong SAR, South Korea, Singapore and Taiwan) and Southeast Asian economies (Indonesia, Malaysia and Thailand) is that steady economic growth and monetary stability[21] are intertwined and reinforcing. Currency crises in several locations around the world, and especially in East-Southeast Asia in the late 1990s and the US-global financial crisis of the late 2000s, further point to problems associated with mismatches between exchange rate regimes, capital flows and monetary policy independence (Frankel, 2011). Therefore the objectives of price stability, balance-of-payments equilibrium and economic growth are interrelated. Any demarcation between the roles of monetary and financial policies in growth and stabilization then seem artificial and may be misleading, especially in developing countries. Nevertheless, the emerging consensus view is that monetary policy cannot target multiple objectives, due to the inefficiency costs imposed by consequent trade-offs and inconsistencies. In addition, having too many objectives assigned to monetary policy is in conflict with the Tinbergen principle.[22]

On the basis of a large body of literature on monetary theory and policy since the 1960s, an emerging consensus view is that the efficient role of monetary policy is the maintenance of price stability. This theme is established by focusing on varied inflationary experiences, including hyperinflations, in Asia, Europe and Latin America. Accordingly, institutionalization of monetary policy has taken place in some developed countries in the form of inflation targeting or some form of a rule-based monetary policy. In doing so, central banks in these countries have gained autonomy, if not independence, in the conduct of monetary policy for price stability. In developing countries, monetary policy is yet to be institutionalized with checks and balances that succeed in efficiently directing the efforts of the monetary authorities at achieving and maintaining price stability. Following the lead of developed countries, several developing countries have recently moved towards rule-based, price-stabilizing monetary policy; some countries imposing on it the additional burden of promoting economic growth, and some not. Consequent on the rapid growth and associated structural change achieved in the three decades following the transition to outward-oriented economic development, the issue of monetary policy for price stability has gained importance relative to the growth-targeted monetary policy in developing countries across East, Southeast and South Asia, in particular (Hossain, 2009).

In contrast to the structuralist view of inflation that was present in the 1950s and 1960s, developing countries have generally accepted the monetary roots of inflation (Corbo, 1974; Hossain, 2009). Monetary expansion is, however, linked to sustained budget deficits in these countries. Consequently, how much control central banks should exercise over money matters to keep inflation within an efficient limit is yet to be resolved. In general, in a market economy, inflation remains outside the direct control of a central bank. What central banks can do is to target various monetary policy instruments at aggregate demand (and possibly aggregate supply) to influence inflationary expectations. The ways in which monetary policy instruments affect the real economy remain uncertain.[23] Understanding of the transmission mechanisms of monetary policy is therefore crucial for the conduct of monetary policy. Further, there are lags between policy actions and impacts on aggregate demand and aggregate supply. The economy also works differently under different economic states; that is, an economy may react variably in boom (expansionary phase of the business cycle) and in recession (contractionary phase) to a given combination of shocks and policy actions (Boivin et al., 2011). Because policymakers work with imperfect information, their actions may have unintended consequences. Political institutions and overlapping organizational arrangements also make it difficult for the authorities, especially fiscal authorities, to demarcate the jurisdiction of the central bank from other institutions in the country.

As part of streamlining the policy-formulation process, an emergent generalized monetary policy framework has now been standardized in the literature. Within the framework, policymakers define variables as either operational or intermediate targets and then manipulate these variables to achieve monetary policy goal(s) either required or agreed by the government. For example, policymakers set an inflation target that is socially acceptable and optimal in economic sense. Whether or not a central bank should, or is able to, conduct monetary policy according to a well-defined rule ultimately depends on the underlying country-specific configuration of relationships among money, output and prices via the interest and exchange rates.

At a basic level, developing countries have accepted the fundamental relations among money, output, prices and exchange rates as suggested by Classical monetary theory. Herein lies the importance of empirical analysis of monetary relations with econometric techniques; for example, time-series econometrics. Historical data now available for a longer period can be used for individual countries separately and then jointly by deploying, say, panel regressions. Case studies of the evolution and conduct of monetary policy in this book and in Hossain (2015) are consistent with this approach to, and the requirements of, improved monetary policymaking. This case-study approach is relevant to rapidly growing developing countries in changing policy environments, as discussed in the next subsection.[24]

Changing Behaviour of Monetary Policy in the Asia-Pacific

Most countries of the Asia-Pacific have experienced low to moderate inflation since the early 1980s, following a period of high inflation in the 1970s originating largely in supply shocks and fuelled by the counterproductive response of monetary accommodation. Although the conduct of monetary policy in most developing countries took the form of monetary targeting from the late 1970s, monetary policy was designed to achieve multiple objectives under a pegged exchange rate system. Exchange rate stability was considered important for both price stability and export promotion. However, due to limited exchange rate flexibility, as well as limited policy control over interest rates, monetary targeting, implicit or explicit, led to inflation volatility (Appendix 7). The consequent high volatilities of real interest and exchange rates adversely affected economic growth and macroeconomic performance.[25]

High-inflation volatility generated high volatilities in both the real interest rate and the real exchange rate as the authorities failed to promptly and fully adjust the corresponding nominal rates. Moreover, although the pegged exchange rate regime was expected to bring monetary-fiscal discipline, some developing countries introduced expansionary monetary and fiscal policies, creating policy-induced inflation and balance-of-payments problems. In turn, a new target for monetary policy became essential: the maintenance of large foreign-exchange reserves. Not until the 1990s was monetary policy eventually released for redirection, at least in principle, at its target of comparative advantage: the maintenance of price stability (Hossain, 2009).

Since the mid 1990s, the pegged exchange rate system has generally been untenable in developing countries of the Asia-Pacific. Some countries in the East-Southeast Asian region attracted large-scale capital inflows due to improved macroeconomic performance and high returns on investment, which subsequently led to the watershed currency financial crisis through 1997–98. This ramified throughout the Asia-Pacific with the abandonment by many countries of exchange rate pegging in favour of a range of more flexible systems, including the full float. A floating exchange rate system permits autonomous conduct of monetary policy using one of a range of intermediate targets, such as monetary aggregates or the (expected) inflation rate. Monetary targeting was not generally adopted, since it had by then become 'unfashionable'. One reason for this was the ascendancy at the time of the argument that the money-demand function had by then been destabilized in developing countries because of the East-Southeast Asian financial crisis and associated financial deregulation and reforms. The sudden spike in the rate of inflation was interpreted as a breakdown of the money-demand relation although this relationship stabilized rather quickly after the crisis was over (Hossain, 2009). Nevertheless, the perception remains that the East-Southeast Asian financial crisis and the subsequent structural and financial reforms have weakened the causal linkage between money supply growth and inflation.

The validity of this proposition remains an empirical issue and is likely to vary from country to country. As a consequence of this uncertain post-crisis stability of the money-demand function, some developing countries in the Asia-Pacific have adopted inflation targeting but have yet to fulfil its key requirements. For example, in Indonesia, a short-term interest rate is used as a policy instrument, although its effectiveness as an instrument of demand management is in doubt. The linkage between the nominal interest rate and inflation is not well defined, as they have a feedback relation. Generally, inflation raises the nominal interest rate with a lag. However, it is not the nominal interest rate but the real interest rate that matters for consumption, investment and trade and capital flows. This is represented in the Taylor principle, which requires a change in the real interest rate to bring changes in aggregate demand, output and prices. The question remains whether the move away from targeting a monetary aggregate to inflation targeting has improved monetary policy in countries which have made this move. The desirability of inflation targeting in other developing countries is an empirical question. Inflation has been low on average in most inflation targeting countries. However, inflation persistence and volatility have remained high. Price stability, in an operational sense, implies low and stable inflation, not low and unstable inflation. This issue is yet to be adequately addressed to draw policy conclusions.

Finally, with increased volatility of capital flows brought about by the deregulation of capital markets in a number of Asia-Pacific countries, financial stability has come to the forefront as an issue in monetary policy. The widely accepted open-economy trilemma states that only two out of the three major monetary policy goals[26] can be achieved simultaneously. One of the theorem's implications is that under a freely floating – and therefore relatively unstable – exchange rate system, monetary policy can be conducted independently with or without freely mobile capital. However, when money and capital markets are shallow, or underdeveloped, as is characteristic in developing countries, freely mobile capital may cause exchange rate volatility, which may lead to banking and financial crises. As large-scale capital flows are triggered by both economic and non-economic factors, they may defy theory formation and ultimate predictability. This explains why inflation targeting[27] in developing countries is conducted within a framework of explicit or implicit targeting of the exchange rate, with or without some capital controls.

Pegging the exchange rate, however, renders the inflation targeting approach to monetary policy 'ineffective' because under a pegged exchange rate system and free capital mobility, the interest rate cannot be delinked from the pegged currency country for deployment as an independent policy instrument. This problem can be resolved somewhat if monetary policy, operating under a floating exchange rate system, is conducted using monetary targeting under capital controls. Administrative or market-based capital controls could be designed to maintain exchange rate stability, while a monetary aggregate, rather than the interest rate, can be used to stabilize the price level.

Developing countries that are not keen to stabilize the exchange rate through capital controls may conduct monetary policy based on the trinity of a flexible exchange rate, an inflation target and a monetary policy rule. Within such a framework, the expected rate of inflation acts as the anchor to prices given the perfect floating of the exchange rate.[28] Inflation targeting is not an alternative to monetary targeting. Taylor (2000) has suggested that under inflation targeting, there is nothing to inhibit substitution of a monetary aggregate for the interest rate as the operational target to achieve the target rate of inflation. Indeed, the use of a monetary aggregate may work better for countries where money and capital markets are not yet sufficiently developed. Money carries information on output and other macroeconomic developments and hence can be useful to forecasting inflation. The recent trend of downgrading the role of money and credit in monetary theory and policy has therefore come under criticism (Issing, 2013).

CONTEMPORARY ISSUES IN MONETARY POLICY

Friedman and Schwartz (1963a, p. 700), in their classic work on the history of monetary policy in the United States, noted that 'One thing of which we are confident is that the history of money will continue to have surprises in store . . . – surprises that [the] student of money and the statesman will ignore at their peril'. This section highlights some of the key contemporary issues in monetary policy in the context of the Asia-Pacific region. Given varied inflation experience, exchange rate arrangement, capital movement and monetary policy strategy, monetary policy issues vary differentially among countries and over time, depending for any given country on its stages of financial and economic development. The case studies on monetary policy in this book and in Hossain (2105) cover some of these issues given their relevance to countries of the Asia-Pacific.

Although there is a perception that the recent global and ongoing European financial crises have made monetary policy ineffective, if not redundant, the key features of monetary policy have remained intact. Some new issues in monetary policy have, however, emerged from an environment in which financial stability is identified with price stability as an objective of monetary policy. Coordination of monetary and macro-prudential policies, within a monetary policy framework, both takes on greater importance and becomes orders of magnitude more difficult when the three objectives of price stability, output stability and financial stability are pursued simultaneously (Mishkin, 2012). The following review of the key overlapping monetary policy issues in an historical context is therefore useful to comprehension of the complexity of policy formulation and implementation and macroeconomic developments in the sample countries.

Price Stability: Key or Sole Objective of Monetary Policy

Most countries now recognize that the key objective of monetary policy is price stability.[29] In reality, policymakers are not keen to deploy monetary policy to maintain price stability alone. Monetary policy is thought to stabilize the economy, which is then included in the list of monetary policy objectives. Monetary policy having both price stability and economic stabilization as objectives leads to a time-inconsistency problem that damages economic efficiency through raised volatility, while simultaneously lowering the credibility and effectiveness of monetary policy in its primary task of price stability maintenance. Targeting monetary policy at multiple objectives gives conflicting signals, confuses the public and compromises price stability by creating inflation bias (Issing, 2013). Nevertheless, many central banks maintain that these twin (conflicting) objectives of monetary policy are compatible with their charters, which are frequently broad and sufficiently vague to legitimize this conclusion.

The US-global financial crisis and its ongoing European ramifications have resulted generally in the addition of financial stability to the list of monetary policy objectives. It is increasingly recognized that the policy of benign neglect of asset price build-up is counterproductive: price stability by itself does not, and cannot, deliver financial stability. Accordingly, it is widely felt that the mandate of monetary policy should be broadened beyond price stability to encompass full macro-financial stability. Within an expanded monetary policy framework, the view that policymakers should be empowered to lean against the build-up of financial imbalances, even if near-term inflationary expectations remain anchored, is gaining ground (Mohanty, 2011). However, a problem arises when monetary policy is burdened with the further target of economic growth and stabilization. This induces a central bank to adopt measures that distort prices and creates economic inefficiency.[30] The growth objective of monetary policy represents a normative view. While the growth objective, by itself, is interpreted as fair from a societal viewpoint, the consensus view of mainstream economics is that monetary policy is inferior as a direct instrument and superior in maintaining the stability needed for real sector expansion to attain maximum efficiency. Ultimately, monetary policy-induced volatility can only interfere with economic growth and stability (Poole and Wheelock, 2008).

Financial Stability: The Role of Regulatory and Supervisory Bodies

Should, indeed, the mandate of monetary policy be broadened to include financial stability? Traditionally, monetary policy maintains price stability, while the prudential regulatory and supervisory bodies maintain financial stability (Svensson, 2011). Some administrations separate responsibility for monetary policy (run by the central bank) from prudential regulation and supervision of financial institutions (run by a separate regulatory body), while maintaining some cross-communication between the two functions. For example, Australian monetary policy is administered by the

Reserve Bank of Australia (RBA), while the chairman of the Australian Prudential Regulation Authority's (APRA) Executive Group sits on the RBA's Payments System Board.

The US-global financial crisis has raised doubt whether a central bank can remain indifferent to events that destabilize the financial sector. Monetary policy actions have their first and strongest impact on the financial system. In the event of a financial crisis, the central bank has responsibility for addressing the problems created by any contributing monetary policy actions and other domestic and external factors. Post-crisis, financial stability is viewed as the responsibility of central banks, although opinion is divided as to what extent it can be considered an objective of monetary policy. There could be a tradeoff between price stability and financial stability when the financial sector remains vulnerable to sharp fluctuations of the interest rate. Therefore, imposing this additional goal upon monetary policy is likely to confuse the public about the central bank's commitment and ability to control price stability (Mishkin, 2012). This explains why financial sector development is essential for conducting a rule-based monetary policy. A deep financial system allows the operation of a rule-based monetary policy where the interest and exchange rates float freely without causing much damage to the economy. In Australia, a sharp fluctuation of the nominal exchange rate since the 1990s has not required the RBA's intervention as the impact of the exchange rate movement on prices has been minimal.

Exchange Rate Stability: Real or Nominal or Both

Full monetary policy independence requires full international capital mobility and a free-floating currency. In developed countries with deep financial markets, exchange rate flexibility exerts benign impact on the price level and financial stability. The Australian case exemplifies the policy implications of operating under a flexible exchange rate system in a well-developed foreign-exchange market and significant capital mobility. Australia has effective monetary control and autonomy in the conduct of monetary policy. The exchange rate has, however, exhibited considerable volatility, which might have affected foreign trade and capital flows. Stevens (2006) maintains that exchange rate volatility has not damaged Australia's economy.

In contrast to Stevens's view and the experiences of Australia, policy-makers in developing countries prefer exchange rate stability as a defence against excessive accumulation of external debt and to maintain financial stability. Consequently, such countries maintain either full peg or managed float exchange rate systems. At the official level, these exchange arrangements are classified as managed or floating. At a policy level, stability of the nominal exchange rate does not guarantee stability of the real exchange rate, noted above as the policy-relevant entity, with the main threat to real exchange rate stability being high-inflation volatility. The real exchange rate affects the volumes of both trade flows and capital flows. Exchange rate stability may stabilize prices in high-inflation economies, but exchange rate flexibility is essential to absorb the periodic shocks to which developing economies are especially vulnerable. In view of all the circumstances, price stability remains the key objective of monetary policy under a flexible exchange rate system. This is achievable through rule-dominated monetary policy formulation. The volatility of real interest rates and real exchange rates under those exchange rate systems that are pegged is an issue of central policy importance for developing countries. The issue is whether the real interest rate and real exchange rate should be kept stable through intervention. For example, within a real exchange rate targeting framework that aims to keep the real exchange rate stable, both inflation and the real interest rate are unbounded, depending on capital restrictions (Calvo et al., 1995).

Asset Prices and Monetary Policy: 'Leaning Against Wind' versus 'Cleaning Bubble' (The Greenspan Doctrine)

Some challenges remain in the conduct of monetary policy under free capital mobility. While capital market liberalization is generally of greater benefit to countries at higher levels of development, most developing countries with thin financial markets have removed some restrictions on capital flows. Under a deregulated financial system, banks borrow heavily from international capital markets. They provide credits to risky borrowers and raise the risk profile of the financial system. A rapid growth of credit, if unchecked by timely regulatory action, can create asset bubbles. No policy prescription is available for the orderly deflation of an accelerating bubble. Sooner or later it must burst, causing damage to the economy.

One of the questions this raises is whether a central bank should use policy to stem the wash-up cost of bubbles by 'pricking' them early. The issue has gained prominence across the globe since the US-global financial crisis.[31] Distinction has been made between credit-led bubbles and equity-type bubbles, in which credit plays only a minor role. Friedman (1981a [1983], 1981b) argued that a credit system is generally unstable. There are two dimensions to this instability. Firstly, the demand function for credit has unstable parameters. Secondly, the supply side of the credit market undergoes frequent shifts because creditors may become over-leveraged and hence go through periods of subsequent retrenchment. Consequently, arguments are made for 'leaning against' credit bubbles and for 'mopping up' in the aftermath of equity bubbles (Mishkin, 2011).[32]

Blinder (2013) suggests that policymakers need to be cautious about 'bubble activism' on the grounds that central banks have generally no information advantage and that they lack appropriate instruments to prick bubbles. Therefore, the costs of collateral damage from monetary intervention could outweigh any benefits. Central banks may, however, have some informational and instrumental advantages in dealing with bank-based credit bubbles, through their supervisorial role in the banking system. This is the basis for the view that central banks should exercise prudential supervision over the banking system. This argument is compatible with the addition of financial stability as a monetary policy objective. Economists therefore, whether intentionally or unintentionally, advise the overburdening of monetary policy and in the process contribute to inefficiencies in monetary policy regimes.[33]

Monetary Policy Strategy

Choice of the strategy of monetary policy has critical significance for the national growth and development experience. Rule-driven monetary policy has comparative advantage in maintaining low and stable inflation, and is at its most effective when low, stable inflation is its sole target. A rule-based monetary policy is often interpreted as a commitment device. It makes monetary policy transparent with a focus on achieving a long-term objective (price stability). A central bank's 'technocratic task' then is to achieve its objective of price stability without requiring justification of its measures while remaining accountable to the public (Issing, 2013). In developing countries, both 'discretionary' exchange rate targeting (nominal or real) and monetary targeting are widely used. Some developing countries have replaced these with inflation targeting over the past decade or so. Considering the complexities of the issues involved, there is no single strategy that has a clear advantage over the others, provided that the strategy chosen is consistently followed through and continuously communicated to the public in a credible and transparent manner. The degree to which any given monetary policy strategy is appropriate depends on economic structure, stage of economic development, level of development of the financial system and the kinds of shocks typically experienced by the economy.

Exchange rate targeting has particular relevance for high-inflationary economies, since it helps to stabilize prices and hence the economy. Monetary targeting is suggested for economies that do not have developed money and capital markets but experience supply shocks more commonly than either monetary shocks or demand shocks. Inflation targeting is suggested for economies that have relatively well-developed money and capital markets capable of absorbing large fluctuations of the exchange rate. For inflation targeting to be at its most effective in minimizing and stabilizing the inflation rate, countries are required to eliminate or reverse the usual dominance of fiscal over monetary policy. Both the monetary targeting and inflation targeting strategies require flexibility of the exchange rate. If a central bank has credibility and the policy rule remains transparent, inflation targeting can be effective in anchoring inflation expectations (Svensson, 2011).

The recent literature emphasizes the importance of monetary policy credibility. It is now received theory, empirically demonstrated, that monetary policy is not effective in boosting employment in the long run. Given the benefits of price stability, the credibility of monetary policy can be enhanced by using a nominal anchor under a well-defined (transparent and routinely communicated to the public) monetary policy regime (Taylor, 1982). An institutional commitment to price stability via adoption of a nominal anchor provides a counterbalance to the time-inconsistency problem under discretionary monetary policy. A long-run policy focus dampens central bank temptation to pursue short-run expansionary policies. Commitment to a nominal anchor can encourage government in the responsible use of fiscal policy to complement, and thereby enhance the effectiveness of, a monetary policy whose key, if not the sole, target is price stability.

Exchange Rate Pegging and Boom-bust Cycles

Some smaller developing countries have consistently, over long periods, pegged their currencies to the US dollar. The policy aim is to maintain international confidence in their exchange rate stability so as to promote trade and investment (Rose, 2000). With no effective controls over capital flows associated with this exchange rate policy and financial integration, these countries sacrifice monetary policy independence, effectively importing the monetary policy of the pegged currency country. While a pegged exchange rate system provides an anchor to domestic prices, the inflation rate often remains high and exhibits high volatility. This is especially so when a country has a large non-tradable goods sector that remains exposed to both demand and supply shocks. Such a configuration can cause a boom-bust cycle if the nominal interest rate and the exchange rate are not regularly adjusted to maintain stability in both the real interest rate and the real exchange rate. Instability in the real interest and exchange rates affects saving, investment and trade flows and destabilizes real output growth. Exchange rate pegging can therefore be problematic for smaller economies, especially ones that are vulnerable to demand-side or supply-side shocks, or both. Most resource-based or oil-exporting economies of the Gulf region, under a pegged exchange rate system, have exhibited high volatility in both inflation and real output since the early 1970s.

Interest Rate Targeting and Money-demand Instability

The role of money in monetary policy has become controversial since the 1990s. The implications of a stable money-demand function are well known since Friedman (1960, 1972) proposed a constant money-growth rule to maintain low and stable inflation. The present debate on monetary policy is whether or not monetary aggregates contain information that can be used to improve inflation predictions under inflation targeting. Economists such as Woodford (2008) argue that they do not, while an alternative view is that monetary aggregates remain important and should be used to improve monetary policy (King, 2002; McCallum and Nelson, 2011). Following the global financial crisis, there is also debate whether a country under recession should follow a monetary policy rule even when the nominal interest rate approaches zero. Taylor (2012) suggests that if, in a recession, a monetary policy rule such as the Taylor rule begins to prescribe a negative target interest rate, then rule-driven policymakers should switch to a money-growth rule.

Lucas (2007) suggests that inflation targeting does not invalidate the view that inflation is a monetary phenomenon and that inflation is linked to money supply growth. Although monetary policy can be conducted without explicit reference to money, there exists in the steady state a causal linkage between money supply growth and inflation. Under inflation targeting, either monetary aggregate or the interest rate can be used to conduct monetary policy. While the use of interest rate may keep inflation at the target level on average, the volatility of money growth arising from deploying the interest rate as an instrument would be reflected in inflation volatility. McCallum and Nelson (2011) suggest that the long-run relation between money supply growth (adjusted for output growth) and inflation, derived from a money-market equilibrium condition, remains valid irrespective of whether or not the money-demand function is stable and whether the money supply is exogenous or endogenous. The role of money in monetary policy therefore cannot be ignored irrespective of the strategy of monetary policy deployed for price stability.

The question of whether the interest rate or a monetary aggregate is more effective as an instrument of monetary policy is a tactical, not a strategic, issue. When shocks are predominantly monetary, the interest rate may perform better while a monetary aggregate may perform better against real shocks, whether to demand or to supply (Poole, 1970). As Poole's analysis suggests, deployment of the interest rate as a policy instrument under inflation targeting is likely to create inflation volatility when the shocks are most commonly real. Inflation volatility has therefore become an issue in monetary policy under flexible inflation targeting as developing economies in particular often experience supply shocks and remain reluctant to adjust both the interest and exchange rates in response to inflationary developments. The resultant inflation volatility may have an independent impact on money demand (Appendix 5).

Use of the interest rate as an instrument of monetary policy, say under inflation targeting, may lead to instrument volatility (high interest rate volatility). This also makes money growth highly volatile. Money-growth volatility is not benign, it remains linked to inflation irrespective of the exchange rate regime and whether money demand is stable or not. Money-growth volatility is reflected in inflation volatility irrespective of the strategy of monetary policy. When the money-demand function is stable, it provides a basis for estimating whether the prevailing money-growth rate is compatible with the inflation target. Any monetary overhang would sooner or later translate into inflation.

Inflation Targeting and Inflation Volatility

While inflation targeting keeps the inflation rate low on average, it does not necessarily lower costly inflation persistence and volatility. By design, inflation targeting attempts to keep inflation within a range over the business cycle. Kilian and Manganelli (2007, 2008) have developed a theoretical framework on the basis of risk management in monetary policy. They observe that a central bank reacts to keep economic growth in line with inflation depending on whether the forecast distribution of inflation lies within the prearranged lower and upper limits. Their empirical results suggest that a central bank does not respond linearly to the conditional mean of inflation. Rather, it allows inflation to fluctuate within a band that remains unknown to the public. This raises inflation uncertainty, especially when the central bank's policy actions lack transparency or, more broadly, the central bank lacks policy credibility (Westelius, 2005).

Some recent theoretical work on monetary policy suggests that central banks operating under inflation targeting adjust their inflation targets non-linearly (Martin and Miles, 2004; Orphanides and Wieland, 2000). They either stabilize or stimulate output when inflation is well within the target range but pursue inflation aggressively when inflation deviates far from the target. Inflation then fluctuates widely at low level and exhibits a random, non-linear character under inflation targeting (Aksoy et al., 2006). Contrary to the expectations, inflation therefore remains highly persistent, with a near unit root characteristic.

Monetary Policy, Inflation Targeting and Supply Shocks

Monetary policy in general, and the inflation targeting strategy in particular, are problematic for economies that experience frequent supply shocks. Adverse supply shocks reduce output and raise prices. If monetary policy is to be targeted at correcting this, then conflicting policy actions are indicated. The loss of supply requires lowering the interest rate for output stabilization; while inflation control requires an increase in the interest rate. If the interest rate is increased, it may lower output that, by then lowering money demand, can raise the price level.

Some economists suggest that if a developing country experiences an adverse supply shock, it should introduce contractionary monetary policy to dampen inflationary expectations (Fender, 2012; Hossain, 2009). Monetary accommodation, following supply shocks, carries the danger of igniting inflation although a rise in the unemployment rate is costly too.

There is a third view: that of the Classicists, who would recommend a policy of neither fiscal nor monetary intervention, since, *ceteris paribus*, the economy will re-equilibrate over a few accounting periods. The optimal monetary policy therefore remains uncertain and subject to judgement (Stevens, 2003). Monetary policy is generally not effective in stabilizing output when an economy suffers from supply shocks and inflationary expectations are built in the system from such shocks. Structural reform and commercial policy may be useful for addressing supply disruptions and their impact on inflation and output. Flexibility of the interest and exchange rates would dampen price instability caused by supply shocks.

Deflation, Inflation Targeting and Zero-bound Interest Rate

Inflation targeting is viewed as a monetary policy strategy that raises policy credibility and keeps inflation low and stable. Problems emerge, however, in the event of a supply shock, as just implied, or when inflation reaches zero or turns negative. The Japanese experience since the early 1990s has raised questions over the conduct of monetary policy in a deflationary environment (Stevens, 2003). This requires some discussion on the problem of how the inflation targeting strategy of monetary policy can respond to deflation.

When an economy exhibits a deflationary trend, the authorities aggressively reduce the interest rate to raise aggregate demand, and hopefully prices, in an attempt to maintain expectations within the target range or return measured inflation to that range. If the nominal interest rate is sufficiently positive, there is scope for the central bank to lower the interest rate, at least a few times, to prevent the economy from falling into deflation. When the nominal interest rate is very low, the real interest rate could remain positive but low if there are deflationary expectations. Low real interest rates are generally expected to raise consumption and investment and hence aggregate demand.

In sharp contrast to the literature on credit rationing when the interest rate is high, low nominal interest rates do not necessarily reduce adverse selection and moral hazard problems, so that they may fail to raise the quality of lending. Low nominal interest rate may lead to excessive risk-taking by financial institutions for at least two reasons. Firstly, low interest rates raise the incentives for asset managers to search for higher yields, thereby increasing the general level of risk-taking in financial markets. Incentives may come from contractual arrangements that compensate asset managers for returns above a minimum level, often zero. With a very low nominal interest rate, only high risk investments bring high compensation for asset managers. Incentives come also from fixed-rate commitments, such as those provided by insurance companies, forcing firms to seek out higher-yielding, riskier investments. Financial risk may, furthermore, have a source in money illusion, whereby investors may treat low nominal rates as low real returns and buy riskier assets to obtain higher returns. Secondly, a low interest rate may promote excessive financial risk-taking through the mechanism of income and valuation effects. When firms borrow short and lend long, low short-term interest rates increase net interest margins. This increases the value of these firms, which raises their leverage and induces them to take on risky assets (Mishkin, 2013).

Monetary policy can encourage risk-taking in two further ways. Relatively more predictable monetary policy action lowers uncertainty, which in turn induces asset managers generally to underestimate risks. Monetary policy designed to clean up financial disruptions by lowering interest rates, named the 'Greenspan put', can fuel the moral hazard problem as financial institutions expect monetary policy to help them recover from bad investments. The Greenspan put increases systemic risk, since it is exercised only when most financial firms are in trouble simultaneously. This encourages many firms to pursue similar investment strategies, which raise the correlation of returns and lowers the advantage of asset diversification (Mishkin, 2011).

This suggests that both very high and very low interest rates raise the incidence of adverse selection and moral hazard problems. The presence of low inflation does not of itself improve the ability of economists to understand the behaviour of inflation. Low but unstable inflation makes both estimating and forecasting it harder. Demand and supply side shocks both impact short-run inflation, and central banks find the prediction of inflationary behaviour challenging.

Then how to conduct monetary policy in the face of a zero nominal interest rate? In such circumstances the Taylor rule, for example, prescribes a negative interest rate target to pursue. Taylor's counter-prescription is that the authorities switch, in a transparent and credible manner, to a constant money-growth rule. Deployment of the interest rate as an instrument of monetary policy, then, necessarily implies a zero interest rate as a potential constraint on monetary policy. There are other alternative instruments of monetary policy that can be used without referring to the nominal interest rate.

McCallum (2000) argues that a realistic policy option for a central bank in an economy when the policy rule has reached zero is to manipulate the nominal exchange rate via large-scale unsterilized foreign-exchange intervention. This option arises from the theoretical framework in which Treasury bills and base money are perfect substitutes at the zero lower bound, but money and foreign exchange are not.

When the interest rate is abandoned as an instrument of monetary policy, the central bank can switch to unconventional monetary policy instruments by adjusting the monetary base to hit the price level target. The message implicitly conveyed to the public by such a policy switch is that the central bank will do whatever is necessary to maintain price stability, including buying assets other than Treasury bills. Until 2014, central banks such as the Fed and the Bank of Japan were heavily engaged in non-traditional monetary policy, whereby they were expanding their respective monetary bases through adding to their traditional portfolio mixes a range of novel assets.

Taylor (2011, 2012) argues that whether or not such programmes ultimately work, the process of implementation has the undesirable effect of compromising the central bank's independence. The programmes are not monetary policy as conventionally defined. Rather, they are in the nature of fiscal policy actions. Other terms that could plausibly describe them include 'credit allocation policy' or 'industrial policy'. These programmes attempt to assist some firms or sectors but not others and are financed through money creation rather than through taxation or public borrowing. Unlike monetary policy, there is no established rationale that such policies should be run by an independent agency of the government. By taking these extraordinary measures, the Fed has risked losing its monetary policy independence.

A further major problem is the risk of inflation. If a central bank such as the Fed finds it politically difficult to reduce the size of its balance sheet as the economy recovers and as the level of government debt rises, then inflationary pressures will emerge. Taylor (2012) argues that rather than a discretionary use of the nominal interest rate, the requirement for rule-driven monetary policy should be legislated. This would bolster central bank independence by increasing its accountability to the public and reducing its ability to implement discretionary policy that is essentially fiscal in nature.

THIS BOOK AND *CENTRAL BANKING AND MONETARY POLICY IN MUSLIM-MAJORITY COUNTRIES*

As reviewed in an earlier section, since the US-global financial crisis, originating in the United States in 2007 and contributing to the development of the ongoing Eurozone malaise, a wide range of issues in monetary policy have come to the forefront of policy debate. The debate is primarily focused on the design and conduct of monetary policy in the United States and its implications for macroeconomic management across the globe. Significantly, most developing countries in the Asia-Pacific have differed from the United States and other developed countries in their policy responses to the global financial crises. Nevertheless, with monetary policy issues now at the forefront of economic analysis, it is at least relevant, if not critical, to review in an historical context the evolution of inflation and monetary policy across a judicious selection of countries.

Key Themes

The countries selected in this book and in Hossain (2105) for a review of inflation and monetary policy have varied characteristics with respect to the stage of development, development strategy, economic openness, inflation history and the strategy of monetary policy. Therefore, these two books do not develop a set of common themes other than highlighting some core areas for discussion in different contexts. Furthermore, rather than becoming prescriptive in most respects, some broad policy issues are reviewed and any consensus reached on those issues is highlighted.

Objectives of Monetary Policy

As highlighted in different contexts, there remains debate on whether monetary policy should attempt to achieve a single or multiple objectives. This debate is more intense in developing countries because it is difficult, if not impossible, to demarcate monetary policy from fiscal policy given the institutional and organizational constraints within underdeveloped political systems (Aghevli and Khan, 1978, 1980). Therefore, monetary policy is not generally viewed in isolation. Fiscal policy remains closely related to the design and conduct of monetary policy. This is essential for maintaining effective coordination between monetary and fiscal policies to establish macroeconomic stability. The key issue is the need for or desirability of monetary accommodation of fiscal deficits and supply shocks as they may lead to a financial, if not an economic, crisis. While fiscal policy is critical for maintaining monetary stability, achieving price stability is not an end in itself; rather, it is seen as a facilitator of steady economic growth. Poole and Wheelock (2008, p. 8) have expressed a firm view on this matter: 'Maintaining low and stable inflation is central to achieving maximum employment and the highest possible rate of economic growth. Price stability also tends to promote financial stability and enhance the central bank's ability to respond to financial disruptions that do occur.'

Problems arise when monetary policy instruments are deployed directly to promote economic growth. Even when an implicit growth objective is targeted, the authorities maintain ambiguity in the design and conduct of monetary policy. This could be 'deliberate', not due to lack of understanding of issues in monetary policy. Experiences of different countries suggest that the multiple objectives of monetary policy, including price stability, financial stability, exchange rate stability and economic growth, lead to ad hoc, faulty design of monetary policy. Most monetary policy issues therefore turn out to be political and institutional rather than technical. Ambiguity in the conduct of monetary policy then becomes acute when monetary policymakers take into account the 'myopic preferences' of political leaders and create a time-inconsistency problem that undermines the central bank's autonomy and its ability to control inflation.

The recent financial crises across different regions have highlighted the importance of financial stability. Although monetary policy has some impact on financial stability, there is debate whether financial stability should be included in the list of monetary policy objectives. Central banks generally have a supervisorial and regulatory responsibility of both banking and non-banking financial institutions. It is not clear how such responsibility can be reconciled with monetary policy for price stability. Although price stability is important for maintaining financial stability, it may not be sufficient because most financial institutions remain exposed to both domestic and external shocks. As most conventional banks are vulnerable to shocks and the sharp movements of the interest rate and exchange rate, there is increasing demand for equity-based financial products. Islamic banks and financial institutions have therefore gained importance in recent years as they provide equity-based and morally, ethically based financial products.

Monetary Policy Strategy

Although many issues in the choice of monetary policy strategy for price stability are yet to be resolved, there is broad consensus that a rule-based monetary policy is superior to discretionary monetary policy. The recent experiences of the United States and Japan suggest that discretionary monetary policy carries the danger of a boom-bust cycle (Ito, 2010). There is, however, no clear choice among the rule-based monetary policy alternatives. A pegged exchange rate-oriented monetary policy is generally considered appropriate for countries that are inflation-prone. The risk is that sustained exchange rate pegging may lead to a boom-bust cycle in an environment when there are large-scale capital flows. Monetary targeting and inflation targeting are considered two alternatives under a flexible exchange rate system. There is no clear choice between these two. The key factor that determines the effectiveness of monetary policy in lowering inflation is the credibility of the central bank in its commitment and ability to maintain low and stable inflation. A rule-based monetary policy generally reduces the time-inconsistency problem and raises the credibility of a central bank.

The main criticism against a rule-based monetary policy is that it may appear rigid and could be costly in terms of a loss of output if inflation is controlled strictly. Friedman (1960) advocated a constant money-growth rule to avoid policy-induced economic uncertainty. He did not consider such a rule optimal but argued it to be necessary for transparency and accountability of central banks in their conduct of monetary policy. McCallum (1989) has suggested a variant of the money-growth rule that allows adjustment of the money-growth rate for any shift in the velocity of money. As the velocity of money may exhibit conditional volatility, it can be accommodated in the money-growth rule to keep inflation low and stable over the long run. Such an adjustment is non-activist; it does not represent an attempt to achieve any pre-set real economic goals (Appendix 10).

Inflation Volatility and Economic Growth

Irrespective of the strategy of monetary policy, one desirable goal of monetary policy is that inflation remains low and stable, not low but unstable. In addition to supply shocks, inflation volatility may originate from the particular strategy of monetary policy adopted to achieve a single or multiple objectives. Supply shocks could be random and raise inflation volatility around a target level that could be maintained over the medium run. Policy-induced inflation volatility is added to volatility originating from any unavoidable exogenous shocks and hence irreducible. Sustained inflation volatility is created when the interest rate and the exchange rate are controlled and when there is monetary accommodation of both demand and supply shocks. Controls over interest and exchange rates prevent the economy from adjusting in the event of supply shocks. Further, a monetary accommodation of supply shocks links the inflationary expectations with shocks that may not otherwise exist under a rule-based monetary policy strategy.

A non-transparent and loose form of monetary targeting may lead to excessively volatile money growth under a pegged or managed float exchange rate system. This is usually the case in most developing countries that operate under a pegged or managed float exchange rate system. In these countries, the monetary base remains linked to balance-of-payments. Large and speculative capital flows, if not effectively sterilized, lead to monetary growth volatility. Furthermore, large budget deficits (often procyclical) lead to excessive money growth and make the authorities' stance on monetary policy unpredictable. Consequently, as inflationary expectations change, inflation becomes unstable and hence unpredictable.

A common theme in the literature is that inflation volatility is costly and should be kept to the 'irreducible' minimum. High inflation and its volatility create economic uncertainty that lowers real investment and retards economic growth. Friedman (2006) argued that there could be a positive, not negative, relation between inflation volatility and economic-growth volatility. As they reflect a sub-optimal monetary policy, it is possible to reduce volatilities of inflation and output growth by improving the design and conduct of monetary policy (Appendix 4).

Inflation volatility is in particular a problem for developing countries. As the interest rate and the exchange rate are not often determined by market forces, the high volatility of inflation in these countries leads to high and volatile real interest rate and real exchange rate (Appendix 6). This makes the people hostile towards both the government and central bank. The central bank then becomes ineffective in controlling inflation and maintaining financial stability. Consequently, high volatility of inflation adversely affects economic growth.

Exchange Rate Flexibility

Monetary policy independence can be gained under a flexible exchange rate system. Monetary policy independence can also be gained under a fixed pegged exchange rate system if there are strict capital controls. Exchange rate flexibility is considered essential for absorbing shocks to an open economy. The main concern is whether a flexible exchange rate system leads to excessive volatility of the exchange rate. Exchange rate volatility in developing countries reflects thin and inefficient foreign-exchange markets that operate unpredictably when there are large-scale capital flows in an uncertain environment. Although the pull factors may be important, aggressive monetary policy in both developed and developing countries makes capital markets unstable. Nevertheless, there is the suggestion that a freely floating exchange rate system is not appropriate for developing countries. A fixed exchange rate system is not again a viable alternative as it may lead to boom-bust cycles when there are no effective restrictions on capital flows. Since the East-Southeast Asian financial crisis of the late 1990s, it is suggested that a managed float exchange rate system, with market-based capital controls, suits a developing economy better. Krugman (1991) suggests that a target zone for the exchange rate is compatible with the uncovered interest rate parity.

Money Growth and Inflation

The money-demand function is generally found to be stable in most countries in the Asia-Pacific. A long-run causal linkage also exists between money supply growth and inflation. Despite these findings, there is an apparent neglect of monetary aggregate in some countries in the design and conduct of monetary policy. To the extent that inflation is determined by money growth, inflation volatility reflects money-growth volatility. Inflation volatility in turn makes the exchange rate volatile. High volatility of inflation affects money demand. This may further raise the volatilities of inflation and the interest rate.

The monetary aggregate and its growth rate have therefore remained important in monetary analysis. A money-growth rule-based monetary policy has some useful properties that can improve the conduct of monetary policy for price stability (McCallum, 2012). Issing (2013) argues in favour of a money-based monetary policy following the US-global financial crisis. Although under inflation targeting the interest rate has been the preferred choice as monetary policy instrument, it is unwise to ignore monetary aggregate to maintain long-run price stability. This is especially the case for developing countries. Even in developed countries the linkage between money growth and inflation is more robust than the linkage between the interest rate and inflation. For example, the Reserve Bank of New Zealand (RBNZ, 1985, p. 627) notes that 'empirical linkages between interest rates and inflation are less well-established than linkages between monetary growth and inflation'. Similarly, Wallich (1985, p. 40) suggested that the 'impact on inflation of a given level of interest rates, nominal or real . . . is far less predictable' than any relationship between inflation and prior monetary growth (McCallum and Nelson, 2011).

Capital Flows, Monetary Policy and Boom-bust Cycles

Foreign capital is highly beneficial for developing countries. Large-scale foreign-capital flows to these countries, however, can create macroeconomic problems. Frankel (2011) has identified three types of problems associated with large-scale capital flows to developing countries. Firstly, capital often flows uphill, that is, from developing to developed countries. Secondly, capital flows are pro-cyclical. Thirdly, capital flows lead to financial crisis.

Recent financial crises across the globe suggest that monetary policy becomes difficult to conduct in an environment that leads to large-scale capital flows. For example, one of the policy measures available for policymakers in developing countries is to sterilize foreign-capital flows to neutralize their impact on the monetary base. Although this could be effective in the short run, they create a quasi-fiscal problem for the central bank that sells government bonds and consequently the interest rate rises. Higher interest rates encourage more foreign capital and create an overheated economy. This problem can be avoided somewhat under a flexible exchange rate system. If this is not adequate, market-based capital control measures may be introduced.

Side-by-side, the financial system would need strengthening, including tightening of prudential supervision and regulation to prevent banks and other financial institutions from taking excessive risk that triggers a credit boom. Aggressive monetary policy actions in developed countries also trigger capital flows to developing countries. Although capital inflows are relatively easy to control, there are no effective controls over capital outflows. Foreign investors generally demonstrate herd behaviour and their sentiment on investment in emerging countries change quickly, without showing much relation with economic fundamentals. How to conduct monetary policy under the condition of freely mobile capital therefore remains an important issue for developing countries.

NOTES

1. Blanchard (1990, p. 785) writes: 'movements in money lead to a slow adjustment of prices and wages, a long-lasting effect on output and little or no movement in real wage along the way'. Here Blanchard argues that money is 'long-run' non-neutral, thereby

flying in the face of the well-established, even in 1990, mainstream theoretical and empirical consensus that money is neutral in the long run. The main policy implication of long-run monetary neutrality is simple and powerful: those short-run 'surprise' policy expansions of the money supply may impose larger economic costs by creating boom-bust cycles than any benefits they confer. For historical discussion on money neutrality, see Patinkin (1972, 1992) and references therein.

2. Inflation uncertainty is usually measured in statistical form. If inflation is a stationary process, then it will have constant unconditional mean and variance. The question is whether the irreducible level of inflation variance, determined mostly by demand and supply shocks, can be brought to the minimum. The conditional variance of inflation may vary widely and change with the rate of inflation. When inflation exhibits high volatility, it cannot be predicted easily. Consequently, the actual outcome of inflation may 'surprise' markets, causing unanticipated capital gains and losses. In such an environment, inflation has real effects via changes in the relative preferences for real assets vis-à-vis financial assets. Real assets in particular become preferred inflation hedgers in an inflationary environment. A consequence is financial disintermediation, in which the financial sector is dominated by fixed-currency value assets. For detailed discussion on this and related issues, see Cagan and Lipsey (1978).
3. For details, see four volumes of *Handbook of Monetary Economics* (Friedman and Hahn, 1990; Friedman and Woodford, 2011).
4. Nelson and Schwartz (2008) have made a review of the contributions of Friedman and his collaborators in monetary theory and policy. Their article lists Friedman's publications in monetary theory and policy.
5. Keynesian economists maintain that monetary expansion is not effective in raising output during recession. An IS-LM model is employed to illustrate this proposition. Within this modelling approach, when the nominal interest rate falls to a very low level, the LM curve becomes highly elastic. This reflects a situation termed the (Keynesian) liquidity trap. In addition, the IS curve is assumed interest inelastic. Under these conditions, monetary expansion exerts little or no effects on either the interest rate or output. Keynesians therefore recommend expansionary fiscal policy, which they expect will shift the IS curve outwards, raising output without raising prices or the interest rate. Monetarists argue, on the contrary, that even at a very low interest rate, monetary expansion raises output through the real balance effect. Higher inflationary expectations also raise the demand for those assets, both real and financial, which are interest-sensitive. For further discussion, see Hossain and Chowdhury (1998).
6. New Classicists argue that, under rational expectations, anticipated monetary expansion does not have any significant impact on output. For details, see Barro (2008).
7. If policymakers do not possess more information than the public, unanticipated monetary changes become uncorrelated with other shocks. This increases noise and makes signal extraction more difficult for individuals and firms, lowering the allocative efficiency of the price system. When policymakers possess more information than the public, money can be used to offset other shocks and improve welfare. However, a more efficient way of achieving this outcome is to make such information available to the public (Blanchard, 1990).
8. Political, institutional and pragmatic reasons are used to justify Friedman's (1960) choice of a constant money-growth rule. It was not meant to be mechanical without scope for modification. The ultimate objective of the money-growth rule was to make monetary policy transparent and predictable, leaving out policymakers' discretion in changing policy stance on political and other grounds. Central banks are viewed as mysterious institutions, having archaic rules and procedures for monetary management, credit allocations and banking regulations. Moreover, central bankers are not elected and remain unaccountable for most of their actions. A constant money-growth rule is therefore considered an improvement to reduce economic volatility over discretionary monetary policy that makes monetary policy non-transparent and ineffective (Friedman, 1962).

9. Some of these studies were undertaken at the University of Chicago within the auspices of the famous Money and Banking Workshop. The monetary interpretation of inflation contradicted with the then prevailing view that inflation in developing countries originates from structuralist sources, often termed the structuralist view on inflation (Corbo, 1974).
10. This included a monetary interpretation of hyperinflations in Europe and other regions (Cagan, 1956; Sachs and Larrain, 1993).
11. Judd and Scadding (1982) have provided the statistical conditions for stability of a money-demand function. Friedman (1956b) refers to Cagan's (1956) study of hyperinflation as an extreme test of stability of money-demand function in a highly unstable condition. Also, see Hossain (2009) for an elaboration of this concept in the context of developing countries of the Asia-Pacific region.
12. In determining the direction of causality, exogeneity of the money supply is determined by observing historical events and statistical techniques. In hyperinflationary episodes, a feedback relation exists between money and prices. McCallum and Nelson (2011) suggest that causality between money growth and inflation does not require the existence of a stable money-demand function or exogenous money supply. A causal relationship between money growth and inflation is given a meaningful long-run interpretation within a cointegration and error-correction modelling framework for variables such as money, output, prices and exchange rates.
13. There is no general agreement that financial deregulation and reforms led to instability in the money-demand function. Various studies suggest one-off change in money holdings due to financial reforms. The long-run money-demand function remained broadly stable although there was some structural change in the money-demand relationship in a deregulated environment as the interest and exchange rates started to play a role in the money-demand function (Hossain, 2009; Laidler, 1986).
14. For further discussion, see Poole (1970) and McCallum and Nelson (2011).
15. If a central bank increases the growth rate of the money supply to lower the rate of unemployment, it may work only if the growth rate of the money supply is significantly higher than what the people expected and then used for entering into wage contracts. This may lower the rate of unemployment in the short run until the people find out the truth and adjust their behaviour and renegotiate wage contracts. Lucas (1996) has summarized this proposition in his Nobel Lecture. Anticipated monetary expansion has an inflation tax effect. It adds inflation premium to the nominal interest rate. In the recent literature, unanticipated monetary changes are shown to have liquidity effects that benefit liquidity-constrained firms who are mostly active in financial markets (Fuerst, 1992; Grossman and Weiss, 1983; Lucas, 1990; Rotemberg, 1984).
16. As Cagan and Lipsey (1978) suggest, instability in inflation in a large part is due to gyrations of aggregate demand management policy in which the economy is first restrained to reduce inflation and then stimulated to overcome the contractionary effect of the restraint imposed earlier.
17. See Buchanan and Wagner (1977), Buchanan et al. (1987) and Buckle and Stemp (1991).
18. See Blackburn and Christensen (1989), Schelling (1982) and Taylor (1982).
19. Most monetary policy rules are not intended to be used in a mechanical way. They transparently and credibly communicate to the public monetary policy decisions and their intended impacts.
20. See Diamond (1982), Cooper and John (1988), Benhabib and Farmer (1994) and Farmer and Guo (1994).
21. Monetary stability is generally defined in a way that is consistent with both internal and external balances. In a limited sense, monetary stability and price stability are used synonymously.
22. The Tinbergen principle requires the number of independent instruments to be equal to the number of objectives to be achieved (Sachs and Larrain, 1993). Monetary policy has a comparative advantage in achieving price stability rather than a real objective alone or jointly with other policies. This indicates that monetary policy should be used to achieve price stability rather than economic growth or employment.

23. This refers to the transmission mechanisms of monetary policy that vary from country to country depending on the structural characteristics and institutional arrangements of the economy.
24. Due to the space constraint, no panel regression analysis is conducted for this study.
25. High volatility of real interest and exchange rates is found to affect real output and its growth under a pegged exchange rate system (Ghosh et al., 1995).
26. Three desirable goals of economic policy are exchange rate stability, monetary policy independence and international capital mobility, implying no sovereign portfolio capital flow controls.
27. The prerequisites for inflation targeting include both a freely floating exchange rate system and developed money and capital markets.
28. One strategy to avoid the open-economy trilemma is to adopt a managed floating exchange rate system and then attempt to achieve all the three objectives simultaneously but only partially. Whether this would improve macroeconomic performance is difficult to predict as such an approach to economic policy creates ambiguity and uncertainty. Most developing countries have introduced managed float, mostly due to 'fear of floating'. The finance ministers and governors of central banks are generally blamed for currency devaluation (Frankel, 2011). Although this was the case until the 1990s, the political sensitivity of exchange rate movement has apparently diminished under the present deregulated environment.
29. There is no clear definition of price stability. Is it zero inflation or 1 to 2 per cent inflation or a much higher rate of inflation? Some economists suggest optimal inflation as a rate that maximizes output or keeps the unemployment rate lowest in a way that avoids a zero-bound nominal interest rate. Schmitt-Grohe and Uribe (2011) have summarized monetary theories and suggest that the optimal rate of inflation ranges from minus the real rate of interest to numbers insignificantly different from zero.
30. The suggested measures include credit allocation and rationing, manipulation of interest rates and exchange rates and capital controls. These measures create financial repression, which retards saving, investment and economic growth (Fry, 1998).
31. Alan Greenspan, former Chairman of the Federal Reserve System, developed the idea that monetary policy should not lean against any asset price bubble but should clean up any mess that is created after the bubble bursts. This doctrine is established on five elements. Firstly, asset price bubbles are difficult to identity. Secondly, any sharp rise in interest rate to prick the bubble may not be effective because the buyers of assets expect higher and higher rates of return from buying bubble-driven assets. Thirdly, many asset prices indicate bubble behaviour at a particular point in time. As monetary policy instruments could be blunt to deal with such situation, monetary policy actions may affect all asset prices rather than solely those in the bubble. Fourthly, a sharp rise in the interest rate may cause a bubble to burst severely and suddenly. This may cause major damage to the economy. Fifthly, as long as policymakers respond in a timely fashion and in an aggressive form after the asset bubble bursts, the harmful effects of a bursting bubble can be kept to a manageable level (Mishkin, 2013).
32. Mishkin (2012) suggests that monetary policy leaning against credit bubbles can be viewed as taking out insurance against the high costs of bubbles when they burst.
33. In Australia, the RBA, for example, takes into account asset prices in its formulation of monetary policy. Over the past decade or so, housing bubbles and commodity booms triggered the RBA to raise the interest rate in a credible fashion to avoid creating boom-bust cycles. The RBA considers such actions pre-emptive and necessary to maintain the economy along the steady path. In the United States, the pre-crisis view was, however, that the housing bubble should continue its course.

REFERENCES

Aghevli, B.B. and M.S. Khan (1978), 'Government budget deficits and inflationary process in developing countries', *IMF Staff Papers*, **25**, 383–416.

Aghevli, B.B. and M.S. Khan (1980), 'Credit policy and the balance of payments in developing countries', in W. Coates and D. Khatkhate (eds), *Money and Monetary Policy in Less Developed Countries: A Survey of Issues and Evidence*, Oxford: Pergamon Press, pp. 347–70.

Aksoy, Y., A. Orphanides, D. Small, V. Weiland and D. Wilcox (2006), 'A quantitative exploration of the opportunistic approach to disinflation', *Journal of Monetary Economics*, **53**, 1877–93.

Alesina, A. and A. Stella (2011), 'The politics of monetary policy', in B.M. Friedman and M. Woodford (eds), *Handbook of Monetary Economics*, Vol. 3B, Amsterdam: Elsevier Science, pp. 1001–54.

Alvarez, F., R.E. Lucas, Jr and W.E. Weber (2001), 'Interest rates and inflation', *American Economic Review*, **9**(2), 219–25.

Ball, L. (2011), 'The performance of alternative monetary regimes', in B.M. Friedman and M. Woodford (eds), *Handbook of Monetary Economics*, Vol. 3B, Amsterdam: Elsevier Science, pp. 1303–43.

Barro, R.J. (1993), *Macroeconomics*, New York: John Wiley and Sons.

Barro, R.J. (2008), *Macroeconomics: A Modern Approach*, Mason, OH: Thomson-South Western.

Benhabib, J. and R. Farmer (1994), 'Indeterminancy and increasing returns', *Journal of Economic Theory*, **63**, 19–41.

Bils, M. and P. Klenow (2004), 'Some evidence on the importance of sticky prices', *Journal of Political Economy*, **112**, 947–85.

Blackburn, K. and M. Christensen (1989), 'Monetary theory and policy credibility', *Journal of Economic Literature*, **27**(1), 1–45.

Blanchard, O.J. (1990), 'Why does money affect output? A survey', in B.M. Friedman and F.H. Hahn (eds), *Handbook of Monetary Economics*, Vol. II, Amsterdam: Elsevier Science, pp. 779–835.

Blinder, A.S. (2013), *After the Music Stopped. The Financial Crisis, the Response and the Work Ahead*, New York: Penguin Press.

Boivin, J., M.T. Kiley and F.S. Mishkin (2011), 'How has the monetary transmission mechanisms evolved over time?', in B.M. Friedman and M. Woodford (eds), *Handbook of Monetary Economics*, Vol.3A, Amsterdam: Elsevier Science, pp. 369–422.

Buchanan, J. and R. Wagner (1977), *Democracy in Deficit*, New York: Academic Press.

Buchanan, J., C. Rowley and R. Tollison (1987), *Deficits*, Oxford: Basil Blackwell.

Buckle, R. and P. Stemp (1991), 'Reserve Bank autonomy and the credibility of monetary policy: a game theoretic approach', *New Zealand Economic Papers*, **25**(1), 51–85.

Cagan, P. (1956), 'The monetary dynamics of hyperinflation', in M. Friedman (ed.), *Studies in the Quantity Theory of Money*, Chicago, IL: University of Chicago Press, pp. 25–117.

Cagan, P. and R.E. Lipsey (1978), *The Financial Effects of Inflation*, Cambridge, MA: Ballinger Publishing.

Calvo, G.A., C.M. Reinhart and C.A. Vegh (1995), 'Targeting the real exchange rate: theory and evidence', *Journal of Development Economics*, **47**, 97–133.
Cline, W. and S. Weintraub (eds) (1981), *World Inflation and Developing Countries*, Washington, DC: Brookings Institution.
Cooper, R. and A. John (1988), 'Coordinating coordination failures in Keynesian models', *Quarterly Journal of Economics*, **103**, 441–63.
Corbo, V.L. (1974), *Inflation in Developing Countries: An Econometric Study of Chilean Inflation*, Amsterdam: North-Holland Publishing.
Corbo, V.L. and J. de Melo (1987), 'Lessons from Southern cone policy reforms', *World Bank Research Observer*, **2**, 111–42.
Cukierman, A. and S.B. Webb (1995), 'Political influence on the central bank: international evidence', *World Bank Economic Review*, **9**(3), 397–423.
Cukierman, A., S. Edwards and G. Tabellini (1992), 'Seigniorage and political instability', *American Economic Review*, **82**(3), 537–55.
Diamond, P. (1982), 'Aggregate demand in search equilibrium', *Journal of Political Economy*, **90**, 881–94.
Dornbusch, R. (1993), *Stabilization, Debt, and Reform: Policy Analysis for Developing Countries*, New York: Harvester Wheatsheaf.
Farmer, R. and J. Guo (1994), 'Real business cycles and the animal spirits hypothesis', *Journal of Economic Theory*, **63**, 42–72.
Fender, J. (2012), *Monetary Policy*, New York: John Wiley and Sons.
Frankel, J. (2011), 'Monetary policy in emerging markets', in B.M. Friedman and M. Woodford (eds), *Handbook of Monetary Economics*, Vol. 3B, Amsterdam: Elsevier Science, pp. 1439–520.
Friedman, B.M. and F.H. Hahn (eds) (1990), *Handbook of Monetary Economics*, Vols I and II, Amsterdam: Elsevier Science.
Friedman, B.M. and M. Woodford (eds) (2011), *Handbook of Monetary Economics*, Vols 3A and 3B, Amsterdam: Elsevier Science.
Friedman, M. (1956a), 'The quantity theory of money: a restatement', in M. Friedman (ed.), *Studies in the Quantity Theory of Money*, Chicago, IL: University of Chicago Press, pp. 3–21.
Friedman, M. (ed.) (1956b), *Studies in the Quantity Theory of Money*, Chicago, IL: University of Chicago Press.
Friedman, M. (1959), 'The demand for money – some theoretical and empirical results', *Journal of Political Economy*, **67**, 327–51.
Friedman, M. (1960), *A Program for Monetary Stability*, New York: Fordham University Press.
Friedman, M. (1962), 'Should there be an independent monetary authority?', in L.B Yeager (ed.), *In Search of a Monetary Constitution*, Cambridge, MA: Harvard University Press, pp. 219–43.
Friedman, M. (1968), 'The role of monetary policy', *American Economic Review*, **58**(1), 1–17.
Friedman, M. (1969), 'The optimum quantity of money', in M. Friedman (ed.), *The Optimum Quantity of Money and Other Essays*, Chicago, IL: Alpine Publishing, pp. 51–67.
Friedman, M. (1972), 'The case of a monetary rule', *Newsweek*, 7 February, 67.
Friedman, M. (1973), *Money and Economic Development*, Toronto: Lexington Books.
Friedman, M. (1981a), 'A memorandum to the Fed', *Wall Street Journal*, 30 January,

20, reprinted in M. Friedman (1983), *Bright Promises, Dismal Performance: An Economist's Protest*, New York: Harcourt Brace Jovanovich, pp. 241–9.

Friedman, M. (1981b), 'An address by Professor Milton Friedman, April 22, 1981', Buttle Wilson and Broadbank Corporation, Wellington, New Zealand.

Friedman, M. (1983), *Bright Promises, Dismal Performance: An Economist's Protest*, New York: Harcourt Brace Jovanovich.

Friedman, M. (1991), *Monetarist Economics*, Oxford: Basil Blackwell.

Friedman, M. (1992), 'Quantity theory of money', in P. Newman, M. Milgate and J. Eatwell (eds), *The New Palgrave Dictionary of Money and Finance*, Vol. III, London: Macmillan, pp. 247–64.

Friedman, M. (2006), 'Tradeoffs in monetary policy', Unpublished manuscript, Stanford University, available at http://web.stanford.edu/~johntayl/Friedman2006.pdf (accessed on 19 March 2015).

Friedman, M. and A.J. Schwartz (1963a), *A Monetary History of the United States, 1867–1960*, Princeton, NJ: Princeton University Press.

Friedman, M. and A.J. Schwartz (1963b), 'Money and business cycles', *Review of Economics and Statistics*, **45**, February, 32–64.

Fry, M. (1998), *Money, Interest, and Banking in Economic Development*, Baltimore, MD: Johns Hopkins University Press.

Fuerst, T. (1992), 'Liquidity, loanable funds, and real activity', *Journal of Monetary Economics*, **29**, 3–24.

Ghosh, A.R., A.M. Gulde and H.C. Wolf (1995), 'Currency boards: more than a quick fix?', *Economic Policy*, **31**, October, 269–335.

Goldfeld, S.M. and D.E. Sichel (1990), 'The demand for money', in B.M. Friedman and F.H. Hahn (eds), *Handbook of Monetary Economics*, Amsterdam: Elsevier Science, pp. 299–356.

Grossman, S. and L. Weiss (1983), 'A transactions-based model of the monetary transmission mechanism', *American Economic Review*, **73**, 871–80.

Hossain, A. (2009), *Central Banking and Monetary Policy in the Asia-Pacific*, Cheltenham, UK and Northampton, MA, USA: Edward Elgar.

Hossain, A. (2015), *Central Banking and Monetary Policy in Muslim-Majority Countries*, Cheltenham, UK and Northampton, MA, USA: Edward Elgar.

Hossain, A. and A. Chowdhury (1998), *Open-Economy Macroeconomics for Developing Countries*, Cheltenham, UK and Northampton, MA, USA: Edward Elgar.

Hume, D. (1752), 'Of money', 'Of interest', and 'Of the balance of trade', reprinted in E. Rotwein (ed.) (1970), *Writings on Economics*, Madison, WI: University of Wisconsin Press, pp. 33–77.

Issing, O. (2013), 'A new paradigm for monetary policy', *International Finance*, **16**(2), 273–88.

Ito, T. (2010), 'Monetary policy and financial stability: is inflation targeting passe?', ADB Economics Working Paper Series No. 206, Manila, the Philippines.

Judd, J.P. and J.L. Scadding (1982), 'The search for a stable money demand function: a survey of the post-1973 literature', *Journal of Economic Literature*, **20**, 993–1023.

Kilian, L. and S. Manganelli (2007), 'Quantifying the risk of deflation', *Journal of Money, Credit and Banking*, **39**, 561–90.

Kilian, L. and S. Manganelli (2008), 'The central banker as a risk manager: estimating the Federal Reserve's preferences under Greenspan', *Journal of Money, Credit and Banking*, **40**, 1103–29.

King, M. (2002), 'No money, no inflation – the role of money in the economy', *Bank of England Quarterly Bulletin*, Summer, 162–77.
Klenow, P.J. and B.A. Malin (2011), 'Microeconomic evidence on price-setting', in B.M. Friedman and M. Woodford (eds), *Handbook of Monetary Economics*, Vol. 3A, Amsterdam: Elsevier Science, pp. 231–84.
Krugman, P.R. (1991), 'Target zones and exchange rate dynamics', *Quarterly Journal of Economics*, **106**(3), 669–82.
Kydland, F.E. and E.C. Prescott (1982), 'Time to build and aggregate fluctuations', *Econometrica*, **51**, November, 1345–70.
Laidler, D. (1986), 'What do we really know about monetary policy?', *Australian Economic Papers*, June, 1–16.
Laidler, D. (1993), *The Demand for Money – Theories, Evidence and Problems*, New York: Harper and Row.
Lucas, R.E., Jr (1980), 'Two illustrations of the quantity theory of money', *American Economic Review*, **70**, 1005–14.
Lucas, R.E., Jr (1990), 'Liquidity and interest rates', *Journal of Economic Theory*, **50**, 237–64.
Lucas, R.E., Jr (1996), 'Noble lecture: monetary neutrality', *Journal of Political Economy*, **104**, August, 661–82.
Lucas, R.E., Jr (2007), 'Mortgages and monetary policy', *Wall Street Journal*, September, available at http://www.wsj.com/articles/SB119017085710932141 (accessed 19 March 2015).
Marquis, M. (1996), *Monetary Theory and Policy*, New York: West Publishing Company.
Martin, C. and C. Miles (2004), 'Modelling monetary policy: inflation targets in practice', *Economica*, **71**, 209–21.
McCallum, B.T. (1989), *Monetary Economics: Theory and Policy*, New York: Macmillan.
McCallum, B.T. (1990), 'Inflation: theory and evidence', in B.M. Friedman and F.H. Hahn (eds), *Handbook of Monetary Economics*, Vol. 2, Amsterdam: North-Holland, pp. 963–1012.
McCallum, B.T. (2000), 'Theoretical analysis regarding a zero lower bound on nominal interest rates', *Journal of Money, Credit and Banking*, **32**, 870–904.
McCallum, B.T. (2012), 'The role of money in New-Keynesian models', Banco Central De Reserve Del Peru, Working Paper Series 2012–019.
McCallum, B.T. and E. Nelson (2011), 'Money and inflation: some critical issues', in B.M. Friedman and M. Woodford (eds), *Handbook of Monetary Economics*, Vol. 3A, Amsterdam: Elsevier Science, pp. 97–153.
Meltzer, A.H. (1998), 'Monetarism: the issues and the outcome', *Atlantic Economic Journal*, **26**, March, 8–31.
Meltzer, A.H. (2012), 'What's wrong with the Federal Reserve?', *Wall Street Journal*, 9 July.
Mishkin, F.S. (2011), 'Over the cliff: from the subprime to the global financial crisis', *Journal of Economic Perspectives*, **25**(1), 49–70.
Mishkin, F.S. (2012), 'Central banking after the crisis', Paper presented at the 16th annual conference of the Central Bank of Chile, Santiago, 15–16 November.
Mishkin, F.S. (2013), *The Economics of Money, Banking, and Financial Markets*, New York: Pearson Education.
Mohanty, D. (2011), 'Lessons for monetary policy from global financial crisis: an

emerging market perspective', Paper presented at the Central Banks conference of the Bank of Israel, Jerusalem, 1 April, available at http://www.rbi.org.in/scripts/BS_SpeechesView.aspx?Id=557 (accessed 19 March 2015).
Nelson, E. and A.J. Schwartz (2008), 'The impact of Milton Friedman on modern monetary economics: setting the record straight on Paul Krugman's "who was Milton Friedman?"', *Journal of Monetary Economics*, **55**(4), 835–56.
Orphanides, A. and V. Wieland, (2000), 'Inflation zone targeting', *European Economic Review*, **44**(7), 1351–87.
Patinkin, D. (1972), 'On the short run non-neutrality of money in the quantity theory', *Banca Nazionale del Lavoro Quarterly Review*, **100**, March, 3–22.
Patinkin, D. (1992), 'Neutrality of money', in P. Newman, M. Milgate and J. Eatwell (eds), *The New Palgrave Dictionary of Money and Finance*, London: Macmillan, pp. 16–23.
Poole, W. (1970), 'Optimal choice of monetary policy instruments in a simple stochastic macro model', *Quarterly Journal of Economics*, **84**(2), 197–216.
Poole, W. and D.C. Wheelock (2008), 'Stable prices, stable economy', *The Regional Economist*, 5–9 January.
Prescott, E. (1986), 'Theory ahead of business cycle measurement', *Federal Reserve Bank of Minneapolis Quarterly Review*, Fall, 9–22.
RBNZ (Reserve Bank of New Zealand) (1985), 'Monetary policy: some questions and answers', *Reserve Bank of New Zealand Bulletin*, **48**, November, 626–9.
Rose, A. (2000), 'One money, one market: estimating the effect of common currencies on trade', *Economic Policy*, **15**(30), 8–45.
Rotemberg, J. (1984), 'A monetary equilibrium model with transactions costs', *Journal of Political Economy*, **92**, 40–58.
Sachs, J. and F. Larrain (1993), *Macroeconomics in the Global Economy*, New York: Harvester Wheatsheaf.
Sargent, T.J. and N. Wallace (1975), 'Rational expectations, the optimal monetary instrument, and the optimal money supply rule', *Journal of Political Economy*, **83**(2), 241–54.
Schelling, T. (1982), 'Establishing credibility: strategic considerations', *American Economic Review*, **72**(2), 77–80.
Schmitt-Grohe, S. and M. Uribe (2011), 'The optimal rate of inflation', in B.M. Friedman and M. Woodford (eds), *Handbook of Monetary Economics*, Vol. 3B, Amsterdam: Elsevier Science, pp. 653–722.
Sorensen, P. and H.J. Whitta-Jacobsen (2005), *Introduction to Advanced Macroeconomics: Growth and Business Cycles*, New York: McGraw Hill.
Stevens, G. (2003), 'Structural change and the conduct of monetary policy', Speech given at the Federal Reserve Bank of Kansas City Economic Symposium, Jackson Hole, 30 August, available at http://www.rba.gov.au/speeches/2003/sp-dg-300803.html (accessed 19 March 2015).
Stevens, G. (2006), 'Capital flows and monetary policy', *Reserve Bank of Australia Bulletin*, 19–25 October.
Svensson, L.E.O. (2011), 'Inflation targeting', in B.M. Friedman and M. Woodford (eds), *Handbook of Monetary Economics*, Vol. 3B, Amsterdam: Elsevier Science, pp. 1237–302.
Taylor, J.B. (1982), 'Establishing credibility: a rational expectations viewpoint', *American Economic Review*, **72**(2), 81–5.
Taylor, J.B. (1993), 'Discretion versus policy rules in practice', *Carnegie-Rochester Conference Series on Public Policy*, **39**(1), 195–214.

Taylor, J.B. (2000), 'Using monetary policy rules in emerging market economies', Paper presented at the 75th Anniversary Conference on Stabilization and Monetary Policy: The International Experience, Bank of Mexico, 14–15 November.

Taylor, J.B. (2011), 'An empirical analysis of the revival of fiscal activism in the 2000s', *Journal of Economic Literature*, **49**, 686–702.

Taylor, J.B. (2012), 'Monetary policy rules work and discretion doesn't: a tale of two era', *Journal of Money, Credit and Banking*, **44**(6), 1017–32.

Taylor, J.B. (2013), 'The effectiveness of central bank independence versus policy rules', available at http://www.johnbtaylor.com/ (accessed 19 March 2015).

Wallich, H.C. (1985), 'U.S. monetary policy in an independent world', in W. Ethier and R.C. Marston (eds), *International Financial Markets and Capital Movements: A Symposium in Honor of Arthur I. Bloomfield*, Princeton, NJ: International Finance Section, pp. 33–44.

Westelius, N.J. (2005), 'Discretionary monetary policy and inflation persistence', *Journal of Monetary Economics*, **52**, 477–96.

Williamson, S. (2008), 'New Keynesian economics: a monetary perspective', *Economic Quarterly*, Federal Reserve Bank of Richmond, **94**, 197–218.

Woodford, M. (1990), 'The optimum quantity of money', in B.M. Friedman and F.H. Hahn (eds), *Handbook of Monetary Economics*, Vol. II, Amsterdam: Elsevier Science, pp. 1067–152.

Woodford, M. (2008), 'How important is money in the conduct of monetary policy?', *Journal of Money, Credit and Banking*, **40**(8), 1561–98.

2. Australia

Australia is an immigrant society numbering about 23 million and dominated by peoples of European ethnicity. Most of Australia is semi-arid or desert, leaving it with a population density of just 3 per square kilometre. Australia is one of the advanced countries of the Asia-Pacific region. Australia's resource-rich, service-oriented economy is the 12th largest in the world. The services sector contributes about 70 per cent of GDP while the agricultural and mineral sectors, which contribute respectively 3 and 5 per cent of GDP, have disproportionately high importance in foreign trade. Consequently, Australia remains a major exporter of agricultural products, namely wheat and wool, minerals, namely iron ore and gold, and energy, namely liquefied gas and coal.[1]

Under a liberal democratic political system, Australia has sustained a high degree of political stability for over a century. The Australian government, irrespective of political persuasion, has demonstrated commitment to improving the quality of macroeconomic management. When political instability and polarization dominate a society, they generally raise inflation and its volatility. Fortunately for Australia, it has escaped both and, in consequence, enjoys bipartisan support for its macroeconomic management strategy of prioritizing price stability while maintaining steady economic growth. This has been institutionalized since the early 1990s in central bank autonomy to conduct monetary policy for price stability. This has been feasible because it has been built on the sound foundation of a large, established, developed financial system and a flexible exchange rate system implemented a decade earlier. Presently, the banking sector is well regulated and supervised and has demonstrated resilience in coping with large-scale capital flows and external shocks.

Australia has achieved a successful, though not painless, transition from moderately high and volatile inflation throughout the 1970s and 1980s to low but unstable inflation since the early 1990s. Since the 1980s the government has deregulated the product and factor markets and privatized many state-owned businesses and enterprises. Economic and financial reforms begun in the early 1980s have transformed the economy into a highly open and efficient one. Australia's overall macroeconomic performance has improved considerably since it adopted inflation targeting in 1993.

Inflation targeting, in particular, has induced improvement in fiscal discipline and consolidation. Consequently, Australia weathered, unscathed almost, the US-global financial crisis of the late 2000s and since then has continued to make steady economic progress.

The remainder of this chapter provides an historical overview of monetary policy in Australia from the early 1950s under different exchange rate arrangements, as summarized in Appendix A. To highlight monetary developments and issues, it uses summary data on key macroeconomic indicators from the early 1950s and draws on findings of some studies on the conduct of monetary policy and the underlying monetary relations with respect to inflation, money demand and the relations among money, output, prices and exchange rates, as reviewed in Appendices B, C, D and E.

MONETARY POLICY AND INFLATION IN AUSTRALIA: AN OVERVIEW

Australia operated under a 'repressed', or heavily regulated, financial system, including capital flow controls, and a fixed pegged exchange rate system throughout the 1950s and 1960s. The currency was successively pegged to the UK pound and the US dollar. Inflation was generally low, but was always unstable, under these exchange rate regimes. While the capital controls left the government some room for independent use of monetary policy as a policy instrument, this was of low significance under the ascendant Keynesian paradigm that determined almost all macroeconomic policy after World War II. In the Keynesian world view, fiscal policy was the preferred and dominant instrument of economic management. Arguably, therefore, monetary policy contributed precious little to Australia's otherwise impressive macroeconomic performance throughout the 1950s and 1960s. It is difficult to demarcate monetary policy from fiscal policy under a repressed financial system, and for Australia this situation obtained until the 1980s. The Keynesian prescription for monetary policy was to supplement fiscal policy ad hoc to maintain both internal and external balance. Price stability was important, but it ranked a long way below growth and employment as an objective of macroeconomic policy until after inflation rose sharply and became a major problem during the 1970s. Moderately high, but highly volatile, inflation henceforth brought monetary policy to the centre-stage of macroeconomic management in general and price stability in particular. However, the extent to which the price stability objective of monetary policy has been achieved and sustained over time remains contentious.

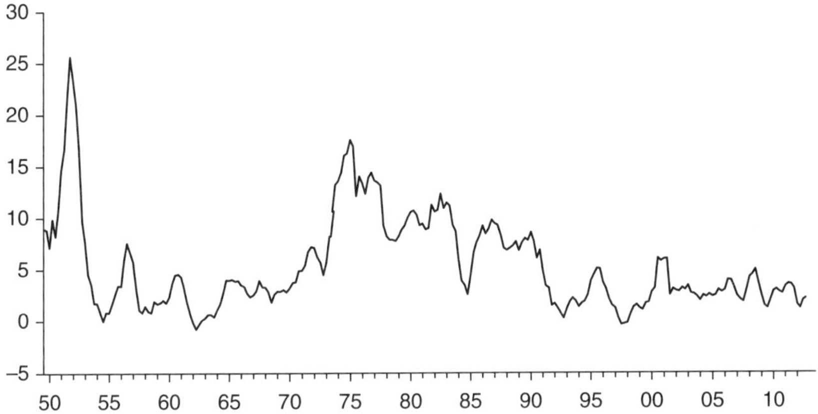

Figure 2.1 *Quarter-on-quarter consumer price index (CPI) inflation in Australia, 1949q3–2012q4*

Figure 2.1 plots the quarter-on-quarter inflation rate in Australia since the end of 1949. It shows that the inflation rate fluctuated widely over time, especially during the 1950s and 1970s. Inflation was tamed in the early 1990s but it has remained volatile (unstable) – that is, it fluctuates by relatively large percentages of its average.

This chapter undertakes an empirical study of the key issues in monetary policy and inflation behaviour in Australia since the 1950s. An empirical analysis of inflation behaviour with a long data series is critical to improved understanding of the role of monetary policy in macroeconomic management. Monetary policy does not operate in isolation, however. Hence the chapter provides an historical account of the evolution of monetary policy under differing political regimes. To inform an assessment of how policy measures have impacted upon macroeconomic variables in general, and inflation in particular, summary data for the key macroeconomic indicators are reported.

The thematic context of the chapter begins with a brief discussion on the socio-economic and political orientations of policymakers and their approaches to macroeconomic management in general and inflation control in particular.

The relatively conservative, centre-right Liberal Party, in coalition with the National Party, governed Australia without interruption over the period 1949–72.[2] The Coalition government, as it was known, mainly under Prime Minister Robert Menzies (1949–66), had presided over a rapidly growing economy in a generally low-inflation environment until the late 1960s. It was eventually replaced in 1972 by the relatively liberal centre-left Australian Labor Party (ALP) government under Prime Minister Gough Whitlam (1972–75). This political change took place at a time of significant, turbulent change in the global economic environment. The new government encountered problems generated by an unprecedented combination of global economic and political developments centred on the OPEC[3] oil price shocks of 1973. Despite its best efforts to deal with a difficult situation, the macroeconomic theory and policy then available to the government were ill-equipped for the task, and macroeconomic performance during the Whitlam era was ultimately judged unsatisfactory with respect to both inflation and unemployment. The Whitlam government was dismissed by the then Governor General in November 1975 on constitutional grounds.

Its replacement by the Fraser Coalition government, following the December 1975 elections, brought a major shift in the core objective of economic policy. The new priority was inflation control without raising unemployment. It replaced Whitlam's emphasis on balance-of-payments stability. In pursuit of this, the instrument of choice was monetary targeting, introduced in 1976. However, the mammoth task was too difficult for the instrument to accomplish within a short period. Inflation was subdued but remained high, and unemployment also remained high. The situation was politically untenable, and it led inexorably to a political change in 1983.

The coalition under Malcolm Fraser lost the March 1983 parliamentary elections to the ALP under Robert Hawke. The newly elected Labor government initially continued the soft form of monetary targeting inherited from the Fraser government, finally abandoning it in February 1985. To begin with, the Hawke government was not enthusiastic about the role of monetary policy in inflation control. Consequently, the conduct of monetary policy under Labor took a regressive turn in the late 1980s when the monetary policy emphasis shifted away from inflation control and towards the reduction of Australia's persistent current account deficits. In the meantime, the Wages and Incomes Accord with the Australian Council of Trade Unions (ACTU) became ineffective in controlling inflation, which only returned to low levels in the early 1990s following a deep recession induced, whether intentionally or otherwise, by tight monetary policy sustained over four years.

Australia adopted inflation targeting as its monetary policy strategy in 1993 and formalized the supporting institutional arrangements in 1996. This policy shift represented a significant break from the past and official recognition of the monetary roots of inflation[4] championed since at least 1976 by Milton Friedman. Although inflation targeting can claim some credit for maintaining low average levels of inflation until the present time, nevertheless Australian inflation retains the characteristics of high persistence and volatility. The central bank, the Reserve Bank of Australia (interchangeably termed the RBA), has been delegated strong statutory operational autonomy in the conduct of monetary policy. However, the high persistence of inflation under its flexible inflation targeting strategy[5] can be taken as an indicator of relatively low commitment by the Bank to steady inflation. This scenario begs the question of whether or not the high persistence and volatility of Australian inflation is due to a time-inconsistency problem created by the flexible inflation targeting approach.

The next section provides a brief description of the organization of the RBA and its role in the design and conduct of monetary policy for price stability. This is followed by further investigation of inflation behaviour in Australia from the 1950s. Thereafter, a review is made of the RBA's conduct of monetary policy and macroeconomic performance under successive policy regimes. The final section offers some concluding remarks based on empirical findings and policy discussion.

THE RBA AND MONETARY POLICY

The RBA assumed the functions of a central bank on the date of effect of the Federal Reserve Bank Act 1959. Until then, the federal government-owned Commonwealth Bank of Australia (CBA), established in 1911, had discharged all such central bank activities as were required. The RBA's current roles and responsibilities, and the details of its governance, are legislated in the 1959 Act, as amended ('the Act').[6] There were no major changes in the legislation, or in the RBA's functions, until Australia effectively abolished exchange and capital flow controls following its floatation of the currency (Australian dollar, A$) in December 1983.

The Reserve Bank Board is responsible for implementing monetary and banking policy. The relationship of the Reserve Bank Board and the government is set out in the Act, which directs that 'the Governor and the Secretary to the Department of the Treasury shall establish a close liaison with each other and shall keep each other fully informed on all matters which jointly concern the Bank and the Department of the Treasury'. Institutionally, the relationship of the RBA with the government is in the form of what the RBA calls 'one of independence with consultation'. This is outlined in RBA documents such as 'Consultation with Government' and 'Accountability to the Parliament' at its website, http://www.rba.gov.au/ about-rba/accountability.html.

The RBA's core responsibility since the early 1990s has been the design and conduct of monetary policy in Australia to pursue the government-set primary monetary policy objective of low inflation, defined as an underlying inflation measure averaging within a loose range of 2 to 3 per cent over the medium term. The objectives of monetary policy as laid out in the RBA Act 1959, subsection 10(2) have remained broad and unchanged. They are '(a) the stability of the currency of Australia; (b) the maintenance of full employment in Australia; and (c) the economic prosperity and welfare of the people of Australia'.[7] In practice, the monetary policy objective (a) is officially interpreted by the government as the maintenance of low inflation for preserving the purchasing power of money, although arguably exchange rate stability remains as a statutory obligation of the RBA, whether or not government or RBA state or include it as a policy objective. Given omission of the stability requirement from the officially stated inflation goal, together with the empirical persistence and volatility problems and the feasibility, both theoretical and applied, of achieving low persistence and volatility of inflation, it is clear that inflation stability is either excluded from the RBA's objective function or is ranked low in the function vector. Indeed, in the early days of implementation, an RBA Governor said as much.[8]

Interpretation of objectives (b) and (c) remains vague. Although monetary policy is no longer subservient to fiscal policy and is not used routinely in attempts to fine-tune the economy, the RBA takes into account the phase of the business cycle for making decisions on monetary policy actions.[9] The rationale for setting a medium-term inflation goal as the primary objective of monetary policy is the hypothesis that low inflation promotes economic growth and raises economic welfare. In its conduct of monetary policy for price stability, the RBA is keen to ensure a high degree of transparency about its goals, decision-making processes and the basis of its policy decisions. Despite volatile short-run inflation, the RBA's focus on a low medium-term rate is useful because it may reduce inflation-uncertainty in an environment of major structural change as the economy responds to, and integrates with, both the globalization 'revolution' and rapid economic progress in most Asian countries. The remainder of the chapter assesses how successful Australia's efforts have been to maintain low and stable inflation with simultaneous economic stability. The next section investigates the trends and dynamics of inflation in Australia and their association with economic growth.

INFLATION, INFLATION VOLATILITY AND ECONOMIC GROWTH

Inflation Trends

Figure 2.2 reports the yearly or the five-year average CPI inflation rate for Australia, 1950–2012.[10] The first five years, 1950–54, averaged about 10 per cent per annum. This high rate had its origins in the commodity boom associated with the Korean War (1950–53). For the second half of the 1950s, average inflation fell to just 3 per cent per annum and remained at that level for a full decade. When, from the late 1960s, the US authorities implemented an expansionary monetary policy in support of the war in Vietnam, the Australian fixed pegged exchange rate system translated it into accelerated Australian inflation. Boosted by the oil price shocks of 1973, inflation in Australia reached a peak during the mid 1970s. It then fell through the late 1970s, resurging in the 1980s. For the remainder of that decade, inflation stayed above 5 per cent. Only in the early 1990s did it return to 1960s levels, falling to 3 per cent in the midst of recession.

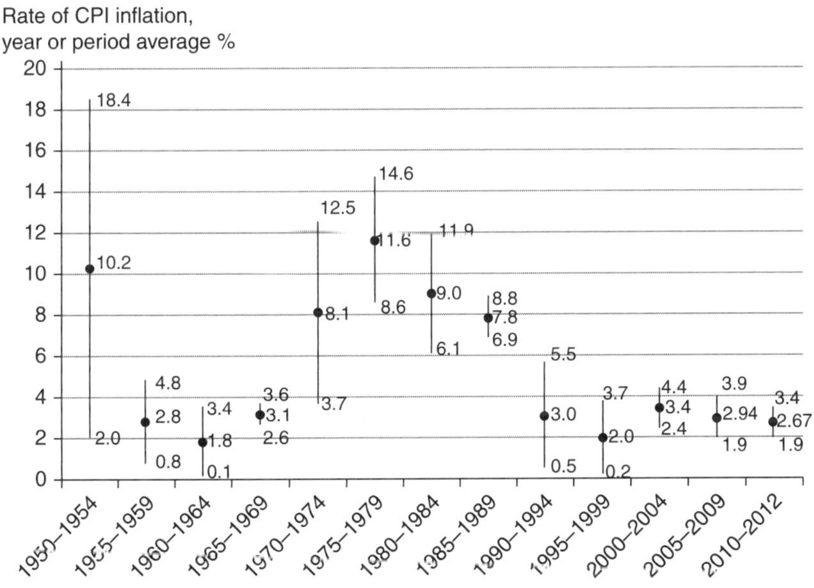

Source: Author's computation based on IMF, *International Financial Statistics*.

Figure 2.2 CPI inflation, period average ± 1 standard deviation in Australia, 1950–2012

This recession was caused by the Hawke-Keating Labor government's implementation of a tight monetary policy aimed at bringing the current account deficit under control. This timely return to low inflation presented the RBA with the opportunity, of which it took full advantage, to suggest to the government that the country follow the lead of New Zealand and Canada and adopt the monetary policy strategy of flexible inflation targeting. This was ultimately implemented from mid 1993 (Stevens, 2003a).

Inflation Volatility

Table 2.1 reports some descriptive statistics of CPI inflation for Australia. The sample period 1950–2012 and several sub-sample periods are covered. Australia operated under fixed exchange rate systems from 1945 to 1974 (Stevens, 2013). The data reveal moderately high average inflation across 1950–71. It reached a peak of over 20 per cent per annum and appears to have then oscillated widely around a mean of about 10 per cent for the decade 1975–84.

Visual inspection of Table 2.1 noting the substantial ratio of inflation's amplitude to its average in all periods suggests that it is relatively volatile. Although variance or standard deviation is used as a measure of inflation variability, an alternative measure is the coefficient of variation of inflation (Katsimbris, 1985; Levi and Makin, 1980). This latter measure better

Table 2.1 Descriptive statistics of CPI inflation in Australia, 1950–2012 (annual average over period, %)

	1950–2012	1970–82	1983–93	1985–92	1993–2012
Mean	8.9	21.8	7.7	6.3	2.7
Median	6.6	12.7	7.4	7.3	2.6
Maximum	69.3	69.3	12.8	9.1	4.6
Minimum	−5.9	−5.3	3.0	1.0	0.3
Standard deviation	13.0	23.7	3.1	2.8	1.2
Coefficient of variation	1.5	1.1	0.4	0.4	0.5
Skewness	3.0	0.8	0.0	−1.1	0.0
Kurtosis	12.4	2.3	2.0	2.7	2.4
Jarque-Bera statistic	323.2	1.7	0.4	1.5	0.3
Probability	0.0	0.4	0.8	0.5	0.8

Source: Author's computation based on IMF, *International Financial Statistics*.

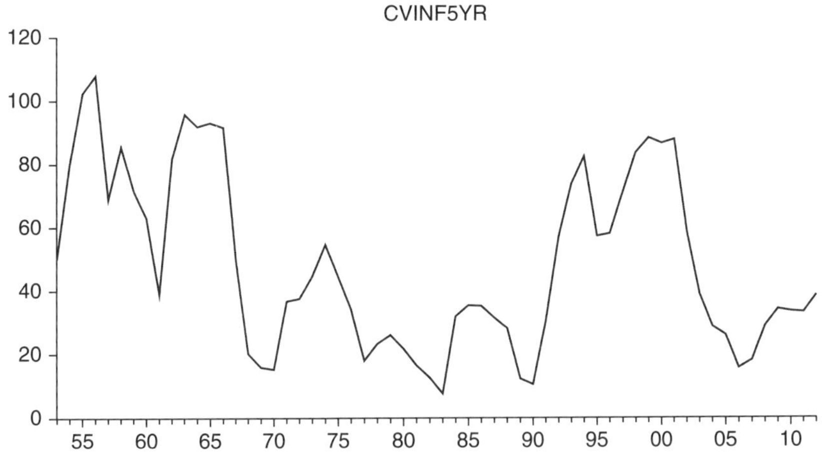

Note: CVINF5YR = five-year rolling moving average of the coefficient of variation of CPI inflation. The coefficient of variation of inflation is defined as the standard deviation of the rate of inflation divided by the rate of annual average inflation over a five-year period, multiplied by 100.

Figure 2.3 Five-year rolling coefficient of variation of inflation in Australia, 1953–2012

captures the deviation of inflation relative to the level of inflation and hence can be used for comparison of inflation variability across countries irrespective of variable inflation levels. Figure 2.3 shows that the coefficient of variation of inflation fell considerably in the 1970s in comparison with that of the previous decade. A decline in the standard deviation of inflation was responsible for this; probably due mainly to the much larger range of inflation rates that occurred in the 1965–74 decade. In the decade subsequent to 1975–84, the annual rate of inflation halved, with only a moderate fall in its standard deviation. Consequently, the coefficient of variation of inflation rose significantly, and remained high until the end of the data set in 2012. It shows that although average inflation in Australia has remained relatively low since inflation targeting was adopted in 1993, inflation volatility has not declined at any time since then and, indeed, exhibits an increasing trend after the mid 2000s.

Inflation Persistence

Inflation in Australia has been highly persistent.[11] Formally, the time-series properties of inflation are investigated within both the linear and non-linear modelling frameworks. Table 2.2 reports the unit root test results. The findings are mixed for the sample period. The ADF (augmented Dickey-Fuller) test rejects the null of a unit root in the inflation series. The findings from the KPSS (Kwiatkowski, Phillips, Schmidt and Shin) test, whose null hypothesis posits inflation as a stationary series, are consistent with those obtained by the ADF test. The Zivot-Andrews test, which incorporates an unknown break in the series, does not reject the null of a unit root in inflation for the sample. The KSS (Kapetanios, Shin and Snell) test, within a non-linear specification, rejects the null of a unit root in inflation for the sample at the conventional 5 per cent level. The overall results suggest that although inflation in Australia exhibits high persistence, it does not have a unit root. It appears that inflation underwent mean-shifts as a result of the transitions from each policy regime to the next (Figure 2.1). This created nonstationarity in the series. Once mean-shift is accounted for, Australian inflation is found to be stationary.

An implication of a near unit root test result is that a shock-induced higher inflation rate will be sustained for a considerable period unless policy efforts are made to return it to sustainably low levels. The finding that inflation does not have a unit root is plausible on both theoretical and empirical grounds. Monetary policy in Australia was conducted under either fixed or adjustable peg exchange rate systems from the 1950s until the early 1980s. Under an exchange rate rule, the anchor country's rate of inflation (US inflation, for example) served as a nominal anchor for inflation in Australia. Australia's mean rate of inflation was not statistically different from that in the United States. This finding is consistent with the purchasing power parity (PPP) proposition. Inflation in Australia was, however, more volatile than in the United States.[12]

The RBA introduced some policy responses to shocks and other macroeconomic developments, even though it had only limited monetary policy independence in controlling inflation and its volatility under the pegged exchange rate systems. Inflation control measures, including incomes policy (wage and price controls), interest rate adjustments and capital controls were eclectic throughout the 1970s and 1980s (with the exception of the removal of capital controls after the currency floatation in December 1983). Only under inflation targeting was monetary policy formalized in the sense of affording the goal of relative price stability as of short-run importance equal to, if not greater than, those of sustaining low and stable unemployment and stability in the balance-of-payments. This suggests that inflation in Australia, especially under inflation targeting, has not developed a stochastic wander; rather, it has demonstrated mean-reversion.

Inflation, Inflation Volatility and Economic Growth

Under its present strategy of monetary policy, Australia has a well-defined nominal anchor to inflationary expectations. The monetary authority utilizes a policy rule to inform its actions, which focus primarily on keeping underlying inflation close to the target rate over the medium term. Despite the inflation target having remained unaltered for two decades, inflation has remained volatile. Figure 2.4a plots a statistically computed series for inflation volatility in Australia for the period 1949q3–2012q4.[13] It shows very high-inflation volatility in the early 1950s, which then fell steadily before rising sharply in the mid 1970s following the 1973 oil price shocks. It again declined until the late 1990s, without ever falling low enough to 'stabilize' inflation, finally rising again and remaining high since the early 2000s.

Figure 2.4b plots a statistically computed series for the volatility of economic growth in Australia for the sample period 1960q3–2012q4. Clearly, economic growth has remained significantly volatile since the introduction of inflation targeting in 1993. This reflects only limited success in stabilizing economic growth and minimizing the rate of unemployment under flexible inflation targeting. It is plausible, even likely, that highly volatile inflation has impacted on volatility in economic growth and hence on the rate of unemployment. Poole and Wheelock (2008) suggest that one of the benefits of price stability is that it makes the economy stable. Economic volatility resulting from such factors as supply shocks is irreducible and can be considered part of the structure of the economy.

Sources of Inflation

Debate continues on the sources of inflation in Australia since the 1950s. It centres on whether inflation in Australia is the result of excessive wage growth or excessive money growth or a combination of the two. A large number of economists suggest that excessive wage growth was the most important source of inflation in Australia, especially from the early 1950s through the 1980s (Boehm and Martin, 1989; Gregory, 1986; Nevile, 1975, 1983). This cost-push view of inflation was developed as an alternative, rather than as a complement, to the monetary view of inflation that considers excessive monetary expansion as the main long-run source of inflation.[14] This monetary view of inflation gained acceptance during the 1970s, when rapid monetary expansion caused inflation to accelerate and kept it high throughout the 1980s. Although there is the perception that inflation targeting does not require either the use or monitoring of monetary aggregates, there is no doubt about the long-run causal linkage

Table 2.2 *The unit root test results for CPI inflation in Australia, 1949q3–2012q4*

Variables	Constant (C); Trend (T)	Optimal lag length (based on AIC) (maximum lag = 15)	ADF test statistic (p-value)	Critical values	Inference at 5% level	The KPSS test statistic			Asymptotic critical values KPSS (1992)	Inference at 5% level
						Constant (C); Trend (T)	Bandwidth: Newey-West	LM statistic		
LCPI	C and T	3	−1.46 (0.84)	CV (5%): −3.43	I(1)	C and T	12	0.248	0.146	I(1)
LCPI	C	3	−1.17 (0.69)	CV (5%): −2.87	I(1)	C	12	2.072	0.463	I(1)
ΔLCPI	C	2	−3.55 (0.01)	CV (5%): −2.57	I(0)	C	11	0.332	0.463	I(0)

The Zivot-Andrews unit root test statistic	Chosen lag length (maximum = 4)	Chosen breakpoint	t-statistic (Zivot-Andrews critical value)	Inference at 5%
Null hypotheses				
ΔLCPI has a unit root with a structural break in the intercept	4	1973q1	−4.31(−4.93)	I(1)
ΔLCPI has a unit root with a structural break in both the intercept and trend	4	1973q1	−4.28(−5.08)	I(1)

The KSS non-linear unit root test for CPI inflation (ΔLCPI)

Lag unadjusted sample period: 1949q3–2012q4	de-meaned t-ratio	de-trended t-ratio	raw data t-ratio
Auxiliary regression with augmentation (p = 4) (with intercept)	−4.04	−4.34	−3.74
Auxiliary regression with augmentation (p = 4) (without intercept)	−3.99	−4.26	−3.52
Asymptotic critical values of t-statistic (5% level)	−2.93	−3.4	−2.22

Note: LCPI = log of the consumer price index (CPI); ΔLCPI = first-order difference of LCPI.

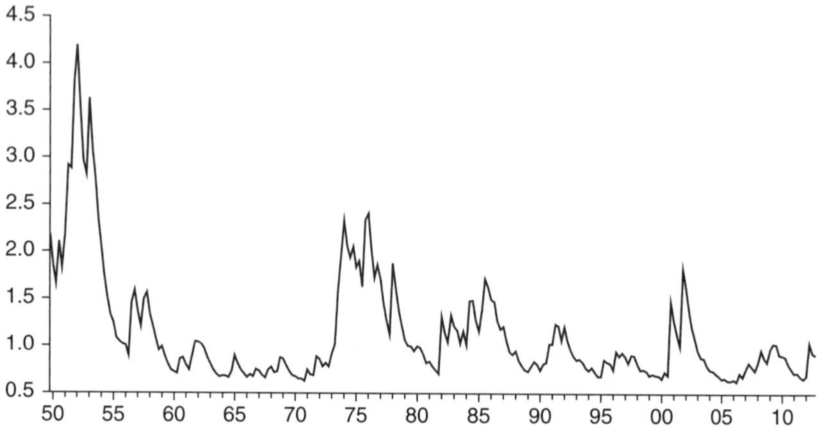

Figure 2.4a *Conditional standard deviation of CPI inflation in Australia, 1949q3–2012q4*

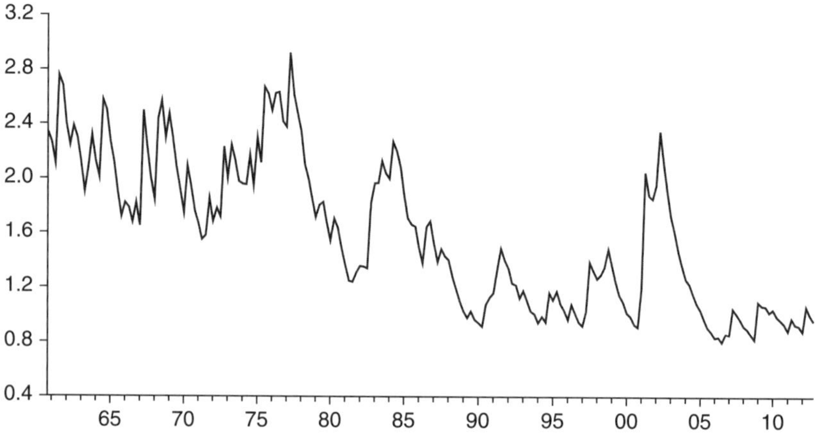

Figure 2.4b *Conditional standard deviation of real output growth in Australia, 1960q3–2012q4*

between money growth and inflation. Nevertheless, although wages growth has been relegated to the status insignificance as a source of inflation, the apparent neglect of a suitable monetary aggregate in the conduct of monetary policy does not fit well with the money growth-inflation relationship.

Inflation and inflation volatility: bidirectional relationship

In the inflation literature, there is a well-known proposition that a rise in inflation raises uncertainty about future inflation. Okun (1971) articulated this idea in the early 1970s. It has gained prominence since Milton Friedman's (1977) Nobel Memorial Lecture of December 1976, entitled 'Inflation and unemployment'. As a critique of the then highly influential idea of the Phillips curve relationship between inflation and unemployment, he postulated that high inflation raises inflation-uncertainty, which in turn lowers investment and economic activity. The rationale behind this proposition is that inflation-uncertainty lowers the price system's efficiency in allocating resources. Friedman (1977, p. 467) stated this as follows: the more uncertain inflation, 'the harder it becomes to extract the signal about relative prices from the absolute prices'. Relative price distortions affect resource allocation and lower economic efficiency and growth. Either very high inflation or hyperinflation invariably leads to economic stagnation. Very low and unstable inflation may also lead to economic stagnation. Japan's low and negative rates of inflation and its sluggish growth across the last two decades exemplify this.

The empirical literature focuses on a feedback relation between inflation and inflation volatility. High inflation generally leads to high volatility of inflation. High-inflation volatility in turn raises the rate of inflation. This subsection investigates such a feedback relationship for Australia using quarterly data from the period 1949q3–2012q4. The empirical results, including the bivariate Granger-causality test results, confirm a feedback relationship between inflation and inflation volatility (Tables 2.3 and 2.4). The results suggest that the rate of inflation has a positive impact on inflation volatility, consistent with the Friedman-Ball hypothesis that inflation raises inflation-uncertainty (Ball, 1992; Friedman, 1977). The empirical results also suggest that inflation shocks exert asymmetric impact on inflation-uncertainty in Australia.[15]

In the reverse direction, the finding that inflation-uncertainty raises inflation in Australia implies that the RBA generates inflation surprises. The inference is plausible, given the full-employment obligation of the monetary authority. It is consistent with the Cukierman-Meltzer hypothesis (Cukierman and Meltzer, 1986), if the politically motivated opportunism driving that hypothesis is interpreted as the RBA's internally motivated efforts to comply with its statutory obligations, rather than as submission to ad hoc or intermittent external pressure from opportunistic political masters. In the Australian case, the opportunism can be thought of as 'built-in' to the monetary authority's charter. Seen in this light, the political-economy implications of this positive relationship between inflation-uncertainty and inflation go to the issues of how of the Reserve Bank's governing statute is 'best' interpreted for policy purposes, and potentially whether or not repeal by parliamentary legislative amendment of its full-employment obligation is, or could be, politically

Table 2.3 The GARCH models for inflation and inflation volatility in Australia, 1949q3–2012q4

	GARCH(1,1)			GARCH(1,1)-in-mean			TGARCH(1,1)-in-mean			EGARCH(1,1)-in-mean		
	coeff.	z-stat.	prob.	coeff.	z-stat.	prob.	coeff.	z-stat.	prob.	coeff.	z-stat.	prob.
Mean equation												
Constant	0.24	3.74	0	0.28	1.77	0.08	−0.01	−0.18	0.86	−45.64	−441.13	0
π(−1)	0.94	50.76	0	0.94	31.09	0	0.99	128.73	0	0.03	2.83	0
log(GARCH)				0.03	0.31	0.76	−0.11	−2.33	0.02			
SQRT(GARCH)										230.85	391.92	0
Variance equation												
Constant	−0.2	−0.8	0.42	−0.02	−0.79	0.43	0.01	1.38	0.17	−3.23	−438.83	0
ARCH(−1)	0.15	1.91	0.06	0.16	1.94	0.05	0.14	4.22	0			
Resid(−1)^2 × Resid (−1)<0							−0.29	−5.63	0			
|ετ − 1| / |στ − 1|										−0.01	−2.16	0.03
ετ − 1 / στ − 1										0.01	5.06	0
GARCH(−1)	0.56	5.08	0	0.55	5.01	0	0.94	43.74	0			
log(GARCH(−1))										0	1.41	0.16
π	0.08	4.3	0	0.08	4.4	0	0.01	4.13	0	0.04	197.08	0
Diagnostics												
Adjusted R^2	0.92			0.92			0.92			0.99		
Durbin-Watson statistic (DW)	1.18			1.17			1.2			0.86		

Note: π = quarter-on-quarter CPI inflation in Australia; TGARCH = threshold GARCH; and EGARCH = exponential GARCH.

Table 2.4 Granger-causality between inflation and inflation volatility in Australia, 1949q3–2012q4

		CPI inflation does not Granger-cause inflation volatility	CPI inflation volatility does not Granger-cause inflation
A. Based on GARCH(1,1) Model			
Order of lag	Number of observations	F-statistic (p-value)	F-statistic (p-value)
2	251	22.83 (0.00)	0.83 (0.44)
4	249	14.89 (0.00)	6.14 (0.00)
6	247	8.90 (0.00)	6.29 (0.00)
8	245	7.54 (0.00)	5.77 (0.00)
10	243	10.52 (0.00)	4.46 (0.00)
12	241	7.55 (0.00)	3.90 (0.00)
B. Based on GARCH(1,1)-in-Mean Model			
Order of lag	Number of observations	F-statistic (p-value)	F-statistic (p-value)
2	251	22.58 (0.00)	0.83 (0.44)
4	249	14.96 (0.00)	6.32 (0.00)
6	247	8.90 (0.00)	6.40 (0.00)
8	245	7.46 (0.00)	5.83 (0.00)
10	243	10.64 (0.00)	4.50 (0.00)
12	241	7.39 (0.00)	3.93 (0.00)

Table 2.4 (continued)

		CPI inflation does not Granger-cause inflation volatility	CPI inflation volatility does not Granger-cause inflation
C. Based on TGARCH(1,1)-in-Mean Model			
Order of lag	Number of observations	F-statistic (p-value)	F-statistic (p-value)
2	251	283.56 (0.00)	4.38 (0.01)
4	249	129.17 (0.00)	5.70 (0.00)
6	247	74.78 (0.00)	2.10 (0.05)
8	245	51.59 (0.00)	2.28 (0.02)
10	243	34.07 (0.00)	1.98 (0.04)
12	241	38.69 (0.00)	2.25 (0.01)
D. Based on EGARCH(1,1)-in-Mean Model			
Order of lag	Number of observations	F-statistic (p-value)	F-statistic (p-value)
2	251	13.83 (0.00)	3.82 (0.02)
4	249	7.99 (0.00)	9.19 (0.00)
6	247	6.42 (0.00)	4.19 (0.00)
8	245	6.36 (0.00)	4.18 (0.00)
10	243	2.71 (0.00)	3.51 (0.00)
12	241	2.63 (0.00)	4.02 (0.00)

Note: TGARCH = threshold GARCH; EGARCH = exponential GARCH.

feasible. Provided that the econometric relationship between inflation and inflation-uncertainty remains robust, it indicates that the monetary authorities behave opportunistically to maintain full employment instead of, having achieved low inflation, then directing policy at minimizing its volatility. This suggests the question: could the full-employment obligation be met more efficiently and effectively in the long run by maintaining low average inflation and adding to this achievement low inflation persistence and low inflation volatility?

Inflation volatility and economic growth: causal linkage

With Australia's low average inflation exhibiting both persistence and volatility, the research question now addressed here is whether inflation volatility adversely impacts economic growth. A simple autoregressive distributed lag model $ARDL_{p,q}$ is estimated for the period 1960q1–2012q4 given data availability, using two lagged terms as suggested by the Schwarz Bayesian Criterion (SBC), to determine any Granger-causality effect of inflation volatility on economic growth. The variable-deletion test results show that there was indeed a Granger-causal impact of inflation volatility on economic growth. The estimated F-statistic value is $F(2,195) = 3.89$ (prob.: 0.02). The forecast error-variance decomposition results show that innovations in inflation volatility contribute about 6 per cent of innovations in economic growth over a ten-period time horizon. Based on an estimated model for 1978q1–2012q4, innovations in inflation volatility are also found to contribute about 9 per cent to innovations in the rate of unemployment.[16] These findings strengthen the argument for low and steady inflation using rule-based[17] monetary policy. The thesis is that a credible rule-based monetary policy, with firm commitment on the part of the authority, maintains low and stable inflation. Monetary policy (with supportive fiscal discipline), by maintaining price stability, then promotes economic growth in a stable economic environment.

PEGGED EXCHANGE RATE SYSTEMS, 1950s TO THE MID 1970s, AND MONETARY TARGETING, 1976–85

According to Macfarlane (1998), the post-World War II monetary policy in Australia has evolved in a number of phases. Australia introduced an adjustable peg exchange rate system with the US dollar after the collapse of the Bretton Woods system in 1971. Frequent adjustment of the exchange rate from the early 1970s made the exchange rate a monetary policy instrument. Macfarlane (1997) suggests that there were at least six exchange rate adjustments from 1971 until the adoption of a crawling peg system in November 1976. This crawling peg system operated until December 1983 when Australia floated the dollar.[18] This was the first in a series of financial and monetary system reforms that proceeded through the following one and a half decades, during which most restrictions on interest rates, capital flows and financial services were removed. A wide range of financial deregulatory measures were also introduced to make the financial system competitive and efficient.[19]

Therefore, economic policy regimes in Australia include successive fixed and then managed exchange rate regimes that started in the late 1940s and lasted until the mid 1970s; a monetary targeting regime from 1976 to 1985; a transitional (eclectic) monetary policy regime from the abandonment of monetary targeting in 1985 until 1992–93; and flexible inflation targeting from 1993. The remainder of the chapter reviews the design and conduct of monetary policy in Australia under these policy regimes.

Successive Fixed and Adjustable Exchange Rate Systems, 1950s to Mid 1970s

The fixed exchange rate arrangement under the Bretton Woods system was the basis for monetary policy in Australia from the late 1940s until the early 1970s. The fixed exchange rate system represents an exchange rate policy that, if capital is internationally mobile, sacrifices monetary policy independence. Australia retained some degree of independence due to its regime of capital controls.[20] However, with policymakers subordinating monetary policy to fiscal policy in a Keynesian framework and using it to smooth out economic fluctuations, it did not have the explicit role of price stabilization. The price-anchoring role of monetary policy did not even come into vogue during the 1950s and 1960s. Australia adopted the British tradition of a subservient central bank operating under the direction of the Treasury, which used it effectively as a regulatory instrument to control interest rates, credit allocation, capital flows and financial institutions.

Australia maintained low inflation under the Bretton Woods system. Australia's inflation was, however, more volatile than inflation in the United States, for example. Policymakers focused on the balance-of-payments as the barometer of policy action. They subscribed to the absorption conception of balance-of-payments theory and interpreted deficits in it as excesses of expenditure over income (Alexander, 1952). Both monetary and fiscal policy were deployed in this framework to maintain internal and external balance, while controls over interest rates, bank credits and the prudential supervision and regulation of financial institutions were deployed as monetary instruments for demand management. However, data for real interest rates and exchange rates suggest that both

Table 2.5 Test results for equality of means and variances of CPI inflation in Australia and the United States, 1958q1–2012q4

	Number of observations	Mean	Standard deviation
1958q1–2012q4			
CPI inflation (Australia)	220	5.00	3.93
CPI inflation (United States)	220	3.93	2.85
1993q1–2012q4			
CPI inflation (Australia)	80	2.66	1.36
CPI inflation (United States)	80	2.50	1.07
Test for equality of means	Degrees of freedom	*t-test statistic*	Probability
1958q1–2012q4	438	3.27	0.00
1993q1–2012q4	158	0.85	0.40
Test for equality of variances	Degrees of freedom	*F-test statistic*	Probability
1958q1–2012q4	(219, 219)	1.90	0.00
1993q1–2012q4	(79, 79)	1.61	0.04

of these became highly volatile due to inflation volatility. The plausible inference is that this volatility affected trade flows and economic activity.

Impressive Economic Performance: 1950s and 1960s

Table 2.6 reports summary data for key macroeconomic indicators in Australia for the period 1950–85. It reveals impressive macroeconomic performance in Australia during the 1950s and 1960s. Australia maintained rapid economic growth in a low-inflationary environment over two decades. Consequently, the unemployment rate was very low from the mid 1950s to the late 1960s.

Economic Turbulence in the Mid 1970s

The macroeconomic environment in Australia changed in the early 1970s. Inflation rose and remained high for the next decade. Political debate began over whether high inflation in the early 1970s originated from domestic sources, from external sources, or from both; and whether inflation was

Table 2.6 Macroeconomic indicators in Australia, 1950–85

Macroeconomic indicators	1950–55	1956–60	1961–65	1966–70	1971–75	1976–80	1981–85
Budget balance (% of GDP)	n.a.	n.a.	n.a.	n.a.	n.a.	−1.3	−2.6
Money-growth rate (%)							
Narrow money growth	8.5	1.8	2.0	6.9	12.8	12.0	7.0
Broad money growth	7.3	4.6	7.5	7.6	16.1	25.1	14.3
Real GDP growth (%)	6.3	11.2	4.5	5.8	2.8	3.0	3.1
Unemployment rate (%)	0.7	1.3	1.7	1.2	1.9	5.7	7.9
Output gap (% of potential GDP)	n.a.	n.a.	n.a.	n.a.	n.a.	1.7	0.6
Real wage index (2005 = 100)	n.a.	n.a.	49.9	57.5	70.9	76.4	78.8
Share price index (2005 = 100)	n.a.	5.0	6.0	9.0	8.8	10.5	15.7
CPI inflation (%)	8.9	3.1	1.8	3.1	10.3	10.6	8.3
Current account balance (% of GDP)	n.a.	n.a.	n.a.	n.a.	n.a.	−2.8	−4.5
Nominal interest rate (%)							
Yield on 3-year Treasury bills	2.8	4.4	4.4	5.2	7.0	9.7	13.6
Yield on 15-year Treasury bills	4.1	5.0	4.9	5.6	7.7	10.1	14.1
Treasury note rediscount rate	n.a.	n.a.	n.a.	6.0	7.2	9.7	13.9

Real interest rate (%)[a]							
Real yield on 3-year Treasury bills	−5.2	1.3	2.6	2.0	−2.9	−0.8	4.9
Real yield on 15-year Treasury bills	−4.0	1.8	3.1	2.4	−2.3	−0.4	5.4
Real Treasury note rediscount rate	n.a.	n.a.	n.a.	2.1	−2.8	−0.8	5.2
External terms of trade[b]	192.4	140.1	137.3	129.2	130.5	102.5	88.1
Nominal exchange rate (A$/US$)	0.9	0.9	0.9	0.9	0.8	0.9	1.1
Nominal effective exchange rate[c]	n.a.	174.1	183.7	192.1	209.3	181.3	164.0
Real effective exchange rate[c]						104.7	110.2

Notes:
n.a. = not available.
a. Real interest rate is estimated as: 100(((1 + interest rate)/(1 + inflation rate))−1) where the interest rate and inflation rate are expressed in decimal.
b. Ratio of export prices to import prices, as per cent.
c. An increase in the index value of the exchange rate represents appreciation.

Source: Authors compilation/computation based on IMF, *International Financial Statistics*; IMF, *World Economic Outlook*; Reserve Bank of Australia's website; Layton (1994); and country-specific publications on the IMF website.

monetary or non-monetary in nature. The available evidence suggests that Australia's high inflation during the 1970s originated from external sources and had monetary roots. A number of factors caused excessive monetary expansion in the early 1970s. Firstly, accumulated foreign reserves, which had originated in earlier commodity booms,[21] were reflected in current account surpluses in 1972–73 (Corden, 1981; Grenville, 1990). Secondly, the OPEC oil shocks raised inflation to relatively high levels, which were subsequently sustained due to monetary accommodation by the RBA on the advice of the Treasury. Thirdly, the government's fiscal policy stance was expansionary. The commodity boom relaxed the balance-of-payments constraint on economic growth, influencing the government to loosen policy discipline. There is a perception that the Whitlam government (1972–75) lost control over fiscal policy. Its 'fiscal extravagance' fuelled a rapid growth of wages in 1974, which further exacerbated the inflation problem.

Monetary Targeting: 1976–85

Friedman (1968) and Phelps (1970) predicted the demise of the Phillips curve relationship at a time when inflation was low in most industrialized countries. Their prediction became a reality in the midst of high inflation across the globe in the mid 1970s. The OECD[22] countries in particular went into recession following the first OPEC oil price shocks of 1973. Policymakers then encountered high rates of inflation and unemployment (stagflation). Options for solving this stagflation were limited, especially when the then new rational expectations hypothesis suggested no sustained impact of expansionary monetary and fiscal policies on output or employment (Lucas, 1973). Some developed countries, such as the United States, West Germany, United Kingdom, Switzerland and Japan, introduced monetary targets to anchor inflationary expectations. By then, Australia was in the grip of high rates of inflation and unemployment and looking for a strategy to simultaneously lower both of them (Argy et al., 1990).

The Fraser Liberal-National Party Coalition government (1975–82) came to power in December 1975 with the policy slogan of 'fight inflation first'. The government's secondary goal was to avoid raising unemployment. As Australian economists by then had acknowledged the monetary roots of inflation, the government introduced monetary targeting in 1976. The monetary targeting strategy, for operational purposes, took the form of announcing in the budget a forecast of the growth rate of broad money (M3) for the next year. Although this represented a shift of policy intent, it was implemented in a casual manner.[23] Nelson (2005) points out that the government's adoption of monetary targeting was not technically sound; for example, it retained a cost-push view of inflation in parallel and supposed complementarity with the monetary 'demand-pull' view. Consequently, the monetary authorities did not interpret the prevailing low real interest rate as originating in loose monetary policy; instead, the cause was seen as an autonomous rise in expected inflation. In hindsight, although inflationary expectations were high and rising at the time, they were not 'autonomous' but were caused by expansionary monetary and fiscal policies introduced since the early 1970s. The non-monetary interpretation of inflation, however, led to the view that it could be lowered by intervention in wage and price setting rather than by raising the nominal interest rate or reducing the money-growth rate.

The monetary targeting approach had some early success in reducing inflation. Inflationary expectations, however, remained high due to continued expansionary fiscal policy, an external volatile economic environment and political uncertainty. There was low political commitment to reducing inflation, despite the 'fight inflation first' slogan, because of the expected rise in unemployment. Inflation was about 11 per cent across 1976–80, much higher than the OECD average (Milbourne, 1990). Meanwhile unemployment, jumping from less than 2 per cent to around 6 per cent in the mid 1970s, also became a policy issue. Policymakers realized that since they lacked policy credibility, an attempt to lower inflation by tightening monetary policy would cause recession (Layton, 1994). In response to some restrictive monetary policy, unemployment rose to 8 per cent in the early 1980s (Pagan and Trivedi, 1983). The government responded to the ensuing political pressure by reverting to expansionary monetary and fiscal policies. The consequence was accelerated inflation with no offsetting reduction in unemployment.

The rising inflation induced in the government a loss of confidence in monetary policy, and in October 1982 it attempted to defeat the inflationary pressure by introducing a six-month wage freeze. By then, monetary targeting had become controversial in the literature as a strategy of monetary policy. Serious questions had been raised, and not resolved, about the stability of the money-demand function and whether there was indeed any linkage between money growth and inflation. The latter doubt arose from an observed weakening of the linkage, arguably originating in financial innovation and deregulation that had been ongoing in Australia since the late 1970s. Financial innovation was initiated by financial institutions to bypass banking regulations and controls dating back to the 1950s. Finally, Australia discarded monetary forecasting in the Federal Budget in February 1985. This marked the complete demise of monetary targeting in Australia. Whether or not the money-demand function in Australia had indeed become unstable at that time and has since stabilized remains an empirical issue, but there is some evidence that this may be the case (Hossain, 2012).

MONETARY POLICY REGIMES SINCE 1983

Monetary Policy Neglect: 1983–93

When the Hawke Labor government came to office in December 1982, it inherited high rates of inflation and unemployment, both around 10 per cent. The new government made a strategic policy shift with respect to inflation control. It reallocated all the major policy instruments away from the Fraser government's strategy of 'fight inflation first without worsening unemployment' to target unemployment. This involved continuation of Fraser-implemented expansionary fiscal policies (Argy, 1992); introduction of a wages and incomes policy; and reorientation of the monetary policy target from inflation control, which then required a generally tightening policy stance, to stimulation of demand (output) growth, requiring monetary expansion. This policy reversal was controversial, since it came just as monetary policy acquired a major boost in its ability to control inflation with the currency float in December 1983.

By the late 1980s, the government had redeployed monetary policy once again to target a ballooning current account deficit. The consequent monetary tightening pushed interest rates to record highs. Sustained for several years, this led in the early 1990s to recession. Furthermore, the government's conduct of monetary policy was asymmetric. Having used tight interest rate policy to cool the economy, it did not include interest rate easing in its formulation of policy to pull the economy out of recession. The policies ultimately implemented were consistent with the Keynesian view that monetary policy is not effective in raising demand during recession. During this period, probably in fear of reigniting 1970s stagflation, and lacking any clear remedy for it in the literature, the government insisted that economic recovery required tight monetary policy to maintain low inflation during recession (Edwards, 1996; Nelson, 2005).

The question has been raised since the late 1980s whether the Hawke government's failure to maintain low and stable inflation was due to its misapplication of monetary policy. The assertion is that Hawke-Keating[24] deployed monetary policy to a real objective, lower unemployment, which it is incapable of achieving in the long run. Consequently, monetary policy-induced recession in the early 1990s became a nemesis for the Labor government and led to the ascendency of a monetary policy framework that took the form of inflation targeting in 1993 under the prime ministership of

Paul Keating (Fraser, 1993; Pitchford, 1990). The adoption of inflation targeting was significant because it rehabilitated monetary policy's role in inflation control while removing the cost-push view of inflation from the scene.

There were complex reasons why the Hawke government did not use monetary policy to control inflation. The government's economic philosophy was a mixture of Keynesian and Classical orthodoxies. It differed from the Fraser government's economic philosophy, which had a Classical-Monetarist twist in intention if not always in practice (Argy, 1992). The main initiative of the Hawke government was a comprehensive Prices and Incomes Accord with the ACTU. The Accord was presented as an instrument of inflation control although the validity of this claim fell into question in later years. The ultimate goal of the Accord was to reduce unemployment by cutting real wages. The prevailing view was that high wages growth during the Whitlam era created real wage overhang, pushing unemployment to high levels. The anti-inflation image of the Accord can therefore be described as something of a camouflage to wrap the government's real intention of restoring low unemployment by cutting real wages. The Accord might otherwise have been opposed by workers (Argy, 1992).

The Accord brought the wages and incomes policy to centre-stage and denied monetary policy the role in which it possesses comparative advantage over other policy instruments: that of price stabilization. The government then looked for an alternative role for monetary policy and found it in the growing current account deficits. The government had continued the expansionary fiscal and monetary policies introduced by the Fraser government. This led, over a period of three or four years, to an overheated economy. Evidence for this can be found in the relatively rapid rate of growth recorded by the economy over 1984–85, causing the current account deficit to blow out to about 6 per cent of GDP in 1985. Reflecting its growing concern over the growing size of current account deficits and its need for a monetary policy target, the government assigned monetary policy the role of lowering current account deficits (Pitchford, 1989). It argued that current account deficits were created by excessive expenditure on traded, implying imported, products, and that to reduce imports a rise in interest rates was required. Many economists opposed the deployment of monetary policy to a current account target. They maintained that monetary policy was not capable of changing investment and saving decisions that are made within an intertemporal framework, pointing out that high interest rate policy for over four years had not lowered current account deficits much, although it had subdued the economy sufficiently to induce a recession by 1990. Furthermore, it was argued, the Prices and Incomes Accord had not much impacted inflation (Nelson, 2005), the target that held comparative advantage for conventional monetary policy.

Summing Up

In summing up, Australia's monetary policy experimentation throughout the 1980s and early 1990s illustrate difficulties inherent in the discretionary manipulation of nominal variables such as interest rates and monetary aggregates in pursuit of real objectives. Australian monetary policy evolution across the period was then, and remains, enigmatic. Initially monetary policy did not have well-defined objectives. Argy (1992) noted that Australia's monetary policy was eclectic, with mixed objectives – at times emphasizing inflation, at times unemployment, at times current account, at times demand pressures and at times exchange rate management. The Prices and Incomes Accord had snatched away the price stabilization role of monetary policy. This led the government to deploy monetary policy to lower current account deficits, caused by expansionary monetary and fiscal policies. Pitchford (1990) and Sjaastad (1989) pointed out that current account deficits after the dollar float were not such a problem for Australia as to require drastic macro-policy interventions. Even if current account deficits were a problem, it was questionable whether a high interest rate policy was appropriate to influence current account balances (Black, 1989).

Inflation Targeting: Since Mid 1993

Monetary policy regained its role in price stabilization in the early 1990s. This represented a widespread recognition, and even adoption, of Friedman's (1973, p. 28) view that 'inflation is always and everywhere a monetary phenomenon'. From this viewpoint, monetary policy was neglected in Australia throughout the 1980s (Nelson and Nikolov, 2004). Australia introduced inflation targeting in 1993, and formalized it in 1996. In December 1989, New Zealand had been the first country to implement inflation targeting as a strategy of monetary policy, formalizing it almost immediately by means of the Reserve Bank of New Zealand (RBNZ) Act of 1989. Canada adopted inflation targeting in February 1991. These developments, New Zealand's move in particular, were instrumental in Australia's decision, but in contrast to the public attention given to the transition in those countries, the shift in Australia was a low key affair.

Bernie Fraser, former Governor of the RBA, talked about holding underlying inflation 'to an average of 2 to 3 per cent over a period of years' in a March 1993 speech (Fraser, 1993, p. 2). Australia announced an inflation target in April 1993. The initial aim was to raise transparency and monetary policy credibility. It was expected that inflation targeting would raise RBA accountability to maintain low inflation. An explicit inflation target was expected to act as a nominal anchor to inflationary expectations. Such an anchor had been missing when the RBA abandoned monetary targeting in February 1985 (Schaechter et al., 2000). The RBA, however, did not signal an abrupt shift in policy. Final agreement was reached between the government and the RBA only in 1996.[25] Until then, the RBA signalled its medium-term inflation target within the then institutional arrangements.

The RBA's articulation of inflation targeting was arrived at after consideration of alternatives debated in public forums. The stage had been under preparation by the RBA since February 1985, following the abandonment of monetary targeting, and through the late 1980s period of 'inappropriate' targeting of monetary policy at the current account deficit. The RBA took the view that the relationship between money growth and inflation became weaker due to financial innovation. It first adopted a 'checklist' approach to monetary policy. Critics pointed out that this approach lacked coherence and failed to achieve monetary policy discipline and credibility. Several alternative regimes came to the forefront for discussion. They included exchange rate pegging, currency board, commodity-standard currency, free-banking regime with competing private currencies, monetary base control and monetary targeting. These diverse proposals were an indication of widespread distrust of the government's discretion over monetary policy (Stevens, 2003b). Inflation targeting is a rule-based monetary policy and its adoption was an acknowledgement of the monetary sources of inflation in Australia (Nelson, 2005).

Inflation Targeting: Design and Implementation

The RBA pursues inflation targeting by taking into account the consequences of monetary policy actions on output and employment. The RBA's view is that inflation control preserves the currency value of the Australian dollar while a low-inflation environment forms the foundation for long-term economic growth. The government has accepted the RBA's recommendation and set the target range for annual underlying average CPI inflation target loosely at 2 to 3 per cent over the course of a business cycle (Stevens, 2003b). This target has not been altered since the implementation of inflation targeting in mid 1993.

The Reserve Bank Board makes decisions on the direction of monetary policy. The Board meets 11 times annually. Its decision on the policy interest rate is communicated promptly to the public. The policy interest rate is termed the cash rate, which is the RBA's target for the rate charged to one another by the banks on loans transacted in the interbank overnight funds market. This 'interbank overnight rate', as it is called, is determined in the market by the interaction of the demand for and supply of overnight funds. The RBA's ability to force the interbank overnight rate to converge to the cash rate every night stems from its control over the supply of funds used by the banks to settle overnight transactions, such as cheque clearing. Each bank is required at law to hold an Exchange Settlement Account (ESA) with the RBA specifically for the purpose of trading in the interbank overnight market. The RBA is then able to predict each bank's supply of or demand for funds and manipulate the ESA balances accordingly so that the loan rate charged is always exactly equal to the cash rate. This was not always the case; until the mid 2000s there was frequently a small margin of error. Since then, however, technical progress has sharpened RBA operations in the ESA accounts to precision point (Figure 2.5).

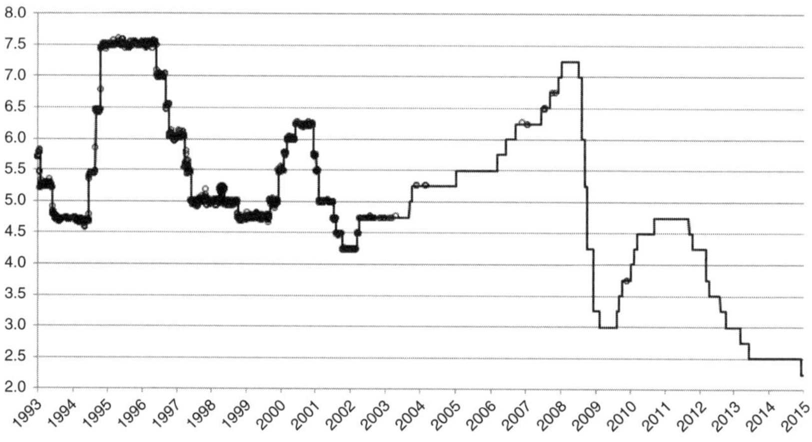

Note: Each annual tick mark denotes 1 March of that year. The solid black line represents the RBA's target for the interbank overnight cash rate (the 'cash rate'). Hollow circles denote days on which the realized interbank overnight cash rate (the 'actual rate') diverged from the RBA target. The unobscured sections of the solid black line denote days on which the two rates coincided. Thus the graph shows that with the exception of 19 and 20 January 2010, the RBA has developed the expertise and technology to materially hit its target rate daily since 1 January 2008.

Source: Current data: http://www.rba.gov.au/statistics/tables/index.html#interest-rates, then page search for 'Interest Rates', Table F1 (from 21 May 2013 to end of February 2015); historical data: http://www.rba.gov.au/statistics/historical-data.html, then page search for 'Interest Rates', Table F1 (to 20 May 2013). Table F1 is the 'Interest Rates' table for both current and historical data sections.

Figure 2.5 The interbank overnight rate ('actual') and the cash rate ('target') in Australia, 1993–2015

To review monetary policy settings the RBA uses information indicators, including the official interest rate (cash rate), other interest rates for borrowers, the exchange rate, the unemployment rate and its trend, economic productivity and capacity, asset prices, credit market conditions and international developments. Officially, the RBA does not follow a monetary policy rule such as the Taylor rule in setting the cash rate. It does, however, make its intention clear to the markets that it stands ready to change the cash rate to the extent necessary to achieve its inflation target 'over the course of the cycle'. Economic observers, however, suspect that the RBA changes the cash rate in a manner that can be described by a Taylor rule with only inflation as its target. Although the RBA is unambiguous about its inflation target, it remains opaque on the issue of whether and how it responds to changes in the unemployment outlook. Blanchard and Sheen (2007) suggest that while it is plausible that the RBA's interest rate rule includes only an inflation target, this would not be consistent with the objectives of monetary policy as set out in the Reserve Bank Act of 1959 (currency stability, employment and welfare optimization). In practice, there is considerable ambiguity about the role of the output gap, and the difficulty of its measurement, in the Taylor rule specification and its implementation.[26]

Transmission Mechanisms of Monetary Policy Under Inflation Targeting

Figure 2.6 exhibits a flowchart of the monetary policy transmission mechanisms under inflation targeting. The transmission mechanisms are based on the assumption of short-term price rigidities, such that changes in nominal interest rates bring about changes in real interest rates. The transmission mechanisms of monetary policy in Australia are commonly understood. Monetary policy actions have, however, lagged and uncertain

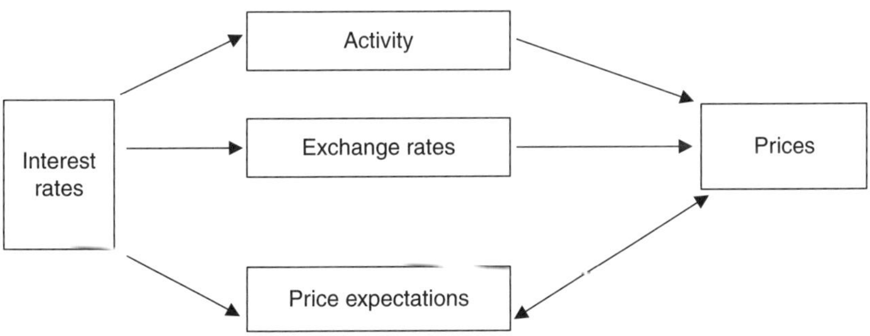

Source: RBA, http://www.rba.org.au.

Figure 2.6 Monetary policy transmission mechanisms in Australia

effects. These effects depend on economic conditions and are inherently changeable over time (hence 'lagged and uncertain'). Initial RBA-caused movements in the cash rate pass through the whole structure of deposit and lending rates with short lags. The consequent changes in the structure of deposit and lending interest rates take some time to impact economic activity and prices, which represent the ultimate target of the initial RBA policy action. There are several distinct channels through which changes in these interest rates affect prices. The RBA suggests that interest rates affect general saving and investment behaviour, the spending behaviour of households, the supply of credit, exchange rates and other asset prices. Within a simple aggregate demand-aggregate supply framework, changes in interest rates influence the level of aggregate demand and, given aggregate supply in the short run, change prices and output. Changes in interest rates affect the exchange rates and through them, import prices. Exchange rate movements alter inflationary expectations, which influence the decisions of consumers, producers and businesses.

A Simple Vector Autoregressive Analysis

As an input to the following subsection assessing Australian macroeconomic performance since the float and through the period of inflation targeting, a brief analysis has been conducted with a vector autoregressive (VAR) model of the following variables: the cash rate; the nominal effective exchange rate; the real effective exchange rate; the real loan rate of interest; real output; and the rate of inflation.

The variables were ordered according to the following provisional hypotheses: (1) an increase in the cash rate contemporaneously impacts the rate of inflation; (2) in the reverse direction, the inflation rate impacts the cash rate with a lag; and (3) the cash rate impacts real output, operating through the exchange rate and the interest rate. Quarterly data for the period 1990q1–2010q4 are used for the analysis. The optimal lag-length selected by the Schwarz Bayesian Criterion (SBC) is seven periods.

Figure 2.7 reports the impulse responses for the variables while Table 2.7 reports the forecast error-variance decomposition results for all variables in the model. It is found that the impact of inflation on the cash rate is significant. The cash rate has some impact on real GDP, which diminishes with time. Other variables that responded to the increase in the cash rate affected the inflation rate. Causality test results based on the VAR model (not reported) suggest that the cash rate has significant impacts on the rate of inflation and real output.

Macroeconomic Performance: 1986–2012

Australia's economic performance was unsatisfactory in the late 1980s. Both inflation and unemployment were high. Tight monetary policy led to recession in the early 1980s. Australia has undergone sustained economic growth with low inflation since 1993 as a result of greater flexibility in the economy under disciplined economic management by successive governments. Credit goes mainly to the combination of the flexible exchange rate since 1983, rule-based monetary policy since 1993 and supporting fiscal discipline. The current monetary policy framework is a far cry from the economic policy regimes of the 1970s and 1980s. The economy of the 1990s and 2000s demonstrated pleasing, perhaps somewhat surprising, resilience to such external shocks as the 1997–98 East-Southeast Asian financial crisis, the 2001 collapse of the dot-com bubble and the US-global financial crisis of 2007–09.

Australia is one of those countries that have embraced financial globalization. With a bipartisan government policy benchmark of continuous improvement in the market orientation of the economy, the following policy achievements have supported the floating currency and policy discipline: open capital accounts; deepened securities markets; and borrowings of global savings to finance real sector investment, especially in the mining sector. Rapid implementation of trade-openness and structural reform policies in the product, labour and capital markets played important roles in raising Australian competitiveness and keeping inflation low. Consequently, commodity booms and supply shocks did not create major imbalances. Commodity booms that began in the mid 2000s continued over the next six or more years, without excessive inflationary pressure and generating substantial budget surpluses. This kept the pressure largely off monetary policy, leaving it free to focus rigorously on its inflation-unemployment targets in the face of contingencies that developed. And some did, as just mentioned. The RBA has been successful in using monetary policy to anchor inflationary expectations. Low inflation has contributed to an environment conducive to real economic activity (Battellino, 2007).

Since 2006, Australia has operated at almost full employment with some signs of capacity constraints, which have put some pressure on inflation. The downturn in Australia after the US-global financial crisis turned out to be milder than expected, with the economy narrowly averting technical recession. However, it is not clear whether expansionary monetary and fiscal policies or the commodity boom (mining in particular) was effective in preventing the economy from falling into a recession. Australia's relatively high real interest rates encouraged foreign-capital inflows. These

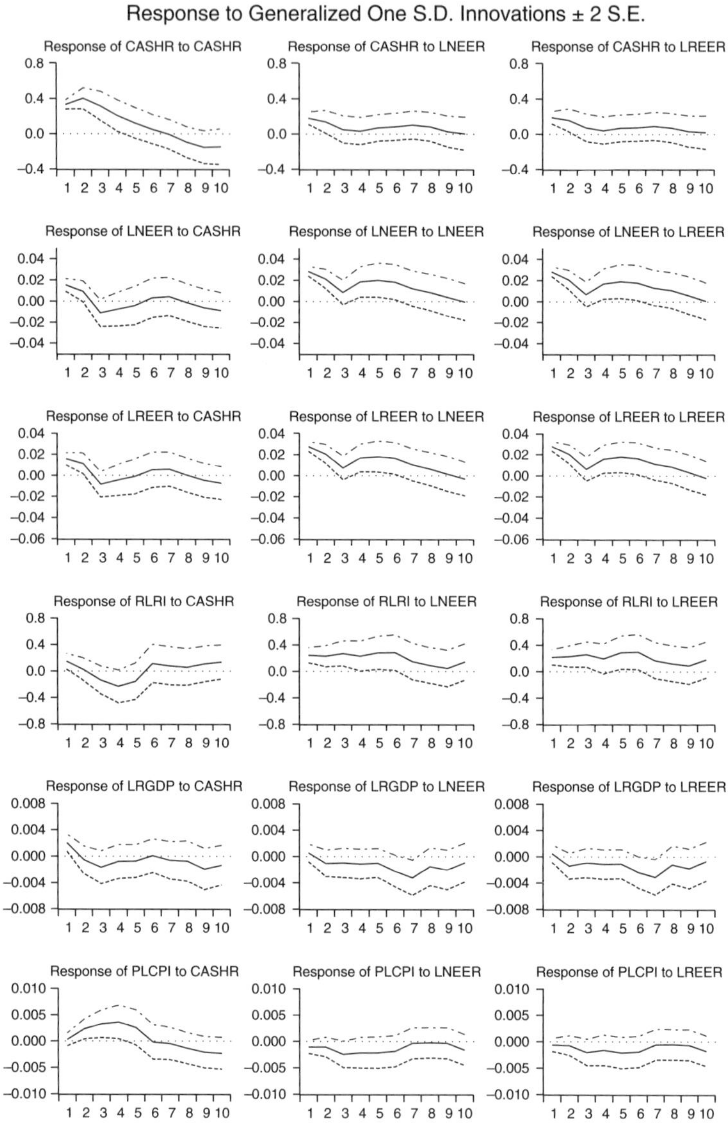

Note: Definitions of variables: CASHR = cash rate of the RBA; LNEER = log of the nominal effective exchange rate of the Australian dollar; LREER = log of the real effective exchange rate of the Australian dollar; RLRI = real lending rate of interest; LRGDP = log of real GDP; PLCPI = ΔLCPI where LCPI is the log of the consumer price index (CPI).

Figure 2.7 Impulse responses for variables in a VAR model for Australia, 1990q1–2010q4

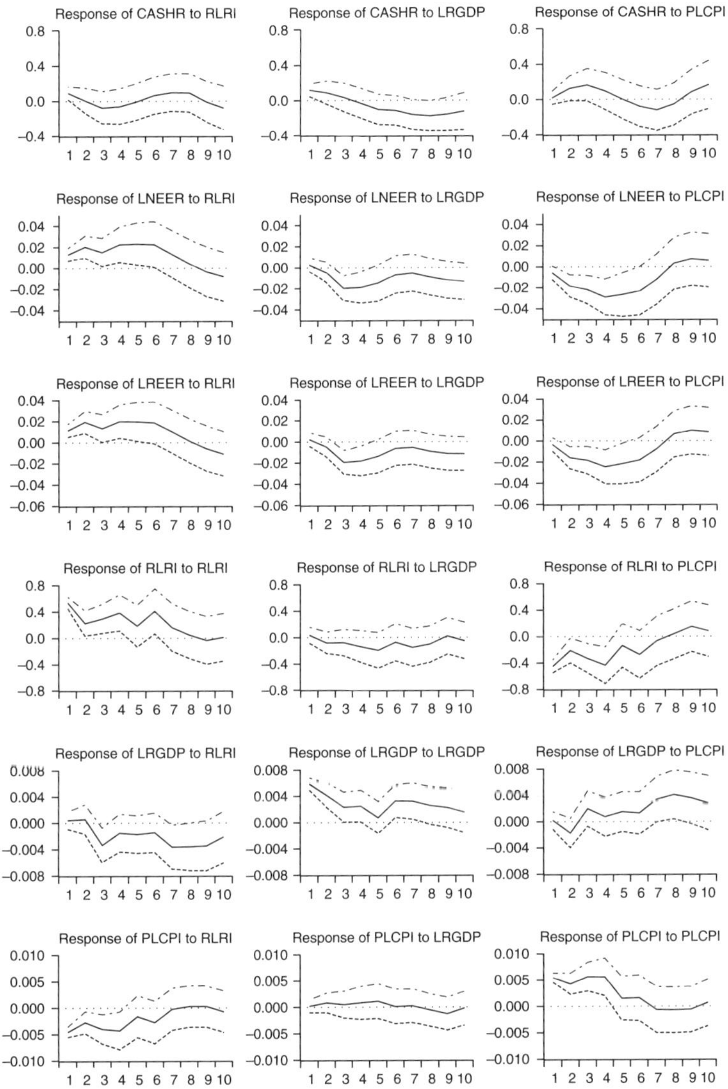

Figure 2.7 (continued)

Table 2.7 Forecast error-variance decomposition of variables in a VAR model for Australia

Variance Decomposition of CASHR:							
Period	S.E.	CASHR	LNEER	LREER	RLRI	LRGDP	PLCPI
1	0.33	100.00	0.00	0.00	0.00	0.00	0.00
2	0.54	93.15	2.98	1.23	1.24	1.28	0.12
7	0.81	64.94	8.64	2.46	4.45	17.34	2.17
10	0.99	49.31	10.89	7.09	3.78	14.05	14.89
Variance Decomposition of LNEER:							
Period	S.E.	CASHR	LNEER	LREER	RLRI	LRGDP	PLCPI
1	0.03	28.93	71.07	0.00	0.00	0.00	0.00
2	0.04	20.97	62.06	1.29	8.22	2.62	4.84
7	0.08	7.98	45.96	2.29	18.86	9.23	15.69
10	0.09	7.91	39.93	12.90	17.16	8.73	13.37
Variance Decomposition of LREER:							
Period	S.E.	CASHR	LNEER	LREER	RLRI	LRGDP	PLCPI
1	0.02	31.8	66.68	1.50	0.00	0.00	0.00
2	0.04	25.66	55.48	0.83	9.93	3.15	4.94
7	0.08	9.28	40.93	2.09	19.88	11.59	16.23
10	0.08	8.59	34.21	13.92	17.89	11.03	14.36
Variance Decomposition of RLRI:							
Period	S.E.	CASHR	LNEER	LREER	RLRI	LRGDP	PLCPI
1	0.54	7.49	13.12	15.65	63.73	0.00	0.00
2	0.64	5.44	25.37	11.53	52.72	0.44	4.49
7	1.31	8.23	42.22	9.78	35.39	1.28	3.08
10	1.42	8.56	36.09	20.03	31.12	1.49	2.71
Variance Decomposition of LRGDP:							
Period	S.E.	CASHR	LNEER	LREER	RLRI	LRGDP	PLCPI
1	0.01	12.13	1.26	4.27	0.80	81.53	0.00
2	0.01	7.09	1.97	19.45	0.62	68.25	2.62
7	0.01	5.52	13.40	10.92	17.50	47.35	5.31
10	0.02	6.51	10.64	12.93	17.42	44.41	8.09
Variance Decomposition of PLCPI:							
Period	S.E.	CASHR	LNEER	LREER	RLRI	LRGDP	PLCPI
1	0.01	0.27	7.37	32.32	45.29	0.18	14.55
2	0.01	9.43	17.38	22.41	32.04	0.14	18.59
7	0.01	16.19	36.60	13.01	22.89	1.57	9.76
10	0.02	18.64	32.14	14.71	19.98	1.83	12.70
The Cholesky Ordering: CASHR LNEER LREER RLRI LRGDP PLCPI							

Note: Definitions of variables: CASHR = cash rate of the RBA; LNEER = log of the nominal effective exchange rate of the Australian dollar; LREER = log of the real effective exchange rate of the Australian dollar; RLRI = real lending rate of interest; LRGDP = log of real GDP; PLCPI = ΔLCPI where LCPI = log of the consumer price index (CPI) and Δ is the first-order difference operator.

raised investment, especially in the mining sector. Sustained economic growth in Asia, China in particular, fuelled this investment-export boom. There has been a suggestion that the mining boom created a two-speed economy in which the rapid expansion of the mining sector and appreciating currency combined to significantly reduce growth of the non-mining sector. In particular, the appreciation of the Australian dollar caused by the large foreign-capital inflows put severe pressure on demand for and pricing of manufacturing and agricultural exports (Corden, 2011; Dornbusch et al., 2013). The appreciating currency prevented the economy from overheating, however. Without the appreciation, Australian inflation and interest rates would have had to rise instead. The unemployment rate declined steadily from the early 1990s, reaching a low of about 5 per cent in 2007 where it has remained (Table 2.8). This is Australia's lowest unemployment rate since the early 1970s (Gruen, 2000; Gruen and Stevens, 2000; Stevens, 2006).

Monetary policy remained the key component of economic policy throughout the global financial crisis during 2007–09. The RBA eased the policy interest rate almost continuously throughout calendar year 2008, from a high of 7.25 per cent at the beginning of 2008 to just 3 per cent by mid 2009. In support, the then Rudd Labor government contributed an expansionary fiscal policy to avert the anticipated recession. The first stage of a large discretionary fiscal stimulus, which totalled around 6 per cent of GDP over several packages, was implemented within three months of the collapse of Lehman Brothers in 2008. Despite early signs of recession and one quarter of negative growth in 2008, the economy had returned to normalcy by 2010. Fiscal stimulus was withdrawn in 2010 as efforts were then made to consolidate fiscal stability over the medium term. The latest IMF publications suggest that Australia remains in a good position to maintain steady economic growth without creating a fiscal crisis. The flexible exchange rate, in particular, plays the critical role in maintaining steady economic growth in the midst of a receding resources boom. The Abbott Liberal-National Federal Coalition government, elected in September 2013, is likely to exercise monetary and fiscal discipline in support of steady economic growth.

SUMMARY, POLICY IMPLICATIONS AND CONCLUDING REMARKS

This chapter has provided an overview of monetary policy conduct in Australia since the 1950s under, successively, fixed peg, managed float and finally free-float exchange rate systems. Until the early 1990s, under

Table 2.8 Macroeconomic indicators, Australia, 1986–2012

Macroeconomic indicators	1986–90	1991–95	1996–2000	2001–05	2006–10	2011	2012
Budget balance (% of GDP)	−0.2	−3.2	0.5	1.6	1.1	−3.4	−2.9
Money-growth rate (%)							
Narrow money growth	13.7	12.5	10.6	6.4	7.5	0.1	3.1
Broad money growth	12.9	3.8	7.5	7.3	11.0	7.6	6.4
Real GDP growth (%)	3.3	2.8	4.2	3.4	2.8	2.4	3.6
Unemployment rate (%)	7.1	9.6	7.5	5.9	4.9	5.1	5.2
Output gap (% of potential GDP)	1.2	−0.8	0.3	−0.2	−0.5	−1.3	−0.9
Real wage index (2005 = 100)	76.8	81.0	88.3	95.6	103.9	109.7	111.0
Share price index (2005 = 100)	34.4	41.7	63.2	80.7	115.6	103.2	100.0
CPI inflation (%)	7.9	2.5	1.9	3.0	3.0	3.4	1.8
Current account balance (% of GDP)	−4.9	−4.0	−4.1	−4.6	−5.6	−3.5	−2.8
Nominal interest rate (%)							
Yield on 3-year Treasury bills	13.6	8.1	6.1	5.1	5.4	4.4	2.8
Yield on 15-year Treasury bills	13.1	9.1	6.6	5.6	5.6	4.9	3.4
Treasury note rediscount rate	15.5	7.0	5.7	5.0	5.3	4.7	3.7
Real interest rate (%)							
Real yield on 3-year Treasury bills	5.2	5.4	4.1	2.1	2.3	0.9	1.0
Real yield on 15-year Treasury bills	4.8	6.4	4.6	2.4	2.5	1.4	1.6
Real treasury note rediscount rate	7.0	4.4	3.7	1.9	2.3	1.3	1.9
External terms of trade (%)	83.5	76.2	75.8	85.9	124.3	152.9	137.3
Nominal exchange rate (A$/US$)	1.4	1.4	1.5	1.6	1.2	1.0	1.0
Nominal effective exchange rate	104.3	95.9	95.6	91.7	103.6	121.7	126.0
Real effective exchange rate	91.9	87.4	86.2	89.1	104.9	115.4	115.4

Note: As for Table 2.6.

Source: See Table 2.6.

the first two types of exchange rate arrangements and significant capital controls, monetary policy in Australia was not conducted independently to ensure price stability. Rather, it was dominated by fiscal policy and targeted at multiple objectives. From the early 1990s, monetary policy has operated under a floating exchange rate system with low capital flow restrictions, and has been directed at low and stable inflation under inflation targeting. Inflation has remained low since then, but there is concern that it has remained unstable and highly persistent. This suggests that a degree of inflation-uncertainty has somewhat compromised the economy's responsiveness to structural change. Hence, firstly, economic growth during the rapid structural change in response to the sustained commodity boom of the early to late 2000s may have been sub-optimal. Secondly, in the face of the receding commodity boom, rapid structural responsiveness is more important than ever as the currency depreciates and investment opportunities in export activity proliferate.

The suggestion is that there is scope for improvement in Australian monetary policy. Monetary policy should focus primarily on inflation and less on smoothing business cycles. Moreover, although the RBA has maintained its autonomy in the conduct of monetary policy and built significant credibility, its secondary full-employment target has left its credibility at a lower level than it could otherwise have attained. The higher credibility alternative was to substitute as its secondary objective an inflation-volatility target using a policy rule. This would confer the advantage of an improved real investment climate while simultaneously meeting the statutory unemployment objective in the long run.

Contrary to the expectations, the adoption of inflation targeting in 1993 did not significantly lower inflation persistence. It is not clear, however, whether Australia's inflation persistence is intrinsic to its average inflation rate or is simultaneously caused by the structural sources that produce the driving process of inflation itself. Higher intrinsic inflation persistence reflects such factors as wage-indexation (implicit or explicit), the price-setting behaviour of firms and small or less frequent changes in the trend rate of inflation. Higher inherited inflation persistence may reflect the persistence of the driving force of inflation, such as the output gap. It is technically difficult to attribute any change in reduced-form inflation persistence to structural sources alone; or to intrinsic sources alone; or, even more difficult, to some combination of both (Fuhrer, 2011), since the shares would then have to be quantified.

The chapter has not investigated this issue further, so that it is possible to draw only some general conclusions. As Australia's reduced-form inflation persistence, evident in the data from 1993 onwards, has not declined significantly over the past two decades, the major policy implications are as follows. Firstly, the RBA should raise its policy commitment, credibility and determination to reduce the amplitude of inflationary oscillations around the average rate. While RBA policy credibility with respect to inflation stability under the flexible inflation targeting regime can by no stretch of the imagination be termed 'low', nevertheless, it should be a highly ranked focus of policy innovation and reform, since the instruments of greater monetary policy communication and transparency, and consequently enhanced RBA credibility, can lower inflation persistence. A focused pursuit by the RBA of its statutory obligation to maintain the stability of the currency, in the sense of maintaining a low and stable rate of inflation (with marginal exchange rate stabilization), are expected to raise its policy credibility and increase its long-run effectiveness in achievement of its other statutory objectives of full employment and the maximization of economic welfare and prosperity. Consultation with the government before implementing such a policy shift would of course be advisable, if not strictly required by law. Secondly, government policy measures are needed in the product and factor markets to make them more flexible in order to reduce intrinsic inflation persistence.

The key issue for Australia's present strategy of monetary policy is inflation volatility. This is partly due to the design of inflation targeting strategy. In particular, the use of a short-term interest rate as the policy instrument has led to inflation volatility. This has happened in the economic environment to which Australia is exposed by its economic structure, in which diverse supply and demand shocks are common (Corden, 2011). Evidence for this is available from the declining decade-long mining boom. The contemporary order of inflation volatility around the measured average rate can be interpreted as a cost that the RBA is prepared to allow in pursuit of its secondary target of output stability. However, the cost of inflation volatility is not immaterial. It affects investment, distorts relative prices and lowers economic efficiency and growth, thereby elevating unemployment. A central bank that earns credibility through maintaining low and stable inflation can generate flow-on effects that make the economy more stable, not less, even in the presence of a commodities-dominated economic structure.

For Australia, the inevitable policy challenge is to maintain low and steady inflation in an environment of rising inflationary expectations from ongoing monetary expansion across the globe. In this environment, the short-term interest rate could be a misleading indicator of the monetary policy stance (Friedman, 2000). The RBA should therefore review favourably the usefulness of the money-growth rate, and its volatility, for forecasting inflation and inflation volatility. The inflation targeting strategy may weaken the long-run linkage between money growth and inflation but it does not eliminate such a relationship. When and how this relation evolves remains a contentious issue in the literature, but it cannot be ignored or put on hold by policy practitioners while academics settle the debate on the usefulness of money in monetary policy (McCallum and Nelson, 2011).

NOTES

1. This section has drawn some information on Australia from Wikipedia, http://en.wikipedia.org/wiki/Australia.
2. The government was headed by Sir Robert Menzies for the period 1949–66.
3. OPEC represents the Organization of Petroleum Exporting Countries.
4. Both the Coalition and Labor governments since then have accepted the monetary interpretation of inflation although under inflation targeting monetary aggregates have been relegated to a lower position while the interest rate has gained dominance as the key policy instrument.
5. See Svensson (2011) for a detailed discussion on the characteristic of flexible inflation targeting and its implications.
6. This is a website description of the RBA's conduct of monetary policy. In detail: 'The Reserve Bank of Australia is Australia's central bank. Its duty is to contribute to the maintenance of price stability, full employment, and the economic prosperity and welfare of the Australian people. It does this by setting the cash rate to meet a medium-term inflation target, working to maintain a strong financial system and efficient payments system, and issuing the nation's banknotes' (http://www.rba.gov.au/about-rba/index.html). For detailed discussion on central banking and monetary policy in Australia, see Beel (2004).
7. See RBA, *Monetary Policy*, http://www.rba.gov.au.
8. Debelle and Stevens (1995), citing Fraser (1994), seem to confirm the circumstantial evidence: 'Numbers of that magnitude for average inflation [2–3 per cent underlying inflation over the medium term] are taken to "equate with reasonable price stability" (Fraser, 1994), in the sense of making any distorting effects of inflation on economic behaviour acceptably small.'
9. This represents the view that inflation responds to output gap when it is positive (overheated economy) but not necessarily when the economy is in recession. Analytically, this suggests the case of a horizontal supply curve until the economy reaches the full-employment level.
10. The figure shows the five-year period mean rate of inflation with ± standard deviation.
11. The reduced-form inflation persistence, measured by the coefficient on one-period lagged rate of inflation in an AR(1) model, is about 0.8. The recursive regression coefficient on the one-period lagged rate of inflation has remained stable.
12. See Table 2.5 for mean and variance equality tests results.
13. This is estimated by GARCH(1,1)-in-mean model, with AR(1) mean equation.
14. Boehm (1984) deployed the Granger-causality test to determine the causal linkage between wage growth and inflation in Australia. He used quarterly data over the period 1954–82 and found Granger causation from wages to prices but not vice versa. Alston and Chalfant (1987) extended Boehm's bivariate study by including money supply growth in their model. They found lagged money supply growth to Granger cause wage growth and inflation. They argued a causal linkage from money to both wages and prices with different time lags.
15. Results obtained by different forms of the GARCH model on an exploratory basis suggest a feedback relation between inflation and inflation volatility. Further research is needed to establish any asymmetric impact of inflation shocks on inflation volatility. For a recent study on this relationship, see Hossain (2014).
16. The empirical results are not reported here.

17. The term 'rule-based' implies a combination of rule and discretion. The rule-dictated or rule-dominated part of policy is prime. Secondarily, policymaker discretion is applied at the margin in either or both of two ways. Firstly, policymakers may use judgement to modify the rule's policy-adjustment recommendations before implementation. Secondly, policymakers may have no choice but to deploy discretion in pursuit of any secondary targets they may have that are not amenable to rule-calculated policy settings. If no discretion is applied, then full transparency requires use of the term 'rule-dictated' policy or something similar.
18. Appendix A makes a brief illustration of exchange rate regimes and their implications on monetary policy in Australia since the 1950s.
19. The Australian banking system has, however, remained oligopolistic.
20. Under a flexible exchange rate system since 1983, the RBA gained monetary policy independence for price stability. Until then, as Australia operated under a fixed pegged exchange rate system, some autonomy in monetary policy depended on whether capital controls were in place and how effective these controls were.
21. Under the fixed pegged exchange rate system, the expansionary fiscal and monetary policies of the United States from the mid 1960s, associated with its financing of war in Vietnam, created excess liquidity across the globe. This contributed to the rapid accumulation of foreign reserves in commodity exporting countries like Australia.
22. OECD represents the Organisation for Economic Co-operation and Development.
23. Nelson (2005) suggests that even the Fraser government's adoption of monetary targeting in 1976 does not change the perception that Australia neglected monetary policy from the 1950s through the early 1990s and that most policymakers and commentators believed in non-monetary sources (cost-push) of inflation until the introduction of inflation targeting. In the absence of effective control over capital flows, the authorities did not have control over monetary aggregates under a pegged exchange rate system. The interest rates were also not market determined. The Treasury set the interest rates and the RBA remained the residual purchaser of Treasury securities in market that were not demanded by the private sector.
24. This government is sometimes referred to as the 'Hawke-Keating' Labor government, for two main reasons: firstly, due to the close political and policy team relationship that developed between Prime Minister Robert Hawke and Treasurer Paul Keating; and secondly, because Keating replaced Hawke as Prime Minister in December 1991 in a Party leadership spill, with Labor still in power. He led this Keating government to a win at the next election in March 1993 and remained in office until the Howard Coalition government was elected in March 1996.
25. In August 1996 inflation targeting was recognized formally as the strategy of monetary policy. An agreement was reached between the Governor of the RBA and the Treasurer of the Commonwealth of Australia. In addition to specifying a numerical inflation target, the agreement established the standards for reporting and accountability of the RBA. This was done through regular policy statements and twice-yearly appearances of the Governor before the Federal House of Representatives Economics Committee (Edey, 2006; Stevens, 2003b).
26. See Appendix C for some empirical results on the interest rate responses to the inflation and output gaps.

REFERENCES

Alexander, S.S. (1952), 'Effects of a devaluation on a trade balance', *IMF Staff Papers*, **2**, June, 263–78.

Alston, J.M. and J.A. Chalfant (1987), 'A note on the causality between money, wages and prices in Australia', *Economic Record*, **63**(181), 115–19.

Argy, V. (1992), *Australian Macroeconomic Policy in a Changing World Environment*, Sydney: Allen and Unwin.
Argy, V., A. Brennan and G. Stevens (1990), 'Monetary targeting: the international experience', *Economic Record*, **66**(192), 37–62.
Ball, L. (1992), 'Why does high inflation raise inflation uncertainty?', *Journal of Monetary Economics*, **29**(3), 371–88.
Battellino, R. (2007), 'Central bank market operations', *Reserve Bank of Australia Bulletin*, September, 19–26.
Beel, S. (2004), *Australia's Money Mandarins: The Reserve Bank and the Politics of Money*, Cambridge: Cambridge University Press.
Black, T. (1989), 'High interest rates: problems and solutions', *Policy*, Spring, 12–16.
Blanchard, O.J. and J. Sheen (2007), *Macroeconomics*, Sydney: Pearson-Education.
Boehm, E. (1984), 'Money wages, consumer prices, and causality in Australia', *Economic Record*, **60**, 236–51.
Boehm, E. and V. Martin (1989), 'An investigation into the major causes of Australia's recent inflation and some policy implications', *Economic Record*, **65**, 1–15.
Bryant, R., P. Hooper and C. Mann (eds) (2003), *Evaluating Policy Regimes: New Research in Empirical Macroeconomics*, Washington, DC: Brookings Institution.
Corden, W.M. (1981), *Inflation, Exchange Rate and the World Economy*, Oxford: Oxford University Press.
Corden, W.M. (2011), 'The Dutch disease in Australia: policy options for a three-speed economy', Working Papers in Trade and Development, Crawford School of Economics and Government, Australian National University, Canberra.
Cukierman, A. and A.H. Meltzer (1986), 'A theory of ambiguity, credibility, and inflation under discretion and asymmetric information', *Econometrica*, **54**, 1099–128.
De Brouwer, G. and J. Gilbert (1998), 'Monetary policy reaction functions in Australia', *Economic Record*, **81**, 124–34.
Debelle, G. and G. Stevens (1995), 'Monetary policy goals for inflation in Australia', Research Discussion Paper No. 9503, Reserve Bank of Australia, Sydney.
Dornbusch, R., P. Bodman, S. Fischer and R. Startz (2013), *Macroeconomics*, Sydney: McGraw Hill.
Edey, M. (2006), 'An Australian perspective on inflation targeting, communication and transparency', BIS Papers No. 31: Monetary Policy in Asia: Approaches and Implementation, Bank for International Settlements, Basel.
Edwards, J. (1996), *Keating: The Inside Story*, Ringwood, Victoria: Viking Penguin.
Fraser, B. (1993), 'Some aspects of monetary policy', *Reserve Bank of Australia Bulletin*, April, 1–7.
Fraser, B. (1994), 'Sustainable growth in Australia', *Reserve Bank of Australia Bulletin*, July, 17–23.
Friedman, M. (1968), 'The role of monetary policy', *American Economic Review*, **78**, 1–17.
Friedman, M. (1973), *Money and Economic Development*, Toronto: Lexington Books.
Friedman, M. (1977), 'Nobel Lecture: Inflation and unemployment', *Journal of Political Economy*, **85**, 451–72.
Friedman, M. (2000), 'Canada and flexible exchange rates', Keynote address, Bank of Canada, available at http://www.bankofcanada.ca/wp-content/uploads/2010/08/keynote.pdf (accessed 27 August 2013).

Fuhrer, J.C. (2011), 'Inflation persistence', in B.M. Friedman and W. Woodford (eds), *Handbook of Monetary Economics*, Vol. 3A, Amsterdam: Elsevier Science, pp. 423–86.

Gregory, R.W. (1986), 'Wages policy and unemployment in Australia', *Economica*, **53**, S53–S74.

Grenville, S.A. (ed.) (1990), *The Australian Macro-economy in the 1980s*, Sydney: Reserve Bank of Australia.

Gruen, D. (2000), 'The Australian economy in the 1990s', *Reserve Bank of Australia Bulletin*, October, 1–6.

Gruen, D. and G. Stevens (2000), 'Australian macroeconomic performance and policies in the 1990s', in D. Gruen and S. Shrestha (eds), *Australian Economy in the 1990s*, Sydney: Ambassador Press, pp. 32–72.

Hossain, A. (2012), 'Modelling of narrow money demand in Australia: an ARDL cointegration approach, 1970–2009', *Empirical Economics*, **42**(3), 767–90.

Hossain, A. (2014), 'Inflation and inflation volatility in Australia', *Economic Papers*, **33**(2), 163–85.

IMF (International Monetary Fund) (various years), *International Financial Statistics*, Washington, DC: IMF.

IMF (International Monetary Fund) (various years), *World Economic Outlook*, Washington, DC: IMF.

Katsimbris, G.M. (1985), 'The relationship between the inflation rate, its variability and output growth variability', *Journal of Money, Credit and Banking*, **17**(2), 179–99.

Layton, A. (1994), *Modern Australian Macroeconomics*, Melbourne: Thomas Nelson Australia.

Leu, S.C.Y and J. Sheen (2006), 'Asymmetric monetary policy in Australia', *Economic Record*, Special Issue, **82**, S85–S96.

Levi, M.D. and J.H. Makin (1980), 'Inflation uncertainty and the Phillips curve: some empirical evidence', *American Economic Review*, **70**(5), 1022–7.

Lucas, R.E., Jr (1973), 'Some international evidence on output-inflation trade-offs', *American Economic Review*, **63**, June, 326–34.

McCallum, B.T. and E. Nelson (2011), 'Money and inflation: some critical issues', in B.M. Friedman and M. Woodford (eds), *Handbook of Monetary Economics*, Vol. 3A, Amsterdam: Elsevier Science, pp. 97–153.

Macfarlane, I.J. (1997), 'Monetary policy regimes: past and future', *Reserve Bank of Australia Bulletin*, October, 20–31.

Macfarlane, I.J. (1998), 'Australian monetary policy in the last quarter of the twentieth century', *Reserve Bank of Australia Bulletin*, October, 6–19.

Milbourne, R. (1990), 'Money and finance', in S. Grenville (ed.), *The Australian Macro-economy in the 1980s*, Sydney: Reserve Bank of Australia, pp. 222–76.

Nelson, E. (2005), 'Monetary policy neglect and the great inflation in Canada, Australia, and New Zealand', *International Journal of Central Banking*, May, 133–79.

Nelson, E. and K. Nikolov (2004), 'Monetary policy and stagflation in the United Kingdom', *Journal of Money, Credit and Banking*, **36**(3), 293–318.

Nevile, J. (1975), 'Fiscal policy and inflation', *Economic Papers*, **50**, 5–14.

Nevile, J. (1983), 'The links between wages, inflation and unemployment', *Economic Papers*, **2**, 28–33.

Okun, A. (1971), 'The mirage of steady inflation', *Brookings Papers on Economic Activity*, **2**, 485–98.

Pagan, A.R. and P.K. Trivedi (1983), *The Effects of Inflation*, Canberra: Centre for Economic Policy Research, Australian National University.

Phelps, E.S. (1970), 'Introduction: the new microeconomics in employment and inflation theory', in E.S. Phelps (ed.), *Microeconomic Foundations of Employment and Inflation Theory*, New York: Norton, pp. 1–23.

Pitchford, J. (1989), 'Does Australia really have a current account problem? And a sceptical view of Australia's current account and debt problem', Discussion Paper No. 214, Centre for Economic Policy Research, Australian National University, Canberra.

Pitchford, J. (1990), *Australia's Foreign Debt: Myths and Realities*, Sydney: Allen and Unwin.

Poole, W. and D.C. Wheelock (2008), 'Stable prices, stable economy', *The Regional Economist*, January, 15–19.

RBA (Reserve Bank of Australia), http://www.rba.gov.au.

RBA (Reserve Bank of Australia), *Monetary Policy*, http://www.rba.gov.au.

RBA (Reserve Bank of Australia) (2014), *The Exchange Rate and the Reserve Bank's Role in the Foreign Exchange Market*, available at http://www.rba.gov.au/mkt-operations/ex-rate-rba-role-fx-mkt.html (accessed 19 March 2015).

Schaechter, A., M.T. Stone and M. Zelmer (2000), 'Adopting inflation targeting: practical issues for emerging market countries', Occasional Paper No. 202, IMF, Washington, DC.

Sjaastad, L. (1989), 'The deficit: a crisis of minor proportions', *Economic Papers*, **8**(4), 19–24.

Stevens, G. (2003a), 'Inflation targeting: a decade of Australian experience', *Reserve Bank of Australia Bulletin*, April, 17–29.

Stevens, G. (2003b), 'Structural change and the conduct of monetary policy', Speech given at the Federal Reserve Bank of Kansas City Economic Symposium, Jackson Hole, 30 August, available at http://www.bis.org/review/r030905e.pdf (accessed 19 March 2015).

Stevens, G. (2013), 'The Australian dollar: thirty years of floating', speech to the Australian Business Economists' Annual Dinner, Sydney, 21 November, available at http://www.rba.gov.au/speeches/2013/sp-gov-211113.html (accessed 19 March 2015).

Stevens, G.R. (2006), 'Capital flows and monetary policy', *Reserve Bank of Australia Bulletin*, October, 19–25.

Svensson, L.E.O. (2011), 'Inflation targeting', in B.M. Friedman and M. Woodford (eds), *Handbook of Monetary Economics*, Vol. 3B, Amsterdam: Elsevier Science, pp. 1237–302.

APPENDIX A: EXCHANGE RATE REGIMES AND MONETARY POLICY INDEPENDENCE IN AUSTRALIA

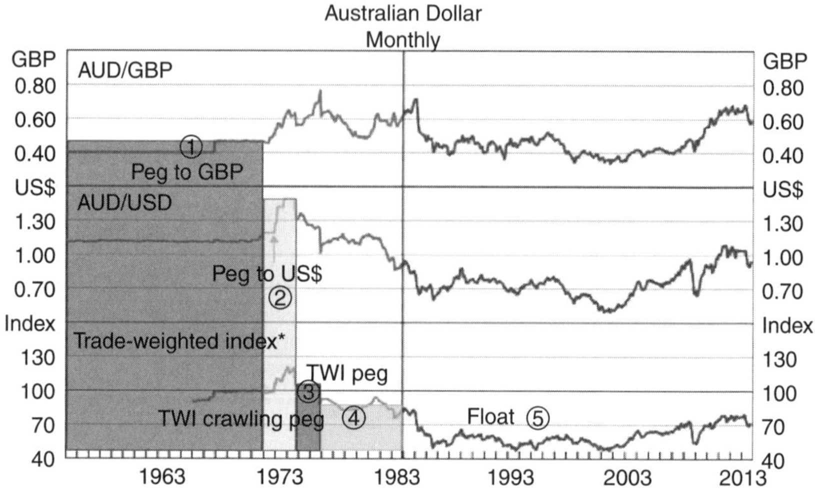

Notes: Based on Stevens (2013, Graph 1) and RBA (2014, Graph 3 and surrounding text), Australia's exchange rate regimes can be inferred as follows:

* May 1970 = 100

1. 1931–late 1971: fixed peg to UK£.
2. Late 1971–late 1974: peg to US$. Macfarlane's (1998, p. 9) treatment, while perhaps somewhat flawed, is suggestive that the peg may have been fixed in the earliest part of this period, but was adjustable thereafter.
3. Late 1974–late 1976: fixed peg to a trade-weighted index (TWI).
4. Late 1976–December, 1983: crawling peg to a TWI.
5. December 1983 →: floating.

Source: Stevens (2013, Graph 1); RBA (2014, Graph 3) and surrounding text; and Macfarlane (1998, p. 9).

Figure 2A.1 Exchange rate regimes in Australia, 1931–2013

Based on Macfarlane (1998), Australia's exchange rate regimes, capital controls and monetary policy independence can be inferred as follows:

Exchange Rate Regimes

1945–71: Macfarlane (1998, p. 9) suggests pegged to US$, but this conflicts with Stevens (2013: Graph 1) and RBA (2014: Graph 3 and surrounding text) (Figure 2A.1). Whether the anchor currency was UK£ or US$, this regime was an exchange rate targeting with capital regulation giving some control over monetary policy.

1971–74: Adjustable peg to US$.

1974–76: Fixed peg to a trade-weighted basket.

1976–83: Crawling peg to a trade-weighted basket.

December 1983: Floating.

Monetary Policy Regimes

Pre-1976: Treasury-conducted exchange rate targeting. Significant national monetary policy independence under high capital regulation; Treasury using its discretionary power to pursue multiple targets; limited transparency (only the exchange rate target).

1976–83: Treasury-conducted monetary targeting. Significant national monetary policy independence under crawling peg to the trade-weighted index (TWI) and high capital regulation; Treasury using its discretionary power to pursue multiple targets; limited transparency (only the monetary target announced annually with the government budget).

1983–85: Treasury-conducted monetary targeting. Full national monetary policy independence following the December 1983 currency float and removal of most capital regulation; Treasury using its discretionary power to pursue multiple targets; limited transparency (only the monetary target announced annually with the government budget).

1985–88: Treasury-conducted 'checklist' approach to monetary policy. Full national monetary policy independence under floating currency and low capital regulation; Treasury using its discretionary power to pursue multiple targets; limited transparency (based on the checklist).

1988–93: Treasury-conducted non-checklist (unfettered) discretionary monetary policy. Full national monetary policy independence under a floating exchange rate with low capital regulation; Treasury using its discretionary power to pursue multiple targets; low transparency.

1993 to date: RBA-conducted, rule-based monetary policy. Full national monetary policy independence under a floating exchange rate with low capital regulation; RBA operational independence to primarily target price stability (by rule) with the secondary target of output stabilization (by discretion); greater transparency than ever before, though still limited.

REFERENCES

Macfarlane, I.J. (1998), 'Australian monetary policy in the last quarter of the twentieth century', *Reserve Bank of Australia Bulletin*, October, 6–19.

RBA (Reserve Bank of Australia) (2014), *The Exchange Rate and the Reserve Bank's Role in the Foreign Exchange Market*, available at http://www.rba.gov.au/mkt-operations/ex-rate-rba-role-fx-mkt.html (accessed 19 March 2015).

Stevens, G. (2013), 'The Australian dollar: thirty years of floating', Speech to the Australian Business Economists' Annual Dinner, Sydney, 21 November, available at http://www.rba.gov.au/speeches/2013/sp-gov-211113.html (accessed 19 March 2015).

APPENDIX B: FLEXIBLE INFLATION TARGETING AND INFLATION PERSISTENCE IN AUSTRALIA

Under flexible inflation targeting the monetary authorities attempt to achieve price stability, meaning low and stable inflation, while stabilizing output around its potential level. The central bank's commitment to maintain price stability is expected to lower inflation persistence. Inflation persistence appears to have declined in inflation targeting countries where price stability has gained priority over other policy objectives. Benati (2008) suggests that intrinsic inflation persistence drops significantly towards zero once a new credible monetary policy regime is embedded into economic policymaking. He found a reduction in inflation persistence across monetary policy regimes that provided credible commitment to price stability. In general, monetary policy credibility depends on transparency, announced policy and visible policy actions, and public perception about successful policy outcomes. This indicates that under credible monetary policy regime, actual inflation consistently resides within a pre-announced range of inflation.

This appendix reports some evidence on high inflation persistence in Australia based on quarterly data over the period 1949q3–2012q4. It examines whether there was significant change in reduced-form inflation persistence over time. The following specification is used for estimation purposes:

$$\pi_t = \alpha + \beta\pi_{t-1} + \varepsilon_t \tag{2B.1}$$

where π_t is defined as $\pi_t = \log(\text{CPI})_t - \log(\text{CPI})_{t-4}$; ε is an error term, representing shocks to inflation and is assumed to be distributed normally with zero mean and a constant variance; α is the intercept term, representing mean inflation determined by the long-term growth of the money supply adjusted for output growth; and β is the persistence coefficient whose value is expected to lie between zero and unity. Gerlach and Tillman (2010) suggest that β can be interpreted as a measure of the importance of permanent inflation shocks relative to the temporary ones. Thus, in economies in which the permanent shocks to inflation dominate, β should be relatively high. When inflation has the characteristic of a unit root, $\beta = 1$. Under inflation targeting or other monetary policy strategy in which the central bank moves the policy interest rate aggressively to offset inflationary shocks to inflation, β should be relatively small, implying that current inflation oscillates with relatively high frequency around the trend rate of inflation.

Although the above model can be specified in a generalized AR(p) form in which the sum of the significant lagged coefficients on the rate of inflation can be used for the interpretation of results, the primary interest is the coefficient on one-period lagged term – which could be the only significant coefficient.

The model is estimated by both the recursive and rolling regression techniques. The parameter of interest is β. The estimated coefficients are based on a regression of the rate of inflation on constant and one lagged term for inflation with data over the period 1949q3–2012q4. Figures 2.B1 and 2.B2

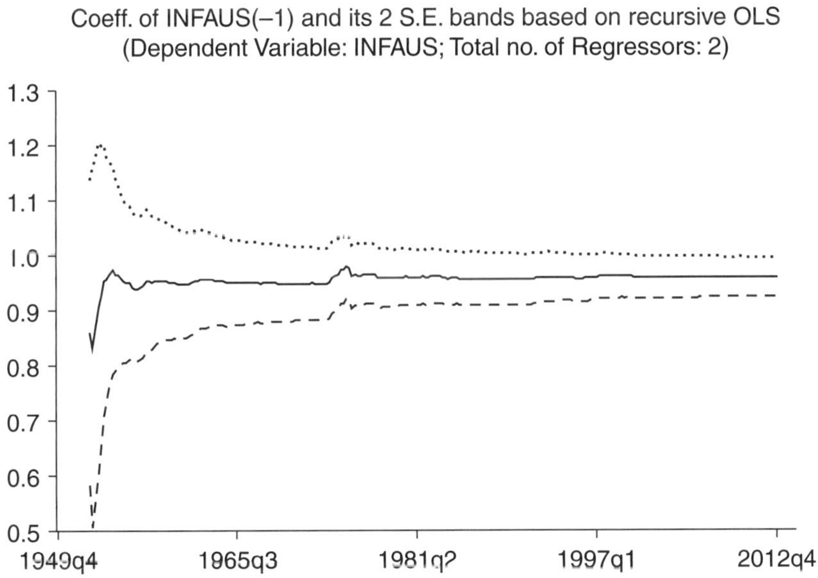

Note: INFAUS = CPI inflation in Australia.

Figure 2B.1 Recursive estimates of the coefficient on the one-period lagged rate of CPI inflation in Australia, 1949q3–2012q4

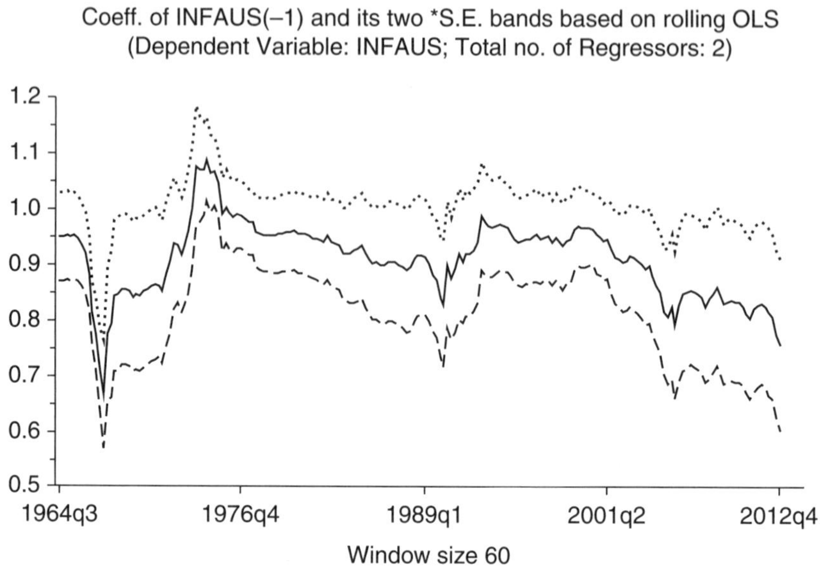

Note: INFAUS = CPI inflation in Australia.

Figure 2B.2 Rolling sample estimates of the coefficient on the one-period lagged rate of CPI inflation in Australia, 1949q3–2012q4

report the recursive and rolling regression coefficients on the one-period lagged rate of inflation.

The recursive coefficient estimates suggest that there was no significant change in the coefficient value on the one-period lagged term of inflation. The rolling sample estimates, however, suggest declining inflation persistence since the mid 2000s. The reasons behind any declining trend of reduced-form inflation persistence are not precise. In the literature, a number of sources are identified to explain any change in reduced-form inflation persistence. One source for changing intrinsic inflation persistence could be the systematic behaviour of central banks that raises its policy credibility. It is expected that the RBA would gradually gain more credibility in maintaining low and stable inflation. This would lower the time-inconsistency problem inherent in the RBA charter that requires it to pursue output stability in the short run.

REFERENCES

Benati, L. (2008), 'Investigating inflation persistence across monetary regimes', *Quarterly Journal of Economics*, **123**(3), 1005–60.
Gerlach, S. and P. Tillman (2010), 'Inflation targeting matters in Asia', available at http://www.voxeu.org/index.php?q=node/5628 (accessed 3 July 2011).

APPENDIX C: INTEREST RATE RESPONSE FUNCTION UNDER INFLATION TARGETING

A Taylor rule for the conduct of monetary policy takes the following form (Taylor, 1993):

$$\mathrm{NIR}_t^p = \pi_t + \mathrm{RIR}^n + \alpha(\pi_t^e - \pi_T) + \beta(y_t^e - y_n) + u_t \qquad (2C.1)$$

where NIR^p is the nominal policy interest rate, RIR^n is the 'long-term natural' real interest rate (assumed constant), π_t^e is the expected rate of inflation given information available at time t, π_T is the pre-set inflation target, y^e is expected real output and y_n is real output at the natural level, u is a random error term and α and β are positive parameters. In this specification, $(\pi_t^e - \pi_T)$ is the expected inflation gap and $(y_t^e - y_n)$ is the expected output gap.[1]

The Taylor principle suggests that the coefficient on the inflation gap (α) should bear a positive sign. This implies that when the expected rate of inflation rises above the inflation target, the central bank raises the interest rate more than proportionately to the rise in inflation. This means that to lower aggregate demand and hence inflation, the central bank should engineer an increase in the real interest rate with the rise in inflation. This gives a positive relation between the real policy interest rate (RIR^p) and the inflation rate. This positive relationship is often shown as Taylor's monetary policy curve. A relation of the following form can be used to examine whether a central bank meets the Taylor principle:

$$\mathrm{RIR}_t^p = \lambda_0 + \lambda_1(\pi_t^e - \pi_T) + \lambda_2(y_t^e - y_n) + v_t \qquad (2C.2)$$

where λ_0 is the long-term natural real interest rate, v is a random error term and λ_1 and λ_2 are positive real interest rate response parameters to the inflation and output gaps.

The Taylor principle requires that λ_1 bears a positive sign. The inclusion of the output gap in the Taylor rule shows the importance that a central bank accords to output (or employment) stability. The output gap is considered a lead indicator of future inflation. A positive output gap represents an economy that operates above full-employment level. The central bank may raise the real interest rate to dampen inflationary pressure in a booming economy. The coefficient on the output gap (λ_2) is expected to bear a positive sign.

Central banks often smooth changes in the interest rate. When it happens, equation (2C.2) can be estimated in a dynamic form with one-period lagged real interest rate, such that an estimable real interest rate reaction function can be specified in the following form:

$$\mathrm{RIR}_t^p = \alpha_0 + \alpha_1 \pi_t^e + \alpha_2 y_t^c + \alpha_3 \mathrm{RIR}_{t-1} + v_t \qquad (2C.3)$$

where the expected rate of inflation can be approximated by: $\pi_t^e = \pi_{t+1} + \varsigma_{t+1}$ with ς_{t+1} representing the random forecast error, and y^c is the output gap, which could be obtained by detrending real output with a Hodrick-Prescott filter. This specification, suitable for estimation purposes, suggests that a central bank raises the real interest rate when the inflation exceeds the target rate and when the output gap is positive.[2] The inclusion of the lagged real interest rate indicates that the central bank follows an interest rate smoothing scheme over time to avoid sharp reversals that may undermine the credibility of a central bank (Enders, 2010). The coefficient value α_3 measures the degree of interest rate smoothing. A slow adjustment of the real interest rate is considered desirable as it may lower the credibility loss from any sudden and large policy reversal. Consequently, this may deliver effective control and stability of inflation and output (Leu and Sheen, 2006).

Provided that the time-series for the variables in the specified model are stationary, it can be estimated preferably by the Generalized Method of Moments (GMM).[3] Table 2C.1 reports some estimates of the interest rate responses to the inflation and output gaps in Australia over the period 1990q1–2012q4. This sample period is chosen depending on data availability and the fact that the RBA conducted monetary policy under inflation targeting (explicit or implicit) over this period. The estimated results obtained by, alternatively, the nominal or real cash rate suggest that the coefficient on one-period lead inflation rate is significant at the 10 per cent level. The coefficient on the output gap, however, is not statistically significant. The residual graph (Figure 2C.1) shows that the fitted value for the real interest rate traces the actual rate closely, implying randomness of the residuals.

NOTES

1. This is a forward-looking interest rate response function, which can be modified and expanded for empirical estimation. For earlier discussion on monetary policy

Table 2C.1 Estimates of coefficients of the interest rate response function in Australia, 1990q1–2012q4

	Ordinary least squares	Generalized method of moments	Generalized method of moments
With nominal cash rate (CASHR)			
	coefficient (t-ratio) [prob.]	coefficient (t-ratio) [prob.]	coefficient (t-ratio) [prob.]
Intercept	0.41 (3.30) [0.00]	0.44 (3.33) [0.00]	0.45 (3.32) [0.00]
CPI inflation(+1)	0.15 (4.79) [0.00]	0.13 (2.26) [0.03]	0.14 (2.75) [0.00]
Lyc	5.98 (1.23) [0.00]	6.98 (0.78) [0.44]	
CASHR(–1)	0.84 (43.56) [0.00]	0.85 (47.86) [0.00]	0.85 (53.35) [0.00]
DW	1.03	1.00	1.00
Adjusted R^2	0.96	0.95	0.95
With real cash rate (RCASHR)			
	coefficient (t-ratio) [prob.]	coefficient (t-ratio) [prob.]	coefficient (t-ratio) [prob.]
Intercept	0.31 (1.33) [0.19]	−0.39 (−1.30) [0.20]	−0.39 (−1.32) [0.19]
CPI inflation(+1)	−0.07 (−1.19) [0.24]	0.17 (1.62) [0.11]	0.16 (1.59) [0.11]
Lyc	9.56 (0.99) [0.32]	−2.68 (−0.17) [0.87]	
RCASHR(–1)	0.93 (21.17) [0.00]	0.96 (17.76) [0.00]	0.96 (21.53) [0.00]
DW	2.35	1.95	1.99
Adjusted R^2	0.84	0.80	0.81

Note: CASHR = cash rate of the RBA; RCASHR = real cash rate of the RBA; and Lyc = cyclical component of log of real GDP.

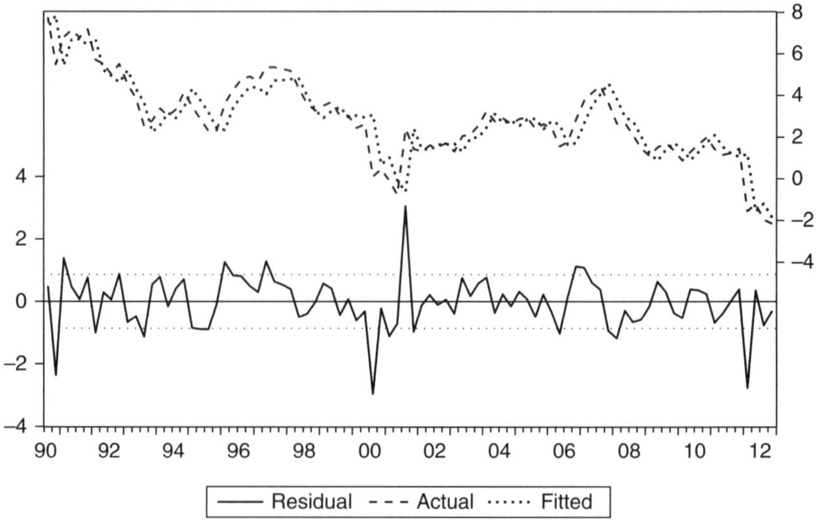

Figure 2C.1 Residual graph of the real cash rate response function in Australia, 1990q1–2012q4

reaction functions in Australia, see De Brouwer and Gilbert (1998) and Leu and Sheen (2006).

2. Some further modification of the above relation can be made by adding such variables as the real exchange rate. A non-linear form of the above specification is another possibility if the central bank reacts asymmetrically depending on whether the inflation gap or output gap is positive or negative. Nevertheless, a simple Taylor rule specification remains popular under inflation targeting (implicit or explicit) as it can trace the interest rate movement for most of the time. Bryant et al. (1993) suggest that if the interest rate responds to both the inflation and output movements, it can deliver the smallest output and price variabilities compared with other policy rules.
3. The GMM is used to estimate the equation due to simultaneity in the specified model.

REFERENCES

Bryant, R., P. Hooper and C. Mann (eds) (1993), *Evaluating Policy Regimes: New Research in Empirical Macroeconomics*, Washington, DC: Brookings Institution.

De Brouwer, G. and J. Gilbert (1998), 'Monetary policy reaction functions in Australia', *Economic Record*, **81**, 124–34.

Enders, W. (2010), *Applied Econometric Time Series*, New York: John Wiley and Sons.

Leu, S.C.Y and J. Sheen (2006), 'Asymmetric monetary policy in Australia', *Economic Record*, Special Issue, 82, S85–S96.

Taylor, J.B. (1993), 'Discretion versus policy rules in practice', *Carnegie-Rochester Conference Series on Public Policy*, **39**(1), 195–214.

APPENDIX D: MONEY-DEMAND RELATIONSHIP IN AUSTRALIA

This appendix reports estimates of an open-economy money-demand function for Australia using annual data for the period 1970–2012.[1] The model specified in the following generic form is used for estimation purposes:

$$\begin{aligned} LRJM_t = \alpha_0 + \alpha_1 Ly_t + \alpha_2 Lw_t + \alpha_3 NIR_t + \alpha_4 FIR_t \\ + \alpha_5 LRER_t + u_t \end{aligned} \quad (2D.1)$$

where LRJM (J = N,B) is the log of real narrow or broad money balances (real narrow money balances are denoted by LRNM while real broad money balances are denoted by LRBM), Ly is the log of real income, Lw is the log of wealth, proxied by the real share price index (Lrspi), NIR is a representative nominal interest rate (for example, the Treasury bill rate, TBR), FIR is a representative foreign nominal interest rate such as the US Treasury bill rate USTBR, LRER is the log of a representative real exchange rate such as the real effective exchange rate (REER), u is a random error term, which captures random money-demand shocks, and α_s are structural parameters to be estimated.

In the above specified equation, the coefficients on real income and the real share price index are expected to bear a positive sign while the coefficients on the domestic and foreign interest rates are expected to bear a negative sign. The coefficient on the real effective exchange rate is indeterminate because it can affect money demand both positively and negatively. The sign of the coefficient on the real exchange rate is, therefore, considered an empirical issue.

One additional variable of interest is inflation volatility, π^v. It is not included in the specification of the model. However, the statistical significance of this variable, measured by the conditional standard deviation of CPI inflation, can be used for investigation of its significance in an error-correction model after taking into account its time-series properties. The ADF and KPSS unit root test results (not reported) suggest that all these variables have a unit root while a measure of inflation volatility either by GARCH(1,1)-in-mean or eight-period rolling standard deviation of inflation is found stationary. This indicates that, except for inflation volatility, all these variables are eligible to form a cointegral relation. Inflation volatility can, however, affect money demand in the short run. This information is used for estimation of the model within a cointegration error-correction modelling framework.

The generic model specified above can be estimated by deploying both the Johansen and ARDL bounds-test approaches. The Johansen maximum-likelihood cointegration approach provides a unified framework for estimation and testing of cointegral relations in the context of vector autoregression error-correction models (VECM). This procedure is considered superior to a single-equation residual-based cointegration test, such as the Engle-Granger residual-based ADF test of cointegration, when there are more than two nonstationary variables in the specified model (Engle and Granger, 1987).

The Johansen Approach

To set up the Johansen test, a number of decisions have been made with respect to the time-series properties of variables, the nature of the intercept/trend in the VAR model and the order of the VAR. In the specified model, three types of variables have been included. Firstly, the nonstationary endogenous variables include LRJM, Ly, Lrspi, NIR and LREER. Secondly, there is one nonstationary exogenous variable, FIR. Thirdly, there is one stationary variable: inflation volatility, π^v. In addition, an intercept term (α_0) and a time trend (T) are added to the regression model. McCallum and Nelson (2011) suggest the inclusion of a trend term that may capture the smooth progress in payments technology. If the financial system develops in a way that allows agents to economise on their money holdings over time, the coefficient on time trend should bear a negative sign. The order of the lag-length in the VAR is set to one from the maximum lag-length four by deploying the SBC. Since annual data are deployed, one lag term is considered reasonable. Inclusion of more than one lag term may create an over-parameterization problem.

Table 2D.1 reports the Johansen cointegration and error-correction results for real narrow money balances.[2] Both the eigenvalue and trace statistics suggest the presence of a cointegral relation. Based on economic theory, this can be interpreted as a long-run money-demand relation. Both the coefficients on real income and the real share price index bear a positive sign. They are statistically highly significant. Although the income elasticity of demand for money is significantly greater than one, the wealth elasticity of demand for money is less than one. The coefficients on the Treasury bill rate and the US Treasury bill rate both act as an opportunity cost of holding money, bear a negative sign and are highly significant. The coefficient on the real exchange rate bears a negative sign and is highly significant. It indicates that an appreciation of the real exchange rate lowers the demand for domestic currency. This finding is consistent with the currency-substitution proposition. In the error-correction model, the

Table 2D.1 The Johansen tests for cointegral real narrow money-demand relationships in Australia, 1970–2012

Hypotheses		Test statistics		Number of cointegrating relationship (based on the Schwarz Bayesian Criterion, SBC)
Null	Alternative	Maximal eigenvalue test statistic	Trace test	
r = 0	r = 1	54.01*	111.05*	r = 1
r <= 1	r = 2	26.20*	57.04*	
r <= 2	r = 3	15.82	30.84	
r <= 3	r = 4	11.21	15.01	
r <= 4	r = 5	3.51	3.81	
r <= 5	r = 6	0.3	0.3	
		Decision: r = 1	Decision: r = 1	
List of eigenvalues: 0.769, 0.559, 0.445, 0.138, 0.042		95% critical value	95% critical value	
		39.83 (r = 1)	95.87 (r ≥ = 1)	
		33.64 (r = 2)	70.49 (r ≥ = 2)	
		27.42 (r = 3)	48.88 (r = 3)	

Variable	Normalized cointegrating vectors			
	Normalized coefficients	Standard errors	Imposed restrictions on cointegrating vectors	Log-likelihood ratio test statistic on restrictions
LRNM	1			$\chi^2_{(1)}$
LRGDP	−1.2	0.03	Coefficient on LRGDP = 0	40.24*
LRSPI	−0.16	0.05	Coefficient on LRGDP = −1	38.56*

Table 2D.1 (continued)

Variable	Normalized coefficients	Standard errors	Imposed restrictions on cointegrating vectors	Log-likelihood ratio test statistic on restrictions
TBR	0.07	0.01	Coefficient on LRSPI = 0	9.33*
LREER	0.4	0.06	Coefficient on TBR = 0	50.65*
USTBR	−0.03	0.01	Coefficient on LREER = 0	36.21*
			Coefficient on USTBR = 0	50.49*
Variable	Error-correction model		The Wald test on restrictions	$\chi^2_{(1)}$
	Coefficient	t-ratio		
Error-correction term(–1)	−0.51	−3.26	Coefficient on error-correction term (–1) = 0	1.36
INFVOL	0.01	1.2	Coefficient on INFVOL = 0	6.38*
Diagnostic statistics for the error-correction model				
DW	2.07	Lagrange multiplier test for serial correlation		F(1, 38) = 2.28
Adjusted R^2	0.22	Ramsey's RESET test of functional form mis-specification		F(1, 38) = 2.72
CUSUM test	stable	Normality of residuals		$\chi^2_{(2)}$ = 10.69
CUSUMSQ test	stable	Heteroskedasticity		F(1, 40) = 0.85

Note: Tests are conducted with restricted intercepts and no trends, and VAR = 1; adjusted sample period: 1970–2012; r represents the number of cointegrating relationship; INFVOL = inflation volatility, measured as the standard deviation of CPI inflation obtained from estimated GARCH(1,1) models; * suggests that the corresponding null hypothesis is rejected at the 95 per cent confidence level; and R^2 is adjusted for the degrees of freedom.

error-correction term is highly significant. The coefficient on inflation volatility bears a negative sign and is significant. The overall results suggest the presence of a long-run cointegral relation among the variables specified. This relationship is confirmed by the presence of a significant error-correction term associated with the cointegral relation. The diagnostic statistics do not suggest any major statistical problem.

The ARDL Approach

The Johansen system-based reduced-rank regression approach involves cases where all the underlying variables are integrated of order one. As most applied researchers face the problem of not knowing with certainty that the variables in the relationship under investigation have a unit root, there is a growing literature that uses the autoregressive distributed lag (ARDL) cointegration approach. The ARDL bounds-testing approach determines the presence of a stable long-run relationship among real money balances, real income, real stock price, the domestic and foreign interest rates, the real effective exchange rate and inflation volatility. The error-correction form of the ARDL model for the above defined variables can be specified in the following generalized log-linear form:

$$\begin{aligned}\Delta LRJM_t &= \alpha_0 + \alpha_1 T + \sum_{i=0}^{l1}\beta_i \Delta Ly_{t-i} + \sum_{i=0}^{l2}\gamma_i \Delta Lrspi_{t-i} + \sum_{i=0}^{l3}\eta_i \Delta NIR_{t-i}\\ &+ \sum_{i=0}^{l4}\lambda_i \Delta FIR_{t-i} + \sum_{i=0}^{l5}\mu_i \Delta LREER_{t-i} + \sum_{i=0}^{l6}\nu_i \Delta \pi^{v}_{t-i} + \sum_{i=1}^{l7}\kappa_i \Delta LRJM_{t-i}\\ &+ \phi_1 LRJM_{t-1} + \phi_2 Ly_{t-1} + \phi_3 Lrspi_{t-1} + \phi_4 NIR_{t-1} + \phi_5 FIR_{t-i}\\ &+ \phi_6 LREER_{t-1} + \phi_7 \pi^{v}_{t-1} + \varepsilon_t \qquad (2D.2)\end{aligned}$$

where the coefficients β_i, γ_i, η_i, λ_i, μ_i, ν_i and κ_i, represent the short-run dynamics of the underlying variables in the ARDL model, the coefficients ϕ_s represent the long-run relationship and ε is a random error term with zero mean and a constant variance. This specification is based on the maintained hypothesis that the time-series properties in the money-demand relationship can be approximated by a log-linear VAR(p) model, augmented with a deterministic intercept (α_0) and a trend (T).

In the specification the value of *i* can be infinity but in practice the number of lags used for estimation with annual data could be one or two. Preliminary estimation results show that one-period lag term is adequate for estimation of the model. Table 2D.2 reports the ARDL test results. The ARDL test results confirm the results obtained by the Johansen approach

Table 2D.2a The ARDL model of long-run real narrow money-demand relationships in Australia

F-statistic	4.27	
W-statistic	25.61	
Critical value bounds	F-test	W-test
90%	(2.58, 3.78)	(15.50, 22.67)
95%	(3.09, 4.46)	(18.52, 26.76)
Regressors	ARDL (2,0,0,0,0,0) (Selected based on SBC) Coefficient (t-ratio) [prob.]	ARDL (2,0,0,0,0,0) Estimated long-run coefficients Coefficient (t-ratio) [prob.]
Intercept	4.19 (9.67) [0.00]	
LRNM(–1)	0.28 (2.60) [0.01]	
LRNM(–2)	0.18 (1.94) [0.06]	
LRGDP	0.60 (6.90) [0.00]	1.13 (18.27) [0.00]
LRSPI	0.15 (4.55) [0.00]	0.27 (4.39) [0.00]
TBR	−0.03 (−7.42) [0.00]	−0.06 (−10.52) [0.00]
USTBR	0.01 (3.62) [0.00]	0.03 (3.92) [0.00]
LREER	−0.22 (−5.65) [0.00]	−0.41 (−4.47) [0.00]
INFVOL	0.01 (1.96) [0.06]	0.01 (1.95) [0.06]

Diagnostics		
Adjusted R^2	0.99	
Lagrange multiplier test for serial correlation	$F(1, 31) = 0.43$	
Ramsey's RESET test of functional form mis-specification	$F(1, 31) = 5.23$	
Normality of residuals	$\chi^2_{(2)} = 0.02$	
Heteroskedasticity	$F(1, 39) = 1.80$	
The Wald test:		
H_O: Coefficient on LRGDP = 0		$\chi^2_{(1)} = 333.87$ [0.00]
H_O: Coefficient on LRGDP = 1		$\chi^2_{(1)} = 4.42$ [0.04]
H_O: Coefficient on LRSPI = 0		$\chi^2_{(1)} = 19.26$ [0.00]
H_O: Coefficient on TB3Y = 0		$\chi^2_{(1)} = 110.69$ [0.00]
H_O: Coefficient on USTBR = 0		$\chi^2_{(1)} = 15.36$ [0.00]
H_O: Coefficient on LREER = 0		$\chi^2_{(1)} = 19.98$ [0.00]
H_O: Coefficient on INFVOL = 0		$\chi^2_{(1)} = 3.81$ [0.05]

Table 2D.2b Error-correction model of real narrow money-demand relationships in Australia

Regressors	ARDL (2,0,0,0,0,0) Coefficient (t-ratio) [prob.]
ΔLRNM(–1)	−0.18 (−1.94) [0.06]
ΔLRGDP	0.60 (6.90) [0.00]
ΔLRSPI	0.15 (5.55) [0.00]
ΔTB3Y	−0.03 (−7.42) [0.00]
ΔUSTBR	0.01 (3.62) [0.00]
ΔLREER	−0.22 (−5.65) [0.00]
ΔINFVOL	0.01 (1.96) [0.06]
error-correction term(–1)	−0.53 (−8.45) [0.00]
The Wald test:	
H_O: Coefficient on ΔLRNM(–1) = 0	$\chi^2_{(1)}$ = 3.77 [0.05]
H_O: Coefficient on ΔLRGDP = 0	$\chi^2_{(1)}$ = 47.56 [0.00]
H_O: Coefficient on ΔLRSPI = 0	$\chi^2_{(1)}$ = 20.70 [0.00]
H_O: Coefficient on ΔTBR = 0	$\chi^2_{(1)}$ = 55.06 [0.00]
H_O: Coefficient on ΔUSTBR = 0	$\chi^2_{(1)}$ = 13.11 [0.00]
H_O: Coefficient on ΔLREER = 0	$\chi^2_{(1)}$ = 31.93 [0.00]
H_O: Coefficient on ΔINFVOL = 0	$\chi^2_{(1)}$ = 3.86 [0.05]
H_O: Coefficient on error-correction term(–1) = 0	$\chi^2_{(1)}$ = 71.40 [0.00]
Adjusted R^2	0.76
Durbin statistic	2.16

and also suggest the significance of inflation volatility as an independent determinant of money demand.

Having determined the order of the lag by the ARDL model, the specified model is estimated for the sample period 1970–2012 by the recursive and rolling regression techniques to examine stability of the estimated coefficients. Except the coefficient on inflation volatility, all other coefficients are found stable over the study period. Figure 2D.1 reports the cumulative sum (CUSUM) and cumulative sum of squared (CUSUMSQ) tests for residuals of the Australian real narrow money-demand function. The figures suggest that the real narrow money-demand function in Australia remained stable over the period 1970–2012.

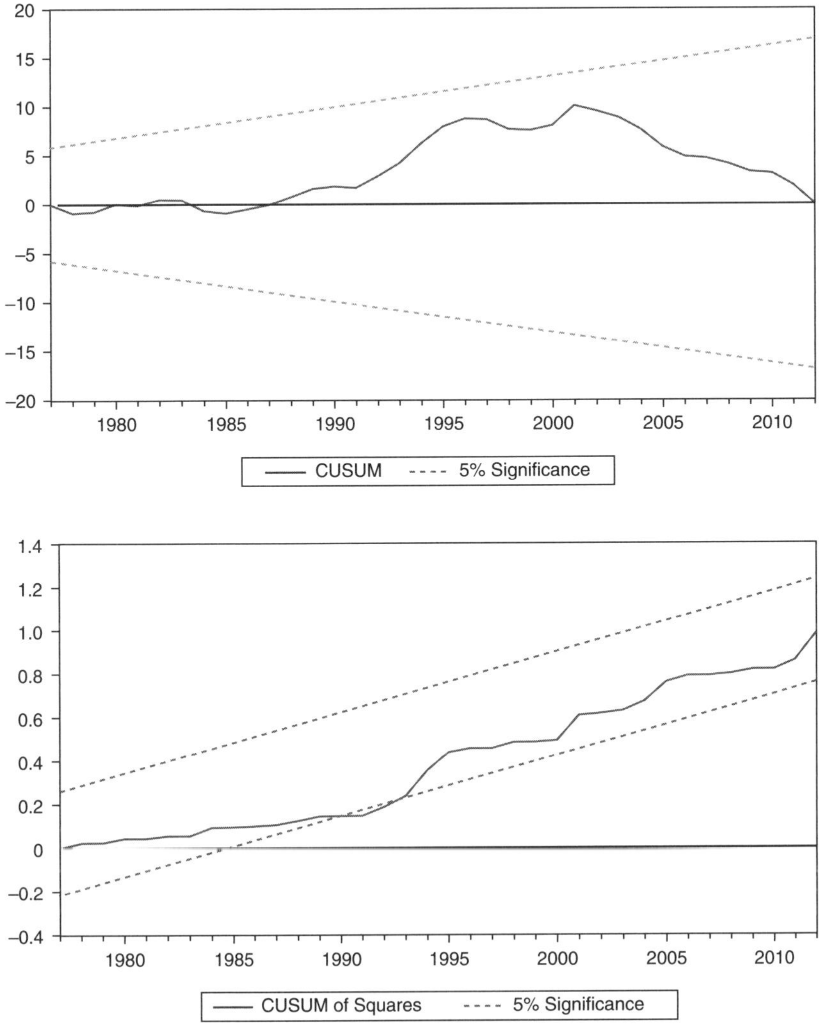

Note: Based on a long-run real narrow money-demand relationship that includes the following determinants of real money balances: real income, real stock price, the Treasury bill rate in Australia, the Treasury bill rate in the United States, the real effective exchange rate of the Australian dollar and inflation volatility measured by the conditional standard deviation of CPI inflation as obtained from a GARCH(1,1) model of inflation.

Figure 2D.1 CUSUM and CUSUMSQ of residuals of long-run real narrow money-demand relationships in Australia

NOTES

1. For earlier studies on money demand in Australia, see Pagan and Volker (1981), Asano (1999), Felmingham and Zhang (2001), Hossain (1994), Valadkhani (2005) and Cusbert and Rohling (2013).
2. Due to space constraints, the results obtained for real broad money balances, which are broadly similar to those obtained for real narrow money balances, are not reported.

REFERENCES

Asano, H. (1999), 'Financial deregulation and stability of money demand: the Australian case', *Australian Economic Papers*, December, 407–21.

Cusbert, T. and T. Rohling (2013), 'Currency demand during the global financial crisis: evidence from Australia', Research Discussion Paper 2013–01, Reserve Bank of Australia, Sydney.

Engle, R.F. and C.W.J. Granger (1987), 'Co-integration and error-correction: representation, estimation, and testing', *Econometrica*, **55**(2), 251–76.

Felmingham, B. and Q. Zhang (2001), 'The long-run demand for broad money in Australia subject to regime shifts', *Australian Economic Papers*, **40**, 146–55.

Hossain A (1994), 'Financial innovation, financial deregulation and the stability of the Australian short run narrow money demand function', *Economic Notes*, **23**(3), 410–37.

McCallum, B.T. and E. Nelson (2011), 'Money and inflation: some critical issues', in B.M. Friedman and M. Woodford (eds), *Handbook of Monetary Economics*, Vol. 3A, Amsterdam: Elsevier Science, pp. 97–153.

Pagan, A.R. and P.A. Volker (1981), 'The short-run demand for transactions balances in Australia', *Economica*, **48**, 381–95.

Valadkhani, A. (2005), 'Modelling demand for broad money in Australia', *Australian Economic Papers*, **44**(91), 47–64.

APPENDIX E: COINTEGRAL RELATIONSHIPS AMONG MONEY, OUTPUT AND PRICES

Given that there exists a stable money-demand function in Australia and that the monetary authorities exercised policy measures to maintain some control over the money stock, it is plausible that the stock of money, prices and real income form a cointegral relationship in Australia. The time-series properties of these variables (not reported) suggest that they have a unit root and are eligible to form a cointegral relationship. The test for cointegration among variables in the cointegrating set (LCPI, LNM or LBM, LRGDP) is essentially a test for a unit root in the residuals of the cointegrating regression. When the nonstationary variables form a cointegral relationship, the residuals should be stationary. The presence of a cointegral relationship is examined within the Engle-Granger cointegration error-correction modelling framework by estimating a regression equation of LCPI (log of the consumer price index) as a dependent variable on real income (Ly) and the nominal money stock (LNM or LBM). Any mis-specification bias that emerges in the cointegration regression as a result of omitted dynamics being forced into the error term is removed by adding to the model the first-difference of one-period lag and lead terms. This is the essence of the dynamic OLS (DOLS) estimation method, which also provides consistent estimates of the parameters in the price level equation.

Table 2E.1 reports the cointegration tests results. The test results suggest that there exists a cointegral relation among money, output and prices in Australia. The coefficient value on money is close to unity.

Engle and Granger (1987) suggest that one of the implications of a cointegral relation between two nonstationary variables is the presence of long-term causality between them running in at least one direction. Table 2E.2 reports the bivariate Granger-causality test results among LCPI, LNM (or LBM) and LRGDP. Given that a cointegral relation exists among money, output and prices, a vector error-correction (VEC) model is estimated. Within a VEC modelling framework, the short-term specification includes an error-correction term that is stationary and other variables in the model appear in a first-difference form. The test results suggest that for Australia, there is causality running from narrow or broad money to prices.

REFERENCES

Engle, R.F. and C.W.J. Granger (1987), 'Co-integration and error-correction: representation, estimation, and testing', *Econometrica*, **55**(2), 251–76.

Table 2E.1 Cointegration test results among money, output and prices in Australia, 1970–2012

Dependent variable: LCPI								
	Fully modified OLS				Dynamic OLS			
					(lead = 1, lag = 1)			
With narrow money (NM)								
Regressor	coefficient	t-ratio	prob.		coefficient	t-ratio	prob.	
Intercept	−0.80	−1.31	0.20		−0.32	−0.31	0.76	
LNM	1.20	4.64	0.00		1.33	3.80	0.00	
LRGDP	−1.97	−2.5	0.02		−2.4	−2.18	0.04	
Sample period	1970–2012				1970–2011			
DW	0.29				0.18			
Adjusted R^2	0.95				0.95			
	tau-statistic	prob.	z-statistic	prob.	tau-statistic	prob.	z-statistic	prob.
The Engle-Granger cointegration tests	−2.02	0.73	−6.89	0.78	−2.02	0.73	−6.89	0.77
The Phillips-Ouliaris cointegration tests	−1.99	0.74	−6.64	0.8	−1.99	0.74	−6.64	0.8
With broad money (BM)								
Regressor	coefficient	t-ratio	prob.		coefficient	t-ratio	prob.	
Intercept	−2.18	−14.82	0.00		−2.18	−11.83	0.00	
LBM	0.67	16.59	0.00		0.67	16.53	0.00	
LRGDP	−0.52	−3.96	0		−0.52	−3.99	0	
Sample Period	1970–2012				1970–2011			
DW	0.42				0.36			
Adjusted R^2	0.99				0.99			
	tau-statistic	prob.	z-statistic	prob.	tau-statistic	prob.	z-statistic	prob.
The Engle-Granger cointegration tests	−1.89	0.78	−9.2	0.61	−1.89	0.78	−9.2	0.61
The Phillips-Ouliaris cointegration tests	−1.92	0.77	−8.1	0.69	−1.92	0.77	−8.1	0.69

Note: Definitions of variables: LCPI = log of the consumer price index; LNM = log of narrow money stock; LBM = log of broad money stock; and LRGDP = log of real GDP.

Table 2E.2 Granger-causality among money, output and prices in Australia, 1950–2012

	Hypotheses No causality runs from:	Chi-square statistic (prob.)	Inference at 5% level
VEC specification (With narrow money, NM)	ΔLNM → ΔLCPI	4.30 (0.12)	Null hypothesis not rejected
	ΔLNM, ΔLRGDP → ΔLCPI	10.67 (0.03)	Null hypothesis rejected
	ΔLCPI → ΔLNM	0.99 (0.61)	Null hypothesis not rejected
	ΔLRGDP → ΔLNM	7.55 (0.02)	Null hypothesis rejected
	ΔLCPI → ΔLRGDP	2.01 (0.37)	Null hypothesis not rejected
	ΔLNM → ΔLRGDP	4.92 (0.09)	Null hypothesis not rejected
VEC specification (With broad money, BM)	ΔLBM → ΔLCPI	11.69 (0.00)	Null hypothesis rejected
	ΔLBM, ΔLRGDP → ΔLCPI	16.67 (0.00)	Null hypothesis rejected
	ΔLCPI → ΔLBM	20.13 (0.00)	Null hypothesis rejected
	ΔLRGDP → ΔLBM	0.50 (0.78)	Null hypothesis not rejected
	ΔLCPI → ΔLRGDP	3.57 (0.17)	Null hypothesis not rejected
	ΔLBM → ΔLRGDP	1.49 (0.47)	Null hypothesis not rejected

Note: Definitions of variables: LCPI = log of the consumer price index; LNM = log of narrow money stock; LBM = log of broad money stock; and LRGDP = log of real GDP. Optimal lag-length = 2 (selected based on the Akaike Information Criterion, AIC).

3. China

The People's Republic of China (PRC)[1] has emerged as the second largest economy in the world since the commencement of economic reforms in 1978,[2] the watershed moment of which was a substantial relaxation of official restrictions on the conduct of international trade and capital transactions – China's 'opening up'. Perhaps the most significant benefits of the opening up process have been sustained economic growth averaging around 9 per cent per annum across the three decades since, associated with impressive economic and social transformation. The three preceding decades had been dominated by central economic planning, following the establishment of the PRC on 1 October 1949. In an historically remarkable achievement, China's investment-led, outward-oriented growth model has pulled out as many as 400 million or 500 million people from the dire straits into which their economic conditions had been sunk, largely by those three decades of central planning.

While Chinese development strategy remains outward-oriented, China has yet to become a fully market economy. Its economic and financial reform programmes have been guided by gradualism. Careful observation of rapid financial deregulation and capital market liberalization in many countries, frequently accompanied by financial crises as an aftermath, has led China into a pragmatic, sequential approach to reforms aimed at rapid economic growth and development while minimizing social and political disruption. The reform process has slowed since 2005, but without major policy reversal or lack of commitment to establish an efficient market economy.[3]

In contrast with other countries in East Asia, the sources of Chinese economic growth have been uncontroversial because unambiguous rapid capital accumulation has played a critical role in Chinese economic growth and transformation. The investment-led, outward-oriented development strategy has been fuelled by a massive pool of surplus labour, and has consequently followed the Lewisian model of development. As predicted by this model, China's export-oriented manufacturing sector employed a large number of workers from the pool, mostly unskilled, at a low wage rate.[4] A relatively slow increase in the real wage rate allowed a massive increase in employment in the manufacturing sector as demand for labour-intensive Chinese products rose across the globe. Partial privatization of agriculture raised both food production and security, creating growth momentum across the tradable sectors. This raised China's profile across the globe and attracted foreign investment, mostly in the form of joint ventures. Low wages and a programme of investment incentives[5] ensured high profit rates for entrepreneurs and businesses.

Starting from the traditional state of an agricultural economy, China has undergone rapid structural change for three decades. A massive rural-urban transfer of workers has led to rapid urbanization and industrialization, leaving little possibility of reversal to any earlier stage of economic development, even if such reversal were desired or politically viable. Two major costs of this policy of growth and development, or economic restructuring, have been sharp rises in, firstly, income and wealth inequality and, secondly, the incidence of corruption. Together these costs have created social and political tension, which has been largely suppressed by the authorities. This development has arguably informed the decisions of policymakers to effect a 'brake' on economic and financial reform, especially across the banking sector and the state-owned enterprises.

With rising income and asset inequality, the significant issues associated with inflation – namely its average level and its volatility, both of which have been endemically high in China – have remained a major economic problem. Chinese inflation is mainly monetary in nature, but is almost routinely exacerbated by official monetary accommodation of real sector shocks sourced either domestically or externally. Most especially, this monetary accommodation of shocks has created volatility in the Chinese money-growth rate and magnified inflation volatility under the fixed peg exchange rate policy. Budget deficits are not considered a source of inflation, but a rapid accumulation of foreign reserves has expanded the money supply despite partial sterilization of foreign-capital inflows.

The People's Bank of China (PBC)[6] is responsible for maintaining price stability. However, it is not independent of the central government of China with respect to either the goals or the instruments of monetary policy. It conducts monetary policy in the context of an investment-led growth model. While price stability remains officially the dominant objective of monetary policy, nevertheless both economic growth and social-political stability share priority in the PBC's design and conduct of monetary policy. To achieve these multiple, government-mandated goals of monetary policy, the PBC uses multiple instruments, including directed lending to the priority sectors and government-owned enterprises through the state-owned commercial and specialized banks. The financial system remains repressed and relatively underdeveloped.[7] Capital flows are controlled but not considered effective. In short, monetary policy has only limited independence for maintaining low and stable inflation.

The Chinese economy is expected to sustain its rapid average growth rate in the near future. The medium-term prospects are not entirely rosy, however. All sectors excepting the financial sector have diversified and become market-oriented. With most advanced economies (namely the United States, Japan and European countries), including China's major customers, currently in the midst of major economic problems, there is concern that these problems directly address the major potential weakness of China's investment-led, outward-oriented growth model, so that its long and extraordinary growth story may not be sustainable for much longer. The 'escape hatch' from this unfortunate position that is currently in debate is financial sector deregulation and reform. The argument is that this would improve economic efficiency and rebalance the Chinese economy by making it more consumer-based. A shift of monetary policy strategy would be required to facilitate this new reform direction, away from growth orientation and towards price stability.

The major prerequisite for this shift, according to the state-of-the-art mainstream economic theory and evidence, is substitution of a flexible exchange rate system with capital mobility for the abandonment of the current fixed peg to the US dollar with some capital controls. Exchange rate flexibility itself, however, requires the deployment of an anchor to inflationary expectations, and therefore to the current and future measured inflation rates (this is frequently abbreviated as 'an anchor to prices'). Under one of the price stability strategies that are available, monetary targeting, a monetary aggregate fulfils the prices-anchor role. Under another available strategy, inflation targeting – popular over the last two decades in both developed and developing countries – a credible inflation target set by a central bank can serve as the required anchor to inflationary expectations. Evidence from inflation targeting countries, currently under discussion in the literature, suggests that policy credibility and transparency has in general not been fully achieved by the central banks concerned, and that doing so is critical for sustaining inflation that is both low and stable.

Presently, the PBC uses both the monetary and credit aggregates as intermediate targets to support the rapid economic growth rate while maintaining low and stable inflation. The question essentially at issue is whether a market-determined interest rate should be harnessed as a key monetary policy instrument for demand management within any revamped monetary policy regime. This raises consequential issues in the choice of exchange rate regime and financial sector reforms. There is an emerging consensus that China should discard its fixed peg in favour of a flexible exchange rate system, or preferably a free float. Although neither is likely to be implemented in the near future, a free-floating currency is the instrument of maximum efficiency to absorb domestic and external shocks and to reduce external imbalances. China's accumulated foreign reserves are enormous. Consequently, its currency, the Chinese yuan, known (analogous with the UK's pound sterling), as renminbi and abbreviated RMB, is perceived to be undervalued. Greater flexibility in the nominal exchange rate would likely lead to an appreciation of the real exchange rate, accelerating the adjustment process of the economy and raising the probability of a soft landing as China's long-standing economic boom slows.

The main problem for the adjustment process originates from the financial sector, which remains unreformed and dominated by inefficient state-owned banks heavily burdened with non-performing loans. While the stock and bond markets have expanded rapidly over the past two decades, they remain relatively underdeveloped, as already mentioned. Under the investment-led growth model, the state-owned banks receive explicit guidance from the PBC on their lending operations. Although the directed-lending programmes were officially terminated in 1998, the PBC maintains administrative control over credit allocation and continues to provide guidance for lending activities. The PBC's lending guidance ensures funding for large state-owned enterprises, including the many commercially unviable ones. This is considered important to employment generation and to provide a socio-economic infrastructure platform for labour, including housing, education, health and pensions. Recognizing that the state-owned banks are burdened with large non-performing loans, the PBC is required to intensify its efforts on banking reforms. Under any revamped monetary policy regime, this would raise the banks' responsiveness to changes in price signals such as exchange rates and interest rates.

China's monetary policy regime is thus in a transitional stage. It is complex and remains integrated with the country's economic growth model. The moot question is whether China should, and can, separate monetary policy from price stability ignoring its linkage with the exchange rate regime and problems associated with financial sector reforms.

The remainder of this chapter gives an overview of monetary policy in China in an historical context. It examines some monetary relations to determine whether China should follow a strict rule-based monetary policy for price stability, such as monetary targeting or, alternatively, inflation targeting that incorporates a monetary aggregate as an instrument. As the Chinese economy's market orientation gradually strengthens, monetary policy is destined to play an increasingly significant role in maintaining low and stable inflation to underpin stable growth at the maximum sustainable rate.

THE PEOPLE'S BANK OF CHINA: ORGANIZATION AND FUNCTIONS[8]

The PBC was established on 1 December 1948, consolidating the Huabei Bank, the Beihai Bank and the Xibei Farmer Bank. In September 1983, the State Council of the PRC declared it the central bank of China. The Law of the PRC on the PBC was passed by the People's Congress on 18 March 1995.[9] This finally gave the PBC legal status as China's central bank. In March 2003, the People's Congress approved the decision on reform of the Organizational Structure of the State Council, separating the supervisory responsibilities of the PBC for banking institutions, asset management companies, trust and investment companies and other depository institutions. Accordingly, the China Banking Regulatory Commission was established to supervise the financial industry. On 27 December 2003 the Standing Committee of the 10th National People's Congress approved at its 6th Meeting the amendment to the Law of the PRC on the PBC. The amended Law is designed to strengthen the role of the PBC in designing and implementing monetary policy, along with safeguarding financial stability and providing financial services in a rapidly growing economy.

The top management of the PBC is composed of the governor and a number of deputy governors. The president appoints the governor. The appointment requires the approval of the National People's Congress. The candidate for the office of governor is nominated by the premier of the State Council, who also appoints the deputy governors. The governor acts as the chief executive of the PBC while the deputy governors assist the governor in performing his or her responsibility. Article 12 of the Law suggests the establishment of a Monetary Policy Committee (MPC), which includes the governor, two deputy governors, a deputy secretary-general of the State Council and others.[10] This Committee plays an important role in macroeconomic management and in the design and implementation of monetary policy. While the MPC is a consultative body for the conduct of monetary policy, it has an advisory role based on a comprehensive research function investigating macroeconomic conditions with the government's economic growth target in mind.

Article 4 of the Law of the PRC on the PBC suggests at least 13 functions and responsibilities. They include:

(a) Issuing and enforcing orders and regulations related to the PBC's functions and responsibilities.
(b) Formulating and implementing monetary policy in accordance with law.
(c) Issuing currency (yuan renminbi, RMB) and controlling its circulation.

(d) Supervising and administering the interbank lending market and interbank bond market.
(e) Controlling foreign exchange and supervising and administering the interbank foreign-exchange market.
(f) Managing the State Treasury.
(g) Guiding and organizing the anti-money laundering work of the financial sector.
(h) Generating financial statistics and conducting surveys, analyses and forecasts.
(i) Participating in international banking operations and performing other functions as prescribed by the State Council.

Article 3 of the Law of the PRC on the PBC states the objectives of monetary policy as 'to maintain the stability of the value of the currency and thereby promote economic growth'. There are two technical interpretations of the 'stability of a currency's value'. Firstly, it can be taken to mean 'price stability', which economists generally define as a low average rate of inflation. A high average inflation rate rapidly reduces a currency's purchasing power, thereby 'destabilizing' it. Furthermore, a high and volatile inflation rate is, as the name suggests, a non-stable rate of decline in a currency's purchasing power. Recent evidence questions the conventional wisdom that low average inflation is also 'stable' in the sense that the costs of uncertainty, especially uncertainty leading to lost investment, that are imposed on an economy by any volatility of the inflation rate can safely be assumed acceptably low (Hossain, 2014).

The second interpretation of currency value stability is perhaps the more intuitive: a depreciating exchange rate reduces the foreign-exchange value of a currency, thereby 'destabilizing' it. Furthermore, a volatile exchange rate denotes a relatively risky currency. The Law, per se, does not distinguish among these four types of risk to the stability of the yuan's value; namely the level and volatility of the inflation rate, and the level and volatility of the exchange rate. Therefore, a black-letter interpretation of the Law would require that the authorities pay attention to them all as their first priority. The economic theory and empirics of these four objectives place them in potential conflict, raising the possibility of a need in practice for policy tradeoffs. As a matter of necessity, then, the four objectives may need to be targeted according to the authorities' own (opaque) objective function. These four primary objectives are followed, under the Law, by the objective of promotion of economic growth.

The Chinese central government sets an economic growth target each year. The target growth rate is expected to generate employment so as to absorb surplus labour that could be freed from the agricultural sector or laid-off workers from the state-owned enterprises. Under Article 2, the PBC is required to formulate and implement monetary policy in a way that minimizes financial risk and maintains financial stability. Exchange rate stability is important to the maintenance of financial stability. Although the PBC is responsible for safeguarding overall financial stability, the Financial Stability Bureau carries out the responsibility of maintaining financial stability by studying issues and designing policies with respect to banking, finance and other related industries. Other regulatory bodies responsible for financial stability include the China Banking Regulatory Commission, the China Insurance Regulatory Commission and the China Securities Regulatory Commission.

The PBC performs its functions and responsibilities without intervention of any kind, including by local governments, government departments at any level, public organizations or by individuals. However, when planning monetary policy operations with respect to the money supply, interest rates, exchange rates and other important matters, the PBC reports its decisions to the State Council for approval before implementation. The PBC is also required to submit 'work reports' to the Standing Committee of the National People's Congress on the conduct of monetary policy and the performance of the financial sector.

EVOLUTION OF MONETARY POLICY

China's monetary policy has changed significantly since it began to implement economic reform policies in 1978. The distance it has come with respect to monetary policy is perhaps best understood by placing the present state of monetary policy in the context of that in the pre-reform phase. Cheng (1988, pp. 404–5) has summarized the monetary policy framework in China prior to financial reforms as follows:

> In conducting the nation's monetary policy, the People's Bank reacted passively to decisions made elsewhere in the economy. This is not to say that the People's Bank had no role in the formulation of China's monetary policy prior to 1979. On the contrary, its role was considerable. The Bank was responsible for drafting and carrying out both the credit plan and the cash plan. Because it regularly monitored payment flows, it was in a position to report current economic and financial conditions to the economic planning authorities in a timely manner. It also had a voice in proposing adjustments in the physical as well as financial plans for achieving macroeconomic balance. Nevertheless, in spite of all this, it was a subordinate agency. It could propose, but not decide; it might dissent, but must carry out decisions made by higher authorities. It is in this sense that its role was essentially a passive, accommodating one, similar to that of a central bank which is obligated to finance all the government debt at fixed interest rates.

In the latter case, too, money is endogenously determined, and monetary policy is essentially passive.

Cheng reveals that Chinese monetary policy before reform did not have separate status with respect to the objective of price stability. Instead, it was part of a macroeconomic policy package that aimed at maintaining a repressed financial system supporting the investment-led, outward-oriented model whose overarching objective was economic growth. The primary instrument was administrative control, and the primary targets were prices and quantities of goods, services and assets. Both economic growth and inflation were low but volatile in nature. The planned economic model with financial repression worked somewhat at the early stage; however, pressure for policy reform built as the economy began to encounter problems from the late 1960s. The impetus for economic reform finally came when, in the early 1970s, the balance of political power shifted away from Mao's hard-line followers to reform-minded members of the Chinese Communist Party led by Deng Xiaoping.[11]

Economic reforms continued steadily, with 'Socialist Market Economy' the designated objective. The economy responded positively to the associated programme of market reforms and incentives. Outward-oriented rapid economic growth created pressure to expand the financial sector. The primacy of monetary policy for price stability was acknowledged, but monetary policy nevertheless remained part of a macroeconomic policy package whose *raison d'être* was economic growth in a low-inflationary environment. In the event, this objective was not achieved as the Chinese economy encountered a series of shocks, whose damaging effects were magnified under China's fixed peg exchange rate system.

In general, the appropriate strategy of monetary policy depends on the exchange rate arrangement and controls over capital flows. Under a fixed peg exchange rate system, monetary policy does not have independence in achieving price stability, or any other goal, unless it is supported by capital controls. Under a floating exchange rate system, there is no distinction between monetary policy and exchange rate policy. While a floating exchange rate system allows the conduct of independent monetary policy, it does not necessarily lead to price stability unless the authorities deploy an anchor, implicit or explicit, to price expectations. Without such an anchor, there is no guarantee that the monetary authorities would remain committed to maintain price stability alone. As monetary policy can be deployed for economic stabilization, the lack of a designated anchor may create a policy inconsistency or a time-inconsistency problem. In turn, time-inconsistent policy creates inflation bias and raises inflation volatility.

Against this framework, the present state of monetary policy in China is now assessed following a review of the evolution of China's exchange rate arrangements and regulation of international capital flows.

Exchange Rate Regime and Capital Controls

China has maintained a fixed peg exchange rate system in one form or another since the early 1970s. Before 1993 the exchange rate, published by the Chinese Statistical Agency, represented the official rate of the currency. The Agency overvalued the exchange rate until 1979, discouraging exports and encouraging imports. As there were limited foreign reserves, imports were controlled, which had the flow-on effect of reducing exports. With the advent of the economic reform era from 1979, the role of the exchange rate in foreign trade began to change. With decentralization of foreign trade, the overvalued exchange rate increasingly imposed disincentives upon exporters. Therefore, an internal settlement rate was established at a level close to the average cost of earning one US dollar in exports. The rate was 2.8 yuan per dollar. This rate was used during 1979–84 for trade-related transactions in place of the official exchange rate. Meanwhile the official exchange rate depreciated towards the internal rate until 1985 when the two rates were merged.

During 1985–93, the multiple exchange rate system reappeared in another form. Because of the existing foreign-exchange controls, foreign-funded enterprises were required to balance their foreign-exchange needs. To avoid creating a constraint on foreign investors, swap markets were established across regions. The swap rates, established for transactions among foreign-funded enterprises, differed from the official exchange rate. In 1994, as part of macroeconomic reform, a national foreign-exchange market was formed that phased out the official rate. By the end of 1996, the RMB became fully convertible for current account transactions (Mehran et al., 1996; Xu, 2000). Since 1996 RMB has maintained a fixed parity of 8.28 yuan per US dollar, despite official classification of China's exchange rate system as a managed float within a narrow band measured against US dollar fluctuations. Since July 2005 the exchange rate of RMB has remained pegged to a basket of currencies. While China appears to follow a policy of gradually allowing RMB to appreciate against the basket, it remains fixed at 8.28 to the US dollar.[12]

In short, China's exchange rate policy since the 1980s has effectively maintained exchange rate stability against the US dollar. This has arguably created an undervalued exchange rate and led to the accumulation of large foreign-exchange reserves. Consequently, the status of RMB has increased, attracting foreign-capital inflows. RMB is now the currency of choice for some categories of international transaction. Importantly, China's success

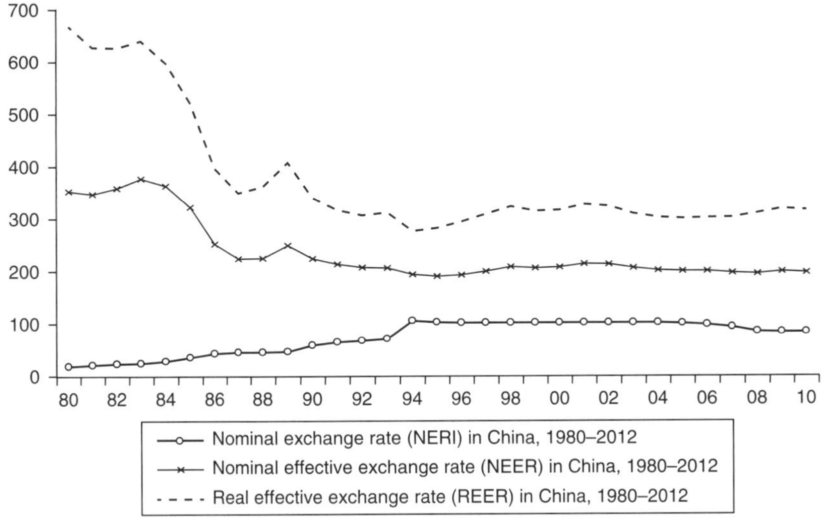

Note: NERI = bilateral exchange rate of yuan renmimbi with the US dollar; a rise in the index value indicates an appreciation of Chinese currency.

Figure 3.1 The exchange rate of yuan renminbi in China, 1980–2012

in achieving exchange rate stability and the consequent accumulation of foreign reserves have arguably raised economic growth by maintaining financial stability, though not via the route of internal price stability, which is the route advocated by the arguments presented in this book.

Figure 3.1 plots the major measures of the exchange rate of RMB. The bilateral nominal exchange rate index with the US dollar (NERI) shows that RMB depreciated steadily until the mid 1990s. It remained stable since then with minor appreciation until recent years. This pattern is evident in the nominal and real effective exchange rates. Since the mid 1990s the real exchange rate has remained roughly stable. This begs the question of whether China adopted a real exchange rate targeting strategy of monetary policy to sustain export-oriented economic growth. As RMB remains pegged to the US dollar and the exchange rates of the US dollar fluctuate against other major currencies, this is reflected in the real and nominal effective exchange rates of RMB. Fluctuations in the real effective exchange rate also reflect the inflation differentials between China and its trading partners, including the United States.

The Chinese government maintains stability of the nominal exchange rate through capital controls. Equity capital flows, in particular, are restricted; and foreign borrowing by corporations and financial institutions is discouraged. Consequently, China's external debt remains low at approximately 3 per cent of GDP. Some components of the balance-of-payments, particularly of the financial account, are open to varying degrees. The item 'net errors and omissions' in the balance-of-payments captures this phenomenon. For example, China has sustained a policy of encouraging foreign direct investment since the early 1990s.

An implication is that the de facto increasing openness of the balance-of-payments' financial account may have made monetary policy less independent under a fixed peg and loose capital controls. This is one reason behind external pressure on China to make its exchange rate regime flexible to retain monetary policy independence while discarding capital controls. Given the size of the Chinese economy, a flexible exchange rate arrangement is considered appropriate for maintaining economic stability. An independent monetary policy can be deployed to maintain price stability under a rule-based monetary policy strategy. Adoption of a real exchange rate targeting approach to monetary policy appears popular but has some undesirable impacts on domestic inflation and the real interest rate.

Conduct of Monetary Policy

Throughout 1978–96 the PBC conducted monetary policy using a credit plan. For individual banks, the PBC set quantitative quotas and lending ceilings, and provided liquidity support to those banks when needed. The allocated credits were distributed among government-sanctioned projects across sectors and sub-sectors. Banks therefore were effectively fiscal agents of the government in the implementation of the monetary policy credit plan policy supporting other policies focused on achievement of the pre-set economic growth target.

Monetary policy under China's investment-based, economic growth development model can be summarized as follows. It conducts a fixed peg exchange rate system with restrictions on capital mobility. Necessarily, then, the open-economy trilemma imposes upon China only a limited degree of monetary policy independence. Following the Law of the PRC on the PBC, monetary policy is deployed to achieve multiple objectives. Several credit control instruments of are used. The key ones are now reviewed in somewhat greater detail.[13]

Standing facilities

The PBC has at least two standing facilities for commercial banks. The first is automatic collateralized lending. Under this arrangement, banks can obtain liquidity from the PBC at a rediscount rate. Under the second standing facility, the PBC allows commercial banks to hold excess reserves.

Open market operations

China began utilizing open market operations in 1993. These were discontinued in 1997 but reintroduced in 1998. The PBC then engaged in 'outright transactions' with banks, involving outright purchase and outright sale of government securities. Later, such transactions were replaced by repurchase transactions, abbreviated as 'repos'. In June 2002, the PBC introduced the use of reverse-repo operations, using Treasury bonds, to sterilize large-scale inflows of foreign capital. In September 2002, when the PBC ran out of Treasury bonds, it started auctioning its own bills. After a transition period, outstanding repos were converted into PBC bills. Since their introduction in 2002, the PBC has used its bills extensively to offset the rise in liquidity in the banking system due to its purchase of foreign currencies. This has led to the informal market description of PBC bills as 'sterilization bonds'. Open market operations are conducted two or three times a week. A primary dealer system in open market operations was implemented in 1998. Since December 2005, the PBC has started using foreign-exchange swaps, including swap arrangements with several central banks across the Asia-Pacific, including Indonesia, Malaysia and Singapore.

Reserve requirements

The PBC conducts large-scale open market operations to reduce or neutralize the impact upon domestic liquidity of its foreign currency purchasing operations. This sterilization operation is supplemented by lifting the required reserves obligations of commercial banks with respect to their deposit balances. This use of the reserve requirement as an active instrument for liquidity management renders it an unreliable indicator of current monetary policy stance, whether easing or tightening.

Interest rate controls

The PBC controls various interest rates by administrative regulation to achieve its monetary policy objectives. The relevant interest rates are the central bank lending rate, the rediscount rate and the interest rates on required and excess reserves. From October 2004, a ceiling on bank loan rates and a floor on deposit rates were eliminated. They were replaced with the converse regulations, with a ceiling imposed on deposit rates and a floor under lending rates.

Special lending schemes and window guidance

In China, firms rely on bank loans as the main source of external financing. The PBC controls liquidity in the banking system as described above and thereby bank lending is believed to have a strong impact on the real economy. In 1998 the PBC evolved the credit plan mechanism into a system whereby it provided guidance for financial institutions on credit growth and its sectoral allocation. Under certain specific eligibility requirements, the PBC provides special funds at a lower cost for a particular group of industries or groups. This 'window guidance' takes the form of moral suasion or indirect pressure through regular meetings with commercial banks so as to influence the quantity and composition of bank credits. Window guidance generally involves provision of guidelines on the volume of lending. It is considered effective because the governor of the PBC is tasked with making this instrument effective. The commercial banks respond to the governor's advice and suggestions on lending operations (Geiger, 2006).

Other administrative measures

On occasion, the PBC induces commercial banks to hold its bills when loan growth is considered sufficiently rapid to create the threat of overheating the economy.

Summing up: the PBC's legal powers and monetary operations incorporate instruments of credit control, including directed lending. The PBC deploys a mixture of indirect market instruments and direct methods to control the volume and composition of bank credits and capital flows. In the absence of market-determined exchange and interest rates, the required reserves on bank deposits and the bank credit channel are the two primary instruments of liquidity and demand management. In contrast with other countries, China's PBC uses the instrument of required reserves extensively to manage domestic liquidity, which is closely linked to China's foreign currency purchasing operations and its accumulation of foreign reserves. Large-scale inflows of foreign capital appear to be at least partly stimulated by an undervalued currency. However, a policy is in place to discourage this component of international capital: the PBC prevents interest rates from rising above a ceiling that it considers appropriate at any given time. This usage of quantity-based instruments in concert with price-based instruments attempts to achieve multiple objectives in an environment where the financial sector operates under allocatively distortionary conditions. Sterilization of large foreign-capital inflows using PBC bills has been relatively easy because of the well-known cultural characteristic of a high household saving rate and the presence of capital controls. Nevertheless, there is generally excess demand for PBC bills despite their high prices and low interest rates.

MACROECONOMIC AND INFLATION PERFORMANCE

Table 3.1 reports data for China's key macroeconomic indicators over the period 1953–2012. It shows that the Chinese economy began growing rapidly from the mid 1960s. Implementation of economic reform policies started in 1979. China has since grown at an impressive pace to become the second-largest economy in the world. Foreign direct investment in labour-intensive products, utilizing advanced production techniques, has been an important contributor to economic growth. Although the wage rate has increased in recent years, China remains one of the lowest cost manufacturing bases in the world. Within three decades, an essentially closed economy has transformed into a highly open, export-oriented economy. Macroeconomic management in China has been impressive for a transition economy at the early stage of development. Unlike other centrally planned economies, the transition of the Chinese economy from a centrally planned economy to a moderately market-driven economy has been smooth.

Figures 3.2a and 3.2b plot data for annual CPI inflation and inflation volatility, as measured by GARCH(1,1) model, in China during 1953–2012. Figure 3.2a shows that China's inflation was low in the 1950s and increased sharply in the early 1960s. Since then it remained low until the early 1980s. Until the financial reform era from 1979, most prices in China had been administered by government agencies and adjusted infrequently. The administered prices were gradually liberalized under the market-oriented 'adjustment and reform policy'. Consequently, the prices of both agricultural and industrial products increased considerably during the early 1980s. Inflation reached high levels during 1985–86 when the economy overheated under rapid expansion of money and domestic credits. Sharp action to control money and bank credits brought the inflation rate down. In 1988, inflation rose rapidly again, this time to about 25 per cent. Once again, sharp policy action reducing both the money supply and bank credits brought the inflation under control.

In 1992, China's paramount leader Deng Xiaoping initiated a rapid economic development programme. To promote investment, the government loosened monetary control, which raised inflation during 1992–94. For a third time, the government implemented measures to control both money and credit volumes and allocations. Chinese inflation has since declined but remained volatile, with three periods of mild deflation across 1998–2000, then 2001–03 and in 2009. The annual average inflation rate over the past decade and a half has been very low. Since the mid 1990s the real exchange rate has remained stable. The sustained low rates of these two

Table 3.1 Macroeconomic indicators, China, 1953–2012

Macroeconomic indicators	1953–54	1955–59	1960–64	1965–69	1970–74	1975–79	1980–84	1985–89	1990–94	1995–99	2000–04	2005–09	2010	2011	2012
Budget balance (% of GDP)	n.a.	n.a.	n.a.	n.a.	n.a.	n.a.	n.a.	−1.8	−2.2	−2.4	−2.6	−1.0	−1.5	−1.2	−1.3
General government gross debt (% of GDP)	n.a.	n.a.	n.a.	n.a.	n.a.	n.a.	1.0	4.2	6.4	8.9	18.2	17.6	33.5	25.8	22.2
Money-growth rate (%)															
Narrow money growth	16.5	25.6	7.0	7.7	8.9	15.2	22.0	19.2	27.6	19.1	15.3	18.5	20.4	8.7	6.5
Broad money growth	10.0	21.2	−0.3	9.6	8.2	14.4	22.2	26.1	32.9	21.0	14.9	20.4	18.9	17.3	14.4
Real GDP growth rate (%)	10.0	11.1	−2.1	8.0	8.5	6.7	9.8	9.7	10.9	9.1	9.2	11.4	10.4	9.3	7.7
GDP per capita, current prices, US dollar	n.a.	n.a.	n.a.	n.a.	n.a.	n.a.	248	326	419	750	1174	2716	4423	5417	6094
CPI inflation rate (%)	2.9	0.7	2.7	−1.0	0.0	1.0	2.9	12.0	10.3	5.2	1.1	2.6	3.3	5.4	2.7
Current account balance (% of GDP)	n.a.	n.a.	n.a.	n.a.	n.a.	n.a.	1.1	−1.6	1.4	1.9	2.4	7.8	4.0	2.8	2.3
Nominal interest rate (%)															
Deposit date of interest	n.a.	n.a.	n.a.	n.a.	n.a.	n.a.	5.6	8.3	9.1	6.0	2.1	2.7	2.8	3.5	3.0

Lending rate of interest	n.a.	n.a.	n.a.	n.a	n.a.	n.a.	6.3	8.8	9.7	8.6	5.6	6.0	5.8	6.6	6.0
Real interest rate (%)[a]															
Deposit rate of interest	n.a.	n.a.	n.a.	n.a.	n.a.	n.a.	2.6	−3.1	−0.7	1.0	1.1	0.1	−0.5	−1.8	0.3
Lending rate of Interest	n.a.	n.a.	n.a.	n.a.	n.a.	n.a.	3.3	−2.6	−0.1	3.5	4.5	3.3	2.4	1.1	3.3
Nominal exchange rate (yuan/US dollar)	n.a.	2.5	2.5	2.5	2.2	1.8	1.9	3.5	6.0	8.3	8.3	7.5	6.8	6.5	6.3
Nominal effective exchange rate[b]	n.a.	n.a.	n.a.	n.a.	232.7	284.1	336.9	211.5	135.8	97.9	107.1	106.6	113.8	114.0	119.8
Real effective exchange rate[b]	n.a.	n.a.	n.a.	n.a.	n.a.	n.a.	275.8	155.0	101.6	105.1	107.2	108.3	118.7	121.9	128.8
Memorandum item:															
Monetary policy stance: (real interest rate plus real exchange rate)	n.a.	n.a.	n.a.	n.a.	n.a.	n.a.	282.2	163.8	111.3	113.7	112.8	114.3	124.5	128.5	134.8

Notes:
n.a. = not available
a. Real interest rate is estimated as: 100(((1 + interest rate)/(1 + inflation rate))−1) where the interest rate and inflation rate are expressed in decimal.
b. An increase in the index value of the exchange rate represents appreciation.

Source: Author's computation based on IMF, *International Financial Statistics*; IMF, *World Economic Outlook*; Asian Development Bank, *Key Indicators of Developing Asian and Pacific Countries*; and country-specific publications on the IMF website.

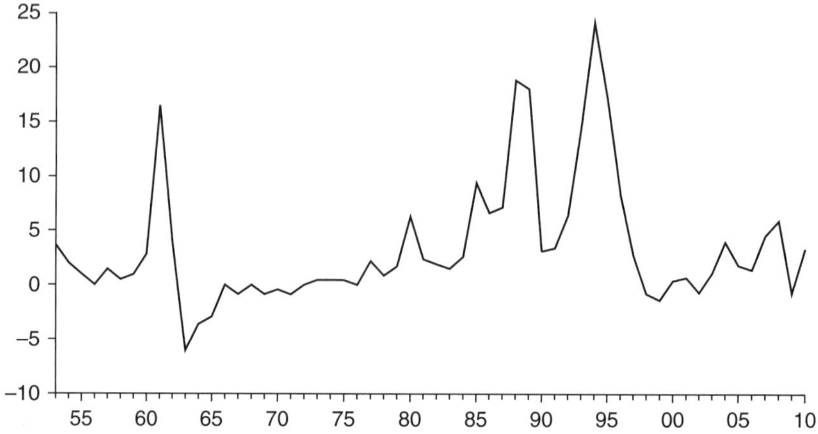

Figure 3.2a CPI inflation in China, 1953–2012

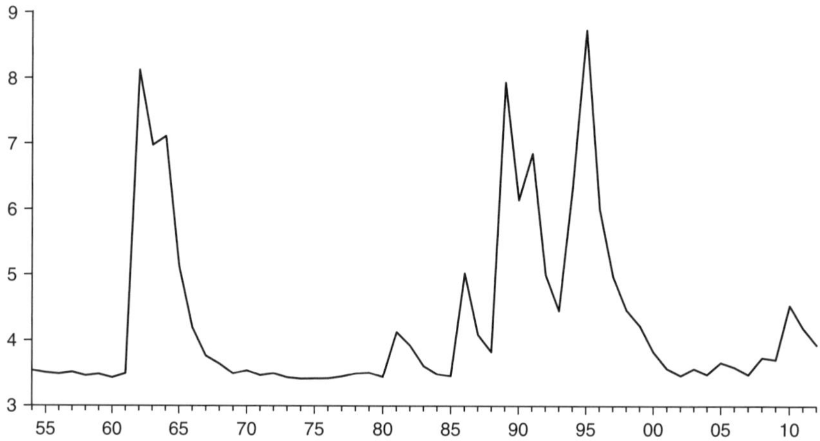

Figure 3.2b Conditional standard deviation of CPI inflation in China, 1953–2012

variables suggest that China has not followed a real exchange rate targeting monetary policy strategy. Rather, the inflation experience in China since the early 1980s demonstrates a stop-and-go approach to monetary policy that led to low but unstable inflation.

Inflation volatility is a common feature in developing countries. There is debate whether inflation volatility is structural, or whether it depends on monetary policy. With structural change in the economy, the nature of shocks to an economy changes. This may affect the degree of inflation volatility. For a rapidly growing economy such as China, changes in both the types of structural shocks and monetary policy may explain changing inflation volatility. Zhang (2010) has showed that the major reason behind the recent reduction in inflation volatility was a smaller number of random shocks. This suggests a need to improve the performance of monetary policy per se in relation to the level and the volatility of inflation.

Over the past two decades, China has opted for a growth-oriented monetary policy in preference to one targeting consistent, sustained inflation control, and has consequently borne the economic costs associated with high and volatile inflation. The question raised here is whether China should move to a monetary policy regime that puts emphasis on low and stable inflation. Goodfriend and Prasad (2006) suggest that the PBC should make low inflation the main objective of monetary policy. They argue that targeting this objective would contribute to macroeconomic stability. Improved macroeconomic stability would, in turn, reduce volatility of economic growth and bolster financial stability.

In the literature there is a view that inflation instability adversely affects economic growth, mainly by reducing the level of investment. This issue is suggested here without detailed theoretical and empirical analysis. The results of a simple causal test (not reported) between Chinese economic growth and inflation volatility suggest a feedback relation, indicating a need for inflation stability. The theory and policy instruments to address this need in the context of an overriding national growth objective are well developed.

Figure 3.3 displays the growth rates of narrow and broad money over the period 1953–2012. They were moderately high and volatile. Inflation and money growth in China are considered causally related. Figure 3.4 displays such a relationship between broad money growth and inflation.[14] Although there is a distinct positive relation between them, there are a number of data points that are outliers. They apparently reflect changes in prices due to administrative price adjustments and supply shocks.

Table 3.2 reports money-growth targets and the realized money-growth rates in China over the period 1994–2012. During this period, the broad money grew consistently at a double-digit rate. The growth rate of broad money has shown higher volatility. In 2009 the growth rates of narrow money and broad money reached historically high levels, 33 per cent and 28 per cent, respectively, when the PBC injected a higher amount of liquidity into the banking system as part of stimulus progress. Since 2007 the PBC has abandoned narrow money targeting. A simple

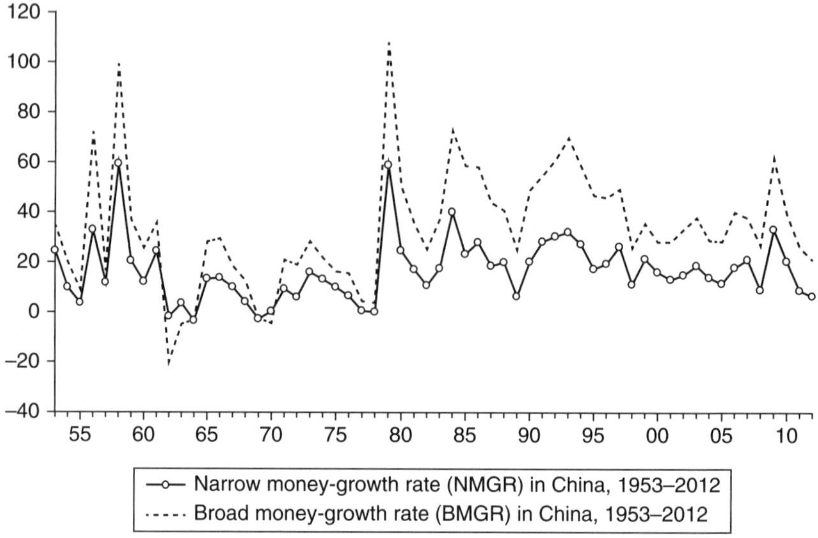

Figure 3.3 *Narrow and broad money-growth rates in China, 1953–2012*

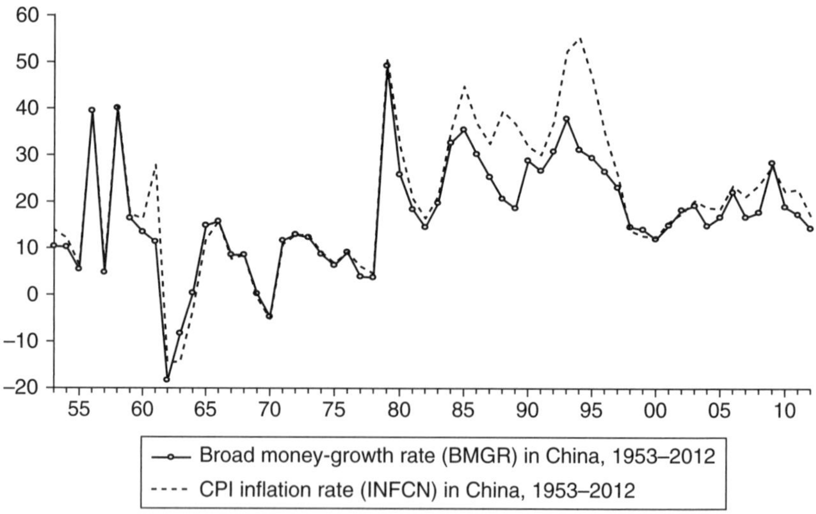

Figure 3.4 *Broad money growth and CPI inflation in China, 1953–2012*

Table 3.2 Targeted and actual growth rates of monetary aggregates in China, 1994–2011

Year	Narrow money (NM), %		Broad money (BM), %	
	Target	Actual	Target	Actual
1994	21	26.2	24	34.5
1995	21–23	16.8	23–25	29.5
1996	18	18.9	25	25.3
1997	18	22.1	23	19.6
1998	17	11.9	16–18	14.8
1999	14	17.7	14–15	14.7
2000	15–17	15.9	14–15	12.3
2001	15–16	12.7	13–14	17.6
2002	13	18.4	13	16.9
2003	16	18.7	16	19.6
2004	17	14.1	17	14.9
2005	15	11.8	15	17.6
2006	14	17.5	16	15.7
2007	n.a.	21	16	16.7
2008	n.a.	9	16	17.8
2009	n.a.	33.2	17	28.4
2010	n.a.	20.4	17	18.9
2011	n.a.	8.7	16	17.3

Note: NM = narrow money stock; BM = broad money stock; n.a. = no target for NM has been announced since 2007.

Source: Chen and Warner (2011) and Sun (2012).

comparison of actual growth rates with the corresponding targets suggests that the PBC frequently missed, or misses, the targets. In most cases, the actual growth rate exceeded target. Possible reasons include the managed float, the build-up of massive reserves, even though partially sterilized, and the accommodation of shocks in money demand.

Despite the apparent 'excess supply' of money over the monetary targeting period, the inflation rate did not rise proportionately. This can be explained on the demand side of the money market. Economic reforms were generally successful as the economy responded positively to incentives. Structural change in the economy created sustained demand for financial services, which brought about significant change in relations within the monetary-financial system. Financial liberalization, in particular, increased demand for money at a rapid rate. Some analysts interpreted this rapid monetization in China as a manifestation of 'forced savings' (Feltenstein and Farhadian, 1987; Portes and Santorum, 1987), and there was concern that this policy would lead to high inflation. The concern was not realized, however, as, in the event, the monetization process was sustained over a long period without causing inflation.

Not unusually for the rapidly growing developing countries, accelerated monetization reflected a sharp increase in demand for money because of the rapid growth rate. Available evidence suggests that this increased demand for 'household money' or transaction balances had at least three sources: (1) rapidly increasing household income and wealth; (2) increasing availability of consumer durables and private housing required preparatory savings; and (3) financial accumulation for small entrepreneurial household businesses (Naughton, 1992). In the discussion of monetary policy and inflation, then, the money demand side has greater relevance and analytical power.

Some discussion on the impact of the fixed peg exchange rate on macroeconomic performance in China is now in order, followed by an examination of inflation behaviour and its linkage to monetary factors.

EXCHANGE RATE PEGGING AND INFLATION AND INTEREST RATES

China fixes the yuan to the US dollar. While it has a large non-tradable goods sector, the question is whether inflation in both China and the United States shares similar patterns and characteristics. Table 3.3 reports the results from some statistical tests that suggest that the volatility of inflation in China in particular was significantly different from that in the United States over the period 1980–2012.

Table 3.3 Means and variances of CPI inflation in China and the United States, 1980–2012

	Observations	Mean	Standard deviation
CPI inflation (China)	33	5.52	6.31
CPI inflation (United States)	33	3.58	2.50
	Degrees of freedom	Statistic	Probability
t-test for equality of means	64	1.64	0.11
	Degrees of freedom	Statistic	Probability
F-test for equality of variances	(32, 32)	6.39	0.00

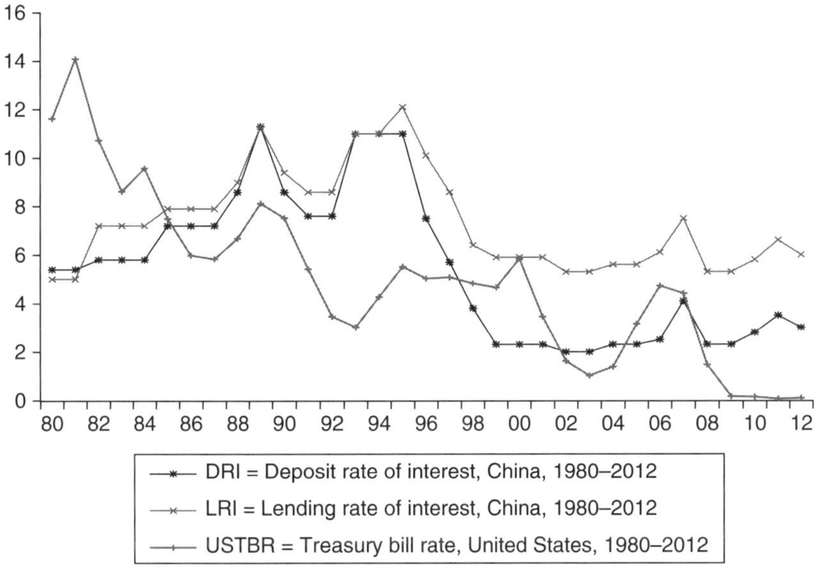

Figure 3.5 Interest rates in China and the United States, 1980–2012

Interest Rate Pass-through

Figure 3.5 displays the deposit and lending interest rates in China and the Treasury bill rate in the United States over the sample period 1980–2012. These interest rates show similar patterns. A monetary policy issue in China is the degree to which its fixed peg exchange rate system with controlled capital mobility reduces its monetary policy independence. With full independence, there should not be any cointegral-causal relation between the US Treasury bill rate and the deposit or lending rate of interest in China. Whether they have a cointegral-causal relation is an empirical issue.

In general, a fixed peg exchange rate system is considered useful when the pegging country fixes its currency to that of a country whose inflation is low and stable. Low, stable measured inflation is expected to exhibit the characteristic of stationarity. The United States is considered such a country. US inflation fell steadily in the 1980s and remained low for more than three decades. In contrast, inflation in China has been low but unstable since the mid 1990s. Inflation rates in China and the United States exhibit somewhat different patterns, but whether they maintain a cointegral-causal linkage depends on the time-series properties of their two measured inflation rates. US inflation is generally found to have high persistence but not a unit root. Table 3.4 reports the unit root test results

Table 3.4 The unit root test results for CPI inflation in China

	Sample period (lag-unadjusted)	Constant (C); Trend (T)	ADF test statistic (SBC-determined lag-length, l)	Inference at 5% level	The KPSS test statistic (Newey-West bandwidth)	Inference at 5% level	Zivot-Andrews	Breakpoint	Inference at 5% level
LCPI	1952–2012	C and T	−1.89 (l = 3)	I(1)	0.199 (6)	I(1)			
LCPI	1952–2012	C	−0.04 (l = 3)	I(1)	0.874 (6)	I(1)	−3.7	1988	1(1)
ΔLCPI	1952–2012	C	−4.08 (l = 1)	I(0)	0.145 (4)	I(0)			
ΔLCPI	1987q1–2012q4	C	−3.01 (l = 5)	I(0)	0.498 (1)	1(1)			

Note: Definitions of variables: LCPI = log of the consumer price index (CPI); ΔLCPI = first-order difference of LCPI; ADF = augmented Dickey-Fuller; KPSS = Kwiatkowski, Phillips, Schmidt and Shin; and SBC = Schwarz Bayesian Criterion.

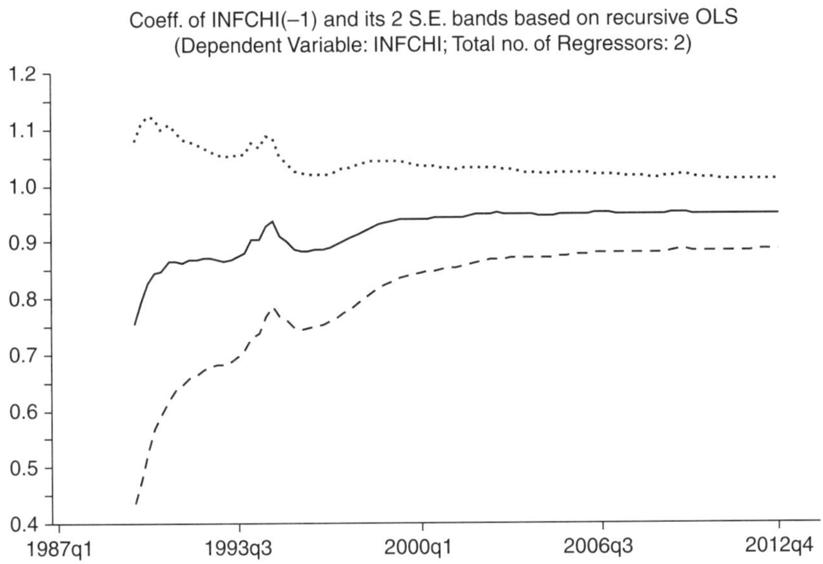

Note: INFCHI = CPI inflation in China.

Figure 3.6a Recursive estimates of the coefficient on the one-period lagged rate of CPI inflation in China

for inflation in China. The test results reject the null hypothesis that inflation in China has a unit root although the Zivot-Andrews breakpoint test results do not reject the null of a unit root. The overall results indicate that the inflation rate in China has high persistence but it does not exhibit the characteristic of a unit root. An implication is that the inflation rates in China and the United States may have a short-term relation but they do not establish a cointegral-causal linkage despite China's fixed peg to the US dollar. Figure 3.6a and Figure 3.6b plot the recursive and rolling regression estimates of one-period lagged rate of inflation in China. The estimates of the coefficient are stable and close to one, implying high persistence.

Table 3.5 reports some empirical results that suggest no significant cointegral-causal relation between the US Treasury bill rate and the deposit rate of interest in China. These interest rates are not causally related although they appear to show similar trends since the late 1980s. This implies that China possesses some monetary policy independence and that changes in monetary policy in the United States do not necessarily lead to a corresponding change in monetary policy in China. Despite the fixed peg exchange rate system, capital controls have allowed China to conduct monetary policy in a somewhat independent manner. The

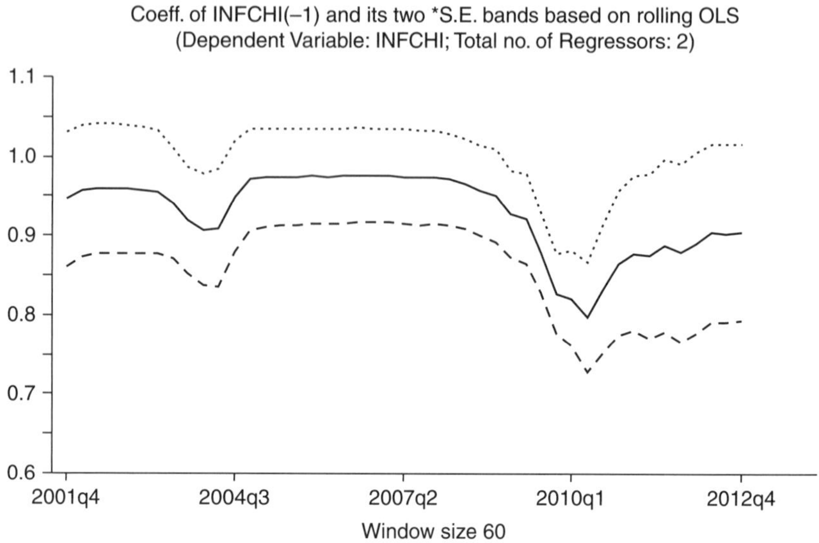

Note: INFCHI = CPI inflation in China.

Figure 3.6b Rolling sample estimates of the coefficient on the one-period lagged rate of CPI inflation in China

effectiveness and significance of this monetary policy independence is an empirical issue.

INFLATION, REAL INTEREST RATE, REAL EXCHANGE RATE AND REAL OUTPUT

One problem in Chinese exchange rate policy is that inflation has remained volatile, albeit on a low average rate, for the past three decades. As the interest rate and the nominal exchange rate in China adjust imperfectly to inflation differentials between China and the United States, high-inflation volatility in China leads to high volatility in both the real interest rate and the real exchange rate. Figure 3.7 reveals such volatility in both the real interest rate and the real exchange rate. One policy issue is whether high volatility in the real interest and exchange rates adversely impacted output. There is debate whether China operated a real exchange rate targeting policy to promote economic growth by keeping its real exchange rate heavily depreciated or undervalued. The data reported earlier demonstrate a steady depreciation of the real exchange rate between the early 1980s and

Table 3.5 *The unit root test results and cointegral relationship between the Treasury bill rate in the United States and the deposit rate of interest in China, 1980–2012*

	Sample (lag-unadjusted)	Constant (C)	ADF test statistic (SBC-determined lag-length, l)	Inference at 5% level	The KPSS test statistic (Newey-West bandwidth)	Inference at 5% level
USTBR	1980–2012	C	−1.87 (l = 1)	I(1)	0.795 (8)	I(1)
ΔUSTBR	1981–2012	none	−4.46 (l = 0)	I(0)	0.04 (6)	I(0)
DRI	1980–2012	C	−1.14 (l = 0)	I(1)	0.80 (8)	I(1)
ΔDRI	1981–2012	none	−4.61 (l = 0)	I(0)	0.05 (4)	I(0)
The Engle-Granger cointegration test results						
Dependent variable	tau-statistic	prob.	z-statistic	prob.		
DRI	−1.57	0.73	−4.35	0.73		
USTBR	−3.80	0.03	−13.15	0.15		

Note: Definitions of variables: USTBR = US Treasury bill rate; DRI = deposit rate of interest; ADF = augmented Dickey-Fuller; KPSS = Kwiatkowski, Phillips, Schmidt and Shin; and SBC = Schwarz Bayesian Criterion.

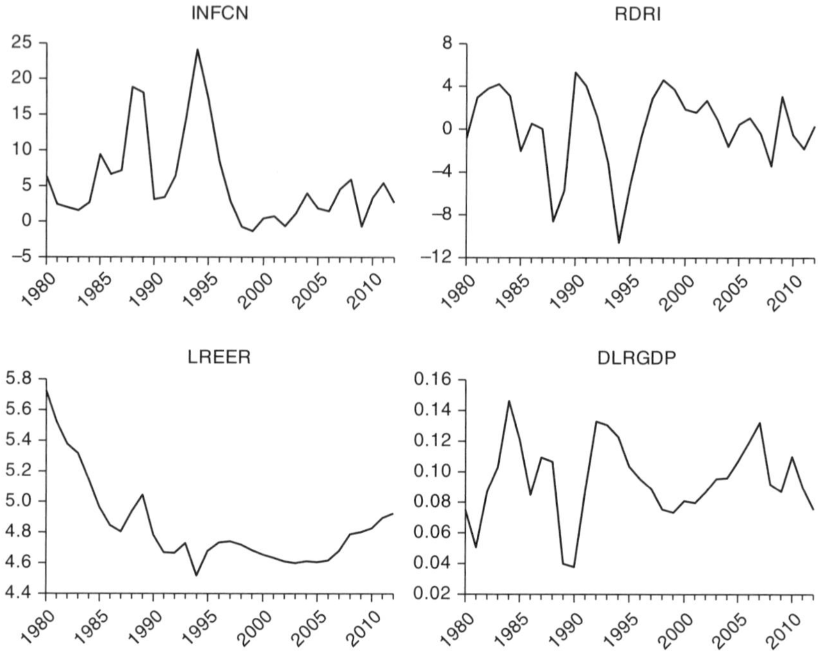

Note: Definitions of variables: INFCN = CPI inflation in China; RDRI = real deposit rate of interest; LREER = log of the real effective exchange rate of Chinese currency; and DLRGDP = first-order difference of the log of real GDP.

Figure 3.7 Data deployed for estimation of the SVAR model for China

the mid 1990s. Since then, the real exchange rate has remained relatively stable, although it has recorded some appreciation in recent years.

A Structural Vector Autoregressive (SVAR) Analysis

Following the discussion in Appendix 5, this subsection, using annual data, estimates a four-variable SVAR model over the period 1980–2012 to examine the interrelationships among inflation, the real deposit rate of interest, the real effective exchange rate and real output. Figure 3.7 plots the data used for estimation purposes.

The model is formulated on the assumption that inflation has a contemporaneous feedback relation with the real interest rate and the real exchange rate. All these variables affect real output. The order of variables in the model is arranged as follows: INFCN, RDRI, LREER and LRGDP where INFCN is the inflation rate in China, RDRI is the real deposit rate of interest, LREER is the log of real effective exchange rate and LRGDP is the log of real GDP. The unit root test results suggest that while inflation, the real deposit rate of interest and the real exchange rate appear stationary, real output is nonstationary. Two versions of the model are then estimated and deployed to generate impulse responses and the forecast error-variance decompositions. The first version of the model is defined as: INFCN, RDRI, LREER and LRGDP while the second version of the model is defined as: INFCN, RDRI, LREER and DLRGDP. In this second version, all the variables are stationary while in the first version real output is nonstationary. Results obtained with the second model are reported.

The impulse responses in Figure 3.8 reveal the interrelations among four variables in the SVAR model. The model does not include the source of inflation. As reviewed in different contexts, high and volatile inflation has monetary roots. When the rate of inflation is low, it is difficult to identify the precise sources of inflation as both demand and supply shocks overwhelm the impact of any core source of inflation such as money growth. The relationship becomes pronounced when inflation remains high. In developing countries, budget deficits become an important source of inflation. The relationships among budget deficits, money growth and inflation are pronounced and detectable. Budget deficits and inflation also maintain a feedback relation. For example, a rise in inflation lowers the real value of tax revenues. This leads to an increase in budget deficits and causes faster money growth and hence inflation.

The impulse responses suggest some expected results. They are indicative, not conclusive. Inflation has a negative impact on economic growth. It lowers the real deposit rate of interest and causes an appreciation of the real exchange rate. The negative real deposit rate is a symptom of financial repression that generally lowers saving, investment and economic growth. The real interest rate responds positively to an appreciation of the real exchange rate. This is because as a grossly appreciated real exchange rate induces capital flight, the real interest rate is required to rise as an inducement to slow down or stop capital flight. This follows the open-economy real exchange rate parity condition. Provided stringent capital controls, there can be short-run deviation of real interest rates across countries, capital controls are not generally effective for most countries irrespective of official regulations and controls. In general, an appreciation of the real exchange rate affects both trade and capital flows while changes in the real interest rate affect saving and investment. Although real appreciation of the currency generally lowers inflation, it may raise inflation via its negative impact on economic growth. The key message that emerges from the empirical results is that inflation and its volatility are not innocuous in so

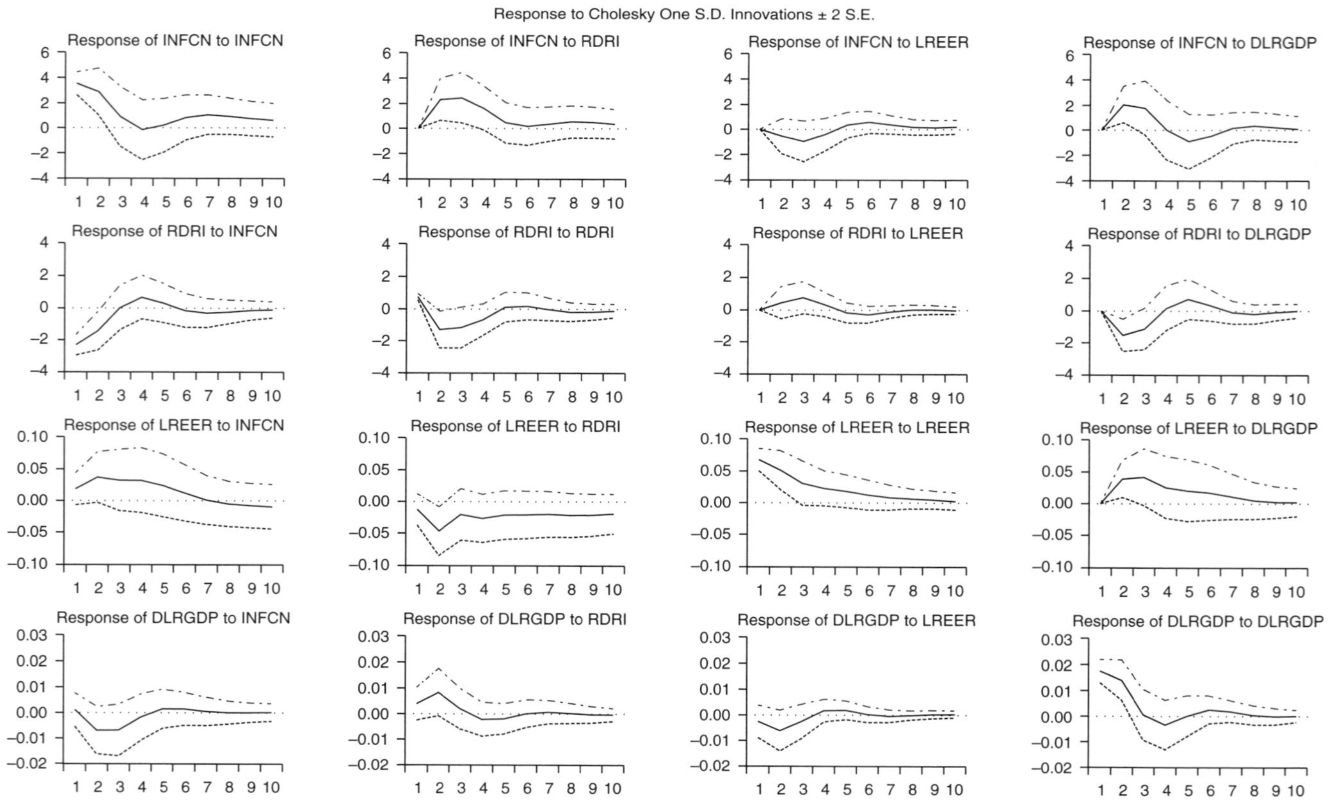

Note: Definitions of variables: INFCN = CPI inflation in China; RDRI = real deposit rate of interest; LREER = log of the real effective exchange rate of Chinese currency; and DLRGDP = first-order difference of the log of real GDP.

Figure 3.8 Impulse responses for variables in the SVAR model for China, 1980–2012

Table 3.6 Forecast error-variance decomposition of variables in the SVAR model for China

Variance Decomposition of INFCN:					
Period	S.E.	INFCN	RDRI	LREER	DLRGDP
1	3.53	100.00	0.00	0.00	0.00
2	5.53	67.85	17.54	0.94	13.67
5	6.74	47.58	31.28	3.28	17.86
10	7.13	49.56	29.60	4.04	16.80
Variance Decomposition of RDRI:					
Period	S.E.	INFCN	RDRI	LREER	DLRGDP
1	2.45	90.35	9.65	0.00	0.00
2	3.51	60.95	18.49	1.67	18.89
5	4.15	46.71	23.80	5.42	24.07
10	4.22	46.36	23.65	5.74	24.25
Variance Decomposition of LREER:					
Period	S.E.	INFCN	RDRI	LREER	DLRGDP
1	0.07	6.73	3.02	90.25	0.00
2	0.11	13.39	18.25	56.41	11.96
5	0.15	20.16	17.99	41.66	20.18
10	0.16	18.87	24.17	37.50	19.46
Variance Decomposition of DLRGDP:					
Period	S.E.	INFCN	RDRI	LREER	DLRGDP
1	0.02	0.40	4.69	1.92	92.99
2	0.03	7.23	12.55	6.46	73.74
5	0.03	13.26	12.71	7.32	66.70
10	0.03	13.36	12.58	7.23	66.81
The Cholesky Ordering: INFCN RDRI LREER DLRGDP					

Note: Definitions of variables: INFCN = CPI inflation in China; RDRI = real deposit rate of interest; LREER = log of the real effective exchange rate of Chinese currency; DLRGDP = first-order difference of the log of real GDP.

far as economic growth is concerned. Inflation affects the real interest rate and the real exchange rate and they have impacts on saving, investment and economic growth. This suggests the need for low and stable inflation for steady economic growth.

Table 3.6 presents the forecast error-variance decompositions of four variables INFCN, RDRI, LREER and DLRGDP. In the table, the numbers represent those percentages of forecast error variance of variables in the model that can be attributed to own innovations and those percentages of forecast error variance that originate from innovations of other variables. The results show that for three of the four variables, the dominant source of the forecast error variance is own innovations, to the extent of 50 per cent for inflation, 24 per cent for the real deposit rate of interest, 38 per cent for the real effective exchange rate and 67 per cent for real output growth over the ten-year time horizon. In the case of real output growth, innovations in the real interest rate and the real exchange rate jointly account for 20 per cent of its forecast error variance. The corresponding share of inflation is 14 per cent. This indicates that real output growth is sensitive to inflation and its volatility through real interest and exchange rate channels.

ISSUES OF MONETARY POLICY AND EXCHANGE RATE POLICY

The empirical results reported above suggest that the Chinese exchange rate system, effectively a fixed peg to the US dollar, leaves it vulnerable to economic shocks. To the extent that Chinese control over capital account transactions weaken, monetary policy changes in the United States are likely to be reflected in Chinese 'involuntary' monetary policy, either creating boom-bust cycles or exacerbating boom-busts of other origins. One way of minimizing such problems is to adopt a flexible, or preferably a floating, exchange rate system. A floating currency allows a sovereign country to independently design and conduct independent monetary policy for price stability. This is particularly appropriate for a relatively large economy, such as China's, with a commensurately large non-tradable goods sector. One shortcoming of a flexible exchange rate system is that it may lead to excess volatility of the exchange rate when the foreign-exchange market is thin. China's financial system is still underdeveloped. However, to the extent that China follows disciplined monetary and fiscal policies and maintains large foreign reserves, its currency is unlikely to display excessive exchange rate volatility.

Provided that China opts for a floating exchange rate system, one policy issue is which strategy of monetary policy China should adopt to maintain price stability. Two strategic options are available in theory: to continue monetary targeting for price stability or to adopt a strategy of fixed or flexible inflation targeting. In the case of inflation targeting, a monetary aggregate, rather than the interest rate, would be the policy instrument of choice.

Stability of the Money-demand Function

Based on the discussion in Appendix 5 a simple money-demand function is estimated for China using real income, the deposit rate of interest, the US Treasury bill rate, the real effective exchange rate and inflation volatility as core determinants of money demand.[15] Both narrow and broad definitions of money have been used for estimation purposes. Preliminary regression results suggest that neither the domestic interest rate nor the real effective exchange rate is statistically significant in the presence of the US Treasury bill rate. In the preferred regression the US Treasury bill rate is retained as the coefficient on this variable is found robust irrespective of the specification and the definition of money used for estimation purposes.

Given the small sample size (1980–2012), the model is estimated using both the ARDL and OLS estimation techniques. As the results obtained by both the narrow and broad definitions of money are qualitatively similar, the results obtained by the narrow definition of money are reported in Table 3.7 for interpretation. They suggest the presence of a weak cointegral relationship among real narrow money balances, real income, the US Treasury bill rate and inflation volatility. The estimated coefficient values are consistent with a priori predictions. The results obtained by the OLS technique are robust. A series of stability tests of the estimated equations suggest that both the narrow and broad money-demand functions remained stable over the sample period. Inflation volatility is found to be a critical variable in the narrow money function. Its exclusion leaves the model somewhat unstable. Inflation instability bears a negative sign in the narrow money-demand function. It implies that as inflation volatility increases, the demand for narrow money decreases. The coefficient on inflation instability is not found significant in the broad money-demand function. Figure 3.9 plots the CUSUM and CUSUMSQ of residuals, suggesting stability of the narrow money-demand function.

Relationships Among Money, Output and Prices

This subsection uses the ARDL bounds-test approach to investigate the relation among money, output and prices. The ARDL bounds-test results suggest the presence of a weak long-run relation among money, output and prices in China (Table 3.8). The coefficient on money in the long-run price level relation is highly significant when broad money is used in the specification. The error-correction model associated with the long-run relation bears a negative sign. Along with the long-run relation among money, output and prices, the money-growth rate has a positive impact on inflation.

Table 3.7 The ARDL and OLS regression results for long-run real narrow money-demand relationships in China, 1980–2012

F-statistic	1.08		
W-statistic	5.42		
Critical value bounds	F-test	W-test	
90%	(2.73, 3.90)	(13.65, 19.49)	
95%	(3.30, 4.67)	(16.48, 23.35)	
Regressors	ARDL (1,0,0,0,1) (Selected based on SBC) Coefficient (t-ratio) [prob.]	ARDL (1,0,0,0,1) Long-run model Coefficient (t-ratio) [prob.]	OLS (Static model) Coefficient (t-ratio) [prob.]
Intercept	2.52 (4.98) [0.00]	3.86 (7.06) [0.00]	4.11 (22.21) [0.00]
LRNM(–1)	0.35 (2.79) [0.10]		
LRGDP	0.81 (5.15) [0.00]	1.23 (31.16) [0.00]	1.19 (38.70) [0.00]
USTBR	−0.01 (−1.98) [0.06]	−0.02 (−2.13) [0.04]	−0.03 (−3.10) [0.00]
LREER	−0.33 (−3.25) [0.00]	0.04 (0.44) [0.66]	
LREER(–1)	0.36 (3.56) [0.00]		
INFVOL	−0.09 (−3.63) [0.00]	−0.14 (3.25) [0.00]	−0.12 (−4.71) [0.00]

Diagnostics			
Adjusted R^2	0.99		0.99
Lagrange multiplier test for serial correlation	$F(1, 25) = 0.92$		$F(1, 28) = 1.57$ [0.22]
Ramsey's RESET test of functional form mis-specification	$F(1, 25) = 0.14$		$F(1, 28) = 2.05$ [0.16]
Normality of residuals	$\chi^2_{(2)} = 0.42$		$\chi^2_{(2)} = 0.18$ [0.91]
Heteroskedasticity	$F(1, 34) = 0.18$		$F(1, 31) = 0.23$ [0.63]
The Wald test:			
H_O: Coefficient on LRGDP = 0		$\chi^2_{(1)} = 970.93$ [0.00]	$\chi^2_{(1)} = 1497.60$ [0.00]
H_O: Coefficient on LRGDP = 1		$\chi^2_{(1)} = 34.90$ [0.00]	$\chi^2_{(1)} = 38.90$ [0.00]
H_O: Coefficient on USTBR = 0		$\chi^2_{(1)} = 4.55$ [0.03]	$\chi^2_{(1)} = 9.63$ [0.00]
H_O: Coefficient on LREER = 0		$\chi^2_{(1)} = 0.19$ [0.66]	
H_O: Coefficient on INFVOL = 0		$\chi^2_{(1)} = 10.57$ [0.00]	$\chi^2_{(1)} = 22.17$ [0.00]

Note: Definitions of variables: LRNM = log of real narrow money balances; LRGDP = log of real GDP; USTBR = US Treasury bill rate; LREER = log of the real effective exchange rate; and INFVOL = inflation volatility.

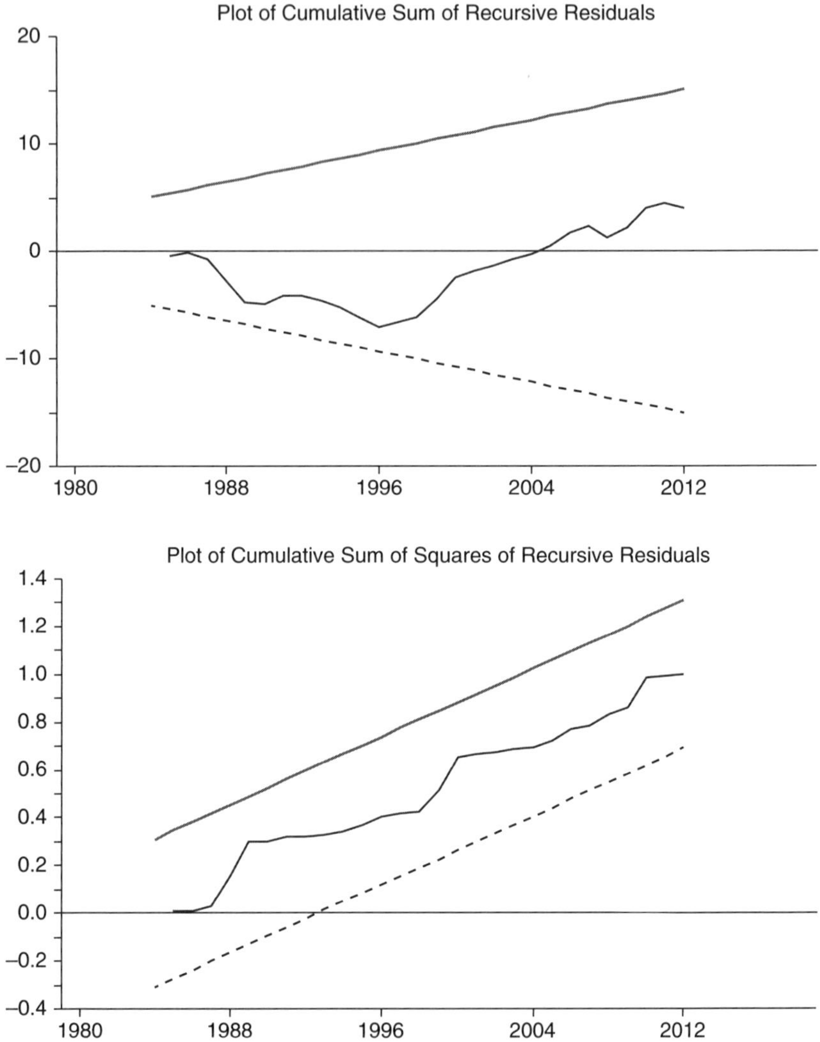

Note: The straight lines represent critical bounds at 5% significance level.

Figure 3.9 CUSUM and CUSUMSQ of residuals for real narrow money-demand relationships in China

Table 3.8 *The ARDL bounds-test results for relationships among money, output and prices in China*

ARDL order selection (SBC)						
		With constant and no time trend F-statistic	ARDL long-run coefficient on LNM/LBM	The Wald test ($\chi^2_{(1)}$) (p-value) Null hypothesis:	ARDL error-correction model (ΔLCPI) (money growth, ΔLNM/ ΔLBM)	ARDL error-correction model (ΔLCPI) (error-correction term, ecm(−1))
	ARDL	Critical value (CV): (lower bound, upper bound)	Coefficient (t-ratio) [prob.]	ARDL long-run coefficient on LNM/LBM = 0	Coefficient (t-ratio)	Coefficient (t-ratio)
With narrow money (NM)						
Sample period: 1980–2012	ARDL(1,0,0)	1.68 CV(95%):{4.18, 5.30} CV(90%):{3.39, 4.40}	1.08 (1.83) [0.08]	3.36 (0.07)	0.14 (0.96)	−0.13 (−1.18)
With broad money (BM)						
Sample period: 1980–2012	ARDL(1,0,0)	2.81 CV(95%):{4.18, 5.30} CV(90%):{3.39, 4.40}	0.86 (9.63) [0.00]	92.77 (0.00)	0.40 (3.70)	−0.46 (−3.76)

Note: Definitions of variables: LNM = log of narrow money stock; LBM = log of broad money stock; ARDL = autoregressive distributed lag; and SBC = Schwarz Bayesian Criterion.

Engle and Granger (1987) have suggested that one of the implications of a cointegral relation between two nonstationary variables is the presence of long-term causality between them running in at least one direction. Table 3.9 reports the bivariate Granger-causality test results among LCPI, LNM (or LBM) and LRGDP. The test results are generated within the vector error-correction (VEC) modelling framework after selecting the optimal lag-length using the AIC. The test results suggest that, for China, there is causality running from money to prices. This is consistent with earlier findings on this relation (Chow, 1987; Hafer and Kutan, 1993; Hasan, 1999).

SUMMARY AND CONCLUDING REMARKS

This chapter has provided an overview of the financial system in China and reviewed the evolution of monetary policy in this country in an historical context. Although China has made impressive economic progress since 1979, its conduct of monetary policy remains integrated with other macroeconomic policy areas. China is yet to recognize and utilize its comparative advantage for targeting and ensuring price stability by monetary policy. China nominally maintains an adjustable peg exchange rate system against a basket of currencies, but because the basket is dominated by the US dollar the peg is effectively fixed and as such has been consistently maintained for some years at 8.28 yuan to the dollar since the mid 2000s. It maintains control over capital flows, enabling it to retain some monetary policy independence although such controls are not fully effective. This is reflected in the absence of a cointegral relation between the interest rates in China and the United States.

One of the problems of the Chinese fixed peg is that it has created high volatilities in at least three key variables: the rate of inflation; real interest rates; and real exchange rates. These three volatilities, in turn, have caused adverse impact on real output or its growth. In general, a fixed peg carries the danger of creating or exacerbating boom-bust cycles.[16] High-inflation volatility also reflects low credibility of monetary policy in so far as its role for achieving price stability is concerned. The people gradually lose confidence in the central bank's ability to keep inflation low and stable. For China, high-inflation volatility arises from multiple objectives of monetary policy and the central bank's limited control over instruments. Various supply shocks do have some impact on China's inflation and its volatility.

The analysis of this chapter implies the radical suggestion that China could gain monetary policy independence, improve the quality of its monetary policy and indeed make the most of the power of modern monetary

Table 3.9 *Granger-causality among money, output and prices in China, 1980–2012*

Sample	Hypotheses No causality runs from:	Chi-square statistic (prob.)	Inference at the 5% level
With narrow money (NM)			
VEC specification	ΔLNM $\rightarrow$ ΔLCPI	13.59 (0.00)	Null hypothesis rejected
	ΔLRGDP $\rightarrow$ ΔLCPI	4.27 (0.23)	Null hypothesis not rejected
	ΔLNM, ΔLRGDP $\rightarrow$ ΔLCPI	19.15 (0.00)	Null hypothesis rejected
	ΔLCPI $\rightarrow$ ΔLNM	7.97 (0.05)	Null hypothesis rejected
	ΔLRGDP $\rightarrow$ ΔLNM	7.41 (0.06)	Null hypothesis not rejected
	ΔLCPI $\rightarrow$ ΔLRGDP	8.50 (0.04)	Null hypothesis rejected
	ΔLNM $\rightarrow$ ΔLRGDP	0.17 (0.98)	Null hypothesis not rejected
With broad money (BM)			
VEC specification	ΔLBM $\rightarrow$ ΔLCPI	27.67 (0.00)	Null hypothesis rejected
	ΔLRGDP $\rightarrow$ ΔLCPI	13.67 (0.00)	Null hypothesis rejected
	ΔLBM, ΔLRGDP $\rightarrow$ ΔLCPI	36.33 (0.00)	Null hypothesis rejected
	ΔLCPI $\rightarrow$ ΔLBM	15.67 (0.00)	Null hypothesis rejected
	ΔLRGDP $\rightarrow$ ΔLBM	13.01 (0.00)	Null hypothesis rejected
	ΔLCPI $\rightarrow$ ΔLRGDP	8.35 (0.04)	Null hypothesis rejected
	ΔLBM $\rightarrow$ ΔLRGDP	0.15 (0.99)	Null hypothesis not rejected

Note: Definitions of variables: LCPI = log of the consumer price index; LNM/LBM = log of narrow/broad money stock; and LRGDP = log of real GDP. Optimal lag = 3 (selected based on the Akaike Information Criterion, AIC).

policy as an economic policy tool, by adopting a flexible, or even a floating, exchange rate system and significantly removing, or completely repealing, its capital controls. A flexible exchange rate would have the added advantage of helping to absorb shocks, both domestic and external. The choice of an exchange rate regime is generally complex and involves tradeoffs. A fixed peg exchange rate system, such as China currently operates, is generally beneficial to small and/or inflationary countries in terms of transparency and policy credibility. High-inflation economies are generally prescribed by the IMF to lower inflation and keep it low credibly. This is expected to start steady economic growth that is often halted during high-inflation episodes. A flexible exchange rate system conferring monetary policy independence is suggested for a large economy. The relatively large size of China's non-tradable goods sector, in relation both to its own and to other economies, reinforces the theoretical appropriateness of a flexible exchange rate system for China. As China does not have deep foreign-exchange markets, there is the fear that the exchange rate may be volatile. This is a possibility but can be tampered by market-oriented capital restrictions to maintain smooth capital flows. Provided that monetary policy is credible, the pass-through of the exchange rate on prices would fall.

There is emerging consensus that China should deploy rule-based monetary policy for price stability. Whether monetary targeting or inflation targeting would be more appropriate remains debatable. Presently, China is using a monetary aggregate along with bank-lending controls as policy instruments to achieve economic growth and price stability. This has created ambiguity. Inflation targeting is probably a long way off in China given its relatively underdeveloped financial system. Its interest rates are not fully market determined and there are restrictions on capital flows. Rule-based monetary targeting is preferable in a developing country until its financial sector is adequately developed. In early stages of development, interest rates are not effective as a policy instrument. Rule-based monetary policy can play an important role for China in creating a stable macroeconomic environment, while a financial reform programme can be devised and implemented to support any exchange rate flexibility adopted and enhance its effectiveness in the monetary policy transmission mechanisms.

An investigation of Chinese money-demand behaviour suggests that there is a stable money-demand function in China, especially when inflation instability is included in the money-demand function. The narrow money-demand function has been found more stable than the broad money-demand function. Although stability of the money-demand function is not a requirement for having a causal linkage between money supply growth and inflation, if present it provides a sound basis for the conduct of monetary policy within a monetary framework. The Granger-causality tests within a VEC model suggest a causal linkage between money supply growth and inflation. The overall empirical results suggest that China can introduce inflation targeting by introducing the use of a monetary aggregate as an instrument of monetary policy to maintain low and stable inflation. A money-growth rule may also be appropriate under a flexible exchange rate regime. Control over the money supply would be more precise and more readily implemented if China effected deep financial reforms and acquired instrument (operational) independence for the conduct of monetary policy.[17]

In an early stage of financial reform, there could be volatility of interest rates and, due to political sensitivity, policymakers may be reluctant to allow an upward movement of the interest rate. Therefore, a monetary aggregate (under the monetary targeting strategy) is considered a superior operating target to a short-term interest rate (under the inflation targeting strategy). However, the monetary targeting approach need not be rigid. Rather, it can be accompanied by monitoring of other indicators provided that the goal of price stability receives monetary policy priority and is communicated to the public with high transparency. There is also a need for firm commitment of the Chinese government to maintain low and stable inflation. This would become more credible if the PBC is given autonomy in conducting monetary policy for price stability.

NOTES

1. This chapter uses the abbreviation PRC or China interchangeably.
2. The market-oriented economic reforms in China were introduced in two stages. The first stage, in the late 1970s and early 1980s, involved decollectivization of agriculture, the opening up of the economy to foreign trade and investment and permission to start private businesses. The second stage, in the late 1980s and 1990s, involved privatization and contracting out of state-owned enterprises, and the removing of price controls, protectionist measures and regulations. The state monopolies were retained in the banking and oil sectors. For further information on economic reforms in China under 'Socialism with Chinese Characteristics', see http://en.wikipedia.org/wiki/Chinese_economic_reform (accessed 19 March 2015).
3. See the statement by Zhou Xiaochuan, former Governor of the Central Bank of China at the IMF, 20 April 2013, available at http://www.imf.org/External/spring/2013/imfc/statement/eng/chn.pdf (accessed 19 March 2015).
4. On the question of the Lewis labour surplus model and the Lewis turning point for China, see IMF (2012, box 1:8) and Das and N'Diaye (2013).
5. Public policy also played a key role in facilitating investment by providing land, subsidized credits and services from public utilities.
6. The People's Bank of China (PBC) is the central bank of China.
7. For discussion on financial repression and its link with exchange rate policy and consequences, see Lardy (2005, 2008).
8. Materials of this section are drawn from various publications of the PBC, including the *People's Bank of China* (http://www.pbc.gov.cn) and *Law of the People's*

Republic of China on the People's Bank of China (http://www.china.org.cn/business/laws_regulations/2007–06/22/content_1214826.htm, accessed 19 March 2015).

9. Before the institutional change in 1983, the PBC performed functions of both a central bank and commercial banks. In 1984 the PBC passed its commercial banking activities to four newly established (or reorganized) state-owned commercial banks, namely the Agricultural Bank of China, the Bank of China, the China Construction Bank and the Industrial and Commercial Bank of China. They are the four largest banks in China and are dubbed the 'Big Four'.
10. The Committee consists of 11 members including the governor and deputy governor of the PBC, representatives from government ministries and agencies, two governors of state-owned banks and independent financial professionals.
11. For details, see *Deng Xiaoping*, available at http://en.wikipedia.org/wiki/Deng_Xiaoping (accessed 19 March 2015).
12. The renminbi was revalued by 2.1 per cent relative to the US dollar on 21 July 2005. The government also announced that the external value of the renminbi would henceforth be set with reference to a basket of currencies. Neither the currency composition of the basket nor the basket weights have been disclosed to the public. The new exchange rate regime allows for some fluctuation around the reference rate. In practice, the exchange rate of the renminbi has not, however, fluctuated much against the dollar since July 2005.
13. Materials of this subsection are mostly drawn from Geiger (2006).
14. Chow (1987) has examined the long-term linkage between money growth and inflation in China with data since the 1950s and found a positive relationship between them. Feyzioglu (2004) has also investigated the inflationary experiences of China within a monetary framework.
15. For earlier studies on money demand in China, see Arize and Malindretos (2000), Bahmani-Oskooee and Wang (2007), Chan et al. (1991), Chen (1997), Hafer and Kutan (2001) and Lee and Chien (2008).
16. Maintenance of an exchange rate regime with limited de facto flexibility exposes the economy to significant risks of macroeconomic instability. While capital controls provide some room for manoeuvre for monetary policy even under such a regime, this room tends to be limited in practice and could result in inadequate control of investment growth and inflationary/deflationary pressures. Furthermore, the effectiveness of capital controls inevitably erodes over time as domestic and international investors find channels, including under invoicing of exports and over invoicing of imports, to evade them.
17. For some early discussion on the exchange rate policy and monetary policy in China, see Xie (2004) and Xu (2000).

REFERENCES

Arize, A.C. and J. Malindretos (2000), 'Does inflation variability affect the demand for money in China? Evidence from error-correction models', *International Economic Journal*, **14**(1), 47–60.

Asian Development Bank (various years), *Key Indicators of Developing Asian and Pacific Countries*, Manila: ADB.

Bahmani-Oskooee, M. and Y. Wang (2007), 'How stable is the money demand in China?', *Journal of Economic Development*, **23**(1), 21–33.

Chan, M.L.L., W. Cheng and R. Deaves (1991), 'Money demand in China revisited: some new empirical evidence', *Journal of Asian Economics*, **2**(1), 137–44.

Chen, B. (1997), 'Long-run money demand and inflation in China', *Journal of Macroeconomics*, **19**(3), 609–17.

Chen, Y. and R.A. Warner (2011), 'The role of monetary aggregates in Chinese monetary policy implementation', *Journal of the Asia Pacific Economy*, **16**(3), 464–88.

Cheng, H.S. (1988), 'Monetary policy and inflation in China', in H.S. Cheng (ed.), *Monetary Policy in Pacific Basin Countries*, Boston, MA: Kluwer Academic Publishers.

Chow, G.C. (1987), 'Money and price level determination in China', *Journal of Comparative Economics*, **11**(3), 319–33.

Das, M. and P. N'Diiaye (2013), 'Chronicle of a decline foretold: has China reached the Lewis turning point?', Working Paper WP 13/26, IMF, Washington, DC.

Engle, R.F. and C.W.J. Granger (1987), 'Co-integration and error-correction: representation, estimation, and testing', *Econometrica*, **55**(2), 251–76.

Feltenstein, A. and Z. Farhadian (1987), 'Fiscal policy, monetary targets, and the price level in a centrally planned economy: an application to China', *Journal of Money, Credit and Banking*, **19**(2), 137–56.

Feyzioglu, T. (2004), 'Price dynamics in China', IMF Occasional Paper No. 232, Washington, DC, 14–20.

Geiger, M. (2006), 'Monetary policy in China (1994–2004): targets, instruments and their effectiveness', Wurzburg Economic Papers No. 68, Universitat Wurzburg.

Goodfriend, M. and E. Prasad (2006), 'A framework for independent monetary policy in China', IMF Working Paper WP/06/111, IMF, Washington, DC.

Hafer, R.W. and A.M. Kutan (1993), 'Further evidence on money, output and prices in China', *Journal of Comparative Economics*, **17**, 701–9.

Hafer, R.W. and A.M. Kutan (2001), 'Economic reforms and long-run money demand in China: implications for monetary policy', *Southern Economic Journal*, **60**(4), 936–45.

Hasan, M.S. (1999), 'Monetary growth and inflation in China', *Journal of Comparative Economics*, **27**, 669–85.

Hossain, A. (2014), 'Monetary policy, inflation and inflation volatility in Australia', *Journal of Post-Keynesian Economics*, **36**(4), 745–79.

IMF (International Monetary Fund) (various years), *International Financial Statistics*, Washington, DC: IMF.

IMF (International Monetary Fund) (various years), *World Economic Outlook*, Washington, DC: IMF.

IMF (International Monetary Fund) (2012), *China: Country Report 12/195*, Washington, DC: IMF.

Lardy, N.R. (2005), 'Exchange rate and monetary policy in China', *Cato Journal*, **25**(1), 41–7.

Lardy, N.R. (2008), 'Financial repression in China', Peterson Institute for International Economics Policy Brief 08–8.

Lee, C.-C. and M.S. Chien (2008), 'Stability of money demand function revisited in China', *Applied Economics*, **40**, 3185–97.

Mehran, H., N. Quintyn, T. Nordman and B. Laurens (1996), 'Monetary and exchange system reforms in China: an experiment in gradualism', Occasional Paper No. 141, IMF, Washington, DC.

Naughton, B. (1992), 'China: monetary and financial system', in P. Newman, M. Milgate and J. Eatwell (eds), *The New Palgrave Dictionary of Money and Finance*, Vol. 1, London: Macmillan, pp. 351–3.

Portes, R. and A. Santorum (1987), 'Money and the consumption goods market in China', *Journal of Comparative Economics*, **11**(3), 354–71.

Sun, R. (2012), 'Does monetary policy matter in China? A narrative approach', Unpublished manuscript, Schumpeter School of Business and Economics, University of Wuppertal, Denmark.

Xie, P. (2004), 'China's monetary policy: 1998–2002', Working Paper No. 217, Stanford Center for International Development, Stanford University, available at http://web.stanford.edu/group/siepr/cgi-bin/siepr/?q=system/files/shared/pubs/papers/pdf/SCID217.pdf (accessed 19 March 2015).

Xu, Y. (2000), 'China's exchange rate policy', *China Economic Review*, **11**, 262–77.

Zhang, C. (2010), 'Inflation uncertainty and monetary policy in China', *China and World Economy*, **18**(3), 40–55.

4. Hong Kong, SAR of China

Hong Kong, Special Administrative Region (SAR) of the People's Republic of China (PRC), is one of the most successful city economies in the world. Starting as an entrepôt, this densely populated city has emerged as one of the major trade and international finance centres in Asia.[1] It has a sophisticated banking sector, which is the second largest in Asia after Japan.[2] Living standards in Hong Kong SAR are very high and are also expected to rise commensurately with the rapid pace of economic growth in mainland China. Over three decades Hong Kong SAR's economy has transformed from manufacturing leader to an affluent service orientation. Tourism, retail trade and financial services have emerged as the key sectors in Hong Kong SAR's economy. Its limited endowment of natural resources confers on Hong Kong SAR a comparative advantage in trade and service activity. Government policy supports this dynamism with minimal economic regulation. The dominance of mercantile trade in Hong Kong's economic structure is reflected in its high degree of economic openness, measured as the ratio of exports plus imports to GDP. For Hong Kong this ratio is among the highest in the world, at greater than 3. Exports from Hong Kong SAR are generally (value-added) re-exports, so that its exports and imports are intertwined. One of Hong Kong SAR's more significant economic activities consists in its role as an intermediary for the mainland's exports and imports. To encourage foreign investment, China maintains low income and consumption taxes in the Hong Kong SAR and does not impose controls on capital movements through it.

Hong Kong SAR's economy has become integrated with that of mainland China, which has progressed rapidly since its international opening in the late 1970s. The opening of the PRC ended a highly closed period following its 1949 victory over the nationalist Chinese forces of General Chiang Kai-Shek. The financial sector, in particular, has expanded rapidly as it integrated with the mainland financial system. Although the Chinese currency renminbi (RMB), of which the basic currency unit is the yuan, is yet to become an international currency, RMB is now used widely along with the Hong Kong SAR dollar (HKD) for payments, deposits and lending in the banking system. It appears that the establishment of an RMB offshore market in Hong Kong SAR is the first step towards the goal of capital account convertibility in mainland China. This is viewed as a natural extension of Hong Kong SAR's key functions in the Chinese economy as a trading port and capital conduit. Hong Kong SAR is then the logical location for activities complementary to trade and free-flowing capital. These include service as a gateway for inwards and outwards foreign investment, management and professional services and technology transfer into mainland China.

Rapid economic growth and transformation in Hong Kong SAR since the 1960s is attributed to a host of factors including free trade, free capital flows and the flexibility of wages and prices. It represents an interesting case study of a low-taxing free market economy where monetary and fiscal policies play a limited role in stabilizing both output and prices. The role of government is confined to a focus on the development and improvement of physical infrastructure and institutions to facilitate trade, business, industries and financial services. As a small open economy, Hong Kong SAR is susceptible to external shocks. However, rather than intervening to neutralize the impacts of those shocks, the government relies on price flexibility (including wage flexibility) to the extent necessary for rapid economic adjustment. There is the perception that the government, by adopting a hands-off approach to economic management, has allowed the economy to prosper without creating large policy-induced distortions. Nevertheless, the following analysis reveals that there are macroeconomic policy issues that, if addressed by some policy adjustments, have the potential to enhance the economy of Hong Kong SAR.

Macroeconomic management in Hong Kong SAR revolves around maintaining the stability of the fixed exchange rate using its 'Linked Exchange Rate System'.[3] The government maintains fiscal discipline through holding large fiscal reserves and committing to a balanced-budget approach over the medium term. Hong Kong SAR has made a policy decision to tradeoff its monetary-policy independence for its fixed peg to the US dollar (USD). For over three decades the Hong Kong currency has been fixed, with only occasional adjustment, at rates between HKD7.7 and HKD7.8 per USD. Hong Kong's Linked Exchange Rate System is essentially a currency board, which is an extreme form of the fixed peg exchange rate system.

There are at least four reasons why the Linked Exchange Rate System is considered appropriate for Hong Kong SAR. Firstly, Hong Kong SAR's economy is flexible; its key markets, namely the labour markets, product markets and the property and retail markets, respond quickly to shocks and changing economic circumstances. The flexibility of these markets is reflected in relatively rapid adjustment of wages and prices, which in turn restores any loss of external competitiveness from the rigidity of the nominal exchange rate. Secondly, Hong Kong SAR's banking sector is highly developed, strong and solvent. Consequently, it copes well with the relatively high volatility of US interest rates, imported into Hongkongese interest rates via the fixed currency peg.[4] Thirdly, the Hong Kong SAR government maintains fiscal discipline given its accumulated fiscal reserves and the target of budgetary balance over the medium term. This removes the danger of budget-deficit monetization originating from fiscal activism or populism. Fourthly, Hong Kong SAR maintains large foreign-exchange reserves to defend its currency board, the Linked Exchange Rate System, in the event of shocks and speculative capital movements.

The Linked Exchange Rate System has served Hong Kong SAR well for three decades, one of the few monetary policy regimes in history that has remained in effect unaltered for so long. There is the suggestion, however, that Hong Kong SAR monetary policy would serve it better under a more flexible exchange rate system, without necessarily floating. The available theory and evidence is likely to make a floating exchange rate system unsuitable for a small, open economy like Hong Kong SAR. Choice of an exchange rate regime is a complex task of high difficulty. Hong Kong SAR is irregularly exposed to external shocks of varying magnitude, an occupational hazard of small, open economies. While flexible exchange rates help to absorb shocks, the associated exchange rate volatility may undermine monetary and financial stability. Hong Kong SAR maintains stability of the nominal exchange rate while sacrificing price stability to some extent, since measured inflation remains volatile and does not necessarily converge to US inflation. The nominal exchange rate does not appear to serve well as an anchor to prices. Hong Kong SAR experienced high inflation in the 1970s and 1990s and deflation after the East-Southeast Asian financial crisis of the late 1990s. Economic growth is also highly volatile, possibly linked to Hong Kong SAR's high volatility of its real interest rates, real exchange rates and real wages. This wide-ranging and costly volatility originates in Hong Kong SAR's volatile inflation, an outcome of the fixed exchange rate arrangement with the US dollar.

Therefore, one of the major shortcomings of the Linked Exchange Rate System is that inflation, deflation and the volatilities of these remain outside government control.[5] As Hong Kong SAR follows a disciplined monetary and fiscal policy, price stability is considered a virtue and an important policy objective. This would require monetary policy independence. In the case of Hong Kong SAR, inflation in the short run does not follow the movement of inflation in the United States, as might be expected of the fixed peg provided all goods and services are tradable. Consequently, the real interest rate, the real exchange rate and real wages are highly volatile. This affects economic growth, employment and the level of economic welfare. The boom-bust cycle, originating in international shocks and the policy responses to them, causes economic distress and creates social problems. In a service-oriented market economy, skilled labour commands high remuneration. This can create social discontent if it leads to large inequalities of income and assets. As productivity growth is low in a service-based economy, real wage growth remains low. This hurts the poor and elderly the most. High and volatile inflation also causes problems for low-income earners. Hongkongese income inequality, as reflected in the Gini coefficient of 0.53, has led Hong Kong SAR to introduce minimum wages and other policy measures to provide some relief to the poor and vulnerable.

The remainder of this chapter provides an overview of Hong Kong SAR's exchange rate system and its implications for key macroeconomic variables, especially inflation, the real interest rate, the real exchange rate and output. Both annual and quarterly data, extending from the early 1980s, are deployed for empirical analysis.

THE HONG KONG MONETARY AUTHORITY

Hong Kong SAR does not have an officially designated central bank. The Hong Kong Monetary Authority (HKMA) performs central banking functions, including maintaining exchange rate stability under the currency board system. It was created on 1 April 1993 in a merger of the Office of the Exchange Fund with the Office of the Commission of Banking. The Exchange Fund Ordinance and the Banking Ordinance govern the functions and responsibilities of the HKMA. The HKMA reports its activities to the financial secretary of the government.

The Exchange Fund was established in 1935 and comprises Hong Kong SAR's official reserves.[6] It provides the backing to safeguard the fixed exchange value of HKD with the USD. A second function is to help preserve the integrity of Hong Kong SAR's monetary-financial system for the purpose of keeping it in demand as an international financial centre. The Exchange Fund is not, however, regarded as an investment fund, nor is it operated as one, though it is invested in a wide range of fixed-income, equity and other assets in international markets. It holds three portfolios: (1) the backing portfolio, to underwrite the monetary base; (2) the investment portfolio, providing the Fund with long-run purchasing power; and (3) the strategic portfolio, containing assets purchased by the Hong Kong government for the account of the Exchange Fund for strategic purposes.

The Exchange Fund Advisory Committee (EFAC) provides advice to the financial secretary on control of the Exchange Fund. The financial secretary is the *ex officio* chairman of the EFAC and appoints other members under the delegated authority of the chief executive of the Hong Kong SAR.

Under the Exchange Fund Ordinance, Chapter 66, subsection 5A(1), the financial secretary of Hong Kong appoints a person to be the Monetary Authority on such terms and conditions as he or she thinks fit. The HKMA itself comes into existence as the office of the Monetary Authority, and the Monetary Authority therefore also has the title of chief executive of the HKMA. The chief executive chairs the Chief Executive's Committee. Its function is to inform the chief executive in two main ways: (1) it reports weekly on the progress of major tasks currently being undertaken by the divisions of the HKMA and (2) it advises on policy matters relating to the operations of the HKMA. This Committee comprises the deputy chief executives, the heads of all the HKMA's divisions and the Hong Kong Mortgage Corporation's chief executive officer. The HKMA under the chief executive performs the following key functions: (a) keeps the fixed HKD/USD exchange rate stable; (b) manages the Exchange Fund in a sound and effective way to maintain monetary and financial stability; (c) promotes the safety of Hong Kong SAR's banking system; and (d) develops Hong Kong SAR's financial structure to promote capital mobility and global financial integration.

Given the status of Hong Kong SAR as an international financial centre, the HKMA emphasizes the banking system's stability through vigilant regulation and supervision. Empowered by the Banking Ordinance, the HKMA ensures that the authorized institutions operate effectively, responsibly, honestly and efficiently and takes measures to protect depositors. The HKMA works closely with the authorities of mainland China and the financial industry to establish Hong Kong SAR as the offshore RMB business centre. Since offshore RMB business began in 2004, Hong Kong SAR has created a RMB financial platform that provides one-stop services, including banking and settlement, financing and wealth management, to corporate and financial institutions. Hong Kong SAR has one of the largest offshore RMB liquidity pools and the potential to be a global hub for RMB trade settlement and bond issuance.

EVOLUTION OF EXCHANGE RATE POLICY

At the time of writing, Hong Kong SAR maintains the Linked Exchange Rate System. Backed by large foreign reserves, it ensures the level of exchange rate stability considered essential for monetary and financial stability. Popularly known as the currency board system, the basic principle is to back both the stock and flow of monetary base with at least 100 per cent foreign reserves, and preferably greater than this, with all changes in the monetary base matched one-for-one in real time by corresponding changes in foreign reserves. This section provides an historical context of the evolution of the present exchange rate system.

From 1845 to 1935 Hong Kong SAR's monetary system participated in the international silver standard. Private commercial banks issued bank notes, which were used as means of transactions. These notes, however, had no legal tender status. In 1895 the Bank Notes Issue Ordinance restricted the issuing of bank notes to the Hong Kong and Shanghai Banking Corporation and the Chartered Bank of India, Australia and China.[7] In November 1935 Hong Kong went off the silver system.

An Exchange Fund was set up under the Exchange Fund Ordinance of 1935. All the note-issuing banks were required to deposit their silver holdings in the Exchange Fund in return for Certificates of Indebtedness, which served as legal backing for bank notes. The Exchange Fund sold silver holdings and invested them in sterling assets. The Hong Kong dollar was then pegged to the sterling at a fixed rate. All note-issuing banks that issued new notes were required to make sterling deposits to the Exchange Fund as full cover for note issues at the same rate. This system was known as the Sterling Exchange Standard. It was a variant of the currency board system that had existed in most British colonies and protectorates.

The Sterling Exchange Standard lasted until June 1972. In July 1972, following the United Kingdom's decision to float its currency, the pound sterling, the Hong Kong government pegged the Hong Kong dollar to the US dollar at the rate of US$1 = HK$5.65. The note-issuing mechanism thereby changed, such that the note-issuing banks were no longer required to pay foreign currency to the Exchange Fund when they issued Hong Kong dollar bank notes. Instead, the backing was provided in Hong Kong SAR dollars, which were issued by the Exchange Fund to acquire foreign currency assets equivalent to the nominal value of notes issued at the then current exchange rate (Jao, 1992).

In November 1974 the US dollar came under speculative attack. The then Hong Kong government, unable to maintain parity of its currency with the US dollar, decided to float. The Hong Kong dollar was by this time a strong currency, so that the floatation led to some appreciation. Although the first two years of the floating regime worked well for Hong Kong, the currency came under pressure after mid 1977. In the absence of a formal central bank and associated appropriate monetary policy instruments, Hong Kong lost control over its money stock. This led to a sharp depreciation of the Hong Kong dollar and raised inflation to double digits over the period 1979–83.

Depreciation of Hong Kong's dollar took a serious turn during 1982–83, when the PRC announced its intention to reclaim sovereignty over Hong Kong's New Territories from the British immediately upon expiry of the 99-year lease on 30 June 1997. Faced with an imminent collapse of its financial system, the then Hong Kong government adopted a two-point currency stabilization plan. The first measure was the reimposition of a foreign-exchange constraint. This required the note-issuing banks to pay in US dollars to the Exchange Fund to obtain the Certificates of Indebtedness (CIs) as cover for their bank notes issued at the fixed rate of USD = HKD7.8. The second was the abolition of 10 per cent withholding tax on interest receipts from HKD-denominated deposits with financial institutions. It removed tax advantage from holding foreign currency deposits. These two measures stabilized the Hong Kong SAR dollar and laid the foundations for the USD-based Linked Exchange Rate System (Hsu, 1985; Jao, 1992; Moreno, 1986, 1988).

The Linked Exchange Rate System has become the external nominal anchor to domestic prices in Hong Kong. The money stock is endogenous, as it responds to balance-of-payment developments. The Hongkongese interest rate is linked to the US interest rate. Dodsworth and Mihaljek (1997, p. 3) have described the present monetary policy framework in Hong Kong SAR as follows:

> Monetary and exchange rate policies have been determined by currency board rules during most of the Hong Kong's history. Under the linked exchange rate system established in 1983, monetary policy has a single, transparent objective: to maintain a stable exchange rate between the Hong Kong and U.S. dollars. The link, together with the freedom from controls on capital flows, implies that Hong Kong's interest rates are essentially determined by U.S. monetary conditions. While the Hong Kong Monetary Authority (HKMA) has some limited tools to influence interbank liquidity and thereby affect local short-term interest rates, these instruments have been used sparingly, mainly to smooth the occasional volatility in overnight interest rates. Such operations, however, have been very much a secondary objective to the primary goal of defending the exchange rate link, which has served Hong Kong well and has provided a firm anchor for financial policies.

MACROECONOMIC DEVELOPMENTS

This section provides a brief discussion of macroeconomic developments in Hong Kong SAR highlighting key policy issues. Table 4.1 shows that real GDP grew at an impressive rate of about 7 per cent per annum during the 1970s and 1980s. This rapid growth was sustained until the mid 1990s. The East-Southeast Asian financial crisis slowed Hong Kong's economic

Table 4.1 Macroeconomic indicators in Hong Kong, 1969–2012

Macroeconomic indicators	1951–55	1956–60	1961–65	1966–70	1971–75	1976–80	1981–85	1986–90	1991–95	1996–2000	2001–05	2006–10	2011	2012
Money-growth rate (%)														
Narrow money growth	n.a.	n.a.	n.a.	n.a.	n.a.	n.a.	n.a.	n.a.	11.6	4.5	12.6	15.5	8.4	14.4
Broad money growth	n.a.	n.a.	n.a.	n.a.	n.a.	n.a.	n.a.	n.a.	11.3	10.0	3.5	10.4	9.8	7.8
Real GDP growth rate (%)	n.a.	n.a.	13.3	5.5	6.6	11.6	5.8	7.8	5.3	2.7	4.3	4.0	4.9	1.5
GDP per capita, current prices, US dollar	n.a.	n.a.	n.a.	n.a.	n.a.	5695	6053	10450	19619	25358	24590	29997	34259	35961
Unemployment rate (%)	n.a.	n.a.	n.a.	n.a.	n.a.	3.8	3.7	1.7	2.2	4.2	6.5	4.4	3.4	3.4
CPI inflation rate (%)		1.3	1.0	4.3	9.0	8.4	9.4	7.5	9.5	1.5	−1.4	2.3	5.3	4.1
Nominal interest rate (%)														
Treasury bill rate	n.a.	n.a.	n.a.	n.a.	n.a.	n.a.	n.a.	n.a.	4.6	5.5	1.3	1.1	0.2	0.1
Lending rate of interest	n.a.	n.a.	n.a.	n.a.	n.a.	n.a.	n.a.	10.0	7.8	9.0	5.6	5.9	5.0	5.0

Real interest rate (%)[a]														
Treasury bill rate	n.a.	n.a.	n.a.	n.a.	n.a.	n.a.	n.a.	n.a.	−4.4	1.6	4.1	−0.1	−2.0	−4.8
Lending rate of interest	n.a.	n.a.	n.a.	n.a.	n.a.	n.a.	n.a.	n.a.	−1.6	4.8	8.4	4.4	2.6	−0.2
Nominal exchange rate (HK$ per US dollar)	5.7	5.7	5.7	5.9	5.3	4.8	6.9	7.8	7.7	7.8	7.8	7.8	7.8	7.8
Nominal effective exchange rate[b]	n.a.	114.8	120.7	121 1	128.1	139.9	119.6	97.5	97.0	105.1	107.5	96.2	89.3	91.4
Real effective exchange rate[b]	n.a.	n.a.	n.a.	n.a.	n.a.	n.a.	75.8	68.2	86.6	122.9	116.0	92.2	88.0	93.7

Notes:
n.a. = not available
a. Real interest rate is estimated as: 100(((1 + interest rate)/(1 + inflation rate))−1) where the interest rate and inflation rate are expressed in decimal.
b. An increase in the index value of the exchange rate represents appreciation.

Source: Author's computation based on IMF, *International Financial Statistics*; IMF, *World Economic Outlook*; ADB, *Key Indicators of Developing Asian and Pacific Countries*; and other country-specific publications on the IMF website growth, followed by gradual recovery for a few years and acceleration to about 7 per cent per annum during 2004–07. Following the onset of the global financial crisis in 2007, adversity struck in the form of a sharp slowdown in 2008 deteriorating to negative economic growth in 2009. Recovery in 2010 has brought with it steady growth of Hongkongese real GDP.

Consequent upon its healthy average rate of economic growth since the early 1980s, the Hong Kong SAR economy has undergone major structural adjustment and associated structural change. It has become increasingly integrated with mainland China and the rest of Asia through the growth of its trade and investment links. The importance of manufacturing to Hong Kong has declined sharply since the 1990s. In its place, a mature service-oriented economy has emerged. Tourism, retail trade and financial services have contributed rapidly increasing shares of GDP in recent years. The transformation has taken place without major disruption in employment. Hong Kong took advantage of, rather than resisted, opportunities for relocation of its production base and the challenge of globalization of businesses and financial operations. Many manufacturing activities previously located in Hong Kong SAR have moved to the southern part of mainland China, while the financial sector has expanded in response to increased demand for financial services from Chinese traders and investors.

Due to its high rates of economic growth for most of the time since the 1970s, Hong Kong's unemployment rate was very low at about 2 per cent throughout the 1970s and 1980s. The rate increased somewhat in the 1990s but has fallen steadily since then. Unemployment rose marginally during the recent global financial crisis. Hong Kong has maintained large current account surpluses since the early 1980s, with the highest recorded having reached about 10 per cent of GDP.

Hong Kong SAR's economic performance has been impressive over a long period, but a problem lingers on the inflation front. It reached double digits during the late 1980s when the economy suffered from a series of asset bubbles. Although the currency board system has apparently kept Hongkongese average inflation relatively low, inflation volatility has created some problems for the economy. Since May 2005 the Linked Exchange Rate System has been refined somewhat. Under the modified system, the HKD is traded within a band. Nevertheless, the question remains whether Hong Kong SAR should adopt a still more flexible exchange rate system, short of a full float, in order to obtain a larger degree of monetary policy independence with which it can then target price stability. This remains the key issue in so far as monetary policy is concerned.

INFLATION AND INTEREST RATES

Figure 4.1a displays quarter-on-quarter inflation in Hong Kong over the period 1981q4–2010q4. Hong Kong experienced moderately high and volatile inflation during the 1980s and 1990s. Inflation declined sharply in the mid 1990s and remained low but unstable henceforth. Figure 4.1b displays the conditional variance of inflation as generated by a GARCH(1,1)

Figure 4.1a Quarter-on-quarter CPI inflation in Hong Kong, 1981q4–2012q4

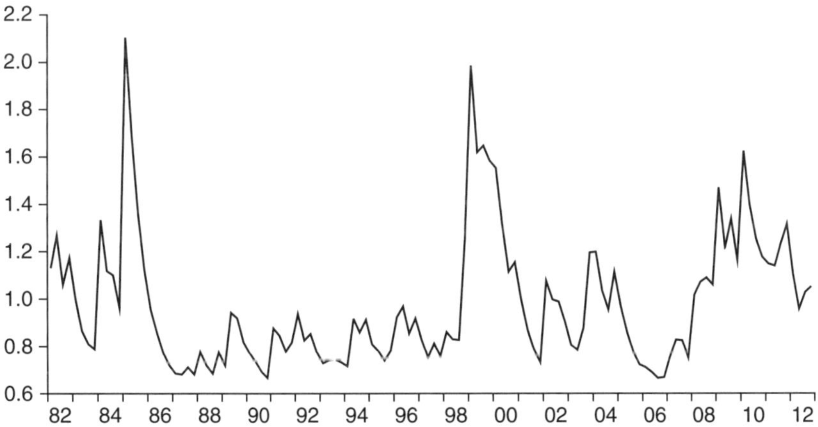

Figure 4.1b Conditional standard deviation of CPI inflation in Hong Kong, 1981q1–2012q4

Table 4.2 Means and variances of inflation in Hong Kong and the United States, 1980q4–2012q4

	Observations	Mean	Standard deviation
CPI inflation (Hong Kong)	117	4.57	4.94
CPI inflation (United States)	117	3.32	2.18
	Degrees of freedom	Statistic	Probability
t-test for equality of means	232	2.50	0.01
	Degrees of freedom	Statistic	Probability
F-test for equality of variances	(116, 116)	5.16	0.00

model. It shows a decade of reduced inflation volatility from the mid 1980s to the mid 1990s, followed by a resurgence of inflation volatility despite a relatively low average rate.

The key question is whether the rates of inflation in Hong Kong and the United States share similar characteristics. Table 4.2 reports results from some statistical tests that suggest that the mean and volatility of inflation in Hong Kong were different from those in the United States across the three decades 1981q4–2010q4. This sample period covers the life of the Linked Exchange Rate System. The evidence suggests significantly higher inflation volatility in Hong Kong than in the United States over the sample period. The conclusion suggested is that, contrary to theory, inflation in Hong Kong has not shown complete convergence to US inflation under the fixed exchange rate system.

Inflation Persistence

Inflation in Hong Kong has high persistence. This is evident in the recursive and rolling regression coefficient estimates on the one-period lagged rate of inflation. Figures 4.2a and 4.2b show that the coefficient on the one-period lagged rate of inflation is close to one.

The fixed peg exchange rate system is considered useful when inflation in the anchor country is low and stable. The United States is considered such a country, since its rate of inflation fell steadily during the 1970s and remained low for more than two decades. As shown earlier, Hong Kong SAR's average inflation rose and remained high from the mid 1980s to the mid 1990s and then fell but has remained unstable throughout. There is clearly a link between the inflation rates in Hong Kong and the United States. Whether any relationship between them is cointegral-causal depends on the time-series properties of inflation rates. Table 4.3 reports the unit root test results for inflation in Hong Kong. The ADF and KPSS test results reject the null hypothesis that inflation in Hong Kong has a unit root.

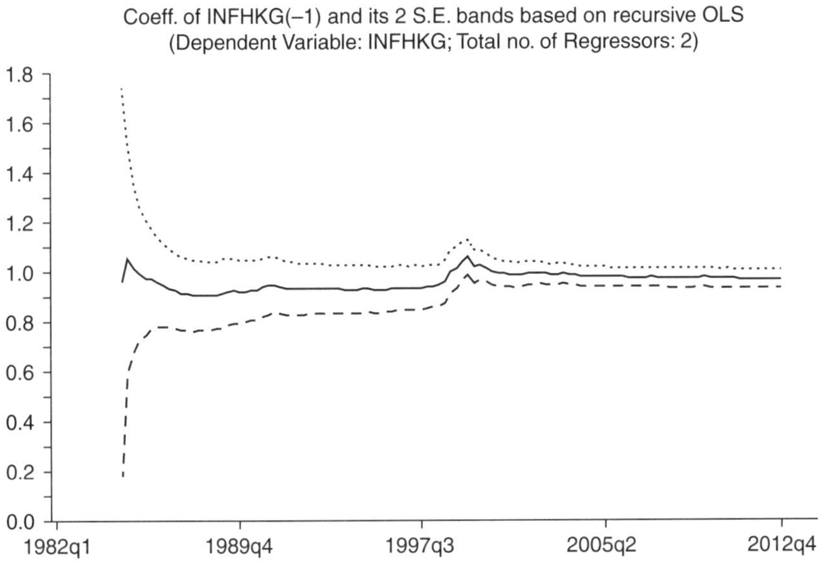

Note: INFHKG = CPI inflation in Hong Kong.

Figure 4.2a Recursive estimates of the coefficient on the one-period lagged rate of CPI inflation in Hong Kong

Interest Rates

Figure 4.3a displays a close linkage between the Treasury bill rate in Hong Kong and the Federal funds rate in the United States over the period 1993q4–2010q4.[8] The scatterplot of the Treasury bill rate in Hong Kong and the Federal funds rate in the United States exhibits perfect correlation between them (Figure 4.3b).

As mentioned, Hong Kong SAR's fixed exchange rate with free capital mobility means that Hong Kong largely imports US monetary policy. The real interest rate parity condition should hold for Hong Kong. Figure 4.3c reports the real interest rates on deposits and Treasury bills in Hong Kong and the real Federal funds rate in the United States. They show a very close linkage, as expected.

Given Hong Kong's dependence on US monetary policy, it is expected that there could be a cointegral-causal relation between the US funds rate and the interest rates in Hong Kong. Table 4.4 reports some empirical results that confirm the presence of a cointegral-causal relation between the Federal funds rate in the United States and the Treasury bill rate in

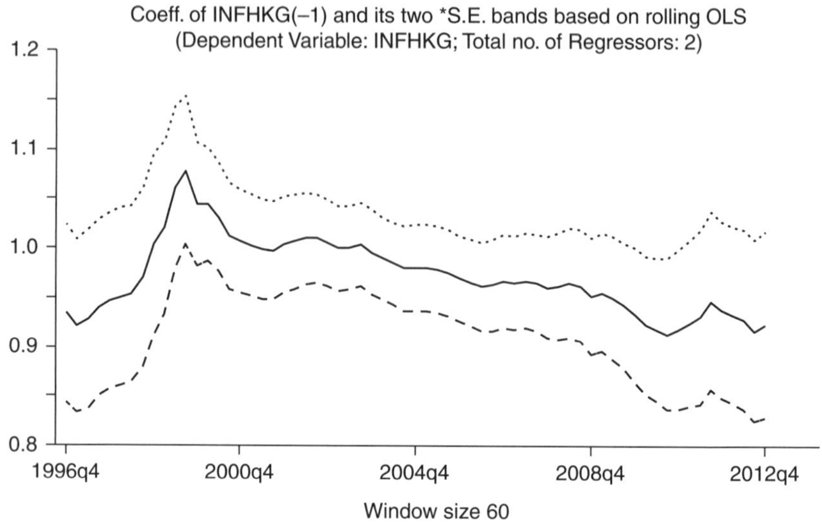

Note: INFHKG = CPI inflation in Hong Kong.

Figure 4.2b Rolling sample estimates of the coefficient on the one-period lagged rate of CPI inflation in Hong Kong

Hong Kong. The causality between these interest rates runs from the Federal funds rate in the United States to the Treasury bill rate in Hong Kong. Although a reverse causality also exists from the Treasury bill rate in Hong Kong to the Federal funds rate, it is not clear whether this makes economic sense as Hong Kong is a relatively small market. The trends of these interest rates reported show a complete pass-through from the Federal funds rate to the Treasury bill rate in Hong Kong. There is also corresponding linkage between the deposit rate of interest and the Federal funds rate. This implies that any change in monetary policy in the United States translates into the deposit and lending rates in Hong Kong.

INFLATION, REAL INTEREST RATE, REAL EXCHANGE RATE AND REAL OUTPUT

One major problem of exchange rate policy in Hong Kong is, as just discussed, its high levels of inflation volatility. High for the last three decades, inflation volatility has risen in recent years.[9] This could be partly due to frequent external shocks and speculation on property markets.

Table 4.3 The unit root test results for CPI inflation in Hong Kong

Variables	Constant (C); None	Optimal lag length (based on SBC)	ADF test statistic (p-value)	Inference at 5% level	The KPSS test statistic			Inference at 5% level
					Constant (C);	Newey-West bandwidth	LM-statistic	
Unadjusted sample period: 1981q4–2010q4		(maximum lag = 12)						
CPI inflation	C	4	−1.60 (0.48)	I(1)	C	9	0.74	I(1)
CPI inflation	None	4	−1.64 (0.09)	I(1)				
ΔCPI inflation	None	3	−6.21 (0.00)	I(0)				

Note: Definitions of variables: LCPI = log of the consumer price index; ΔLCPI = first-order difference of LCPI; SBC = Schwarz Bayesian Criterion; and KPSS = Kwiatkowski, Phillips, Schmidt and Shin.

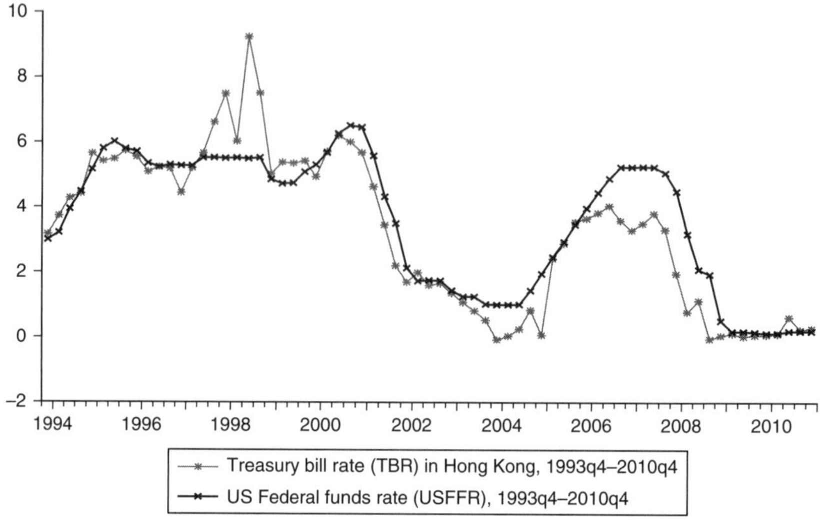

Figure 4.3a *The Treasury bill rate in Hong Kong and the Federal funds rate in the United States, 1993q4–2010q4*

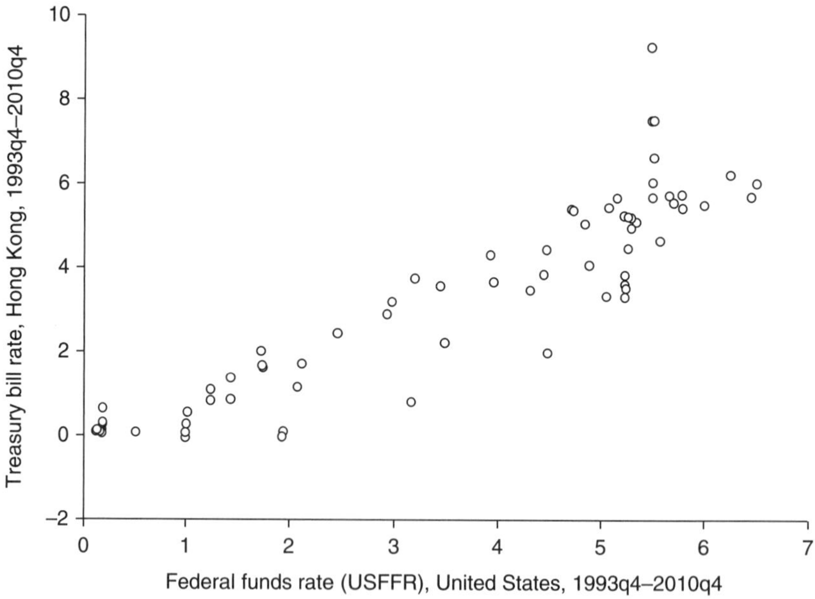

Figure 4.3b *The Treasury bill rate in Hong Kong plotted against the Federal funds rate in the United States, 1993q4–2010q4*

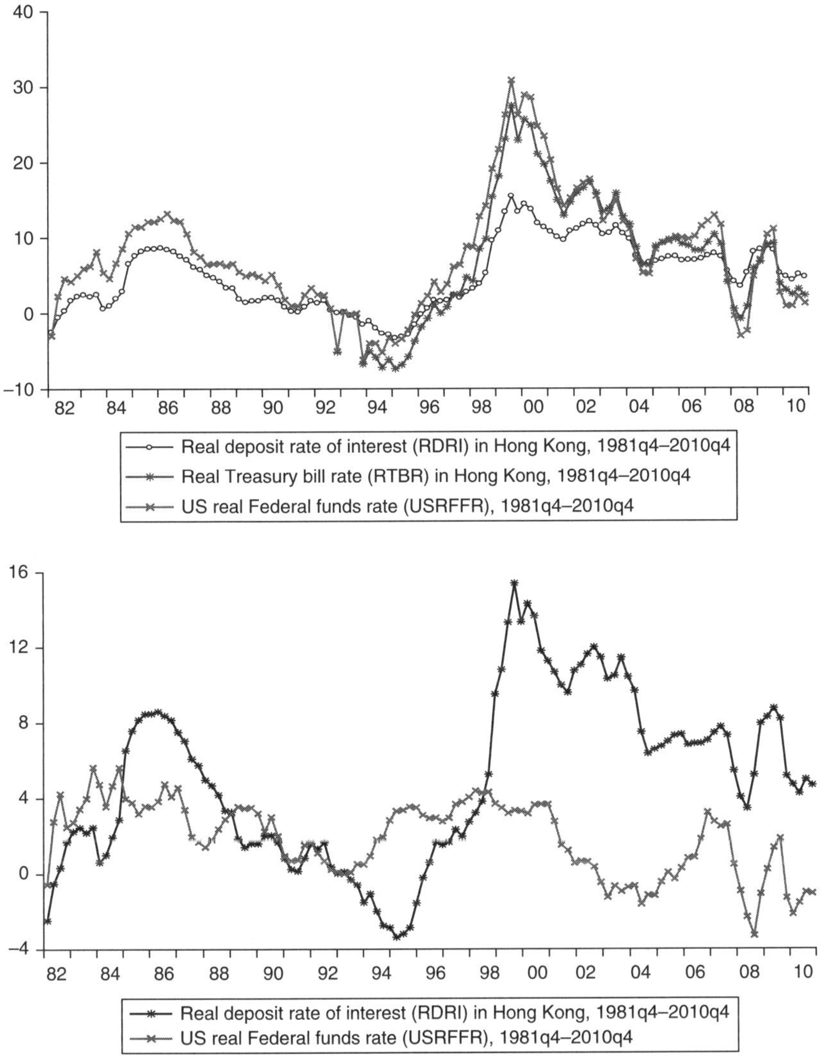

Figure 4.3c Real interest rates in Hong Kong and the United States: the real interest rates on deposits and Treasury bills in Hong Kong and the real Federal funds rate in the United States, 1981q4–2010q4

Table 4.4 Unit root and cointegration test results for the Federal funds rate in the United States and the Treasury bill rate in Hong Kong, 1980–2012

	Sample period (lag-unadjusted)	Constant (C)	ADF test statistic (SBC-determined lag-length, l)	Inference at 5% level	The KPSS test statistic (Newey-West bandwidth)	Inference at 5% level
USFFR	1981q4–2010q4	C	−2.05 (l = 11)	I(1)	1.03 (9)	I(1)
ΔUSFFR	1981q4–2010q4	none	−4.46 (l = 0)	I(0)	0.17 (6)	I(0)
TBR	1994q1–2010q4	C	−1.17 (l = 0)	I(1)	0.70 (6)	I(1)
ΔTBR	1994q2–2010q4	none	−8.66 (l = 0)	I(0)	0.12 (4)	I(0)
The Engle-Granger cointegration test results						
Dependent variable	tau-statistic	prob.*	z-statistic	prob.*		
TBR	−3.21	0.08	−18.59	0.06		

Note: Definitions of variables: USFFR = US Federal funds rate; TBR = Treasury bill rate; ADF = augmented Dickey-Fuller; KPSS = Kwiatkowski, Phillips, Schmidt and Shin; and SBC = Schwarz Bayesian Criterion.

Since the interest rate and the nominal exchange rate in Hong Kong do not adjust completely to the inflation differential between Hong Kong and the United States, high volatility of inflation in Hong Kong leads to high volatility in its real interest rate and its real exchange rate. Data reported in Table 4.1 reveal this volatility. Volatile Hongkongese real interest rates and real exchange rates can, via the investment channel, significantly reduce the growth rate of real output. Since the early 2000s the US interest rate has remained low and volatile. Inflation in Hong Kong SAR has been low and even more volatile. Consequently, Hong Kong SAR's real interest rate became low and volatile. This might have inflicted boom-bust cycles.[10]

The Structural Vector Autoregressive (SVAR) Analysis

This subsection, following the discussion in Appendix 5, uses annual data to estimate a four-variable SVAR model examining the interrelationships among inflation, the real interest rate, the real exchange rate and real output.[11] Figure 4.4 plots the data used for estimation purposes.

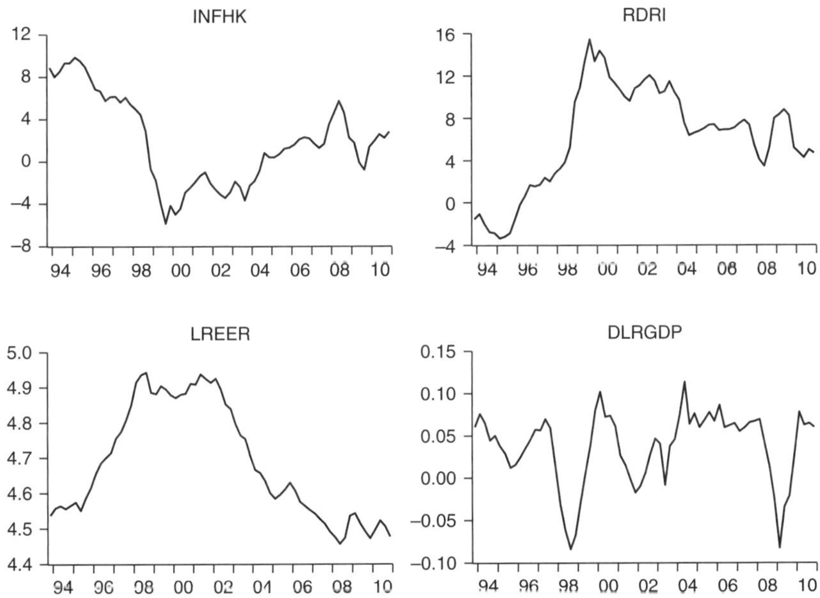

Note: Definitions of variables: INFHK = CPI inflation in Hong Kong; RDRI = real deposit rate of interest; LREER = log of the real effective exchange rate of the Hong Kong dollar; and DLRGDP = first-order difference of the log of real GDP.

Figure 4.4 Data deployed for estimation of the SVAR model for Hong Kong

The model is formulated on the assumption that inflation has a contemporaneous feedback relation with the real interest rate and the real exchange rate. All these variables affect real output. The order of variables in the model can then be arranged as follows: INFHK, RIR, LREER and LRGDP where INFHK is the inflation rate in Hong Kong, RIR is the real interest rate, LREER is the log of the real effective exchange rate and LRGDP is the log of real GDP. The unit root test results suggest that inflation, the real interest rate and the real exchange rate are stationary while real output is nonstationary. Two versions of the model are then estimated and deployed to generate impulse responses and the forecast error-variance decompositions. The first version of the model is defined as: INFHK, RIR, LREER and LRGDP while the second version of the model is defined as: INFHK, RIR, LREER and DLRGDP. In the second version of the model, all the variables are stationary while in the first version real output is nonstationary. To conserve space, results obtained by the second version of the model are reported.

The impulse responses in Figure 4.5 reveal the interrelations among four variables in the SVAR model. The impulse response results are indicative, not conclusive. As expected, a rise in inflation lowers the real rate of interest. It indicates that the nominal interest rate responds slowly to any rise in inflation. Although a decrease in the real interest rate is expected to raise investment, this may not always be true in developing or transition economies. In these countries, a very low or negative real interest rate, caused by say high inflation given unchanged nominal interest rates, creates financial repression that lowers saving, investment and economic growth. High and volatile inflation may also create other macroeconomic problems. A rise in inflation appreciates the real exchange rate, which in turn affects inflation and economic growth. The real interest rate in particular responds positively to an appreciation of the real exchange rate. This is because as a grossly appreciated real exchange rate induces capital flight, the real interest rate is required to rise as an inducement to slow down or stop capital flight. This follows the open-economy real exchange rate parity condition. In general, an appreciation of the real exchange rate affects both trade and capital flows while changes in the real interest rate affect saving and investment.

The overall results suggest significant interrelations among inflation, the real interest rate, the real exchange rate and output growth. Although it is not investigated here, an expanded model is expected to show the impacts of the real interest and exchange rates on saving, investment and both trade and capital flows. The key message that emerges from the empirical results is that inflation and its volatility are not innocuous in so far as economic growth is concerned. Inflation affects the real interest rate and the real exchange rate

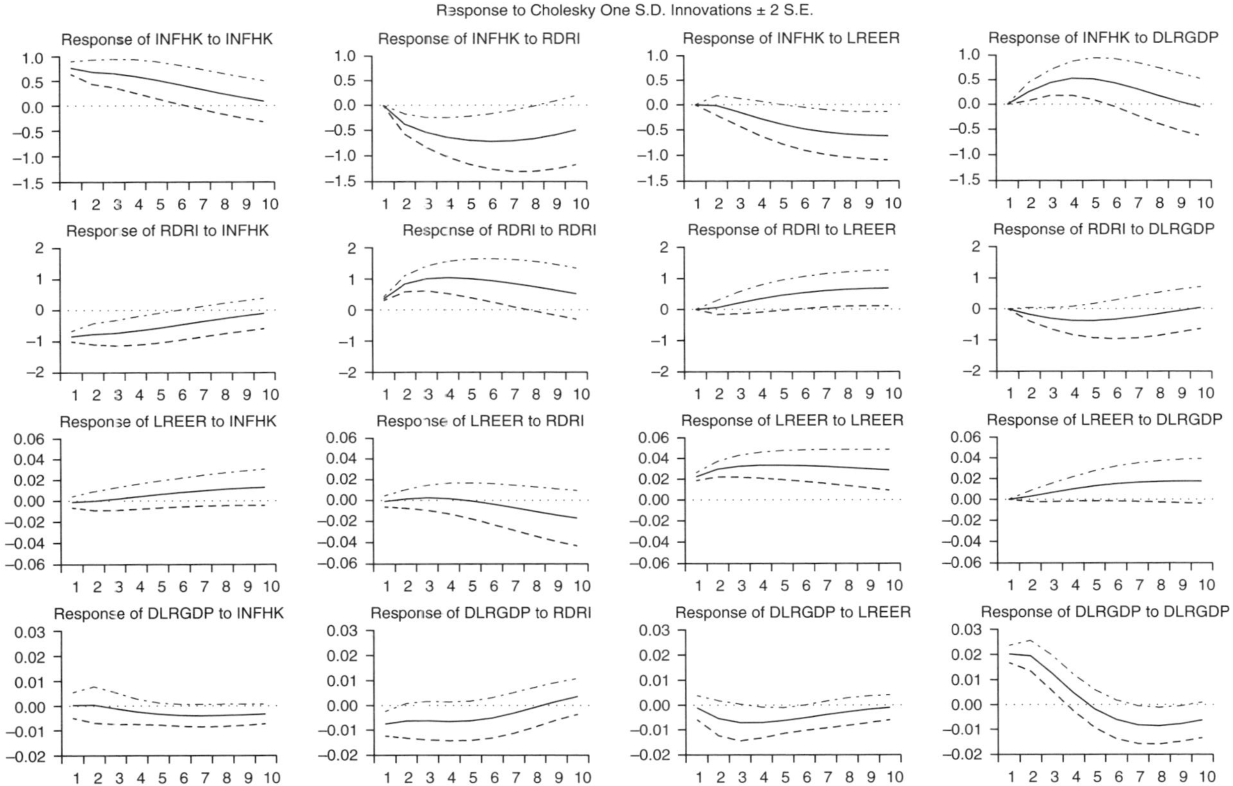

Note: Definitions of variables: INFHK = CPI inflation in Hong Kong; RDRI = real deposit rate of interest; LREER = log of the real effective exchange rate of the Hong Kong dollar; and DLRGDP = first-order difference of the log of real GDP.

Figure 4.5 Impulse responses for variables in the SVAR model for Hong Kong

Table 4.5 *Forecast error-variance decomposition of variables in the SVAR model for Hong Kong*

Variance Decomposition of INFHK:					
Period	S.E.	INFHK	RDRI	LREER	DLRGDP
1	0.77	100.00	0.00	0.00	0.00
2	1.12	83.56	11.17	0.02	5.25
5	2.11	46.87	29.65	5.45	18.03
10	2.98	27.96	38.10	21.11	12.83
Variance Decomposition of RDRI:					
Period	S.E.	INFHK	RDRI	LREER	DLRGDP
1	0.91	84.43	15.57	0.00	0.00
2	1.47	59.56	38.79	0.17	1.49
5	2.72	35.53	53.80	4.99	5.67
10	3.61	24.06	52.86	18.18	4.91
Variance Decomposition of LREER:					
Period	S.E.	INFHK	RDRI	LREER	DLRGDP
1	0.03	0.23	0.16	99.61	0.00
2	0.04	0.08	0.17	99.12	0.62
5	0.07	1.08	0.23	92.36	6.33
10	0.11	5.12	5.38	75.77	13.73
Variance Decomposition of DLRGDP:					
Period	S.E.	INFHK	RDRI	LREER	DLRGDP
1	0.02	0.01	12.11	0.23	87.65
2	0.03	0.02	10.48	3.31	86.19
5	0.04	1.34	15.74	12.50	70.42
10	0.04	4.88	14.66	12.34	68.13
The Cholesky Ordering: INFHK RDRI LREER DLRGDP					

Note: Definitions of variables: INFHK = CPI inflation in Hong Kong; RDRI = real deposit rate of interest; LREER = log of the real effective exchange rate of the Hong Kong dollar; and DLRGDP = first-order difference of the log of real GDP.

and they have impacts on saving, investment and economic growth. This suggests the need for low and stable inflation for steady economic growth.

Table 4.5 presents the forecast error-variance decompositions of variables for two versions of the model: one using the real value of output (INFHK, RIR, LREER and LRGDP); and the other using real output growth (INFHK, RIR, LREER and DLRGDP). In the table, the numbers represent those percentages of forecast error variance of variables in the model that can be attributed to own innovations and those percentages of forecast error variance that originate from innovations of other variables. The results show that the dominant source of the forecast error variance for all four variables is own innovations. The magnitudes are 60 per cent for inflation, 40 per cent for the real interest rate, 68 per cent for the real exchange rate and 53 per cent for real GDP over the ten-year time horizon. In the case of real output growth, innovations in the real interest rate and the real exchange rate jointly account for 22 per cent of real output growth's forecast error variance. The corresponding share of inflation is 24 per cent. This shows that real output growth is highly sensitive to both the average rate of inflation and its volatility. Inflation affects the real interest rate and the real exchange rate, which in turn affect real output growth. The overall results suggest that US monetary policy has pervasive importance for inflation, external competitiveness and real output growth in the Hong Kong SAR. Inflation instability affects economic growth adversely. A simple Granger-causality test is conducted between economic growth and inflation instability for Hong Kong. The results (not reported) suggest a feedback relation between them.[12]

MONETARY AND EXCHANGE RATE POLICY ISSUES

The empirical results reported above suggest that the Hong Kong economy, due largely to its fixed peg exchange rate system (its Linked Exchange Rate System), remains vulnerable to external economic shocks and exposed to US discretionary monetary policy changes. The empirical evidence suggests that the fixed peg causes US monetary policy to have a major impact on the Hong Kong economy through both the real interest rate and the real exchange rate channels. One way of minimizing this problem is to adopt a less rigid exchange rate system. This allows a country to design and conduct an independent monetary policy, which in turn creates policy space to target price stability. A shortcoming of flexible exchange rate systems for small economies with a thin foreign-exchange market is that they may create excess exchange rate volatility. To the extent that Hong Kong follows disciplined monetary and fiscal policies and maintains large foreign reserves, the HKD exchange rate is unlikely to show excess volatility. The question is which strategy of monetary policy Hong Kong may adopt to maintain price stability under a floating exchange rate system. Hong Kong SAR faces two policy alternatives. It can introduce (1) monetary targeting or (2) inflation targeting with a monetary aggregate as an instrument of monetary policy.

Until recently the prevailing view was that monetary targeting for price stability requires a stable money-demand function to establish a causal linkage between money supply growth and inflation. The recent literature suggests that a causal relation exists between money growth and inflation irrespective of the exchange rate regime and irrespective of whether or not a stable money-demand function pertains (McCallum and Nelson, 2011). Nevertheless, this section examines whether or not Hong Kong SAR has a stable money-demand function.[13] For estimation purposes, an open-economy money-demand function is specified as follows:

$$LRJM_t = \alpha_0 + \alpha_1 Ly_t + \alpha_2 NIR_t + \alpha_3 LER_t + \alpha_4 \pi_t^v + \varepsilon_t \quad (4.1)$$

where LRJM (J = N, B) is the log of real money balances (LRNM for narrowly defined money or LRBM for broadly defined money), Ly is the log of real income, NIR is a representative domestic interest rate, LER is the log of a representative nominal or real exchange rate such as the nominal or real effective exchange rate, π_t^v is a measure of inflation volatility and ε_t is a random error term.

In this specification, real income represents a scale variable and its coefficient is expected to bear a positive sign. The Hong Kong economy has grown rapidly since the 1960s. There has also been a rapid monetization of the economy since then. Consequently the income elasticity of demand for money may exceed unity. The coefficient on the interest rate is expected to bear a negative sign. However, as reviewed in Appendix 5, the signs of the coefficients on the real exchange rate and inflation volatility remain indeterminate a priori.

The unit root test results suggest that all the variables in the model have a unit root. Consequently, they are eligible to form a cointegral relationship. Table 4.6 reports the ARDL results, which suggest that a cointegral relationship is indeed present. The estimated coefficient values are consistent with a priori predictions. A series of stability tests is conducted that suggest that the narrow money-demand function is more stable than the broad money-demand function. Inflation volatility appears not to be a determinant of narrow money demand. Narrow money demand became unstable in the 1990s but has stabilized since then (Figures 4.6a and 4.6b). The broad money demand has remained unstable. The coefficients on the nominal effective exchange rate and the deposit rate of interest are significant. Inflation instability bears a positive sign in the broad money function. It implies that as inflation instability increases, there is an increase in demand for real broad money balances.

Relationships Among Money, Output and Prices

The ARDL bounds-test results suggest that money, output and prices have a cointegral relationship (Table 4.7). The bounds-test results suggest

Table 4.6 The ARDL and OLS regression results for long-run real narrow money-demand relationships in Hong Kong

F-statistic	3.65			
W-statistic	18.27			
Critical value bounds	F-test	W-test		
90%	(2.26, 3.62)	(11.28, 18.10)		
95%	(2.85, 4.50)	(14.27, 22.49)		
Sample period: 1992–2012	ARDL (0,0,1,0,0) (Selected based on SBC)	ARDL (0,0,1,0,0) Long-run model	OLS (Static model)	OLS (Dynamic model)
Regressors	Coefficient (t-ratio) [prob.]	Coefficient (t-ratio) [prob.]	Coefficient (t-ratio) [prob.]	Coefficient (t-ratio) [prob.]
Intercept	−5.68 (−5.35) [0.00]	−5.68 (−5.35) [0.00]	−5.95 (−5.59) [0.00]	−4.26 (−3.09) [0.01]
LRNM(−1)				0.26 (1.52) [0.15]
LRGDP	1.70 (15.53) [0.00]	1.70 (15.53) [0.00]	1.71 (15.75) [0.00]	1.25 (3.49) [0.00]
USFFR	−0.06 (−3.83) [0.00]	−0.09 (−7.77) [0.00]	−0.08 (−6.37) [0.00]	−0.06 (−4.30) [0.00]
USFER(−1)	−0.04 (−2.53) [0.02]			
LRER	0.86 (3.36) [0.00]	0.87 (3.36) [0.00]	0.90 (4.02) [0.00]	0.66 (2.33) [0.03]
INFVOL	0.01 (0.95) [0.36]	0.01 (0.95) [0.36]	0.01 (0.29) [0.77]	0.003 (0.27) [0.79]
Diagnostics				
Adjusted R^2	0.99		0.98	0.98

Table 4.6 (continued)

Lagrange multiplier test for serial correlation	F(1, 14) = 2.08 [0.17]		F(1, 16) = 0.10 [0.76]	F(1, 14) = 2.10 [0.17]
Ramsey's RESET test of functional form mis-specification	F(1, 14) = 0.65 [0.44]		F(1, 16) = 3.63 [0.08]	F(1, 14) = 0.30 [0.59]
Normality of residuals	$\chi^2_{(2)} = 1.08$ [0.58]		$\chi^2_{(2)} = 2.77$ [0.25]	$\chi^2_{(2)} = 1.21$ [0.55]
Heteroskedasticity	F(1, 19) = 0.01 [0.94]		F(1, 20) = 0.98 [0.34]	F(1, 19) = 0.82 [0.38]
The Wald test:				
H_O: Coefficient on LRGDP = 0		$\chi^2_{(1)} = 241.09$ [0.00]	$\chi^2_{(1)} = 248.13$ [0.00]	
H_O: Coefficient on LRGDP = 1		$\chi^2_{(1)} = 40.67$ [0.00]	$\chi^2_{(1)} = 42.97$ [0.00]	
H_O: Coefficient on USFFR = 0		$\chi^2_{(1)} = 60.39$ [0.00]	$\chi^2_{(1)} = 40.53$ [0.00]	
H_O: Coefficient on LRER = 0		$\chi^2_{(1)} = 11.26$ [0.00]	$\chi^2_{(1)} = 16.12$ [0.00]	
H_O: Coefficient on INFVOL = 0		$\chi^2_{(1)} = 0.90$ [0.34]	$\chi^2_{(1)} = 0.09$ [0.77]	

Note: Definitions of variables: LRNM = log of real narrow money balances; LRGDP = log of real GDP; USFFR = US Federal funds rate; ARDL = autoregression distributed lag; and SBC = Schwarz Bayesian Criterion.

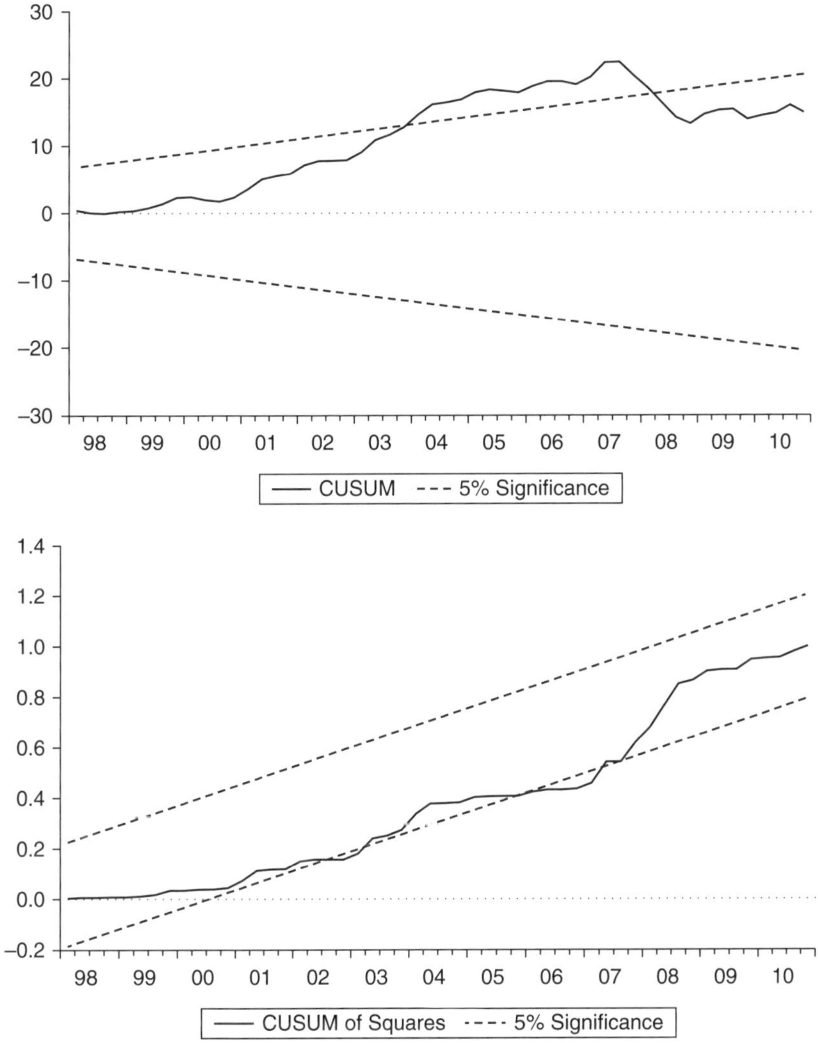

Figure 4.6a *CUSUM and CUSUMSQ of residuals for real narrow money-demand relationships in Hong Kong*

the presence of a long-run relation among money, output and prices in Hong Kong. The error-correction model associated with the long-run relation bears a negative sign. Along with the long-run relation among money, output and prices, the money-growth rate has a positive impact on inflation.

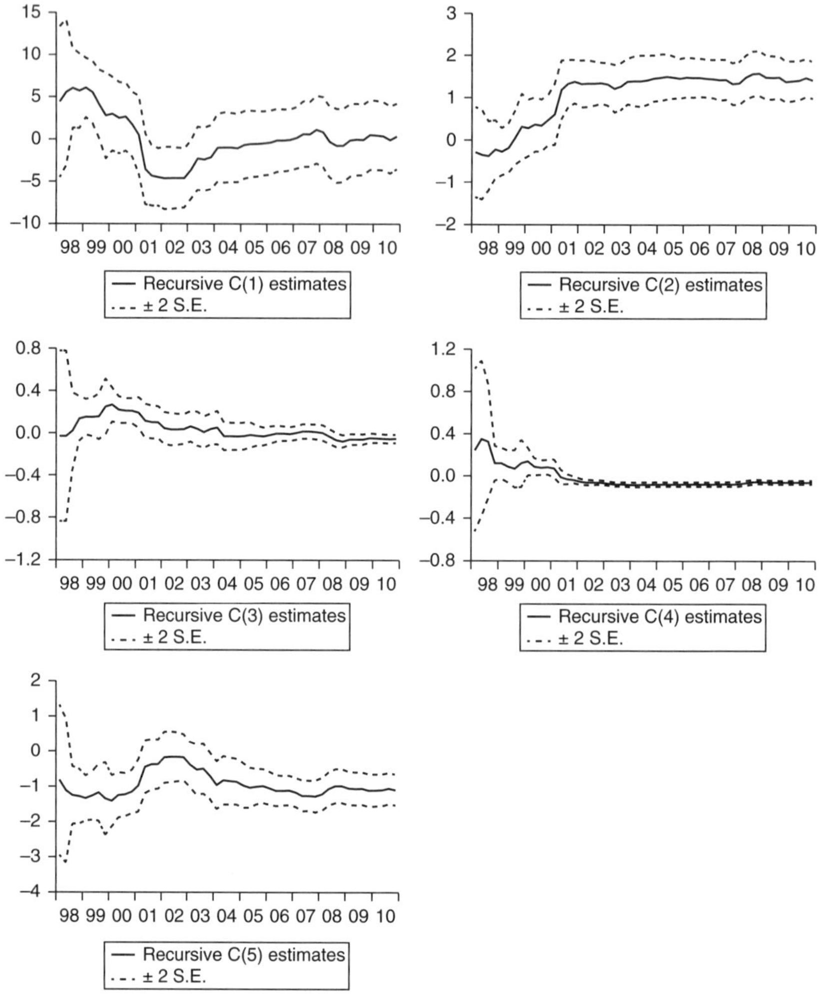

Figure 4.6b Recursive estimates of the coefficients on the determinants of real narrow money-demand relationships in Hong Kong

Engle and Granger (1987) have suggested that one of the implications of a cointegral relation between two nonstationary variables is the presence of long-term causality between them running in at least one direction. Table 4.8 reports the bivariate Granger-causality test results among LCPI, LNM (or LBM) and LRGDP. Test results are generated within a vector error-correction (VEC) modelling framework after selecting the optimal lag-length using the SBC. The test results suggest that for Hong Kong,

Table 4.7 The ARDL bounds-test results among money, output and prices in Hong Kong

ARDL order selection: SBC						
		With constant and no time trend		The Wald test ($\chi^2_{(1)}$) (p-value)	ARDL error-correction model (ΔLCPI)	ARDL error-correction model (ΔLCPI)
		F-statistic	ARDL long-run coefficient on LNM/LBM	Null hypothesis: ARDL long-run coefficient on LNM/LBM = 0	(money growth, ΔLNM/ΔLBM)	(error-correction term, ecm(−1))
	ARDL	Critical value (CV): (lower bound, upper bound)	Coefficient (t-ratio) [prob.]		Coefficient (t-ratio)	Coefficient (t-ratio)
With narrow money (NM)						
Sample period: 1992–2012	ARDL(1,0,0)	4.62 CV(95%):{4.59, 5.81} CV(90%):{3.59, 4.72}	−0.14 (−0.68) [0.50]	0.46 (0.50)	−0.04 (−0.67)	−0.26 (−3.50)
With broad money (BM)						
Sample period: 1992–2012	ARDL(1,0,0)	18.04 CV(95%):{4.59, 5.81} CV(90%):{3.59, 4.72}	11.56 (0.47) [0.64]	0.22 (0.64)	−0.24 (−1.41)	0.04 (0.44)

Note: Definitions of variables: LCPI = log of the consumer price index; LNM = log of narrow money stock; LBM = log of broad money stock; LRGDP = log of real GDP; ARDL = autoregressive distributed lag; and SBC = Schwarz Bayesian Criterion.

Table 4.8 Granger-causality among money, output and prices in Hong Kong, 1991–2012

	Hypotheses No causality runs from:	Chi-square statistic (prob.)	Inference at 5% level
With narrow money (NM)			
VEC specification	ΔLNM → ΔLCPI	3.20 (0.07)	Null hypothesis not rejected
	ΔLRGDP → ΔLCPI	11.06 (0.00)	Null hypothesis rejected
	ΔLNM, ΔLRGDP → ΔLCPI	11.29 (0.00)	Null hypothesis rejected
	ΔLCPI → ΔLNM	1.19 (0.28)	Null hypothesis not rejected
	ΔLRGDP → ΔLNM	6.45 (0.01)	Null hypothesis rejected
	ΔLCPI → ΔLRGDP	1.53 (0.22)	Null hypothesis not rejected
	ΔLNM → ΔLRGDP	0.62 (0.43)	Null hypothesis not rejected
With broad money (BM)			
VEC specification	ΔLBM → ΔLCPI	0.70 (0.40)	Null hypothesis not rejected
	ΔLRGDP → ΔLCPI	0.12 (0.73)	Null hypothesis not rejected
	ΔLBM, ΔLRGDP → ΔLCPI	1.66 (0.44)	Null hypothesis not rejected
	ΔLCPI → ΔLBM	12.27 (0.00)	Null hypothesis rejected
	ΔLRGDP → ΔLBM	13.60 (0.00)	Null hypothesis rejected
	ΔLCPI → ΔLRGDP	3.95 (0.05)	Null hypothesis rejected
	ΔLBM → ΔLRGDP	1.96 (0.16)	Null hypothesis not rejected

Note: Definitions of variables: LCPI = log of the consumer price index; LNM/LBM = log of narrow/broad money stock; and LRGDP = log of real GDP. Optimal lag = 1 (selected based on the Akaike Information Criterion, AIC).

there is only weak causality running from narrow or broad money to prices.

SUMMARY AND CONCLUSION

This chapter has reviewed the key features of exchange rate policy in the Hong Kong SAR and examined the impact with which the volatility of Hongkongese inflation influences its real interest rate, real exchange rate and growth rate of real output, using data back to the early 1980s. Hong Kong SAR operates under a currency board system, in which its currency is pegged to the US dollar. The main objective of this arrangement is to maintain monetary and financial stability. A major cost of this policy has been price instability. Hong Kong does not have monetary policy independence and prices are determined by the purchasing power parity condition. While this keeps the prices of tradables in Hong Kong SAR linked to their prices on international markets, the non-tradables' prices are determined by heterogeneous factors. Hong Kong SAR's average rate of inflation has remained moderately low since the early 1990s, but the volatility of Hongkongese inflation has remained high. This has created highly volatile real interest and exchange rates and affected the economy.

Hong Kong SAR has a large non-tradable goods sector and consequently there is an inflation differential between Hong Kong SAR and the United States. Hong Kong can stabilize its price level by reducing the rigidity of its exchange rate system. Given that Hong Kong maintains fiscal discipline, it is plausible that a more flexible exchange rate would remain stable.[14] Nevertheless, as a small, open economy, its exchange rate is vulnerable to volatility imposed by external shocks. Perhaps Hong Kong SAR's most important intermediate target is to sustain a stable real exchange rate to maintain its competitiveness. Financial stability is essential to Hong Kong SAR as an international financial centre. It has a developed financial system and hence some exchange rate instability is unlikely to cause problems.

This chapter has investigated the relationships among inflation, the real interest rate, the real exchange rate and real output. It is found that the volatility of inflation has reduced real output or its growth. The empirical results suggest that the narrow money-demand function in Hong Kong SAR is stable while the broad money-demand function is unstable. There is also weak causality between money supply growth and inflation.

Based on the empirical results, it is possible to argue that Hong Kong SAR should make the exchange rate more flexible, enhancing its monetary policy independence in order to target monetary policy at price stability. Given that Hong Kong SAR is committed to monetary and fiscal discipline, an increase in flexibility of the exchange rate would give the Monetary Authority some scope for targeting price stability. The pegged exchange rate system has not ensured price stability. Rather, it has destabilized Hong Kong SAR's real economy while maintaining stability of the nominal exchange rate. Although wages and prices are flexible and adjustment to external economic shocks is resilient, these do not necessarily translate into improved macroeconomic conditions if the impact on volatile inflation and economic growth are considered. This does not necessarily mean that Hong Kong SAR should float its currency, given that Hong Kong SAR is a small, open economy susceptible to external economic shocks; and given that its dependence on foreign trade and financial services make exchange rate stability critical. Sustained stability of real interest rates and real exchange rates are fundamental for Hong Kong SAR, since financial stability remains a cornerstone of its increasing dominance as an international financial centre. One danger for targeting the real exchange rate is that it may lose control over inflation or the real interest rate depending on the degree of capital mobility. Under the pegged exchange rate system, the role of fiscal policy is limited.[15]

NOTES

1. There are a number of factors behind the establishment of Hong Kong SAR as an international financial centre. They include strategic location, sophisticated and modern communication, free capital movements, developed and efficient legal system and effective and transparent rules and regulations.
2. Hong Kong SAR has about 154 licensed banks, 48 restricted licensed banks and 61 deposit-taking institutions from over 40 countries. They are collectively known as authorized institutions.
3. Hong Kong SAR's exchange rate system is called a Linked Exchange Rate or currency board. It was established in 1983, with some modifications in later years.
4. Under the currency board system, the interest rate rather than the exchange rate adjusts with the inflows or outflows of capital. The monetary base increases when the foreign currency is sold to the currency board for domestic currency (capital inflows). Similarly, the monetary base contracts when the foreign currency is bought from the currency board by exchanging domestic currency (capital outflows). The expansion or contraction in the monetary base is reflected in the interest rate for domestic currency. In the process, increased (decreased) money supply is matched by increased (decreased) money demand originating from the fall (rise) in the interest rate and the increase (decrease) of real output. This keeps the monetary condition in an equilibrium state, which maintains exchange rate stability. This automatic adjustment mechanism is the essence of the currency board system.
5. Chiu (2003, p. 2) explains this phenomenon: 'Economic theory also tells us that inflation can be restrained by a policy to reduce money supply through raising interest rates and deflation can be mitigated by a policy to increase money supply through a reduction

in interest rates. However, under the linked exchange rate system, interest rates in Hong Kong have to follow the interest rates in the United States. In other words, no discretionary monetary policy can be employed to tackle the problems of inflation and deflation in Hong Kong. However there is a self-adjustment mechanism inherent in the linked rate system. When there is inflation exports will fall. The fall in exports will lead to lower employment and lower inflation. When there is deflation, exports will increase. The increase in exports will lead to higher employment and lower inflation.'

6. The government started transferring fiscal reserves to the Exchange Fund in 1976 to increase the rate of return on fiscal reserves. This was also to strengthen the resources of the Fund needed for maintaining stability of the Hong King dollar. Before 1 April 1998, fiscal reserves were placed with the Fund to receive a fixed rate of investment return. To achieve a higher long-term return for fiscal reserves, the annual rate of return for fiscal reserves was linked to the rate achieved by the entire Exchange Fund over the period 1998–2007. This arrangement was known as the income-sharing arrangement. The investment income of fiscal reserves is an important source of revenue for the government. However, it was volatile under the income-sharing arrangement. Therefore, to make the government's investment income predictable, the financial secretary introduced a new fee arrangement between fiscal reserves and the Exchange Fund on 1 April 2007. Under the new arrangement, the return on fiscal reserves is calculated based on the average annual rate of return of the Exchange Fund's investment portfolio over the past six years.
7. The latter bank was renamed the Standard Chartered Bank.
8. This sample period is chosen due to data availability.
9. Inflation in Hong Kong does not match one-for-one with that in the United States. High volatility of inflation in Hong Kong is apparently due to high volatility of non-tradable prices.
10. Bentour and Razzak (2009) have highlighted this problem under a pegged exchange rate system. When the domestic inflation rate (π) exceeds the foreign inflation rate (π^*), the domestic real interest rate (r) becomes much lower than the foreign real interest rate (r^*). This suggests that if the foreign real interest rate falls to a very low, say, zero, level, the domestic real interest rate becomes negative. This may generate a boom-bust cycle.
11. As Hong Kong operates under a pegged exchange rate system, a sustained deviation of inflation in Hong Kong from US inflation affects contemporaneously the real exchange rate. Real exchange rate misalignment in turn may affect the rate of inflation by changing the demand for, and hence the prices of, non-tradables. As the nominal interest rate mimics the US interest rate, any sustained deviation of inflation in Hong Kong from US inflation also affects the real interest rate and in turn saving, investment and economic growth.
12. Yellen (2010, p. 1) has summarized the issue that Hong Kong now faces as other adopters of a pegged system: 'The Hong Kong economy was quite exposed to the global downturn due to its heavy dependence on external trade and financial services . . . The recovery has been facilitated by expansionary monetary and fiscal policies in Hong Kong and by China's robust recovery. For all practical purposes, Hong Kong delegated the determination of its monetary policy to the Federal Reserve through its unilateral decision in 1983 to peg the Hong Kong dollar to the US dollar in an arrangement known as a currency board . . . While Hong Kong's recovery has undoubtedly benefitted from the Fed's easy monetary policy, there is concern that the stimulus may soon prove excessive and inflationary if the recovery in Asia proceeds more rapidly than the in the United States and other developed countries. There is substantial concern in Asia that easy monetary policies in the United States and other developed economies are triggering another round of bubble activity, particularly in Hong Kong real estate prices.'
13. For an earlier study on the money-demand behaviour in Hong Kong, see Bahmani-Oskooee and Wing Ng (2002).
14. Yam (2012, p. 29) has expressed this sentiment: 'While the monetary system of the United States can survive a deficit to GDP ratio of 10% and a debt ratio of 100% (although

there is now serious doubt in the case of the euro zone), much lower corresponding numbers would be death warrants for the monetary system of Hong Kong . . . I hope Hong Kong does not go down that slippery slope towards large government, persistent budget deficits, heavy public debt, financial meltdown and monetary crisis.'

15. In the absence of monetary policy independence under the currency board, fiscal policy remains one of the tools for demand management. However, Hong Kong SAR does not deploy fiscal policy for economic stabilization to avoid undermining credibility of the Linked Exchange Rate System. As Hong Kong SAR's economy remains volatile, the government's fiscal revenue is pro-cyclical. This requires adjustment of spending to avoid creating sustained fiscal deficits. According to the Basic Law, Hong Kong SAR follows a balanced budget approach over the medium term. In fact, it has accumulated fiscal reserve of about 25 per cent of GDP as a key source of revenue to stabilize the fiscal sector. The fiscal reserve is part of the Exchange Fund used for maintaining monetary and financial stability. Therefore, any indication of fiscal activism for economic stabilization is indicative and not substantive and sustained.

REFERENCES

Asian Development Bank (various years), *Key Indicators of Developing Asian and Pacific Countries*, Manila: ADB.

Bahmani-Oskooee, M. and R.C. Wing Ng (2002), 'Long-run demand for money in Hong Kong: an application of the ARDL model', *International Journal of Business and Economics*, **1**(2), 147–55.

Bentour, E.M. and W.A. Razzak (2009), 'Real interest rates, bubbles and monetary policy in the GCC countries', Unpublished manuscript, Arab Planning Institute.

Chiu, P. (2003), 'Hong Kong's experience in operating the currency board system', Unpublished manuscript, Hong Kong Monetary Authority.

Dodsworth, J. and D. Mihaljek (1997), 'Hong Kong, China: growth, structural change, and economic stability during the transition', Occasional Paper 152, IMF, Washington, DC.

Engle, R.F. and C.W.J. Granger (1987), 'Co-integration and error-correction: representation, estimation, and testing', *Econometrica*, **55**(2), 251–76.

Hsu. J.C. (1985), 'Exchange rate management without a central bank: the Hong Kong experience', *Hong Kong Economic Papers*, **16**, 14–26.

IMF (International Monetary Fund) (various years), *International Financial Statistics*, Washington, DC: IMF.

IMF (International Monetary Fund) (various years), *World Economic Outlook*, Washington, DC: IMF.

Jao, Y.C. (1992), 'Hong Kong monetary and financial system', in P. Newman, M. Milgate and J. Eatwell (eds), *The New Palgrave Dictionary of Money and Finance*, Vol. 2, London: Macmillan, pp. 314–16.

McCallum, B.T. and E. Nelson (2011), 'Money and inflation: some critical issues', in B.M. Friedman and M. Woodford (eds), *Handbook of Monetary Economics*, Vol. 3A, Amsterdam: Elsevier Science, pp. 97–153.

Moreno, R. (1986), 'Monetary control without a central bank: the case of Hong Kong', Federal Reserve Bank of San Francisco, *Economic Review*, Spring, 17–37.

Moreno, R. (1988), 'Exchange rates and monetary policy in Singapore and Hong

Kong', in H.S. Cheng (ed.), *Monetary Policy in Pacific Basin Countries*, Boston, MA: Kluwer Academic Publishers, pp. 381–99.

Yam, J. (2012), 'The future of the monetary system of Hong Kong', Working Paper No. 9, Institute of Global Economics and Finance, The Chinese University of Hong Kong.

Yellen, J.L. (2010), 'Hong Kong and China and the global recession', *FRBSF Economic Letter*, **2010–04**, February, 1–5.

5. India

Since Independence from Britain in 1947 India has achieved an order of economic and social progress that sets it well on the way to becoming one of the world's major economies. Its post-Independence economic history, however, provides a case study in comparison and contrast between the inward-oriented and the outward-oriented strategies of development. India began the period with a strategy of forced industrialization emphasizing heavy industry, public ownership and import substitution, dominated as it was by the Soviet Union model of centrally planned growth and development (Ahluwalia and Little, 1998).

While this inward-focused development strategy created a foundation for Indian industrialization, it failed to ignite the sustained growth of output necessary for economic transformation and poverty alleviation. Indeed, the economy performed poorly. There was no major change in Indian industrialization policy until after the beginning of the Soviet Union breakdown in the late 1980s. Joshi and Little (1996) have pointed out that the Indian overall development strategy proceeded on such self-defeating, impoverishing ideas as contempt for the price mechanism, the belief that competition was harmful, a phobia against foreign investment and a keen desire for self-sufficiency in all respects. This 'Fabian socialism', when processed through the Indian cultural and political machine, came out as a kind of 'permit raj' economic regime with complex rules, regulations and bureaucratic regulatory controls over the factor and product markets (Bhagwati, 1992, 1993).

Despite a relatively high manufacturing growth rate, the overall rate of real output growth remained low, around 3.5 per cent per annum. This was not high enough to dent India's massive poverty and socio-economic inequality. Under the centrally planned system, economic efficiency was negligible. The financial system in particular was regulation-repressed within the import-substituting industrialization model. Coincidentally and simultaneously, it served the purpose of financing large government budget deficits. A challenge to this dirigistic economic model came in the late 1980s when the Rajiv Gandhi government, following the passing of the former Prime Minister, his mother Indira Gandhi, indicated the intention of undertaking the reforms necessary to create a dynamic, open economy. India's 1991 balance-of-payments crisis, originating largely in weak economic fundamentals, provided the final push, opening the door to India's reform agenda (Ahluwalia, 2002; Chopra et al., 1995).

The opening up of the Indian economy has been slow, but it has been associated with a wide range of reforms in foreign trade, banking, exchange rate policy and financial account transactions. The aim of reform has been to create a more efficient private sector-dominated economy with more flexible prices and wages. There has been, however, no enthusiasm among political leaders or policymakers for establishing a fully flexible 'laissez-faire' economy, flowing from the recognition that fully deregulated private sector domination may be less efficient than central planning. Throughout the reform exercise, there are indications that policymakers may also have maintained the view that rapid and comprehensive deregulation would lead to economic crisis in the manner of both Latin American (early 1980s) and East Asian (1997) experiences. Russia (or former Soviet Union), with which India (had) has long historic ties, had apparently influenced decision-making in India. The outcome of the Russian sudden deregulation since the early 1990s led to economic crisis and the creation of a few oligarchic warlords. In India, together with rapid deregulation, large inflows of foreign investment have been regarded with suspicion. Consequently, the idea of self-sufficiency has retained a presence in all reform initiatives and measures that were gradual, cautious and, to date, only partial. The most visible reforms undertaken have been in foreign trade and the financial sector.

Following long decades of regulatory repression and stagnant economic growth, the early supply response to economic reform was swift and considerable. India's economy grew at about 5.5 per cent per annum in the 1990s, accelerating to about 8 per cent per annum in the mid 2000s. For some time during the 2000s, India and China found themselves in something of a growth race, although it was effectively 'no contest'. India's growth rate, while rapid, remained at all times lower than China's and was in any event considered unsustainable due to structural weaknesses. Nevertheless, rapid economic growth for over two decades has brought some structural change in India's economy and lowered its poverty incidence significantly. Since the global financial crisis of 2007–09, India's economic growth rate has slowed sharply. With only partial economic reform, the economy appears to have lost momentum after its annual growth rate peaked in mid 2005.

The remainder of this chapter is organized as follows. The next section provides an overview of financial reform and inflation in India. This is followed by discussion of the evolution of India's monetary policy framework. Macroeconomic developments and inflation performance in India are then reviewed and analysed with historical data. To determine whether rule-based monetary policy can be introduced in India, the money-demand behaviour and the money growth-inflation relationship are then investigated. The concluding section summarizes the key findings and draws a conclusion.

FINANCIAL REFORMS AND MONETARY POLICY[1]

Until implementation of financial reforms from the mid 1980s, a wide range of controls over interest rates, credits, capital flows and exchange rates repressed the financial system of India. These measures of regulatory repression were used to promote India's import-substituting industrialization strategy. The commercial banks had been nationalized in 1969 and most of them remained in the public sector. They were used by the government to target multiple socio-economic objectives. Budget deficits were high, around 8 per cent of GDP, and sustained under a pegged exchange rate system until the financial crisis emerged in 1991. Excessive money supply growth, generated by almost automatic government monetization of its budget deficits, fed high and volatile inflation. Consequently, the real exchange rate became overvalued, which inflated the Indian current account deficit. With private capital inflows drying up, official reserves eventually became depleted to such an extent that highly radical policy measures were required. These included import suppression and external borrowing from international financial institutions.

The precarious economic conditions came under further stress from increasingly frequent supply shocks. Given the pegged exchange rate system with capital controls, there were no effective policy instruments to neutralize the impacts of supply shocks on inflation, trade flows and economic growth. By the mid 1980s India became a classic case of financial repression, à la McKinnon-Shaw. It was only one notch behind some of the contemporarily crisis-afflicted Latin American countries under government policy regimes known as 'macroeconomic populism' (Dornbusch and Edwards, 1990, 1991). The Indian forced-industrialization development policy, a component of the inward-looking import-substituting strategy mentioned earlier, thus became a variation on the Latin American model of structuralism and consequent economic stagnation.

Consequently, Indian policymakers came under heavy criticism from some prominent economists working in and on India, including Jagdish Bhagwati. Beyond the professional criticism, a second 'push' factor moving India's affections away from its inward-looking industrialization strategy was the collapse of the former Soviet Union towards the end of the 1980s. While this may have been the final deciding event, a third influence in the ultimate decision to discard the strategy was a 'pull factor': the experience of sustained rapid economic growth and associated restructuring undergone by some East-Southeast Asian developing countries. This phenomenon had for some time beckoned Indian policymakers towards the outward-oriented, market-driven model of development. The process of deciding to adopt this model has been called India's 'look East policy'.

India is considered a relatively low-inflation economy. However, Indian inflation remains highly volatile and this has been a major problem since the 1950s. Average inflation rates were moderately high during the 1970s and 1980s. They fell in the 1990s and have remained low, but the instability has remained throughout. During the period of moderately high average inflation, Indian policymakers generally accepted the monetary source of inflation; however, supply shocks received greater importance in their policy discussion and debate. Although policymakers remained concerned about inflation, they did not commit on a sustained basis to a monetary policy strategy targeting price stability. Their focus on economic growth and poverty alleviation continued, and they perhaps adopted the view, prominent at the time, that there exists a stable tradeoff between inflation and economic growth. Following Structuralist tradition, a moderate rate of inflation is considered inevitable due to supply shocks and structural rigidities in the economy. Politically, it is costly to maintain a commitment to price stability through disciplined fiscal and monetary policies.

During the period under discussion, therefore, from the 1960s through the 1980s, the conduct of monetary policy took the form of passive fiscal accommodation of supply shocks. This led to sustained budget deficits of about 8 per cent of GDP, and they accumulated to create a major public debt challenge for monetary policy. This distracted monetary policy away from its comparative advantage role of targeting price stability. Instead, it was directed towards economic growth and stability, with accompanying repressive regulatory policies and measures allocating and controlling bank credit. During this period, then, credit aggregates were accorded great importance as the key indicator of the official monetary policy stance and its impact on output growth. Money growth was controlled to the extent necessary to keep inflation at single-digit levels.

Financial reforms begun in the mid 1980s were accelerated in the 1990s. Reform in the banking sector was, however, limited. There was no push for privatization of state banks or other financial institutions. In India, the state banks have been used to achieve socio-economic objectives. Consequently, profit has not been a key indicator of bank performance. Banking efficiency was a consideration for financial reform, but was considered ownership-neutral and subordinate, as mentioned, to socio-economic objectives. The state banks therefore remain dominant in the Indian banking sector.

Financial reform generally manifested as deregulation of interest rates and bank credits. These measures were aimed at subjecting the banking sector to competitive pressure. The government has also undertaken some measures to develop money markets for government securities. A number of financial instruments have been developed to broaden and deepen money markets. Treasury bills of varying maturities, bearing market interest rates, have been introduced. This maximizes sales of government securities to the public, simultaneously minimizing sales to the central bank and consequent budget deficit monetization (Macfarlane, 1998). The government has converted the Reserve Bank of India's (RBI) holdings of non-marketable treasury bills into securities bearing market interest rates. Some changes have been made in the stock market. A major reform in liberalizing the pricing of shares in capital markets has been the repeal of the Capital Issues (Control) Act of 1947 and the abolition of the Office of the Controller of Capital Issues. Companies are now free to issue securities and to price them subject to the general guidelines of the Securities and Exchange Board. These measures have expanded money and capital markets and enhanced investment confidence and credibility in the financial system.

The persistence of inflation at moderately high levels has generated concern that the slowdown of economic growth in the early 2010s had structural causes, not cyclical. If so, then an acceleration of the (structural) reform process is indicated. However, political leaders show no great reform enthusiasm, with no major efforts underway to remove existing supply bottlenecks or to introduce the deep structural reforms needed to raise economic efficiency. Fiscal deficits have remained at about 8 per cent of GDP. This is one of the highest, even by developing country standards. Fiscal consolidation is therefore considered an essential task, not only for sustained economic growth but also complementary to any shift of monetary policy targeting to price stability, if contemplated by the Indian authorities. The target for which monetary policy possesses comparative advantage is price stability. Price stability is necessary for maintaining macroeconomic stability to sustain steady economic growth. Low, stable inflation also has a social dimension. Low inflation reduces stress on the poor and vulnerable in society. Monetary and fiscal policies, therefore, are technically integrated if the policy objectives are macroeconomic stability in general and price stability in particular. Monetary policy alone cannot create an environment for steady economic growth in the midst of fiscal indiscipline.

The RBI does not have autonomy in the design and implementation of monetary policy. The key monetary policy issues for India remain: (a) the choice of a monetary policy strategy for price stability and (b) the question of whether, under Indian conditions, price stability and economic growth can be achieved simultaneously. There is at the very least a need to streamline the objectives and instruments of monetary policy to raise monetary policy transparency and credibility. High volatility of inflation reflects low credibility in monetary policy and could be costly for any developing economy. Empirically, the real interest rate and the real exchange rate both track inflation closely. High volatility of inflation therefore has an adverse impact on real output or its growth.

There are at least three areas needing financial reform prior to any potential introduction of a rule-based monetary policy, such as inflation targeting. Firstly, India's financial system remains underdeveloped. Most public banks are relatively inefficient and unresponsive to market signals. They operate under government instructions within a social cost-benefit framework and are not subject to the level of market discipline present in efficient financial systems. Consequently, it is difficult to implement sophisticated monetary policy strategy requiring the presence of a strong interest rate exchange rate channel of the monetary policy transmission mechanism. Moreover, capital market development is an important requirement for any interest-based transmission mechanism of monetary policy.

Secondly, along with fiscal consolidation, full monetary policy independence to target price stability requires a freely floating currency. A managed floating exchange rate confers some monetary policy independence under capital controls. Financial account liberalization benefits the causes both of raising foreign investment inflows and improving economic efficiency. A flexible exchange rate is needed to absorb external shocks to sustain economic stability and control current account deficits.

Thirdly, there is a need for autonomy of the RBI with respect to the design and implementation of monetary policy for price stability. Volatile prices in an environment of high inflation have damaged India in several ways. Firstly, they have created economic uncertainty. This, in turn, has further repressed investment in productive capacity, which was already crippled by infrastructure bottlenecks and rigidities in both the factor and product markets as a result of India's heavy regulatory regime. Secondly, this same volatility-generated economic uncertainty has created scope for excessive speculative activity. Some such activity is efficient, but an excess of it is not conducive to long-term productive investment and technological progress. Thirdly and finally, they have distorted the growth paths of assets both financial and real. For example, the demand for gold has risen rapidly in India as an inflation hedge. Low and stable inflation would raise investment and productive capacity.

EVOLUTION OF MONETARY POLICY FRAMEWORK[2]

Monetary Policy Objectives

Monetary policy in India has evolved around the RBI Act of 1934. It has stated the tasks of the RBI as follows:

> to regulate the issue of bank notes and keeping of reserves with a view to securing monetary stability in India and generally to operate the currency and credit system of the country to its advantage.

This is a broad statement and subject to multiple interpretations. Monetary stability is generally interpreted as price stability (internal) and exchange rate stability (external). As already discussed, India's current strategy of monetary policy uses exchange rate pegging as the primary instrument targeting the goal of financial stability. The RBI at its website states the objectives of monetary policy as: 'maintaining price stability and ensuring adequate flow of credit to productive sectors'. India's fixed or managed float exchange rate policy suggests that the second of these two objectives has priority over price stability, since the exchange rate risk to capital inflows is minimized by a stable exchange rate. An alternative interpretation of the two stated objectives is that monetary policy in India aims primarily to achieve price stability and broad-based sustainable economic growth. These twin objectives of monetary policy have apparently governed the conduct of monetary policy in India since the 1950s.

The relative emphasis placed by successive policymakers on these objectives has, however, varied over time under different exchange rate and capital mobility regulatory regimes. Maintaining an appropriate balance between economic growth and price stability is difficult; in particular, it is not clear how economic growth can be enhanced by direct policy action in a deregulated financial environment. The RBI has not resolved any conflict between them; nor has it announced any priority of one objective over the other. Some authors, such as Reddy (1999, 2002, 2007), point out that the judicious balance between these objectives is heavily tilted towards price stability, meaning an acceptable rate of inflation. While ever India maintains a pegged or managed float exchange rate, this interpretation is unlikely to be valid. If it is true, however, then price stability can be considered a key (if not the sole) objective of monetary policy in India and it remains only for policymakers to devise policy to achieve it given India's unique configuration of economic structure, dynamics and conditions.

The key issue is autonomy in the conduct of monetary policy for price stability. Following the tradition of the Bank of England until the 1990s, the RBI coordinates its monetary policy with the Ministry of Finance. The RBI has limited autonomy and has not to date argued publicly against the multiple-objective strategy of monetary policy. The responsibility of monetary policy decisions effectively rests with the Ministry of Finance. This has not, however, always been the case. The RBI had considerable de facto power and influence in the 1950s and early 1960s. Its position was eroded in 1969 when the government of Indira Ghandi nationalized all commercial banks and financial institutions. Joshi and Little (1994) have mentioned that the RBI became politicized during the 1970s and lost credibility in maintaining price stability. Monetary policy then took the form of 'automatic' accommodation of large fiscal deficits with allocation of credits across interest groups and economic sectors. Fiscal deficits became a chronic threat to sustained macroeconomic stability. With fiscal policy targeted as a political instrument at socio-political objectives, fiscal consolidation became excluded from the policy options. As monetary policy became accommodative, socio-political objectives were added to its multiple conflicting targets. These developments effectively downgraded the role of monetary policy in price stability.

The remainder of this chapter reviews exchange rate arrangements and capital mobility in India in an historical context. They are important to determine the extent to which the RBI has had the ability, if not necessarily the ambition, to conduct an independent monetary policy for price stability.

Institutional Arrangements

Exchange rate regime

From 1947 and continuously until September 1975, the Indian rupee was pegged to the British pound sterling. In September 1975, the pound sterling was abandoned as the anchor currency and a basket of reference currencies was adopted instead. The weights on the individual currencies were left within the discretion of the RBI. In practice, the nominal exchange rate of the rupee remained pegged to the US dollar until 1991. With the US dollar designated the intervention currency by the Indian authorities, the rupee exchange rate with the US dollar was occasionally realigned. In July 1991 the rupee was devalued by 17.4 per cent cumulatively when India experienced a major balance-of-payments crisis.

In March 1993, the government inaugurated what was officially called a 'market-determined unified exchange rate' regime. This quasi-market-determined exchange rate imparted a degree of exchange rate flexibility, although the RBI intervened actively, often heavily, in the foreign-exchange market to stabilize both the nominal and real exchange rates. The nominal exchange rate was generally kept stable with the US dollar. There was occasional depreciation of the rupee to correct for any overvaluation of the real exchange rate. In 1999 the nominal exchange rate became determined by a 'managed float' under the Foreign Exchange Management Act of 1999. RBI stabilizing interventions in the foreign-exchange market experienced peaks in the mid 1990s and mid 2000s in response to large-scale capital inflows, which put pressure on the real exchange rate. Sen (2007) points out that the RBI's intervention took the form of sterilized intervention by selling government securities. Because of pervasive controls over capital flows and interest rates, the RBI was able to perform sterilization and maintain stability of the real exchange rate (Table 5.1).The relatively low volatility of the nominal exchange rate and a higher volatility of interest rates, monetary base and foreign-exchange reserves confirm that India's exchange rate regime in recent years has been much closer to a fixed rather than a floating one (Joshi and Sanyal, 2004).

Capital controls[3]

India imposed capital controls in the late 1950s. They had become comprehensive by the early 1970s. Capital controls were selectively liberalized during the early 1990s. In the terms of India's 'Article IV' agreement with the IMF, the rupee was made convertible for current account transactions in 1994. Associated with this, controls were relaxed over external borrowing to finance current account deficits, including short-term borrowing. Since the 1990s, controls over debt-creating inflows, particularly short-term inflows, have been tightened while those on non-debt-creating inflows have been allowed.

Foreign direct investment

Foreign investment is regarded with suspicion in India. Before 1991, restrictions on foreign investment were stringent. Proposals were reviewed case-by-case. Consequently, foreign investment was negligible. Since 1992 there has been some relaxation of controls over foreign investment. Although small majority shareholdings not too much greater than 50 per cent are allowed without review for investment in a range of industries, proposals for a larger share of foreign majority ownership are considered by the Foreign Investment Promotion Board. In 1996 the list of industries eligible for foreign direct investment was expanded. In a few cases, foreign equity up to 74 per cent has been approved. While this paints a bright picture of liberalization of foreign investment, various restrictions remain at the state and local levels. In comparison with East Asian countries such

Table 5.1 Exchange rate regimes in India, 1947–2012

Year	Foreign-exchange market and the exchange rates
1947–71	Par value system of exchange rate. Rupee's external par value was fixed in terms of gold with the pound sterling as intervention currency.
1971	Breakdown of the Bretton Woods system and the floatation of major currencies. Rupee was linked to the pound sterling in December 1971.
1975	To ensure stability of the external value of the rupee, and to avoid weaknesses associated with a single currency peg, the rupee was pegged to a basket of currencies. Currency selection and the weight assignment was left to the discretion of the Reserve Bank.
1978	RBI allowed the domestic banks to undertake intra-day trading in foreign currencies.
1978–92	Commercial banks began to start quoting two-way prices against the rupee as well as in other currencies. Foreign-exchange markets were still highly regulated with several restrictions on external transactions, entry barriers and transaction costs. Foreign exchange transactions were controlled through the Foreign Exchange Regulations Act.
1990–91	India suffered a major balance-of-payments crisis.
July 1991	To stabilize the exchange rate market, a two-step downward exchange rate adjustment was done (9 per cent and 11 per cent). This was the end to the pegged exchange rate regime.
March 1992	To ease the transition to a market-determined exchange rate system, a liberalized exchange rate management system was put in place, which used a dual exchange rate system. This was a transitional arrangement.
March 1993	The dual rates converged and a market-determined exchange rate regime was introduced. All foreign-exchange receipts became convertible at market-determined exchange rates.
Since 1994	Since August 1994 the rupee has been convertible on the current account and the process of integration of the Indian financial market with the rest of the world has been underway. Capital account convertibility is allowed for foreigners, foreign-based corporate and non-resident Indians. Several types of exchange controls have been dismantled and the Indian rupee is no longer pegged.

Source: Author's adaptation based on Dua and Sinha (2007, 2008).

as Singapore, Hong Kong SAR, Malaysia and Indonesia, India remains far behind in its outlook towards foreign investment.

Foreign portfolio investment

Foreign portfolio investment was not allowed until 1991. Since 1992, foreign institutional investors, namely pension funds and mutual funds, have been allowed to invest in listed securities (equities and bonds, excluding government bonds) in primary and secondary markets provided they meet regulatory requirements. Since 1997 portfolio investment has been permitted in government securities and Treasury bills. Furthermore, institutional investors may repatriate capital, income and capital gains at the market exchange rate.

External commercial borrowing

The door is open for Indian companies to borrow in the form of commercial bank loans and Eurobonds subject to approval of the Ministry of Finance. In general, the Ministry of Finance exercises case-by-case control over external borrowing. Short-term borrowing beyond the needs of trade credit is not encouraged. There is also an overall annual ceiling on approvals for external commercial borrowing.

Non-resident Indian deposits

In the 1990s the Indian government began to encourage bank deposits from non-resident Indians. Higher interest rates were offered for their deposits as well as exchange rate guarantees. As these deposits were found volatile during the 1991 crisis, the exchange rate guarantee has been withdrawn and the interest rate incentives have been progressively reduced.

Foreign currency-denominated deposits and loans

Commercial banks are prohibited from accepting deposits or extending loans denominated in foreign currencies. Strict controls are maintained on commercial banks' foreign asset and liability positions. There are restrictions on domestic currency lending to non-residents. This aims at reducing the opportunities for direct short-selling of the rupee. The swap and forward markets are also tightly controlled. This aims to reduce speculation against the rupee by circumventing restrictions on direct lending in rupees to non-residents. Consequently, the swap and forward markets do not have adequate liquidity and depth.

Capital outflows

Repatriation of capital is allowed for foreign institutional investors and non-resident Indian investors who invest in the country under recognized schemes. Capital outflows by residents are prohibited with minor exceptions.

Summing up

Although India has removed some restrictions on capital flows, major restrictions remain. The government controls offshore borrowings by Indian companies case-by-case, and maintains annual ceilings on external commercial borrowings. Commercial banks may not maintain deposits or make loans in foreign currencies. Their foreign assets and liabilities are controlled. Offshore trading of the rupee is prohibited. Policy is also directed towards limiting forward trading in the foreign-exchange market for hedging current account transactions. The forward market thus lacks depth and remains liquidity deficient. Much scope remains, therefore, for further liberalization of capital accounts. The pressure for such reform is limited as the idea of the free market is still resisted by policymakers. Nor do strong pressure groups, such as the banking sector and the business sector, advocate effectively for capital account convertibility.

Monetary Policy Strategy

Pre-reform period

Before 1991 the RBI maintained a Monetarist view on inflation and kept control over money growth by deploying both direct and indirect policy instruments. Monetary policymakers were generally conservative and tried to keep inflation low. However, because one target of monetary policy was the promotion of economic growth, policy inconsistencies were inevitable. Monetary policy strategy in India for maintaining price stability was formalized during the 1980s. Under the fixed or pegged exchange rate system, India considered the exchange rate of the rupee as an anchor to prices, despite the fact that India has a large non-tradable goods sector. Stringent trade and capital controls allowed India to use measures to control credits and interest rates as instruments of monetary policy. From the mid 1980s India finally formalized its monetary policy framework in the form of money-growth targeting to control inflation.

From the mid 1980s to 1997–98, the RBI monetary policy framework was characterized as 'monetary targeting with feedback'. It was established in 1985 on the lines as recommended in the *Report of the Committee to Review the Working of the Monetary System*, popularly known as the Chakravarty Committee ('Chakravarty'). The Committee suggested a formal structure of coordination, proposing an agreement between the central government and the RBI on the level of monetary expansion and the extent of monetization of the fiscal deficit. Chakravarty did not suggest a rigid monetary growth target rule but its recommendation was that the targeted money-growth rate should be modified on the basis of available information on expected output growth and a tolerable rate of inflation around 4 per cent per annum. A broad money (M3) growth rate became the anchor to inflation. Bank reserves and reserve money were used, respectively, as operating instrument and operating target to influence M3 growth. This monetary policy framework was best described as a flexible monetary targeting approach.[4] As recommended by Chakravarty, some new financial instruments were created, including 182-day Treasury bills, Certificates of Deposit, commercial paper and participation certificates, and institutions developed to support monetary targeting.

The validity of this monetary targeting framework depended on the degree of control that the RBI could exert on monetary-base growth under the then pegged exchange rate system. The money-demand function in India was considered stable. It made monetary targeting appropriate in principle even if there was the problem of monetary control under the pegged exchange rate system. Implicit in the monetary targeting framework was a monetary policy transmission mechanism that relied heavily on the credit channel. The monetary growth rate target was therefore associated with a credit-growth target. Interest rates did not play a major role in the monetary policy transmission mechanism. Most credits were allowed through the state banks. Political factors played a major role in the allocation of credit across sectors.

Multiple-indicator approach to monetary policy

Since April 1998 India has introduced what is known as the multiple-indicator approach to monetary policy. Concerns about stability of the money-demand function caused the shift from monetary targeting with feedback to a multiple-indicator approach. Yet there is evidence suggesting that India's long-run money-demand function did not become unstable in the 1990s (Hossain and Rashid, 1996). Under the multiple-indicator approach, the monetary aggregate has become one of many indicators of monetary policy. This has diluted the importance of the monetary aggregate as an intermediate target, reflecting the view that some weakening of the (perennial) link between money growth and changes in the price level has occurred.

Acceptance of the multiple-indicator approach has effectively spelt, for India, the end of the monetary aggregate as an anchor to prices. Under the multiple-indicator approach, the RBI has not nominated any other anchor as replacement of money. In the technical parlance, the absence of such a nominal anchor renders monetary policy 'clueless', or 'policy on the run'. Such irresponsible monetary policy can be criticized first and foremost as counter to the public interest. It can also be criticized for its lack of transparency and for its inability to anchor to inflationary expectations. In some developed countries, especially in the United States, the void left by the absence of a nominal monetary anchor has been filled by inflationary expectations as the implicit anchor to prices. Policies are adjusted to control inflationary expectations and keep them close around some administratively determined, unannounced target or acceptable rate of inflation. This does not seem to be the case in India since, in effect, economic growth has priority over price stability. There is a perception that the RBI's inflation projections represent a 'soft form' of inflation targeting. This also does not seem to be the case because, under the multiple-indicator approach, monetary policy aims to achieve the following set of objectives: (1) low and stable inflation; (2) financial stability to promote economic growth; (3) stability of the exchange rate; and (4) stability of the interest rate.

Under the multiple-indicator approach, the RBI uses short-term interest rates for demand management. The Indian money and capital markets remain underdeveloped, so that the transmission mechanisms of monetary policy are not well known. The RBI claims that in recent years the interest rate channel has become ascendant over other channels in demand management, especially over the credit and exchange rate channels. The exchange rate channel, in particular, is not strong because the Indian economy is only very partially open (Reddy, 1999, 2002).

Within the present multiple-indicator approach to monetary policy, most monetary indicator variables, including the monetary aggregates, have causal relationships with output or prices. This suggests that pre-announced economic and financial variables generally remain eligible to serve as policy indicators. However, this approach to monetary policy is non-transparent. A more transparent monetary policy strategy is inflation targeting. To avoid a resurgence of inflation, the RBI needs to make a firm commitment to maintain low and stable inflation. This would require institutional and operational changes.

Before the advent of financial reform, the RBI applied direct policy instruments such as interest rate regulations, selective credit controls, the cash reserve ratio and the liquidity reserve ratio. These instruments were used to neutralize the monetary impact of government budgetary operations. Since financial reform, some indirect instruments of monetary policy have been adopted. These include open-market operations. A Liquidity Adjustment Facility (LAF) has been implemented for liquidity management and as a signalling device for interest rates in overnight markets. The RBI uses the repurchase and reverse repurchase agreements for short-run liquidity management. The bank rate (discount rate) has been restored as a signalling instrument of monetary policy. To raise the degree of competition among the commercial banks, there has been a phased reduction in the cash reserve ratio and the statutory liquidity requirement ratio (Dua and Sinha, 2007; Mohan, 2008).

Analysis of India's multiple-indicator approach begs the question of why India chose it over inflation targeting, which is considered by many to be perhaps the most effective tool to maintain low and stable inflation without generating growth volatility. A raft of serious impediments prevents the implementation of inflation targeting in India. Firstly, inflation has generally been low, though unstable. Secondly, political leaders rate too high the political costs of major change in the monetary policy framework. Such major change would include: public declaration of the numerical value of the inflation target; making price stability the sole objective of monetary policy; transferring management of the other 'indicators' – really, they are policy objectives – to targeting by more appropriate policy instruments; withdrawal of controls over wages and prices; and the end of routine official interventions in the foreign-exchange market. Thirdly, inflation targeting requires central bank operational autonomy in pursuing the inflation target. If the RBI is not granted that autonomy, there is concern that inflation targeting would further reduce its already low credibility since, in all likelihood, the inflation target would consistently not be achieved. An associated fear is that supply shocks, a common phenomenon, and India's entrenched fiscal profligacy, would compromise the RBI's stance on inflation (Bhattacharya, 2005). Conversely, were the government to grant to the RBI the full measure of the necessary autonomy, this would number the days of almost automatic central bank monetization of the fiscal deficit. Such a scenario represents anathema to the culture of macroeconomic populism that has been embedded for decades in Indian politics. Fourthly, the absence of a well-developed monetary policy transmission mechanism – that is, one dominated by the interest rate and the exchange rate channels – makes inflation targeting difficult.

The multiple-indicator approach to monetary policy is therefore considered a compromise choice. However, its appropriateness remains in doubt against the standard macroeconomic principle of one instrument, one target. The multiple-indicator approach uses information on the monetary aggregates, rates of return on financial assets and movements in real variables to indicate (discretionary) policy decisions.

In sum, monetary policy in India is in transition. It has been conducted under an increasingly deregulated financial system. However, the institutional set-up remains only weakly configured for the conduct of monetary policy. The RBI does not yet have the necessary level of operational autonomy to conduct an independent monetary policy to achieve price stability.

Both price stability and economic growth remain the stated objectives of monetary policy. The empirics suggest that the growth objective is primary and it has general appeal. Whether manipulation by monetary policy of nominal instruments can achieve this real objective is another matter.

Monetary policy in transition

India needs a sharp break in the choice of monetary policy strategy. Progress amenable to introduction of rule-based monetary policy has been made in some areas. Exchange rate flexibility has gradually risen. However, under the current managed float, the RBI intervenes in the foreign-exchange market to stabilize the exchange rate. This compromises somewhat the independence of Indian monetary policy to target price stability. To maintain exchange rate stability, there are restrictions on capital movements. Overall, monetary policy remains in the shadow of fiscal and exchange rate management policies. Its role in price stability is, therefore, not transparent.

Despite recent economic deregulation and financial reform, India's economy operates under a substantial regime of economic controls and regulations. Trade barriers, both tariff and non-tariff, are high. Problems associated with state ownership of the banking system remain unresolved. Under the regulated system, monetary policy instruments were direct and somewhat bland. Under the deregulated system, some indirect instruments of monetary control have been used. However, their usefulness has been hampered by the habitual policy monetization of unpredictably large budget deficits. Restrictions remain on international capital transactions. A widely held view is that economic controls (including capital controls) have protected India's economy from external shocks, most especially from the 1997 East-Southeast Asian financial crisis, by limiting external indebtedness.

During the mid 2000s large inflows of foreign capital created problems for Indian monetary and exchange rate management. Capital inflows have had at least three major effects: (1) appreciation of the real exchange rate; (2) accumulation of large foreign reserves given the economy's limited absorptive capacity; and (3) excess liquidity, caused by reserves accumulation despite sterilization measures by the RBI. With the swell of capital inflows, tensions in the monetary policy framework have emerged between exchange rate stability, monetary independence and financial openness. Increased exchange rate flexibility, strengthened monetary operations and effective communication with markets are expected to strengthen monetary policy effectiveness in a more financially open environment (IMF, country reports on the website, several years).

MACROECONOMIC DEVELOPMENTS AND INFLATION PERFORMANCE

As reviewed earlier, for most of the period since Independence from the British Raj, India has combined a highly interventionist and inward-oriented development strategy with supportive macroeconomic policies. The key aim of the development strategy has been to build a publicly owned, heavy industry sector. The consumer goods sector and agriculture have been left for the private sector. The inward-oriented development strategy suppressed import demand and discouraged exports. To promote import-substituting industries, policymakers relied on industrial licensing, trade-protection barriers of both tariff and non-tariff types and controls over credits, interest rates and capital flows. Macroeconomic policies were aimed at promoting economic growth and maintaining low and stable inflation. However, as there was automatic monetization of budget deficits, monetary expansion remained high and volatile, which led to volatile inflation. The administered interest rates were generally low. High and volatile inflation led to very low or negative real interest rates (discussion in this section uses the data provided in Table 5.2). Under a branch banking system, the state banks were allowed to increase bank branches across the country. This increased the pace of monetization and raised financial savings.

India's economy grew, on average, about 4 per cent per annum over the period 1950–70. The manufacturing sector, which expanded rapidly under the import-substituting industrialization strategy, made a significant contribution to output growth. Agricultural output grew at roughly 2 per cent per annum. Agriculture dominated the economy, keeping overall economic growth relatively low. India maintained low but unstable inflation throughout the 1950s and 1960s. The public position of Indian policymakers remained generally committed to low inflation. However, without an appropriate monetary policy strategy, there was no effective way of controlling inflation under the then fixed pegged exchange rate system. Inflation was difficult to control in an agricultural economy that frequently suffered from supply shocks. Policymakers tried to reduce budget deficits and keep the money-growth rate low. Their policy measures were, however, ad hoc as there was no institutional control over budget deficits and money growth. India experienced high inflation during the 1970s and 1980s. Budget deficits and money growth were high. Supply shocks played a role in raising inflation during the 1970s.

India experienced a balance-of-payments crisis during 1990–91, due to a combination of internal economic weaknesses and external shocks. Joshi and Sanyal (2004) suggest that it was caused primarily by weak

Table 5.2 Macroeconomic indicators, India, 1950–2012

Macroeconomic indicators	1951–55	1956–60	1961–65	1956–70	1971–75	1976–80	1981–85	1986–90	1991–95	1996–2000	2001–05	2006–10	2011	2012
Budget balance (% of GDP)	n.a.	n.a.	n.a.	n.a.	n.a.	n.a.	n.a.	−5.3	−6.2	−7.3	−9.5	−7.9	−9.0	−9.5
General government gross debt (% of GDP)	n.a.	n.a.	n.a.	n.a.	n.a.	n.a.	n.a.	n.a.	74.9	69.4	82.0	74.1	67.0	67.6
Money-growth rate (%)														
Narrow money growth	2.4	5.8	9.5	9.5	12.6	11.6	15.1	15.7	17.4	13.2	15.7	17.2	6.7	6.7
Broad money growth	3.3	9.1	8.7	11.1	15.6	19.7	17.3	16.7	16.7	17.4	15.3	21.2	16.0	11.1
Real GDP growth rate (%)	4.0	4.1	3.7	4.5	2.9	3.2	5.4	5.9	5.4	6.0	6.8	8.7	6.2	5.0
GDP per capita, current prices, US dollar	n.a.	n.a.	n.a.	n.a.	n.a.	266	293	358	345	435	571	1071	1514	1592
Unemployment rate (%)	n.a.	n.a.	n.a.	n.a.	n.a.	n.a.	n.a.	n.a.	2.6	2.7	3.1	2.5	n.a	n.a
CPI inflation rate (%)	−0.9	5.2	6.2	6.5	12.2	4.2	9.3	7.8	10.5	7.6	4.0	8.7	8.9	9.3
Current account balance (% of GDP)	n.a.	n.a.	n.a.	n.a.	n.a.	−1.3	−1.5	−2.2	−1.1	−1.1	0.4	−1.9	−3.4	−3.8

Table 5.2 (continued)

Macroeconomic indicators	1951–55	1956–60	1961–65	1966–70	1971–75	1976–80	1981–85	1986–90	1991–95	1996–2000	2001–05	2006–10	2011	2012
Nominal interest rate (%)														
Lending rate of interest	n.a.	n.a.	n.a.	n.a.	n.a.	14.8	16.5	16.5	16.7	13.6	11.4	11.6	10.2	10.6
Call money rate	2.1	3.1	4.4	4.6	8.3	9.0	8.8	11.3	13.2	8.2	8.8[c]	9.5	8.8	9.3
Real interest rate (%)[a]														
Lending rate of interest	n.a.	n.a.	n.a.	n.a.	n.a.	7.7	6.6	8.1	5.6	5.7	7.2	2.7	1.2	1.2
Call money rate	3.2	−2.0	−1.5	−1.6	−2.9	5.2	−0.4	3.3	2.4	0.1	0.1[c]	0.2	−0.1	0.0
Nominal exchange rate (rupee per US dollar)	4.8	4.8	4.8	7.3	7.9	8.4	10.4	14.6	28.6	40.2	46.4	44.9	46.7	53.4
Bilateral real exchange rate with US dollar[b]	45.3	43.1	38.0	44.5	43.5	49.4	58.2	66.8	99.9	104.6	107.8	88.4	73.7	78.8

Notes:
n.a. = not available
a. Real interest rate is estimated as: 100(((1 + interest rate)/(1 + inflation rate))−1) where the interest rate and inflation rate are expressed in decimal.
b. An increase in the index value of the exchange rate represents depreciation.
c. Due to a lack of data the call money rate entries for the period 2001–05 are interpolated.

Source: Author's computation based on IMF, *International Financial Statistics*; IMF, *World Economic Outlook*; and other country-specific publications on the IMF website.

fundamentals, in particular fiscal and current account deficits. The trigger for the crisis was the brief spike in oil prices that followed the Iraqi invasion of Kuwait. There was associated political instability in India. The Gulf War reduced overseas remittances from the Gulf region and stepped up pressure on the balance-of-payments. The global slowdown during the period impacted India's exports. Under these circumstances, investors lost confidence in the government's ability to handle the expected economic crisis (Dua and Sinha, 2007). When the crisis broke, there was an outflow of non-resident deposits and a cut-off of short-term external loans. For a time the country was on the edge of debt default. The fundamental problems were fiscal and monetary. High budget deficits were linked to money creation, which led to high inflation and balance-of-payments problems. The pegged exchange rate system led to an overvalued economy, raising current account deficits. The crisis was resolved by a combination of devaluation, deflation and borrowing from the IMF. Simultaneously with stabilization measures, the government embarked on economic deregulation and reforms.

India's economy grew rapidly throughout the 1990s as economic reform proceeded. There was, however, no break in the old fiscal and monetary policymaking habits. The key components of ongoing policy were: (1) the managed float; (2) capital controls; (3) state banks; (4) regulated interest rates and credit allocations; and (4) high budget deficits. The combination was arguably appropriate to avoid the 'open-economy trilemma', in which theory allows, for a given macroeconomy, the simultaneous achievement of two only from the following three elements of a desirable policy configuration: full and free international capital mobility; a stable exchange rate; and independent monetary policy. India's economy sustained economic growth for about a decade and escaped from the adverse effects of the East-Southeast Asian and the US-global financial crises.

Inflation Behaviour

Figure 5.1a displays quarter-on-quarter CPI inflation in India over the period 1958q1–2012q4. As discussed above, it shows that except in the 1970s, inflation in India remained moderately low but unstable. Figure 5.1b shows that inflation volatility in India has somewhat diminished since the mid 2000s.

Because of inflation volatility and limited adjustment of the interest rate, there was high volatility of the real interest rate. Figure 5.2 displays the real call money rate, some data gaps in the 1990s are filled by the lending rate. It shows that the real call money rate was highly volatile throughout the period 1950–2010.

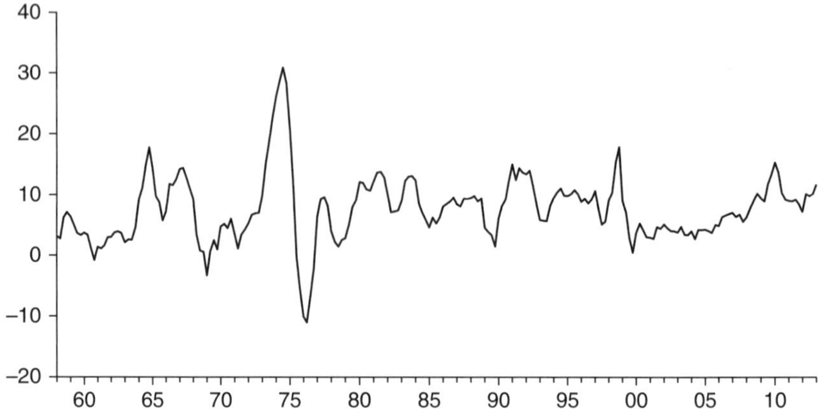

Figure 5.1a Quarter-on-quarter CPI inflation in India, 1958q1–2012q4

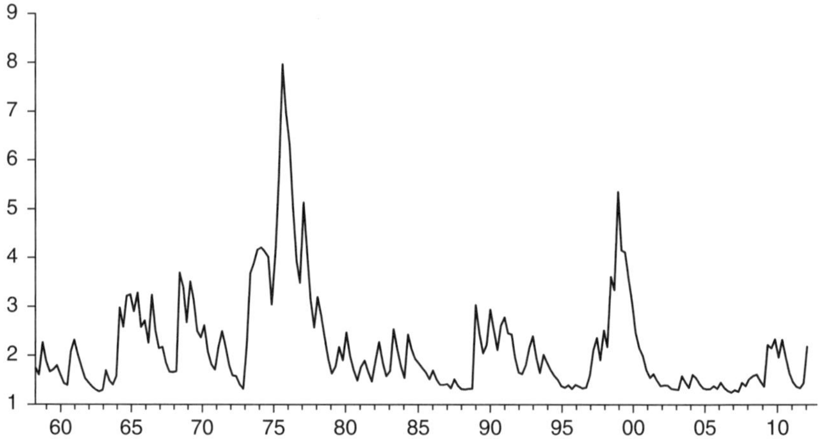

Figure 5.1b Conditional standard deviation of CPI inflation in India, 1958q1–2012q4

Figure 5.3 displays the real effective exchange rate of the Indian rupee over the period 1970–2010. It shows that the real exchange rate, which was heavily overvalued in the 1970s, depreciated sharply in the early 1990s and has remained stable over the last two decades.

Figure 5.4 shows a close relation between the real call money rate in India and the real Treasury bill rate in the United States. This is indicative that a real interest rate parity condition holds between India and the United States. The time-series properties (not reported) suggest that both

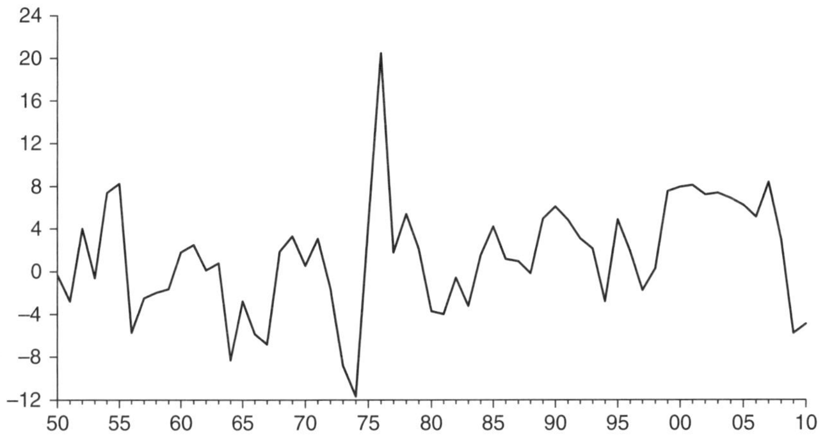

Figure 5.2 The real call money rate in India, 1950–2010

these series are stationary, implying that they have a short-term relation but no long-term cointegral-causal relation.

Inflation persistence

Inflation in India is highly persistent. This is reflected in the estimated coefficient value on the one-period lagged rate of inflation, obtained by both the recursive and rolling regression techniques (Figures 5.5a and 5.5b). Table 5.3 reports the unit root test results for inflation in India. The ADF tests reject the null hypothesis that inflation in India has a unit root, leading to the conclusion that there is no cointegral-causal relation between the inflation rates in India and the United States.

INFLATION, REAL INTEREST RATE, REAL EXCHANGE RATE AND REAL OUTPUT

One problem for exchange rate policy in India is high-inflation volatility. Inflation has fallen since the mid 1990s. With it, inflation volatility has decreased. Since the interest rate and the nominal exchange rate in India do not adjust completely to the inflation differential between India and the United States, inflation volatility in India leads to volatility in both the real interest rate and the real exchange rate, as revealed by Table 5.2. Inflation in India behaves differently from that in the United States, so that the real interest rate and the real exchange rate in India can affect real output. Since the early 2000s the US interest rate has remained low and volatile. Inflation

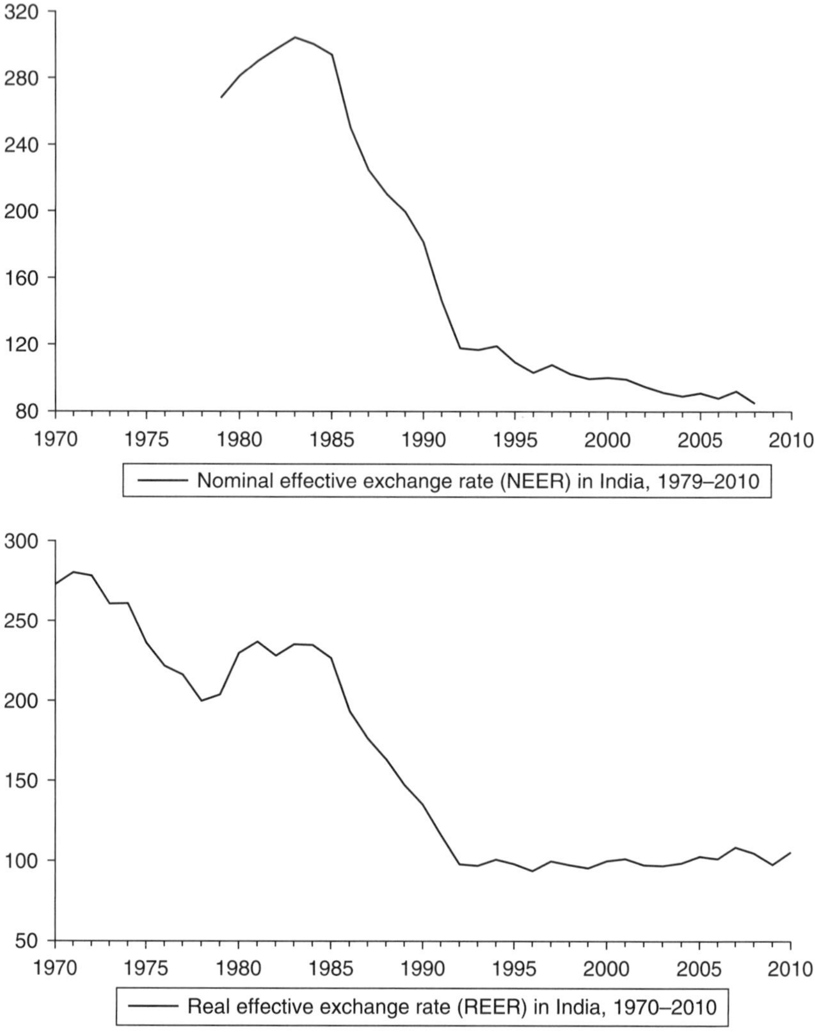

Note: An increase in the index value indicates an appreciation of Indian rupee.

Source: IMF, *International Financial Statistics*; other country-specific publications on the IMF website; and J.P. Morgan.

Figure 5.3 Nominal and real effective exchange rates in India, 1970–2010

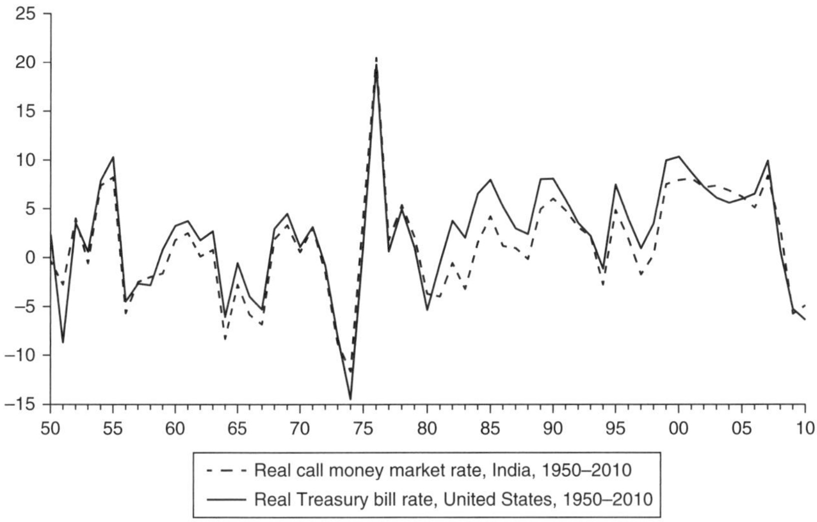

Figure 5.4 The real call rate of interest in India and the real Treasury bill rate in the United States, 1950–2010

in India was low, but more volatile. Consequently India's real interest rate became low and volatile, perhaps to such an extent as to have caused boom-bust cycles.[5]

The Structural Vector Autoregressive (SVAR) Analysis

This subsection uses annual data to estimate a four-variable SVAR model to examine the interrelationships among inflation, the real interest rate, the real exchange rate and real output.[6] The model is formulated on the assumptions that: (1) inflation has a contemporaneous feedback relation with the real interest rate and the real exchange rate and (2) all three of these variables affect real output. The order of variables in the model can then be arranged as follows: INFIN, RCMR, LREER and LRGDP where INFIN is the rate of inflation in India, RCMR is the real call money rate, LREER is the log of the real effective exchange rate and LRGDP is the log of real GDP. The unit root test results suggest that inflation, the real interest rate and the real exchange rate are stationary, while real output is nonstationary. Based on this information, two versions of the model are estimated and deployed to generate impulse responses and the forecast error-variance decompositions for all the above variables. The first version of the model is defined as: INFIN, RCMR, LREER and LRGDP while the second version of the model is defined as: INFIN, RCMR, LREER

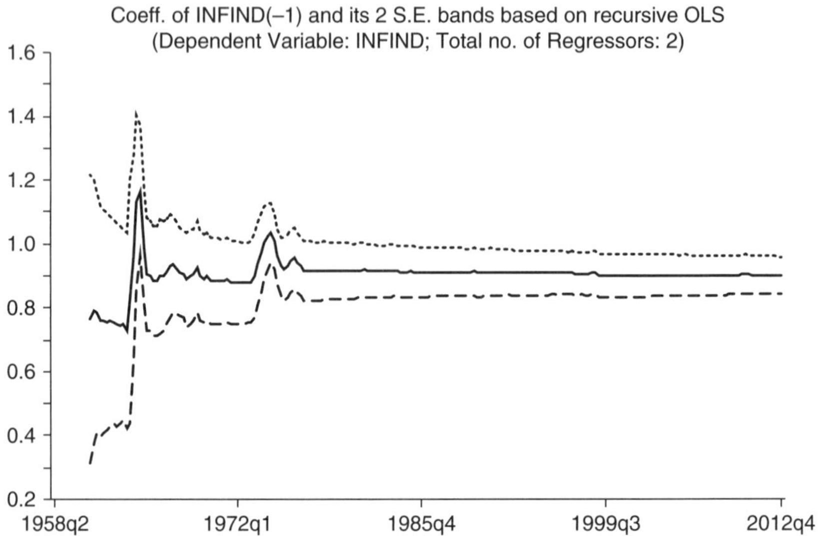

Note: INFIND = CPI inflation in India.

Figure 5.5a Recursive estimates of the coefficient on the one-period lagged rate of CPI inflation in India

and DLRGDP. In the second version of the model, all the variables are stationary while in the first version real output is nonstationary. Results obtained from the second model are reported and used for interpretation. Figure 5.6 plots the data used for estimation purposes.

The impulse response results in Figure 5.7 reveal the interrelations among four variables in the SVAR model. The model does not include the source of inflation. As reviewed in different contexts, high and volatile inflation have monetary roots. When the inflation rate is low, it is difficult to identify the sources of inflation as both demand and supply shocks overwhelm the impact of core sources of inflation such as money growth. The relationship becomes pronounced when inflation is high and sustained. In developing countries, budget deficits are considered a key source of inflation. The relationships among budget deficits, money growth and inflation are pronounced and detectable. Budget deficits and inflation also maintain a feedback relation. For example, a rise in inflation lowers the real value of tax revenues. This leads to an increase in budget deficits and causes faster money growth and hence inflation.

The impulse response results are indicative, not conclusive. As expected, a rise in inflation lowers the real rate of interest. It indicates that the

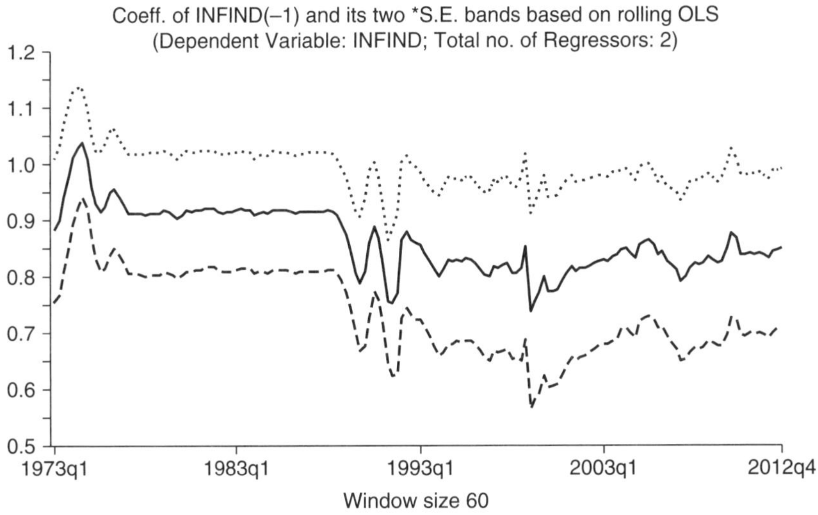

Note: INFIND = CPI inflation in India.

Figure 5.5b Rolling sample estimates of the coefficient on the one-period lagged rate of CPI inflation in India

nominal interest rate responds slowly to a rise in inflation. Although a decrease in the real interest rate is expected to raise investment, this is unlikely in developing countries. In these countries, a very low or negative real interest rate, caused by high inflation given unchanged nominal interest rates, creates financial repression that lowers saving, investment and economic growth. Low economic growth may raise inflation given money supply growth. High and volatile inflation also may create other macroeconomic problems. A rise in inflation appreciates the real exchange rate, which in turn affects inflation and economic growth. The real interest rate in particular responds positively to an appreciation of the real exchange rate. This is because as a grossly appreciated real exchange rate induces capital flight, the real interest rate is required to rise as an inducement to slow down or stop capital flight. This follows the open-economy real exchange rate parity condition. Provided stringent capital controls, there can be short-run deviation of real interest rates across countries, capital controls are not generally effective for most countries irrespective of official regulations and controls. In general, an appreciation of the real exchange rate affects both trade and capital flows while changes in the real interest rate affect saving and investment.

The overall results suggest significant interrelations among inflation, the

Table 5.3 The unit root test results for CPI inflation in India

Variables	Constant (C); Trend (T); None	Optimal lag-length (based on SBC)	ADF test statistic (p-value)	Inference at 5% level	The KPSS test statistic		LM-statistic	Inference at 5% level
					Constant (C); Trend (T)	Newey-West bandwidth		
Unadjusted sample period: 1949–2010		(maximum lag = 10)	ADF					
LCPI	C and T	1	−3.31 (0.08)	I(1)	C and T	5	0.2	I(0)
LCPI	C	1	1.08 (1.00)	I(1)	C	6	0.98	I(1)
ΔLCPI	C	1	−4.78 (0.00)	I(0)	C	3	0.43	I(0)
ΔLCPI	None	0	−2.64 (0.01)	I(0)				
The Zivot-Andrews unit root test statistic		Sample period: 1950–2010	Chosen lag-length (maximum = 4)	Chosen breakpoint	t-statistic	Inference at 5% level		
Null hypotheses:								
ΔLCP has a unit root with a structural break in the intercept			4	1983	−4.5	I(1)		
ΔLCPI has a unit root with a structural break in both the intercept and trend			4	1991	−4.22	I(1)		

Note: Definitions of variables: LCPI = logarithm of the consumer price index; ΔLCPI = first-order logarithm difference of the consumer price index; ADF = augmented Dickey-Fuller; KPSS = Kwiatkowski, Phillips, Schmidt and Shin; and SBC = Schwarz Bayesian Criterion.

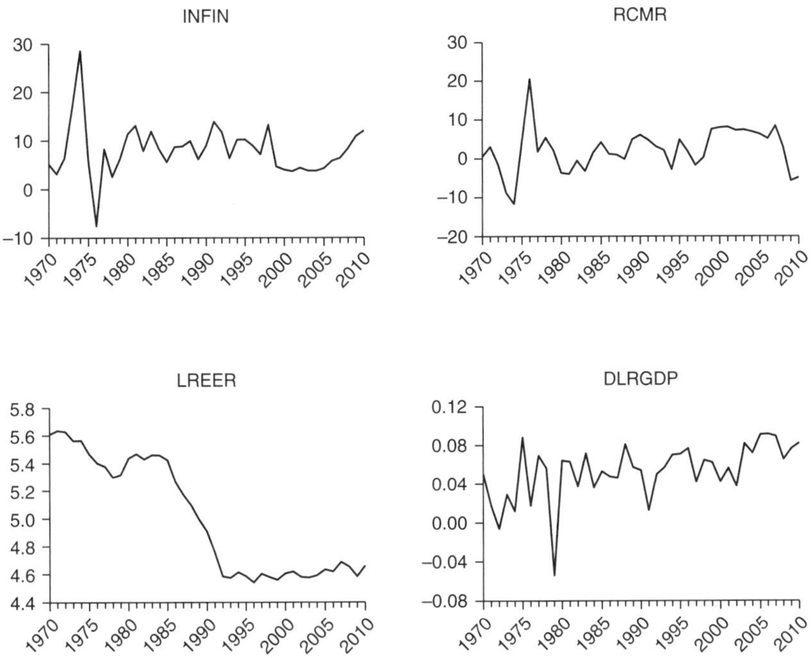

Note: Definitions of variables: INFIN = inflation rate in India; RCMR = real call money-market rate; LREER =log of the real effective exchange rate; and DLRGDP = first-order difference of the log of real GDP.

Figure 5.6 Data deployed for estimation of the SVAR model for India

real interest rate, the real exchange rate and output growth. Although it is not investigated here, an expanded model is expected to show the impacts of the real interest and exchange rates on saving, investment and both trade and capital flows. The key message that emerges from the empirical results is that inflation and its volatility are not innocuous with respect to economic growth. Inflation affects the real interest rate and the real exchange rate and they have impacts on saving, investment and economic growth. This suggests the need for low and stable inflation for steady economic growth.

Table 5.4 presents the forecast error-variance decompositions of variables in the second version of the SVAR model. In the table, the numbers represent those percentages of forecast error variance of variables in the model that can be attributed to own innovations and those percentages of forecast error variance that originate from innovations of other variables. The results show that for all the four variables, the dominant source of the forecast error variance is own innovations, to the extent of 64 per cent

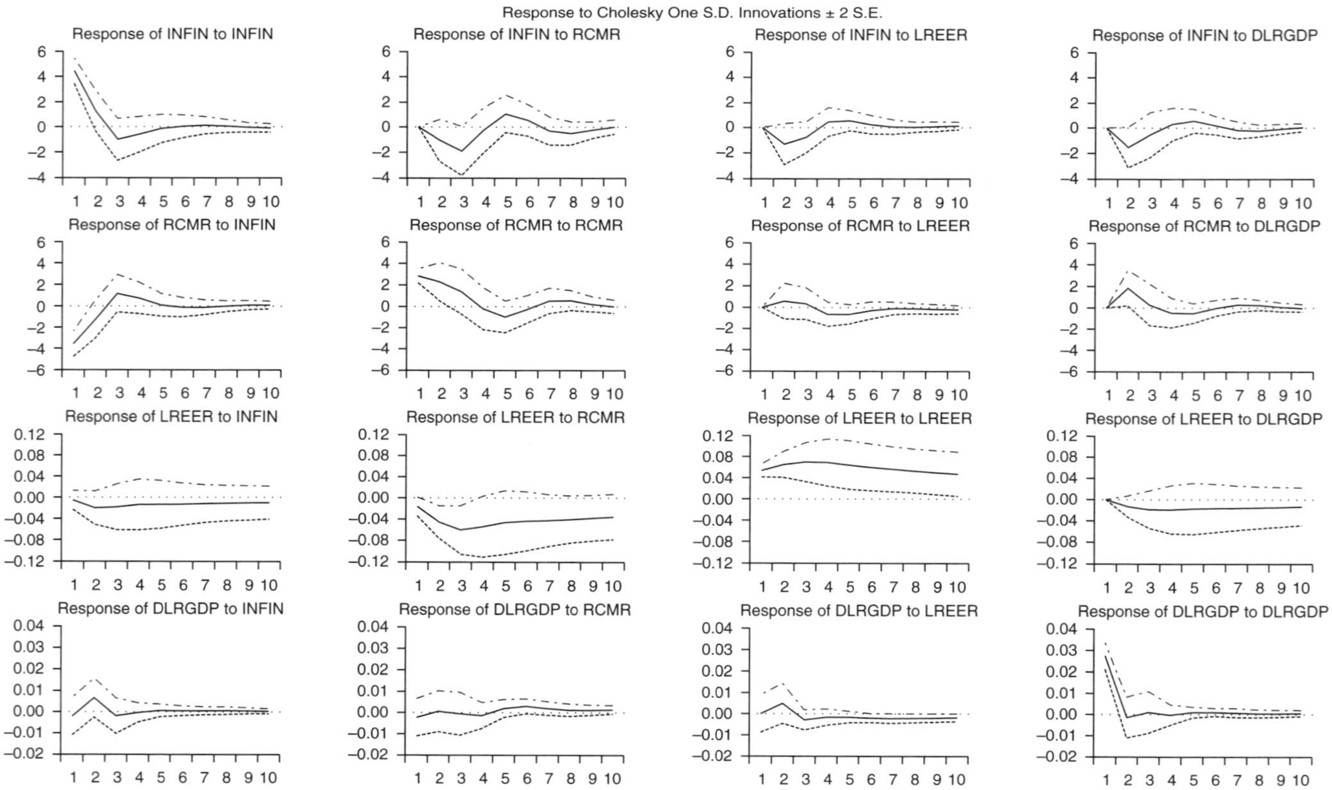

Note: Definitions of variables: INFIN = CPI inflation in India; RCMR = real call money market rate; LREER = log of the real effective exchange rate of the rupee; and DLRGDP = first-order difference of the log of real GDP.

Figure 5.7 Impulse responses for variables in the SVAR model for India

Table 5.4 Forecast-error-variance decomposition of variables in the SVAR model for India

Period	S.E.	INFIN	RCMR	LREER	DLRGDP
Variance Decomposition of INFIN:					
1	4.45	100.00	0.00	0.00	0.00
2	5.16	80.38	4.24	6.42	8.95
5	5.88	65.83	17.16	8.11	8.89
10	5.96	64.14	18.70	8.13	9.03
Variance Decomposition of RCMR:					
1	4.57	61.39	38.61	0.00	0.00
2	5.61	45.91	42.29	1.03	10.76
5	6.15	43.13	42.95	3.46	10.47
10	6.24	42.04	43.58	3.81	10.56
Variance Decomposition of LREER:					
1	0.056	0.89	8.37	90.74	0.00
2	0.010	4.33	23.21	70.71	1.75
5	0.185	3.35	32.52	60.59	3.53
10	0.242	3.08	33.08	59.78	4.06
Variance Decomposition of DLRGDP:					
1	0.028	0.58	0.67	0.00	98.75
2	0.029	5.68	0.65	2.85	90.81
5	0.029	5.99	1.36	4.33	88.32
10	0.030	5.84	3.21	6.43	84.52
The Cholesky Ordering: INFIN RCMR LREER DLRGDP					

Notes: INFIN = CPI inflation in India; RCMR = real call money market rate; LREER = log of the real effective exchange rate; DLRGDP = first-order difference of the log of real GDP.

for inflation, 44 per cent for the real interest rate, 60 per cent for the real exchange rate and 85 per cent for real GDP growth over the ten-year time horizon. In the case of real output growth, innovations in the real interest rate and the real exchange rate jointly account for 9 per cent of real output's forecast error variance. The corresponding share of inflation is 6 per cent. Real output growth is thus found mildly sensitive to inflation and its volatility.

MONETARY AND EXCHANGE RATE POLICY ISSUES

The empirical results reported above suggest that India's economy, under the pegged exchange rate system, remains sensitive to external shocks. The empirical evidence suggests that under the pegged system, US monetary policy has some impact on the Indian economy through its impact on the real interest rate and the real exchange rate. One way of minimizing this problem is to adopt a flexible exchange rate system, which then frees a country to design and conduct an independent monetary policy, the comparative advantage target being price stability. One shortcoming of a flexible exchange rate system is that it is vulnerable to excess volatility when the foreign-exchange market is thin. To the extent that Indian economic reform embeds disciplined monetary and fiscal policies and accumulates large foreign reserves, a floating rupee is unlikely to be excessively volatile. With these fundamentals in place, the issue becomes a choice of the least cost, or most efficient, monetary policy India can adopt to establish and maintain price stability under a floating exchange rate system. Two options stand out for India. It could either continue with its present 'multiple-indicator approach' to monetary policy or adopt inflation targeting, despite the presence of weak transmission channels as mentioned above. In the latter case, there is scope for using a monetary aggregate as an instrument of monetary policy.

Until recently the prevailing view was that monetary targeting for price stability requires a stable money-demand function to establish a causal linkage between money supply growth and inflation. The recent literature suggests that a causal relation exists between money supply growth and inflation irrespective of the exchange rate regime, and whether or not the money-demand function is stable (McCallum and Nelson, 2011). Nevertheless, this section examines whether there exists a stable money-demand function in India.[7] For estimation purposes, an open-economy money-demand function is specified as follows:

$$\begin{aligned} LRJM_t = \alpha_0 + \alpha_1\, Ly_t + \alpha_2\, NIR_t + \alpha_3\, FIR_t \\ + \alpha_4\, LER_t + \alpha_5 \pi_t^v + u_t \end{aligned} \quad (5.1)$$

where LRJM (J = N, B) is the log of real narrow or broad money balances (LRNM represents the log of real narrow money balances and LRBM represents the log of real broad money balances), Ly is the log of real income, NIR is a representative nominal interest rate, FIR is a representative foreign interest rate such as the US Federal funds rate, LER is the log of the exchange rate (nominal or real), π_t^v is a measure of inflation volatility and u_t is a random error term with zero mean and a constant variance. In this specification, real income represents the scale variable and the coefficient on it is expected to bear a positive sign. Since the 1960s, the Indian economy has grown steadily and there has been rapid monetization of the economy. Consequently, the income elasticity of demand for money may exceed unity.

The coefficients on the interest rates are expected to bear a negative sign. However, as reviewed in Appendix 5, the signs of the coefficients on the exchange rate and inflation volatility remain indeterminate a priori.

The unit root test results suggest that each variable in the model has a unit root, rendering them eligible to be tested for cointegration. The model was initially estimated by the Johansen cointegration techniques. The test results indicate the presence of at least one cointegral relation among these variables. However, the coefficient values of the variables are found highly sensitive to the inclusion of trends, intercepts and lag terms. The model is then estimated using both the ARDL and OLS/DOLS. Although both the narrow and broad definitions of money are used for estimation purposes, the results obtained by the narrow definition of money are used for interpretation. The test results are reported in Table 5.5. Although both the ARDL and OLS results are similar, the results obtained by the ARDL technique are used for interpretation. The test results suggest the presence of cointegration among real narrow money balances, real income and the foreign interest rate. The coefficients on the real exchange rate and inflation volatility are not statistically significant.

A series of stability tests, including the CUSUM and CUSUMSQ of residuals (Figure 5.8), is conducted which suggests that the narrow money-demand function is more stable than the broad money-demand function. Narrow money demand became unstable in the 1990s but has stabilized.

Relationships Among Money, Output and Prices

The ARDL bounds-test results suggest that money, output and prices have a cointegral relationship (Table 5.6). The bounds-test results suggest the presence of a long-run relation among money, output and prices in India. The error-correction model associated with the long-run relation bears a negative sign. Along with the long-run relation among money, output and prices, the money-growth rate has a positive impact on inflation.

Engle and Granger (1987) suggest that one of the implications of a cointegral relation between two nonstationary variables is the presence of long-term causality between them running in at least one direction. Table 5.7 reports the bivariate Granger-causality test results among LCPI, LNM (or LBM) and LRGDP. Test results are generated within both these

Table 5.5 The ARDL and OLS regression results for long-run real narrow money-demand relationships in India

F-statistic	3.2			
W-statistic	15.99			
Critical value bounds	F-test	W-test		
90%	(2.56, 3.73)	(12.80, 18.64)		
95%	(3.07, 4.33)	(15.37, 21.64)		
Sample period	1957–2012	1957–2012	1955–2012	1955–2012
	ARDL (1,0,0,0,0)	ARDL (1,0,0,0,0)	OLS	OLS
	(Selected based on SBC)	Long-run model	(Static model)	(Dynamic model)
Regressors	Coefficient (t-ratio) [prob.]	Coefficient (t-ratio) [prob.]	Coefficient (t-ratio) [prob.]	Coefficient (t-ratio) [prob.]
Intercept	2.30 (3.32) [0.00]	4.39 (14.54) [0.00]	4.54 (26.86) [0.00]	1.81 (2.95) [0.01]
LRNM(−1)	0.48 (3.44) [0.00]			0.57 (4.56) [0.00]
LRGDP	0.56 (3.67) [0.00]	1.07 (26.40) [0.00]	1.06 (44.10) [0.00]	0.45 (3.39) [0.00]
USFFR	−0.01 (−1.94) [0.06]	−0.01 (−2.15) [0.04]	−0.01 (−4.32) [0.00]	−0.01 (−2.07) [0.04]
LRER	−0.06 (−1.04) [0.30]	−0.11 (−1.22) [0.23]	−0.14 (−2.82) [0.00]	0.02 (0.36) [0.72]
INFVOL	0.01 (0.73) [0.47]	0.02 (0.72) [0.48]	0.03 (1.57) [0.12]	0.02 (1.24) [0.22]
Diagnostics				
Adjusted R^2	0.99		0.98	0.99

Lagrange multiplier test for serial correlation	$F(1, 49) = 0.12$ [0.73]		$F(1, 52) = 9.46$ [0.00]	$F(1, 51) = 0.02$ [0.90]
Ramsey's RESET test of functional form mis-specification	$F(1, 49) = 1.35$ [0.25]		$F(1, 52) = 8.60$ [0.01]	$F(1, 51) = 3.75$ [0.06]
Normality of residuals	$\chi^2_{(2)} = 3.21$ [0.20]		$\chi^2_{(2)} = 0.28$ [0.87]	$\chi^2_{(2)} = 7.28$ [0.03]
Heteroskedasticity	$F(1, 54) = 0.36$ [0.35]		$F(1, 56) = 0.05$ [0.82]	$F(1, 56) = 0.77$ [0.38]
The Wald test:				
H_O: Coefficient on LRGDP = 0		$\chi^2_{(1)} = 696.73$ [0.00]	$\chi^2_{(1)} = 1944.8$ [0.00]	
H_O: Coefficient on LRGDP = 1		$\chi^2_{(1)} = 3.37$ [0.07]	$\chi^2_{(1)} = 5.62$ [0.02]	
H_O: Coefficient on USFFR = 0		$\chi^2_{(1)} = 4.63$ [0.03]	$\chi^2_{(1)} = 18.70$ [0.00]	
H_O: Coefficient on LRER = 0		$\chi^2_{(1)} = 1.49$ [0.22]	$\chi^2_{(1)} = 7.94$ [0.01]	
H_O: Coefficient on INFVOL = 0		$\chi^2_{(1)} = 0.52$ [0.47]	$\chi^2_{(1)} = 2.45$ [0.12]	

Note: Definitions of variables: LRNM = log of real narrow money balances; LRGDP = log of real GDP; USFFR = US Federal funds rate; LRER = log of the bilateral real exchange rate against the US dollar; INFVOL = inflation volatility; ARDL = autoregressive distributed lag; and SBC = Schwarz Bayesian Criterion.

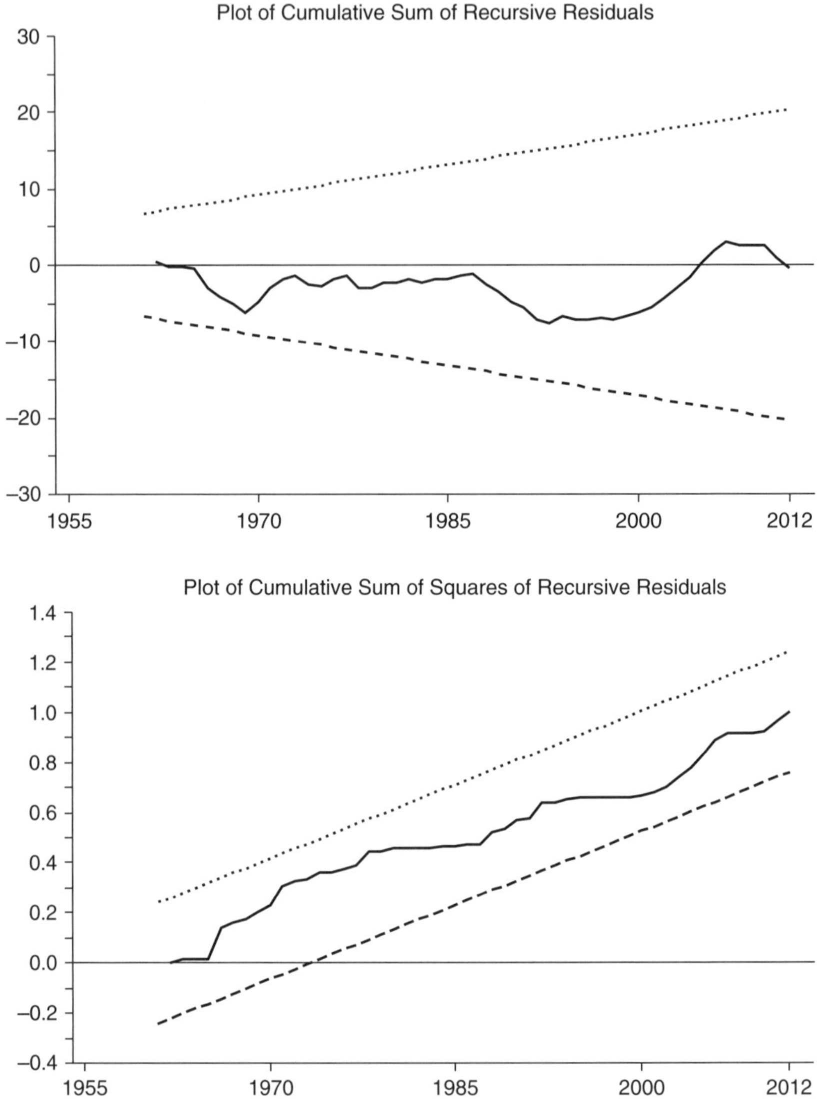

Note: The straight lines represent critical bounds at 5% significance level.

Figure 5.8 CUSUM and CUSUMSQ of residuals for real narrow money-demand relationships in India

Table 5.6 The ARDL bounds-test results among money, output and prices in India

Dependent variable = LCPI								
	Fully modified OLS				Dynamic OLS			
With narrow money (NM)					(lead = 1, lag = 1)			
Regressor	coefficient	t-ratio	prob.		coefficient	t-ratio	prob.	
Intercept	1.04	3.92	0.00		1.48	4.88	0.00	
LNM	1.03	10.49	0.00		1.14	11.17	0.00	
LRGDP	−1.19	4.88	0		−1.48	−5.79	0	
Sample period	1970–2012				1970–2011			
DW	1.14				0.63			
Adjusted R^2	0.99				0.99			
	tau-statistic	prob.	z-statistic	prob.	tau-statistic	prob.	z-statistic	prob.
The Engle-Granger cointegration tests	−3.48	0.13	42.47	0.99	−3.48	0.13	42.47	0.99
The Phillips-Ouliaris cointegration tests	−3.57	0.11	−21.36	0.06	−3.57	0.11	−21.36	0.06
With broad money (BM)					(lead = 1, lag = 1)			
Regressor	coefficient	t-ratio	prob.		coefficient	t-ratio	prob.	
Intercept	0.37	1.36	0.18		0.69	2.05	0.05	
LBM	0.64	7.81	0.00		0.64	7.42	0.00	
LRGDP	−0.48	−2.02	0.05		−0.47	−1.89	0.07	
Sample	1970–2012				1970–2011			
DW	0.52				0.4			
Adjusted R^2	0.99				0.99			
	tau-statistic	prob.	z-statistic	prob.	tau-statistic	prob.	z-statistic	prob.
The Engle-Granger cointegration tests	−2.46	0.52	−10.82	0.5	−2.46	0.52	−10.82	0.5
The Phillips-Ouliaris cointegration tests	−2.64	0.43	−12.77	0.4	−2.64	0.43	−12.8	0.37

Note: Definitions of variables: LCPI = log of the consumer price index; LNM = log of narrow money stock; LBM = log of broad money stock; and LRGDP = log of real GDP.

Table 5.7 Granger-causality among LCPI, LNM/LBM and LRGDP, 1950–2012

	Hypotheses No causality runs from:	Chi-square statistic (prob.)	Inference at 5% level
VEC specification	ΔLNM $\rightarrow$ ΔLCPI	7.20 (0.03)	Null hypothesis rejected
(With narrow money, NM)	ΔLNM, ΔLRGDP $\rightarrow$ ΔLCPI	22.26 (0.00)	Null hypothesis rejected
	ΔLCPI $\rightarrow$ ΔLNM	13.45 (0.00)	Null hypothesis rejected
	ΔLRGDP $\rightarrow$ ΔLNM	0.64 (0.73)	Null hypothesis not rejected
	ΔLCPI $\rightarrow$ ΔLRGDP	2.87 (0.24)	Null hypothesis not rejected
	ΔLNM $\rightarrow$ ΔLRGDP	7.60 (0.02)	Null hypothesis rejected
VEC specification	ΔLBM $\rightarrow$ ΔLCPI	4.94 (0.08)	Null hypothesis not rejected
(With broad money, BM)	ΔLBM, ΔLRGDP $\rightarrow$ ΔLCPI	21.75 (0.00)	Null hypothesis rejected
	ΔLCPI $\rightarrow$ ΔLBM	2.09 (0.35)	Null hypothesis not rejected
	ΔLRGDP $\rightarrow$ ΔLBM	4.25 (0.12)	Null hypothesis not rejected
	ΔLCPI $\rightarrow$ ΔLRGDP	0.25 (0.88)	Null hypothesis not rejected
	ΔLBM $\rightarrow$ ΔLRGDP	2.06 (0.36)	Null hypothesis not rejected

Note: Definitions of variables: LCPI = log of the consumer price index; LNM = log of narrow money stock; LBM = log of broad money stock; and LRGDP = log of real GDP. Optimal lag-length = 2 (selected based on the Schwarz Bayesian Criterion).

modelling frameworks after selecting the optimal lag-length using the Schwarz Bayesian Criterion (SBC). The results suggest that for India, there is causality running from narrow or broad money to prices.

SUMMARY AND CONCLUSION

India's economy is in transition. Since the early 1990s India has moved away from a heavily regulated, slow-growing economy to a deregulated, high-growth, flexible, open economy. This chapter has provided an overview of the design and conduct of Indian monetary policy in an historical perspective. Although India is a relatively low-inflation country and policymakers are generally conservative, inflation has remained moderately high and volatile. India followed monetary targeting from the mid 1980s until the late 1990s. Under its pegged exchange rate system, monetary policy would have been dictated by that of the anchor country (the United States), had capital controls not conferred upon it some limited independence. One major problem faced by India is volatile inflation although inflation remains low on average. It originates from multiple sources, especially an ad hoc nature of monetary policy and monetization of frequent supply shocks. Since financial reform began in the early 1990s, price stability has emerged as one of the pressing objectives of monetary policy while emphasis remains on economic growth.

India moved on financial reform following the balance-of-payments crisis of 1991. The main goal of this reform was to improve the efficiency of the financial sector and the economy; and to provide a solid foundation for a monetary policy transmission mechanism comprised of strong interest rate and exchange rate channels. Accordingly, interest rates have been made somewhat flexible and some controls over credit allocations have been removed. The nominal exchange rate is yet to be fully market determined. The monetary authorities appear to follow a monetary policy of real exchange rate targeting with the goal of enhancing exports. Financial stability is considered an important objective of monetary policy. The Indian banking system is dominated by state banks, which remain inefficient and, despite reform, still substantially take government instructions on credit allocation. The RBI is not anxious to adopt inflation targeting, for several reasons. Firstly, the structure of India's economy exposes it to frequent supply shocks, thereby reducing the efficacy of inflation-targeted monetary policy for India. This is due to the significant role that structural factors and supply shocks are thought to play in generating inflation. Secondly, large budget deficits dominate monetary policy and management.[8] Thirdly, the interest rate channel of the monetary transmission mechanism remains weak. Fourthly, limitations on the availability of high-frequency data constrain the adoption of inflation targeting, which requires reliable inflation forecasts.

This chapter has investigated money-demand behaviour in India. The narrow money-demand function is found to be stable relative to the broad money-demand function. Inflation volatility is not found significant in the narrow money-demand function. Further empirical results suggest a strong causal link between narrow money growth and inflation. The question remains whether India should switch to inflation targeting. There is a strong case for such a move because, if fully implemented, it would raise monetary policy's transparency, contribute towards price stability and create an optimal environment in which India could pursue a maximum efficient rate of long-term growth and development. However, for India, the interest rate may not be effective as an instrument of monetary policy. Monetary aggregates could be used as an instrument of monetary policy while implementing a floating exchange rate system.

As there is the possibility, at least in the transitional process, of high exchange rate volatility, market-based capital controls could be an option. The aim of such controls would be to smooth the volatility of capital flows, not to stop them altogether. For sustained economic growth, capital mobility is ultimately required for long-term capital accumulation and technical progress. Despite wide-ranging reforms, the government remains cautious on convertibility of the capital account.[9]

NOTES

1. Some general discussion on central banking and monetary policy in India is drawn from various publications available on the website of the Reserve Bank of India (RBI), http:/ www.rbi.org.in/home.aspx, Joshi and Little (1994), Reddy (1999, 2002, 2007), Hossain and Rashid (1996) and Rangarajan (2009).
2. Some general information on the RBI is drawn from the Reserve Bank of India, available at http://en.wikipedia.org/wiki/Reserve_Bank_of_India (accessed 19 March 2015).
3. This subsection is based on Joshi and Little (1996).
4. Joshi and Little (1994, p. 244) summed up India's monetary policy stance during pre-reform period as follows: 'Monetary policy in India is not wholly subsidiary to fiscal policy nor is it heavily constrained by the balance of payments. Though there is a link between fiscal deficits and the supply of money, this can be weakened by instruments at the disposal of the authorities. The exchange rate is managed (and has sometimes been fixed for long periods) but exchange controls on capital movements have been effective enough to permit substantial monetary independence.'
5. Bentour and Razzak (2009) have highlighted this problem under a pegged exchange rate system. When the domestic inflation rate (π) exceeds the foreign inflation rate (π^*), the domestic real interest rate (r) becomes much lower than the foreign real interest rate (r^*). This suggests that if the foreign real interest rate falls to very low levels or even zero, then the domestic real interest rate becomes negative. This may generate a boom-bust cycle.

6. As India operates under a pegged exchange rate system, a sustained deviation of inflation in India from US inflation affects contemporaneously the real exchange rate. Real exchange rate misalignment in turn may affect the rate of inflation by changing the demand for, and hence the prices of, non-tradables. As the nominal interest rate mimics the US interest rate, any sustained deviation of inflation in India from US inflation also affects the real interest rate and in turn saving, investment and economic growth.
7. For some earlier studies on money demand in India, see Moosa (1992), Bhattacharya (1995), Das and Mandal (2000) and Rao and Singh (2006).
8. The significance of market rate sales of Treasury securities is that the volume of securities necessary to finance the budget deficit is sold to the public, and the government pays the going market price for its borrowings. As an alternative method of financing the budget deficit, the government still prepares a volume of securities sufficient to finance its budget deficit. However, it sets the rate that it wishes to pay on this debt and is therefore unable to sell to the public any more than the volume that the public demands at that rate. To minimize their borrowing costs, governments invariably set the rate on their securities below the going market rate. Public demand for government securities is therefore limited and some government securities remain unsold. To meet the looming shortfall in financing the budget deficit, governments sell the undemanded leftover bonds to the central bank, thereby printing money to finance the budget deficit or monetizing the budget deficit. This causes an expansion in the money supply that is generally thought to be inflationary.
9. As suggested in the text, current account transactions were made currency-convertible in 1994. Foreign direct investment has been allowed only since 1991. Some foreign portfolio investment by institutional investors (such as pension funds and mutual funds) has been allowed since 1991. Such funds are permitted to invest in both primary and secondary markets for equities and bonds of publicly listed companies. Since 1997 foreign institutional investors have been allowed to invest in government securities and Treasury bills. Capital income and capital gains are allowed to be repatriated at the market exchange rates.

REFERENCES

Ahluwalia, I.J. and I.M.D. Little (eds) (1998), *India's Economic Reforms and Development*, Delhi: Oxford University Press.

Ahluwalia, M. (2002), 'Economic reforms since 1991: has gradualism worked?', *Journal of Economic Perspectives*, **16**(3), 67–88.

Bentour, E.M. and W.A. Razzak (2009), 'Real interest rates, bubbles and monetary policy in the GCC countries', Unpublished manuscript, Arab Planning Institute.

Bhagwati, J.N. (1992), *India's Economy: The Shackled Giant*, Oxford: Clarendon Press.

Bhagwati, J.N. (1993), *India in Transition: Freeing the Economy*, Oxford: Clarendon Press.

Bhattacharya, K. (2005), 'Monetary policy approaches in India', BIS Papers No. 31, Monetary Policy in Asia: Approaches and Implementation, Bank for International Settlements, Basel.

Bhattacharya, R. (1995), 'Cointegrating relationships in the demand for money in India', *Indian Economic Journal*, **43**(1), 69–75.

Chopra, A., C. Collyns, R. Hemming and K. Parker (1995), 'India: economic reform and growth', Occasional Paper No. 134, International Monetary Fund, Washington, DC.

Das, S. and K. Mandal (2000), 'Modeling money demand in India: testing weak, strong and super exogeneity', *Indian Economic Review*, **35**(1), 1–19.

Dornbusch, R. and S. Edwards (1990), 'The macroeconomics of populism in Latin America', *Journal of Development Economics*, **32**, 247–77.

Dornbusch, R. and S. Edwards (1991), *The Macroeconomics of Populism in Latin America*, Chicago, IL: University of Chicago Press.

Dua, P. and A. Sinha (2007), 'Insulation of India from the East Asian crisis: an analysis', *Singapore Economic Review*, **52**(3), 419–43.

Dua, P. and A. Sinha (2008), 'Insulation of India from the East Asia crisis: an analysis', in P.S.L. Yip (ed.), *Exchange Rate Systems and Policies in Asia*, Singapore: World Scientific, pp. 135–59.

Engle, R.F. and C.W.J. Granger (1987), 'Co-integration and error-correction: representation, estimation, and testing', *Econometrica*, **55**(2), 251–76.

Hossain, A. and S. Rashid (1996), *In Quest of Development: The Political Economy of South Asia*, Dhaka: University Press Limited.

IMF (International Monetary Fund) (various years), *International Financial Statistics*, Washington, DC: IMF.

IMF (International Monetary Fund) (various years), *World Economic Outlook*, Washington, DC: IMF.

IMF (International Monetary Fund) (various years), Country and consultation reports, available at http://www.imf.org.

Joshi, V. and I. Little (1994), *India: Macroeconomics and Political Economy*, New Delhi: Oxford University Press.

Joshi, V. and I. Little (1996), *India's Economic Reforms 1991–2001*, New Delhi: Oxford University Press.

Joshi, V. and S. Sanyal (2004), 'Foreign inflows and macroeconomic policy in India', *India Policy Forum*, **1**, 135–79.

McCallum, B.T. and E. Nelson (2011), 'Money and inflation: some critical issues', in B.M. Friedman and M. Woodford (eds), *Handbook of Monetary Economics*, Vol. 3A, Amsterdam: Elsevier Science, pp. 97–153.

Macfarlane, I.J. (1998), 'Australian monetary policy in the last quarter of the twentieth century', *Reserve Bank of Australia Bulletin*, October, 6–19.

Mohan, R. (2008), 'Monetary policy transmission in India', BIS Papers No. 35, Bank for International Settlements, Basel, 259–307.

Moosa, I. (1992), 'The demand for money in India: a cointegration approach', *Indian Economic Journal*, **40**(1), 101–15.

Rangarajan, C. (2009), *India: Monetary Policy, Financial Stability and Other Essays*, New Delhi: Academic Foundation.

Rao, B.B. and R. Singh (2006), 'Demand for money in India: 1953–2003', *Applied Economics*, **38**(11), 1319–26.

RBI (Reserve Bank of India), http://www.rbi.org.in/home.aspx.

Reddy, Y.V. (1999), 'Monetary policy in India', *BIS Review* **621**.

Reddy, Y.V. (2002), 'Parameters of monetary policy in India', *BIS Review* **3**.

Reddy, Y.V. (2007), 'Evolving role of the Reserve Bank of India – recent developments', Speech by Dr Y.V. Reddy, Governor of the Reserve Bank of India, Jaipur, 30 June.

Sen, P. (2007), 'Capital inflows, financial repression, and macroeconomic policy in India since the reforms,' *Oxford Review of Economic Policy*, **23**(2), 292–310.

6. Japan

Japan comprises about 7000 islands situated off the east coast of China, Korea and Russia. It is located on a vast volcanic zone that all but encircles the Pacific Ocean, known as the Pacific Ring of Fire. All of Japan is therefore exposed with relatively high frequency to earthquakes, tsunami and volcanic eruptions.[1] Japan is relatively land-scarce in so far as productive capacity is concerned. About 73 per cent of its land mass is forested mountains unsuitable for agricultural, industrial or urban settlement. Consequently, most habitable zones are located on coastal plains.

Japan's social, cultural and economic institutions, deep-rooted in ancient cultural traditions, guide its otherwise modern economy. Japanese society is generally viewed as homogeneous, socially conservative and cohesive. This cultural capital contributed powerfully to Japan's rapid economic growth and dynamism during its 'industrial takeoff' phase of development from the 1950s through the 1980s. However, the Japanese economic slowdown from the early 1990s has called into question the strength of social conformities on most matters of economic organization, management and decision-making.

Japan became the second largest economy in the world in the 1980s and remained so until surpassed in the mid 2000s by China. Nevertheless, Japan's post-World War II economic history remains important and fascinating for understanding economic growth dynamics in developing countries. It was the first Asian country to gain the status of a developed country within just one generation. Japan has also played a leadership role and remained so in facilitating rapid economic growth in most countries in Southeast and East Asia (Ichimura, 1993; Ito, 1997). As a consequence of its development success, the Japanese economy is now heavily integrated with most countries in the Asian-Pacific region.

Having encountered a host of damaging economic, social and political problems since the 1990s, and following numerous attempted solutions, Japan has yet to devise effective strategies to tackle these problems and set back on track the future course of its economy, society and polity.

One of the major problems is demographic. Japan's present population numbers about 127 million, while its population density is one of the highest in the world, at about 337 per square kilometre. It is an ageing population, with a life expectancy averaging 84 years; again one of the world's highest. The consequent rapid change in the Japanese demographic structure has created economic and social problems.

A second major concern for policymakers has been Japan's economic stagnation since the early 1990s. Japan confronts a challenging macro-financial environment that is considered inimical to economic growth. Deflationary pressure remains, growth is sluggish and public debt and budget deficits are massive. In this deflationary environment, a high real interest rate has led to reduced demand for credit. Investment has dried up due to a dearth of feasible projects, or reluctance to initiate cost-benefit analyses on potential projects, or both. A flat yield curve indicates the possibility of falling prices and the consequent low corporate profitability and investment (Ito, 2004a, 2006).

Problems and issues in Japanese macroeconomic management in general have therefore become an important focus of monetary policy research. The roles of fiscal and monetary policies in economic recovery have indeed generated interest among researchers and policymakers across the globe. The remainder of this chapter provides an overview of the evolution of monetary policy in Japan in the context of its economic growth dynamics since the 1960s. Issues in the design and conduct of monetary policy for price stability are then highlighted.

OVERVIEW OF JAPAN'S RECENT ECONOMIC AND POLITICAL HISTORY

The foundations of the modern Japanese economy were laid following the Meiji restoration of 1868, at the end of the Tokugawa shogunate. The pace of Japan's economic progress from the 1960s through the 1980s was so impressive that it was considered a post-war 'economic miracle'. Perhaps the most significant element of the Japanese 'miracle' is the fact that most of Japan's modern infrastructure had been destroyed in World War II, leaving Japanese society devastated and its economy with it.

While Japan remains the world's third largest economy by gross GDP, in terms of the purchasing power parity (PPP) measure it ranks fourth after the United States, China and India. Considerable debate remains over the sources of Japan's modern economic growth, but there is consensus that the sources of the Japanese economic miracle can be found largely in its implementation of the export-oriented development strategy. This strategy took anything but a laissez-faire approach. Rather, there was government regulation of imports and capital flows until the 1980s. The financial system was repressed and used until the 1980s to implement government measures targeted at rapid industrialization and growth. Only since the 1990s has Japan opened up its economy to imports and foreign investment in some sectors (Suzuki, 1981, 1985, 1992). Presently Japan is the fourth largest exporter and fourth largest importer in the world.

In addition to building the most advanced industrial economy in Asia, Japan has emerged as a major investor in East Asia. Its investment in European and North American countries is substantial and increasing. In global trade and direct investment, Japanese companies dominate in the fields of electronics, automobiles, heavy machinery, earthquake engineering, industrial robotics, optics, chemicals, semiconductors and metals.

As an outcome of the large scale of its industrialization and associated economic growth, the Japanese economy has undergone major structural change since the 1960s. A full three quarters of Japan's GDP now originate in the services sector. This sector's productivity growth, however, remains far lower than that of the tradable sector, manufacturing in particular. Much of the difference can be attributed to policy protection of the services sector from foreign competition. A fundamental question has therefore emerged, in the context of its two decade-long stagnation, as to whether Japan's growth model has structural weaknesses.

The Japanese model of economic organization possesses the distinctive features of *keiretsu* enterprises, lifetime employment and seniority-based career advancement. Until the 1980s these features of industrial organization and labour markets were considered pillars of economic strength and a model of economic growth with equity. In more recent times they are viewed as the major constraints on Japan's prospect of economic recovery from deep recession in a deflationary environment. The economic vibrancy that was once a hallmark of the Japanese economy has been in decline since the 1980s. Japan's economic difficulties have exposed possible structural flaws in Japanese society. Japanese ethnic homogeneity, an ageing population, together with cultural customs such as social conformity, consensus-oriented economic and political leadership and its patriarchical-societal norms have all come under scrutiny for possible roles in the economic malaise. Such considerations suggest the fundamental notion that Japan's growth problem may be structural, not cyclical.

One common perception is that to regain growth momentum, Japan could undertake deep labour market reform, major financial sector reform and open up the agricultural and services sectors for foreign investment and competition. Japan's demographic problems, in particular, may be fundamental and could be long-lasting, requiring large-scale immigration from developing countries of the Asia-Pacific region. The major impacts of this upon Japanese society and culture are likely to create social tension and political instability. Resolution could not then emerge until and unless

Japanese society became prepared to revisit and reconstruct its foundations in such a way as to lead to a consensus among the various stakeholders in the society on some fundamental issues in the Japanese economy, society and polity in a global context.[2]

Struggling as it is to recover from the recession that started in the early 1990s, there is debate on the roles of monetary and fiscal policies in economic growth and stabilization. The role of the exchange rate remains critical for the operation of the ongoing outward-oriented growth model. Historically, the major breakthrough in Japan's economic growth came in the 1960s with the emergence of its export-oriented development strategy. At the time it appeared that this was facilitated by an undervalued yen[3] real exchange rate. Throughout the post-World War II reconstruction that yielded rapid economic growth in Europe and North America, the Korean War (1950–53) and the protracted American War in Vietnam, Japanese labour-intensive exportable products continued in high demand in those countries until the early 1970s. This large stimulus kick-started the Japanese economy and led to its rapid economic growth and an associated high degree of transformation in its economic structure. Japan then experienced sustained economic growth averaging around 9 per cent per annum in 1956–70.

This rate fell sharply, however, roughly halving over the period 1971–90. Recession in Western economies, originating from the OPEC oil price shocks, and a secular appreciation of Japan's real exchange rate lowered its exports and hence reduced economic growth. Japanese authorities waited until the early 1980s, when the lower average growth over the 1970s looked like declining further, to implement an expansionary monetary policy. The policy was sustained sufficiently to create an asset bubble that finally emerged during the late 1980s. Sharp contractionary monetary policy burst this bubble. For example, the broad money-growth rate during 1986–90 was 10.4 per cent per annum, which fell to 2.1 per cent per annum during 1991–95. Since early 1990s, however, Japan's corporate and financial sectors have experienced massive problems, such as reduced demand and low profitability and loan defaults, and the economy has remained moribund in a deflationary environment. Annual average inflation over the period 1991–2012 was close to zero (Table 6.1).

Since the early 1990s both the recession, and policy attempts to generate recovery have persisted. Fiscal policy was deployed heavily from the onset of the recession. The principal consequence has been steady accumulation of public debt to more than 230 per cent of GDP. This is the highest level of public debt in an advanced country and has emerged as a major constraint on continued use of fiscal policy as an instrument of economic recovery. Facing the limits of fiscal policy, the government turned to expansionary

Table 6.1 Macroeconomic indicators, Japan, 1950–2012

Macroeconomic indicators	1951–55	1956–60	1961–65	1966–70	1971–75	1976–80	1981–85	1986–90	1991–95	1996–2000	2001–05	2006–10	2011	2012
Budget balance (% of GDP)	n.a.	n.a.	n.a.	n.a.	n.a.	−4.8	−3.4	0.3	−1.8	−6.3	−6.5	−5.9	−9.8	−10.0
General government gross debt (% of GDP)	n.a.	n.a.	n.a.	n.a.	n.a.	50.6	62.5	69.4	77.9	119.0	170.9	197.3	229.6	236.6
Money growth rate (%)														
Narrow money growth	n.a.	13.5	19.5	15.8	18.7	7.0	5.1	6.1	7.5	7.7	15.3	0.8	5.1	3.5
Broad money growth	n.a.	19.2	19.9	16.2	18.9	11.9	8.3	10.4	2.1	3.3	2.2	2.0	2.7	2.5
Real GDP growth rate (%)	n.a.	8.8	7.1	11.0	4.4	4.8	4.3	5.0	1.4	0.9	1.2	0.4	−0.6	2.3
GDP per capita, current prices, US dollar	n.a.	n.a.	n.a.	n.a.	n.a.	9312	10423	22305	35233	35006	33979	37633	45870	46896
Unemployment rate (%)	n.a.	n.a.	n.a.	n.a.	n.a.	2.0	2.5	2.5	2.6	4.0	5.0	4.4	4.6	4.3
Output gap (% of potential GDP)	n.a.	n.a.	n.a.	n.a.	n.a.	−6.5	−3.6	0.7	0.4	−0.5	−1.3	−2.3	−4.0	−2.2
CPI inflation rate (%)	6.7	1.5	6.1	5.5	11.6	6.6	2.8	1.3	1.4	0.3	−0.4	−0.1	−0.3	0.0
Current account balance (% of GDP)	n.a.	n.a.	n.a.	n.a.	n.a.	−1.0	1.8	2.7	2.5	2.4	3.1	3.7	2.0	1.6

Table 6.1 (continued)

Macroeconomic indicators	1951–55	1956–60	1961–65	1966–70	1971–75	1976–80	1981–85	1986–90	1991–95	1996–2000	2001–05	2006–10	2011	2012
Nominal interest rate (%)														
Lending rate of interest	9.1	8.3	7.9	7.5	8.0	7.4	7.1	5.7	5.2	2.3	1.8	1.8	1.5	1.4
Government bond yield	n.a.	n.a.	n.a.	7.0	7.9	7.8	7.5	5.2	4.3	1.7	1.3	1.5	1.1	0.8
Treasury bill rate	n.a.	n.a.	n.a.	n.a.	n.a.	n.a.	n.a.	n.a.	n.a.	n.a.	0.0	0.3	0.1	0.1
Real interest rate (%)[a]														
Lending rate of interest	5.0	6.8	1.8	1.9	−2.9	0.7	4.3	4.3	3.8	2.0	2.3	1.8	1.8	1.4
Government bond yield	n.a.	n.a.	n.a.	1.5	−3.0	1.1	4.6	3.8	2.9	1.4	1.7	1.6	1.4	0.9
Treasury bill rate											0.5	0.4	0.4	0.1
Nominal exchange rate (yen per dollar)	360.4	360.0	360.0	360.0	302.9	244.3	236.6	144.8	113.8	116.5	116.3	103.8	79.8	79.8
Nominal effective exchange rate[b]	n.a.	21.0	23.0	24.4	28.5	36.0	43.8	70.5	94.8	101.0	103.3	104.3	129.8	133.5
Real effective exchange rate[b, c]	36.4	37.4	43.4	49.2	67.2	91.6	77.3	113.6	132.5	116.1	100.8	99.7	119.1	116.6

Notes:
n.a. = not available
a. Real interest rate is estimated as: 100(((1 + interest rate)/(1 + inflation rate))−1) where the interest rate and inflation rate are expressed as decimal.
b. A rise in the index value of the exchange rate represents appreciation.
c. Real exchange rate: data for the period 1951–70 represents the bilateral real exchange rate of the Japanese yen against the US dollar.

Source: Author's computation based on IMF, *International Financial Statistics*; IMF, *World Economic Outlook*; and country-specific publications on the IMF website.

monetary policy as a last resort while attempting fiscal consolidation. The conduct of monetary policy, however, has been half-hearted in commitment and non-transparent with respect to its goal. In an environment of very low or negative inflation, the real interest rate has remained positive and high for most of the recessionary period. Broad money growth has averaged around 2.5 per cent per annum over the period 1991–2012.[4]

At least two reasons may explain why Japan has not conducted sustained expansionary monetary policy since the late 1990s. Firstly, both the IMF and the US government put pressure on the Japanese government not to depreciate the yen. The argument was that a sharp depreciation of Japanese currency would slow economic recovery in East-Southeast Asia, then in devastation under the financial crisis of 1997–98. Furthermore, a sharp depreciation of Japan's real exchange rate would raise its trade surplus with the United States, potentially leading to trade friction between them. In the event, the real exchange rate depreciated somewhat during the mid 2000s but has shown an appreciating trend since 2011 (see Table 6.1). Secondly, Japan's central bank, the Bank of Japan (BOJ), was delegated some degree of monetary policy autonomy in 1998. It has consequently been reluctant to risk losing control over inflation by implementing expansionary monetary policy. It is suggested that monetary expansion would undermine BOJ policy credibility, and thereby its status as a conservative institution with responsibility to maintain price stability (Ito, 2004a). Consequently, inflation has remained low or negative, with the authorities failing to, or refusing to, generate higher inflationary expectations. Instead, the restrictive stance of monetary policy has been manifested in low asset prices, especially the prices of corporate shares and of land. Naturally this has been problematic, both for the corporate and for the financial sectors.

In the midst of deep recession, the debate continues over the extent to which Japan's ongoing deflation is due primarily to demand or to supply factors. Also in question is whether deflation was the cause or the consequence of economic recession and stagnation. In its early stages, 1997–99, deflation was considered good for consumers and for the economy. Two related arguments supported this view. Firstly, it was considered a global phenomenon; a benefit of the technological revolution. The argument went that technical progress in information and communications technology had lowered the prices of most goods and services. This was the 'New Economy' argument being put forward to explain the 'great moderation' in the United States, which sustained for around two decades rapid economic growth in a low-inflation environment. Secondly, cheap imports from China and South Korea, consequential partly on the technological revolution and partly on Japan's pioneering success in export-oriented development policy, were considered beneficent as a further downward influence on Japanese prices.

These interpretations have since been discredited. Firstly, the relative price changes that technical progress brought did not lead to deflation. Technological innovation mostly lowered the relative prices of products made using heavy inputs of information and communication technologies. The prices of all goods and services, reflected in the general price level, derived from other factors, especially from the stance of monetary policy and from the general level of income. Secondly, although the debate continues, the argument can be made that deflation was not a supply-side phenomenon. Assuming normal aggregate demand and aggregate supply curves, a *ceteris paribus* shift of the supply curve to the right would raise output and lower prices. In Japan, the decline in the general price level was associated with a decrease in output. In short, the Japanese experience has been recession and deflation, not boom and deflation as would be expected from a technological revolution.

In the midst of such macroeconomic developments and scenarios, then, what are the efficient, comparative advantage roles of fiscal and monetary policies in raising and sustaining economic growth in a low-inflationary environment? This issue can usefully be considered in an historical context. During Japan's high-growth phase, through the 1950s and 1960s, monetary policy was subordinate to fiscal and commercial policies as economic growth was prioritized above other policy objectives. Monetary policy has risen in importance since the late 1990s, partly because the BOJ has been reluctant to apply the policy autonomy that it gained in 1998 to expansionary monetary policy. This stance has become controversial. Japan has now entered into a state of economic stagnation where there is a danger that the BOJ may lose its policy autonomy unless it undertakes monetary policy measures to facilitate economic recovery. A question that may exercise the minds of the BOJ board is whether or not monetary policy is sufficiently powerful to bring sustainable economic recovery in the presence of both economic and political constraints.

A further BOJ policy stance has come under scrutiny. In implementing its brief to target low, stable inflation, the BOJ does not deploy rule-based monetary policy to maintain low and stable inflation (Ito, 2004b). While it may pursue some implicit inflation target, its discretionary conduct of monetary policy has failed to generate inflationary expectations sufficiently high to generate economic recovery. Japan has encountered the limits to fiscal policy, but expansionary monetary policy also has its limits. While technically a large monetary policy easing could kick-start a long-awaited recovery by means of significant currency depreciation, it could not do so without attracting retaliation from its major trading partners, especially the United States. While the United States has managed to depreciate its currency steadily following the US-global financial crisis, Japan is in no position to follow suit.

Having failed for so long to generate high-inflationary expectations from a two decade-long deflation trap (IMF, 1988), the BOJ in 2013 set a 2 per cent inflation target in a new initiative to rescue the economy using as the instrument a massive monetary expansion, to be implemented across a timeframe of about two years. The monetary expansion is to be brought about through large-scale purchases of both government bonds and private assets that include commercial papers, corporate bonds, exchange-traded funds and real estate investment trusts. To lend credibility to the initiative, the BOJ has strengthened its public communication operations and used them in an attempt to create the market opinion that it will continue monetary easing as long as necessary to raise inflationary expectations. Joint policy statements by the BOJ and the government have been designed to promote the credibility and effectiveness of monetary policy. Whether these unprecedented, long-term measures will succeed in raising inflationary expectations will, at the time of writing, not be known for some time.

THE BANK OF JAPAN AND MONETARY POLICY[5]

The BOJ's founding legislation, the BOJ Act, was promulgated in June 1882 during the Meiji restoration. The BOJ was reorganized during World War II under the BOJ Law of 1942 to reflect wartime conditions and expectations. For example, Article 1 of the Law stated the objectives of the Bank as follows:

> the regulation of the currency, control and facilitation of credit and finance, and the maintenance and fostering of the credit system, pursuant to national policy, in order that the general economic activities of the nation might adequately be enhanced.

Following the war, the BOJ Law of 1942 was amended several times. These amendments included the establishment in June 1949 of a Policy Board as the Bank's highest decision-making body, and this provision remains in place today. The Policy Board now consists of the governor, two vice governors and six outside members appointed by the Cabinet and approved by the Parliament. All serve five-year terms of office. The Policy Board determines the BOJ's monetary policy stance. The Law of 1942 was revised completely in June 1997 under two principles, namely 'independence' and 'transparency'. The revised BOJ Law came into effect on 1 April 1998. Several factors led to the 1997 revision. They included:

(1) the property bubble of the late 1980s; (2) bad debts and insolvency of financial institutions; (3) rapid development and integration of financial and capital markets across the globe; (4) the shift from the fixed exchange rate regime to a floating currency; (5) bulk issues of government bonds; and (6) financial deregulation and reforms, including liberalization of interest rates and capital controls (Hossain, 2009).

The 1998 Law specifies two pillars: 'the pursuit of price stability, contributing to the sound development of the national economy' (Article 2); and 'maintenance of an orderly financial system' (Article 1). While clearly price stability is the putative primary target, nevertheless it would appear that these Articles together are worded broadly enough to allow discretionary substitution of alternative policy targets, such as economic growth, full employment or exchange rate stability. Financial stability remains the shared responsibility of the BOJ and the government. Somewhat unusually, the Ministry of Finance retains the power to influence exchange rate movements. As Japan operates under a floating exchange rate system, the Ministry of Finance's forex operations have the potential to compromise the ability of the putatively independent BOJ to maintain price stability. Under a floating exchange rate system, monetary policy and exchange rate policy are not separate, since exchange rate movements substantially reflect money supply movements.

The Law of 1998 granted increased independence to the BOJ, both in terms of instruments and goals. Before the enactment of this Law, the government had two voting members on the BOJ Policy Board, one from the Ministry of Finance and the other from the Economic Planning Agency. The 1998 Law removed the government representatives' voting rights at Policy Board meetings. However, they can request the delay of the board's monetary policy decisions. The Ministry of Finance under the new Law lost its authority to oversee BOJ operations, particularly with respect to its right to dismiss senior officials of the BOJ. The government can no longer dismiss either the governor or Policy Board members unless they are found to be physically or mentally incapacitated as determined by an appropriate body. Their terms of appointment are five years. Nevertheless, the Ministry of Finance maintains some control over the BOJ's budget items that are not related to its conduct of monetary policy. The Ministry of Finance's veto power over the BOJ's budget is viewed as a potential channel of influence compromising the BOJ's independence. Whether or not the BOJ compromises monetary policy decisions in response to government budgetary control is not known, but the potential exists.

The Policy Board of the BOJ meets twice a month and announces its policy decisions at a press conference following each meeting, with publication of the meeting's minutes about a month later. These actions, together with frequent public speeches by nine board members and the posting of significant publications on the BOJ website, ensure that the financial markets and the public remain well informed on the monetary policy stance in Japan vis-à-vis other major countries. To meet its obligation of accountability to the public, the BOJ prepares and submits to the Diet (Japanese Parliament) a semi-annual report in June and December each year on currency and monetary control. Furthermore, the governor and other executives appear before the Diet committees if requested and then answer questions on monetary policy and its operations and issues.

Cecchetti (2008) suggests that the BOJ's system of independence, accountability, transparent communication and the overall monetary policy framework meet the requirements of a modern, independent central bank. The key issue, however, is whether the BOJ, in its conduct of monetary policy for price stability, takes into account the ongoing recession in Japan. Political leaders appear to be of the opinion that it does not. The Law states that 'The Bank of Japan's autonomy regarding currency and monetary control shall be respected'. As there is the suggestion that monetary policy and the government's overall economic policy stance need to be harmonious, the Law stipulates further that the Bank shall 'always maintain close contact with the government and exchange views sufficiently'. This indicates that a consensus is yet to emerge in Japan on some vital issues with respect to the effective, transparent conduct of monetary policy for price stability.

EVOLUTION OF MONETARY POLICY

During Japan's industrial takeoff, the financial system was highly seller-concentrated and repressively regulated. Money and capital markets were underdeveloped and the interest rates were administratively controlled. The yen was pegged against the US dollar, with extensive controls over foreign exchange transactions (Suzuki, 1981). The monetary policy stance during this high-growth phase was generally expansionary, to accommodate and sustain rapid economic growth. Suzuki (1992, p. 167) has described the transmission mechanisms of monetary policy in Japan during its high-growth phase as follows:

> During the high-growth period, when deposit rates were regulated, lending rates were rigid and the bond market was underdeveloped, the transmission channel was rather simple. It started with rationing of credit by the central bank at its discount window. This caused large fluctuations in inter-bank money rates and significantly affected the lending behaviour of banks, since lending rates were inflexible compared with inter-bank money rates. This policy channel was

> supplemented by 'Window Guidance', whereby the Bank of Japan used moral persuasion to influence the amount of increase in private bank loans.

Monetary policy in Japan has changed since the mid 1970s. With relaxation of the objective of exchange rate stability, the conduct of monetary policy has been affected by gradual liberalization of the Japanese financial system. Liberalization measures included decontrol of interest rates, development of financial instruments and financial markets, and relaxation of constraints on the asset and liability choices of investors, borrowers and financial institutions. Suzuki (1992, p. 167) has reviewed this aspect as part of the development of the financial system in Japan:

> After the high growth period ended, large-scale government bond issues led to the development of the bond market. Exchange controls were lifted in order to open up the financial market following the shift to the floating exchange rate system. Japan also began to move towards financial deregulation, internationalization and computerization. These changes, together with resultant innovations, were manifested in the formation of numerous financial instruments and markets. In this context, the Bank of Japan began to use market operations more than lending, and transmission channel have since multiplied.

Some economists attribute the low but steady growth in Japan, and a sharp decline in inflation, from the late 1970s to the mid 1980s to BOJ's adoption of a monetarist policy framework that posits a causal linkage between money supply growth and inflation (Friedman, 1982, 1985). While the BOJ monetary targeting approach was not strict, it did demonstrate recognition that the main source of inflation in Japan is monetary, thereby requiring monetary measures to control inflation on a sustained basis (Hutchison, 1986; Ito, 1989). In 1978 the BOJ began announcing at the beginning of each quarter forecasts of its monetary target, defined as 'broad money (M2) plus Certificates of Deposit (CDs)'. The BOJ lowered the 'M2 plus CDs' growth rate after the second OPEC oil price shock in 1979. This starkly contrasted against the expansionary monetary policy pursued following the first oil price shock in 1973–74, with an associated rise in the money-growth rate. Perhaps lessons were taken from this episode and applied in the similar circumstances that arose five years later. Under this strategy of monetary policy, the interbank interest rate was deployed as an operating target on a daily basis to achieve the money-growth target.

The BOJ continued its use of monetary targeting into the 1980s. By the early 1980s, inflation had been brought under control through a significant reduction in the money-growth rate (Greenwood, 1984; Hutchison, 1986; Meltzer, 2000). The BOJ remained committed to monetary targeting; however, financial innovation and deregulation in Japan through the 1980s arguably diminished the relevance of monetary aggregates, such as 'M2 plus CDs', as indicators of monetary policy. To avoid recession in the early 1980s, the BOJ opted to depreciate the yen through rapid monetary expansion. Later, in response to the yen appreciation through 1987–89, the BOJ increased the growth rate of the money supply. This pushed interest rates to low levels and depreciated the yen nominal exchange rate. It did not, however, bring depreciation of the real exchange rate, which could have raised the growth rate of exports. Japan did not, or could not, sustain a real exchange rate targeting approach to monetary policy to spur economic growth. High-inflation volatility was transmitted to the real exchange rate, whose high volatility then dampened Japan's trade flows and economic growth (Ito, 2004c).

Monetary expansion was a contributing factor to the asset bubble of the 1980s. Stock and land prices skyrocketed. In an attempt to contain runaway speculation in these two markets, the BOJ tightened monetary policy in 1989. This can be observed to some degree in the sharp decline in the annual growth rate of the broad money supply from 10.4 per cent over 1986–90 to 2.1 per cent for 1991–95. Consequently, stock and land prices then declined sharply. This bust of the asset bubble in the early 1990s heralded a decline into recession, and ultimately the economy's fall into the deflation trap in which it remains at the time of writing in the mid 2010s. The long economic malaise has led to a loss of policy direction and efficacy. The question of what went wrong with Japanese monetary policy has therefore vitally engaged policymakers and researchers across the globe (Ito and Hayashi, 2004; Ken and Popper, 1997; Olivei, 2002).

The BOJ defines price stability as the rate of inflation that does not distort economic decision-making. Despite this, it conducted monetary policy for years in the absence of a numerical target for inflation as a guide. Initially, a short-term interest rate was deployed as the instrument of monetary policy. This ultimately stopped working after reaching some critically low level. There has since been no clear strategy in place to conduct the effectively expansionary monetary policy needed in support of other stimulatory policy aimed at lifting Japan out of the deflation trap. This can be seen in a short account of BOJ conduct of monetary policy since it successfully burst the late 1980s asset price bubble. It immediately then began to ease monetary policy again. The evidence for this is an observed fall in the BOJ discount rate from a full 6 per cent in June 1991 to just one-half (½) per cent in September 1995. As intended, the lending rate of interest fell correspondingly, but the money supply failed to respond as intended and expected. As already noted, broad money growth fell from 10.4 per cent to just 2.1 per cent for the half-decade to 1995 and only 2.5 per cent for the entire decade to 2000. Perversely, expansionary monetary policy, indicated in the fall in the discount rate, was followed by monetary contraction. This may go some way towards explaining why, despite a sharp decrease in the nominal interest rate, prices continued to fall and ultimately held the real interest rate in positive territory at around 2 per cent. In 1999–2000, the BOJ adopted a zero nominal interest rate policy. This time the economy failed almost completely to respond and little or nothing was achieved in the way of economic recovery. From March 2001 to 2006, the BOJ implemented a first trial of quantitative-easing policy. The strategy was to raise the money supply growth rate in the hope of generating an aggregate demand-led economic recovery. The money-growth data, however, suggest the depth of the stagnation. For example, while narrow money growth totalled 15 per cent for 2001–05, broad money growth struggled to total 2.2 per cent (Table 6.1). In an uncertain economic environment, there was a sharp rise in demand for the most liquid form of money. Both the narrow and broad money-growth rates have fallen sharply since the mid 2000s.

Under quantitative-easing policy, the BOJ engaged in purchasing Japanese government bonds to achieve an operating target of current account balances (bank reserves) held by financial institutions with the BOJ. Despite the development of signs that the economy might be on the way to an escape from the deflation trap, the BOJ exited quantitative-easing policy in March 2006. The reason was the BOJ concern over excessive equipment investment by corporations. The quantitative-easing exit was followed in July 2006 by the BOJ's exit from zero interest rate policy. In November 2006, it raised the uncollaterized overnight call rate to 0.25 per cent. Consequently, the lending rate rose from 1.6 per cent in March 2006 to 1.74 per cent in late 2006. There is the suggestion that the BOJ's exit from quantitative easing in 2006 was premature. The economy relapsed into stagnation and deflation once the quantitative-easing policy had been discarded.

The BOJ resumed quantitative easing following the US-global financial crisis, 2007–09, purchasing Japanese government bonds and implementing some unconventional measures to promote financial stability. In October 2010, the BOJ undertook comprehensive monetary policy easing that attempted to resurrect inflation expectations from their deflationary state. Operations under this policy included BOJ's purchases of government securities and private financial assets, such as corporate bonds, commercial paper, exchange-traded funds and real estate investment trusts (Ueda, 2011).

Quantitative easing is an expansionary monetary policy aimed at raising inflation from negative to positive levels; however, there has been no formalization of this policy in terms of setting a target rate as a guide to monetary policy. The BOJ's announcement of its aim to achieve a positive inflation rate is not backed by firm BOJ and government commitment to achieve and sustain a low, positive rate of inflation under a well-designed inflation targeting strategy. Many economic commentators suggest that Japan should discard discretionary monetary policy and introduce inflation targeting as a strategy of monetary policy.

The BOJ remains sceptical of inflation targeting as a solution to deflation. It appears to doubt, on the solid ground of well-documented recent Japanese history, its ability to influence inflationary expectations. There can be little doubt that its credibility would suffer enormously if it attempted and failed to achieve and sustain the set and publicly announced inflation target. Further, there is well-founded apprehension that once positive inflationary expectations are generated, the associated release of pent-up demand could overwhelm BOJ policy to contain them. There are other reasons for the BOJ's reluctance to introduce inflation targeting. Firstly, it interprets calls for inflation targeting as potentially having the ulterior motive of inflating away the non-performing loans of the banking sector. Secondly, a rise in inflation may delay implementation of the financial reform needed to sustain economic recovery. Thirdly, at the institutional level there is a suggestion that the BOJ has fallen into what has been called an 'independence trap'. That is, a putative BOJ objective to retain government-granted independence at almost any cost. Given such an objective, then, it is rational for the BOJ to avoid actions and policy that could lead to loss of independence, whether or not those actions are technically appropriate; and to undertake actions and policy that do not lead to the loss of BOJ independence, even if those actions and policy are policy-inappropriate.

Notably, the BOJ has been reluctant to take bold monetary action since it was delegated independence in 1998. Before this, the prevailing view was that it is relatively easy to quickly reduce the interest rate, but raising it is so difficult, at least politically, that doing so is likely to take a long time. With the acquisition of policy independence, the BOJ has become more conservative. It is not willing to risk any failure of bold monetary initiatives. Its maintenance of a steady monetary policy course suggests that it intends to establish simultaneous policy credibility and effectiveness. However, rather than following a monetary policy rule, it has maintained a discretionary approach to policy. This creates policy opacity and ambiguity, with consequent public confusion (economic uncertainty), loss of policy credibility and ultimate monetary policy ineffectiveness (Ito, 2010; Ito and Hayashi, 2004; Speigel, 2000).

Since 2012 Japanese political leaders have become restless due to the continuing economic stagnation and deflation. Under political pressure, the BOJ agreed to raise the annual inflation target to 2 per cent in 2013 and pursue it by deployment of appropriately expansionary monetary policy. While this was a positive step, the BOJ did not share the enthusiasm of Japan's political leaders, because of the 'fear of failure' described above, and because of the long-term implications of inflationary stimulus. The idea of lowering the debt burden using the inflationary mechanism has the danger that it may further harm the Japanese public's confidence in the ability of the BOJ to maintain price stability. Furthermore, on experience grounds the BOJ does not share the view that expansionary monetary policy alone is effective in raising economic growth.

With a debt-GDP ratio in excess of 230 per cent, the government faces a fiscal challenge that renders fiscal policy incapable of supporting expansionary monetary policy, whether that be the 2012-initiated quantitative-easing programme or the targeting of a positive inflation rate. How much additional debt the Japanese public is prepared to hold is a matter of contention. A budget deficit as high as 10 per cent of GDP is unusual for advanced economies. On this matter, the European debt-afflicted countries could be a pointer. One of the BOJ's multitude of concerns is that even if massive monetary stimulus is ultimately perceived as successful in leading Japan to economic recovery, future governments may create economic havoc by attempting to deploy monetary policy as a cure for all economic ills. The government may then not feel pressured to implement the structural reforms necessary to make the Japanese economy more resilient and competitive in the present competitive world.[6]

MACROECONOMIC DEVELOPMENTS AND INFLATION PERFORMANCE

Japan experienced sustained rapid economic growth from the mid 1950s and throughout the 1960s (Table 6.1). The high average rate of growth was sustained internally by high corporate investment in plant and equipment as Japan continued to build its post-World War II economy. This post-war reconstruction was driven by a rapidly expanding exportable sector as demand for Japan's labour-intensive products in Europe and North America rose steadily.

From the 1950s to the mid 1970s the role of monetary policy in Japan was to facilitate economic growth while maintaining price stability, meaning low and stable inflation. During Japan's rapid growth phase in the 1950s and 1960s inflation averaged about 5 per cent per annum. This was considerably higher than the inflation rates of other countries in the Asia-Pacific region. However, the rate of economic growth was so high that this moderately high inflation represented a relatively low and tolerable

Table 6.2 Tools of open market operations in Japan

Operational target	Policy instruments and action
Provision of short-term funds	Purchase of Treasury bills/financing bills under repurchase agreements Outright purchases of Treasury bills/financing bills Borrowing of Japanese government bonds against cash collaterals Outright purchase of bills Purchases of commercial paper under repurchase agreements
Absorption of funds over a short term	Sales of Treasury bills/financial bills under repurchase agreements Outright sales of Treasury bills/financial bills Outright sales of bills issued by the Bank of Japan
Provision of long-term funds	Outright purchases of Japanese government bonds

Source: Olivei (2002).

cost. The situation began to change in the early 1970s when the first of the OPEC oil price shocks raised the Japanese rate of inflation to about 20 per cent in 1974. The oil price shock came on top of an expansionary monetary policy that, in 1973, had raised the money supply in excess of 20 per cent. Incontrovertibly, therefore, the monetary policy stance in Japan was expansionary through the early 1970s (Table 6.2). The main source of the 1973 monetary expansion was rapid accumulation of foreign reserves from large and sustained external surpluses. A secondary source was BOJ monetary accommodation of the then Tanaka government's plan to sustain rapid economic growth in the 1970s. Although inflation was high, economic growth received policy priority over inflation throughout the 1970s. Nevertheless, in contrast with an average of around 9 per cent for the 1960s, economic growth across the 1970s decelerated to average just 4 per cent. This rate of growth then persisted until the asset bubble collapsed in the late 1980s. Since then the Japanese economy has averaged less than 1 per cent per annum. Japan's recession since the early 1990s has been longer and more severe than any recession in the industrialized countries since the Great Depression of the 1930s.

No consensus analysis has yet emerged of the factors underlying Japan's sharp economic slowdown in the early 1990s and subsequent, ongoing recession. Nevertheless, several plausible causes have been identified. Firstly, the 1990–91 collapse of the bubble in asset markets simultaneously deflated the balance sheet of the corporate sector and reduced household wealth and spending. Secondly, the government did not introduce the financial reforms necessary to facilitate restoration of the corporate sector's balance sheet. Thirdly, the government failed to comprehend the nature of the business cycle, and introduction of fiscal and monetary measures was half-hearted, uncoordinated and inadequate. BOJ conduct of monetary policy before the mid 2000s was neither systematic nor effective. Asset prices since then, however, have remained low, fuelling persistent doubt that monetary policy has been sufficiently expansionary.

The interlocking nature of the corporate and financial sectors in Japan blurs the boundaries between the real sector and the financial sector of the economy. The sharp decline of land and other real estate values in the 1990–91 bust of the asset price bubble rendered many mortgages valueless. This created the problem of a large volume of non-performing loans in the financial sector (Altunbas et al., 2000). The quantum was so huge as to render the banks unable to write off a significant volume of these loans. In addition, the banks were required to raise the shareholders' equity, and to limit lending to fulfil a requirement of the Bank for International Settlements (BIS) that banks maintain their capital adequacy ratios around 8 per cent of asset values. Similarly, share prices had declined sharply in the bust, leaving many securities companies saddled with bad debts. Naturally enough, there were consequent bank and corporate bankruptcies. The gravity of the problem in the financial institutions was not sufficiently recognized by the Ministry of Finance and the BOJ until it was too late.

The Japanese economy began a gradual and tentative recovery in the early 2000s. By 2006 the deflationary pressure had eased somewhat. The rate of inflation, however, remained at less than 1 per cent per annum, despite the expansionary monetary policy measures discussed above. There were mixed signals on the strength of the economy. Private investment was rising rapidly. Export growth remained high despite an appreciation of the real exchange rate. Private consumption demand, however, remained weak for several reasons: (1) slow wage growth; (2) expectations of tax increases to finance large budget deficits; and (3) the combination of Japan's slow population growth and ageing population further contributed to the consumption problem. Fiscal policy options were exhausted, leading to increased pressure on the BOJ to at least continue, and preferably step up, expansionary monetary policy in ongoing official pursuit of the long-sought positive but low-inflationary environment. The BOJ resisted such pressure on a sustained basis.

Inflation and Inflation Volatility

Figures 6.1a and 6.1b display inflation and its volatility in Japan over the period 1958q1–2012q4, as represented by the conditional standard deviation of inflation obtained by application of the GARCH(1,1) model. Both reveal the highly volatile nature of inflation in Japan until the mid 1980s. Since then, inflation volatility has subsided with the fall in inflation.

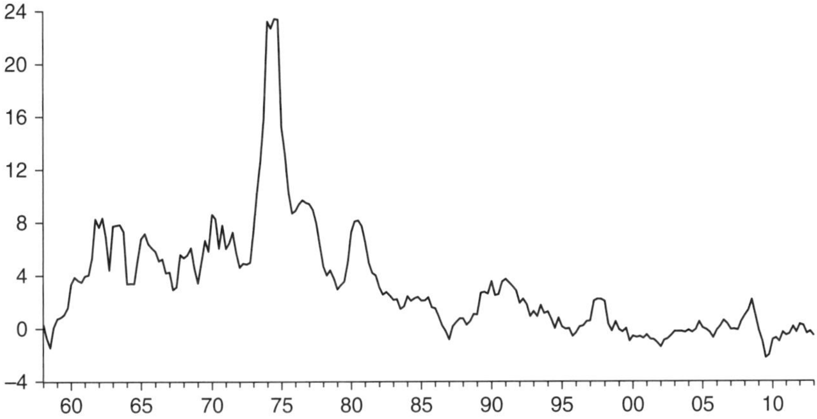

Figure 6.1a *Quarter-on-quarter CPI inflation in Japan, 1958q1–2012q4*

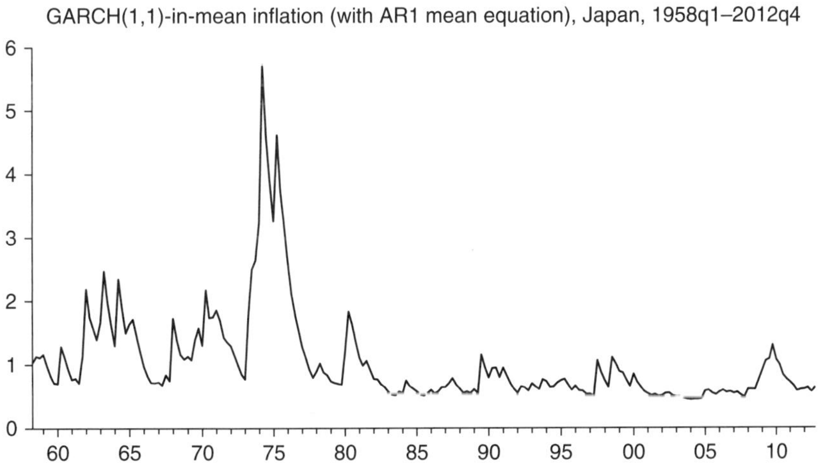

Figure 6.1b *Conditional standard deviation of CPI inflation in Japan, 1958q1–2012q4*

Empirically, inflation volatility is generally found to have an adverse effect on economic growth. The results (not reported) of a simple Granger-causality test show that Japan is no exception, suggesting the presence of a feedback relationship between the two in this country.

Inflation Persistence

Inflation in Japan has exhibited a high degree of persistence. This is reflected in the high and stable coefficient value on the one-period lagged rate of inflation in an autoregressive model AR(1), estimated by both the recursive and rolling regression techniques (Figures 6.2a and 6.2b). Rolling estimates of coefficient of the one-period lagged rate of inflation show a declining trend in the coefficient value since the early 2000s. High values of measured persistence of inflation are generally associated with low credibility of monetary policy. These results support the hypothesis that monetary policy in Japan, despite the appearance of BOJ autonomy in goal and instrument selection to conduct monetary policy, has low credibility in maintaining low and stable inflation. Japan's high inflation-persistence indicates that monetary policy has not been effective in changing inflationary expectations and keeping it low but positive and stable.

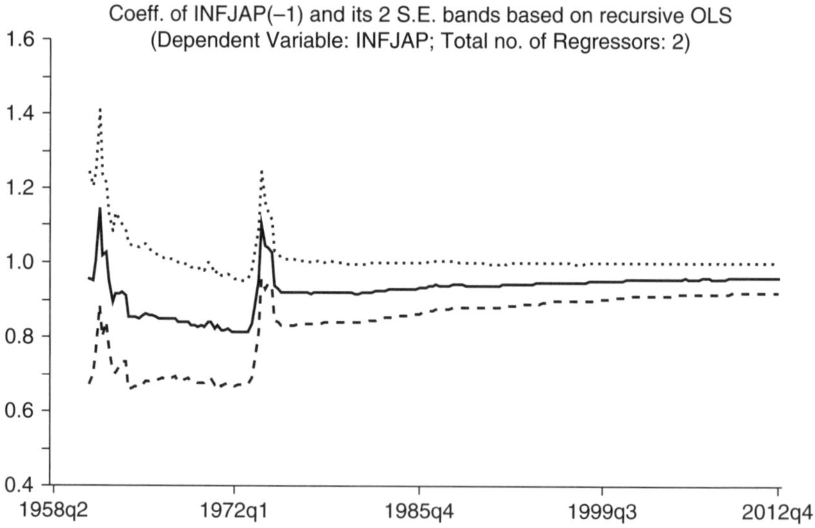

Note: INFJP = quarter-on-quarter CPI inflation in Japan.

Figure 6.2a *Recursive estimates of the coefficient on the one-period lagged rate of inflation in Japan*

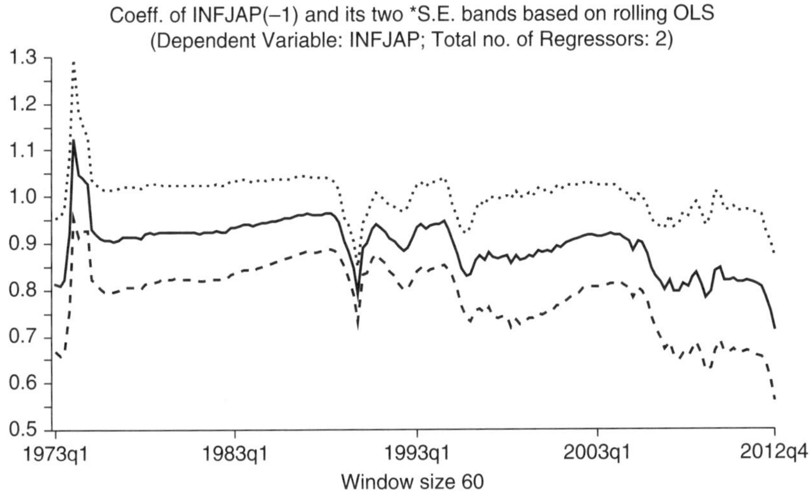

Note: INFJP = quarter-on-quarter CPI inflation in Japan.

Figure 6.2b *Rolling sample estimates of the coefficient on the one-period lagged rate of CPI inflation in Japan*

Interest Rates

The financing bill rate in Japan and the Treasury bill rate in the United States exhibit very different behaviours (Figure 6.3a), indicating that Japan has maintained monetary policy independence from the United States. Due to high volatility of inflation, Japanese real interest rates have exhibited high volatility. Since the early 2000s the United States has maintained a very low interest rate policy that created negative real interest rate during 2003–06; while Japan has maintained positive real interest rate since the 1980s (Figure 6.3b). This indicates that Japanese monetary conditions were more restrictive than those in the United States, as suggested by the fact that the real interest rate in Japan was higher than that in the United States; this occurred despite several BOJ monetary policy easings. Facing sustained economic stagnation in a deflationary environment, there was pressure on the BOJ to bring the real interest rate to zero or a negative level with the expectation that this would create a stimulatory environment. Figure 6.3c shows that Japan sustained highly volatile real deposit and lending rates since the 1950s through the 1980s. During the 1970s the real interest rates were very low or negative and this created financial repression. In contrast, the real interest rates in Japan have remained significantly positive since the

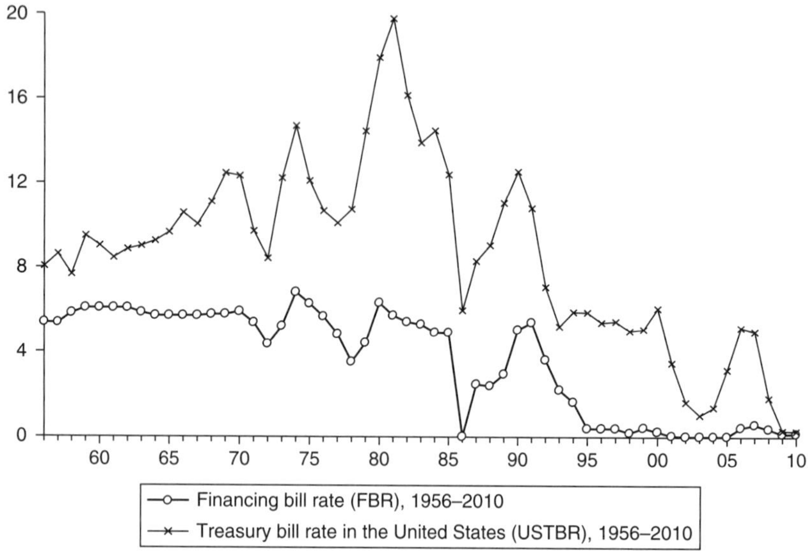

Figure 6.3a Financing bill rate in Japan and the Treasury bill rate in the United States

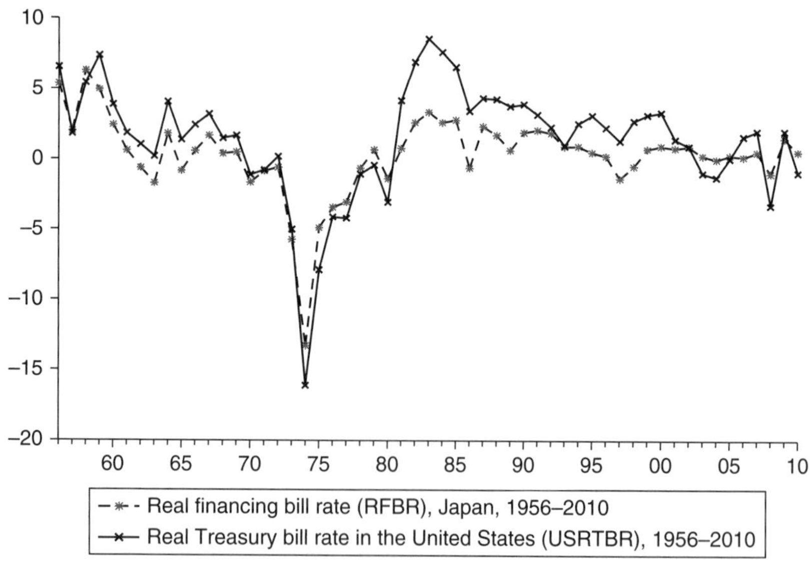

Figure 6.3b Real financing bill rate in Japan and real Treasury bill rate in the United States

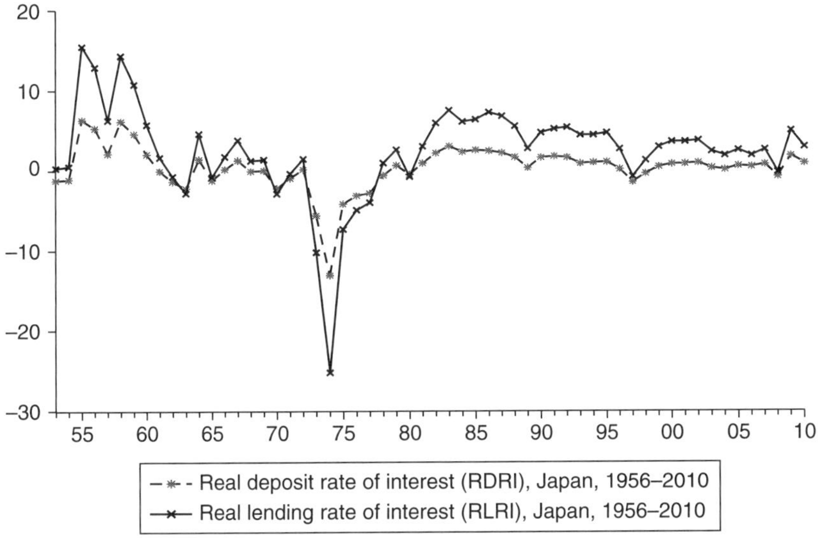

Figure 6.3c *Real deposit rate of interest and real lending rate of interest in Japan, 1956–2010*

1980s despite historically low nominal interest rates since the late 1990s. In short, Japan has failed to maintain real interest rates as low and stable. This was one of the contributors to boom-bust cycles in this country.

Exchange Rates

Figure 6.4 plots the nominal and real effective exchange rates in Japan for 1975q1–2010q4. It shows that although the nominal effective exchange rate has depreciated steadily since the early 1980s, the real effective exchange rate remains highly volatile due to inflation volatility. This can be interpreted as evidence that Japan has not deployed a real exchange rate targeting approach to monetary policy to promote exports; at least, not after 1975. It is plausible that high volatility of the real exchange rate has adversely affected Japan's export flows and economic growth.

INFLATION, REAL INTEREST RATE, REAL EXCHANGE RATE AND REAL OUTPUT

The key problem of monetary policy in Japan is low but unstable inflation and its impact on volatility, both of the real exchange rate and the

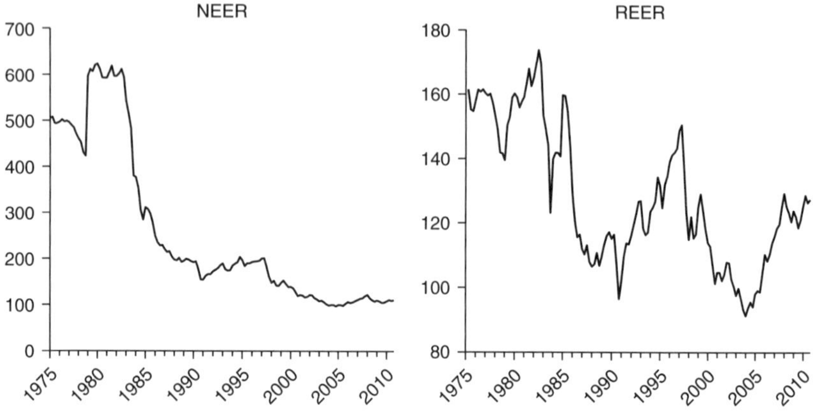

Note: Definitions of variables: NEER = nominal effective exchange rate of Japanese yen; REER = real effective exchange rate of Japanese yen. A rise in the index value represents an appreciation of the Japanese yen.

Figure 6.4 Nominal and real effective exchange rates of Japanese yen, 1975q1–2010q4

real interest rate. Under discretionary monetary policy, Japan has failed to keep inflation stable – a standard weakness of the discretionary approach to monetary policy formulation and implementation. This instability has been transmitted to the real interest rate. The main mechanism of this transmission is the dynamic that the nominal interest rate does not always adjust to inflation due to rigidities in the Japanese banking system. Inflation, the real interest rate, the real exchange rate and real output are therefore intertwined. Their interrelations are therefore appropriately investigated within the framework of a structural vector autoregression (SVAR) model.

This section, using annual data, estimates a four-variable SVAR model to examine the interrelationships among inflation, the real interest rate, the real exchange rate and real output. Figure 6.5 plots the data used for estimation purposes.

The model is formulated on the assumption that inflation has contemporaneous feedback with the real interest rate and the real exchange rate. All these variables exert lagged effects upon real output. The order of variables in the model is arranged as: INFJP, RLRI, LREER and LRGDP where INFJP is the inflation rate in Japan, RLRI is the real lending rate of interest, LREER is the log of the real effective exchange rate and LRGDP is the log of real GDP. The unit root test results suggest that while inflation,

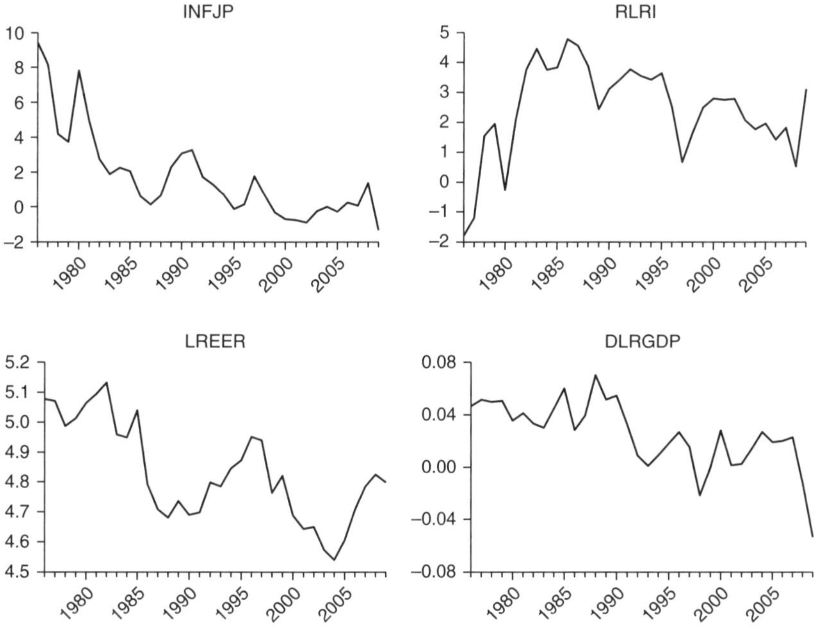

Note: Definitions of variables: INFJP = CPI inflation in Japan; RLRI = real lending rate of interest; LREER = log of the real effective exchange rate of the Japanese yen; and DLRGDP = first-order difference of the log of real GDP.

Figure 6.5 Data deployed for estimation of the SVAR model for Japan, 1976–2009

the real lending rate of interest and the real effective exchange rate are stationary, real output is nonstationary (stochastic). Two versions of the model are then estimated and deployed to generate impulse responses and forecast error-variance decompositions. The first version of the model is defined as: INFJP, RLRI, LREER and LRGDP while the second version of the model is defined as: INFJP, RLRI, LREER and DLRGDP. In the second version of the model, all the variables are stationary while in the first version real output is nonstationary. To conserve discussion space, results obtained by the second model only are reported as they are qualitatively similar to those obtained with the first model.

The impulse responses in Figure 6.6 demonstrate the interrelations among four variables in the SVAR model. The model does not include the source of inflation. The impulse response results are indicative, not conclusive. As expected, a rise in inflation lowers the real lending rate of interest. It indicates that the nominal lending rate of interest responds

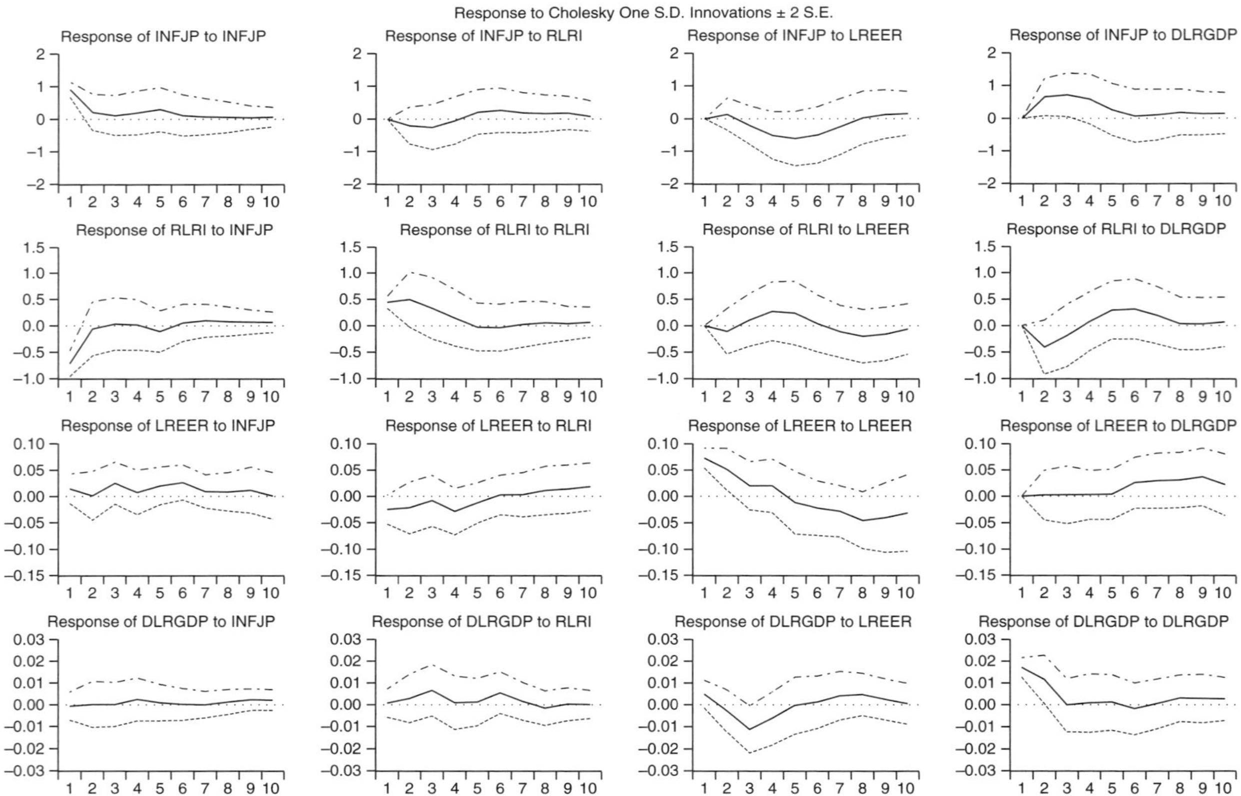

Note: Definitions of variables: INFJP = CPI inflation in Japan; LRLRI = real lending rate of interest; LREER = log of the real effective exchange rate of the Japanese yen; and DLRGDP = first-order difference of the log of real GDP.

Figure 6.6 Impulse responses for variables in the SVAR model for Japan slowly to a rise in inflation. However, it has no significant impact on output growth. Rises in output growth raise inflation, which appreciates the real exchange rate. The appreciated real exchange rate in turn is found to exert downward pressure on inflation and output growth. So there are feedback relations among inflation, real interest rate, real exchange rate and output growth. The real lending rate of interest responds positively to an appreciation of the real exchange rate. This is because as an appreciated real exchange rate induces capital flight, the real interest rate is required to rise as an inducement to slow down or stop capital flight. This follows the open-economy real exchange rate parity condition. In general, an appreciation of the real exchange rate affects both trade and capital flows while changes in the real interest rate affect saving and investment. The overall results suggest significant interrelations among inflation, the real interest rate, the real exchange rate and output growth. Although it is not investigated here, an expanded model is expected to show the impacts of the real interest and exchange rates on saving, investment and both trade and capital flows. The key message that emerges from the empirical results is that inflation and its volatility are not innocuous in so far as economic growth. Inflation affects the real interest rate and the real exchange rate and they have impacts on saving, investment and economic growth. This suggests the need for low and stable inflation for steady economic growth.

Table 6.3 presents the forecast error-variance decompositions for INFJP, RLRI, LREER and DLRGDP. In the table, the numbers represent those percentages of forecast error variance of variables in the model attributable to own innovations and those that originate from innovations of other variables. The results show that for all four of the model's variables, the dominant source of the forecast error variance is own innovations, to the extent of 27 per cent for inflation, 32 per cent for the real interest rate, 61 per cent for the real exchange rate and 57 per cent for real GDP growth over the ten-year time horizon. In the case of real output growth, innovations in the real lending rate of interest and the real exchange rate jointly account for 41 per cent of its forecast error variance, while inflation accounts for just 2.3 per cent. This shows that while real output growth is not very sensitive to changes in Japan's low average rate of inflation, it is highly sensitive to the volatility of inflation through the impact that inflation volatility exerts on the real interest rate and the real exchange rate. High volatility of the real exchange rate in particular is found to have a major impact on real output growth, alone contributing 30 per cent of its innovations.

Table 6.3 Forecast error-variance decomposition of variables in the SVAR model for Japan

Variance Decomposition of INFJP:					
Period	S.E.	INFJP	RLRI	LREER	DLRGDP
1	0.903	100.00	0.00	0.00	0.00
2	1.159	63.88	3.13	1.39	31.60
5	1.792	30.96	4.80	22.21	42.03
10	1.963	26.51	8.36	27.76	37.37
Variance Decomposition of RLRI:					
Period	S.E.	INFJP	RLRI	LREER	DLRGDP
1	0.842	72.37	27.63	0.00	0.00
2	1.065	45.56	38.69	0.98	14.76
5	1.244	34.18	36.87	9.90	19.05
10	1.347	30.70	32.12	13.01	24.16
Variance Decomposition of LREER:					
Period	S.E.	INFJP	RLRI	LREER	DLRGDP
1	0.078	3.41	10.27	86.31	0.00
2	0.096	2.28	11.98	85.69	0.05
5	0.111	10.46	17.46	71.79	0.29
10	0.156	9.40	11.60	61.11	17.89
Variance Decomposition of DLRGDP:					
Period	S.E.	INFJP	RLRI	LREER	DLRGDP
1	0.017	0.15	0.15	7.50	92.20
2	0.021	0.11	1.79	6.76	91.34
5	0.026	1.06	7.89	28.50	62.57
10	0.028	2.29	11.03	30.00	56.68
The Cholesky Ordering: INFJP RLRI LREER DLRGDP					

Note: Definitions of variables: INFJP = CPI inflation in Japan; RLRI = real lending rate of interest; LREER = log of the real effective exchange rate of the Japanese yen; and DLRGDP = first-order difference of the log of real GDP.

MONETARY AND EXCHANGE RATE POLICY ISSUES

The empirical results reported above suggest that the Japanese economy has languished in a moribund state since the early 1990s. There is debate on the sources and resolution of the problem. There is, however, no doubt that, like the United States, Japan conducts monetary policy under discretion, which lacks credibility and is not transparent and effective. This is reflected in Japan's high persistence of inflation. Unlike that of the United States, the Japanese financial sector is relatively underdeveloped. The challenge for Japan going forward is to achieve a steadily growing economy with low and stable inflation. Without diminishing the importance of fiscal discipline and financial reform issues, a third major issue remains the design, implementation and conduct of a rule-based monetary policy to replace the demonstrated deeply flawed discretionary policy process characterized by legislated channels of influence to the BOJ from the government through the Ministry of Finance. While in the 1970s the real interest rate became negative and highly volatile, it has remained above zero since recession began in the early 1990s. This has occurred in the context of a nominal interest rate that was, at best, only partially adjusted to inflation. This partial interest rate adjustment has fuelled the boom-bust to which the Japanese economy is perennially exposed.

In contemplating, against the benchmark of comparative advantage, which strategy of monetary policy is most efficient or effective for Japan to maintain price stability under a floating exchange rate system, two options appear appropriate. It can introduce either monetary targeting or inflation targeting. Under inflation targeting, the interest rate or a monetary aggregate can be used as an instrument of monetary policy. The relevance and effectiveness of a short-term interest rate as an instrument of monetary policy remains controversial when the interest rate declines to very low levels, as in Japan's case.

This section provides some empirical results on key monetary relations that are linked to the conduct of a rule-based monetary policy such as monetary targeting. Until recently the prevailing view was that monetary targeting for price stability requires a stable money-demand function to establish a causal linkage between money supply growth and inflation. The recent literature suggests that a causal relation can exist between money supply growth and inflation, irrespective both of the exchange rate regime and whether or not the money-demand function is stable (McCallum and Nelson, 2011).

This section examines whether there exists a stable money-demand function in Japan.[7] For estimation purposes, an open-economy money-demand function is specified as follows:

$$LRJM_t = \alpha_0 + \alpha_1 Ly_t + \alpha_2 NIR_t + \alpha_3 FIR_t + \alpha_4 LRER_t + \alpha_5 \pi_t^v + u_t \quad (6.1)$$

where LRJM (J = N, B) is the log of real money balances (LRNM for narrowly defined money or LRBM for broadly defined money), Ly is the log of real income, NIR is a representative nominal interest rate, FIR is a representative foreign interest rate such as the US Federal funds rate

(USFFR), LRER is the log of a representative real exchange rate such as the real effective exchange rate (REER), π_t^v is a measure of inflation volatility and u_t is a random error term.

In this specification, real income represents a scale variable and its coefficient is expected to bear a positive sign and have a magnitude not significantly different from unity. The coefficients on NIR and FIR, which represent the opportunity cost variables, are expected to bear a negative sign. As reviewed in Appendix 5, the sign of the coefficient on the real exchange rate remains indeterminate. The sign of the coefficient on inflation volatility also remains indeterminate.

The unit root test results suggest that all the variables in the specified model have a unit root. They are therefore eligible to form a cointegral money-demand relationship. However, preliminary estimation results for a longer sample period, 1957–2012, suggest that when NIR is proxied by either the deposit rate or the lending rate of interest in Japan, and FIR is proxied by the US Federal funds rate (USFFR), their coefficients become significant only when one of them is used in the model. The model is then estimated using the USFFR as the opportunity cost variable. The USFFR is considered more appropriate as it is largely market determined throughout the sample period, while the Japanese deposit or lending interest rate was institutionally determined until the 1990s.

Table 6.4 reports both the ARDL and OLS results for the real narrow money-demand function (LRNM). Once again to conserve discussion space, the results obtained by a broad definition of money are not reported. The results obtained by the ARDL model are found superior to those obtained by OLS/DOLS. The results suggest the presence of a weak form of long-run cointegral relationship among real narrow money balances, real income, the US Federal funds rate, the real exchange rate and inflation volatility. The estimated coefficient values are consistent with a priori predictions. A series of stability tests, including CUSUM and CUSUMSQ of residuals (Figure 6.7), is conducted, which suggests that the narrow money-demand function remains stable over the study period.

As expected, real income remains the core determinant of narrow money demand in Japan. The income elasticity of demand for real narrow money balances is greater than one. This is theoretically unexpected for advanced countries such as Japan. Inflation volatility is not highly significant in the model but, importantly, its exclusion makes the model unstable. Inflation instability bears a positive sign in the narrow money-demand function. It implies that as inflation instability increases, there is an increase in demand for the most highly liquid form of money. As expected, the US Federal funds rate bears a negative sign and is statistically highly significant. It is noted earlier that the domestic interest rate does not become significant

Table 6.4 The ARDL and OLS regression results of real narrow money-demand relationships in Japan

	F-statistic 2	W-statistic 10.02		
Critical value bounds	F-test	W-test		
90%	(2.56, 3.73)	(12.80, 18.64)		
95%	(3.07, 4.33)	(15.37, 21.64)		
Sample period	1957–2012 ARDL (2,0,1,1,0) (Selected based on SBC)	1957–2012 ARDL (1,2,0,0,0) Long-run model	1960–2012 OLS (Static)	1961–2012 OLS (Dynamic model)
Regressors	Coefficient (t-ratio) [prob.]	Coefficient (t-ratio) [prob.]	Coefficient (t-ratio) [prob.]	Coefficient (t-ratio) [prob.]
Intercept	−0.87 (−2.01) [0.05]	−10.19 (−2.29) [0.03]	6.11 (10.29) [0.00]	1.95 (1.96) [0.06]
LRNM(−1)	1.21 (9.19) [0.00]			0.53 (4.40) [0.00]
LRNM(−2)	−0.30 (−2.36) [0.02]			
LRGDP	0.19 (2.96) [0.01]	2.20 (5.83) [0.00]	1.41 (48.30) [0.00]	0.65 (3.79) [0.00]
USFFR	−0.01 (−3.79) [0.00]	−0.13 (−3.84) [0.00]	−0.01 (−2.60) [0.01]	−0.01 (−0.38) [0.71]
LRER	0.12 (2.08) [0.04]	1.44 (2.28) [0.03]	0.02 (0.20) [0.84]	0.21 (1.60) [0.12]
INFVOL	0.02 (1.32) [0.19]	0.19 (1.27) [0.21]	−0.04 (−1.66) [0.10]	0.02 (1.24) [0.22]
Diagnostics				
Adjusted R^2	0.99		0.99	0.99

Table 6.4 (continued)

	F-statistic	W-statistic		
Lagrange multiplier test for serial correlation	F(1, 48) = 0.23 [0.63]		F(1, 47) = 31.69 [0.00]	F(1, 45) = 3.74 [0.06]
Ramsey's RESET test of functional form mis-specification	F(1, 48) = 0.04 [0.84]		F(1, 47) = 0.62 [0.43]	F(1, 45) = 0.68 [0.41]
Normality of residuals	$\chi^2_{(2)} = 2.75$ [0.25]		$\chi^2_{(2)} = 1.17$ [0.56]	$\chi^2_{(2)} = 4.53$ [0.10]
Heteroskedasticity	F(1, 54) = 0.13 [0.72]		F(1, 51) = 3.02 [0.09]	F(1, 50) = 2.07 [0.16]
The Wald test:				
H_O: Coefficient on LRGDP = 0		$\chi^2_{(1)} = 33.97$ [0.00]	$\chi^2_{(1)} = 2332.9$ [0.00]	
H_O: Coefficient on LRGDP = 1		$\chi^2_{(1)} = 10.13$ [0.00]	$\chi^2_{(1)} = 195.59$ [0.00]	
H_O: Coefficient on USFFR = 0		$\chi^2_{(1)} = 14.71$ [0.00]	$\chi^2_{(1)} = 6.77$ [0.01]	
H_O: Coefficient on LRER = 0		$\chi^2_{(1)} = 5.21$ [0.02]	$\chi^2_{(1)} = 0.04$ [0.84]	
H_O: Coefficient on INFVOL = 0		$\chi^2_{(1)} = 1.60$ [0.21]	$\chi^2_{(1)} = 2.77$ [0.10]	

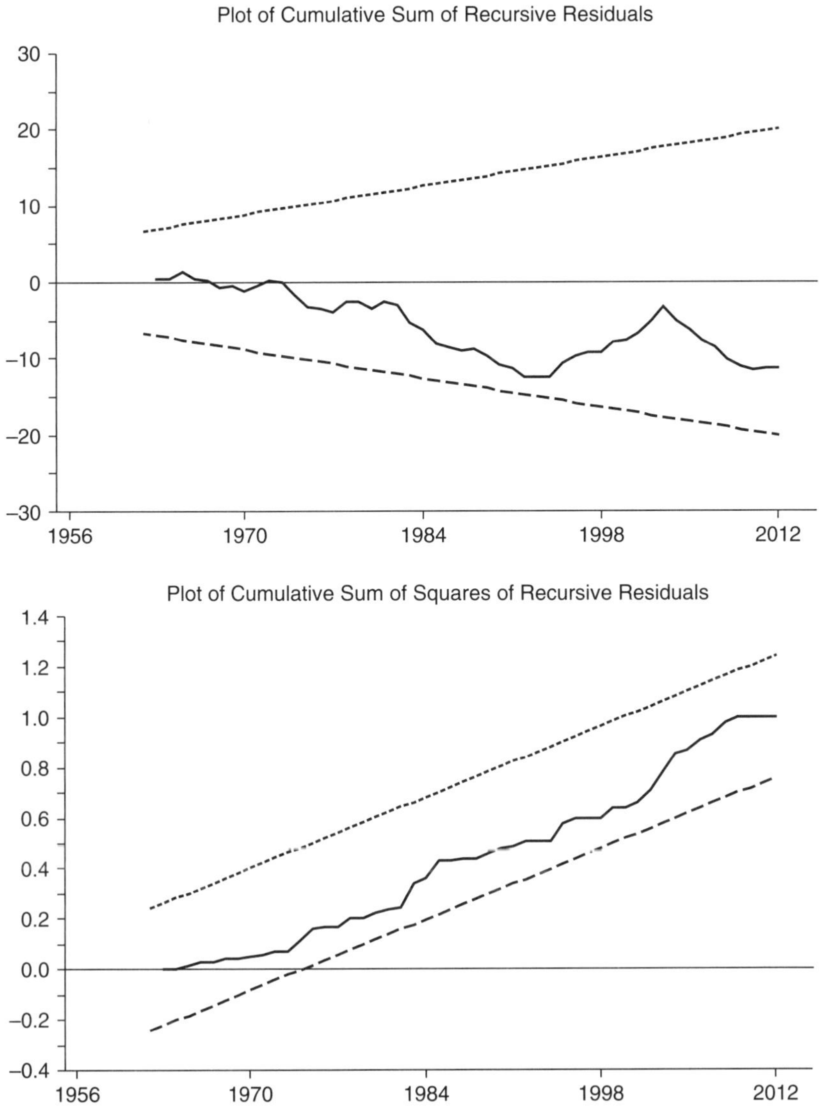

Note: The straight lines represent critical bounds at 5% significance level.

Figure 6.7 CUSUM and CUSUMSQ of residuals of real narrow money-demand relationships in Japan in the presence of the foreign interest rate. The real effective exchange rate bears a positive sign. As discussed in Appendix 5, a theory-informed expectation about the sign of the coefficient on the exchange rate cannot be formed a priori. In an open economy with freely mobile capital, the impact of the exchange rate on real narrow money balances is theoretically indeterminate because an appreciation of the exchange rate simultaneously exerts both upward and downward pressure on real balances. The net effect in any given case then depends on which of the two directions of impact is empirically dominant in the given case. The mechanisms are as follows. In an open economy with freely mobile capital, wealth-holders have an option to hold both domestic and foreign assets in their portfolios. They adjust their portfolios in the event of changes in the expected rates of return on domestic and foreign assets. For those wealth-holders who evaluate their portfolios in terms of domestic currency, a currency appreciation lowers their money demand as they adjust their portfolios by using domestic currency to purchase now cheaper foreign currency-denominated assets. In contrast, for those wealth-holders who, despite the recent appreciation, believe that the domestic currency remains undervalued and may appreciate further, or who evaluate their portfolios in foreign currency terms, a currency appreciation raises their money demand as they adjust their portfolios by converting foreign asset holdings into domestic currency-denominated assets. The empirically dominant effect from this three-way interplay, where a potential wealth effect opposes an opposite wealth effect and a currency-substitution effect, determines the net outcome of exchange rate changes on money demand. Therefore, the net effect of currency appreciation on money demand is considered an empirical issue.

Relationships Among Money, Output and Prices

Table 6.5 reports the cointegration test results among money, output and prices. The results obtained for a broad definition of money are found more robust than those obtained for a narrow definition of money. The Engle-Granger cointegration test results suggest a weak form of cointegral relationship among money, output and prices. The dynamic OLS (DOLS) estimates suggest that the broad money is highly significant in the price level equation and that the coefficient value of broad money is not significantly different from one. As expected, real output bears a negative sign and is statistically highly significant.

Engle and Granger (1987) suggest that one of the implications of a cointegral relation between two nonstationary (stochastic) variables is the presence of long-term causality between them running in at least one direction. Table 6.6 reports the bivariate Granger-causality test results

Table 6.5 *Cointegration test results among money, output and prices in Japan*

Dependent variable: LCPI								
	Fully modified OLS				Dynamic OLS			
					(lead = 1, lag = 1)			
With narrow money (NM)								
Regressor	coefficient	t-ratio	prob.		coefficient	t-ratio	prob.	
Intercept	0.11	0.17	0.87		0.90	1.34	0.19	
LNM	−0.10	−1.05	0.30		−0.14	−1.48	0.15	
LRGDP	1.12	4.61	0		1.02	4.5	0	
Sample period	1970–2012				1970–2011			
DW	0.14				0.42			
Adjusted R^2	0.84				0.9			
	tau-statistic	prob.	z-statistic	prob.	tau-statistic	prob.	z-statistic	prob.
The Engle-Granger cointegration tests	−2.66	0.42	−6.19	0.82	−2.66	0.42	−6.19	0.82
The Phillips-Ouliaris cointegration tests	−2.67	0.42	8.58	0.66	−2.67	0.42	−8.58	0.66
With broad money (BM)								
Regressor	coefficient	t-ratio	prob.		coefficient	t-ratio	prob.	
Intercept	5.16	6.66	0		5.92	6.31	0	
LBM	1.10	5.73	0		1.09	4.62	0	
LRGDP	−1.68	−3.83	0		−1.82	−3.66	0	
Sample	1970–2012				1970–2011			
DW	0.25				0.24			
Adjusted R^2	0.94				0.96			
	tau-statistic	prob.	z-statistic	prob.	tau-statistic	prob.	z-statistic	prob.
The Engle-Granger cointegration tests	−0.96	0.97	−3.22	0.96	−0.96	0.97	−3.22	0.96
The Phillips-Ouliaris cointegration tests	−1.22	0.94	−4.55	0.91	−1.22	0.94	−4.55	0.91

Note: Definitions of variables: LCPI = log of the consumer price index; LNM = log of narrow money stock; LBM = log of broad money stock; and LRGDP = log of real GDP.

Table 6.6 *Granger-causality among money, output and prices in Japan, 1955–2012*

	Hypotheses No causality runs from	Chi-square statistic (prob.)	Inference at 5% level
VEC specification (With narrow money, NM)	ΔLNM → ΔLCPI	5.57 (0.06)	Null hypothesis not rejected
	ΔLNM, ΔLRGDP → ΔLCPI	15.79 (0.00)	Null hypothesis rejected
	ΔLCPI → ΔLNM	0.49 (0.78)	Null hypothesis not rejected
	ΔLRGDP → ΔLNM	0.08 (0.96)	Null hypothesis not rejected
	ΔLCPI → ΔLRGDP	0.26 (0.88)	Null hypothesis not rejected
	ΔLNM → ΔLRGDP	5.02 (0.08)	Null hypothesis not rejected
VEC specification (With broad money, BM)	ΔLBM → ΔLCPI	22.34 (0.00)	Null hypothesis rejected
	ΔLBM, ΔLRGDP → ΔLCPI	41.01 (0.00)	Null hypothesis rejected
	ΔLCPI → ΔLBM	4.14 (0.13)	Null hypothesis not rejected
	ΔLRGDP → ΔLBM	10.39 (0.00)	Null hypothesis rejected
	ΔLCPI → ΔLRGDP	0.06 (0.97)	Null hypothesis not rejected
	ΔLBM → ΔLRGDP	6.77 (0.03)	Null hypothesis rejected

Note: Definitions of variables: LCPI = log of the consumer price index; LNM = log of narrow money stock; LBM = log of broad money stock; and LRGDP = log of real GDP. Optimal lag-length = 2 (selected based on the Schwarz Bayesian Criterion, SBC).

among LCPI, LNM (LBM) and LRGDP. Test results are generated within a vector error-correction (VEC) modelling framework after selecting the optimal lag-length using the SBC. The test results suggest that, for Japan, there is strong causality running from both narrow and broad money growth to inflation. Broad money growth is also found to have a strong causal impact on output growth.

SUMMARY AND CONCLUSION

This chapter has provided an overview of monetary policy in Japan from an historical perspective. Japan sustained a repressed financial system from the 1950s through the 1970s. Fiscal policy dominated monetary policy and the central bank remained a subservient institution. Consequently, monetary policy was used to promote economic growth by providing subsidized credit to the priority sectors. Nominal interest rates were controlled and stable over long periods. Real interest rates then became low or negative as inflation was moderately high and volatile, especially during the 1970s. High inflation was due mainly to supply shocks and accommodative monetary policy that raised money supply growth.

During the 1980s monetary policy was somewhat expansionary. This led to a depreciation of the real exchange rate and subsequent boom-bust cycle. Since the early 1990s the BOJ has maintained restrictive monetary policy in a deflationary environment while fiscal policy was deployed to pull the economy out of recession. As the nominal interest rate was sustained at very low levels, monetary policy was widely regarded as expansionary while, in reality, it effectively remained restrictive until the mid 2000s (Figure 6.8). In consequence, the Japanese economy has since the 1990s remained stagnant and standards of living have fallen or remained unchanged. Some economists suggest that Japanese monetary policy is to be blamed for Japan's poor economic performance since the 1990s. Under political pressure, the BOJ began implementing some expansionary monetary policy from the mid 2000s, with little improvement in the situation. There is a suggestion that the BOJ may lose its independence in conducting monetary policy if the present recession continues for very much longer.

Mishkin (2013) has drawn some policy lessons from the Japanese monetary policy experience. Firstly, low nominal interest rates do not necessarily imply loose monetary policy as discussed above. Japan's short-term interest rate was lowered in the late 1990s. It fell to, and remained near, zero until the early 2000s. Although the BOJ assumed that monetary policy was expansionary, this view was incorrect because of the very low or

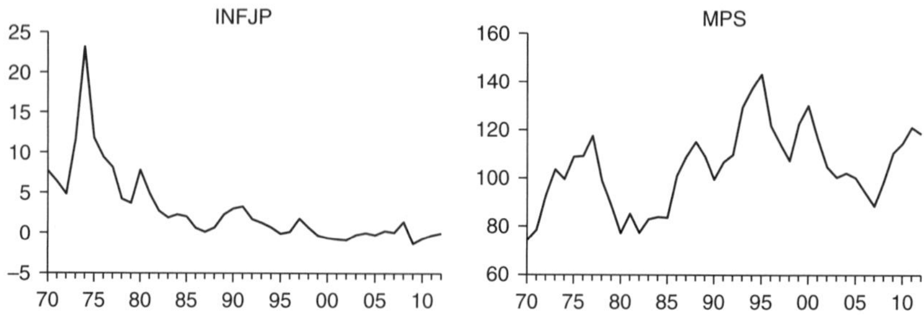

Note: Definitions of variables: INFJP = CPI inflation in Japan; MPS = monetary policy stance (defined as the sum of the real financing bill rate and the real effective exchange rate of Japanese yen). A rise in the value of MPS represents an increase in restrictiveness of monetary policy.

Figure 6.8 Monetary policy stance in Japan, 1970–2012

negative inflation rate that kept the real interest rate significantly positive and sometimes high. There is the suggestion that a much more expansionary monetary policy could have led to economic recovery much earlier. Secondly, asset prices should be considered an indicator of monetary policy stance. When nominal interest rates were falling in Japan, stock and real estate prices were collapsing as well. Had the BOJ recognized this indicator that monetary policy had remained contractionary despite its interest rate easing, this would have put it in a position to implement further expansionary measures. Figure 6.9 shows that the real share price index, which peaked in the late 1980s, showed a falling trend until the mid 2000s and then it rose sharply until the US-global financial crisis. Thirdly, monetary policy can be effective even if the short-term interest rate is zero or near zero. The BOJ has the option of purchasing foreign currency-denominated assets to boost aggregate demand when the domestic securities and money are treated as perfect substitutes. McCallum (2000) points out that domestic money and foreign currency assets are not necessarily perfect substitutes. The issue is whether Japan would be able to depreciate its currency sufficiently to generate some stimulus to its stagnant economy. Fourthly, price stability remains important for economic efficiency and growth. Deflation is damaging to an economy and inconsistent with the goal of price stability. Inflation targeting can avoid unexpected deflation provided that the BOJ commits to maintain a low but stable positive inflation and that its policy acquires sufficient credibility and transparency to be effective in changing inflationary expectations.

After more than a decade-long deflation, the BOJ has apparently accepted implicit inflation targeting. Although this is a positive development, on its

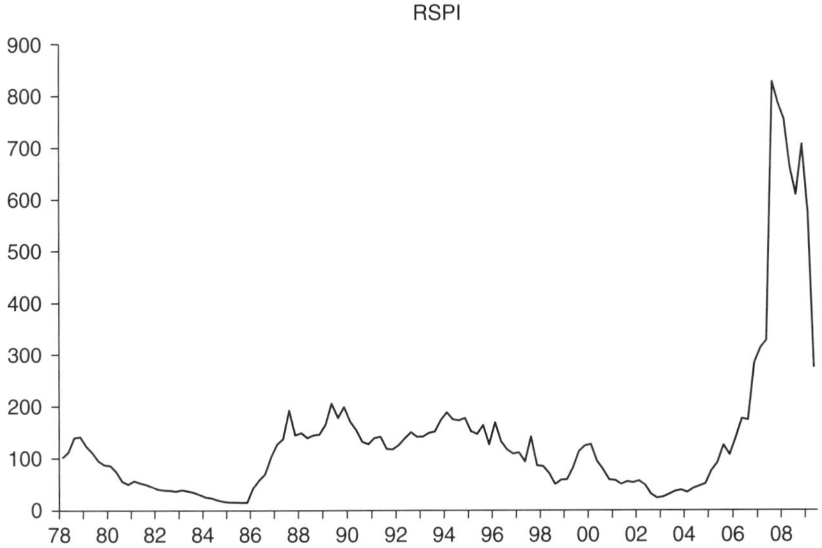

Figure 6.9 Real share price index in Japan, 1978q1–2009q2

own it may not be enough to achieve economic recovery.[8] Greater exchange rate flexibility is needed to raise the efficacy of inflation targeting. Japan has long maintained an overvalued real exchange rate to avoid creating trade friction with the United States. This has made Japanese products overpriced relative to the prices of similar products from South Korea and China. Due to high-inflation volatility, the real exchange rate has remained volatile. As Japan remains export-oriented, a rapid expansion of the monetary base, through a purchase of foreign currency-denominated assets, can cause a sharp depreciation of the yen. Such aggressive exchange rate policy is not generally supported by the IMF and the United States. Nevertheless, it has been suggested that such a policy may be justified on the ground that it would raise demand for Japanese products in the region. Steady economic growth in Japan is important to sustained economic growth in East-Southeast Asia.

The policy problem in this case is that of engineering a sharp depreciation of the yen in Japan when the BOJ remains reluctant to implement expansionary monetary policy. This suggests a need for coordination of monetary policy with the Ministry of Finance. In Japan, large foreign-exchange intervention remains the responsibility of the Ministry of Finance. However, under a floating exchange rate system, monetary policy and exchange rate policy would become equivalent, enabling the BOJ to intervene in the foreign-exchange market to depreciate the yen. This may represent an element of non-conventional monetary policy. In short, the BOJ and the Ministry of Finance may coordinate their exchange rate interventions, together with other measures, to conduct in combination an expansionary monetary policy that achieves a positive inflation rate at a level that strengthens the Japanese economy. While such a policy regime may generate large current account surpluses on a sustained basis, this is not the policy intention. Rather, it is an activist policy regime required for economic recovery on a sustained basis.

Over the long term, the exchange rate should be more flexible, with monetary policy conducted following a monetary policy rule. The aim is to keep inflation low and stable. In support of this, Japan should relax at least some restrictions on capital flows, especially inflows of foreign capital aimed at investment in the services sectors. Large-scale capital outflows may return the real exchange rate closer to its long-run value, which will make the economy more competitive. This value is the one that sustainably supports the export-led development strategy. Contemporarily, the overvalued real exchange rate has lowered economic efficiency as the non-tradable goods sector has gained more importance; but it remains protected. There are signs and expectations that the BOJ can be more effective in its conduct of monetary policy for price stability; recovery from the ongoing economic slump. A positive development is that Japan's financial system has improved with reform, and has subsequently demonstrated resilience through the US-global financial crisis. The sooner Japan achieves sustained, robust economic recovery, the better for the health of the global economy.

NOTES

1. Some general discussion on Japan is based on information drawn from multiple sources, including http://en.wikipedia.org/wiki/Japan and country information on the IMF website, http://www.imf.org/external/country/JPN/index.htm.
2. Information on contemporary issues in Japan is drawn from country-specific publications available on the IMF website, http://www.imf.org/external/country/JPN/index.htm.
3. The yen is the Japanese currency unit.
4. For discussion on contemporary monetary policy and macroeconomic developments, see Bernanke (2000, 2003), Hayashi and Prescott (2002), Hetzel (1999, 2003), Ito and Mishkin (2006), Ito and Harada (2005), Ito (2010), Miyao (2000, 2002) and Bank of Japan, http://www.boj.oro.jp/em/.
5. Some information on this section is drawn from the website on the Bank of Japan available at http://en.wikipedia.org/wiki/Bank_of_Japan.
6. For latest information on macroeconomic developments and policy issues in Japan, see IMF's country reports available at the IMF website, http://www.imf.org.
7. For earlier studies on money demand in Japan, see Amano and Wirjanto (2000), Bae et al. (2006), Bahmani-Oskooee (2001), Bahmani-Oskooee and Shabsigh (1996), Corker (1990), Nagayasu (2003), Fujiki (2002) and Fujiki et al. (2002).

8. The BOJ maintains the view that monetary policy can have only limited impact in the battle against persistent deflation and stagnation. Pumping unlimited amounts of cash into the banking system or underwriting government debts would thrust Japan into a financial crisis. Apparently, BOJ policymakers' experience with past bouts of asset bubbles and price inflation has left deep impressions difficult to discard.

REFERENCES

Altunbas, Y., M. Liu, P. Molyneau and R. Seth (2000), 'Efficiency and risk in Japanese banking', *Journal of Banking and Finance*, **24**, 1605–28.

Amano, R.A. and T.S. Wirjanto (2000), 'On the stability of long-run M2 demand in Japan', *Japanese Economic Review*, **51**(4), 536–43.

Bae, Y., V. Kakkar and M. Ogaki (2006), 'Money demand in Japan and nonlinear cointegration', *Journal of Money, Credit and Banking*, **38**(6), 1659–67.

Bahmani-Oskooee, M. (2001), 'How stable is M2 money demand function in Japan?', *Japan and the World Economy*, **13**, 455–61.

Bahmani-Oskooee, M. and G. Shabsigh (1996), 'The demand for money in Japan: evidence from cointegration analysis', *Japan and the World Economy*, **8**, 1–10.

Bank of Japan, https://www.boj.or.jp/en/.

Bernanake, B.S. (2000), 'Japanese monetary policy: a case of self-induced paralysis?', in R. Mikitani and A.S. Posen (eds), *Japan's Financial Crisis and its Parallels to US Experience*, Washington, DC: Institute for International Economics, pp. 149–66.

Bernanke, B.S. (2003), 'Some thoughts on monetary policy in Japan', Speech before the Japan Society of Monetary Economics, Tokyo, available on the Federal Reserve Board home page.

Cecchetti, S.G. (2008), *Money, Banking and Financial Markets*, New York: McGraw-Hill.

Corker, R. (1990), 'Wealth, financial liberalization, and the demand for money in Japan', *IMF Staff Papers*, **37**(2), 418–32.

Engle, R.F. and C.W.J. Granger (1987), 'Co-integration and error-correction: representation, estimation, and testing', *Econometrica*, **55**(2), 251–76.

Friedman, M. (1982), 'Monetary policy: theory and practice', *Journal of Money, Credit and Banking*, **14**, 98–118.

Friedman, M. (1985), 'Monetarism in rhetoric and in practice', in A. Ando, H. Eguchi, R. Farmer and Y. Suzuki (eds), *Monetary Policy in Our Times*, Cambridge, MA: MIT Press, pp. 15–28.

Fujiki, H. (2002), 'Money demand near zero interest rate: evidence from regional data', *Monetary and Economic Studies*, **20**(2), 25–41.

Fujiki, H., C. Hsiao and Y. Shen (2002), 'Is there a stable money demand function under the low interest rate policy? A panel data analysis', *Monetary and Economic Studies*, **20**(2), 1–23.

Greenwood, J. (1984), *Japanese Experiment in Monetarism 1974–1984*, Manhattan Report on Economic Policy No. 4.

Hayashi, F. and E.C. Prescott (2002), 'The 1990s in Japan: a lost decade', *Review of Economic Dynamics*, **5**, 206–35.

Hetzel, R.L. (1999), 'Japanese monetary policy: a quantity theory perspective', *Federal Reserve Bank of Richmond Economic Quarterly*, **85**(1), 1–25.

Hetzel, R.L. (2003), 'Japanese monetary policy and deflation', *Economic Quarterly*, **89**, 21–52.
Hossain, A. (2009), *Central Banking and Monetary Policy in the Asia-Pacific*, Cheltenham, UK and Northampton, MA, USA: Edward Elgar.
Hutchison, M. (1986), 'Japan's "money focused" monetary policy', *Federal Reserve Bank of San Francisco Economic Review*, **3**, Summer, 33–47.
Ichimura, S. (1993), *The Role of Japan in Asia*, San Francisco, CA: ICS Press.
IMF (International Monetary Fund) (various years), *International Financial Statistics*, Washington, DC: IMF.
IMF (International Monetary Fund) (various years), *World Economic Outlook*, Washington, DC: IMF.
IMF (International Monetary Fund) (1988), 'Japan's liquidity trap' (box 4.1), *World Economic Outlook*, Washington, DC: IMF.
Ito, T. (1989), 'Is the Bank of Japan a closet monetarism? Monetary targeting in Japan, 1978–1988', NBER Working Paper 2874, NBER, New York.
Ito, T. (1997), 'How can developing countries learn from East Asia's economic growth?', in *Annual World Bank Conference on Development Economics 1997*, Washington, DC: World Bank, pp. 183–200.
Ito, T. (2004a), 'Inflation targeting and Japan: why has the Bank of Japan not adopted inflation targeting?', in C. Kent and S. Guttmann (eds), *The Future of Inflation Targeting*, Sydney: Reserve Bank of Australia, pp. 220–67.
Ito, T. (2004b), 'Debt, deflation, and declining growth: new challenges of the Japanese economy', in R. Solow (ed.), *Structural Reform and Economic Policy*, London: Palgrave Macmillan, pp. 131–69.
Ito, T. (2004c), 'The *Yen* and the Japanese economy 2004', in C.F. Bergsten and J. Williamson (eds), *Dollar Adjustment: How Far? Against What?*, Washington, DC: Institute for International Economics, pp. 171–96.
Ito, T. (2006), 'Japanese monetary policy: 1998–2005 and beyond', BIS Papers No. 31, Monetary Policy in Asia: Approaches and Implementation, Bank for International Settlements, Basel, 15–132.
Ito, T. (2010), 'Monetary policy and financial stability: is inflation targeting passe?', ADB Economics Working Paper Series No. 206, Manila, the Philippines.
Ito, T. and K. Harada (2005), 'Japan premium and stock prices: two mirrors of Japanese banking crises', *International Journal of Finance and Economics*, **10**, 195–211.
Ito, T. and T. Hayashi (2004), 'Inflation targeting in Asia', HKIMR Occasional Paper No. 1, Hong Kong Institute for Monetary Research, Hong Kong Monetary Authority, Hong Kong.
Ito, T. and F.S. Mishkin (2006), 'Two decades of Japanese monetary policy and the deflation problem', in T. Ito and A. Rose (eds), *Monetary Policy with Low Inflation in the Pacific Rim*, Chicago, IL: University of Chicago Press, pp. 131–93.
Ken, K. and H. Popper (1997), 'Monetary policy in Japan: a structural VAR analysis', *Journal of the Japanese and International Economics*, **11**(3), 275–95.
McCallum, B.T. (2000), 'Theoretical analysis regarding a zero lower bound on nominal interest rates', *Journal of Money, Credit and Banking*, **32**, 870–904.
McCallum, B.T. and E. Nelson (2011), 'Money and inflation: some critical issues', in B.M. Friedman and M. Woodford (eds), *Handbook of Monetary Economics*, Vol. 3A, Amsterdam: Elsevier Science, pp. 97–153.
Meltzer, A.H. (2000), 'Monetary policy in the new global economy: the case of Japan', *Cato Journal*, **20**(1), 69–72.

Mishkin, F.S. (2013), *The Economics of Money, Banking, and Financial Markets*, New York: Pearson Education.
Miyao, R. (2000), 'The role of monetary policy in Japan: a break in the 1990s', *Journal of the Japanese and International Economics*, **14**, 366–84.
Miyao, R. (2002), 'The effects of monetary policy in Japan', *Journal of Money, Credit and Banking*, **34**, 376–92.
Nagayasu, J. (2003), 'A re-examination of the Japanese money demand function and structural shifts', *Journal of Policy Modeling*, **25**, 359–75.
Olivei, G.P. (2002), 'Japan's approach to monetary policy', *New England Economic Review*, Second quarter, 39–43.
Speigel, M.M. (2000), 'Inflation targeting for the Bank of Japan', *Federal Reserve Bank of San Francisco Economic Letter*, No. 2000–11.
Suzuki, Y. (1981), 'Why is the performance of the Japanese economy so much better?', *Journal of Japanese Studies*, **7**(2), 403–13.
Suzuki, Y. (1985), 'Japan's monetary policy over the past 10 years', *Bank of Japan Monetary and Economic Studies*, **3**(2) 1–9.
Suzuki, Y. (1992), 'Bank of Japan', in P. Newman, M. Milgate and J. Eatwell (eds), *The New Palgrave Dictionary of Money and Finance*, Vol. 1, London: Macmillan, pp. 167–9.
Ueda, K. (2011), 'The effectiveness of non-traditional monetary policy measures: the case of the Bank of Japan', CARF Working Paper, CARF-F-252.

7. South Korea

South Korea is one of the major economies of East Asia. Having made impressive economic and social progress since the 1960s, it joined the OECD in 1996. This transformation of the South Korean economy is viewed as a test case in economic development, comparable with the 'economic miracle' of the Japanese development 'take-off' that preceded it by several decades.

South Korea has an ancient history and culture. It is an ethnically homogeneous society with a population size of about 50 million and has one of the highest population densities in the world, averaging about 491 persons per square kilometre. The beginnings of South Korea's contemporary economic and political history can be traced to the mid 1940s when, as an outcome of the Japanese defeat in World War II, it gained independence from Japan. Since then South Korea's impressive economic performance and social progress have drawn interest among development economists and policymakers across the globe.

Like many developing countries of the Asia-Pacific region, South Korea underwent intermittent, major political upheaval throughout the twentieth century. Having suffered from repression by the Japanese colonial regime for much of the first half of the twentieth century, South Korea was then devastated by a three year-long war with North Korea, 1950–53, which took the lives of 1.2 million people. South Korea has sustained tense political-military relations with North Korea since partition of the Korean Peninsula post-World War II. Following military rule from the 1960s through the mid 1980s, South Korea has established a presidential form of democracy that appears to have worked well so far. In so far as politics is concerned, the country is moving ahead steadily with the processes of democratization, together with associated institutional development, needed for sustaining the steady economic growth of an advanced market economy.

Following a long period of sustained economic and social progress since the 1960s, South Korea was perhaps the nation hardest-hit by the East-Southeast Asian financial crisis, 1997–98. Although the economy suffered heavily and took a number of years to recover, the crisis turned out to be a blessing in disguise for the quality of South Korean macroeconomic management. Under an IMF-supported stabilization and structural adjustment programme, the government introduced a wide range of post-crisis deregulatory measures and financial reforms. The main aim of the reform measures has been to establish efficiency and associated resilience of the financial system, such that it can both absorb external shocks and more readily channel funds to productive sectors of the economy according to demand. For institutionalization of rule-based monetary policy for price stability, in 1998 South Korea floated the exchange rate of its currency (the Korean won), complementarily relaxed its regulation of international capital flows and adopted inflation targeting as its monetary policy strategy of choice. This was significant because South Korea is one of the major countries in Asia that sustained rapid economic growth, beginning from the 1960s through the mid 1990s, in an inflationary environment. Policymakers in South Korea allowed economic growth to override price stability as the key objective of policy. The potency of monetary policy had, however, been limited under its preceding exchange rate regime – a fixed peg exchange rate system with restricted capital flows (Dueker and Kim, 1999).

Under inflation targeting since the financial crisis, South Korea has maintained low average inflation, at about 3 per cent per annum. While economic growth has slowed somewhat since the financial crisis, South Korea has nevertheless maintained a relatively substantial economic growth rate of 4 per cent per annum or thereabouts. This can be considered satisfactory for an advanced economy such as South Korea, with a difficult period of global economic turbulence forming its environment, especially through the US-global financial crisis followed by the continuing European debt crisis.

In a comparative sense, unlike Japan, South Korea has mostly managed to escape the adverse consequences of the US-global financial crisis. Fiscal prudence and the consequent low level of public debt have allowed policymakers in South Korea to focus on inflation control to sustain economic growth, albeit at a reduced pace (see Table 7.1) in comparison with headier times. In contrast, macroeconomic management in Japan remains difficult as it has been overwhelmed by a rapidly rising public debt in an economy beseiged by prolonged recession. South Korea's fiscal prudence is attributed to the standing commitment of the government, especially since the financial crisis, to achieve budget balance over the business cycle (Oh, 2012). This is an almost unprecedented political achievement, since it requires new political resolve every few years. The inference from it is that budget balance has become part of South Korea's political landscape and achievement of it is useful, or indeed essential, to the government's efforts to be re-elected at each national election. Nevertheless, South

Table 7.1 Macroeconomic indicators, South Korea, 1951–2012

Macroeconomic indicators	1951–55	1956–60	1961–65	1966–70	1971–75	1976–80	1981–85	1986–90	1991–95	1996–2000	2001–05	2006–10	2011	2012
Budget balance (% of GDP)	n.a.	n.a.	n.a.	n.a.	n.a.	n.a.	n.a.	n.a.	2.4	2.4	1.8	1.4	1.8	2.0
General government gross debt (% of GDP)	n.a.	n.a.	n.a.	n.a.	n.a.	n.a.	n.a.	13.8	11.5	14.1	22.4	31.8	34.2	33.5
Money-growth rate (%)														
Narrow money growth	n.a.	n.a.	25.3	38.1	29.5	32.1	26.2	25.0	18.2	15.0	11.3	5.8	3.3	6.3
Broad money growth	73.3	22.3	28.1	52.9	29.1	37.0	26.6	28.1	20.6	14.1	7.7	10.2	5.5	4.8
Real GDP growth rate (%)	5.0	3.4	6.5	10.4	7.6	7.0	7.8	9.7	7.8	4.9	4.5	3.8	3.7	2.0
GDP per capita, current prices, US dollar	n.a.	n.a.	n.a.	n.a.	n.a.	1689	2152	4530	8995	10629	13756	19559	22424	23021
Unemployment rate (%)	n.a.	n.a.	n.a.	n.a.	n.a.	5.2	4.3	3.1	2.7	4.7	3.7	3.5	3.4	3.3
Output gap (% of potential GDP)	n.a.	n.a.	n.a.	n.a.	n.a.	−2.8	−1.1	0.2	−0.2	−0.3	−0.2	−0.8	−0.1	−1.0
CPI inflation rate (%)	119.9	11.4	15.4	12.6	15.6	17.4	7.3	5.4	6.2	4.0	3.3	3.0	4.0	2.2
Current account balance (% of GDP)	n.a.	n.a.	n.a.	n.a.	n.a.	−8.3	−2.4	4.2	−0.9	2.9	2.4	2.1	2.4	1.9

Nominal interest rate (%)														
Deposit rate of interest	n.a.	n.a.	n.a.	22.8	14.9	17.5	10.3	10.0	9.2	9.5	4.5	4.6	4.2	3.7
Money-market rate	n.a.	n.a.	n.a.	n.a.	n.a.	19.8	13.2	11.1	13.7	10.2	4.0	3.6	3.1	3.1
Real interest rate (%)[a]														
Deposit rate of interest	n.a.	n.a.	n.a.	7.5	−0.2	0.3	3.0	4.4	2.8	5.3	1.1	1.5	0.1	1.5
Money-market rate						1.8	5.7	5.4	7.0	5.9	0.6	0.5	−0.9	0.8
Nominal exchange rate (won per US dollar)	19.6	52.6	173.0	233.4	405.4	508.7	772.8	762.9	778.3	1095.4	1180.6	1083.8	1108.3	1126.5
Nominal effective exchange rate[b]	n.a.	2214.7	906.7	497.4	323.2	240.5	176.2	149.2	131.3	102.7	93.8	91.7	80.1	80.7
Real effective exchange rate[b, c]	220.2	201.1	98.5	97.8	97.8	114.2	98.0	101.0	112.5	91.9	86.7	96.4	96.9	95.4

Notes:
n.a. = not available
a. Real interest rate is estimated as: 100(((1 + interest rate)/(1 + inflation rate))−1) where the interest rate and inflation rate are expressed in decimal.
b. A rise in the index value of the exchange rate represents appreciation.
c. Real exchange rate: data for the period 1951–70 represents the bilateral real exchange rate of the South Korean won against the US dollar.

Source: Author's computation based on IMF, *International Financial Statistics*; IMF, *World Economic Outlook*; and other country-specific publications on the IMF website.

Korea introduced some countercyclical expansionary monetary and fiscal policies that provided some stimulatory impact on South Korea's economy during the US-global financial crisis. Apparently, these were due to the encouragement of the IMF. The measures were considered useful to minimize the adverse consequences of the US-global financial crisis (Alp et al., 2011) and deployed within the (IMF) framework of medium-term fiscal planning and consolidation. The policy measures were not, however, critical for maintaining economic growth at a moderately high level given the economy's strong economic fundamentals. The IMF has complimented the South Korean government on the resilience of its economy, on its maintenance of a low level of public debt and on the accumulation of large fiscal reserves to cope with global economic uncertainty, including the possibility of further unexpected sudden future deteriorations in the global economy.

The remainder of this chapter provides an overview of the issues in central banking and monetary policy in South Korea in an historical context, and examines some monetary relations that underwrite the design of rule-based and conduct of monetary policy for price stability. To put the discussion into perspective, the next section provides a brief review of the recent economic and political history of South Korea. In particular, this discussion focuses on the evolution of the role of South Korea's financial system in its rapid, sustained economic growth.

SOUTH KOREA'S RECENT ECONOMIC AND POLITICAL HISTORY

South Korea was one of the poorest countries in Asia until the 1950s. Until the East Asian currency financial crisis, rapid economic growth brought significant structural change in South Korea's economy. This has been associated with social progress and rapid urbanization of the country. Unlike most countries in Latin America, South Korea managed to sustain rapid economic growth in the midst of a high-inflation environment. The question of how it achieved this has attracted the attention and interest of development economists and policymakers across the globe.

After a period of economic and political instability during the 1950s, South Korea's economy reached the 'take-off' stage of economic development in the mid 1960s. History recognizes General Park Chung-hee, who took power in 1961 in a military *coup d'état*, as the architect of this take-off. His regime laid a sound foundation for the modernization, rapid economic growth and transformation of the South Korean economy from the early 1960s through the 1970s (Amsden, 1989; Song, 1990).

Like Japan, South Korea's endowment of natural resources is limited.

In the import-substituting development model, such endowment is considered an important ingredient in 'take-off' and subsequent rapid economic development. Economic breakthrough in South Korea came in the mid 1960s when it partially moved away from the import-substituting strategy of industrialization and became successful in raising the exports of labour-intensive products to Western industrialized countries. In particular, exports took off in 1964 in response to a sharp devaluation of the won under an IMF-supported stabilization and structural adjustment programme. For example, exports rose about 37 per cent in US dollar terms in 1964. This was followed by a sharp increase in exports of about 47 per cent in 1965 (Eichengreen, 2012). Textiles, lumber, plywood and steel and metal products accounted for most of this export expansion. The major export products were labour- and resource-intensive, with substantial imported inputs. After 1965, South Korea was able to add a few more products to its export basket. The new products, which relied heavily on imported parts and components, included consumer electronics, electrical machinery, household appliances and transport equipment.

While South Korea thereby became dependent on imports of raw materials and intermediate products to maintain its impressive export growth, it continued with protectionist policies throughout the late 1960s and the 1970s. Consequently, South Korea's trade policies became complex, designed as they were to support both the import-substituting and export-oriented industries; especially some weak and inefficient ones (Dornbusch and Park, 1987; Song, 1990). Over the years, the trade composition and the policy focus and environment have changed. Imports have now become as important as exports for maintaining steady economic growth, albeit at a much lower level. Presently, South Korea is the sixth largest exporter and the tenth largest importer in the world.

South Korea's export-oriented development strategy, in the midst of protectionist import policies, was in operation in the presence of a repressed financial system from the 1960s through the mid 1980s. The financial environment started to become repressive following the nationalization of banks and other financial institutions in 1961. From that time, the government imposed controls on interest rates, bank credits and capital flows. The main task of nationalized banks and other financial institutions was to channel preferential and subsidized credits both to import-substituting and to export-oriented industries. Consequently, South Korean money and capital markets remained thin and underdeveloped. This affected saving, investment and economic growth (Cho, 1989; Fry, 1985).

In the midst of import restrictions and financial repression, then, the South Korean government's development strategy emphasized export-oriented industrialization. As a savings-scarce country, from 1962, with the passage of the Act for Payment Guarantee for Foreign Loans, South Korea became involved in foreign borrowing by export-oriented firms. The government in particular guaranteed all foreign loans obtained by domestic firms. However, to avoid creating a moral hazard problem, the authorities monitored the operations of those firms that borrowed from overseas and whose loans were guaranteed by the government. Moreover, all firms intending to borrow from abroad were required to obtain approval from the Economic Planning Board. This Board had the authority to limit the size of borrowing and to dictate end use of borrowed funds. Finally, the Ministry of Finance took responsibility for monitoring the usage of borrowed funds from overseas and their repayment as per agreed contracts (Eichengreen, 2012; Emery, 2001).

During the mid 1970s, South Korea switched its development strategy from rapid export growth of labour-intensive products to the establishment of heavy and chemical industries. To implement this strategy of industrialization, the monetary authorities imposed greater repression on the financial system, with tightened control over banks and the specialized allocation and distribution of credits across industrial sectors selected by policymakers as 'winners'. Although South Korea experienced high and volatile inflation throughout the 1970s, the monetary authorities kept the interest rate unchanged and consistently below the rate of inflation. Consequently, the real deposit rate of interest, for example, hovered around very low and positive, and even negative levels. This created a shortage of investible funds, leading the government to instruct the banks to ration financial credits and direct them to selective projects on a priority basis. To facilitate this administrative control over credit distribution, the Bank of Korea (BOK), which is the central bank of South Korea, provided all commercial banks with refinancing facilities for their policy-linked loans. Consequently, during the early years of the introduction of subsidized credit schemes in the 1970s, about 70 per cent of bank loans went to heavy and chemical industries. In parallel with these measures, the authorities provided tax concessions and maintained import restrictions to support the establishment of the desired heavy and chemical industries (Fry, 1998).

For several reasons, the government's industrial policy to establish heavy and chemical industries did not work well. Firstly, the heavy industrialization policy rested on policymakers' optimistic assumption of foreign demand for heavy industrial and chemical products. This led to an excess of investment, in relatively inefficient form. Secondly, as high priority was accorded to the promotion of heavy industries, this in effect was a neglect of labour-intensive export industries where South Korea had a comparative advantage. In particular, as the real exchange rate of the won appreciated sharply in the late 1970s due to high and volatile inflation, South

Korea lost some of its competitiveness for the exportation of labour-intensive products. Moreover, the growth of exports fell because there were domestic shortages of basic products, which sustained high inflationary pressure throughout the 1970s. Thirdly, the rapid expansion of credits to the heavy industry sector was associated with large-scale inflows of foreign capital, originating mostly from the construction boom in the Gulf region where the South Korean construction firms had participated. As most of these capital inflows were unsterilized, they expanded the money supply and accelerated inflation. The consequent appreciation of the real exchange rate lowered exports, raised current account deficits and, subsequently, created a balance-of-payments crisis after the second OPEC oil shock of 1979.

Having encountered such macroeconomic problems in the 1970s, there was a major shift of economic policy in South Korea in the 1980s. An IMF-supported comprehensive stabilization programme was introduced, which included some restrictions on the conduct of fiscal and monetary policies. The main objectives of restrictive and disciplined monetary and fiscal policies were to lower and stabilize inflation and sustain rapid economic growth, without raising the levels of current account deficits and external debt. With trade liberalization measures, the government implemented some financial deregulation measures, such as the removal of controls over both interest rates and the credit allocation and distribution across sectors.

Before 1982 there was a plethora of differential and regulated interest rates, which the monetary authorities adjusted only partially and occasionally to any rise in inflation. The first major attempt to deregulate interest rates was in December 1988. This was a time when inflation was moderately low and stable. The deregulatory measures undertaken made the real deposit rate of interest significantly positive and hence lowered the degree of financial repression. Meanwhile, South Korea, being the fourth largest borrower of foreign funds among developing countries, prioritized improvement of its balance-of-payments situation by making the exchange rate more flexible. In addition, some policy measures were undertaken that led to a depreciation of both the nominal and real effective exchange rates. They restored the competitiveness of key exportable products that South Korea had lost in its 1970s policy push to establish its heavy and chemical industries.

However, the overall financial sector reform in South Korea fell short of the requirements for creating a market-oriented financial system. Financial institutions, used to following directions from the government for both the adjustment of interest rates and credit distribution, were unready for competition in a deregulated financial environment. Consequently, the government continued to provide guidance on interest rate policy. Its main purpose was to avoid steep rises in interest rates. Therefore, interest rates remained largely unresponsive to market conditions until inflation targeting was implemented following the 1997 financial crisis (Amsden and Euh, 1993; Fry, 1998). The crisis had originated in Thailand in July 1997, and the thin, underdeveloped financial system in South Korea could not cope with large-scale capital flows that it generated. The South Korean economy was consequently engulfed.

THE BANK OF KOREA (BOK): ORGANIZATION AND ACTIVITIES

South Korea first attempted to create a central banking system in November 1909, with the establishment of the Bank of Korea. Its first functions included the issuing of banknotes and coins and the management of the National Treasury, which until then had been handled by the Japanese Daiichi Bank. This first iteration of the Bank of Korea was reorganized and renamed the Bank of Chosun on 1 August 1911. The Bank of Chosun performed some central banking functions such as the issuing of banknotes and coins and the management of the national Treasury. It continued to act as the central bank when South Korea gained independence from Japan after World War II. Expanded functions of the Bank of Chosun then taken up included the issuing of banknotes and coins, the managing of the national Treasury, the holding of foreign reserves and the offering of rediscount loan facilities to the commercial banks.

South Korea made considerable preparation for the establishment of a formal central bank in the midst of economic and political uncertainties during the late 1940s. The present Bank of Korea Act was promulgated on 5 June 1950. As the country's central bank, the Bank of Korea (BOK) commenced operations on 12 June 1950. The BOK now acts as the note issuing authority, banker to the private sector banking system ('banker to the banks') and the government's bank. It is also responsible for the design and conduct of monetary and credit policies and for the management of foreign reserves of the country (BOK, 2000).

The Monetary Policy Committee (MPC) is the policymaking body of the BOK. It makes policy decisions on such matters as the operations of the Bank and the designing and conducting of monetary and credit policies. The MPC is composed of the following members:

(a) the governor of the BOK
(b) one member recommended by the minister of finance and economy

(c) one member recommended by the chairman of the Financial Supervisory Commission
(d) one member recommended by the president of the Korea Chamber of Commerce and Industry
(e) one member recommended by the chairman of the Korea Federation of Banks
(f) one member recommended by the Chairman of the Korea Securities Dealers Association.

The governor is an *ex officio* member of the MPC, which is appointed by the President of the Republic, following the deliberation of the State Council. The State Council is the supreme policy deliberation body of the government. On the recommendation of each of the pertinent organizations listed above, the President appoints other members of the Committee. The appointed members have a four-year term and remain eligible for reappointment for a single consecutive term. The governor serves as chairman of the MPC.

The governor has a four-year term of office. It may be extended for a single consecutive term. The governor has a guarantee that he or she will not be discharged from office against his or her will during any four-year term, except under certain conditions as codified in the relevant laws. The governor appoints the deputy governor and assistant governors as his or her assistants. In addition, the BOK has an auditor, who is independent of the Bank's executive organs. The auditor is appointed by the President on the recommendation of the minister of finance and economy.

The BOK Act of 1950 was revised by the Supreme Committee for the National Reconstruction and enacted in May 1962. The revised Act changed the role of the MPC from devising policies on monetary, credit and foreign exchange to a new role for the development of policies on monetary and credit operations and management. The responsibility for both foreign-exchange policy and foreign reserve management was transferred from the BOK to the government. Moreover, any policy decisions arrived at by the MPC were made conditional on a reconsideration request from the minister of finance and economy. If such a request for reconsideration of policy was rejected, the responsibility for making the final decision was given to the Cabinet. The government thereby clearly retains final authority to make decisions on monetary and credit operations and management. The government already had taken control over both exchange rate policy and foreign reserve management.

The financial markets in South Korea have undergone a rapid structural change from the 1990s. Some of the recent financial reforms have been triggered by the East-Southeast Asian financial crisis of the late 1990s, which heavily affected South Korea's economy despite its strong economic fundamentals. Major reforms included the deregulation of interest rates, the opening up of the banking and financial sector and the liberalization of exchange and capital markets. The most far-reaching reform undertaken by the government was institutionalization of the conduct of monetary policy. Under a revised central banking Act effective from 1 April 1998, the BOK has assumed responsibility for price stability under inflation targeting. With inflation targeting a forward-looking, pre-emptive strategy of monetary policy, the BOK has improved its organizational set-up for inflation forecasting and the monitoring of economic and financial variables. The BOK monitors those economic and financial variables that are considered useful to inflation forecasting and for improved understanding of monetary policy actions that are taken by the MPC for maintaining price stability.

The next section provides further discussion on the evolution of monetary policy in South Korea and reviews related policy issues in an historical context.

EVOLUTION OF MONETARY POLICY[1]

South Korea has conducted its monetary policy under a succession of economic policy regimes since the late 1950s. At that time, it introduced a Fiscal Financial Stabilization Plan, which provided a macroeconomic framework for achieving and maintaining price stability for sustained economic growth. This plan reduced the inflation rate from moderately high levels, which had originated in the monetization of large and sustained budget deficits during the Korean War, in which China-backed, communist North Korea attempted to invade and subjugate the US-backed South Korea. In addition, the post-war reconstruction of the economy led to a rapid monetary expansion that kept inflation high and unstable. Under the Fiscal Financial Stabilization Plan, the narrow money-growth rate was set with an upper limit and was pre-announced quarterly or yearly. Monetary policy independence for price stability, however, depended on the exchange rate arrangements and the effectiveness of capital controls in place to maintain financial stability.

South Korea maintained a de facto US dollar pegged exchange rate regime from the 1950s through the end of the 1970s. It was called a unified floating exchange rate system from 1965. Within this system, the nominal exchange rate of the won against the US dollar was adjusted occasionally when the real exchange rate became overvalued and, as a consequence, reduced the competitiveness of exportable items in international markets.

Accordingly, large devaluations of South Korean currency took place in 1971, 1974 and 1980. This bilateral pegged exchange rate arrangement with the US dollar was abandoned in the early 1980s. An alternative system was then introduced in which the exchange rate of the won was pegged to a basket of hard currencies. The basket currency pegged exchange rate system was designed mostly to achieve stability of the real exchange rate of the won. This was necessary as some currencies exhibited large fluctuations under a floating exchange rate system, and this created a danger of real exchange rate misalignment for the won in South Korea (Dooley et al., 2001).

In March 1990, South Korea introduced a new exchange rate system after replacing the multi-currency basket peg system. The new system was called the Market Average Exchange Rate system. Under this system the exchange rate of the won against the US dollar was allowed to be determined in the market within an intervention band. The intervention band was set around the weighted average of the interbank exchange rates of the won of the previous day. The cross rates of the won against other currencies were determined by the US dollar exchange rates against those currencies in the foreign-exchange markets. This system created some flexibility of the exchange rate of the won. It was intended to stabilize the exchange rate while creating an environment for any future move towards a freely floating exchange rate for the won.

South Korea continued with capital controls from the 1950s through the 1980s. This created some potency for monetary policy in South Korea under a pegged exchange rate system. As discussed above, monetary policy in South Korea was accommodative since the 1960s, in the sense that it was supportive of the government's export-led development strategy, the grain-support programme and the promotion of heavy and chemical industries (Amsden, 1989). Fry (1985) explained this monetary accommodation policy as follows: 'loans for export activities have been heavily subsidised through an automatic rediscount mechanism. A rapid increase in exports and, hence, export credit has caused a rapid expansion of high-powered money in the form of increased export rediscount' (p. 300). Consequently, the money-growth rate, narrow or broad, was maintained at a high level, well above 20 per cent per annum, until the mid 1990s (see Table 7.1). This caused high and volatile inflation and breached IMF conditionality under stabilization and structural adjustment programmes.

Historically, South Korea has maintained close relations with the IMF. After running large current account deficits for a number of years in the early 1960s, South Korea accepted a standby credit agreement with the IMF. This agreement required South Korea to set a concrete figure for the money-growth target in consultation with the IMF. Despite such an arrangement with the IMF in later years, South Korea was the only East Asian industrializing country that accorded high priority to economic growth over price stability. Policymakers in South Korea had broad consensus as a matter of principle on promoting economic growth provided that inflation does not exceed a tolerable rate. For example, Park (1983, p. 323) pointed out that '[a]ll groups including business in Korea . . . have seldom been willing to put up with the possible setbacks to growth that price stability may require'. This explains why price stability did not gain such importance in South Korea as to introduce a rule-based monetary policy until the country was hit by the East-Southeast Asian financial crisis during 1997–98. This was, however, an issue that came to the forefront of discussion from the late 1970s.

After the second OPEC oil price shock in 1979, South Korea switched its monetary policy objective from rapid economic growth to price stability. Cole and Park (1983, p. 214) observed that '[r]ecently . . . inflation has become the most important issue in Korea, and there is some indication that both the government and the general public would be willing to trade 1 or 2 per cent growth for greater stability of prices'. Accordingly, the money-growth rate, both narrow and broad, was lowered during the early 1980s. The BOK used indirect monetary policy instruments to control the money-growth rate during the first half of the 1980s. During the second half of the 1980s, the BOK introduced direct measures to control the money supply such as the reduction of preferential discounting for export industries, raising both the reserve requirement ratio and the rediscount rate, and the reintroduction of marginal reserve requirements. In addition, some credit control measures were taken to supplement open market operations for monetary control and management (BOK, 2000).

South Korea suffered heavily from the 1997–98 financial crisis. As a result, it came under an IMF-stabilization and structural adjustment programme, which included a package of policy conditionality such as the floatation of the exchange rate of the won, opening up the financial sector for foreign investment and liberalization of capital accounts in the balance-of-payments. Pursuant to a revision of the BOK Act in April 1998, the BOK adopted inflation targeting for price stability. Following standard practice around the world, the BOK sets the inflation target in consultation with the government. Article 1, Clause 1 of the BOK Act stipulates that the purpose of this Act is 'to contribute to the sound development of the national economy by pursuing price stability through the formulation and implementation of efficient monetary policy'. Accordingly, the BOK takes price stability as the most important objective of monetary policy. Article 1, Clause 2 of the BOK Act, however, stipulates that 'the Bank of

Korea needs to pay attention to financial stability in the implementation of monetary policy'. This raises the question of the extent, if any, to which the MPC takes into account the impact of any change in the interest rate on the exchange rate and the consequent impact on financial stability. In a developing country, in particular, exchange rate stability is considered important for maintaining financial stability. This is because any sharp volatility of the exchange rate may trigger large-scale capital flows. It is not clear whether this remains an issue in South Korea given that it has accumulated a large volume of foreign reserves since the East-Southeast Asian financial crisis. The suggested linkage between monetary policy and fiscal policy indicates that the Bank of Korea does not consider the volatility of the exchange rate benign.

During 1998–99 the BOK used CPI inflation as the benchmark indicator for inflation targeting. This headline measure of inflation was used because of its familiarity to the public and its consequent potential, in the early stages of inflation targeting, to maximize the credibility of inflation targeting among the broader public beyond the markets. Since 2000 a measure of core CPI inflation has been chosen as the benchmark indicator for inflation targeting. This definition of CPI excludes the prices of petroleum and agricultural products, excluding cereals. The reason for excluding the prices of these products is that they are susceptible to the supply shocks and hence cannot be controlled through monetary policy measures. Based on Article 6, Clause 1 of the BOK Act, the BOK sets the mid-term inflation target for three years in consultation with the government. Presently, South Korea's inflation target is within the range 2.5 to 3.5 per cent per annum.

Some amendment has been made to the use of the monetary policy instrument since the 2000s. Initially, to achieve the announced inflation target under the revised Act of the Bank of Korea, the growth rate of a broad monetary aggregate (M3) was used as an operational target. This arrangement was similar to the two-pillar monetary system of the European Central Bank (ECB). The target inflation rate was expected to act as an anchor to inflation expectations. The BOK then set the broad money-growth target because it was concerned about any sudden drop of the M3 aggregate as an instrument of monetary policy. During 2001–02 the M3 growth rate was not set but only monitored. In 2003 the M3 growth rate was discontinued altogether. This ended the transition from the two-pillar monetary system to full-fledged inflation targeting. Under the present form of inflation targeting, the BOK deploys a policy interest rate as an instrument of monetary policy. The question then arises whether jettisoning the monetary aggregate as an instrument of monetary policy was somewhat premature. The recent literature suggests that there is scope for using a monetary aggregate as an instrument of monetary policy under inflation targeting. After all, the linkage between money growth and inflation remains strong for most countries, including South Korea. The relative effectiveness of the interest rate in demand management, when it is already very low, is another contentious issue. A large body of literature has emerged on the issue, especially in the context of Japan's prolonged recession in a deflationary environment.

Presently, the MPC of the BOK sets the base interest rate every month after taking into consideration price movements, economic activity and financial market conditions. Then the BOK steers the call rate in the interbank market to converge on the newly set base rate by making itself available for borrowing from, and lending to, participating institutions in the interbank market. Changes in the call rate of interest affect the market interest rates such as the yields on the Certificates of Deposits and Treasury bonds and the deposit and lending rates of interest. Any change in real interest rate brought about monetary policy affects consumption and investment spending. This changes aggregate demand and hence both output and prices given the level of aggregate supply.

South Korea's inflation targeting strategy for price stability has been broadly successful in maintaining inflation within the target range (Kim and Park, 2006). It has also maintained economic growth of about 4 per cent per annum. Importantly, since the introduction of inflation targeting, monetary policy operations have become transparent. The chairman of the MPC publicly explains the background of monetary policy decisions once they are made. To ensure its accountability, the BOK submits a monetary policy report to the Congress every year. In addition, the chairman of the MPC, its members and other high officials inform the public on monetary policy stance and future policy directions through public addresses, interviews and conference presentations (Kim and Park, 2006). How much credibility the BOK has for maintaining price stability is, however, not yet clear. Achieving policy credibility is a time-consuming process. High persistence of inflation in South Korea indicates that the Bank of Korea has limited credibility of monetary policy despite its gaining autonomy in conducting monetary policy for price stability.

MONETARY POLICY TRANSMISSION MECHANISMS

Open market operations are the main instrument of monetary policy in South Korea. The BOK carries out open market operations to steer the overnight call rate in the interbank market around the base interest rate that it sets every month. Changes of the base rate induce financial institutions to adjust their temporary surpluses or shortfalls of funds. During any financial turmoil, the BOK takes measures to maintain stability of the financial system. It does so by changing the liquidity condition through open market operations. In undertaking such functions, the BOK conducts monetary operations in three ways: (1) through transaction of government securities; (2) through issuance and repurchase of monetary stabilization bonds; and (3) through the commercial banks' deposits at the Monetary Stabilization Accounts.

The BOK's adjustment of the base interest rate affects the economy through different channels of the transmission of monetary policy. For example, if the BOK raises the base rate of interest, the very short-term interest rate, such as the overnight call rate, rises immediately. The deposit and lending rates of interest rise subsequently depending on any restrictions imposed by the authorities on their movements. The long-term interest rates may also come under upward pressure depending on the future inflationary expectations. The movements of the interest rates may change aggregate demand by influencing the decisions of economic agents with respect to both consumption and investment spending. A rise in the real interest rate generally lowers consumption or raises saving. A rise in the real interest rate also raises the cost of borrowing and hence may lower investment. Provided that the level of aggregate supply remains unchanged, any decrease in aggregate demand would lower both output and prices.

Here follows some further elaboration of the key channels of the transmission mechanisms of monetary policy in South Korea. To facilitate this discussion, Figure 7.1 provides a simplified sketch of the monetary policy transmission mechanisms in this country, as illustrated by the BOK on its website.

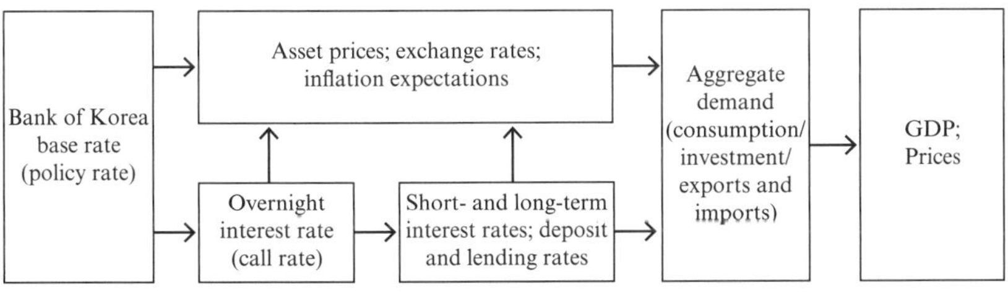

Source: Adapted based on Bank of Korea website, http://www.bok.or.kr/eng/.

Figure 7.1 Monetary policy transmission mechanisms in South Korea

Asset Price Channel

A change in the base rate of interest influences asset prices including the prices of stocks, bonds and real estate. For instance, if the base rate of interest rises, the present value of future profits from holding the stocks, bonds and real estate declines. This lowers the current prices of these assets. The consequent decrease in wealth lowers consumption spending. A rise in the interest rate, by depressing the asset prices, also lowers the net worth of a firm. This diminishes the firm's ability to borrow for investment.

Credit Channel

Any weakening of the balance sheet of a firm due to a rise in the interest rate raises the asymmetric information problem. This lowers the firm's ability to borrow for investment. For a bank, a rise in the interest rate raises credit risk, which in turn raises the lending rate of interest. This lowers the demand for loans for investment. This shows that any adjustment of the base rate of interest can affect the banks' lending behaviour. Further, a rise in the interest rate can lower credit-based consumption demand by households.

Exchange Rate Channel

Ceteris paribus, an increase in the base rate of interest may lead to an appreciation of the exchange rate. For instance, if the base rate of interest rises in South Korea while the interest rates in other countries remain unchanged, the relative rates of returns on South Korean won-denominated assets would increase. This may attract foreign capital and appreciate the domestic currency. An appreciated currency usually lowers net exports and hence domestic activity and prices.

Inflation Expectations Channel

An increase in the base rate of interest may lower inflation expectations and hence current prices. For example, an increase in the base rate of interest may be interpreted as the BOK's resolve to lower inflation from a high level. Provided that the BOK's actions are credible, inflation expectations would fall. This may influence the firms' decisions on setting the product prices low and the workers' decisions on acceptance of lower wages. The outcome could be a decline in inflation. In general, the higher the credibility of a central bank in controlling inflation, the more effective could be the impact of the interest rate on inflation through the inflation expectations channel.

Summing Up

The above channels of the transmission mechanisms of monetary policy in South Korea are indicative. They remain speculative in a changing economic environment. Consequently, like other central banks, the BOK monitors all plausible channels and strives to ensure that the impulses of monetary policy actions are transmitted through the economy and that they bring the expected outcomes with respect to output and prices within a shorter time horizon. The transmission mechanisms of monetary policy ultimately depend on the validity of the assumption of short-term rigidities of wages and prices and the prevailing rates of inflation and inflationary expectations. Monetary policy transmission mechanisms generally operate better when the money and capital markets are highly developed and when economic agents remain sensitive, and respond quickly, to market signals.

MACROECONOMIC DEVELOPMENTS AND INFLATION PERFORMANCE

South Korea has maintained an impressive economic performance since the late 1950s. From the early 1960s to the mid 1990s, economic growth remained high. The South Korean economy in particular managed to grow rapidly in the midst of double-digit inflation since the mid 1950s through the 1970s (Dornbusch and Park, 1987). Inflation was reduced to single-digit level in the early 1980s. As an oil-importing country, South Korea suffered from large current account deficits during the 1970s following two oil price shocks. Due to high and volatile inflation, the real exchange rate appreciated and became misaligned. Since the mid 1980s through the mid 1990s, the real exchange rate remained mostly stable. During this period South Korea maintained current account surpluses at the rate of about 6 per cent of GDP. This indicates that the 1997–98 financial crisis that hit the South Korean economy was not due to large and unsustainable currency account deficits originating from an overvalued exchange rate. The real exchange rate during the period was quite likely tracked closely to a level determined by the fundamentals of Korea's economy.

Under IMF-supported structural adjustment programmes, the real exchange rate depreciated sharply and facilitated the recovery process of the South Korean economy. It has performed well since its rapid recovery, sustaining output growth rate at around 4 per cent per annum since the early 2000s. The flexible exchange rate system, in particular, has played a key role as a shock absorber following the US-global financial crisis. While a growth rate averaging 4 per cent is respectable for an advanced economy, there is some concern that economic growth in South Korea has trended downward since 2005. Given strong fundamentals, the economy is expected to grow at about the 4 per cent level in the near future in a moderately low-inflation environment.

Although the real exchange rate has showed an appreciating trend since the mid 2000s, this has apparently not caused a problem for the current account of the balance-of-payments. South Korea introduced major structural reforms after the East-Southeast Asian financial crisis. Doubtless this has been at least partly responsible for an observed significant improvement in the health of both the corporate and financial sectors. Since the crisis, South Korea has accumulated considerable foreign-exchange reserves as an anchor to financial stability; these have indeed lowered South Korea's vulnerability to shocks from external sources. The accumulation provides South Korea with strong support for its liberalization, as part of its IMF-sponsored structural adjustment programme, of the capital account of its balance-of-payments. Consequently, South Korea has attracted large-scale capital inflows, especially since interest rates in the United States entered their current low period. This has led to an appreciation of the real exchange rate of the won since the late 2000s. To redress the excessive inflows and encourage capital outflows, the BOK has taken some steps in the form of providing incentives to South Korean firms to undertake foreign direct investment projects, especially around the Asia-Pacific region. In short, South Korea has improved its macroeconomic management since the East-Southeast Asian financial crisis. Its handling of the US-global financial crisis has been outstanding, since it was able to avoid raising fiscal imbalances and external debt.

Inflation and Inflation Volatility

South Korea experienced a very high rate of inflation in the early 1950s due to its three year-long war with North Korea. By the late 1950s, however, the rate of inflation had been controlled (Table 7.1). Figures 7.2a and 7.2b display quarter-on-quarter inflation and inflation volatility, measured by the conditional standard deviation of inflation as obtained by GARCH (1,1) model, over the period 1971q1–2012q4. Figure 7.2b shows that inflation in South Korea was highly volatile from the early 1970s through the early 2000s. The volatility was mainly due to a series of external shocks, including the OPEC oil price shocks of the early 1970s, the

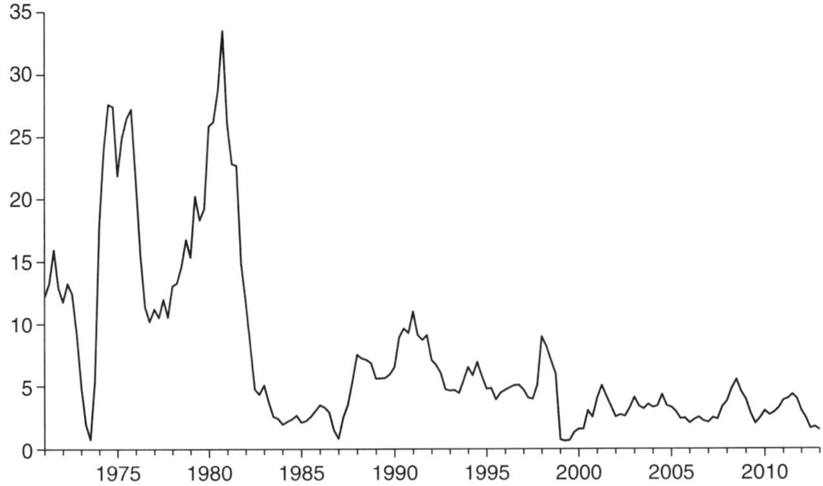

Figure 7.2a *Quarter-on-quarter CPI inflation in South Korea, 1971q1–2012q4*

GARCH(1,1) in-mean inflation (with AR1 mean equation), South Korea, 1971q1–2012q4

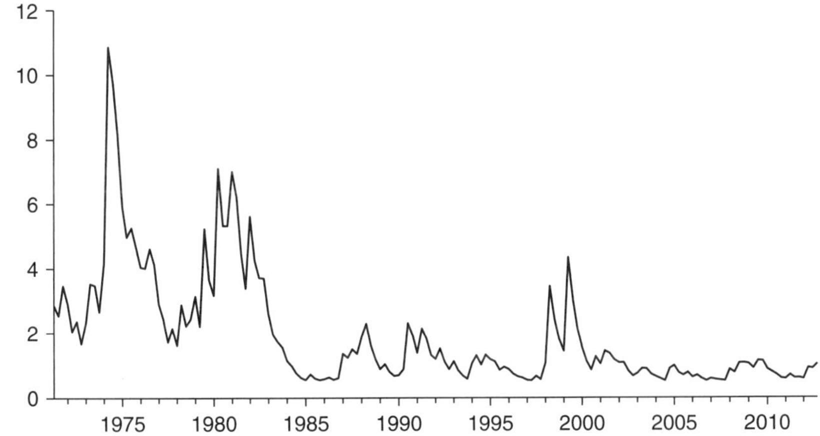

Figure 7.2b *Conditional standard deviation of CPI inflation in South Korea, 1971q1–2012q4*

Latin American debt crisis of the early 1980s and the East Asian currency financial crisis discussed earlier. Since the early 2000s, inflation volatility in South Korea has diminished while the inflation rate has remained around 3 per cent per annum.

Inflation Persistence

Inflation in South Korea exhibits a high degree of persistence. This is reflected in the high and stable value of the coefficient on the one-period lagged rate of inflation in an autoregressive model AR(1), as estimated by both the recursive and the rolling regression techniques (Table 7.3a and Table 7.3b). The rolling estimates of the one-period lagged rate of inflation suggest that the coefficient value has shown a mildly declining trend since the early 2000s. High measured persistence of inflation is generally associated with low credibility of monetary policy. A further contributor to measured inflation persistence is the presence of rigid institutional arrangements for price setting, including the indexation of wages. Given high and volatile inflation from the early 1970s through the early 2000s, monetary policy in South Korea was unable to gain much credibility,

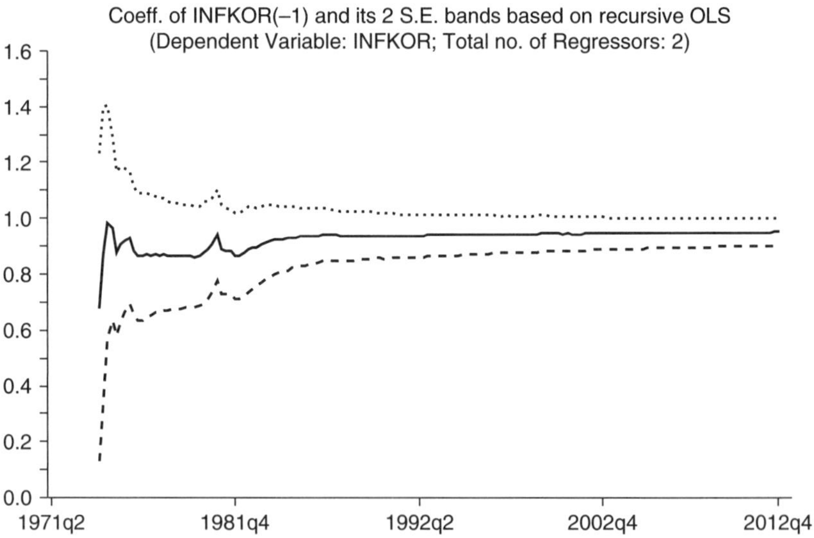

Note: INFKOR = CPI inflation in South Korea.

Figure 7.3a Recursive estimates of the coefficient on the one-period lagged rate of CPI inflation in South Korea

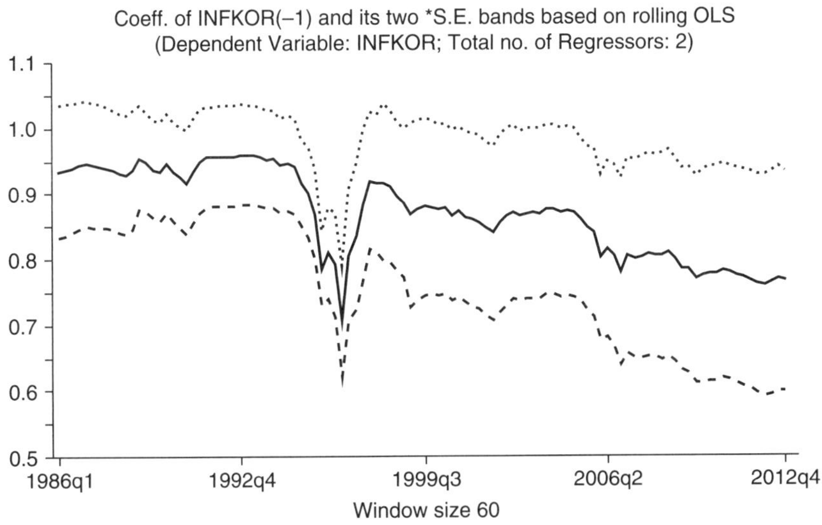

Note: INFKOR = CPI inflation in South Korea.

Figure 7.3b Rolling sample estimates of the coefficient on the one-period lagged rate of CPI inflation in South Korea

although the BOK has since been granted some autonomy in conducting monetary policy under inflation targeting.

Table 7.2 reports the unit root test results for inflation in South Korea over the period 1950–2012. The ADF test rejects the null hypothesis that inflation in South Korea has a unit root. The KPSS test, however, rejects the null of stationarity of the inflation rate. The Zivot Andrews test for the unit root suggests that the inflation rate does not have a unit root. The overall results suggest that although inflation in South Korea has high persistence, it does not have a unit root.

Real Deposit Rate of Interest

Figure 7.4 shows that the real deposit rate of interest in South Korea was highly volatile over the period 1969–2012. This reflects the impact of high and volatile inflation on the deposit and lending rates of interest, which were mainly determined institutionally until the East-Southeast Asian financial crisis. As these interest rates were not adjusted fully to high and volatile inflation, the real deposit and lending rates of interest exhibited high volatility.

Table 7.2 The unit root test results for CPI inflation in South Korea

	Sample (adjusted)	Constant (C); Trend (T)	ADF test statistic (SBC-determined lag-length, l)	Inference at 5% level	The KPSS test statistic (Newey-West bandwidth)	Inference at 5% level	Sample (unadjusted)	Zivot-Andrews test statistic	Breakpoint	Inference at 5% level
LCPI	1951–2012	C and T	−4.26 (l = 1)	I(0)	0.262 (5)	I(1)	1952–2010	−3.89	1973	I(0)
LCPI	1951–2012	C	−2.22 (l = 1)	I(1)	0.977 (6)	I(1)	1952–2010	−4.18	1987	I(0)
ΔLCPI	1951–2012	C	−4.06 (l = 0)	I(0)	0.598 (5)	I(1)	1953–2010	−3.02	1988	I(0)

Note: Definitions of variables: LCPI = log of the consumer price index; ΔLCPI = first-order difference of LCPI; SBC = Schwarz Bayesian Criterion; ADF = augmented Dickey-Fuller; and KPSS = Kwiatkowski, Phillips, Schmidt and Shin.

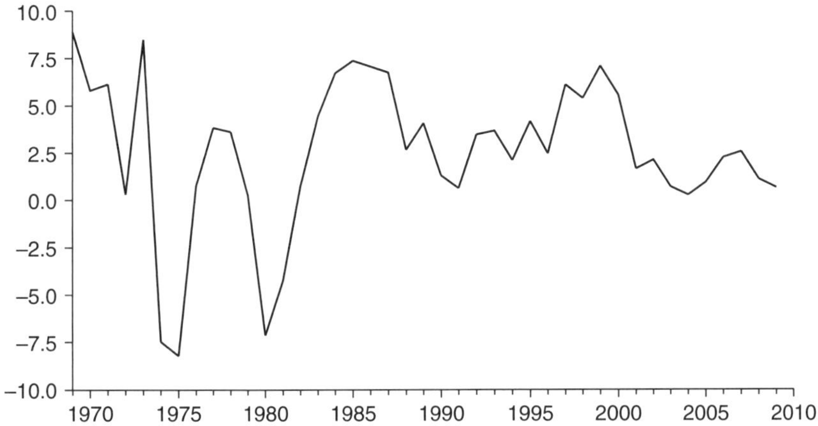

Figure 7.4 Real time deposit rate of interest (RTDR) in South Korea, 1969–2010

Exchange Rates

Figure 7.5 plots the nominal and real effective exchange rates in South Korea over the period 1980–2010. It shows that both the nominal and real effective exchange rates depreciated steadily, beginning in the early 1980s. The real exchange rate, in particular, exhibited some volatility, implying that South Korea did not attempt to introduce a real exchange rate targeting approach to monetary policy as a strategy to promote exports and hence economic growth. South Korea was one of the major Asian economies adversely affected by the US-global financial crisis of 2008–09. Anticipating a downturn in the economy, the BOK allowed the real exchange rate to depreciate as capital flowed out due to a sharp cut in the base rate of interest. Some country-specific IMF studies suggest that in the absence of a flexible exchange rate regime and the introduction of some countercyclical monetary policy measures within inflation targeting, the impact of the US-global financial crisis could have been severe on the South Korean economy. Inflation targeting allowed the BOK to implement countercyclical and discretionary interest cuts that depreciated the exchange rate and facilitated the absorption of external shocks.

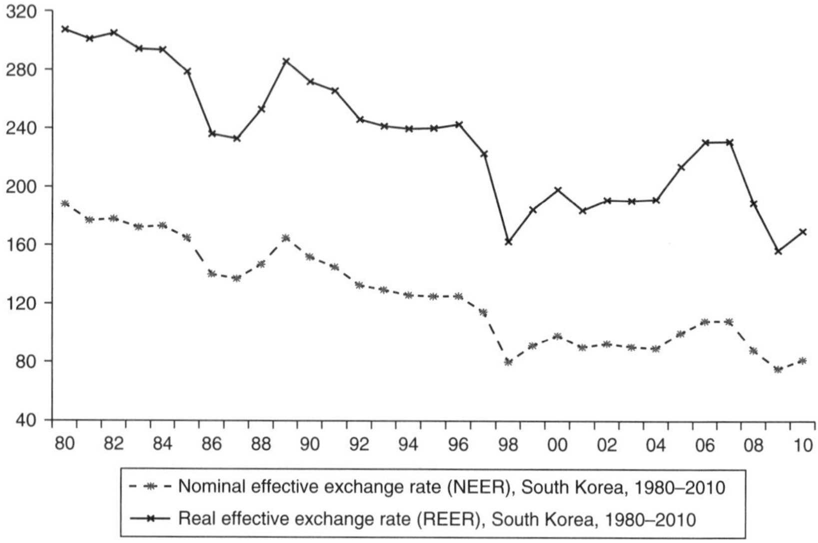

Figure 7.5 Nominal and real effective exchange rates in South Korea, 1980–2010

INFLATION, REAL INTEREST RATE, REAL EXCHANGE RATE AND REAL OUTPUT

In South Korea, the key monetary policy issue is the volatility of the real exchange rate and the real interest rate. While it is true that inflation has remained relatively low since the mid 2000s, at the 3 per cent level, it had been consistently high and volatile until the early 2000s. Presently, South Korea's adopted strategy of monetary policy is flexible inflation targeting. This has raised inflation volatility in an attempted policy tradeoff for lower output volatility (and putative associated better aggregate employment outcomes). The use of the interest rate as an instrument of monetary policy, when the interest rate is already low, contributes to inflation volatility in a low-inflation environment. The question is whether inflation volatility has any adverse impact on output growth and whether it raises output growth volatility.

The Structural Vector Autoregressive (SVAR) Analysis

Using annual data for 1980–2010, this subsection estimates a four-variable SVAR model to examine the interrelationships among inflation, the real interest rate, the real exchange rate and real output. The model is formulated at a basic level on the assumption that inflation has a contemporaneous feedback relation with both the real interest rate and the real exchange rate. All three variables affect real output and its growth. The order of variables in the model is arranged as follows: INFKR, RTDR, LREER and LRGDP. The variables are defined as: INFKR is the inflation rate in South Korea, RTDR is the real time deposit rate of interest in South Korea, LREER is the log of the real effective exchange rate and LRGDP is the log of real GDP. The ADF and KPSS unit root test results suggest that inflation, the real interest rate and the real exchange rate are stationary, while real output is nonstationary. Based on this information, two versions of the model are estimated and deployed to generate impulse responses and the forecast error-variance decompositions of all the above variables. The first version of the model is defined as: INFKR, RTDR, LREER and LRGDP, while the second version of the model is defined as: INFKR, RTDR, LREER and DLRGDP. In the second version of the model, all the variables are stationary while in the first version real output is non-stationary. To conserve space, the results obtained by the second model only are reported and interpreted, as the results obtained by both models are qualitatively similar. Figure 7.6 plots the data used for estimation purposes.

The impulse responses in Figure 7.7 suggest the interrelations among four variables in the SVAR model. The impulse response results are indicative, not conclusive. The indications are as follow. As expected, a rise in inflation lowers the real rate of interest. It indicates that the nominal interest rate responds slowly to a rise in inflation. High and volatile inflation also create other macroeconomic problems. A rise in inflation appreciates the real exchange rate, which in turn affects inflation and economic growth. The real interest rate also responds positively to an appreciation of the real exchange rate. This is because as a grossly appreciated real exchange rate induces capital flight, the real interest rate is required to rise as an inducement to slow down or stop capital flight. This follows the open-economy real exchange rate parity condition. In general, an appreciation of the real exchange rate affects both trade and capital flows while changes in the real interest rate affect saving and investment. The overall results suggest significant interrelations among inflation, the real interest rate, the real exchange rate and output growth. Although it is not investigated here, an expanded model is expected to show the impacts of the real interest rate and the exchange rate on saving, investment and both trade and capital flows. The key message that emerges from the empirical results is that inflation and its volatility are not innocuous in so far as the rate and volatility of economic growth. Inflation affects the real interest

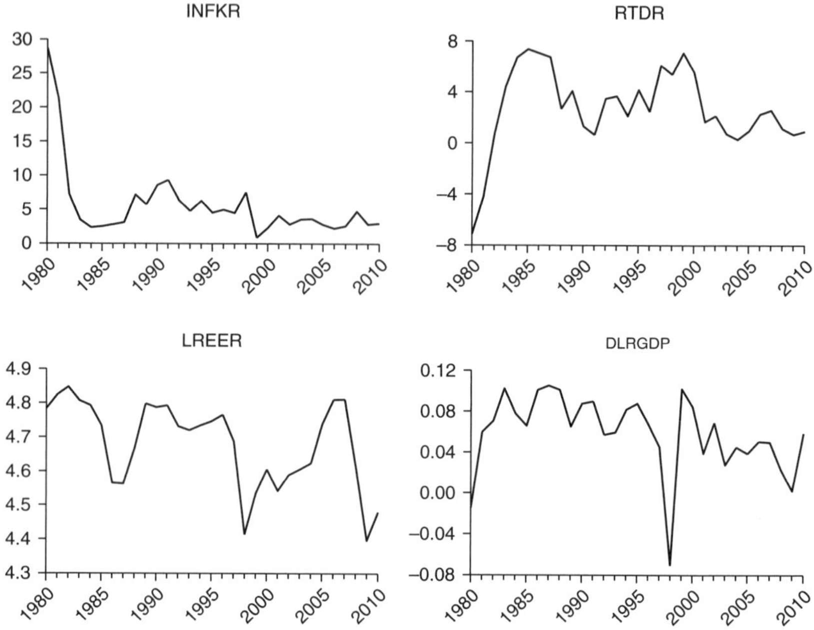

Note: Definitions of variables: INFKR = CPI inflation in South Korea; RTDR = real time deposit rate of interest; LREER = log of the real effective exchange rate of the won; and DLRGDP = first-order difference of the log of real GDP.

Figure 7.6 Data deployed for estimation of the SVAR model for South Korea, 1980–2010

rate and the real exchange rate and they impact on saving, investment and growth. This suggests the need for low and stable inflation for steady economic growth.

Table 7.3 reports the forecast error-variance decompositions for INFKR, RTDR, LREER and DLRGDP. In the table, the numbers represent those percentages of forecast error variance of variables that can be attributed to own innovations and those percentages of forecast error variance of variables that originate from innovations of other variables in the system. The results show that for all four of the variables, the dominant source of the forecast error variance is own innovations, to the extent of 59 per cent for inflation, 47 per cent for the real deposit rate of interest, 85 per cent for the real effective exchange rate and 13 per cent for real GDP growth over the ten-year time horizon. In the case of real output growth, innovations in the real deposit rate of interest and the real effective exchange rate jointly account for 79 per cent of real output growth's

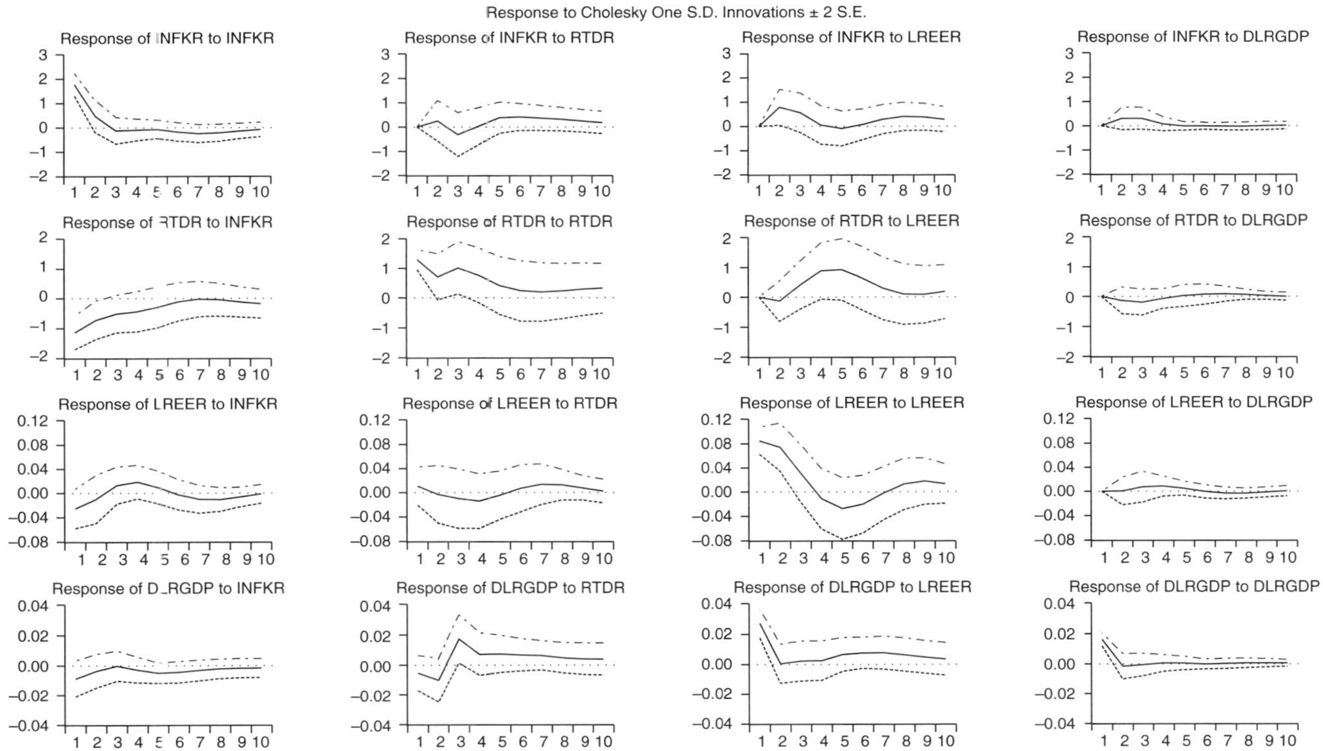

Note: Definitions of variables: INFKR = CPI inflation in South Korea; RTDR = real time deposit rate of interest; LREER = log of the real effective exchange rate of the won; and DLRGDP = first-order difference of the log of real GDP.

Figure 7.7 Impulse responses for variables in the SVAR model for South Korea

Table 7.3 Forecast error-variance decompositions of variables in the SVAR model for South Korea

Variance Decomposition of INFKR:					
Period	S.E.	INFKR	RTDR	LREER	DLRGDP
1	1.769	100.00	0.00	0.00	0.00
2	2.030	81.19	1.54	14.99	2.28
5	2.198	69.93	6.37	19.66	4.03
10	2.442	59.39	13.41	23.90	3.29
Variance Decomposition of RTDR:					
Period	S.E.	INFKR	RTDR	LREER	DLRGDP
1	1.725	43.88	56.12	0.00	0.00
2	2.010	45.45	53.70	0.41	0.43
5	2.865	29.13	47.87	22.27	0.73
10	3.024	26.82	46.51	25.83	0.84
Variance Decomposition of LREER:					
Period	S.E.	INFKR	RTDR	LREER	DLRGDP
1	0.089	8.26	1.47	90.27	0.00
2	0.117	5.63	0.93	93.44	0.00
5	0.128	8.19	2.70	88.17	0.95
10	0.135	8.85	4.95	85.23	0.97
Variance Decomposition of DLRGDP:					
Period	S.E.	INFKR	RTDR	LREER	DLRGDP
1	0.033	7.145	2.66	66.52	23.67
2	0.035	7.59	10.86	59.99	21.56
5	0.042	7.46	31.06	46.03	15.45
10	0.046	8.18	32.13	46.98	12.71
The Cholesky Ordering: INFKR RTDR LREER DLRGDP					

Note: Definitions of variables: INFKR = CPI inflation in South Korea; RTDR = real time deposit rate of interest; LREER = log of the real effective exchange rate of the won; and DLRGDP = first-order difference of the log of real GDP.

forecast error variance. The corresponding share of inflation is 8 per cent. The overall results show that real output growth is highly sensitive to inflation and its volatility. Inflation affects both the real deposit rate of interest and the real effective exchange rate. These, in turn, affect real output and its growth.

MONETARY AND EXCHANGE RATE POLICY ISSUES

Inflation performance in South Korea has been broadly satisfactory since it adopted inflation targeting in the wake of the East-Southeast Asian financial crisis. South Korea has maintained a flexible exchange rate system. This has been instrumental in absorbing external shocks and sustaining rule-based monetary policy. However, since the South Korean financial system is not yet adequately developed, the monetary policy transmission mechanisms, via the interest rate and exchange rate channels, are considered moderately effective and remain somewhat speculative. Other channels of the monetary policy transmission mechanisms, such as the credit channel, the asset price channel and the expectations channel, remain important. The question remains whether a monetary aggregate has a role to play in the monetary policy transmission mechanisms given that a linkage exists between money growth and inflation.

One of the reasons behind the adoption of inflation targeting was, arguably, instability in the money-demand function, which might have been caused by financial deregulation and reform over time. The empirical results generally suggest that the money-demand function in most developing countries remained stable despite financial deregulation and reform throughout the 1980s and 1990s. Even if there were some instability in the money-demand function during any particular financial reform episode, it subsequently stabilized and behaved like a stable money-demand function. Importantly, until recently the prevailing view was that monetary targeting for price stability requires a stable money-demand function to establish a causal linkage between money growth and inflation. The recent literature suggests that a causal relation exists between money growth and inflation irrespective both of the exchange rate regime and whether or not the money-demand function is stable (McCallum and Nelson, 2011). This raises the issue of the role of the monetary aggregates in the monetary policy transmission mechanisms under inflation targeting. There is no inconsistency in using a monetary aggregate as an instrument of monetary policy under inflation targeting. They have an especially useful, even critical, role to play when the interest rate approaches zero. The presence of a stable money-demand function allows the estimation of monetary overhang that can affect future inflation. Such a prediction is useful to improve the conduct of monetary policy under inflation forecasting.

This section examines whether there exists a stable money-demand function in South Korea.[2] For estimation purposes, a generic open-economy money-demand function is specified as follows:

$$LRJM_t = \alpha_0 + \alpha_1 Ly_t + \alpha_2 NIR_t + \alpha_3 FIR_t + \alpha_4 LRER_t + \alpha_5 \pi_t^v + u_t \quad (7.1)$$

where LRJM (J = N, B) is the log of real money balances (LRNM represents the log of narrowly defined real narrow money balances or LRBM represents the log of real broad money balances), Ly is the log of real income, NIR is a representative nominal interest rate, FIR is a representative foreign interest rate such as the US Federal funds rate (USFFR), LRER is the log of the real exchange rate such as the real effective exchange rate (REER), π_t^v is a measure of inflation volatility and u_t is a randomly distributed error term with zero mean and constant variance.

In this specification, real income represents a scale variable and its coefficient is expected to bear a positive sign and have a value not significantly different from one. Since the 1960s, the South Korean economy has grown steadily and there has been rapid monetization of the economy. Consequently, the income elasticity of demand for money may exceed unity.

The coefficients on both the domestic and foreign interest rates are expected to bear a negative sign. However, as reviewed in Appendix 5, the signs of the coefficients on the real exchange rate and inflation volatility remain a priori indeterminate.

The unit root test results suggest that all the variables in the specified model have a unit root. Consequently, they are eligible to form a cointegral money-demand relationship. Preliminary estimation results for a shorter sample period suggest that the deposit rate of interest in South Korea and the US Federal funds rate become significant when one of them is used in the model. The model is then estimated for a longer sample period 1962–2012 using the USFFR as the opportunity cost variable. The USFFR is considered more appropriate for this study as it is largely market determined.

Table 7.4 reports both the autoregressive distributed lag (ARDL) and ordinary least squares (OLS) results for the real narrow money-demand function. To conserve space, the results obtained by a broad definition of money are not reported. The results obtained by the ARDL model are found superior to those obtained by OLS/dynamic OLS (DOLS). The results suggest the presence of a strong form of cointegral relationship among real narrow money balances, real income, the real exchange rate and inflation volatility. The estimated coefficient values are consistent with a priori predictions. The CUSUM (cumulative sum) of residuals and CUSUMSQ (cumulative sum of squared) residuals in Figure 7.8 show that the real narrow money-demand function remained stable over the study period.

As expected, real income remains the core determinant of narrow money demand in South Korea. The income elasticity of demand for real narrow money balances is greater than one. This is significant for an

Table 7.4 *The ARDL and OLS regression results for long-run real narrow money-demand relationships in South Korea*

F-statistic	6.75			
W-statistic	33.77			
Critical value bounds	F-test	W-test		
90%	(2.61, 3.75)	(13.03, 18.74)		
95%	(3.15, 4.38)	(15.76, 21.92)		
Sample period	1962–2012 ARDL (2,0,1,1,0) (Selected based on SBC)	1962–2012 ARDL (1,2,0,0,0) Long-run model	1960–2012 OLS (Static model)	1961–2012 OLS (Dynamic model)
Regressors	Coefficient (t-ratio) [prob.]	Coefficient (t-ratio) [prob.]	Coefficient (t-ratio) [prob.]	Coefficient (t-ratio) [prob.]
Intercept	2.29 (2.79) [0.01]	3.61 (3.88) [0.00]	6.11 (10.29) [0.00]	1.95 (1.96) [0.06]
LRNM(−1)	0.57 (4.75) [0.00]			0.53 (4.40) [0.00]
LRNM(−2)	−0.20 (−1.88) [0.07]			
LRGDP	0.89 (6.28) [0.00]	1.40 (45.34) [0.00]	1.41 (48.30) [0.00]	0.65 (3.79) [0.00]
USFFR	−0.01 (−1.77) [0.08]	0.01 (0.72) [0.47]	−0.01 (−2.60) [0.01]	−0.01 (−0.38) [0.71]
LRER	−0.12 (−0.87) [0.39]	0.56 (2.76) [0.01]	0.02 (0.20) [0.84]	0.21 (1.60) [0.12]
INFVOL	−0.04 (−2.52) [0.02]	−0.06 (−2.62) [0.01]	−0.04 (−1.66) [0.10]	0.02 (1.24) [0.22]
Diagnostics				
Adjusted R^2	0.99		0.99	0.99

Table 7.4 (continued)

Lagrange multiplier test for serial correlation	$F(1, 41) = 0.36$ [0.55]		$F(1, 47) = 31.69$ [0.00]	$F(1, 45) = 3.74$ [0.06]
Ramsey's RESET test of functional form mis-specification	$F(1, 41) = 0.06$ [0.81]		$F(1, 47) = 0.62$ [0.43]	$F(1, 45) = 0.68$ [0.41]
Normality of residuals	$\chi^2_{(2)} = 0.17$ [0.92]		$\chi^2_{(2)} = 1.17$ [0.56]	$\chi^2_{(2)} = 4.53$ [0.10]
Heteroskedasticity	$F(1, 49) = 0.33$ [0.57]		$F(1, 51) = 3.02$ [0.09]	$F(1, 50) = 2.07$ [0.16]
The Wald test:				
H_O: Coefficient on LRGDP = 0		$\chi^2_{(1)} = 2056.21$ [0.00]	$\chi^2_{(1)} = 2332.9$ [0.00]	
H_O: Coefficient on LRGDP = 1		$\chi^2_{(1)} = 170.06$ [0.00]	$\chi^2_{(1)} = 195.59$ [0.00]	
H_O: Coefficient on USFFR = 0		$\chi^2_{(1)} = 0.52$ [0.47]	$\chi^2_{(1)} = 6.77$ [0.01]	
H_O: Coefficient on LRER = 0		$\chi^2_{(1)} = 7.64$ [0.01]	$\chi^2_{(1)} = 0.04$ [0.84]	
H_O: Coefficient on INFVOL = 0		$\chi^2_{(1)} = 6.87$ [0.01]	$\chi^2_{(1)} = 2.77$ [0.10]	

Note: Definitions of variables: LRNM = log of real narrow money balances; LRGDP = log of real GDP; USFFR = US Federal funds rate; LRER = log of the bilateral real exchange rate with the US dollar; INFVOL = inflation volatility; and SBC = Schwarz Bayesian Criterion.

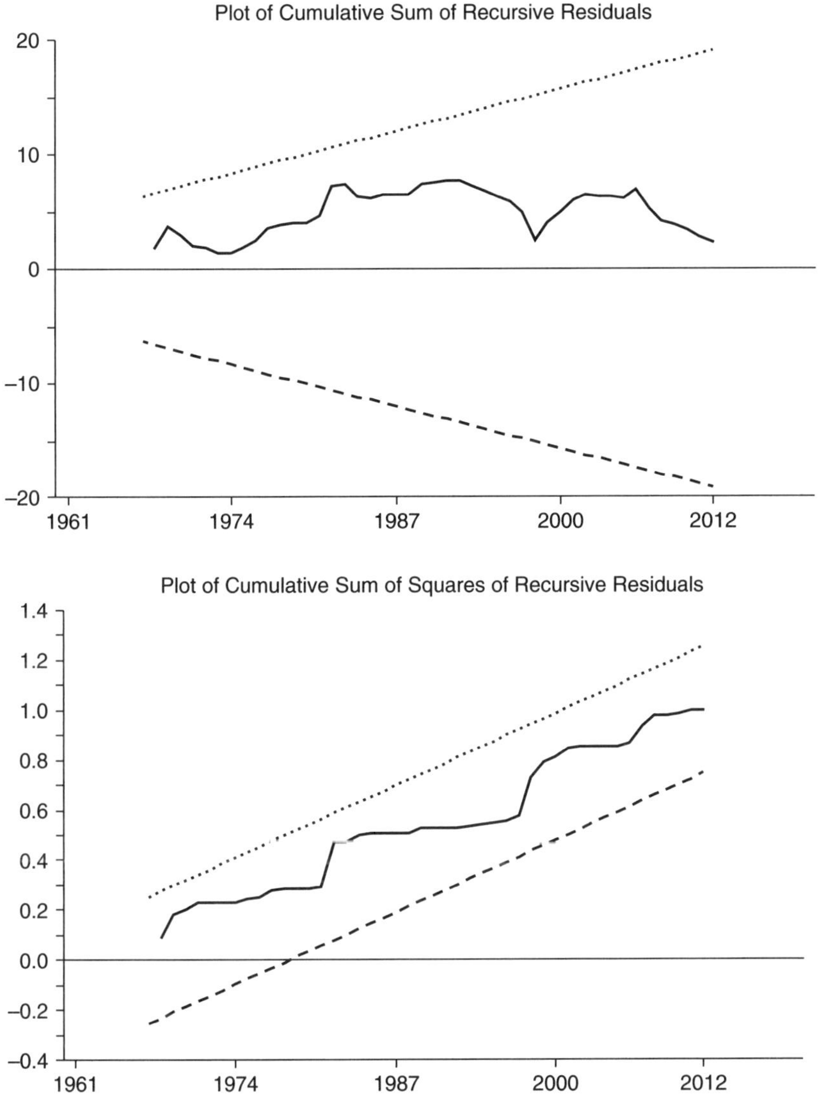

Note: The straight lines represent critical bounds at 5% significance level.

Figure 7.8 CUSUM and CUSUMSQ of residuals for real narrow money-demand relationships in South Korea advanced economy such as South Korea. The real exchange rate bears a positive sign and is highly significant. Inflation volatility is found an important determinant of money demand in South Korea. The coefficient bears a negative sign and is statistically highly significant. It implies that as inflation volatility increases, there is a decline in the demand for real narrow money balances. An implication is that by lowering narrow money demand, inflation volatility can raise inflation. This in turn can affect the real interest rate and the real exchange rate. Inflation volatility should therefore be a focus of monetary policy, especially when the interest rate becomes less effective in maintaining inflation as low and stable. This happens when the interest rate falls to a very low level in a deflationary environment.

Relationships Among Money, Output and Prices

According to Classical monetary theory, there exists a long-run relation among money, output and prices. The validity of this proposition can be investigated by estimating a cointegral relation among these variables. Table 7.5 reports the cointegration test results among these variables for the period 1970–2012. The results are similar irrespective of the definition of money. The Engle-Granger cointegration test results suggest a weak form of cointegral relationship among money, output and prices. The DOLS estimates suggest that either the narrow or the broad definition of money is highly significant in the price level equation. The coefficient value on the monetary aggregate is estimated lower than one. As expected, real output bears a negative sign and is statistically highly significant.

Engle and Granger (1987) suggest that one of the implications of a cointegral relation between two nonstationary variables is the presence of long-term causality between them running in at least one direction. Table 7.6 reports the bivariate Granger-causality test results among LCPI, LNM (LBM) and LRGDP for the period 1960–2012. Test results are generated within a vector error-correction (VEC) modelling framework after selecting the optimal lag-length using the Schwarz Bayesian Criterion (SBC).

The test results suggest that for South Korea, a strong causality runs both from narrow and from broad money growth to inflation. Broad money growth is also found to have a strong causal impact on output growth. The results obtained are consistent with the predictions of Classical monetary theory. The overall results reinforce the importance of monetary aggregates in the design and conduct of monetary policy.

Table 7.5 *Cointegration test results among money, output and prices in South Korea*

Dependent variable: LCPI								
	Fully modified OLS				Dynamic OLS			
With narrow money (NM)					(lead = 1, lag = 1)			
Regressor	coefficient	t-ratio	prob.		coefficient	t-ratio	prob.	
Intercept	−0.16	−1.61	0.11		0.30	1.24	0.23	
LNM	0.79	9.73	0.00		0.88	11.32	0.00	
LRGDP	−1.14	−5.03	0		−1.47	−6.22	0	
Sample period	1970–2012				1970–2011			
DW	0.76				0.54			
Adjusted R^2	0.99				0.99			
	tau-statistic	prob.	z-statistic	prob.	tau-statistic	prob.	z-statistic	prob.
The Engle-Granger cointegration tests	−2.95	0.29	−14.84	0.25	−2.95	0.29	−14.84	0.25
The Phillips-Ouliaris cointegration tests	−2.95	0.29	−14.87	0.25	−2.95	0.29	−14.87	0.25
With broad money (BM)								
Regressor	coefficient	t-ratio	prob.		coefficient	t-ratio	prob.	
Intercept	−0.42	−3.61	0.00		−0.55	−1.30	0.20	
LBM	0.71	8.49	0.00		0.72	6.75	0.00	
LRGDP	−1.06	−4.23	0		−1.06	−2.94	0.01	
Sample period	1970–2012				1970–2011			
DW	0.35				0.38			
Adjusted R^2	0.99				0.99			
	tau-statistic	prob.	z-statistic	prob.	tau-statistic	prob.	z-statistic	prob.
The Engle-Granger cointegration tests	−2.07	0.71	−7.47	0.74	−2.07	0.71	−7.47	0.74
The Phillips-Ouliaris cointegration tests	−2.18	0.66	−8.42	0.67	−2.18	0.66	−8.42	0.67

Note: Definitions of variables: LCPI = log of the consumer price index; LNM = log of narrow money stock; LBM = log of broad money stock; and LRGDP = log of real GDP.

Table 7.6 Granger-causality among money, output and prices in South Korea, 1960–2012

	Hypotheses No causality runs from:	Chi-square statistic (prob.)	Inference at 5% level
VEC specification (With Narrow Money, NM)	ΔLNM → ΔLCPI	2.90 (0.23)	Null hypothesis not rejected
	ΔLNM, ΔLRGDP → ΔLCPI	3.64 (0.46)	Null hypothesis not rejected
	ΔLCPI → ΔLNM	12.31 (0.00)	Null hypothesis rejected
	ΔLRGDP → ΔLNM	0.51 (0.78)	Null hypothesis not rejected
	ΔLCPI → ΔLRGDP	1.55 (0.50)	Null hypothesis not rejected
	ΔLNM → ΔLRGDP	4.12 (0.13)	Null hypothesis not rejected
VEC specification (With Broad Money, BM)	ΔLBM → ΔLCPI	7.57 (0.02)	Null hypothesis rejected
	ΔLBM, ΔLRGDP → ΔLCPI	12.05 (0.02)	Null hypothesis rejected
	ΔLCPI → ΔLBM	5.24 (0.07)	Null hypothesis not rejected
	ΔLRGDP → ΔLBM	5.70 (0.06)	Null hypothesis not rejected
	ΔLCPI → ΔLRGDP	2.38 (0.30)	Null hypothesis not rejected
	ΔLBM → ΔLRGDP	4.32 (0.12)	Null hypothesis not rejected

Note: Definitions of variables: LCPI = log of the consumer price index; LNM = log of narrow money stock; LBM = log of broad money stock; LRGDP = log of real GDP; Optimal lag length = 2 (selected based on the Schwarz Bayesian Criterion).

SUMMARY AND CONCLUSION

Due to sustained economic growth over several decades since the 1960s, South Korea's economy has undergone major structural change and transformation into a major, open, market economy. After some experimentation with the import-substituting model of industrialization in the 1950s and 1960s, it began the pursuit of an export-oriented development strategy from the mid 1960s. This strategy operated in the midst of financial repression while the authorities maintained protectionist policies to support both import-substituting and export-oriented industries. Consequently, the financial system remained underdeveloped until the 1990s. This affected saving, investment and economic growth which, while relatively high until 1997, could no doubt have been even higher. Whether such an approach to industrialization was appropriate remains a matter of contention (Nam, 1995).

South Korea introduced financial reforms in the 1980s. Its economy was one of the major casualties of the East-Southeast Asian financial crisis of the late 1990s. Although this crisis affected South Korea's economy heavily, this was a blessing in disguise in so far as macroeconomic management. It conferred on South Korea the opportunity to undertake much needed economic reforms, including the floatation of the exchange rate of its currency, the won, and the introduction of inflation targeting for price stability. The financial reform measures improved the financial system and made it more resilient to shocks.

Although South Korea was an inflation-prone economy from the 1950s through the early 2000s, its inflation performance has improved significantly under inflation targeting. This new strategy of monetary policy has provided South Korea a sounder basis for targeting price stability. The economy has grown steadily, albeit at the slower, but still very sound, pace of about 4 per cent per annum over the past decade. The flexible exchange rate system has apparently worked well for South Korea. It has minimized the impacts of external shocks on the economy and facilitated the efficient conduct of rule-based monetary policy for price stability. Inflation in South Korea, while relatively low, has, however, remained volatile and persistent. This raises the question of whether monetary activism is consistent with the spirit of inflation targeting, which works most efficaciously when aimed at maintaining low and stable inflation. Inflation volatility remains one of the contributory factors to the volatility of both the real exchange rate and output growth.

South Korea is expected to continue with inflation targeting[3] for maintaining price stability, yet a question remains whether the interest rate, which is presently used as an instrument of monetary policy, leads to price instability and hence should be supplemented by a monetary aggregate given that inflation maintains a strong relation with money growth. The neglect of money growth in the formulation of monetary policy has apparently contributed to inflation volatility. Inflation volatility is not benign but affects real output and its growth, via raising the volatility of both the real interest rate and the real exchange rate. This chapter has investigated some monetary relations, including the question of whether the money-demand function in Korea was stable over the study period and whether any linkage existed between money supply growth and inflation. The empirical results suggest that the narrow money-demand function in South Korea remained stable over the study period and that there existed a causal linkage between money supply growth and inflation.

Another concern is the danger of high volatility of the exchange rate under a floating exchange rate system. At a policy level, the question is whether any high volatility of the exchange rate in an emerging market economy such as South Korea should be considered benign for financial stability. In developing countries, any sharp movement of the exchange rate is likely to have some impact on financial stability. This raises the question of whether some market-based capital controls need to be introduced to keep the exchange rate stable until the financial system becomes sufficiently developed. If monetary and fiscal policies are conducted conservatively, some administrative capital controls could be effective in stabilizing the exchange rate. This is unlikely to adversely impact the development of money and capital markets.

NOTES

1. Some information on this section is based on BOK (2000, 2008, 2012). On aspects of monetary policy, inflation targeting and financial system in Korea, see Choi (2003) and Park (1992).
2. For early studies on money demand in Korea, see Bahmani-Oskooee and Rhee (1994), Lee and Keun (1995) and Banafea (2012).
3. For further analysis of monetary policy, see Chung et al. (2007) and Hoffmaister (2001).

REFERENCES

Alp, H., S. Elekdag and S. Lass (2011), 'Did Korean monetary policy help soften the impact of the global financial crisis of 2008–09?', Working Paper WP/12/5, IMF, Washington, DC.

Amsden, A. (1989), *Asia's Next Giant: South Korea and Late Industrialization*, New York: Oxford University Press.

Amsden, A. and Y. Euh (1993), 'South Korea's 1980s financial reforms: good-bye

financial repression (maybe), hello institutional restraints', *World Development*, **21**(3), 379–90.
Bahmani-Oskooee, M. and H.J. Rhee (1994), 'Long-run elasticities of the demand for money in Korea: evidence from cointegration analysis', *International Economic Journal*, **8**(2), 83–93.
Banafea, W.A. (2012), 'Essays on structural breaks and stability of the money demand function', PhD dissertation, Kansas State University, available at https://krex.k-state.edu/dspace/handle/2097/14869 (accessed 19 March 2015).
BOK (Bank of Korea), *Monetary Policy*, available at http://www.bok.org.kr/ (accessed 20 June 2015).
BOK (Bank of Korea) (2000), *The Bank of Korea: A History of Fifty Years*, Seoul: Bank of Korea.
BOK (Bank of Korea) (2008), *Monetary Policy in Korea*, Seoul: Bank of Korea.
BOK (Bank of Korea) (2012), *Monetary Policy in Korea*, available at http://www.bok.or.kr/ (accessed 20 March 2012).
Cho, T.J. (1989), 'Finance and development: the Korean approach', *Oxford Review of Economic Policy*, **5**(4), 88–102.
Choi, G. (2003), 'Structural changes and the scope of inflation targeting in Korea', *International Economic Journal*, **17**, 113–42.
Chung, J., Y. Jung and D. Yang (2007), 'Optimal monetary policy in a small open economy: the case of Korea', *Journal of Asian Economics*, **18**, 125–43.
Cole, D. and Y.C. Park (1983), *Financial Development in Korea, 1945–1978*, Cambridge, MA: Harvard University Press.
Dooley, M.R., R. Dornbusch and Y.C. Park (2001), 'A framework for exchange rate policy in Korea', Paper presented at the KIEP/IMF conference Korea Crisis and Recovery, Seoul, 17–19 May.
Dornbusch, R. and Y.C. Park (1987), 'Korean growth policy', *Brookings Papers on Economic Activity*, **2**, 389–444.
Dueker, M. and G. Kim (1999), 'A monetary policy feedback rule in Korea's fast-growing economy', *Journal of International Financial Markets, Institutions and Money*, **9**, 19–31.
Eichengreen, B. (2012), 'Government, business and finance in Korean industrial development', *International Economic Journal*, **26**(3), 357–77.
Emery, R.F. (2001), *Korean Economic Reform: Before and Since the 1997 Crisis*, London: Ashgate Publishing.
Engle, R.F. and C.W.J. Granger (1987), 'Co-integration and error-correction: representation, estimation, and testing', *Econometrica*, **55**(2), 251–76.
Fry, M. (1985), 'Financial structure, monetary policy, and economic growth in Hong Kong, Singapore, Taiwan and South Korea, 1960–1983', in V. Corbo, A. Krueger and F. Ossa (eds), *Export-Oriented Development Strategies: The Success of Five Newly Industrializing Countries*, Boulder, CO: Westview Press.
Fry, M. (1998), *Money, Interest, and Banking in Economic Development*, Baltimore, MD: Johns Hopkins University Press.
Hoffmaister, A. (2001), 'Inflation targeting in Korea: an empirical exploration', *IMF Staff Papers*, **48**, 317–43.
Kim, S. and Y.C. Park (2006), 'Inflation targeting in Korea: a model of success', BIS Papers No. 31, Monetary Policy in Asia: Approaches and Implementation, Bank for International Settlements, Basel.
Lee, T.H. and J.C. Keun (1995), 'Further results on the long-run demand for money in Korea: cointegration analysis', *International Economic Journal*, **9**(3), 103–113.

McCallum, B.T. and E. Nelson (2011), 'Money and inflation: some critical issues', in B.M. Friedman and M. Woodford (eds), *Handbook of Monetary Economics*, Vol. 3A, Amsterdam: Elsevier Science, pp. 97–153.

Nam, S.W. (1995), 'Korea's financial markets and policies', in S.N. Zahid (ed.), *Financial Sector Development in Asia: Country Studies*, Manila: Asian Development Bank.

Oh, G.W. (2012), 'Public debt and monetary policy in Korea', BIS Papers No. 67, Monetary Policy in Asia: Approaches and Implementation, Bank for International Settlements, Basel, 217–32.

Park, S.H. (1992), 'South Korea: monetary and financial system', in P. Newman, M. Milgate and J. Eatwell (eds), *The New Palgrave Dictionary of Money and Finance*, Vol. 3, London: Macmillan, pp. 490–92.

Park, Y.C. (1983), 'Inflation and stabilization policies in Korea, 1960–1980', Paper presented at the Conference on Inflation in East Asian Countries, Chung-Hua Institution for Economic Research, Taipei.

Song, B.N. (1990), *The Rise of the Korean Economy*, Hong Kong: Oxford University Press.

8. New Zealand

New Zealand is a small, open economy in the Southwestern Pacific Ocean, population approximately 5 million. It is situated about 1500 kilometres across the Tasman Sea to the east of Australia's southern coastline. Like Australia, New Zealand is a developed country with membership in both the OECD and other major international organizations. As at the 2013 national census, the large majority of the New Zealand population is of eclectic European ethnicity, culture and tradition with a significant level of integration between the European background and indigenous Maori populations. New Zealand's largest ethnic minorities comprise immigrants from Asia and the Pacific.

New Zealand had the sixth highest per capita income in the world during the 1950s and 1960s. High demand for its agricultural products in particular, mainly from the United Kingdom and the United States, resulted in achievement of one of the highest standards of living until the 1960s. Since then New Zealand's ranking in terms of per capita income has fallen to the lower end of the OECD countries. Moreover, New Zealand's economic progress is sometimes compared with that of Australia to assess its relative performance. This comparison supports the impression of a decline in New Zealand's economic standing within the Australasian region.[1]

Until the 1980s New Zealand maintained a highly regulated, protection ist policy regime to provide the economy with stability. Government played an active role in controlling inflation and keeping unemployment low. Its interventionist policies followed the then prevailing wisdom on macroeconomic management, targeting stabilization of an economy vulnerable to shocks of both domestic and external origin. New Zealand's economy retains this characteristic today, and the prevailing wisdom remains stabilization; but advances in the technologies of macroeconomic management have led mainstream economists nowadays to recommend less interventionist policy instruments. In general, the stabilization strategy followed the Keynesian paradigm, with the Phillips curve relation embedded in determination of the policy stance and direction and moderately high inflation thought to be a driver of growth and employment.

New Zealand can take pride in being the birthplace of A.W. Phillips, discoverer in the late 1950s of the Phillips curve relation. Later, the relation was interpreted as a policy menu for the choice of a politically optimal combination of the rates of inflation and unemployment. Manipulation of the monetary and fiscal policy instruments was then considered effective in achieving real objectives, such as raising the rate of economic growth in order to reduce the unemployment rate. Hence it featured prominently in policy discussion. When, in the 1970s, high rates of inflation became associated with high rates of unemployment in most advanced countries, the heyday of the Phillips curve relation was over. An early casualty of the change in policy thinking was the idea of inflation as a facilitator of economic growth. It was gradually accepted that inflation hurts rather than promotes economic growth. In consequence, since the 1970s, many countries have prioritized inflation control, via rule-based monetary policy, over other potential objectives such as sustaining economic growth and economic stabilization.

Here again, New Zealand has made a pioneering contribution as the birthplace of inflation targeting, perhaps the most influential of the contemporary monetary policy strategies. As it implemented this strategy in 1990, New Zealand's inflation was viewed as a cost-push phenomenon with a causal link to trade union militancy or industrial unrest. Incomes policy aimed more at limiting wages growth than prices growth was therefore considered more important than monetary policy to restore price stability. Consequently, monetary policy was considered superfluous or short term in nature and was assigned the role of providing cheap credit to boost the national level of investment. Brash (1995, p. 24) has described this phenomenon as follows:

> At one time or another, governments around the world have tried to use monetary policy to achieve almost every conceivable economic objective, and some social objectives as well. Economic growth and employment have often been high on the list of objectives for monetary policy. New Zealand's experience over the 1970s and early 1980s provides as good an example as any of this shotgun approach to monetary policy. The former Reserve Bank legislation, in place until 1989, required that monetary policy be directed toward enhancing economic and social welfare. In doing so, attention was to be given to promoting the highest level of production, trade, and full employment, and to maintaining a stable price level. The act did not define these objectives. Moreover, the Reserve Bank was given little operational independence to achieve them. Legally, the responsibility for monetary policy rested almost entirely upon the minister of finance.

New Zealand had low but volatile inflation during the 1960s. Inflation accelerated and then remained high and volatile throughout the 1970s and early 1980s, caused primarily by expansionary monetary and fiscal policies in the midst of the global oil price shocks of the time. As high, volatile inflation was associated with low, volatile economic growth, the unemployment rate rose from as low as 1 per cent in the early 1970s to about 5 per cent in the early 1980s (Brash, 1995, 2000).

In 1984, facing high inflation, slow economic growth and high unemployment – together known as 'stagflation' – the government introduced and began implementing a comprehensive package of economic reforms under the then newly elected centre-left Labour government. This political change was significant in most respects. The centre-right National Party had governed New Zealand for almost 30 years of the period 1949–84, having lost power for only a few years at a time in 1957–60 and 1972–75. Throughout 1984–85 the newly elected Labour Party, having been starved of government office, had accumulated a backlog of economic reform policies encompassing all sectors, and it now set about implementing them. In particular, for achieving and maintaining macroeconomic stability, the government instructed the Reserve Bank of New Zealand (RBNZ) to reduce inflation substantially, even at the cost of raising the unemployment rate.

It took longer than expected to achieve this goal, but by 1991 the high inflation of the early 1980s had been controlled. This two-year transition to low inflation was not costless, however. It was associated with a sharp rise in unemployment that peaked at 10 per cent across 1991–92. However, as inflation had exhibited a declining trend from the late 1980s, the RBNZ grasped the opportunity presented by this period of falling inflation to introduce the new strategy of monetary policy for price stability, that is, inflation targeting (Brash, 2000; Debelle, 1996).

Replacing the discretion of politicians and technocrats with monetary policy by technical rule, the government passed into law the RBNZ Act 1989, which made price stability the single goal of monetary policy (Brash, 1998, p. 3) and described the policy as inflation targeting. Implementation began in 1990. 'Price stability' was defined as 'low and stable inflation', so that the specific aim set for inflation targeting was to keep inflation within the range zero to 2 per cent per annum over the medium term. The Act did not specify a definition of price stability; rather, it was part of an agreement between the minister of finance and the governor of the RBNZ. The agreement has been known as the Policy Targets Agreement (PTA). The PTA has been renegotiated at each RBNZ governorship appointment. The latest PTA defines price stability as inflation within the range 1 to 3 per cent over the medium term.[2]

To complement the new monetary policy regime, the government institutionalized fiscal discipline five years later through the Fiscal Responsibility Act, 1994. The Act directs government spending and taxation policy within a medium-term planning horizon. Its main aim is to prevent government from attempting to pump-prime the economy to generate employment gains. Enactment of this statute effectively removed fiscal dominance over monetary policy in New Zealand. Fundamentally, legislation of price stability and fiscal discipline constituted official recognition in New Zealand, both of the monetary origin of inflation and the importance of fiscal discipline in the operation of monetary policy.

Until the advent of inflation targeting in 1990, monetary factors had been ignored as the key source of inflation in New Zealand. Wages growth and other cost-push factors, for example, oil prices, were viewed both as originators and propagators of inflation. Other possible drivers of New Zealand inflation included wage indexation, government sector wage-fixing arrangements, corporate monopoly power and currency devaluation (Nelson, 2005). Inflation targeting, therefore, represented a major change in New Zealand's approach to inflation control within a monetary framework. Following the lead of New Zealand, Australia later introduced inflation targeting in 1993.

Having successfully applied inflation targeting to contain inflation within the target range over two decades, the RBNZ has become involved in economic stabilization by deployment of monetary policy instruments. This represents something of a reversal by the RBNZ away from its earlier strict stance on inflation control towards flexible inflation targeting in which the RBNZ takes into account the unemployment rate and other factors when making monetary policy decisions. This reflects the suggestion in the current PTA that in pursuing price stability, monetary policy should 'seek to avoid unnecessary instability in output, interest rates and the exchange rate'. This hints at a gradualist approach to the conduct of monetary policy control inflation, but it falls short of assigning monetary policy an activist role in stabilizing the economy. Nevertheless, the role of monetary policy in New Zealand has been broadened to target economic stabilization since the US-global financial crisis (2007–09).

The New Zealand economy experienced a decade-long boom, 1998–2007, followed by recession, 2008–09. The boom originated mainly in an expanded immigration policy, an improvement in the external terms of trade and a rapid increase in government spending. Large immigration, predominantly from Asian countries, raised house prices as banks and other financial institutions were able and willing to make large loans available to an expanding housing sector. Following deregulation of the capital account in the balance-of-payments from the late 1980s, the banking sector gained access to foreign capital for lending in the booming housing sector. The downside of capital market liberalization has, predictably, been the volatility that is a property of unrestricted capital flow. The immediate and direct consequence is increased volatility in the exchange rate and, through it, more volatile rates of investment and economic growth.

New Zealand floated its currency, the NZ dollar (NZD), in 1985. Since then both the nominal and real effective exchange rates have been highly volatile. In particular, large-scale capital inflows during the housing boom appreciated the currency sharply. There was an expectation that the RBNZ would tighten monetary policy to dampen the inflationary pressure built up in an overheated economy. The expectation was largely realized. With the tightening of monetary policy, further large-scale capital inflows attracted by higher New Zealand interest rates led to an appreciation of the real exchange rate. This put pressure on the tradable goods sector and created a Dutch Disease-type problem. Consequent large current account deficits raised the level of external debt. On the positive side, the long duration of New Zealand's housing-led economic boom kept unemployment down at around 4 per cent until the US-global financial crisis emerged. New Zealand's boom had come to an end by the time the United States was engulfed in its 2007 sub-prime mortgage crisis. By 2009 New Zealand's unemployment rate had reached about 7 per cent.

The events described suggest that macroeconomic management in New Zealand has been a difficult task for most of the past four decades. Its economy is small and endemically exposed to a wide range of potential shocks of both domestic and foreign origin. Exports account for a quarter of GDP. The principal export industries are agriculture, horticulture, fishing, forestry and mining, all vulnerable to international commodity price movements. Since 1990 and inflation targeting, the question has been asked whether inflation targeting has significantly improved national macroeconomic performance. Unlike Australia's moderately high and steady economic growth since the early 1990s, New Zealand's growth has remained low and unstable. Further, while inflation has been low on average, it remains highly persistent and volatile. Economic uncertainty, caused by inflation volatility, has adversely affected economic growth. In the midst of high volatility of both inflation and economic growth, the real exchange rate in particular became unstable. Large-scale capital flows exacerbated this problem. Altogether, inflation targeting played a role in New Zealand's low inflation without bringing the expected dividend of sustained economic growth. There is the suggestion that deep structural reform in both the product and factor markets is needed to spur and sustain economic growth. The rationale is that structural reform makes an economy more resilient to shocks of all origins. This works by reducing the 'downward stickiness' of wages and prices. Structural reform extends to raising the level of discipline in monetary and fiscal policies promoting macroeconomic stability in general, price stability in particular, thereby simultaneously reducing the magnitude and duration of shocks that necessitate downward wage and price flexibility. The corollary of this reduced economic volatility and uncertainty is increased stability of both the real interest rate and the real exchange rate. The outcome is an enhanced national investment environment highly attractive to domestic and international investors.

The remainder of this chapter overviews New Zealand's inflation and monetary policy in an historical context. It analyses the key issues in monetary policy and reports empirical results obtained for some monetary relations. Both annual and quarterly data are used for empirical analysis.

THE RESERVE BANK OF NEW ZEALAND: ORGANIZATION AND ACTIVITIES[3]

The RBNZ was established in 1934 and has similarity with other central banks with respect to the assigned functions and responsibilities. Three main functions of the RBNZ are:

(a) operating monetary policy to maintain price stability
(b) promoting and maintaining a sound and efficient financial system
(c) meeting the currency needs of the public.

The RBNZ performs other central banking functions. For example, it:

(d) acts as banker to the banks, providing interbank settlement facilities and related payment services
(e) manages foreign-exchange reserves and, if required, intervenes into foreign-exchange markets to stabilize the exchange rate
(f) provides cash and debt management services to the government
(g) advises the government on the operation of the financial system
(h) provides secretariat services to New Zealand's Overseas Investment Commission.

The governor, as the chief executive officer, exercises the powers of the RBNZ. The 1989 Act stipulates that it is the duty of the governor to ensure that the Bank carries out its central banking functions. The minister of finance, on the recommendation of the Board of Directors, appoints the governor for a five-year term. The Board has no executive authority over the Bank, with the governor remaining solely responsible for the conduct of monetary policy in accordance with the provisions of the Act. The reason for making the governor responsible for achieving price stability has been to raise the credibility of monetary policy in the sense that monetary policy cannot be deployed to achieve other objectives. A general concern is that this may lead to an aggressive form of monetary policy to maintain price stability at the cost of economic growth.

Price stability, however, does not lead to exchange rate stability. As a small economy, New Zealand's foreign-exchange market is not deep and the consequent active engagement with the international capital market is perhaps the major driver of exchange rate volatility. To help smooth excessive exchange rate peaks and troughs, the RBNZ maintains large foreign reserves for intervention in the forex market if and as required. In New Zealand, exchange rate stability is indeed considered important to financial stability. In managing foreign reserves, the RBNZ maintains the overriding objective of meeting liquidity needs for intervention. Therefore the Bank attempts to strike a balance between liquidity maintenance and minimization of the costs of holding excess reserves in liquid form ready for foreign-exchange interventions.

EVOLUTION OF MONETARY POLICY

It was suggested earlier that New Zealand's macroeconomic performance was essentially dismal during the 1970s and early 1980s. In 1984, the then newly elected Labour government instructed the RBNZ to reduce inflation which, while it had plummeted from 10 per cent to under 4 per cent during 1983, was on the rise and threatening to get out of hand again. In the event, and in retrospect because the RBNZ lacked the tools to put a lid on it, inflation was back up to 8 per cent by the end of 1984 and had reached 16 per cent by mid 1985. This damaging level of volatility contributed to the new government's determination to formulate and implement comprehensive economic and financial reform aimed at making the New Zealand economy more efficient and resilient to shocks.

New Zealand operated under a fixed peg exchange rate system until 1985 when it floated its currency. By definition, it maintained complementary capital controls. Until the mid 1980s, capital controls underwrote New Zealand's monetary policy with some potency, although fiscal policy generally dominated monetary policy in the pursuit of macroeconomic stability in general and external stability in particular. As decisions over monetary policy were generally the responsibility of the minister of finance, the RBNZ did not exercise control over monetary policy to achieve price stability. Moreover, the government maintained a cost/wage-push view of inflation, with inflation linked to trade union militancy and industrial unrest. To control inflation, the government introduced incomes policy controls over wages and prices whilst allowing the money growth rate to remain high and volatile. Consequently, despite the intrusive incomes policy, inflation was high and volatile for most of the time from the 1950s through the 1980s.

The New Zealand dollar was floated in March 1985. This was accompanied by a deregulation of interest rates and capital flows. To spur and sustain rapid economic growth, consensus emerged among the political leaders that the New Zealand economy required both price stability and greater efficiency and resilience to domestic and external shocks. The view on price stability was formalized with the passing of the RBNZ Act 1989. It contains the 'economic objective of achieving and maintaining stability in the general level of prices'. In the Act, the provision of price stability is explicit and non-negotiable. The RBNZ thus departed from the earlier role of monetary policy to support fiscal policy and gained autonomy in conducting monetary policy for price stability alone.

Prior to the 1989 legislation, the RBNZ's role was essentially that of adviser to the government. It was subject to ministerial directions for monetary policy and other responsibilities. RBNZ decisions were subject to the discretion of the minister of finance. Ministerial directions to the RBNZ were confidential and priorities shifted frequently as political factors dominated policy decisions. Monetary policy was regarded as an instrument that could achieve multiple objectives. As such, it was (mis)applied to targets that were often inherently conflicting, such as short-run inflation and unemployment.

Inflation targeting has brought a degree of monetary policy transparency to New Zealand. This also emerged as a key feature of the monetary policy framework. Provisions in the 1989 Act require transparency and accountability to enhance monetary policy credibility and therefore effectiveness. Transparency is indeed used as a device to moderate central banks' incentives to create inflation bias. Transparency is viewed as a key component of accountability of the RBNZ. The RBNZ Act requires that the Bank publish a monetary policy statement at least every six months. In addition, a Select Committee of the Parliament reviews the Bank's statements on monetary policy and its handling of monetary policy. The Act also establishes the governor's sole accountability for decisions on implementation of monetary policy. The assignment of authority and the responsibility of monetary policy to a single individual, rather than a committee, is uncommon and has been contentious in central banking (Walsh, 1995a, 1995b, 1996). In practice, the governor has an advisory committee that provides advice to the governor prior to making monetary policy decisions. The advisory committee, however, does not bear responsibility for policy decisions made by the governor and their impacts on the economy.

Policy Targets Agreement

The RBNZ Act requires that the operational details of the Bank's inflation target be made public in a separate agreement between the governor and the minister of finance. This is known as the Policy Targets Agreement. It contains specific details about inflation targeting and its operational procedure. The RBNZ is given responsibility for implementing monetary policy in the manner it thinks appropriate to achieve its policy objectives. Below is a part of the latest Agreement between the minister of finance and the governor on the key objective of monetary policy and its achievement.

This Agreement between the minister of finance and the governor of the RBNZ (the Bank) is made under Section 9 of the RBNZ Act 1989 (the Act). The minister and the governor agree as follows:

Price stability

(a) Under Section 8 of the Act the Reserve Bank is required to conduct monetary policy with the goal of maintaining a stable general level of prices.

(b) The government's economic objective is to promote a growing, open and competitive economy as the best means of delivering permanently higher incomes and living standards for New Zealanders. Price stability plays an important part in supporting this objective.

Policy target

(c) In pursuing the objective of a stable general level of prices, the Bank monitors prices, including asset prices, as measured by a range of price indices. The price stability target is defined in terms of the All Groups consumer price index (CPI), as published by Statistics New Zealand.

(d) For the purpose of this Agreement, the policy target is to keep future CPI inflation outcomes between 1 per cent and 3 per cent on average over the medium term, with a focus on keeping future average inflation near the 2 per cent target midpoint.

Monetary Policy Design and Implementation

Inflation targeting experience in New Zealand over the past two and a half decades has shown some flexibility in both design and implementation. Firstly, the target range has been modified: from 0–2 per cent in 1990, to 0–3 per cent in 1996 and then to 1–3 per cent in 2002. While inflation targeting was regarded as strict in an operational sense during the early years of its introduction, economic stabilization has entered into the objective function of monetary policy since the late 2000s following the US-global financial crisis. Inflation targeting is now regarded as flexible or accommodative to the goal of economic stabilization. Secondly, the RBNZ emphasizes that the inflation floor of the target range should be as binding as the ceiling of the range. Nominally, then, there is no asymmetry in the RBNZ's policymaking approach to the conduct of monetary policy for price stability, irrespective of whether inflation crosses the set ceiling or floor of the inflation target. The danger of deflation thereby receives equal weight to that of inflation in so far as determining the stance of monetary policy. Accordingly, the Bank has eased monetary policy as required to prevent any threatened sharp fall in inflation below the target range. Thirdly, the monetary authorities have an 'escape clause' that allows the RBNZ to accommodate specific shocks to inflation, including significant changes in the external terms of trade, changes in indirect taxes that affect prices and supply shocks such as, for example, a livestock epidemic.

This flexibility contrasts with New Zealand's inflation targeting in its early years, namely the one-year horizon for the inflation target, and a potential penalty for the governor if the inflation target was breached by even a small amount. These rigid elements allegedly led to two problems. Firstly, they led to instrument instability, that is, a wide swing of the interest rate or exchange rate to maintain price stability in the event of shocks to inflation. Secondly, they led to output volatility (with employment consequences) because of the need to maintain inflation within the range almost continuously given the short (annual) time horizon. The PTA has changed the inflation range a few times. Although the range remains 2 percentage points, the inflation targeting approach has become flexible in the sense that it allows monetary policy to try and fine-tune the economy when inflation remains within the target or does not seem to pose problems for the economy in other respects.

Monetary Policy Transmission Mechanisms

Since 17 March 1999 the RBNZ has used the official cash rate to influence short-term market interest rates, including variable floating mortgage interest rates. The RBNZ has the option to alter the official 'cash rate' (interbank overnight rate) eight times a year by manipulating the (potential) supply of funds into the interbank overnight market. The cash rate influences the short-term interest rates in the following way. When the official cash rate is announced, the RBNZ stands ready to pay commercial banks an interest rate that is ¼ per cent below the official cash rate for funds deposited at their settlement accounts. The Bank also remains ready to provide overnight cash to commercial banks against good securities, charging an interest rate ¼ per cent above the official cash rate. The Bank sets no limit on the amount of cash it is willing to take in or lend out provided that the interest rate is at ¼ per cent below or above the official cash rate. Therefore, the official cash rate works by setting effective upper and lower limits for borrowing and lending in interbank markets. Banks are unlikely to lend overnight with interest rates less than they can receive from the RBNZ, nor would they borrow with rates that are higher than they can pay for funds from the RBNZ. Competitive pressure from banks similarly puts upper and lower limits for interest rates on other forms of overnight borrowing and lending.

By influencing the overnight rates, the RBNZ's decisions on the policy rate have a strong impact on short-term market interest rates such as the 90-day bill rate and the floating mortgage rate given that loans of different maturities are considered substitutable. By controlling short-term interest rates, the Bank influences aggregate demand and hence prices provided that the level of aggregate supply remains unchanged. Changes in interest rates affect aggregate expenditure, comprising consumption and investment spending. As New Zealand is a small, trade-oriented economy, exchange rate movements due to changes in interest rates affect trade flows and domestic prices. For example, a depreciation of the New Zealand dollar may lead to an increase in the prices of imported goods and hence the level of domestic prices. Exchange rate movements also have an indirect effect on the rate of inflation. When the dollar depreciates, export income rises. This may raise domestic demand and hence prices. Both these influences work in the opposite direction when the dollar appreciates. Over the medium term interest rates, exchange rates, trade flows and output maintain feedback relations in a dynamic sense, implying that the short-term policy interest rate (the cash rate) loses its status as an exogenous policy variable and becomes linked to inflationary developments in the economy (Stock and Watson, 2012).

Figure 8.1 is a flowchart of the monetary policy transmission mechanisms in New Zealand. The official cash rate affects short-term interest rates and exchange rates. The effect of the cash rate on the exchange rate is imprecise. Changes in real interest rates affect intertemporal decisions on borrowing and lending of investible funds while changes in real exchange rates, which represent changes in the prices of foreign goods in terms of domestic goods, affect trade and capital flows. Changes in both real interest rates and exchange rates thus affect aggregate demand with a lag of perhaps one year. Changes in aggregate demand initially affect output and then inflation down the track.

However, the variable timing and magnitude with which changes in the interest rate ultimately impact output and prices are presently not

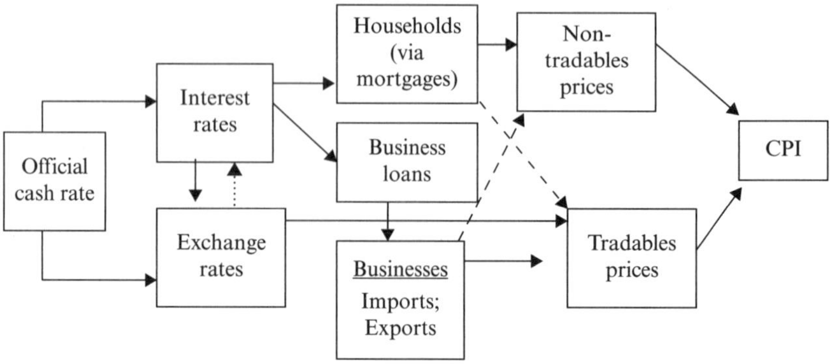

Source: Adapted from Bollard and Karagedkli (2006).

Figure 8.1 Monetary policy transmission mechanisms in New Zealand

knowable with precision, partly because of the complex nature of the economy and partly because of the lag itself. The timing and extent of the inflation response to changes in the interest rate are dependent on a variety of factors that include the prevailing inflationary expectations. The uncertainty is reflected in the degree of volatility in interest rates. This raises the question of how appropriate the interest rate can be as the instrument of monetary policy in a small, open economy such as that of New Zealand.

MACROECONOMIC DEVELOPMENTS AND INFLATION PERFORMANCE

Monetary policy in New Zealand has undergone some structural change since inflation targeting began in 1990. Until then the conduct of monetary policy in New Zealand was similar to that in Australia. New Zealand maintained low inflation and steady economic growth in the 1950s and 1960s. Inflation and unemployment then rose in the 1970s and early 1980s, delivering unsatisfactory macroeconomic performance throughout the period (Table 8.1). Political change seemed inevitable and in hindsight it was. After defeating the conservative National Party, the Labour Party came to power in 1984 and began a much needed process of economic and financial reform. Most of the financial reforms were implemented during 1984–85, including replacement of direct controls over money, credit, interest rates and capital flows with less direct instruments of economic management.

The aim of this comprehensive programme of economic and financial reform during the mid 1980s was to increase the economy's flexibility and

Table 8.1 Macroeconomic indicators, New Zealand, 1951–2012

Macroeconomic indicators	1951–55	1956–60	1961–65	1966–70	1971–75	1976–80	1981–85	1986–90	1991–95	1996–2000	2001–05	2006–10	2011	2012
Budget balance (% of GDP)	n.a.	n.a.	n.a.	n.a.	n.a.	n.a.	−5.1	−2.0	−0.8	0.9	2.8	−0.6	−5.8	−4.8
General government gross debt (% of GDP)	n.a.	n.a.	n.a.	n.a.	n.a.	n.a.	67.1	62.7	55.9	35.6	25.9	23.1	38.2	38.6
Money-growth rate (%)														
Narrow money growth	5.2	4.3	1.0	2.0	15.7	8.0	10.2	16.3	4.4	8.7	24.4	0.3	10.0	7.3
Broad money growth	4.6	4.5	1.3	5.2	20.6	17.1	18.0	34.2	6.0	5.9	6.4	8.1	4.0	6.1
Real GDP growth rate (%)	3.9	4.0	4.9	2.8	4.0	0.7	2.5	3.3	3.0	3.1	4.0	1.0	2.2	2.1
GDP per capita, current prices, US dollar	n.a.	n.a.	n.a.	n.a.	n.a.	7190	7113	11 714	13 366	15 880	20 039	29 408	35 973	37 401
Unemployment rate (%)	n.a.	n.a.	n.a.	n.a.	n.a.	4.0	5.1	5.8	9.2	7.0	4.7	4.9	6.5	6.6
Output gap (% of potential GDP)						0.9	1.7	1.1	−0.8	0.2	1.4	−0.6	−1.7	−1.4
CPI inflation rate (%)	6.1	2.9	2.7	5.0	10.2	14.8	12.1	9.4	2.1	1.6	2.3	2.8	4.4	0.9
Current account balance (% of GDP)	n.a.	n.a.	n.a.	n.a.	n.a.	−4.0	−6.6	−3.9	−4.1	−5.3	−4.7	−6.2	−4.2	−5.4

Table 8.1 (continued)

Macroeconomic indicators	1951–55	1956–60	1961–65	1966–70	1971–75	1976–80	1981–85	1986–90	1991–95	1996–2000	2001–05	2006–10	2011	2012
Nominal interest rate														
Money-market rate	n.a.	n.a.	n.a.	n.a.	n.a.	n.a.	24.7	16.2	7.6	6.8	5.8	5.6	2.5	2.5
Government bond yield	3.8	4.8	5.1	5.5	5.9	10.6	13.6	14.3	8.0	6.9	6.0	5.7	4.0	3.1
Real interest rate[a]														
Money-market rate	n.a.	n.a.	n.a.	n.a.	n.a.	n.a.	8.1	6.3	5.4	5.1	3.4	2.7	−1.9	1.6
Government bond yield	−2.1	1.9	2.4	0.5	−3.9	−3.7	1.5	4.6	5.8	5.3	3.6	2.8	−0.4	2.2
Nominal exchange rate (NZ$ per US$)	0.7	0.7	0.7	0.8	0.8	1.0	1.6	1.7	1.7	1.8	1.8	1.5	1.3	1.2
Nominal effective exchange rate[b]	n.a.	263.6	271.0	244.1	230.5	182.4	143.8	107.2	83.1	88.6	88.9	92.2	96.1	101.1
Real effective exchange rate[b, c]	67.2	74.3	77.7	72.0	83.2	85.0	71.1	90.2	87.8	84.0	80.9	98.4	116.9	118.5

Note:
n.a. = not available
a. Real interest rate is estimated as: 100(((1 + interest rate)/(1 + inflation rate))−1) where the interest rate and inflation rate are expressed as decimal.
b. A rise in the index value of the exchange rate represents appreciation.
c. Real exchange rate: data for the period 1951–70 represents the bilateral real exchange rate of the New Zealand dollar against the US dollar.

Source: Author's computation based on IMF, *International Financial Statistics*; IMF, *World Economic Outlook*; and other country-specific publications on the IMF website.

thereby render it more resilient to shocks (Walsh, 1998a, 1998b). Economic growth in New Zealand fell during the late 1980s due to contractionary monetary and fiscal policies that reduced the rate of inflation. With slower economic growth, the unemployment rate rose. These conditions did not begin to recede until 1993, when the economy began to experience steady economic expansion. This accelerated from 1998 into a decade-long economic boom fuelled by rising foreign demand. By the time the US-global financial crisis emerged in 2007, the unemployment rate was down around 4 per cent. Inflationary pressures developed, inducing the RBNZ to raise short-term interest rates using the procedures described above. The increased domestic interest rates created large differentials against international rates. This attracted large-scale foreign-capital inflows that, in combination with a coincidental sharp rise in world prices for commodities, caused the real exchange rate to appreciate. Some asset prices, especially housing and shares, rose sharply. The appreciated real exchange rate raised the level of current account deficits to about 8 per cent of GDP. Consequently, the net foreign liabilities of the country rose to about 90 per cent of GDP.

New Zealand's high interest rate policy, however, was not very effective in dampening demand. Competition in the housing market, in part reflecting banks' access to abundant international capital until the US-global financial crisis, weakened the transmission of the official interest rate into flexible mortgage rates. As a result, the housing boom, initially coinciding with an immigration spurt, remained resilient, raising household wealth and hence domestic demand. Searching for high yields, international investors responded to a sustained wide interest rate differential.

Inflation and Inflation Volatility

Figure 8.2a plots quarter-on-quarter inflation in New Zealand for 1958q1–2012q4. A rising trend is evident from the early 1960s, peaking in the 1970s and effectively plateauing until the mid 1980s. It began falling from the late 1980s and has remained low and relatively unstable since then. Figure 8.2b plots the estimated conditional standard deviation of inflation for the period 1958q1–2012q4. From it the argument can be put that New Zealand inflation was highly volatile from the late 1950s until the mid 1990s, after which inflation volatility remained moderately low until the mid 2000s, with a rising trend evident since then.

Inflation Persistence

Inflation in New Zealand has been highly persistent over the study period, as is reflected in the estimated coefficient value on the one-period lagged

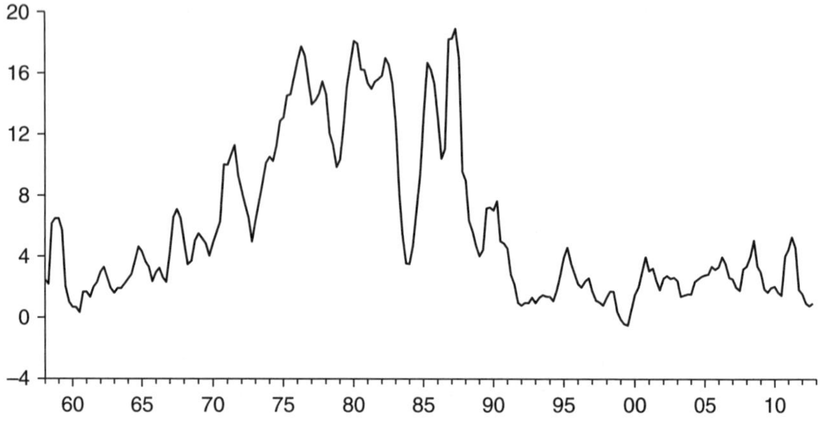

Figure 8.2a Quarter-on-quarter CPI inflation in New Zealand, 1958q1–2012q4

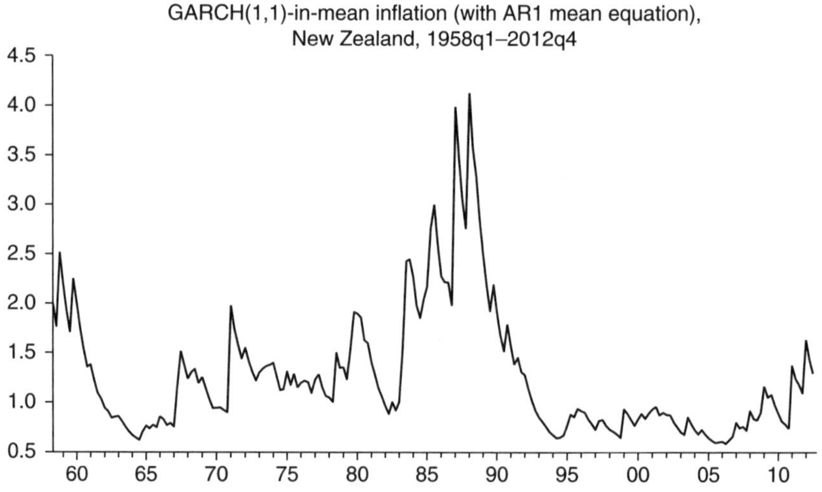

Figure 8.2b Conditional standard deviation of CPI inflation in New Zealand, 1958q1–2012q4

rate of inflation in an autoregressive model AR(1) (Figures 8.3a and 8.3b). The model is estimated by both the recursive and rolling regression techniques. High persistence of inflation is an indicator of low monetary policy credibility, and this result is suggestive of limited RBNZ ability to maintain low, stable inflation. Inflation persistence originates in several

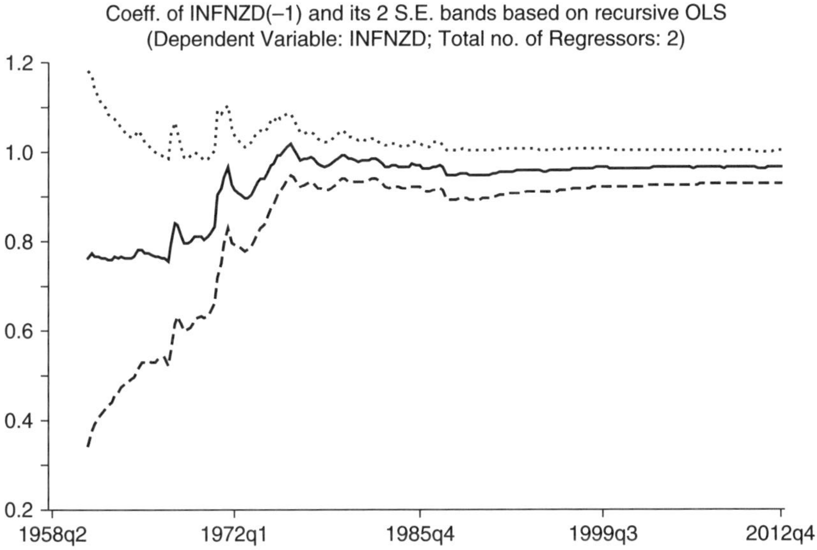

Note: INFNZD = CPI inflation in New Zealand.

Figure 8.3a Recursive estimates of the coefficient on the one-period lagged rate of inflation in New Zealand

intrinsic sources, such as the structural determinants of inflation. This evidence suggests further that inflation targeting has, at best, marginally reduced inflation persistence in New Zealand in the past two decades. This is exhibited in the rolling sample estimates of the coefficient on the one-period lagged rate of inflation. This raises the question of whether or not New Zealand inflation has a unit root.

Table 8.2 reports the unit root test results for inflation. While the ADF test results suggest the presence of a unit root, the KPSS test results contradict this. The Zivot-Andrews breakpoint test results also suggest no unit root in the inflation series. The overall results suggest that although inflation in New Zealand is highly persistent, it does not have a unit root.

Interest Rates and Exchange Rates

Figures 8.4 and 8.5 plot the nominal and real Treasury bill rates of New Zealand and of the United States for 1978q1–2010q4. These two rates are taken in the remaining discussion as proxies for short-term interest rates in the two countries. Figure 8.4 reveals that the New Zealand rate exhibited

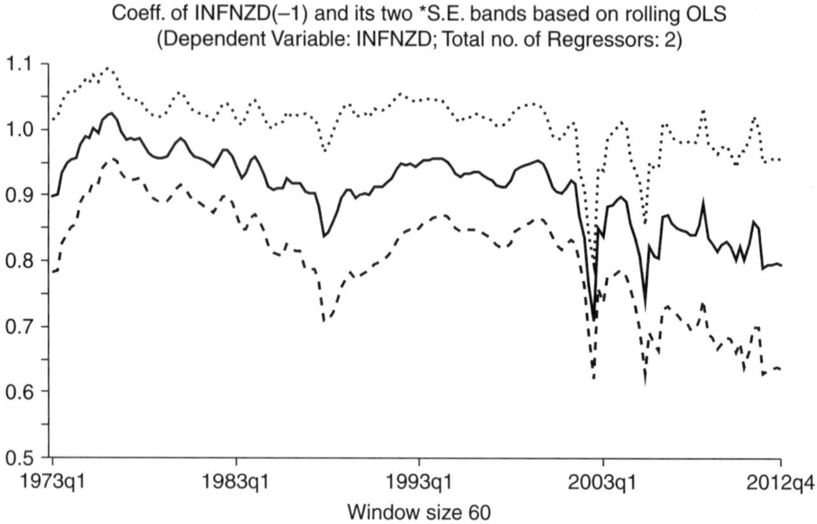

Note: INFNZD = CPI inflation in New Zealand.

Figure 8.3b Rolling sample estimates of the coefficient on the one-period lagged rate of inflation in New Zealand

a differing pattern and movement from that of the United States until the mid 2000s. Figure 8.5 shows that the countries' short-term real interest rates moved broadly together, which is consistent with the real interest rate parity condition. This is expected to hold in an open economy with freely mobile capital. The real interest rates in both countries were, however, highly volatile. Figure 8.6 shows that both the nominal and real effective exchange rates in New Zealand were highly volatile over 1975q1–2010q4.

INFLATION, REAL INTEREST RATE, REAL EXCHANGE RATE AND REAL OUTPUT

As reviewed above, New Zealand's inflation was high and volatile much of the time until the mid 1990s. Before inflation targeting (1990), New Zealand did not conduct a credible, rule-based monetary policy to maintain low and stable inflation. Both monetary and fiscal policies were used to manage aggregate demand. They were deployed mostly to smooth economic fluctuations, caused by shocks and other factors. The exchange rate remained pegged or was determined under a managed float system.

Table 8.2 The unit root test results for CPI inflation in New Zealand, 1949–2012

	Constant (C); Trend (T)	ADF test statistic (SBC-determined lag-length, l)	Inference at 5% level	The KPSS test statistic (Newey-West bandwidth)	Inference at 5% level	Zivot-Andrews test statistic	Breakpoint	Inference at 5% level
LCPI	C and T	−3.95 (l = 5)	I(0)	0.171 (6)	I(1)	−4.05	1974	I(0)
LCPI	C	−1.38(l = 1)	I(1)	0.20 (6)	I(0)	−4.18	1985	I(0)
ΔLCPI	C	−2.36 (l = 0)	I(1)	0.20 (6)	I(0)	−3.81	1988	I(0)

Note: Definitions of variables: LCPI = log of the consumer price index; ΔLCPI = first-order difference of LCPI; SBC = Schwarz Bayesian Criterion; ADF = augmented Dickey-Fuller; and KPSS = Kwiatkowski, Phillips, Schmidt and Shin.

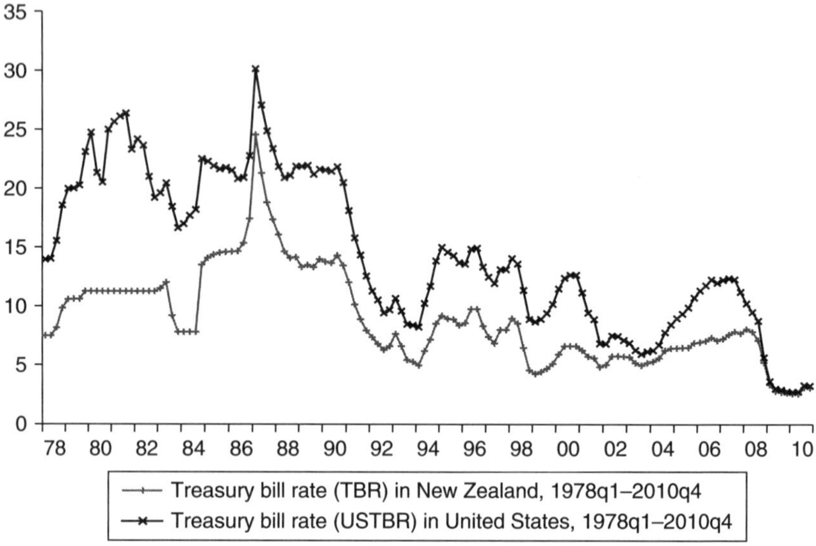

Figure 8.4 Treasury bill rate in New Zealand and Treasury bill rate in the United States 1978q1–2010q4

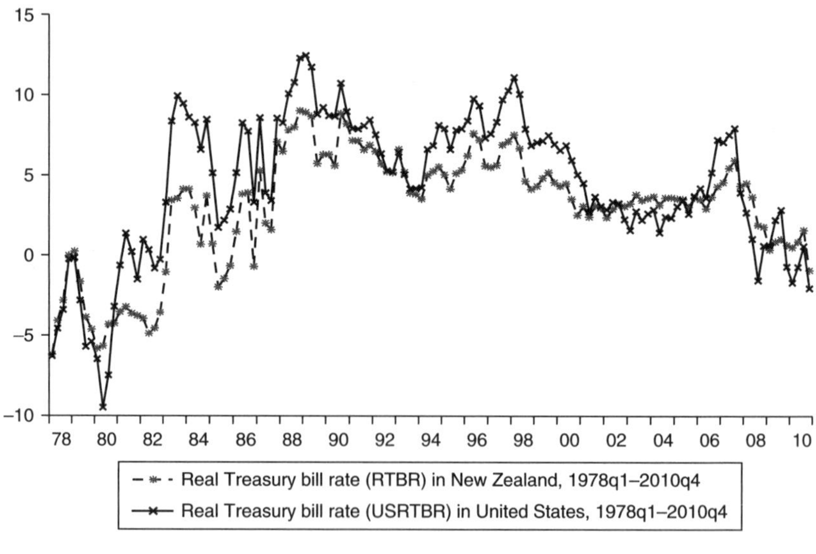

Figure 8.5 Real Treasury bill rate in New Zealand and real Treasury bill rate in the United States, 1978q–2010q4

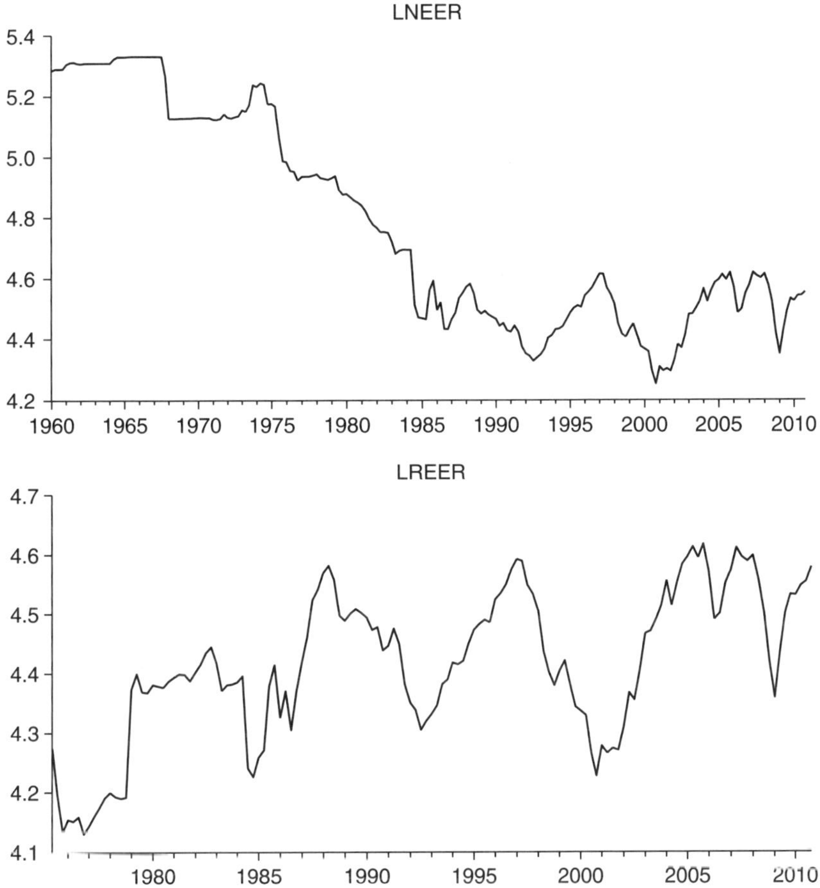

Note: LNEER = log of the nominal effective exchange rate of New Zealand dollar, 1960q1–2010q4; LREER = log of the real effective exchange rate of New Zealand dollar, 1975q1–2010q4.

Figure 8.6 Nominal and real effective exchange rates of New Zealand dollar

The fixed peg exchange rate system reduced the shock-absorbing capacity of exchange rates. Consequently, inflation volatility affected output and its rate of growth, transmitting volatility to both the real interest rate and the real exchange rate. Therefore, the key issue in monetary policy in New Zealand remains the maintenance of low and stable inflation despite the policy change in the early 2000s from a focused inflation targeting strategy to a flexible variation of the strategy that aims to keep inflation low but not necessarily stable, through the adoption of secondary goals for monetary policy that may expose the monetary authority to time-inconsistency problems.

The Structural Vector Autoregressive (SVAR) Analysis

This subsection, using quarterly data, estimates a four-variable SVAR model to examine the interrelationships among inflation, the real interest rate, the real exchange rate and real output. Figure 8.7 plots the data deployed for estimation of the SVAR model.

The model is formulated on the assumption that inflation has a contemporaneous feedback relation with the real interest rate and the real exchange rate. All these variables affect real output. The order of variables in the model is arranged as follows: INFNZ, RTBR, LREER and

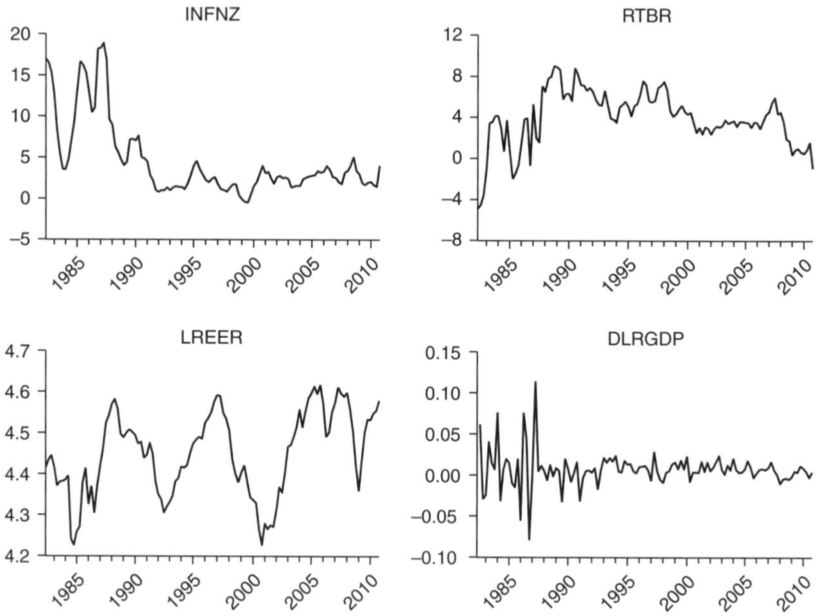

Note: Definitions of variables: INFNZ = CPI inflation in New Zealand; RTBR = real Treasury bill rate; LREER = log of the real effective exchange rate of New Zealand dollar; and DLRGDP = first-order difference of the log of real GDP.

Figure 8.7 Data deployed for estimation of the SVAR model for New Zealand, 1982q2–2010q4

LRGDP, where INFNZ is the New Zealand inflation rate, RTBR is the real Treasury bill rate, LREER is the log of the real effective exchange rate and LRGDP is the log of real GDP. The unit root test results suggest that while inflation, the real Treasury bill rate and the real effective exchange rate are stationary, real output is nonstationary. Two versions of the model are then estimated and deployed to generate impulse responses and the forecast error-variance decompositions. The first version is defined as: INFNZ, RTBR, LREER and LRGDP while the second version is defined as: INFNZ, RTBR, LREER and DLRGDP. In this second version, all the variables are stationary. To conserve space, only the results generated by the second version of the model are reported, since the results obtained by both versions are qualitatively similar.

The impulse responses in Figure 8.8 reveal the interrelations among four variables in the SVAR model. The impulse response results are indicative, not conclusive. As expected, a rise in inflation dampens the real rate of interest, indicating that the nominal interest rate responds slowly to a rise in inflation. Increased inflation, in turn, appreciates the real exchange rate. The real interest rate responds positively to an appreciation of the real exchange rate because, as an appreciated real exchange rate induces capital flight, the real interest rate is required to rise as an inducement to slow down or stop capital flight. This follows the open-economy real exchange rate parity condition. Provided stringent capital controls are in place, there can be short-run deviation of real interest rates across countries. However, capital controls are not generally effective for most countries irrespective of official regulations and controls. In general, an appreciation of the real exchange rate affects both trade and capital flows while changes in the real interest rate affect saving and investment. The overall results suggest significant interrelations among inflation, the real interest rate, the real exchange rate and output growth. Although it is not investigated here, an expanded model is expected to show the impacts of changes in the real interest rate and the real exchange rate on saving, investment and both trade and capital flows.

Table 8.3 presents the forecast error-variance decompositions of INFNZ, RTBR, LREER and DLRGDP. In the tables, the numbers represent those percentages of forecast error variance of variables in the model that can be attributed to own innovations and those percentages of forecast error variance that originate from innovations of other variables. The results show that for all four variables, the dominant source of the forecast error variance is own innovations, to the extent of 66.5 per cent for inflation, 43 per cent for the real interest rate, 91 per cent for the real exchange rate and 68 per cent for real output growth over the ten-year time horizon. In the case of real output growth, innovations in

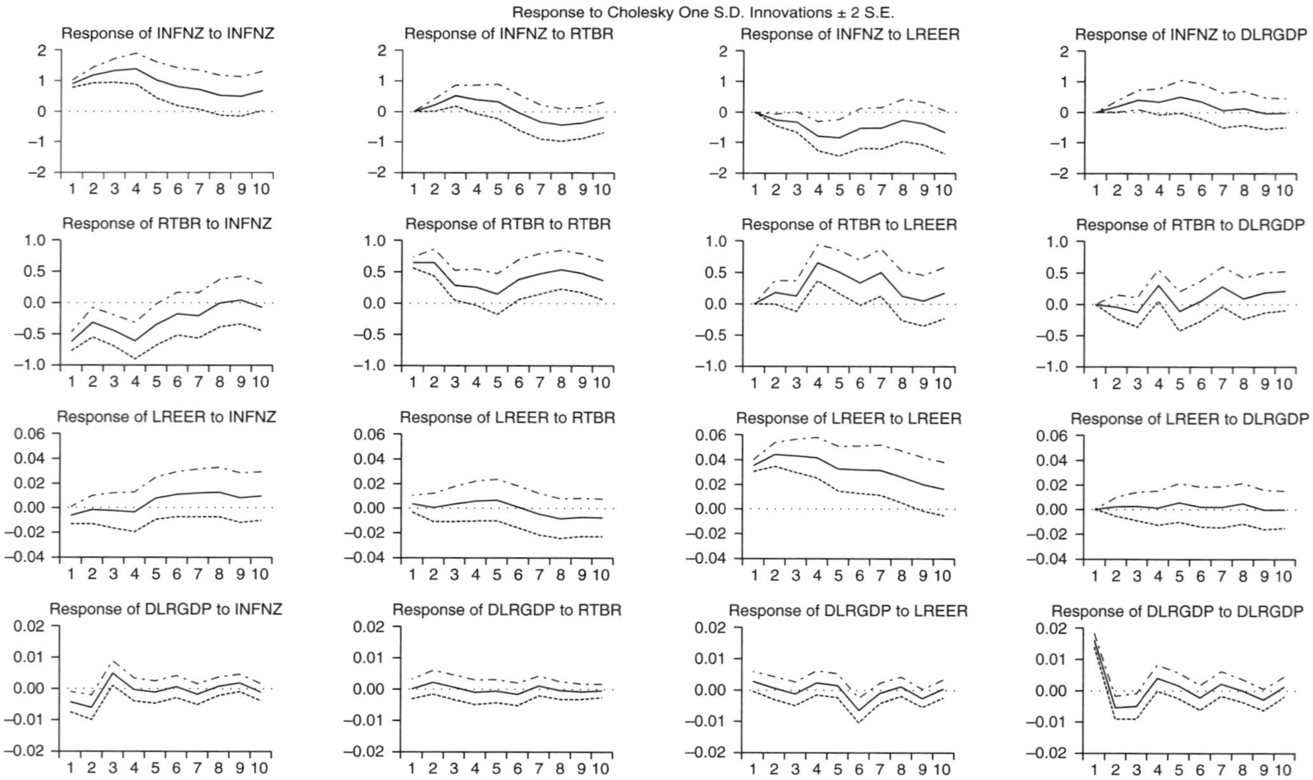

Note: Definitions of variables: INFNZ = CPI inflation in New Zealand; RTBR = real Treasury bill rate; LREER = log of the real effective exchange rate of New Zealand dollar; and DLRGDP = first-order difference of the log of real GDP.

Figure 8.8 Impulse responses for variables in the SVAR model for New Zealand

Table 8.3 *Forecast error-variance decomposition of variables in the SVAR model for New Zealand*

Period	S.E.	INFNZ	RTBR	LREER	DLRGDP
Variance Decomposition of INFNZ:					
1	0.901	100.00	0.00	0.00	0.00
2	1.543	93.53	2.01	2.86	1.60
5	3.112	72.06	5.98	15.87	6.10
10	3.698	66.54	7.79	20.27	5.40
Variance Decomposition of RTBR:					
Period	S.E.	INFNZ	RTBR	LREER	DLRGDP
1	0.900	47.96	52.04	0.00	0.00
2	1.168	35.76	61.64	2.49	0.12
5	1.752	38.68	32.93	24.35	4.04
10	2.182	26.61	42.61	24.49	6.29
Variance Decomposition of LREER:					
Period	S.E.	INFNZ	RTBR	LREER	DLRGDP
1	0.036	2.88	1.00	96.11	0.00
2	0.057	1.22	0.41	98.22	0.15
5	0.090	1.42	1.27	96.75	0.55
10	0.111	5.71	2.52	91.14	0.62
Variance Decomposition of DLRGDP:					
Period	S.E.	INFNZ	RTBR	LREER	DLRGDP
1	0.017	6.30	0.00	2.56	91.12
2	0.019	15.32	1.30	2.17	81.21
5	0.021	18.23	1.45	3.75	76.57
10	0.023	16.97	2.15	12.83	68.04
The Cholesky Ordering: INFNZ RTBR LREER DLRGDP					

Note: Definitions of variables: INFNZ = CPI inflation in New Zealand; RTBR = real Treasury bill rate; LREER = log of the real effective exchange rate of New Zealand dollar; and DLRGDP = first-order difference of the log of real GDP.

the real interest rate and the real exchange rate jointly account for 15 per cent of its forecast error variance. The corresponding share of inflation is 17 per cent. This shows that real output growth is sensitive to the rate of inflation as well as to volatility in that rate. Inflation affects the real interest rate and the real exchange rate, which in turn affect the rate of real output growth. The overall results suggest that inflation significantly impacts the real exchange rate, real interest rate and real output growth in New Zealand.

MONETARY AND EXCHANGE RATE POLICY ISSUES

The empirical results reported above suggest that New Zealand's economy remains vulnerable to external shocks. In its conduct of monetary policy, New Zealand uses a short-term interest rate. It does not use any monetary or credit aggregate as an indicator of monetary policy. It has been suggested by some writers that these aggregates do not provide any new information beyond that contained in the interest rate (Woodford, 2003). However, since the US-global financial crisis, most countries have started monitoring monetary and credit aggregates. There is continuing debate as to whether or not monetary aggregates remain useful to countries that conduct monetary policy under inflation targeting.

Under inflation targeting money supply is demand determined, since the interest rate is used as a policy instrument and therefore cannot be market determined, at least in the short run. The interest rate is, however, affected by inflation and output gaps, as revealed in a monetary policy reaction function. Therefore, the interest rate and inflation are considered to have a feedback relation. This implies that as money supply growth maintains a stable causal link with inflation, the use of the interest rate as an instrument of monetary policy leads to instability in the rate of money growth. Money-growth instability then makes inflation volatile, and this volatility can feed into less stable (short-term) interest rates. Interest rate instability changes money demand, thereby feeding back into the inflation rate itself. The point is that money-growth instability can lead to instability both of inflation and the interest rate. The role of the interest rate in the implementation of monetary policy therefore remains controversial. At very low levels of the short-term interest rate instrument, it has been found in the recent literature to be ineffective in changing aggregate demand.

Then the question arises as to whether or not a monetary aggregate has any role at all to play in the conduct of monetary policy in a country like New Zealand and, if so, what is the nature and weighting of that role in the decision-making processes? Until recently the prevailing view was that monetary targeting for price stability requires a stable money-demand function to establish a causal linkage between money supply growth and inflation. The recent literature suggests that a causal relation exists between money supply growth and the rate of inflation, irrespective of the exchange rate regime and whether or not the money-demand function is stable (McCallum and Nelson, 2011).

This section tests for the presence of a stable money-demand function in New Zealand.[4] For estimation purposes, an open-economy money-demand function is specified as follows:

$$\text{LRJM}_t = \alpha_0 + \alpha_1\text{Ly}_t + \alpha_2\text{NIR}_t + \alpha_3\text{FIR}_t + \alpha_4\text{LRER}_t + \alpha_5\pi_t^v + u_t \quad (8.1)$$

where LRJM (J = N, B) is the log of real money balances (LRNM for narrowly defined money or LRBM for broadly defined money), Ly is the log of real income, NIR is a representative nominal interest rate, FIR is a representative foreign interest rate such as the US Federal funds rate (USFFR), LRER is the log of a representative real exchange rate such as the real effective exchange rate (REER), π_t^v is a measure of inflation volatility and u_t is a random error term. In this specification, real income represents a scale variable and its coefficient is expected to bear a positive sign and have a value not significantly different from one. The coefficients on the domestic and foreign interest rates are expected to bear a negative sign. Following the discussion in Appendix 5, the coefficients on the real exchange rate and inflation volatility remain a priori indeterminate.

The unit root test results suggest that all the variables in the specified model have a unit root. Consequently, they are eligible to form a cointegral money-demand relation. However, preliminary estimation results for a longer sample period 1957–2012 suggest that the deposit or lending rates of interest in New Zealand, and the US Federal funds rate become significant when one of them is used in the model. The model is then estimated using the USFFR as the opportunity cost variable. The USFFR is considered more appropriate as it was market determined in the main, while the New Zealand deposit interest rate was institutionally determined until the mid 1980s. Table 8.4 reports both the autoregressive distributed lag (ARDL) and ordinary least squares (OLS) results obtained for the real broad money-demand function. To conserve space, the results obtained by the narrow definition of money are not reported. As the ARDL and OLS estimation techniques provide similar results, the results obtained by the ARDL technique are deployed for interpretation. The results suggest the presence of a strong form of long-run cointegral relationship among real broad money balances, real income, the US Federal funds rate, the real exchange rate and inflation volatility. The estimated coefficient values are consistent with a priori predictions.

As expected, real income remains the core determinant of broad money demand in New Zealand. The income elasticity of demand for real broad money balances is greater than one. This is significant for an advanced economy like New Zealand. The US Federal funds rate bears a negative sign and is statistically significant. The real effective exchange rate bears a positive sign. As discussed in Appendix 5, the sign of the coefficient on the real exchange rate is not known a priori. Although inflation volatility is not highly significant in the model, it is retained as its exclusion makes the model unstable. Contrary to expectations, inflation instability bears

Table 8.4 The ARDL and OLS regression results for real broad money-demand relationships in New Zealand

F-statistic	6.05			
W-statistic	30.25			
Critical value bounds	F-test	W-test		
90%	(2.56, 3.73)	(12.80, 18.64)		
95%	(3.07, 4.33)	(15.37, 21.64)		
Regressors	Sample: 1957–2012 ARDL (1,2,0,0,0,0) (Selected based on SBC) Coefficient (t-ratio) [prob.]	Sample: 1957–2012 ARDL (1,2,0,0,0) Long-run model Coefficient (t-ratio) [prob.]	Sample: 1955–2012 OLS (Static model) Coefficient (t-ratio) [prob.]	Sample: 1955–2012 OLS (Dynamic model) Coefficient (t-ratio) [prob.]
Intercept	−0.78 (−1.97) [0.06]	−8.44 (−1.33) [0.19]	−0.71 (−0.65) [0.52]	−0.87 (−2.11) [0.04]
LRBM(−1)	0.91 (17.96) [0.00]			0.87 (17.99) [0.00]
LRGDP	1.18 (2.29) [0.03]	1.75 (3.09) [0.00]	1.50 (11.61) [0.00]	0.18 (1.98) [0.05]
LRGDP(−1)	0.10 (0.13) [0.89]			
LRGDP(−2)	−1.12 (−2.09) [0.04]			
USFFR	−0.01 (−1.77) [0.08]	−0.09 (−1.72) [0.09]	−0.06 (−4.76) [0.00]	−0.01 (−1.79) [0.08]
LREER	0.24 (1.73) [0.09]	2.63 (1.59) [0.12]	1.29 (3.70) [0.00]	0.36 (2.56) [0.01]
INFVOL	0.05 (2.63) [0.01]	0.53 (1.35) [0.19]	−0.03 (−0.62) [0.54]	0.02 (1.24) [0.22]
Diagnostics				
Adjusted R^2	0.99		0.94	0.99

Lagrange multiplier test for serial correlation	F(1, 47) = 0.38 [0.54]		F(1, 52) = 82.64 [0.00]	F(1, 51) = 0.09 [0.76]
Ramsey's RESET test of functional form mis-specification	F(1, 47) = 0.00 [0.97]		F(1, 52) = 0.36 [0.55]	F(1, 51) = 0.88 [0.35]
Normality of residuals	$\chi^2_{(2)}$ = 272.01 [0.00]		$\chi^2_{(2)}$ = 3.28 [0.19]	$\chi^2_{(2)}$ = 526.94 [0.00]
Heteroskedasticity	F(1, 54) = 0.09 [0.77]		F(1, 56) = 0.01 [0.92]	F(1, 56) = 0.04 [0.85]
The Wald test:				
H_O: Coefficient on LRGDP = 0		$\chi^2_{(1)}$ = 9.53 [0.00]	$\chi^2_{(1)}$ = 134.74 [0.00]	
H_O: Coefficient on LRGDP = 1		$\chi^2_{(1)}$ = 1.75 [0.19]	$\chi^2_{(1)}$ = 15.12 [0.00]	
H_O: Coefficient on USFFR = 0		$\chi^2_{(1)}$ = 2.96 [0.09]	$\chi^2_{(1)}$ = 22.69 [0.00]	
H_O: Coefficient on LREER = 0		$\chi^2_{(1)}$ = 2.51 [0.11]	$\chi^2_{(1)}$ = 13.66 [0.00]	
H_O: Coefficient on INFVOL = 0		$\chi^2_{(1)}$ = 1.81 [0.18]	$\chi^2_{(1)}$ = 0.38 [0.54]	

Note: Definitions of variables: LRBM = log of real broad money balances; LRGDP = log of real GDP; USFFR = US Federal funds rate; LREER = log of the real effective exchange rate of New Zealand dollar; INFVOL = inflation volatility; SBC = Schwarz Bayesian criterion; and ARDL = autoregressive distributed lag.

a positive sign in the broad money-demand function. It implies the following. As inflation instability rises, there is an increase in demand for a broader definition of money. An interpretation is that inflation volatility raises economic uncertainty, deterring investment. Potential investors may then hold interest-bearing fixed deposits until the investment condition improves. This is an interpretation that is suggested for financially repressed economies where investors accumulate investible funds for investment. A series of stability tests is conducted that suggest that the broad money-demand function is more stable than the narrow money-demand function (Figure 8.9).

Relationships Among Money, Output and Prices

Table 8.5 reports the cointegration test results among money, output and prices. The results obtained for a broad definition of money are found more robust than those obtained for a narrow definition of money. The Engle-Granger cointegration test results suggest a weak form of cointegral relationship among money, output and prices. The dynamic OLS (DOLS) estimates suggest that broad money is highly significant in the price level equation and that the coefficient value of broad money is significantly lower than one. As expected, real output bears a negative sign and is statistically highly significant.

Engle and Granger (1987) have suggested that one of the implications of a cointegral relation between two nonstationary variables is the presence of long-term causality between them running in at least one direction. Table 8.6 reports the bivariate Granger-causality test results among LCPI, LNM (LBM) and LRGDP. Test results are generated within a vector error-correction (VEC) modelling framework after selecting the optimal lag-length using the Schwarz Bayesian Criterion (SBC). The test results suggest that for New Zealand, there is weak short-term causality running from narrow or broad money growth to inflation. Money-growth rate (narrow or broad) is not found to have any strong short-term causal impact on output growth.

SUMMARY AND CONCLUSION

New Zealand is a small, trade-oriented, developed country. Although it was one of the richest countries in the world in the 1950s and 1960s, New Zealand's economic ranking fell in the 1970s as it lost export markets for its agricultural products. The macroeconomic performance of New Zealand deteriorated sharply during the 1970s and early 1980s. This induced political change in 1984 and, with it, the policymakers in the newly

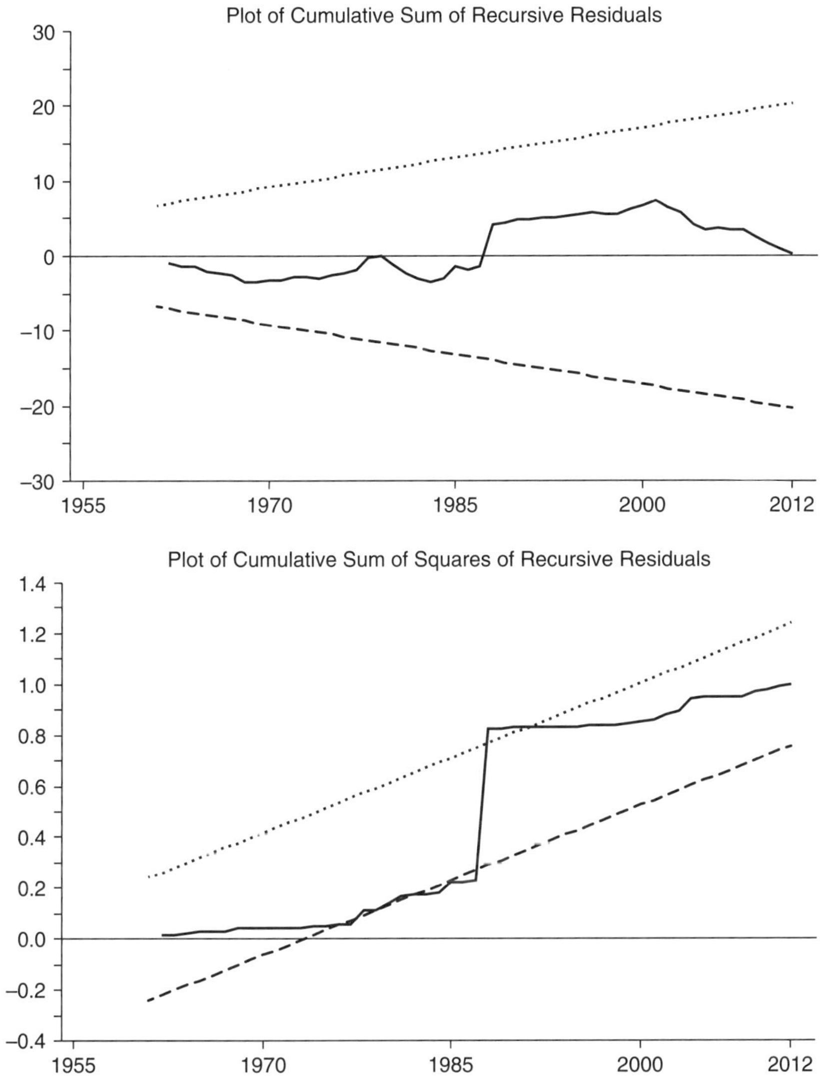

Note: The straight lines represent critical bounds at 5% significance level.

Figure 8.9 CUSUM and CUSUMSQ of residuals of real broad money-demand relationships in New Zealand

Table 8.5 Cointegration test results among money, output and prices in New Zealand, 1970–2012

	Fully modified OLS				Dynamic OLS			
					(lead = 1, lag = 1)			
With narrow money (NM)								
Regressor	coefficient	t-ratio	prob.		coefficient	t-ratio	prob.	
Intercept	3.95	1.52	0.14		4.69	1.48	0.15	
LNM	1.63	3.76	0.00		1.74	3.35	0.00	
LRGDP	−3.51	−2.29	0.03		−3.93	−2.12	0.04	
Sample period	1970–2012				1970–2011			
DW	0.45				0.34			
Adjusted R^2	0.87				0.89			
	tau-statistic	prob.	z-statistic	prob.	tau-statistic	prob.	z-statistic	prob.
The Engle-Granger cointegration tests	−1.88	0.78	−6.24	0.82	−1.89	0.78	−2.03	0.72
The Phillips-Ouliaris cointegration tests	−2.03	0.72	−7.48	0.74	−6.24	0.82	−7.48	0.74
With broad money (BM)								
Regressor	coefficient	t-ratio	prob.		coefficient	t-ratio	prob.	
Intercept	0.74	0.98	0.34		0.52	0.61	0.55	
LBM	0.72	9.84	0.00		0.73	9.86	0.00	
LRGDP	−1.02	−2.94	0.01		−0.98	−2.72	0.01	
Sample period	1970–2012				1970–2011			
DW	0.39				0.33			
Adjusted R^2	0.97				0.98			
	tau-statistic	prob.	z-statistic	prob.	tau-statistic	prob.	z-statistic	prob.
The Engle-Granger cointegration tests	−2.15	0.67	−8.22	0.69	−2.15	0.67	−8.22	0.69
The Phillips-Ouliaris cointegration tests	−2.23	0.63	−8.91	0.64	−2.23	0.63	−8.91	0.64

Note: Definitions of variables: LNM = log of narrow money stock; LBM = log of broad money stock; and LRGDP = log real GDP.

Table 8.6 Granger-causality among money, output and prices in New Zealand, 1954–2012

	Hypotheses No causality runs from:	Chi-square statistic (prob.)	Inference at 5% level
VEC specification	ΔLNM → ΔLCPI	1.45 (0.49)	Null hypothesis not rejected
(With narrow money, NM)	ΔLNM, ΔLRGDP → ΔLCPI	6.69 (0.15)	Null hypothesis not rejected
	ΔLCPI → ΔLNM	0.40 (0.82)	Null hypothesis not rejected
	ΔLRGDP → ΔLNM	0.17 (0.92)	Null hypothesis not rejected
	ΔLCPI → ΔLRGDP	1.17 (0.56)	Null hypothesis not rejected
	ΔLNM → ΔLRGDP	1.03 (0.60)	Null hypothesis not rejected
VEC specification	ΔLBM → ΔLCPI	1.19 (0.57)	Null hypothesis not rejected
(With broad money, BM)	ΔLBM, ΔLRGDP → ΔLCPI	3.74 (0.44)	Null hypothesis not rejected
	ΔLCPI → ΔLBM	4.96 (0.08)	Null hypothesis not rejected
	ΔLRGDP → ΔLBM	7.76 (0.02)	Null hypothesis rejected
	ΔLCPI → ΔLRGDP	0.89 (0.64)	Null hypothesis not rejected
	ΔLBM → ΔLRGDP	0.10 (0.95)	Null hypothesis not rejected

Note: Definitions of variables: LCPI = log of the consumer price index, LNM = log of narrow money stock; LBM = log of broad money stock; and LRGDP = log of real GDP. Optimal lag-length = 2 (selected based on the Schwarz Bayesian Criterion).

elected Labour government to devise and implement a package of comprehensive economic and financial reforms. The aim of the reforms was to make New Zealand's economy more efficient and resilient to shocks, both domestic and external. Price stability was identified as a priority policy goal to raise investment and achieve sustained economic growth.

To maintain price stability, the role of monetary policy was redefined in the RBNZ Act 1989. To institutionalize the key objective of monetary policy (price stability), New Zealand introduced inflation targeting in 1990. This was an innovative approach to the conduct of monetary policy for price stability. It followed the backdrop of instability in the money-demand function that allegedly loosened the linkage between money supply growth and inflation. Inflation targeting was implemented once the RBNZ was successful in lowering inflation from about 10 per cent in the mid 1980s to less than 2 per cent by 1991. This sharp reduction of inflation proved costly, raising the unemployment rate to around 10 per cent.

Since it adopted inflation targeting, New Zealand's macroeconomic performance has been mediocre at best. It experienced a long boom lasting over a decade (1998–2007), sourced from large-scale immigration, an improvement in its external terms of trade and higher government spending. A recession followed, originated in and driven by the US-global financial crisis in 2007. Earlier, there was an appreciation of the real exchange rate, which was caused by large-scale inflows of foreign capital. The economy has recovered from the recession since 2010.

Under inflation targeting, New Zealand's average inflation rate remained within the target range of 1 to 3 per cent; however, inflation volatility has not diminished much. Inflation persistence has also remained high. This evidence suggests limited RBNZ monetary policy credibility. In the early years of inflation targeting, New Zealand adopted a strict version of inflation targeting. The conventional wisdom is that this led to high economic volatility. In the early 2000s the monetary authorities moved to a more flexible version of inflation targeting. This suggests the question of whether or not the RBNZ has diluted its stance on inflation and allows monetary policy to also target business cycle smoothing. The question of how successful, or otherwise, monetary policy can potentially be in stabilizing output in a small, open economy is another matter. A negative outcome of flexible inflation targeting is the possibility of high-inflation volatility. The use of a short-term interest rate for the conduct of monetary policy makes money growth unstable and hence raises inflation volatility.

Since the start of the US-global financial crisis in 2007, financial stability has become an important consideration of monetary policy in many countries, including New Zealand. As New Zealand is a small, open economy and its foreign-exchange market is not deep, the elevated level of exchange rate volatility in a deregulated system has become a matter of concern. A further factor is that New Zealand's banking sector is dominated by foreign banks. This has made the New Zealand economy more vulnerable to external shocks relative to domestic monetary disturbances. In theory, a high degree of interest rate volatility, combined with exchange rate instability exacerbated by New Zealand's thin money and capital markets, triggers large capital flows and creates a boom-bust cycle.[5] Consequently, many problems that New Zealand experienced with respect to macroeconomic management before inflation targeting in 1990 have re-emerged.

Monetary policy has not been effective in dealing with shocks originating from external sources. This reflects difficulty in conducting monetary policy in a small economy that deploys monetary policy to achieve multiple objectives. The question is whether New Zealand, being a small and open economy, can manage monetary policy autonomy in the face of large-scale capital flows that make the exchange rate volatile. High volatility of exchange rates reflects high volatility of capital movements. Large capital movements could be triggered by any aggressive monetary policy stance that the RBNZ may need to take to maintain inflation within the target range. The addition of economic stabilization as a simultaneous objective of monetary policy has raised the level of ambiguity in the conduct of monetary policy. This has diluted the power of monetary policy to maintain low and stable inflation (Walsh, 2009).

High volatility of inflation has raised volatility in output growth in New Zealand. Although monetary policy has been deployed on occasions during the boom period, it was not effective in stabilizing the economy. The sharp appreciation of the exchange rate created problems for the tradable goods sector. An emerging policy issue is whether New Zealand should introduce market-based capital controls to maintain exchange rate stability.

A further concern for New Zealand is the role of money under inflation targeting. It is by now well established in mainstream theory and evidence that high and volatile money supply growth impacts on inflation and its volatility. This chapter has investigated the money-demand behaviour in New Zealand and examined the linkage between money supply growth and inflation within a vector error-correction (VEC) modelling framework. The empirical results suggest the presence of a stable broad money-demand function in New Zealand. However, there is only a weak form of short-run causal linkage between money supply growth and inflation.

Although it is unlikely that New Zealand would switch from inflation targeting to monetary targeting (or exchange rate targeting), there remains scope for improving inflation targeting for price stability. The main point is whether or not the RBNZ should follow the prevailing orthodoxy and ignore inflation volatility. Inflation volatility generally retards the rate of economic growth and raises unemployment. Razzak (2000) has provided evidence that the relationship between money supply growth and inflation has weakened in New Zealand under inflation targeting. The empirical results reported in this chapter confirm Razzak's finding. The finding is, however, inconsistent with the view that the relationship between money supply growth and inflation could be robust irrespective of the monetary policy regime and whether or not the money-demand function is stable. Nevertheless, Razzak (2000) suggests the need for monitoring money for its linkage with real output but not with inflation. Poole (1999, 2007) suggests that ignoring monetary aggregates could be a mistake because of the historical linkage between money supply growth and inflation. Further investigation is required to establish linkages among money, output, prices and exchange rates in New Zealand.

NOTES

1. General information on New Zealand is based on http://en.wikipedia.org/wiki/New_Zealand.
2. For aspects of monetary policy and inflation targeting, see Buckle and Stemp (1991), Fischer (1993), Walsh (1995a, 1995b, 1996) and West (2003).
3. Some information on this section is drawn from the RBNZ website, http://www.rbnz.govt.nz/.
4. For early studies on money-demand behaviour in New Zealand, see Choi and Oxley (2004) and Valadkhani (2002).
5. High volatility of interest rates is a symptom of unstable demand and supply conditions in credit markets. Credit market risks are translated into interest rates, credit rationing and the availability of funds for lending. Macroeconomic stability is therefore critical for maintaining stable demand and supply of loanable funds in credit markets. This is expected to maintain stability in interest rates.

REFERENCES

Bollard, A. and O. Karagedikli (2006), 'Inflation targeting: the New Zealand experience and some lessons', Paper presented at Inflation Targeting: Performance and Challenges Conference at the Central Bank of the Republic of Turkey, Istanbul, 19–20 January.

Brash, D.T. (1995), 'The role of monetary policy; where does unemployment fit in?', *Federal Reserve Bank of Kansas City*, First quarter, 23–30.

Brash, D.T. (1998), 'Inflation targeting in New Zealand: experience and practice', Seminar paper No. 641, Institute for International Economic Studies, Stockholm University.

Brash, D.T. (2000), 'Inflation targeting in New Zealand, 1988–2000', Speech to the Trans-Tasman Business Cycle, Melbourne, 9 February.

Buckle, R. and P. Stemp (1991), 'Reserve Bank autonomy and the credibility of monetary policy: a game theoretic approach', *New Zealand Economic Papers*, **25**(1), 51–85.

Choi, D. and L. Oxley (2004), 'Modelling the demand for money in New Zealand', *Mathematics and Computers in Simulation*, **64**, 185–91.

Debelle, G. (1996), 'The ends of three small inflations: Australia, New Zealand and Canada', *Canadian Public Policy*, **21**(1), 56–78.

Engle, R.F. and C.W.J. Granger (1987), 'Co-integration and error-correction: representation, estimation, and testing', *Econometrica*, **55**(2), 251–76.

Fischer, A.M. (1993), 'Inflation targeting: the New Zealand and Canadian cases', *Cato Journal*, **13**, Spring/Summer, 1–27.

IMF (International Monetary Fund) (various years), *International Financial Statistics*, Washington, DC: IMF.

IMF (International Monetary Fund) (various years), *World Economic Outlook*, Washington, DC: IMF.

McCallum, B.T. and E. Nelson (2011), 'Money and inflation: some critical issues', in B.M. Friedman and M. Woodford (eds), *Handbook of Monetary Economics*, Vol. 3A, Amsterdam: Elsevier Science, pp. 97–153.

Nelson, E. (2005), 'Monetary policy neglect and the great inflation in Canada, Australia, and New Zealand', *International Journal of Central Banking*, May, 133–79.

Poole, W. (1999), 'Monetary policy rules?', *Federal Reserve Bank of St. Louis Review*, March/April, 3–12.

Poole, W. (2007), 'Understanding the Fed', *Federal Reserve Bank of St. Louis Review*, **89**, 3–13.

Razzak, W. (2000), 'Inflation: is it a unit root or a long-memory process?', available at http://www.razzakw.net/paper2.pdf (accessed 19 March 2015).

Stock, J.H. and M.W. Watson (2012), *Introduction to Econometrics*, New York: Pearson-Addison Wesley.

Valadkhani, A. (2002), 'Long and short-run determinants of money demand in New Zealand: evidence from cointegration analysis', *New Zealand Economic Papers*, **36**, 235–50.

Walsh, C.E. (1995a), 'Optimal contracts for central bankers', *American Economic Review*, **85**(1), 150–67.

Walsh, C.E. (1995b), 'Is New Zealand's Reserve Bank Act of 1989 an optimal central bank contract?', *Journal of Money, Credit and Banking*, **27**(4), 1179–91.

Walsh, C.E. (1996), 'Accountability in practice; recent monetary policy in New Zealand', *Federal Reserve Bank of San Francisco Economic Letter*, No. 96–25, 9 September.

Walsh, C.E. (1998a), *Monetary Theory and Policy*, Cambridge, MA: MIT Press.

Walsh, C.E. (1998b), 'Financial deregulation and monetary policy in New Zealand', in H.S. Cheng (ed.), *Monetary Policy in Pacific Basin Countries*, Boston, MA: Kluwer Academic Publishers.

Walsh, C.E. (2009), 'Using monetary policy to stabilize economic activity', in Federal Reserve Bank of Kansas City (ed.), *Financial Stability and Macroeconomic Policy*, Kansas City, MO: Federal Reserve Bank of Kansas City, pp. 245–96.

West, K.D. (2003), 'Monetary policy and the volatility of real exchange rates in New Zealand', *New Zealand Economic Papers*, **37**(2), 175–96.

Woodford, M. (2003), *Interest and Prices: Foundations of a Theory of Monetary Policy*, Princeton, NJ: Princeton University Press.

9. The Philippines

The Philippines, formally the Republic of the Philippines, is an archipelago in Southeast Asia, comprising about 7000 islands bordering the Western Pacific Ocean and situated on the Pacific Ring of Fire between about 5 and 20 degrees north latitude. It is resource-rich, but vulnerable to earthquakes, typhoons and other natural disasters. The population of the Philippines is about 100 million. Religiously, the population is overwhelmingly Roman Catholic of varied ethnicity. The Philippines is a political democracy. In some southern islands of the country, Muslims form the majority and therefore exercise some autonomy in political affairs. In modern colonial times, the Philippines has a long past dating to the sixteenth century when it was part of the Spanish East Indies. Hence, it has inherited complex, heavily European-influenced economic, social and political institutions, with English as the major external language supplementing Spanish and local languages. The Philippine Islands moved from the Spanish to the US sphere of influence at the end of the nineteenth century following the Spanish-American War (1898). Its recent political history dates from the end of World War II when it gained full independence from the United States. The United States still plays a key role in the economic, social and political affairs of the Philippines.[1]

The Philippines is a major economy in Southeast Asia. It gained the status of a middle-income country in the mid 1990s. This achievement was not, however, an uninterrupted progression. In the 1950s the Philippines had one of the highest per capita incomes in Asia. At that moment in history, it had the potential for development 'takeoff' and embarked on the 'miraculous' pathway to economic development first taken by Japan and later by South Korea and the other 'Asian Tigers'. However, the economic and social ranking of the Philippines fell sharply during the 1970s and 1980s under the repressive monarch-like rule of Ferdinand and Imelda Marcos. It was not until 1986 that the country's political dynamics were released to begin the process of its democratic transition. Since then the Philippines has gained political stability, although there have been occasional political upheavals and setbacks over the past two and a half decades with various 'pretenders to the throne' undermining democratization and economic development processes in misguided attempts to return the country to various retarded forms of autocratic rule. On the economic front, the Philippines has managed, despite the political sideshows, a successful transition from low growth and high inflation to a moderately high-growth, low-inflation economy. As the economic fundamentals have improved in this country over the past two decades, the country is expected to make further economic progress provided it can sustain economic and political stability. The transition of the Philippine economy is significant when examined from an historical perspective (Vos and Yap, 1996).

The Philippine economy was heavily regulated and controlled until the early 1980s. It introduced IMF-supported stabilization and structural adjustment programmes during the late 1980s and 1990s. These reforms were effective in creating a more flexible and resilient economy, able to absorb shocks, both internal and external, and rebound resiliently. Large-scale capital inflows, such as overseas remittances the equivalent of about 20 billion US dollars, by more than 12 million Filipinos, are particularly important as capital flows remain volatile and pro-cyclical. The Philippines has also undertaken major institutional reforms in central banking and monetary policy to maintain price stability. Consequently, the Philippines escaped, largely unscathed, both the East-Southeast Asian financial crisis of the late 1990s and the US-global financial crisis of 2007–09. These crises were, however, instrumental to ongoing economic and financial reforms creating an environment for sustained economic growth in a low-inflation environment (IMF, 2011).

Presently, the Philippines operates under a managed float exchange rate system. The central bank of the Philippines, Bangko Sentral ng Pilipinas (BSP), has the option to intervene in the foreign-exchange market to stabilize the exchange rate to sustain financial stability. The BSP also maintains some administrative controls over capital flows to sustain financial stability. The degree to which these controls are effective is not known. Significantly, in a reform aimed at institutionalizing monetary policy for price stability, the Philippines adopted inflation targeting in 2002. This forward-looking monetary policy strategy, with a numerical inflation target, has been useful to anchor inflationary expectations and keep inflation close to the target level (Lim, 2006).

Macroeconomic performance of the Philippines has improved significantly over the past decade, and can now be described as largely successful at first glance. However, the presence of high persistence of inflation in the Philippines suggests that the BSP's credibility in maintaining low and stable inflation has not improved significantly. Presently, there is no significant inflationary pressure in the Philippines from monetary overhang, caused by any expansionary monetary and fiscal policies. Supply shocks, however, remain a frequent phenomenon, and this phenomenon is one of the Philippines's major sources of inflation volatility (Lim, 1987, 2008).

Despite such shocks, a low-inflation environment has emerged in the Philippines since 2010. This has been associated with moderately rapid economic growth of about 5 per cent per annum. The external sector balance in the Philippines has also improved. The current account of the balance-of-payments has been in surplus since the early 2000s. This was mostly due to large-scale workers' remittances, originating from the Middle East and East Asian countries. In addition, the Philippines has diversified its export composition; especially, it has increased the exports of manufacturing products. This is an indicator that the Philippines does not operate under a foreign-exchange constraint on its economic growth. Its external debt level is also at a low level and sustainable.

Macroeconomic management therefore plays a leading role in the sustenance of steady economic growth in the Philippines. A key factor, in play since the East-Southeast Asian financial crisis of the late 1990s, is the attraction of increased levels of long-term, large-scale foreign investment into the Philippines. This has eventuated partly in response to major financial reforms undertaken to reduce the vulnerability of the financial sector to external shocks through firm commitment by the Philippine authorities to maintain the managed float exchange rate system, with complementary administrative controls over capital flows. For example, during the US-global financial crisis, rather than following a strict form of inflation targeting, the Philippines deployed expansionary monetary and fiscal policies to foster economic recovery. This was essentially in response to the suggestion of the IMF and other international organizations. However, to avoid creating unsustainable fiscal imbalances, the BSP unwound liquidity support measures early in 2010, once the economic recovery was underway. To continue with inflation targeting, the BSP sets the inflation target range over the medium term within 3 to 5 per cent per annum. Although this target range is relatively high, it is considered realistic and appropriate for the Philippine circumstances as a developing country operating under some institutional and organizational rigidities. A further justification for this relatively high target band for inflation is its ability to contribute to output maximization (Khan and Senhadji, 2001).

THE BANGKO SENTRAL NG PILIPINAS: ORGANIZATION AND ACTIVITIES[2]

Bangko Sentral ng Pilipinas is usually abbreviated to BSP or simply Bangko Sentral. Previously known as the Central Bank of the Philippines

(CBP), it was established on 3 January 1949. The policy objectives of the CBP were contained in the Republic Act (RA) No. 265. This Act guided the CBP in its discharge of such functions as the promotion of economic development and the maintenance of internal and external monetary stability. The RA No. 265 was amended by Presidential Decree (PD) No. 72 to make the CBP's actions more responsive to changing economic conditions. The PD No. 72 emphasized the maintenance of monetary stability as the primary objective of the CBP. The CBP was renamed BSP on 3 July 1993 pursuant to the provisions of the 1987 Philippine Constitution and the New Central Bank Act of 1993 (Republic Act No. 7653).

The BSP enjoys both fiscal and administrative autonomy from the government of the Philippines in pursuit of its assigned responsibilities, especially maintaining monetary stability. The New Central Bank Act maintains price stability as the primary objective of monetary policy. Although price stability is not defined precisely, the implication is of low and stable inflation. Following the extant literature, price stability is expected to promote balanced and sustainable economic growth. In addition to maintaining price stability, the BSP is committed to establish a sound and efficient financial system to ensure exchange rate stability. This indicates that BSP conduct of monetary policy is expected to achieve a set of objectives that are broad but useful to maintain macroeconomic stability. Exchange rate stability implies the maintenance of low volatility of the exchange rate under a managed float exchange rate system. The BSP has the responsibility of promoting and preserving monetary stability so that the Philippine currency (peso) remains convertible against some hard currencies, especially the US dollar and the Japanese yen.

A duly constituted Monetary Board exercises the powers and functions of the BSP. It is composed of seven members who are appointed by the president of the Philippines for a maximum term of six years. The governor of the BSP is the chairman of the Monetary Board. Five of the remaining six members work full time and are appointed from the private sector. The remaining member is appointed by the president from the Cabinet. Out of the five private members who are appointed from the private sector, three are appointed for a term of six years while the remaining two members are appointed for a term of three years.

The governor is the chief executive of the BSP and remains responsible for the direction and supervision of the Bank's operations and administration. The governor designates a deputy governor to act as his or her alternative whenever the governor is unable to attend any meeting of the Monetary Board. The Monetary Board meets at least once a week. Subject to some constraints, in an emergency the governor has the authority to make decisions on any matter or take any action within the authority of the Board. The Monetary Board publishes and submits a number of reports on economic and financial matters of the BSP to the president and to the Congress as per some time restrictions.

The governor of the BSP, with the approval of the Monetary Board, appoints not more than three deputy governors and assigns them duties and responsibilities. At the time of writing, a deputy governor heads each of the three operating sectors of the BSP. These sectors are:

(a) The monetary stability sector, which takes charge of the formulation and implementation of monetary policy, including serving the needs of all commercial banks through accepting deposits, servicing withdrawals and extending credits through rediscounting facilities.
(b) The supervision and examination sector, which enforces and monitors the compliance of the banking laws to promote a sound and healthy banking system.
(c) The resource management sector, which serves the human, financial and physical resource needs of the BSP.

EVOLUTION OF MONETARY POLICY IN THE PHILIPPINES

The Philippines maintained moderately high economic growth in 1950–80. This was a time when the Philippine economy grew rapidly, commensurately with other economies in the region, including Japan and the four 'Asian Tigers': South Korea, Taiwan, Hong Kong and Singapore. However, the Philippines experienced lacklustre economic performance throughout the 1980s and mid 1990s when the country suffered major political instability in a difficult process of transition to a more enlightened system of government amenable to releasing the wealth-creation energies and talents of citizens. From the late 1990s the Philippines has improved its macroeconomic performance and emerged as a rapidly growing market economy. It weathered the East-Southeast Asian financial crisis of the late 1990s better than other countries in the region; indeed, the crisis was turned to advantage and became instrumental in strengthening the financial institutions of the Philippines. Consequently, the Philippines has maintained an impressive record of successful crisis management over the past one and a half decades. In particular, unlike some other countries in the region, the 2007–09 US-global financial crisis did not impact the Philippine economy very widely or deeply, apart from perhaps in the most significant way: acting as a salutary confirmation of the Philippine policymakers' earlier wisdom in putting in place macroeconomic policy measures that conferred the economy with protective resilience against the two major economic crises of the late twentieth and early twenty-first centuries.

Underpinning the recent economic transformation in the Philippines has been the development of institutions for improved decision-making on monetary policy. Until the early 1980s monetary policy in the Philippines was dominated by fiscal policy. It lacked clear focus and objectives. This led to a loss of control over the money-growth rate, which caused high and volatile inflation and a balance-of-payments crisis during the late 1970s. Implementation of monetary policy began to improve with the establishment of the BSP in 1993. The old Central Bank of the Philippines had rendered itself insolvent in bailing out some domestic banks that had run into financial difficulties (Baunto et al., 2011). Consequently, the BSP was established with a fresh balance sheet, capitalized by the Philippine government. Under the New Central Bank Act of 1993, the mandate of the BSP was amended to pursue price stability as the primary objective of monetary policy. Consequently, the BSP has become the sole formulator and executor of monetary policy for price stability. To impose restrictions on the government's borrowing from the BSP, the Act imposes limits on the amount and maturity of BSP credits to the government. The aim is to diminish fiscal dominance over monetary policy. This is a key requirement for successful operation of inflation targeting for maintaining low and stable inflation.

From 1993 to 2002 the BSP conducted monetary policy within the IMF financial programming framework. This framework had, indeed, been in place since 1984 when the then CBP introduced the managed float exchange rate system. Monetary policy under financial programming revolved around monetary base programming. This programme is based on the premise that there exists a linkage between money, output and prices in the Philippines (Bautista, 1983; Gochoco-Bautista, 2006; Reyes and Yap, 1993). Assuming constant velocity of money, it suggests a causal linkage between money supply growth and inflation. There was, however, limited control over the money supply especially under the pegged exchange rate system put in place in 1996–97. During this period the Philippines experienced an externally financed, credit-led economic boom. The Philippines peso then came under strong pressure to depreciate when the East-Southeast Asian financial crisis emerged. On 11 July 1997 the peso was floated to relieve the pressure, while the monetary policy focus shifted from price stability to exchange rate stability. It was expected that a stable exchange rate would anchor prices and hence mitigate the adverse impact of the currency crisis on the Philippine economy by containing inflation.

While the economy did not suffer much from the crisis, the Philippines switched to inflation targeting in principle in January 2000 to embed in its macroeconomic management programme a monetary policy strategy that had proven itself in difficult circumstances. It adopted inflation targeting more formally in January 2002. The stated reason for the switch from monetary targeting to inflation targeting was alleged instability in the money-demand function. Instability of the money-demand function arguably originated in financial deregulation and liberalization. It was suggested that this had weakened the causal relationship between money supply growth and inflation since 1994. Financial liberalization, it was argued, had also made the money multiplier unstable, leaving the money-multiplier model inappropriate to explain the money supply process. Accordingly, a modified monetary targeting policy was introduced. This allowed the money-growth rate to exceed the target growth rate of the money supply as long as the inflation target was met. The introduction of inflation targeting appears, therefore, to have been the policy outcome of the suspected breakdown of the monetary base targeting framework that had been in place since the mid 1980s.

To complement its adoption of inflation targeting under a flexible exchange rate system, the government liberalized the capital account of the balance-of-payments. This was intended to encourage foreign-capital inflows. Large-scale capital flows, which remain episodic and speculative, however, continue to create some pressure on the exchange rate of the peso given that the foreign-exchange market in the Philippines is still thin and underdeveloped.

At the time of writing, the Philippine government, through the Development Budget Coordinating Committee, sets the inflation target, based on the headline consumer price index, two years ahead in consultation with the BSP. The BSP announces the inflation target and sets the course of monetary policy measures to achieve the inflation target. The BSP has changed the target range of inflation a number of times. During 2000–13 the flexible inflation target ranged between 3.5 to 6 per cent. This range was significantly wider than usual, but considered appropriate for a developing country like the Philippines. The Philippine economy remains exposed to myriad supply shocks that generate inflation spikes. Consequently, the BSP's monetary policy framework provides exemption clauses with the view that there are limits to the effectiveness of monetary policy and that there could be occasional breaches of inflation target due to factors that remain beyond the control of the BSP.

As Table 9.1 shows, the BSP broadly achieved the inflation target during 2002–12. The average annual inflation rate was close to the midpoint average rate within the target range. In 2008, the inflation target was missed due to both the sharp rise in commodity prices in international

Table 9.1 Macroeconomic indicators, Philippines, 1950–2012

Macroeconomic indicators	1951–55	1956–60	1961–65	1966–70	1971–75	1976–80	1981–85	1986–90	1991–95	1996–2000	2001–05	2006–10	2011	2012
Budget balance (% of GDP)	n.a.	n.a.	n.a.	n.a.	n.a.	n.a.	n.a.	n.a.	−0.2	−1.2	−3.1	−1.1	−0.8	−1.9
General government gross debt (% of GDP)	n.a.	n.a.	n.a.	n.a.	n.a.	n.a.	n.a.	n.a.	64.1	55.4	63.0	45.6	41.9	41.5
Money-growth rate (%)														
Narrow money growth	0.6	7.4	9.2	10.9	19.2	17.0	11.3	20.6	16.1	15.7	9.4	17.5	10.9	7.4
Broad money growth	3.9	8.9	13.4	14.2	16.7	22.8	23.9	17.9	21.9	16.1	7.0	14.2	5.3	7.0
Real GDP growth rate (%)	n.a	1.6	5.2	4.6	5.8	6.1	−1.1	4.7	2.2	3.6	4.6	5.0	3.9	6.6
GDP per capita, current prices, US dollar	n.a.	n.a.	n.a.	n.a.	n.a.	744	717	706	975	1136	1063	1792	2345	2462
Unemployment rate (%)	n.a.	n.a.	n.a.	n.a.	n.a.	n.a.	11.1	9.9	9.7	9.6	11.4	7.5	7.0	7.0
CPI inflation rate (%)	−0.8	2.2	4.8	6.1	17.4	12.4	21.4	7.3	9.8	6.5	4.3	4.9	4.6	3.2
Current account balance (% of GDP)	n.a.	n.a.	n.a.	n.a.	n.a.	−6.9	−2.4	−0.7	−3.0	−2.6	0.3	4.2	3.1	3.0

Table 9.1 (continued)

Macroeconomic indicators	1951–55	1956–60	1961–65	1966–70	1971–75	1976–80	1981–85	1986–90	1991–95	1996–2000	2001–05	2006–10	2011	2012
Nominal interest rate (%)														
Treasury bill rate	n.a.	n.a.	n.a.	n.a.	n.a.	11.3	19.2	16.9	14.9	12.0	6.9	4.3	1.3	1.5
Government bond yield	n.a.	n.a.	n.a.	n.a.	n.a.	n.a.	n.a.	n.a.	13.8	13.8	9.9	6.4	na	na
Real interest rate (%)[a]														
Treasury bill rate	n.a.	n.a.	n.a.	n.a.	n.a.	−0.9	−1.0	9.0	4.7	5.2	2.5	−0.6	−3.2	−1.6
Government bond yield	n.a.	n.a.	n.a.	n.a.	n.a.	n.a.	n.a.	n.a.	5.8	6.9	5.4	2.1	n.a.	n.a.
Nominal exchange rate (peso per US$)	2.0	2.0	3.5	4.3	6.8	7.4	12.6	21.6	26.4	36.0	53.6	46.9	43.3	42.2
Nominal effective exchange rate[b]	n.a.	n.a.	n.a.	975.6	758.5	638.0	462.5	204.2	180.2	160.2	108.0	110.1	108.3	112.2
Real effective exchange rate[b]	n.a.	n.a.	n.a.	n.a.	n.a.	158.9	163.9	119.5	127.7	132.4	101.8	119.5	126.7	132.8

Notes:
n.a. = not available
a. Real interest rate is estimated as: 100(((1 + interest rate)/(1 + inflation rate))−1) where the interest rate and inflation rate are expressed in decimal.
b. An increase in the index value of the exchange rate represents appreciation.

Source: Author's computation based on IMF, *International Financial Statistics*; IMF, *World Economic Outlook*; and other country-specific publications on the IMF website.

markets and the US-global financial crisis. Inflation targeting appears to have been effective in anchoring inflationary expectations, signalling as it does the intention of the BSP to maintain price stability. The implication drawn by the public is one of low inflation on average, given the familiar and frequent supply shocks.

Under these monetary policy arrangements, the BSP has gained some respect and, possibly, a modicum of policy credibility. Further financial reforms and fiscal consolidation are expected to make inflation targeting more effective in keeping inflation low and stable, and perhaps reduce the level of inflation persistence. Some potential problems remain with inflation targeting; especially, the BSP's deployment of a short-term interest rate as the instrument of monetary policy. Both the interest rate and the exchange rate channels of the monetary policy transmission mechanism are not fully developed. As a compromise, the BSP monitors monetary and credit aggregates to assist its efforts to prevent the generation of inflationary pressures. It is shown below that a strong causal relation indeed exists between money supply growth and inflation in the Philippines. This relation holds irrespective both of whether or not the money-demand function is stable, and of whether money is exogenous or endogenous under different exchange rate arrangements (McCallum and Nelson, 2011).

Transmission Mechanisms of Monetary Policy in the Philippines

Figure 9.1 exhibits a flowchart of the monetary policy transmission mechanisms in the Philippines. In implementing monetary policy for price stability, the BSP brings about changes in reserve money by deploying a set of monetary policy instruments. They include the policy interest rate, the reserve requirement rate, deposits in the special deposit account of banks and trust entities, the rediscount rate and open market operations. The BSP's primary monetary policy instruments are the overnight reverse repurchase (borrowing) rate and overnight repurchase (lending) rate. Changes in the level of liquidity in the system, effected through open market operations, alter the interest rate and the exchange rate; both of these alter aggregate demand and, subsequently, output and the price level. For example, changes in domestic liquidity affect the 91-day Treasury bill rate, which alters the term structure of interest rates. Given the interest rate parity condition, any change in the 91-day Treasury bill rate brings about changes in the exchange rate. This makes monetary policy equivalent to exchange rate policy under a floating exchange rate system. Changes in the exchange rate affect the domestic prices of importable goods and hence the price level. Inflation, in turn, has a feedback impact on the exchange rate given the purchasing power parity relationship. The transmission

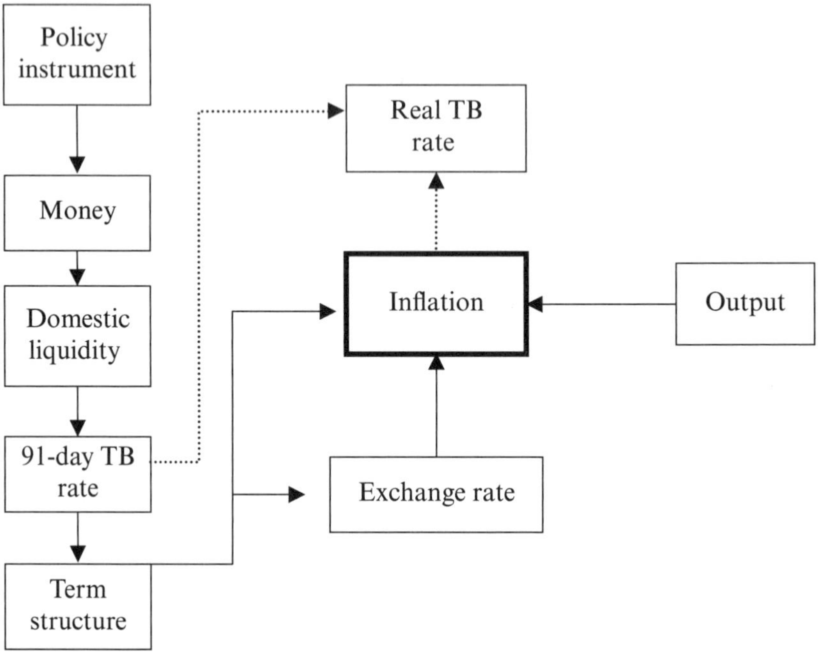

Source: Adapted based on Guinigundo (2008).

Figure 9.1 Monetary policy transmission mechanisms in the Philippines

mechanisms of monetary policy suggested here rely heavily on the assumption of short-run wage and price rigidities. Under this assumption, changes in both the nominal interest rate and the exchange rate bring changes in both the real interest rate and the real exchange rate. Changes in the real interest rate and the real exchange rate then feed into changes in aggregate demand and, consequently, both output and prices.[3]

MACROECONOMIC DEVELOPMENTS AND INFLATION PERFORMANCE

The Philippine economy was an underperformer for over five decades from the 1950s when its record is compared with the economic performance of other countries in the East-Southeast Asian region. Political instability and the associated, relatively unsound, macroeconomic policies in the Philippines were not conducive to steady economic growth. Throughout the 1960s and 1970s, the main thrust of economic policy was to develop an industrial sector deploying the import-substituting strategy of economic development. The Philippine government's interventionist policy stance in economic affairs was reflected in the provision of various fiscal incentives to import-substituting firms, subsidized credits to the priority sectors and the promotion of capital-intensive industries in an otherwise labour-abundant country. These policies continued throughout the 1970s and mid 1980s until the Marcos regime came to an end. Throughout these decades, inflation remained high and volatile, which in turn compromised the rate of economic growth and left it unbalanced and volatile (Montes and Lim, 1996; Yap, 1996).

From 1986 the government reoriented economic policies to establish a market-oriented economy. The Aquino government came to power in 1986 when the Marcos government was overthrown by the well-known, largely bloodless, 'people-power' revolution. The Aquino government adopted an economic reform agenda that included trade and financial reform. Quantitative restrictions on imports were phased out and the tariff structure was rationalized and simplified. To encourage the level of foreign investment needed for industrialization, a liberal 'Foreign Investment Act' was passed. Some public corporations were privatized to attract foreign investment and make them competitive. To bring some structural change to the rural economic and political structure, the government introduced a land-reform programme as part of what was called the Comprehensive Agricultural Reform programme. From the beginning of this much needed reform, there has been powerful political resistance to it. As time has passed, some of the reform measures implemented early in the programme have subsequently been reversed or watered down. Political instability has been the main impediment to implementation of the land-reform programme. To date, then, no major success has therefore been achieved with respect to both economic and political structure.

The government of General Ramos assumed office in 1992. It adopted various economic reforms to steer the economy towards a steady growth path. The key reforms were the removal of restrictions on both the current and capital accounts of the balance-of-payments. On the financial sector, the BSP Act 1993 was passed, which established price stability as the primary objective of monetary policy. The Act also strengthened the legal framework for the improvement of bank supervision and the regulation of banks and non-bank financial institutions to deal with the potential for financial crisis.

Economic reform undertaken by both the Aquino and the Ramos governments has positively impacted economic growth. Productivity growth rose and the industrial sector showed signs of dynamism. Historically, economic growth in the Philippines had been uneven.

Economic performance in the Philippines has improved markedly since the early 2000s. Investor confidence has grown with government initiatives to consolidate the fiscal balance and demonstration of the BSP's ability to exercise its independence from the government and maintain low and stable inflation. Foreign remittances of about 12 million Filipinos have been a major contributor to the Philippine current account surpluses. Since the introduction of a managed float exchange rate system in the late 1990s, the exchange rate has been stable in the sense that there are no signs of real exchange rate misalignment. Moreover, the BSP intervenes in the foreign-exchange market, as needed, to smooth exchange rate volatility. Over time, the BSP has accumulated considerable foreign reserves. These have reduced the country's vulnerability to external shocks. The BSP is likely to accumulate further reserves as self-insurance against any future speculative attacks on the peso. The BSP has sterilized much of the reserves build-up and thereby avoided excessive monetary expansion to sustain price stability. This has increased sterilization costs because of the interest differential between domestic and foreign financial products. The authorities have liberalized controls over capital outflows, paid down some external debt and implemented some macro-prudential measures to maintain financial stability. Effective from January 2012, the BSP has raised the market risk weights for the banks' non-deliverable forward positions because they are considered large in size and speculative in nature. This represents a macro-prudential measure to forestall any systemic risk in the financial system from exchange rate volatility.

The near-term economic outlook of the Philippines seems bright. Annual inflation remains around 4 per cent. An appreciating peso and prudent monetary policy have kept inflation close to target. There is no immediate inflationary pressure from monetary overhang. Inflation targeting continues to work well, although some reforms would be useful to reduce the volatility of inflation. Fiscal consolidation efforts should be sustained, for example, to create fiscal space for the budget to respond to the future shocks that history demonstrates will occur with a probability of unity. The authorities' stated intention is to reduce budget deficits to about 2 per cent of GDP. The associated strategy comprises a greater tax effort, a reorientation of expenditure towards social sectors and infrastructure investment and a debt management strategy that reduces national reliance on external debt. Fiscal consolidation is expected to reduce sovereign risk and enhance investment. It would also lower the debt service burden of the government.

Finally, the BSP remains committed to its mandate of maintaining price stability while allowing monetary policy to facilitate non-inflationary economic growth. It also remains committed to a flexible exchange rate system, provided that the currency does not exhibit excessive volatility in the Philippines' relatively thin foreign-exchange market. Exchange rate flexibility is expected to absorb external shocks. Therefore, the BSP intervenes in the market to smooth sharp fluctuations of the exchange rate provided that these are not responses to rapid changes in economic fundamentals. The monetary authorities continue to use a range of measures to manage large-scale inflows of foreign capital, including the option of reserve accumulation and the appreciation of the exchange rate. Some prudential and regulatory measures are also deployed to smooth capital flows and to minimize their negative implications for monetary policy and financial stability.

Inflation and Inflation Volatility

Figure 9.2a and Figure 9.2b display quarter-on-quarter inflation and inflation volatility in the Philippines over the period 1958q1–2012q4. Inflation volatility is measured by the conditional standard deviation of inflation as obtained by a generalized autoregressive conditional heteroskedasticity GARCH (1, 1) model. It shows that inflation in the Philippines was highly volatile since the 1970s through the 1990s. Since the mid 2000s inflation volatility has diminished along with a decline in the rate of inflation. The Philippines has maintained a CPI inflation rate of about 3 per cent per annum over the period 2006–12. This is considered a remarkable achievement for a developing country.

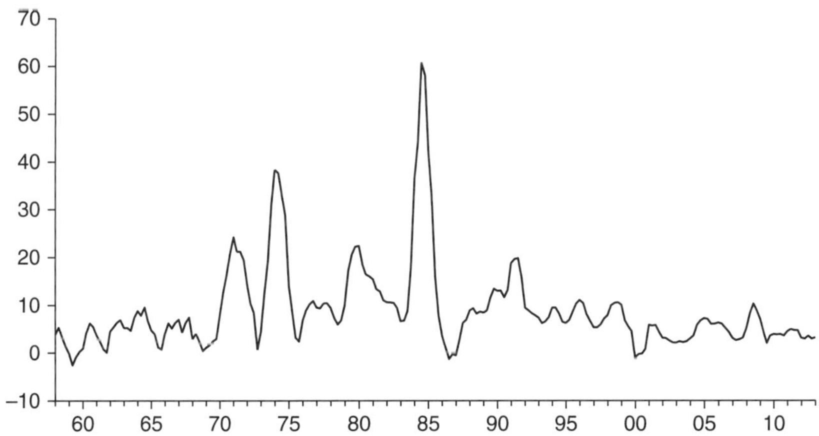

Figure 9.2a Quarter-on-quarter CPI inflation in the Philippines, 1958q1–2012q4

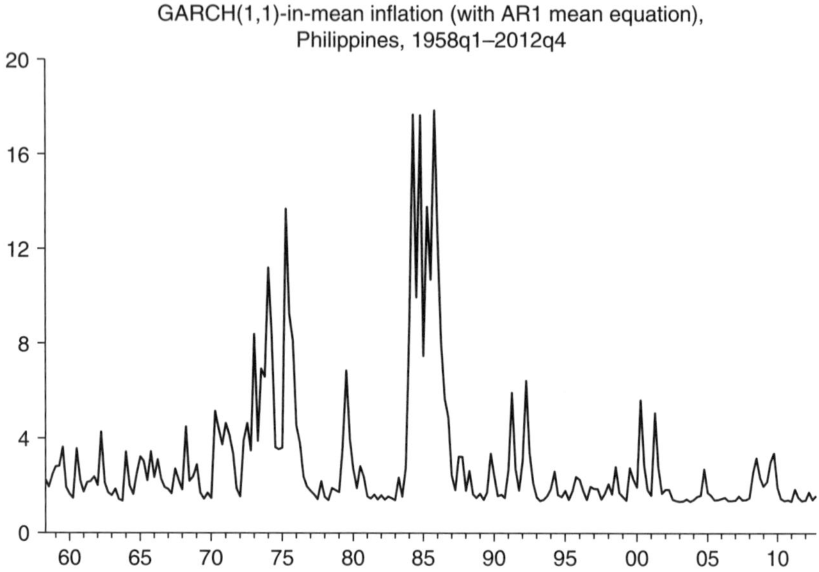

Figure 9.2b Conditional standard deviation of CPI inflation in the Philippines, 1958q1–2012q4

Inflation Persistence

Inflation in the Philippines has exhibited a high degree of persistence. This is reflected in the high and stable coefficient value on the one-period lagged rate of inflation in an autoregressive model AR(1), estimated by both the recursive and rolling regression techniques (Figures 9.3a and 9.3b). Rolling-estimates of the coefficient on the one-period-lagged rate of inflation suggest that the coefficient value has shown only a mild declining trend since the early 2000s. High persistence of inflation is generally associated with low credibility of monetary policy. High and volatile inflation in the Philippines until the early 2000s indicates that monetary policy in the country did not gain much credibility in maintaining low and stable inflation although the BSP has gained autonomy in conducting monetary policy since the early 1990s. Table 9.2 reports the unit root test results for inflation in the Philippines, 1950–2012. Both the ADF and KPSS tests reject the null hypothesis that inflation in the Philippines has a unit root. The Zivot-Andrews test for the unit root, however, suggests that the inflation rate has a unit root. The overall results suggest that although inflation in the Philippines has high persistence, it does not have a unit root.

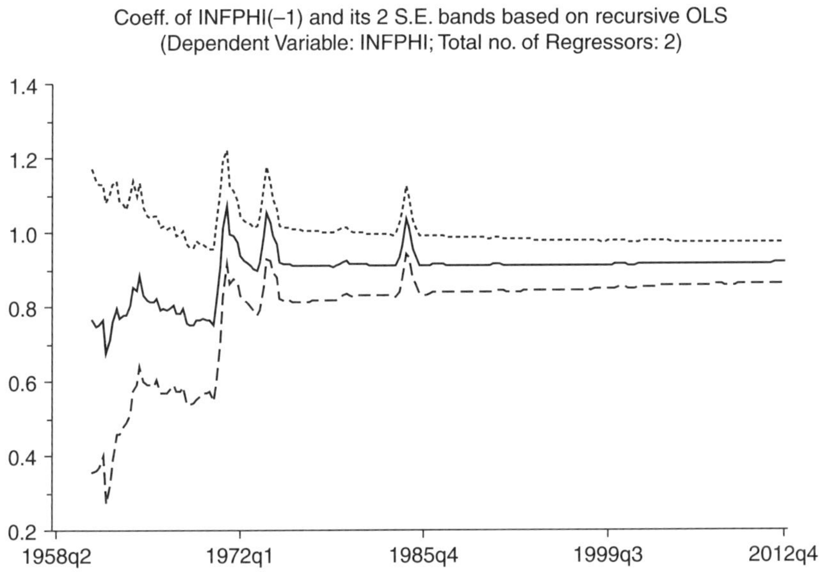

Note: INFPHI = CPI inflation in the Philippines.

Figure 9.3a Recursive estimates of the coefficient on the one-period lagged rate of CPI inflation in the Philippines

The Nominal and Real Treasury Bill Rates in the Philippines and the United States

Figures 9.4a and 9.4b report both the nominal and real Treasury bill rates in the Philippines and the United States over the period 1976–2010. They were highly volatile and have shown similar trends. This suggests that the real interest rate parity proposition holds for the Philippines, despite restricted capital flows.

Exchange Rates

Figure 9.5 plots the nominal and real effective exchange rates in the Philippines. It shows that nominal and real effective exchange rates have steadily depreciated since the mid 1980s. The real exchange rate has shown some mild volatility. This reflects the volatility of inflation as the nominal exchange rate adjusts only partially. This raises the question of whether the Philippines attempted to introduce a real exchange rate targeting approach to monetary policy.

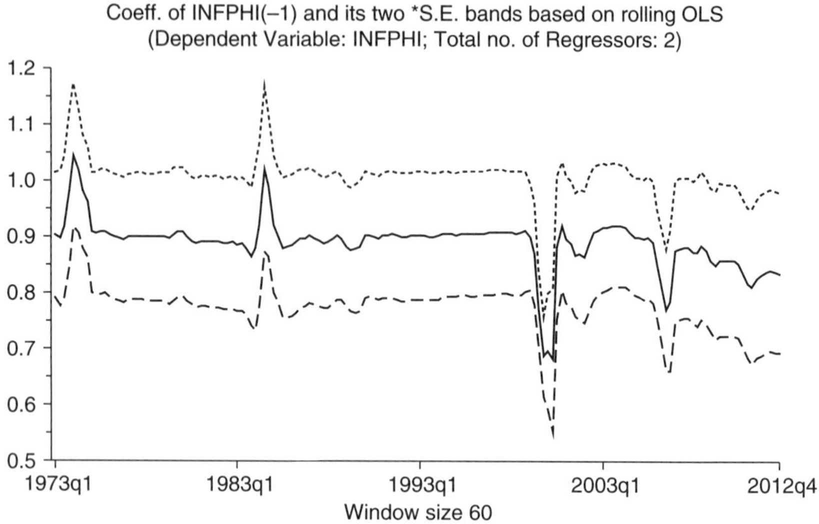

Note: INFPHI = CPI inflation in the Philippines.

Figure 9.3b *Rolling sample estimates of the coefficient on the one-period lagged rate of CPI inflation in the Philippines*

INFLATION, REAL INTEREST RATE, REAL EXCHANGE RATE AND REAL OUTPUT

The Philippines experienced moderately high and unstable inflation from the 1970s through the late 1990s. Although inflation volatility has declined since inflation targeting began in 2002, it remains problematic under a flexible inflation targeting strategy intended to emphasize economic growth *and* stabilization. As the interest rate and the nominal exchange rate in the Philippines do not adjust fully to any inflation differential between the Philippines and, for example, the United States, high-inflation volatility in the Philippines leads to high volatility, both in the real interest rate and the real exchange rate, as exhibited in Table 9.1

The Structural Vector Autoregressive (SVAR) Analysis

This subsection uses annual data to estimate a four-variable SVAR model to examine interrelationships among inflation, the real interest rate, the real exchange rate and real output in the Philippines. The model is formulated on the assumption that inflation has a contemporaneous feedback

Table 9.2 The unit root test results for CPI inflation in the Philippines

	Sample (adjusted)	Constant (C); Trend (T)	ADF test statistic (SBC-determined lag-length, l)	Inference at 5% level	The KPSS test statistic (Newey-West bandwidth)	Inference at 5% level	Sample (unadjusted)	Zivot-Andrews test statistic	Breakpoint	Inference at 5% level
LCPI	1951–2012	C and T	−2.01 (l = 1)	I(1)	0.138 (6)	I(0)	1949–2012	−3.32	1979	I(0)
LCPI	1951–2012	C	0.08 (l = 1)	I(1)	0.994 (6)	I(1)	1949–2012	−3.32	1984	I(0)
ΔLCPI	1951–2012	C	−4.74 (l = 0)	I(0)	0.278 (5)	I(0)	1949–2012	−4.7	1970	I(0)

Note: Definitions of variables: LCPI = log of the consumer price index; ΔLCPI = first-order difference of LCPI; SBC = Schwarz Bayesian Criterion; ADF = augmented Dickey-Fuller; and KPSS = Kwiatkowski, Phillips, Schmidt and Shin.

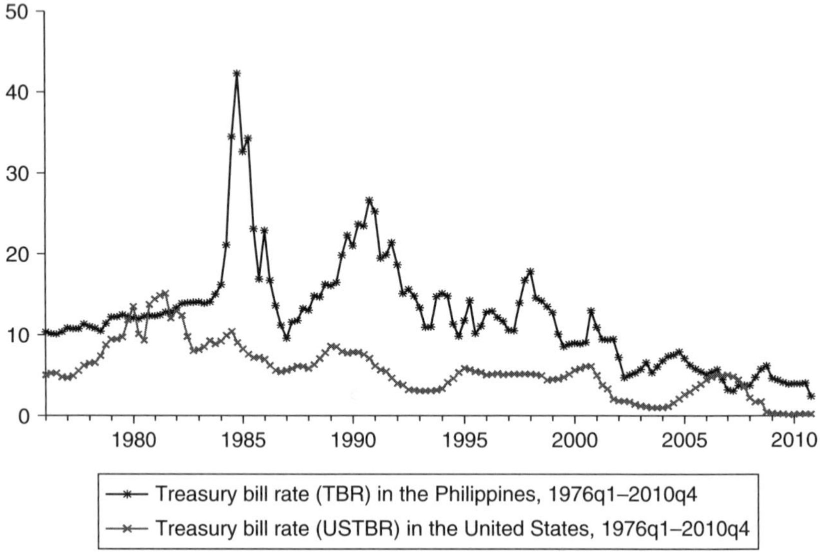

Figure 9.4a *The Treasury bill rate in the Philippines and the Treasury bill rate in the United States, 1976q1–2010q4*

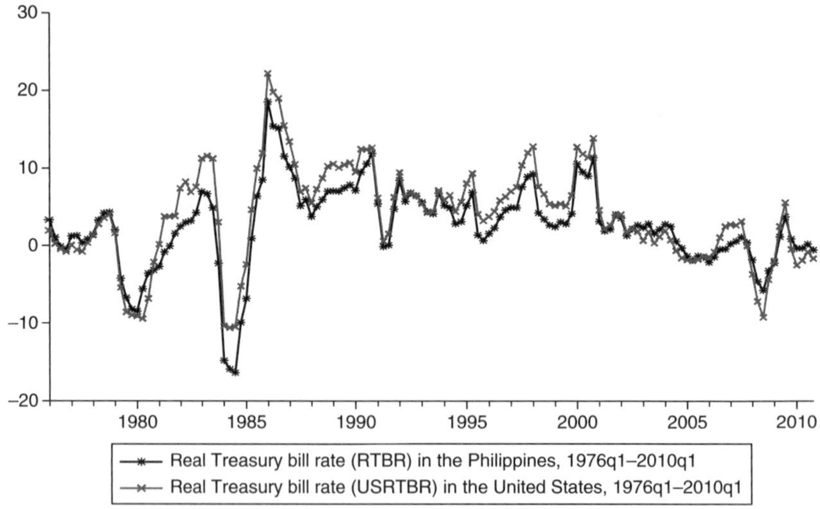

Figure 9.4b *Real Treasury bill rates in the Philippines and the United States, 1976q1–2010q4*

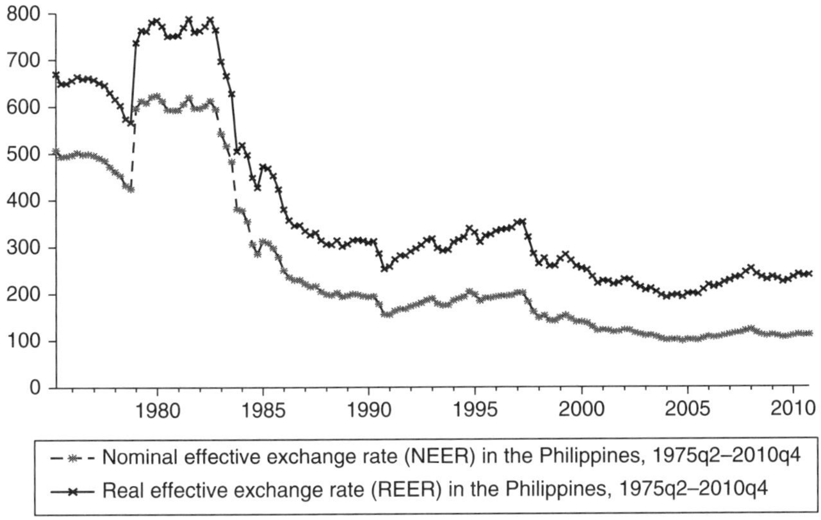

Figure 9.5 Nominal and real effective exchange rates in the Philippines, 1975q2–2010q4

relation with the real interest rate and the real exchange rate. All these variables affect output and its growth. The order of variables in the model is arranged as follows: INFPH, RTBR, LREER and LRGDP where INFPH is the inflation rate in the Philippines, RTBR is the real interest rate, LREER is the log of the real effective exchange rate and LRGDP is the log of real GDP. The unit root test results suggest that while inflation, the real interest rate and the real exchange rate are stationary, output is nonstationary. Two versions of the model are then estimated and deployed to generate impulse responses and forecast error-variance decompositions. The first version of the model is defined as: INFPH, RTBR, LREER and LRGDP while the second version of the model is defined as: INFPH, RTBR, LREER and DLRGDP. In the second version of the model, all the variables are stationary while in the first version real output is nonstationary. To conserve space, the results generated with the second model are reported. The results obtained by both models are qualitatively similar. Figure 9.6 plots data deployed for estimation purposes

The impulse responses in Figure 9.7 suggest the interrelations among four variables in the SVAR model. The model does not include the source of inflation. As reviewed in a range of contexts, high and volatile inflation are well established to have monetary sources. When the inflation rate is low, it is difficult to identify the precise sources of inflation as both

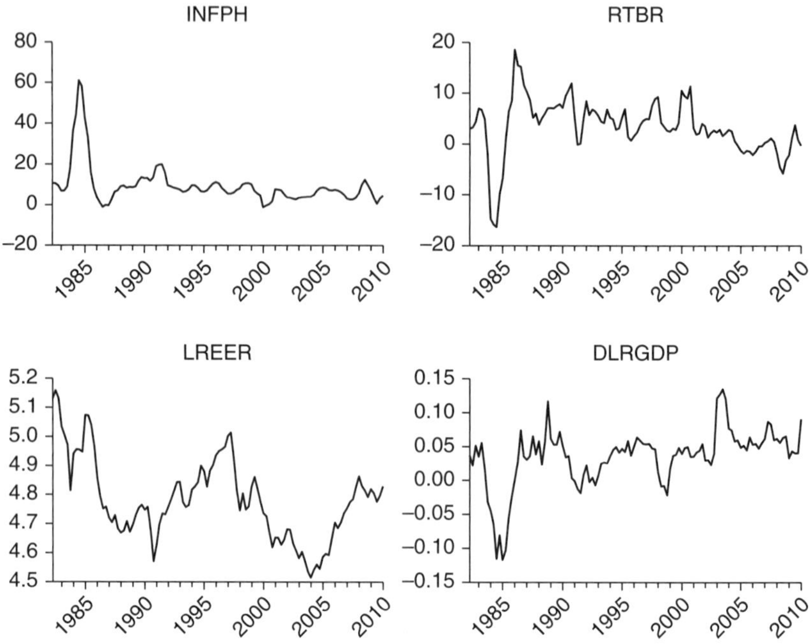

Note: Definitions of variables: INFPH = CPI inflation in the Philippines; RTBR = real Treasury bill rate; LREER = log of the real effective exchange rate of the peso; and DLRGDP = first-order difference of the log of real GDP.

Figure 9.6 Data deployed for estimation of the SVAR model for the Philippines

demand and supply shocks overwhelm the impact of the perennial, core sources of inflation such as money growth. The relationship becomes pronounced when inflation is high and sustained. In developing countries, budget deficit monetization is a common source of inflation. The relationships among budget deficits, money growth and inflation are pronounced and detectable. Furthermore, budget deficits and inflation also maintain a feedback relation. For example, a rise in inflation lowers the real value of tax revenues. This presents fiscal policymakers with an incentive to further increase the budget deficit, leading to faster money growth and consequent higher inflation.

The impulse response results are indicative, not conclusive. As expected, a rise in inflation lowers the real rate of interest. It indicates that the nominal interest rate responds slowly to a rise in inflation. Although a decrease in the real interest rate is expected to raise investment, this is unlikely in developing countries. In these countries, a very low or

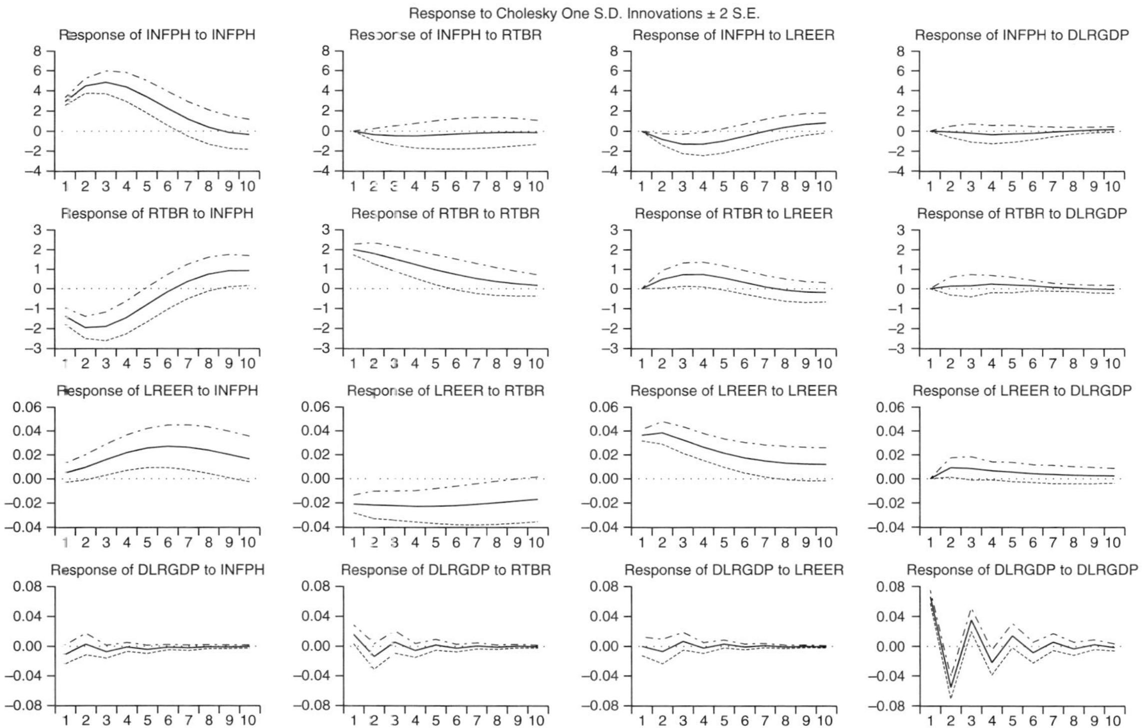

Note: Definitions of variables: INFPH = CPI inflation in the Philippines; RTBR = real Treasury bill rate; LREER = log of the real effective exchange rate of the peso; and DLRGDP = first-order difference of the log of real GDP.

Figure 9.7 Impulse responses for variables in the SVAR model for the Philippines negative real interest rate, caused by high inflation – given unchanged nominal interest rates – creates financial repression that reduces saving, investment and economic growth. High and volatile inflation creates other macroeconomic problems. A rise in inflation appreciates the real exchange rate, which in turn affects inflation and economic growth. The real interest rate also responds positively to an appreciation of the real exchange rate. The mechanism is as follows. A grossly appreciated real exchange rate induces capital flight, requiring the real interest rate to rise as an inducement to slow down or stop this capital flight. This follows the open-economy real exchange rate parity condition. In general, an appreciation of the real exchange rate affects both trade and capital flows, while changes in the real interest rate affect domestic saving and investment.

The overall results suggest significant interrelations among inflation, the real interest rate, the real exchange rate and output growth. Although it is not investigated here, an expanded model is expected to show the impacts of both the real interest rate and the real exchange rate on saving, investment and both trade and capital flows. The key message that emerges from the empirical results is that inflation and its volatility are not innocuous in so far as economic growth is concerned. Inflation affects the real interest rate and the real exchange rate and they have impacts on saving, investment and economic growth. This suggests the need for low and stable inflation for steady economic growth.

Table 9.3 presents the forecast error-variance decompositions of INFPH, RTBR, LREER and DLRGDP. In the table, the numbers represent those percentages of forecast error variance of variables in the model that can be attributed to own innovations and those percentages of forecast error variance that originate from innovations of other variables. The results show that for all four of the specified variables, the dominant source of forecast error variance is own innovations, to the extent of 92 per cent for inflation, 45 per cent for the real interest rate, 40 per cent for the real exchange rate and 92 per cent for real GDP growth over the ten-year time horizon. In the case of real output growth, innovations in the real interest rate and the real exchange rate jointly account for 6 per cent of real output growth's forecast error variance. The corresponding share of inflation is 2 per cent. This implies that real output growth in the Philippines is not highly sensitive to inflation and its volatility. It appears that supply shocks, unsurprisingly, play the dominant role in output fluctuations in the Philippines. This creates difficulty in stabilizing output through monetary policy. Although there is debate whether there is scope for developing monetary and fiscal policies, policymakers could be better advised to deploy fiscal policy, as needed, under extreme situations such as supply shocks, for stabilization

Table 9.3 Forecast error-variance decomposition of variables in the SVAR model for the Philippines

Variance Decomposition of INFPH:					
Period	S.E.	INFPH	RTBR	LREER	DLRGDP
1	2.945	100.00	0.00	0.00	0.00
2	5.429	97.27	0.42	2.29	0.02
5	9.411	93.30	0.81	5.63	0.26
10	9.85	92.07	0.93	6.66	0.34
Variance Decomposition of RTBR:					
Period	S.E.	INFPH	RTBR	LREER	DLRGDP
1	2.44	31.96	68.03	0.00	0.00
2	3.647	43.03	55.11	1.71	0.14
5	5.101	46.50	46.84	6.13	0.53
10	5.447	48.88	44.55	6.00	0.58
Variance Decomposition of LREER:					
Period	S.E.	INFPH	RTBR	LREER	DLRGDP
1	0.042	1.40	24.53	74.08	0.00
2	0.063	2.96	23.31	71.53	2.20
5	0.096	16.28	26.65	54.51	2.56
10	0.122	27.91	29.77	40.40	1.93
Variance Decomposition of DLRGDP:					
Period	S.E.	INFPH	RTBR	LREER	DLRGDP
1	0.069	2.53	5.21	0.00	92.26
2	0.090	1.58	5.47	0.64	92.31
5	0.101	2.03	4.99	1.08	91.90
10	0.102	2.09	5.01	1.09	91.80
The Cholesky Ordering: INFPH RTBR LREER DLRGDP					

Note: Definitions of variables: INFPH = CPI inflation in the Philippines; RTBR = real Treasury bill rate; LREER = log of the real effective exchange rate of the peso; and DLRGDP = first-order difference of the log of real GDP.

of the economy; while avoiding the creation of major fiscal imbalances over the medium term.

MONETARY AND EXCHANGE RATE POLICY ISSUES

Monetary aggregates remain an important variable in the conduct of monetary policy in the Philippines, in spite of the ascendancy of inflation targeting as the official policy strategy, embedded in statute. Even under present inflation targeting, the BSP manages system liquidity by deploying a range of instruments of monetary policy to stabilize the price level. Until recently, the prevailing view was that monetary targeting for price stability requires a stable money-demand function to establish a causal linkage between money supply growth and inflation. The recent literature suggests that causality runs from money supply growth to inflation, irrespective of the exchange rate regime and of whether or not the money-demand function is stable (McCallum and Nelson, 2011).

This section examines whether there exists in the Philippines a stable money-demand function.[4] For estimation purposes, a generic open-economy money-demand function is specified as follows:

$$LRJM_t = \alpha_0 + \alpha_1 Ly_t + \alpha_2 NIR_t + \alpha_3 FIR_t + \alpha_4 LRER_t + \alpha_5 \pi_t^v + u_t \quad (9.1)$$

where LRJM (J = N, B) is the log of real money balances (LRNM for narrowly defined money or LRBM for broadly defined money), Ly is the log of real income, NIR is a representative nominal interest rate, FIR is a representative foreign interest rate such as the US Federal funds rate (USFFR), LRER is the log of a representative real exchange rate such as the real effective exchange rate (REER), π_t^v is a measure of inflation volatility and u_t is a random error term with zero mean and a constant variance. In this specification, real income represents a scale variable and its coefficient is expected to bear a positive sign. The Philippine economy has grown steadily since the 1990s. There has also been rapid monetization of the Philippine economy since then. Consequently, it is possible that the income elasticity of demand for money exceeds one. The coefficients on the domestic and foreign interest rates are expected to bear a negative sign. However, as reviewed in Appendix 5, the signs of the coefficients on the real exchange rate and inflation volatility remain indeterminate a priori.

The unit root test results suggest that all the variables in the specified model have a unit root. Consequently, they are eligible to be tested for cointegration. Preliminary estimation results for a shorter sample period, given data availability, suggest that the deposit rate of interest in the Philippines and the US Federal funds rate become significant when one of them is used in the model. The model is then estimated using the USFFR as the opportunity cost variable. The USFFR is considered more appropriate as it is mostly market determined while the Philippine deposit interest rate was institutionally determined until the 1990s.

Table 9.4 reports both the autoregressive distributed lag (ARDL) and ordinary least squares (OLS) results for real narrow money-demand function. To conserve space, the results obtained by a broad definition of

Table 9.4 The ARDL and OLS regression results for real narrow money-demand relationships in the Philippines

F-statistic	5.34			
W-statistic	26.7			
Critical value bounds	F-test	W-test		
90%	(2.61, 3.74)	(13.06, 18.68)		
95%	(3.13, 4.33)	(15.64, 21.67)		
Sample period	1960–2012 ARDL (1,1,0,0,0) (Selected based on SBC)	1960–2012 ARDL (1,1,0,0,0) Long-run model	1958–2012 OLS (Static model)	1959–2012 OLS (Dynamic model)
Regressors	Coefficient (t-ratio) [prob.]	Coefficient (t-ratio) [prob.]	Coefficient (t-ratio) [prob.]	Coefficient (t-ratio) [prob.]
Intercept	0.16 (0.32) [0.75]	0.33 (0.33) [0.75]	1.67 (2.61) [0.01]	0.85 (1.52) [0.14]
LRNM(−1)	0.51 (5.87) [0.00]			0.49 (4.96) [0.00]
LRGDP	2.18 (5.57) [0.00]	1.15 (18.73) [0.00]	1.08 (26.58) [0.00]	0.56(5.05) [0.00]
USFFR	−0.01 (−3.30) [0.00]	−0.03 (−3.19) [0.00]	−0.02 (−3.11) [0.03]	−0.01 (−2.40) [0.02]
LREER	0.15 (1.96) [0.06]	0.30 (1.96) [0.06]	0.11 (1.18) [0.25]	0.06 (0.74) [0.46]
INFVOL	−0.08 (−2.42) [0.02]	−0.15 (−2.84) [0.00]	−0.19 (−5.73) [0.00]	−0.11 (−3.38) [0.00]
Diagnostics				
Adjusted R^2	0.98		0.97	0.98

Table 9.4 (continued)

Lagrange multiplier test for serial correlation	F(1, 44) = 4.66 [0.04]		F(1, 48) = 31.94 [0.00]	F(1, 46) = 0.45 [0.51]
Ramsey's RESET test of functional form mis-specification	F(1, 44) = 2.51 [0.12]		F(1, 48) = 24.66 [0.00]	F(1, 46) = 4.79 [0.03]
Normality of residuals	$\chi^2_{(2)} = 2.13$ [0.35]		$\chi^2_{(2)} = 2.38$ [0.31]	$\chi^2_{(2)} = 2.65$ [0.27]
Heteroskedasticity	F(1, 50) = 0.29 [0.59]		F(1, 52) = 0.29 [0.59]	F(1, 51) = 0.01 [0.99]
The Wald test:				
H_O: Coefficient on LRGDP = 0		$\chi^2_{(1)} = 350.88$ [0.00]	$\chi^2_{(1)} = 706.29$ [0.00]	
H_O: Coefficient on LRGDP = 1		$\chi^2_{(1)} = 5.86$ [0.02]	$\chi^2_{(1)} = 3.59$ [0.06]	
H_O: Coefficient on USFFR = 0		$\chi^2_{(1)} = 10.21$ [0.00]	$\chi^2_{(1)} = 9.64$ [0.00]	
H_O: Coefficient on LREER = 0		$\chi^2_{(1)} = 3.84$ [0.05]	$\chi^2_{(1)} = 1.38$ [0.24]	
H_O: Coefficient on INFVOL = 0		$\chi^2_{(1)} = 8.08$ [0.00]	$\chi^2_{(1)} = 32.77$ [0.00]	

Note: Definitions of variables: LRNM = log of real narrow money balances; LRGDP = log of real GDP; USFFR = US Federal funds rate; LREER = log of the real effective exchange rate; INFVOL = inflation volatility; ARDL = autoregressive distributed lag; and SBC = Schwarz Bayesian Criterion.

money are not reported. The results obtained by the ARDL model are found superior to those obtained by OLS/dynamic OLS (DOLS). The results suggest the presence of a strong form of long-run cointegral relationship among real narrow money balances, real income, the US Federal funds rate, the real exchange rate and inflation volatility. The estimated coefficient values are consistent with a priori predictions and the model is found stable, as shown by the CUSUM and CUSUMSQ of residuals (Figure 9.8).

As expected, real income remains the core determinant of narrow money demand. The income elasticity of demand for real narrow money balances is marginally greater than one. This is expected for a developing country like the Philippines. The real effective exchange rate bears a positive sign but is not significant. The coefficient on the US Federal funds rate bears a negative sign and is statistically significant. The coefficient on inflation volatility bears a negative sign and is highly significant. This indicates that as inflation volatility increases, there is diminishing demand for real narrow money balances.

Relationships Among Money, Output and Prices

Classical monetary theory suggests that there exists a stable linkage among money, output and prices. Table 9.5 reports the cointegration test results among money, output and prices. The results obtained for a broad definition of money are found more robust than those obtained for a narrow definition of money. The Engle-Granger cointegration test results suggest a weak form of cointegral relationship among money, output and prices. The DOLS estimates suggest that either the narrow or broad money is highly significant in the price level equation and that the coefficient value of narrow money is not significantly different from one. As expected, in a price level equation, real output bears a negative sign and is statistically highly significant.

Engle and Granger (1987) suggest that an implication of a cointegral relation between two nonstationary variables is the presence of long-term causality between them running in at least one direction. Table 9.6 reports the bivariate Granger-causality test results among LCPI, LNM (LBM) and LRGDP. Test results are generated within a vector error-correction (VEC) modelling framework after selecting the optimal lag-length using the Schwarz Bayesian Criterion (SBC). The test results suggest that for the Philippines, there is strong causality running both from narrow and broad money growth to inflation. Broad money growth is also found to have strong causal impact on output growth.

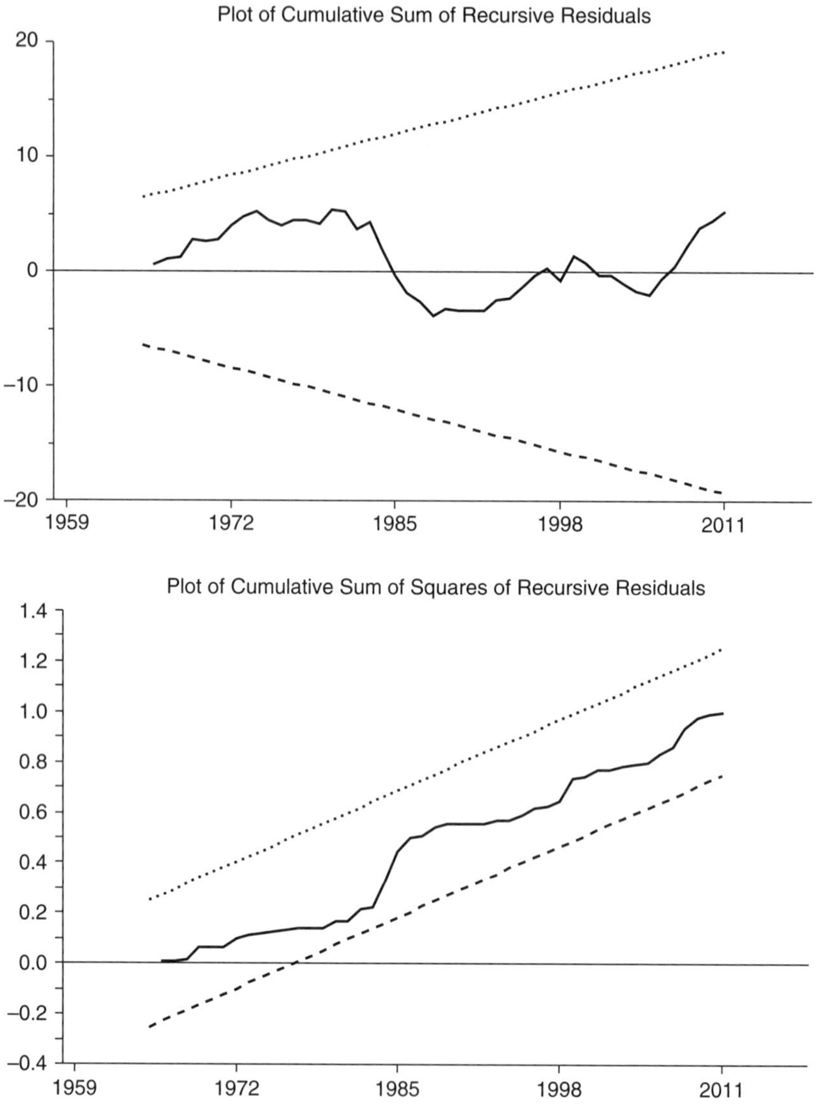

Note: The straight lines represent critical bounds at 5% significance level.

Figure 9.8 CUSUM and CUSUMSQ of residuals for real narrow money-demand relationships in the Philippines

Table 9.5 Cointegration test results among money, output and prices in the Philippines

Dependent variable: LCPI								
	Fully modified OLS				Dynamic OLS			
					(lead = 1, lag = 1)			
With narrow money (NM)								
Regressor	Coefficient	t-ratio	prob.		Coefficient	t-ratio	prob.	
Intercept	3.82	2.31	0.03		3.69	−1.80	0.08	
LNM	0.94	7.68	0.00		0.92	6.48	0.00	
LRGDP	−1.14	−2.15	0.04		−1.05	−1.66	0.11	
Sample period	1970–2011				1970–2010			
DW	0.22				0.36			
Adjusted R^2	0.97				0.98			
	tau-statistic	prob.	z-statistic	prob.	tau-statistic	prob.	z-statistic	prob.
The Engle-Granger cointegration tests	−2.21	0.64	−6.63	0.8	−2.21	0.64	−6.63	0.8
The Phillips-Ouliaris cointegration tests	−2.17	0.66	−6.19	0.82	−2.17	0.66	−6.19	0.82
With broad money (BM)								
Regressor	Coefficient	t-ratio	prob.		Coefficient	t-ratio	prob.	
Intercept	2.05	2.02	0.05		1.65	1.46	0.15	
LBM	0.73	11.00	0.00		0.71	9.74	0.00	
LRGDP	−0.71	−2.12	0.04		−0.59	−1.57	0.13	
Sample period	1970–2011				1970–2010			
DW	0.27				0.55			
Adjusted R^2	0.98				0.99			
	tau-statistic	prob.	z-statistic	prob.	tau-statistic	prob.	z-statistic	prob.
The Engle-Granger cointegration tests	−3.03	0.26	−9.23	0.61	−3.03	0.26	−9.23	0.61
The Phillips-Ouliaris cointegration tests	−3.04	0.26	−10.04	0.55	−3.04	0.26	−10.04	0.55

Note: Definitions of variables: LCPI = log of the consumer price index; LNM = log of narrow money stock; LBM = log of broad money stock; LRGDP = log of real GDP; and SBC = Schwarz Bayesian Criterion.

Table 9.6 Granger-causality among money, output and prices in the Philippines, 1958–2011

	Hypotheses No causality runs from:	Chi-square statistic (prob.)	Inference at 5% level
VEC specification	ΔLNM → ΔLCPI	11.58 (0.00)	Null hypothesis rejected
(With narrow money, NM)	ΔLNM, ΔLRGDP → ΔLCPI	16.75 (0.01)	Null hypothesis rejected
	ΔLCPI → ΔLNM	0.82(0.85)	Null hypothesis not rejected
	ΔLRGDP → ΔLNM	0.54 (0.91)	Null hypothesis not rejected
	ΔLCPI → ΔLRGDP	12.79 (0.01)	Null hypothesis rejected
	ΔLNM → ΔLRGDP	2.00 (0.57)	Null hypothesis not rejected
VEC specification	ΔLBM → ΔLCPI	10.11 (0.02)	Null hypothesis rejected
(With broad money, BM)	ΔLBM, ΔLRGDP → ΔLCPI	14.82 (0.02)	Null hypothesis rejected
	ΔLCPI → ΔLBM	5.84 (0.12)	Null hypothesis not rejected
	ΔLRGDP → ΔLBM	3.09 (0.38)	Null hypothesis not rejected
	ΔLCPI → ΔLRGDP	10.46 (0.02)	Null hypothesis rejected
	ΔLBM → ΔLRGDP	13.19 (0.00)	Null hypothesis rejected

Note: Definitions of variables: LCPI = log of the consumer price index; LNM = log of narrow money stock; LBM = log of broad money stock; and LRGDP = log of real GDP. Optimal lag-length = 2 (selected based on the Schwarz Bayesian Criterion).

SUMMARY AND CONCLUSION

This chapter has provided an overview of issues in central banking and monetary policy in the Philippines in an historical context. It has also reviewed macroeconomic developments and policies in the Philippines since the 1950s. After going through major economic and political oppression and upheaval across several decades, the Philippines finally broke its mediaeval political shackles to emerge as a successful wealth-creating, industrializing economy in Southeast Asia. This is highly significant when the evolution of economic and social development in the Philippines is viewed in an historical context.

In the 1950s, the Philippines had one of the highest per capita incomes in Asia. Although it was expected to perform better than other countries in the region, it fell far short of potential, especially during the 1970s and 1980s, in the midst of economic and political oppression and instability. Contemporaneously, the Philippines underwent high and volatile inflation. Economic growth was low and unstable. High and volatile inflation created high volatility of both the real interest rate and the real exchange rate, which affected real output and its growth. High volatility of inflation was mostly due to unsteady money-growth rate, which was linked to large and sustained budget deficits. Although the Philippines adopted monetary targeting of one form or the other from the mid 1980s until the introduction of inflation targeting in 2002, it was soft and ad hoc in nature. Consequently, the BSP was not able to control money growth and inflation, which made output growth volatile.

The Philippines has made a transition from a low-growth, high-inflation economy to a rapid-growth, low-inflation economy since the early 2000s. Following the East-Southeast Asian financial crisis, the Philippines implemented financial reform to create the more efficient and resilient financial system needed to absorb shocks, especially those originating from external sources. It adopted inflation targeting in 2002, and has successfully sustained inflation within the target range by managing to anchor the public's inflation expectations. Over the past decade, annual average inflation in the Philippines has remained within the target band set by the BSP. Inflation remains volatile under inflation targeting; however, this strategy of monetary policy is considered an improvement over the preceding strategies, such as monetary targeting and exchange rate targeting, deployed until the late 1990s. Until the 1990s, monetary policy had been largely erratic, stumbling to pursue multiple objectives, including economic growth.

The Philippines conducts its monetary policy under a managed float exchange rate system. In general, the conduct of independent monetary policy requires the presence of a flexible exchange rate system. The rationale behind the adoption of the managed float is the potential risk of exchange rate overshooting carried by the floating exchange rate system in the presence of a thin, underdeveloped foreign-exchange market. This is sometimes used to justify deployment of market-based capital controls until the financial markets become sufficiently developed to cope with potentially excessive volatility of exchange rates. Although administrative-based capital controls are found inefficient, there is general acceptance of market-based capital controls in emerging market economies provided that such controls are useful to sustain exchange rate stability. When the financial system becomes more developed and the exchange rate responds predominantly to economic fundamentals, then sharp fluctuations of the exchange rate tend to absorb economic shocks, rather than damaging the economy.

Under a floating exchange rate system, a central bank can exercise either discretionary or rule-based monetary policy. In the case that a central bank adopts rule-based monetary policy, one issue remains. That is the issue of whether a short-term interest rate, or a monetary aggregate, or some combination of both, should be used as an instrument of monetary policy. The use of an interest rate as an instrument of monetary policy has the potential to make both money growth and inflation unstable. A suitable monetary aggregate remains eligible to replace the interest rate as an instrument of monetary policy. The question remains whether the linkage between money growth and inflation is strong enough to use a monetary aggregate as an instrument of monetary policy. Although the presence of a stable money-demand function is not necessary to establish a linkage between money supply growth and inflation, it remains a core relation that can be deployed to improve inflation forecasting. This chapter has investigated some core monetary relations for the Philippines. The empirical results suggest that the narrow money-demand relation in the Philippines remained stable over the study period and that there existed a casual linkage between money growth and inflation.

Provided that the BSP remains committed to maintain discipline in monetary policy and the government remains committed to maintain fiscal discipline, the deployment of a monetary aggregate as an instrument of monetary policy would ensure price stability over the business cycle. The recent experience suggests that central banks prefer to use the interest rate as an instrument of monetary policy, irrespective of whether the shocks to the economy are real or monetary or both. The effectiveness of the interest rate in demand management is, however, limited in countries that do not have developed money and capital markets. In general, the more developed the financial system, the more effective is the interest rate as an instrument of monetary policy. Provided that the exchange rate remains flexible to absorb shocks in a well-developed financial institutional framework, monetary policy is not required to address supply shocks, which by definition are random and transitory. To ensure financial stability, there is scope for improvement of the financial sector through improved prudential regulation and supervision.

NOTES

1. Some general information on the Philippines is based on http://en.wikipedia.org/wiki/Philippines.
2. For detailed discussion on aspects of central banking, monetary policy and exchange rate policy in the Philippines, see BSP, http://www.bsp.gov.ph, BSP, the New Central Bank Act No. 7653, Lamberte (2002), Inoguchi (2008), Gochoco-Bautista (1993, 2005, 2006), Gochoco-Bautista and Bautista (2005) and Gochoco-Bautista and Canals (2003).
3. For a detailed discussion on the transmission mechanisms of monetary policy, see Guinigundo (2005, 2008), McNelis and Bagsic (2006) and IMF (2011).
4. For earlier studies on money-demand behaviour in the Philippines, see Arize (1989), Ariff and Khalid (2000) and Tang (2007).

REFERENCES

Ariff, M. and A.M. Khalid (2000), *Liberalization, Growth and the Asian Financial Crisis*, Cheltenham, UK and Northampton, MA, USA: Edward Elgar.

Arize, A.C. (1989), 'An econometric investigation of money demand behavior in four Asian developing countries', *International Economic Journal*, **3**(4), 79–93.

Baunto, A.L., C. Bordes, S. Maveyraud and P. Rous (2011), 'Money growth and velocity with structural breaks: evidence from the Philippines', *Philippine Management Review*, **18**, 71–81.

Bautista, R.M. (1983), 'Determinants of inflation in the Philippines', School of Economics Discussion Paper 9115, University of the Philippines, Manila.

BSP (Bangko Sentral ng Pilipinas), http://www.bsp.gov.ph.

BSP (Bangko Sentral ng Pilipinas), The New Central Bank Act, Republic Act No. 7653, Republic of the Philippines.

Engle, R.F. and C.W.J. Granger (1987), 'Co-integration and error-correction: representation, estimation, and testing', *Econometrica*, **55**(2), 251–76.

Gochoco-Bautista, M.S. (1993), 'Are money, interest rates, output and the exchange rate cointegated? Implications for monetary targeting', *The Philippine Review of Business and Economics*, **333**(1), 91–101.

Gochoco-Bautista, M.S. (2005), 'An assessment of the usefulness of money for policy in the Philippines', Discussion Paper No. 0508, School of Economics, University of the Philippines.

Gochoco-Bautista, M.S. (2006), 'An assessment of the usefulness of money for policy in the Philippines', *Asian Economic Papers*, **5**(1), 142–76.

Gochoco-Bautista, M.S. and C.C. Bautista (2005), 'Monetary policy and exchange market pressure: the case of the Philippines', *Journal of Macroeconomics*, **27**(1), 153–68.

Gochoco-Bautista, M.S. and D. Canals (2003), 'Monetary and exchange rate policy', in A. Balisacan and H. Hill (eds), *The Philippine Economy: Development, Policies, and Challenges*, New York: Oxford University Press, pp. 77–105.

Guinigundo, D.C (2005), 'Inflation targeting: the Philippine experience', Unpublished manuscript, BSP, Manila.

Guinigundo, D.C (2008), 'Transmission mechanisms of monetary policy in the Philippines', BIS Papers No. 35, Monetary Policy in Asia: Approaches and Implementation, Bank for International Settlements, Basel, 413–26.

IMF (International Monetary Fund) (various years), *International Financial Statistics*, Washington, DC: IMF.

IMF (International Monetary Fund) (various years), *World Economic Outlook*, Washington, DC: IMF.

IMF (2011), 'Forecasting and monetary policy analysis system for the Philippines', Philippines: Selected Issues Paper, *IMF Country Report No. 11/58*, Washington, DC: IMF.

Inoguchi, M. (2008), 'Central bank operating procedures in Thailand and the Philippines', Center for Contemporary Asian Studies Working Paper No. 19.

Khan, M.S. and A.S. Senhadji (2001), 'Threshold effects in the relationship between inflation and growth', *IMF Staff Papers*, **48**(1), 1–21.

Lamberte, M. (2002), 'Central banking in the Philippines: then, now and the future', Philippine Institute of Development Studies Discussion Paper No. 2002–10.

Lim, J. (1987), 'The new structuralist critique of the monetarist theory of inflation: the case of the Philippines', *Journal of Development Economics*, **25**(1), 45–61.

Lim, J. (2006), 'Philippine monetary policies: a critical assessment and search for alternatives', Political Economy Research Institute Discussion Paper No. 10.

Lim, J. (2008), 'Central banking in the Philippines: from inflation targeting to financing development', *International Review of Applied Economics*, **22**(2), 271–85.

McCallum, B.T. and E. Nelson (2011), 'Money and inflation: some critical issues', in B.M. Friedman and M. Woodford (eds), *Handbook of Monetary Economics*, Vol. 3A, Amsterdam: Elsevier Science, pp. 97–153.

McNelis, P.D. and C.B. Bagsic (2006), *Output-gap for Inflation Forecasting: The Case of the Philippines*, Report prepared for the Bangko Sentral ng Pilipinas, Manila.

Montes, M.F. and J.Y. Lim (1996), 'Macroeconomic volatility, investment anemia and environmental struggles in the Philippines', *World Development*, **24**(2), 341–57.

Reyes, C. and J. Yap (1993), 'Money and prices in the Philippines, 1981–1992: a cointegration analysis', *Journal of Philippine Development*, **20**(1), 57–78.

Tang, T.C. (2007), 'Money demand function for Southeast Asian countries: an empirical view from expenditure components', *Journal of Economic Studies*, **34**(6), 476–96.

Vos, R. and J. Yap (1996), *The Philippine Economy: East Asia's Stray Cat? Structure, Finance and Adjustment*, London: Macmillan.

Yap, J. (1996), 'Inflation and economic growth in the Philippines', Discussion Paper Series No. 96–11, Philippine Institute for Development Studies, Manila.

10. Singapore

Singapore is a geographically small city-state of 710 square kilometres located across the narrow Johor Strait off the southernmost coast of the eastern edge of the Asian continent. It comprises 63 islands, having a multi-ethnic, multi-religious population size of about 5.3 million. The dominant ethnic groups are Chinese, Malay and Indian; while the dominant 'religions' or philosophies are Buddhist, Christian, Muslim, Tao and 'secularism'. Singapore has four official languages: Mandarin, English, Malay and Tamil.[1] Mainly an immigrant society, Singapore's core population comprises 3.3 million citizens; the remainder are permanent residents and temporary foreign workers. From its beginning as a British crown colony in the early nineteenth century, Singapore has evolved as a prominent international port and trade centre. Early immigrants to Singapore came from southern China to work in British rubber plantations across the various states of what is present-day Malaysia, and in the shipping services and trading activities in the port city of Singapore. By the end of the 1880s, Singapore was an international rubber-exporting centre.[2]

Singapore's political and strategic importance became evident during World War II. Until 1942, Singapore was the largest British stronghold in Southeast Asia, when the Imperial Japanese army overran the British within a week in February 1942 and occupied Singapore for the remainder of the war, with 130000 captives from Singapore and the Malay Peninsula, until Japan surrendered to the Allied Forces in August 1945. Although the British repossessed Singapore after Japan's surrender in 1945, it eventually acceded to demands for self-governance. Singapore gained the status of internal self-governing state in 1959 with Lee Kuan Yew as its first Prime Minister.

On 31 August 1963 Singapore became fully independent and afterwards joined with Malaya, Sabah and Sarawak to establish the New Federation of Malaysia. For Singapore, this union of convenience did not last long. Singapore was expelled from the Federation of Malaysia in 1965. Strong-willed Lee Kuan Yew had major disagreements with Malay nationalist leaders on managing the economic and political affairs of the Federation of Malaysia. After its expulsion from Malaysia, Singapore charted its own course of economic development under the leadership of Lee Kuan

Yew. This was a challenging task for any political leadership in an island economy that does not have exploitable natural resources for economic development, especially in its early stages. Lee Kuan Yew, to his great credit, succeeded in changing the face of Singapore and established himself as a formidable leader in possession of the requisite foresight, dedication and commitment to build a small, independent, multi-ethnic nation.

Singapore has made impressive economic and social progress since the early 1960s. Presently, Singapore has the third highest per capita income in the world. The high standards of living in this city-state are reflected in most economic and social indicators. For instance, the life-expectancy is 80 years for males and 85 years for females. The basic amenities of life, namely housing, safe water, sanitation and medical facilities, are available to all Singaporean citizens. Singapore's rapid economic and social development to such a high level, within the lifespan of just one generation, has therefore been viewed by many as a 'miracle', or at least an ideal for emulation by other countries in the region (Bercuson, 1995).

To maintain its high standard of living, Singapore relies heavily on foreign trade and investment, tourism and other services, especially education and health. Although the Singaporean economy remains vulnerable to external shocks, its economic prosperity is assured; it has demonstrated adeptness in utilizing its strategic locational advantage between two major economies, namely Malaysia and Indonesia, and having trade and investment links with most rapidly growing economies in the Asia-Pacific region. One area of concern, however, remains the ethnic and religious aspects of its relations with its Muslim-majority neighbours. Malaysia and Indonesia, in particular, have been 'ambivalent', if not hostile. Consequently, until the late 1960s, Singapore's survival as an independent state remained in some doubt. This led Singapore to establish strategic relations with most Western countries and their allies in the Asia-Pacific region, and remains a bone of contention in Southeast Asian diplomacy.

Although Singapore is yet to become a true nation-state, rather than a multi-cultural assembly of communities, it has made significant progress in establishing a Singaporean identity for its people by installing a meritocratic form of governance and a determination to improve the standards of living of its citizens. Moreover, under the able and determined leadership of Lee Kuan Yew from 1959 to 1989, Singapore maintained social and political stability by deploying quasi-authoritarian measures and by introducing compulsory national service for all able-bodied men of appropriate age groups. This overall strategy of nation-building of a multi-cultural society has succeeded, as the government has been able to stimulate rapid economic growth under a state-led, export-oriented development strategy. With the rapid expansion of the national economic pie, the government has been able to provide tangible benefits to all communities comprising Singaporean society, given their participation in economic activity.

Why and how Singapore managed to succeed where other multi-ethnic countries have failed has become an area of widespread research interest. Unlike many multi-ethnic societies across the globe, which remain in perpetual conflict, Lee Kuan Yew accorded high priority to social and political stability for rapid economic and social progress. Political stability, however, was achieved at the cost of political freedom and of limited tolerance for dissenting voices. A strong judicial system has been established that accords top priority to maintaining law and order in the unique milieu of a strongly multi-ethnic society. Some minor political reforms have been undertaken by post-Lee Kuan Yew governments under Goh Chok Tong and Lee Hsien Loong. Singapore is, however, unlikely to become a liberal democracy with free speech to foster an unfettered market economy. It remains a quasi-market economy, operating under strong government guidance, regulation and supervision.[3] The government retains its role as the largest stakeholder in the economy through myriad public sector enterprises. These enterprises operate largely on competitive profit-making principles and by deploying management best-practice in a rapidly changing global environment.

Singaporean economic prosperity remains dependent on the sustenance of an open trade and investment regime. Trade openness, as measured by the exports-plus-imports-to-GDP ratio, remains very high, around 4, meaning that inwards-plus-outwards trade exceeds 400 per cent of GDP. The major exports include electronics, chemicals, engineering and biomedical products. Significantly, since the 1970s Singapore has attracted large-scale foreign direct investment. Factors playing a role in Singapore's attractiveness on this score include its strategic location, high-quality infrastructure, low tax regime, low levels of official corruption, skilled workforce and financial stability. Moreover, Singapore's monetary policy, exchange rate policy and fiscal discipline have created a financial infrastructure highly appealing from a locational perspective to major multinational companies across the globe. Presently, more than 7000 multinational corporations operate in Singapore. This makes Singapore effectively a large corporate entity; and it has colloquially been dubbed 'Singapore, Inc.' As the economy progresses and matures, Singapore researches and identifies areas where it has a comparative advantage or has the ability to acquire competitive advantage. For example, since the late 1990s it has become a hub in several major sectors of economic activity: Singapore is today known as a 'financial hub', an 'education hub' and a 'health-services hub'. The establishment of these core centres of activity in these sectors has been facilitated by government encouragement of the recruitment of skilled workers and professionals from around the globe.

Singapore's overall development strategy includes the encouragement of foreign investment while allowing free capital mobility. This is reflected in the empirical observation that the real interest rate parity condition is fulfilled in the long run, although real rates of return on financial assets may deviate from it significantly in the short run. Inflation volatility therefore plays an important role in the movement of capital. Consequently, the level of foreign investment and its volatility significantly impact Singaporean economic growth and its volatility.

Having achieved, with the other three so-called 'Asian Tiger' economies, the status of a developed economy, Singapore is no doubt intent upon sustaining and promoting its economic progress and stability by several means, including continuous improvement in macroeconomic management. To begin with, Singapore follows conservative but flexible fiscal and monetary management practices. Consequently, inflation was low in the 1960s, increased somewhat during the mid 1970s due to the OPEC oil shocks and, since then, has remained moderately low, though unstable. Monetary policy in Singapore has been unique since 1981 in the sense that it uses its nominal exchange rate as the intermediate target to anchor domestic prices. It remains a matter of contention how effective for price stability this strategy has been (MAS, 2001; Parrado, 2004).

The relation between the nominal exchange rate and inflation in Singapore is bidirectional. The monetary authorities appreciate the exchange rate in order to reduce inflation while, operating in the opposite direction, low inflation itself, in an otherwise rapidly growing economy, mitigates appreciation pressure on the nominal exchange rate. Nevertheless, the use of the nominal exchange rate to control inflation has volatilized both the nominal and real exchange rates. There is a suggestion that the exchange rate and trade flows in Singapore are not causally related. This makes the exchange rate available as a monetary policy instrument for the monetary authorities to deploy in operations designed to achieve policy targets for both output and prices, to the extent that exchange rate movements affect aggregate demand.

This line of argument is not, however, satisfactory; because, empirically, the real exchange rate and its volatility do, in fact, influence trade and capital flows. Inflation in Singapore has remained relatively low since the 1980s. However, it is unstable due mainly to external shocks. To the extent that inflation is volatile, the real exchange rate becomes volatile if the nominal exchange rate does not adjust fully to maintain the stability of the real exchange rate. Similarly, if the real interest rate exhibits volatility due to inflation volatility, it may contribute some volatility to trade and capital flows. This is a less than desirable channel of influence to exacerbate, since trade and capital flows are closely linked to investment, output and employment in Singapore.

In a long-run context, the real exchange rate in Singapore has not appreciated as much as might be expected, that is, rapidly growing given the rapid growth rate of the Singapore economy. A sustained low rate of inflation has crowded out any possibility of sustained appreciation of the real exchange rate. It is therefore highly unlikely that Singapore has ever seriously undertaken a real exchange rate targeting approach to monetary policy to promote output growth through export promotion. Its access to overseas workers has helped to keep its real wage rate low and to quickly redress skill shortages as they appear. This mechanism has militated strongly against any appreciation pressures on the real exchange rate rapidly growing that might be generated by the impressively rapid growth of the economy.

For a small, open economy with free capital mobility such as Singapore, the potency of monetary policy is minimal under a pegged exchange rate system. There is little doubt that price stability should remain the goal of monetary policy in Singapore. The question is whether there is scope for independent monetary policy under a floating exchange rate system. This question is made all the more significant for Singapore, exposed as its economy is to shocks, mainly from external sources. Where, as is the case in Singapore, a country's financial system operates within a mature institutional framework and has deep capital markets, a floating exchange rate system is considered both effective and useful as a shock absorber.

As Singapore has a developed financial system, one research question is whether Singapore should consider inflation targeting to maintain price stability under a floating exchange rate system. Given that monetary and fiscal policies in Singapore remain conservative in nature and that its financial system has developed over the past three decades, the exchange rate is likely to remain stable between shocks, while its flexibility would protect the economy in the (relatively frequent) event of an external shock. This is important for sustaining macroeconomic stability given the status of Singapore as an international financial centre.

The remainder of this chapter provides an overview of monetary policy in Singapore in an historical context. To examine the feasibility of independent monetary policy under a flexible exchange rate system, it investigates Singaporean money-demand behaviour and tests for the presence of any causal linkage between money supply growth and inflation. Following the recent literature, it is expected that there would exist such a relation, irrespective of whether or not there exists a stable money-demand function, and whether Singapore's money is endogenous or exogenous under any exchange rate arrangement.

THE FINANCIAL SYSTEM[4]

Singapore has a well-developed financial system dominated by the banking sector. Local and foreign banks operate in Singapore. Foreign banks enjoy high visibility in Singapore, but local banks have majority market share. All foreign banks, individually, have small market shares. The total number of commercial banks in Singapore is 122. Five are local banks and the remaining 117 are foreign. The five local banks are owned by three banking groups. All local banks maintain high liquidity and are well capitalized and profitable. They follow conservative banking management practices to minimize financial risk. Of the 117 foreign banks, 27 are full banks, 53 are wholesale banks and 37 are offshore banks. These designations reflect different privileges and restrictions that the Monetary Authority of Singapore (MAS), the central bank of Singapore, has imposed on these banks as licensing conditions for operations in Singapore. While the local banks have license to undertake the full range of banking activities, foreign banks operate under varying restrictions on their domestic retail operations.

Like the banking sector, the insurance sector is well capitalized and profitable. As Singapore's economy is vulnerable to external shocks, the MAS has put in place a stringent regulatory and supervisory framework. Consequently, the Singapore financial sector has weathered with minimal disruption all major economic shocks since the mid 1990s. Key in the soundness of Singapore's financial sector is the conscientious exercise of best-practice in the political governance of the city-state, together with a sensible, responsible form of government entrepreneurship in leading the society and the economy forward. Flowing from this, partly following the government's example and partly bound by fully enforced law and regulation, particularly anti-corruption measures, are the following critical pillars of any financial system: an efficient legal system; high accounting standards; and the application of best-practice corporate governance. The presence of foreign banks has raised the efficiency of local banks and boosted the resilience of the financial system against the endemic external shock property of the Singapore economy. Above all, Singapore has led the field in the acquisition of technical competency in globalized banking. It has established the institutional infrastructure essential to the effective regulation and prudential supervision of a developed financial system that includes many foreign banks and financial institutions. The task ahead is to consolidate Singapore's status as an international financial centre.

This process has begun since the East-Southeast Asian financial crisis during 1997–98, which triggered a process of financial reform in Singapore, and has led to major regulatory change with the objective of putting Singapore's status as the world's foremost financial hub beyond dispute. The key measures in this respect included: (1) increasing foreign bank accessibility to the banking industry; (2) the implementation of prudential regulation and supervision and disclosure-based regulation of international best-practice standards; (3) the development of deep and liquid fixed-income and equity markets; (4) promotion of the asset management industry; (5) liberalization of restrictions on internationalization of the Singapore dollar; and (6) consolidation of local banks. Such measures, in the presence of political stability, the highly developed legal system and strong macroeconomic fundamentals, have all contributed synergistically to the stated goal of embedding Singapore's financial hub status.

The main component of this status is the Asian eurodollar market that intermediates large cross-border interbank credit flows. Given the small size of the domestic economy, the main operations of foreign commercial banks in Singapore are in eurocurrencies. Three local banking groups dominate the retail banking sector. Since the 1997–98 East-Southeast Asian financial crisis, there has indeed been a structural change in the Asian eurocurrency market. Beginning in the early 1980s, and through to the onset of the crisis, this market mainly intermediated capital flows from Europe, North America and the Middle East to the rapidly growing economies of Southeast Asia. During the crisis, there was a reversal of capital flow intermediation, so that capital then flowed from Southeast Asian countries back to Europe, North America and the Middle East. Presently, the Asian dollar market intermediates flows in both directions as the global economy works through the current period of uncertainty while some major economies engage in loose monetary and fiscal policies in their desperation to end recession. This has heightened the unpredictability of capital movements across countries and sectors.

In the context of developing Singapore as an international financial centre, the government has designated a priority the development of bond markets by issuing significant volumes of official debt securities, in parallel with its sustained maintenance of budget surpluses. The corporate bond market has, however, not developed much given sustained excess liquidity in the banking system. Finance companies enjoy only a relatively small market share in Singapore's financial system. The MAS supervises these companies, which generally finance small-scale projects such as mortgage loans and consumer credit. Presently, Singapore has about 162 insurers, representing direct insurers and reinsurers, and 70 insurance brokers. The insurance sector accounts for about 6 per cent of financial sector assets.

Islamic Banking and Finance

Singapore's efforts to establish a dominant position as a financial centre would fall short of comprehensive if it ignored the strong emergence of Islamic banking and finance in recent decades. Accordingly, Singapore has included promotion of Islamic banking and finance in its expansion programme. In 2001, Singapore launched its own *sukuk* (bonds) and has signalled its intention to expand into such areas as Islamic-principled hedge funds, property investment, *sukuk*, *takaful* and wealth management. Since the early 2000s Singapore has established collaboration with major Islamic financial institutions across the world in innovation and specialization in Islamic banking and finance. As an international financial centre, Singapore is well placed to offer Islamic financial products to large corporate and individual investors undertaking diversification of asset and liability portfolios.

Since around mid 2005, Islamic banking and finance activities have steadily increased. In 2005, Malaya Islamic Bank (May Bank Singapore) launched Islamic banking operations in Singapore. Other financial institutions, including the Overseas Chinese Banking Corporation (OCBC), Kuwait Finance House (KFH), Development Bank of Singapore (DBS), Hong Kong and Shanghai Banking Corporation (HSBC) and National Trades Union Congress (NTUC), have begun sales of Islamic financial products, including Islamic insurance. In 2005, the Singapore Stock exchange introduced its first Islamic index (Lion 30), comprising 33 companies whose operations were fully *shariah*-compliant. In February 2006, the Singaporean Stock Exchange launched the first FTSE-SGX Asia sharpie 100 index. The index composed 100 stocks of companies across Asia whose operations were in full compliance with Islamic *shariah* principles. Overall, the MAS remains committed to implement any changes needed to ensure the growth and development of Islamic banking and financial institutions, including changes to Singapore's taxation, regulatory and prudential supervision policies and the provision of training for local Islamic scholars.

THE MONETARY AUTHORITY OF SINGAPORE: ORGANIZATION AND ACTIVITIES

The MAS is the de facto central bank of Singapore. The MAS was established under the MAS Act of 1970. It commenced operations on

1 January 1971, collecting together central bank functions that had earlier been performed by several different government departments and agencies. In April 1977, the government brought the regulatory task of the insurance industry under the wing of the MAS. In September 1984 the regulatory functions enshrined in the Securities Industry Act 1973 were transferred to the MAS. Following its merger with the Board of Commissioners of Currency on 1 October 2002, the MAS has become responsible for the issuance of currency notes of Singapore.

The MAS is governed by a Board of Directors consisting of the chairman, deputy chairman, managing director and five other members. The managing director is the chief executive, who is entrusted with the MAS's operations and administration. A deputy managing director and a team of assistant managing directors, executive directors and directors assist the managing director in performing its functions.

Presently, the main functions of the MAS are: to issue currency notes; to conduct monetary policy and exchange rate policy; to manage official foreign-exchange reserves; and to issue government securities. The MAS regulates and prudentially supervises the financial sector and plays a leading and powerful role in the development and promotion of Singapore as an international financial centre.

MONETARY POLICY FRAMEWORK IN SINGAPORE

The main objective of monetary policy in Singapore is to maintain 'price stability conducive to sustainable growth of the economy'. To achieve this objective, the MAS uses the nominal effective exchange rate (NEER) as an instrument of monetary policy under what is known as the basket-band-crawl (BBC) approach. The key parameters of this framework are undisclosed but include (1) the 'basket' (a trade-weighted set of currencies); (2) the 'bandwidth' within which the NEER is allowed to fluctuate; and (3) the 'crawl or slope' (the rate by which the band's limits and mid-point change over time, dependent on the rate of structural change of the economy and on global financial developments.

Singapore, as a small, open economy, does not seem to have the ability to conduct independent monetary policy to smooth business cycles. However, it can adjust the exchange rate to maintain low inflation and allow free capital mobility to encourage foreign investment. The interest rate parity condition suggests that an active adjustment of the nominal exchange rate implies an active adjustment of the nominal interest rate given the foreign interest rate. Singapore maintains the real exchange rate parity condition to avoid the development of capital flows so rapid as to put pressure on the exchange rate and threaten a boom-bust cycle. The conclusion is that Singapore has an exchange rate policy, which is for all intents and purposes its monetary policy, to maintain price stability. Singapore does not have control over the domestic interest rate in the absence of a market-determined exchange rate system. Under a floating exchange rate system, a central bank would acquire control over monetary policy for price stability. Under the current system, in which Singapore controls the exchange rate within a policy band of acceptable values, the MAS loses control of the domestic interest rate, which must necessarily mimic the foreign interest rate. Meanwhile, domestic prices maintain a link with foreign prices through the (MAS-controlled) exchange rate under the purchasing power parity mechanism, which has been empirically observed to hold in the long run.

This provides a potential explanation as to why the MAS might consider price stability the objective of its policy of fixing the exchange rate under perfect capital mobility. Price stability, which remains overtly undefined by the MAS, is understood in the broader applied macroeconomics community to mean low and stable inflation. Following the extant literature, Singapore considers price stability necessary to sustainable economic growth. This view is reflected in the MAS's Exchange Rate Policy statement (Parrado, 2004, p. 4):

> The primary objective of monetary policy is to ensure low inflation as a sound basis for sustained economic growth. In Singapore, monetary policy is centred on the management of the exchange rate, rather than money supply or interest rates. This reflects the fact that, in the small and open Singapore economy, the exchange rate is the most effective tool in maintaining price stability.

As a tactic to keep domestic prices low, Singapore generally keeps the Singapore dollar strong vis-à-vis its trading partners. The MAS intervenes in the foreign-exchange market to appreciate or depreciate the trade-weighted exchange rate of the Singapore dollar, depending on whether it perceives net inflationary pressure to be strong or weak. Foreign-exchange market intervention is supplemented by money-market operations designed to maintain an appropriate level of liquidity in the banking system. The money-market tools deployed for the purpose include foreign-exchange swaps, direct lending to or borrowing from banks and open-market operations, including repurchase agreements involving Singapore government securities and MAS bills. Singapore generally maintains a strong dollar policy to primarily contain inflation and then as a secondary operation intervenes in the foreign-exchange market to maintain the exchange rate at a level considered consistent with economic fundamentals. High economic growth and low unemployment allow the MAS to pursue this policy without creating a time-inconsistency problem. Another

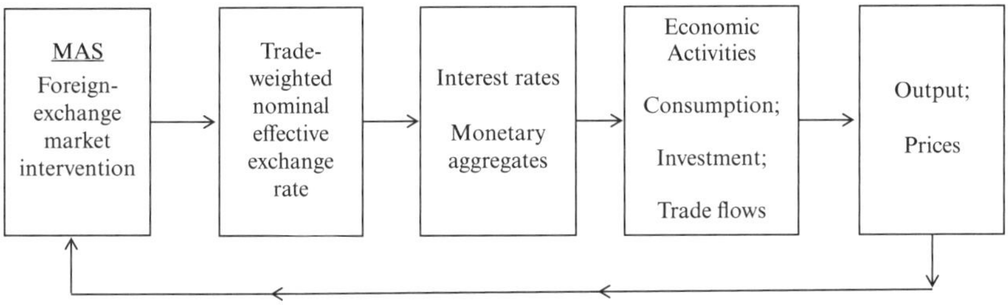

Figure 10.1 Monetary policy transmissions mechanisms in Singapore

consideration behind the 'strong Singapore dollar' policy is to sustain the confidence of the public to hold Singapore currency-denominated assets (including the currency itself). Freely mobile capital and the strong currency policy are the twin pillars sustaining Singapore's status as an international financial centre.

Monetary Policy Transmission Mechanisms

Figure 10.1 exhibits a flowchart illustrating the major components of the monetary policy transmission mechanism in Singapore. Intervention in the foreign-exchange market changes the trade-weighted nominal exchange rate, which affects the domestic prices of both goods and assets. Depending on the degree of pass-through, exchange rate movements are associated with changes in the domestic interest rate. Singapore is a small, open economy, limiting the effectiveness with which MAS intervention in the foreign-exchange market impacts foreign interest rates. Given the domestic interest rate, the money stock adjusts to establish equilibrium in the money market. Assuming a stable money-demand function, changes in the money stock, flowing from changes in the interest rate, impact aggregate demand. This alters output and prices. Output and price changes induce the MAS to bring about policy changes in the exchange rate, if required. A further channel by which exchange rate movements impact on domestic prices is through the ability of exchange rate changes to alter aggregate demand via net trade flows affecting economic activity. In general, these transmission mechanisms of monetary policy depict the procedure deployed by the MAS for short-run macroeconomic management. The MAS (1999, p. 12) argues that monetary policy has only short-term impact on the economy and cannot be deployed to raise long-term economic growth:

> While it can ensure price stability for sustainable economic growth, monetary policy *per se* cannot affect the long-term growth capacity of the economy. In the

long-run, the growth of an economy is determined by supply-side factors such as technological progress, capital accumulation, and the size and quality of the labour force. Some government policies may be able to influence these supply-side factors, but monetary policy generally cannot do so directly. By providing a sound and stable macroeconomic environment, however, monetary policy can ensure the smooth and efficient functioning of the economy, thereby sustaining its growth.

MACROECONOMIC DEVELOPMENTS AND INFLATION PERFORMANCE

Singapore has established an impressive macroeconomic management record since the mid 1970s. It has effectively deployed macroeconomic policy (fiscal policy, monetary/exchange rate policy and wages policy) to sustain both macroeconomic stability and economic growth. This has led to the accumulation of large-scale foreign capital in Singapore and created an environment for export-oriented economic growth. To facilitate this growth, Singapore has applied exchange rate-centred monetary policy to maintain price stability. As Singapore allows free capital mobility, the government maintains supporting fiscal discipline and generally records budget surpluses despite Singaporean tax rates, which are the lowest in the Asia-Pacific region.

In 1985 Singapore suffered a recession caused by a deterioration in its export competitiveness in combination with a cyclical downturn in electronic exports and the collapse of the construction boom. The policy response, attempting to stimulate recovery from the recession, included the following. The government adjusted the exchange rate, brought about wage cuts and reduced the mandatory rate of employer contribution to the Central Provident Fund. Similar policy measures have been deployed in response to other shocks, namely the East-Southeast Asian financial crisis and the US-global financial crisis.

The exchange rate is ostensibly adjusted to stabilize aggregate demand and output in the event of external shocks, while attempting to maintain price stability. There is the suggestion, however, of an appreciation bias inherent in the management of Singapore's exchange rate management, since appreciation of the Singapore dollar does not hurt Singapore's export-oriented economy. On the contrary, an appreciated currency encourages Singaporean companies to move up the value chain and then gain competitive advantage in higher value-added industries. As Singapore's exports have become simultaneously technology-, skill- and capital-intensive, exchange rate movements do not have much impact on demand in international markets. Nevertheless, this remains an empirical issue.

At this point, a broad overview of Singapore's key macroeconomic indicators will be useful (Table 10.1).

Inflation and Inflation Volatility

Figures 10.2a and 10.2b display inflation and inflation volatility in Singapore for 1962q–2012q4. They show inflation high and volatile in the 1970s and unstable also in the mid 1980s. After that inflation remained relatively stable until the mid 2000s, but since the mid 2000s it has exhibited high volatility. Figure 10.2c shows that inflation in Singapore mimics the US inflation rate. This is expected in a small economy operating an adjustable peg.

Inflation Persistence

Inflation in Singapore has exhibited a high degree of measured persistence. This is reflected in the high and stable coefficient value on the one-period lagged rate of inflation in an autoregressive model AR(1), estimated by both the recursive and rolling regression techniques (Figures 10.3a and 10.3b). The rolling estimates of coefficients on the one-period lagged rate of inflation suggest that the coefficient value has recorded volatility from the mid 1980s onwards, depending on inflation shocks. High persistence of inflation is generally associated with low credibility of monetary policy. The indication is that Singapore's exchange rate-based monetary policy has failed to establish credibility in achieving the publicly stated objective of monetary policy; namely price stability. Table 10.2 reports the unit root test results for inflation in Singapore. The ADF and KPSS tests reject the null hypothesis that inflation in Singapore has a unit root. This suggests that although Singapore has high inflation persistence, it does not have a unit root.

Interest Rates

Figures 10.4a and 10.4b show the movements of the nominal and real Treasury bill rate in Singapore and the nominal and real Federal funds rate in the United States. Visual inspection suggests that they have similar characteristics since the mid 1990s. Figure 10.4b suggests a high degree of correlation between the real Treasury bill rate in Singapore and the real Federal funds rate in the United States, implying that they maintain real interest rate parity, as expected under free capital mobility according to the purchasing power parity condition. With a highly volatile real interest rate, including a record of some negative values, Singapore has experienced

Table 10.1 Macroeconomic indicators, Singapore, 1951–2012

Macroeconomic indicators	1951–55	1956–60	1961–65	1966–70	1971–75	1976–80	1981–85	1986–90	1991–95	1996–2000	2001–05	2006–10	2011	2012
Budget balance (% of GDP)	n.a.	n.a.	n.a.	n.a.	n.a.	n.a.	n.a.	11.3	12.9	6.9	5.7	6.4	7.3	5.2
General government gross debt (% of GDP)	n.a.	n.a.	n.a.	n.a.	n.a.	n.a.	n.a.	71.1	71.1	77.4	95.8	94.7	107.6	106.2
Money-growth rate (%)														
Narrow money growth	n.a.	n.a.	2.4	13.4	16.8	12.1	7.7	11.7	10.9	5.7	6.9	19.6	16.1	7.7
Broad money growth	n.a.	n.a.	5.4	18.5	16.4	14.7	12.1	17.1	10.5	11.4	5.2	13.0	10.0	7.2
Real GDP growth rate (%)	n.a.	n.a.	5.9	12.9	9.6	8.6	6.3	8.1	9.0	6.3	4.8	6.7	5.2	1.3
GDP per capita, current prices, US dollar	n.a.	n.a.	n.a.	n.a.	n.a.	4756	6347	9210	18 373	23 139	24 195	37 395	49 271	49 936
Unemployment rate (%)	n.a.	n.a.	n.a.	n.a.	n.a.	5.8	5.7	2.4	1.7	2.2	3.3	2.4	2.0	2.1
CPI inflation rate (%)	n.a.	n.a.	1.0	1.2	9.7	3.8	3.3	1.3	2.6	0.9	0.6	2.6	5.3	4.5
Current account balance (% of GDP)	n.a.	n.a.	n.a.	n.a.	n.a.	−13.1	−4.6	5.2	12.2	16.0	17.5	21.0	21.9	21.0

Nominal interest rate (%)														
Treasury bill rate	n.a.	n.a.	n.a.	n.a.	3.9	4.3	3.5	3.3	1.8	1.8	1.2	1.4	0.3	0.3
Deposit rate of interest	n.a.	n.a.	n.a.	n.a.	n.a.	6.1	7.2	3.5	3.3	3.0	0.7	0.4	0.2	0.1
Real interest rate (%)[a]														
Treasury bill rate	n.a.	n.a.	n.a.	n.a.	−9.0	0.6	0.3	2.0	−0.8	0.9	0.6	−1.2	−4.7	−4.1
Deposit rate of interest	n.a.	n.a.	n.a.	n.a.	n.a.	0.9	3.9	2.2	0.7	2.1	0.1	−2.1	−4.8	−4.2
Nominal exchange rate (S$ per US dollar)	3.1	3.1	3.1	3.1	2.6	2.3	2.1	2.0	1.6	1.6	1.7	1.5	1.3	1.2
Nominal effective exchange rate[b]	n.a.	n.a.	n.a.	60.8	65.9	69.2	82.9	76.6	92.4	103.4	100.9	107.6	116.1	118.9
Real effective exchange rate[b]	n.a.	n.a.	n.a.	n.a.	n.a.	113.9	118.1	97.7	110.3	114.7	104.0	106.0	117.4	122.8

Notes:
n.a. = not available
a. Real interest rate is estimated as: 100(((1 + interest rate)/(1 + inflation rate))−1) where the interest rate and inflation rate are expressed in decimal.
b. An increase in the index value of the exchange rate represents appreciation.

Source: Author's computation based on IMF, *International Financial Statistics*; IMF, *World Economic Outlook*; and other country-specific publications on the IMF website.

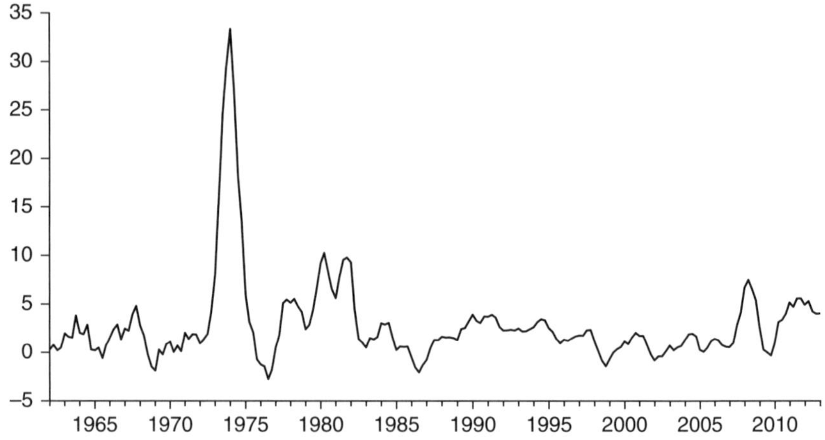

Figure 10.2a Quarter-on-quarter CPI inflation in Singapore, 1962q1–2012q4

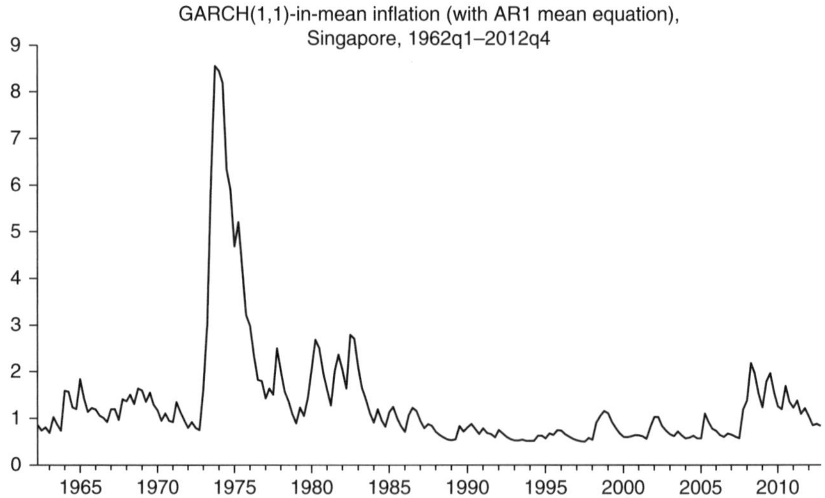

Figure 10.2b Conditional standard deviation of CPI inflation in Singapore, 1962q1–2012q4

boom-bust cycles. In Singapore a negative real interest rate, in particular, raises demand for assets, especially houses. Also, as Singapore is a regional safe haven for foreign capital of questionable sources, house prices in Singapore remain volatile, dependent as they are upon capital flows.

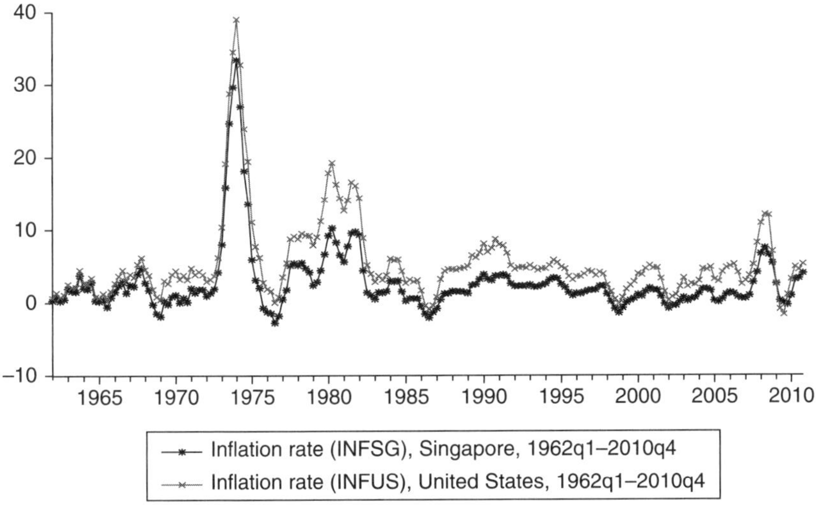

Figure 10.2c Quarter-on-quarter CPI inflation rates in Singapore and the United States, 1962q1–2012q4

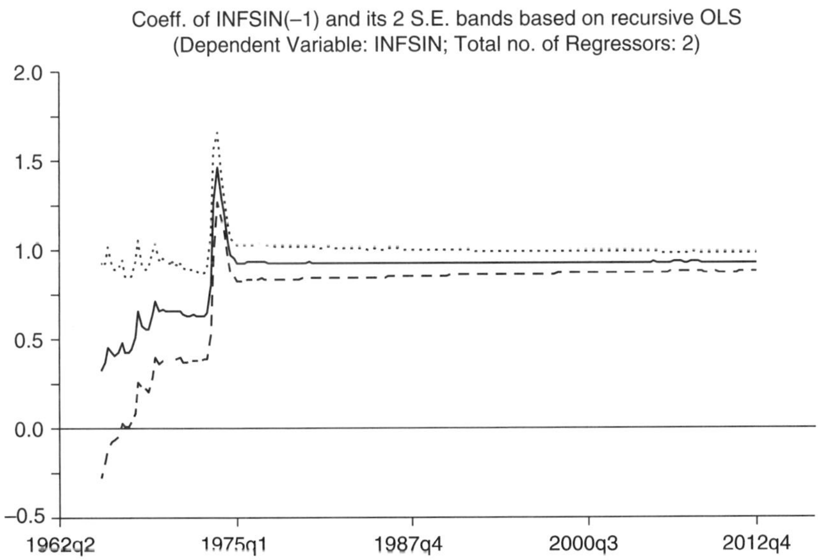

Note: INFSIN = CPI inflation in Singapore.

Figure 10.3a Recursive estimates of the coefficient on the one-period lagged rate of CPI inflation in Singapore

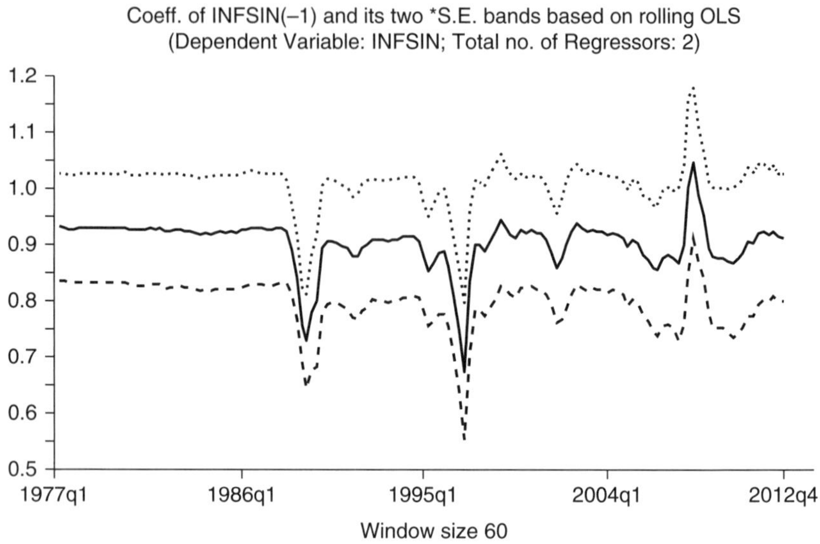

Note: INFSIN = CPI inflation in Singapore.

Figure 10.3b Rolling sample estimates of the coefficient on the one-period lagged rate of CPI inflation in Singapore

Exchange Rates

Figure 10.5 plots the nominal and real effective exchange rates in Singapore. Both the nominal and real effective exchange rates appear to have been highly volatile since the early 1980s. As discussed, the nominal effective exchange rate is the instrument deployed to stabilize prices. The high volatility of the nominal effective exchange rate demonstrates the instrument instability required to stabilize aggregate demand and hence the general price level. The real effective exchange rate also reflects this, given short-run price rigidities. One key issue is whether, and to what extent, this volatility of the real exchange rate has impacted trade and capital flows and consequently the level of output and its growth.

INFLATION, REAL INTEREST RATE, REAL EXCHANGE RATE AND REAL OUTPUT

Under the present exchange rate-based monetary policy, inflation, the real interest rate and the real exchange rate have remained volatile. Although

Table 10.2 The unit root test results for CPI inflation in Singapore

	Sample (lag-unadjusted)	Constant (C); Trend (T)	ADF test statistic (SBC-determined lag-length, l)	Inference at 5% level	The KPSS test statistic (Newey-West bandwidth)	Inference at 5% level
LCPI	1963–2012	C and T	−1.17 (l = 2)	I(1)	0.207 (5)	I(1)
LCPI	1963–2012	C	−1.24 (l = 2)	I(1)	0.819 (6)	I(1)
ΔLCPI	1963–2012	C	−5.33 (l = 1)	I(0)	0.161 (1)	I(0)

Note: Definitions of variables: LCPI = log of the consumer price index; ΔLCPI = first-order difference of LCPI; SBC = Schwarz Bayesian Criterion; ADF = augmented Dickey-Fuller; and KPSS = Kwiatkowski, Phillips, Schmidt and Shin.

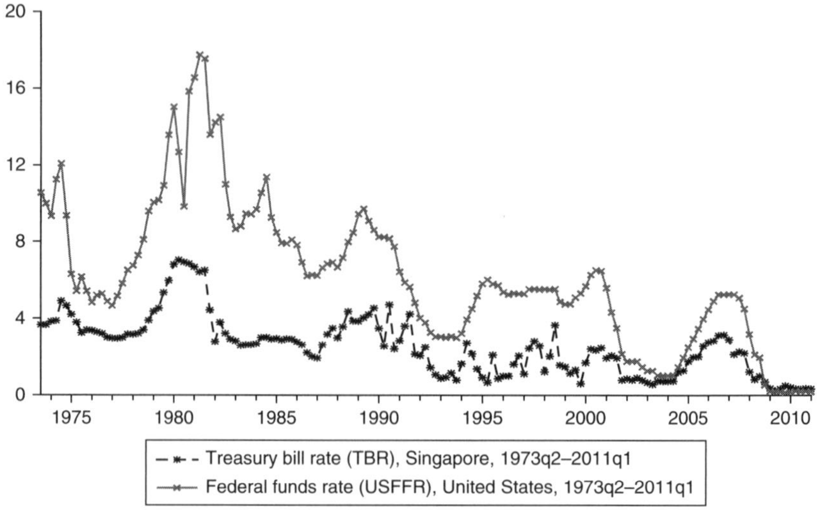

Figure 10.4a The Treasury bill rate in Singapore and the Federal funds rate in the United States, 1973q2–2011q1

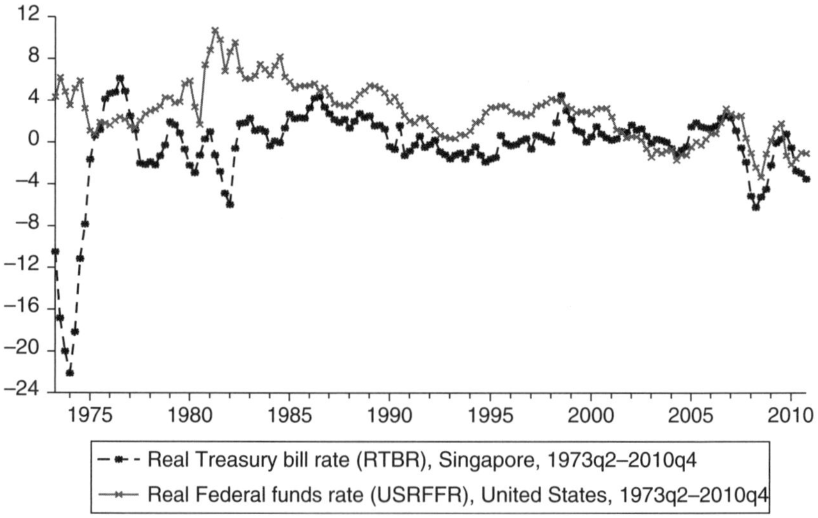

Figure 10.4b The real Treasury bill rate in Singapore and the real Federal funds rate in the United States, 1973q2–2010q4

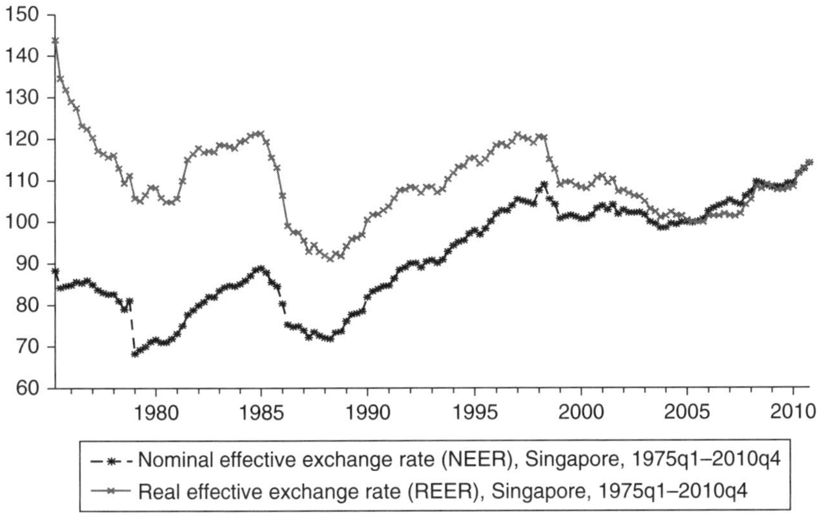

Figure 10.5 *Nominal and real effective exchange rates in Singapore, 1975q1–2010q4*

inflation volatility declined between the mid 1980s and the early 2000s, it has resurged in recent years. Neither the interest rate nor the nominal exchange rate in Singapore adjust completely to the inflation differential between Singapore and its trading partners. The relatively high-inflation volatility in Singapore has led to high volatility in both the real interest rate and the real exchange rate.

The Structural Vector Autoregressive (SVAR) Analysis

This subsection, using annual data, estimates a four-variable SVAR model to examine the interrelationships among inflation, the real interest rate, the real exchange rate and real output. The model is formulated on the assumption that inflation has a contemporaneous feedback relation with the real interest rate and the real exchange rate. All these variables affect real output with a lag. The order of variables in the model is arranged as follows: INFSG, RTBR, LREER and LRGDP, where INFSG is the inflation rate in Singapore, RTBR is the real Treasury bill rate, LREER is the log of the real exchange rate and LRGDP is the log of real GDP. The unit root test results suggest that while inflation, the real interest rate and the real exchange rate appear stationary, real output is nonstationary. Two versions of the model are then estimated and deployed to generate impulse responses and the forecast error-variance decompositions. The

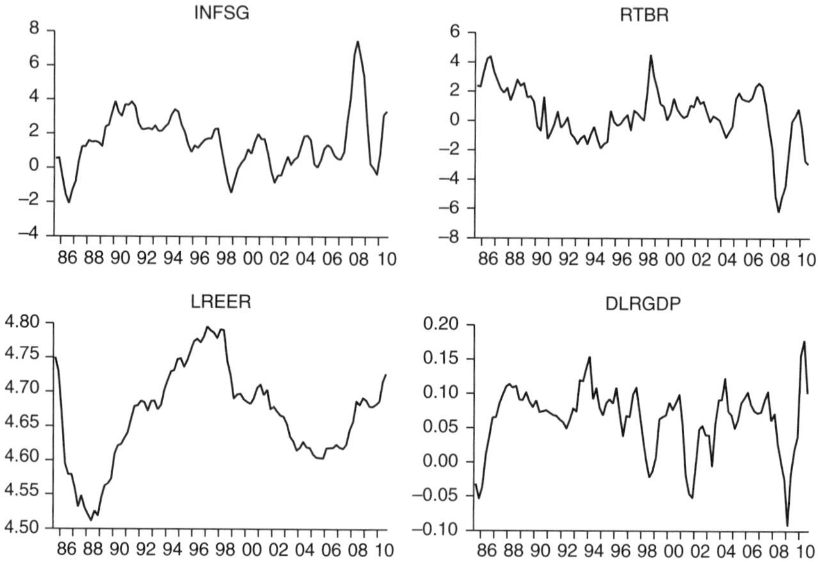

Note: Definitions of variables: INFSG = CPI inflation in Singapore; RTBR = real Treasury bill rate; LREER = log of the real effective exchange rate of the Singapore dollar; and DLRGDP = first-order difference of the log of real GDP.

Figure 10.6 Data deployed for estimation of the SVAR model for Singapore

first version of the model is defined as: INFSG, RTBR, LREER and LRGDP while the second version of the model is defined as: INFSG, RTBR, LREER and DLRGDP. In the second version of the model, all the variables are stationary while in the first version real output is nonstationary. The results obtained from the second model are reported, as results obtained by both models are broadly similar. Figure 10.6 plots the data used for estimation purposes.

The impulse responses in Figure 10.7 suggest the interrelations among four variables in the SVAR model. The impulse response results are indicative, not conclusive. As expected, a rise in inflation reduces the real rate of interest, indicating that the nominal interest rate responds slowly to a rise in inflation. A rise in inflation appreciates the real exchange rate, which in turn affects inflation and economic growth. The real interest rate also responds positively to an appreciation of the real exchange rate because, as a grossly appreciated real exchange rate induces capital flight, the real interest rate is required to rise as an inducement to slow down or stop capital flight. This requirement is a prediction of the open-economy

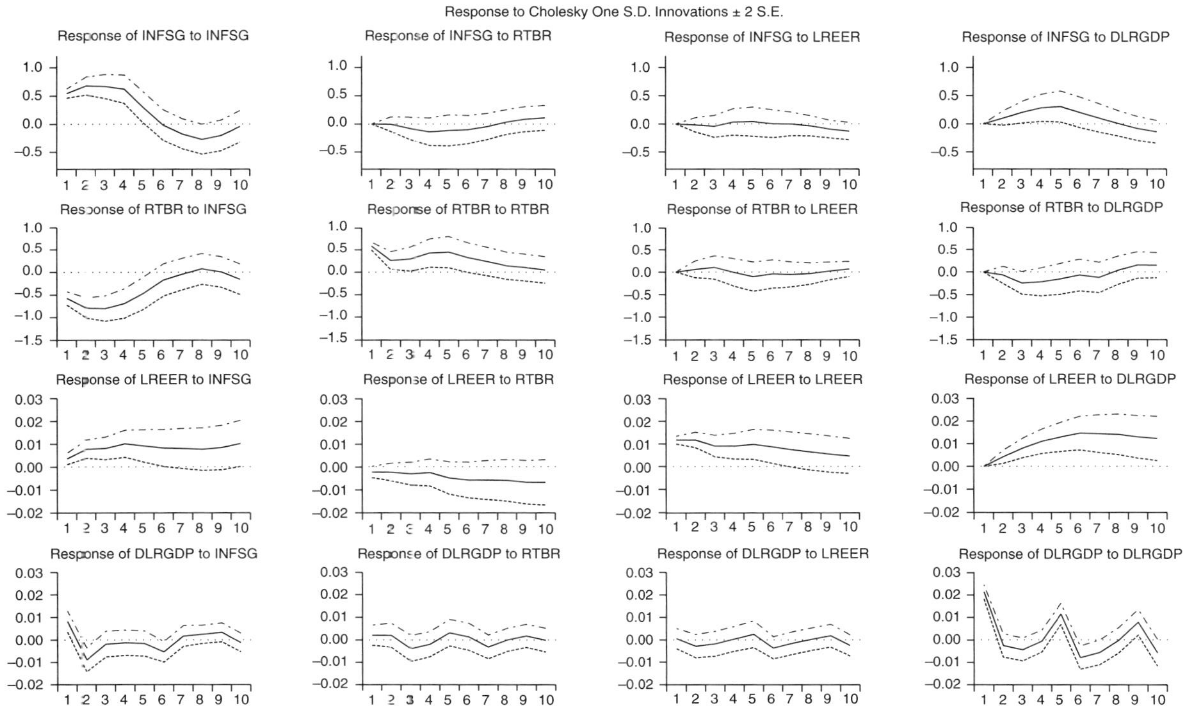

Note: Definitions of variables: INFSG = CPI inflation in Singapore; RTBR = real Treasury bill rate; LREER = log of the real effective exchange rate of the Singapore dollar; and DLRGDP = first-order difference of the log of real GDP.

Figure 10.7 Impulse responses for variables in the SVAR model for Singapore real exchange rate parity condition. In general, an appreciation of the real exchange rate affects both trade and capital flows while changes in the real interest rate affect saving and investment.

The overall results suggest significant interrelations among inflation, the real interest rate, the real exchange rate and output growth. Although it is not investigated here, an expanded model is expected to show the impacts of the real interest and exchange rates on saving, investment and on flows of both real sector trade and financial sector capital. The key message to emerge from the empirical results is that inflation and its volatility are not innocuous in so far as economic growth is concerned. Inflation affects the real interest rate and the real exchange rate and they have impacts on saving, investment and economic growth. This suggests the need for low and stable inflation for steady economic growth.

Table 10.3 presents the forecast error-variance decompositions of INFSG, RTBR, LREER and DLRGDP. In the table, the numbers represent those percentages of forecast error variance of variables in the model that can be attributed to own innovations and those percentages of forecast error variance that originate from innovations of other variables. The results show that, for all four of the specified variables, the dominant source of the forecast error variance is own innovations, to the extent of 82 per cent for inflation, 29 per cent for the real interest rate, 25 per cent for the real exchange rate and 73 per cent for real GDP growth over the ten-year time horizon. In the case of real output growth, innovations in the real interest rate and the real exchange rate jointly account for 9 per cent of real output growth's forecast error variance. The corresponding share of inflation is 19 per cent. This shows that real output growth in Singapore is highly sensitive to inflation and its volatility.

MONETARY AND EXCHANGE RATE POLICY ISSUES

The empirical results reported above suggest that the Singapore economy remains vulnerable to external shocks. Under its present exchange rate-based monetary policy, US monetary policy has a major influence on the Singapore economy. One way of minimizing this problem could be the introduction of a flexible exchange rate system, which would allow Singapore to conduct an independent monetary policy for price stability while the exchange rate would absorb shocks. One shortcoming of such a flexible exchange rate system for a small economy like Singapore is that it may generate excess volatility of the exchange rate in an underdeveloped foreign-exchange market. To the extent that a country like Singapore follows disciplined monetary and fiscal policies and maintains large

Table 10.3 Forecast error-variance decomposition of variables in the SVAR model for Singapore

Variance Decomposition of INFSG:					
Period	S.E.	INFSG	RTBR	LREER	DLRGDP
1	0.542	100.00	0.00	0.00	0.00
2	0.871	98.65	0.00	0.03	1.32
5	1.387	86.04	2.00	0.26	11.70
10	1.486	81.61	3.21	1.41	13.77
Variance Decomposition of RTBR:					
Period	S.E.	INFSG	RTBR	LREER	DLRGDP
1	0.824	49.00	50.99	0.00	0.00
2	1.177	69.62	29.81	0.26	0.32
5	1.832	68.97	26.25	0.74	4.04
10	1.921	64.41	29.11	0.96	5.51
Variance Decomposition of LREER:					
Period	S.E.	INFSG	RTBR	LREER	DLRGDP
1	0.012	8.45	3.49	88.0	0.00
2	0.019	19.88	2.92	72.46	4.74
5	0.036	25.57	4.04	41.34	29.04
10	0.055	23.16	8.33	24.92	43.59
Variance Decomposition of DLRGDP:					
Period	S.E.	INFSG	RTBR	LREER	DLRGDP
1	0.023	13.01	0.82	0.05	86.11
2	0.025	23.83	1.32	1.33	73.52
5	0.029	19.14	4.53	2.16	74.17
10	0.033	18.90	4.73	3.91	72.47
The Cholesky Ordering: INFSG RTBR LREER DLRGDP					

Note: Definitions of variables: INFSG = CPI inflation in Singapore; RTBR = real Treasury bill rate; LREER = log of the real effective exchange rate of the Singapore dollar; and DLRGDP = first-order difference of the log of real GDP.

foreign reserves, the exchange rate of the Singapore dollar is unlikely to show excess volatility.

The question is the choice of monetary policy strategy that Singapore may adopt to maintain price stability under a floating exchange rate system. There are two options for Singapore. It can introduce either monetary targeting or inflation targeting while using monetary aggregate as an instrument of monetary policy.

Until recently the prevailing view was that monetary targeting for price stability requires a stable money-demand function to establish a causal linkage between money supply growth and inflation. The recent literature suggests the presence of a causal relation between money supply growth and inflation, irrespective both of the exchange rate regime and whether the money-demand function is stable or not (McCallum and Nelson, 2011).

This section examines whether there exists a stable money-demand function in Singapore.[5] For estimation purposes, an open-economy money-demand function of the following restricted form is specified:

$$\mathrm{LRJM}_t = \alpha_0 + \alpha_1 \mathrm{Ly}_t + \alpha_3 FIR_t + \alpha_4 \mathrm{LRER}_t + \alpha_5 \pi_t^v + u_t \qquad (10.1)$$

where LRJM (J = N, B) is the log of real money balances (LRNM for narrowly defined money or LRBM for broadly defined money), Ly is the log of real income, FIR is a representative foreign interest rate, LRER is the log of a real exchange rate such as the real effective exchange rate (REER), π_t^v is a measure of inflation volatility and u_t is a random error term. In this specification, real income represents a scale variable and its coefficient is expected to bear a positive sign and have a value not significantly different from one. Given perfect capital mobility, the domestic interest rate approximates the foreign interest rate, so that both cannot be used simultaneously in the money-demand function. The coefficient on the foreign interest rate is expected to bear a negative sign. Following the discussion in Appendix 5, the coefficients on the real exchange rate and inflation volatility remain a priori indeterminate.

The unit root test results suggest that all the variables in the specified model have a unit root. Consequently, they are eligible to be tested for cointegration. Given that Singapore operates under a pegged exchange rate system, the US Federal funds rate is used as the opportunity cost variable. Table 10.4 reports both the ARDL and OLS results for real broad money-demand function. To conserve space, the results obtained using the narrow definition of money series are not reported. The results obtained by the ordinary least squares (OLS) model are found superior to those obtained by the ARDL model. The results suggest the presence of a weak form of long-run cointegral relationship among real broad money balances, real income, the Federal funds rate and the real exchange rate. The estimated coefficient values are consistent with a priori predictions. As expected, real income remains the core determinant of broad money demand. The income elasticity of demand for real broad money balances is greater than one. This is significant for an advanced country like Singapore. The real effective exchange rate bears a negative sign and is statistically significant. The coefficient on inflation volatility is not significant. The CUSUM and CUSUMSQ of residuals in Figure 10.8 suggest

Table 10.4 The ARDL and OLS regression results of real broad money-demand relationship in Singapore

F-statistic	1.56			
W-statistic	7.81			
Critical value bounds	F-test	W-test		
90%	(2.60, 3.75)	(13.02, 18.75)		
95%	(3.14, 4.42)	(15.71, 22.09)		
Sample period	1965–2012	1965–2012	1963–2012	1964–2012
	ARDL (1,0,0,0,0)	ARDL (1,0,0,0,0)	OLS	OLS
	(Selected based on SBC)	Long-run model	(Static model)	(Dynamic model)
Regressors	Coefficient (t-ratio) [prob.]	Coefficient (t-ratio) [prob.]	Coefficient (t-ratio) [prob.]	Coefficient (t-ratio) [prob.]
Intercept	2.71 (2.59) [0.01]	10.79 (4.68) [0.00]	8.65 (15.54) [0.00]	2.91 (3.03) [0.00]
LRBM(−1)	0.75 (6.39) [0.00]			0.73 (6.58) [0.00]
LRGDP	0.30 (2.05) [0.05]	1.18 (27.46) [0.00]	1.22 (111.54) [0.00]	0.32 (2.35) [0.02]
USFFR	−0.01 (−0.96) [0.34]	−0.01 (−1.21) [0.23]	−0.02 (−5.15) [0.00]	−0.01 (−0.99) [0.33]
LREER	−0.19 (−1.66) [0.10]	−0.76 (−1.55) [0.13]	−0.40 (−3.37) [0.00]	−0.21 (−2.39) [0.02]
INFVOL	−0.01 (−0.28) [0.79]			
Diagnostics				
Adjusted R^2	0.99		0.99	0.99

Table 10.4 (continued)

Lagrange multiplier test for serial correlation	$F(1, 41) = 0.41$ [0.53]		$F(1, 45) = 16.15$ [0.00]	$F(1, 43) = 0.65$ [0.43]
Ramsey's RESET test of functional form mis-specification	$F(1, 41) = 1.92$ [0.17]		$F(1,45) = 7.36$ [0.01]	$F(1, 43) = 1.80$ [0.19]
Normality of residuals	$\chi^2_{(2)} = 19.25$ [0.00]		$\chi^2_{(2)} = 1.26$ [0.53]	$\chi^2_{(2)} = 21.84$ [0.00]
Heteroskedasticity	$F(1, 46) = 0.15$ [0.70]		$F(1, 48) = 1.46$ [0.23]	$F(1, 47) = 0.20$ [0.66]
The Wald test:				
H_O: Coefficient on LRGDP = 0		$\chi^2_{(1)} = 754.06$ [0.00]	$\chi^2_{(1)} = 12441.9$ [0.00]	
H_O: Coefficient on LRGDP = 1		$\chi^2_{(1)} = 19.21$ [0.00]	$\chi^2_{(1)} = 417.39$ [0.00]	
H_O: Coefficient on USFFR = 0		$\chi^2_{(1)} = 1.46$ [0.23]	$\chi^2_{(1)} = 26.50$ [0.00]	
H_O: Coefficient on LREER = 0		$\chi^2_{(1)} = 2.40$ [0.12]	$\chi^2_{(1)} = 11.38$ [0.00]	
H_O: Coefficient on INFVOL = 0		$\chi^2_{(1)} = 0.07$ [0.79]		

Note: Definitions of variables: LRBM = log of real broad money balances; LRGDP = log of real GDP; USFFR = US Federal funds rate; LREER = log of the real effective exchange rate; INFVOL = inflation volatility; ARDL = autoregressive distributed lag; and SBC = Schwarz Bayesian Criterion.

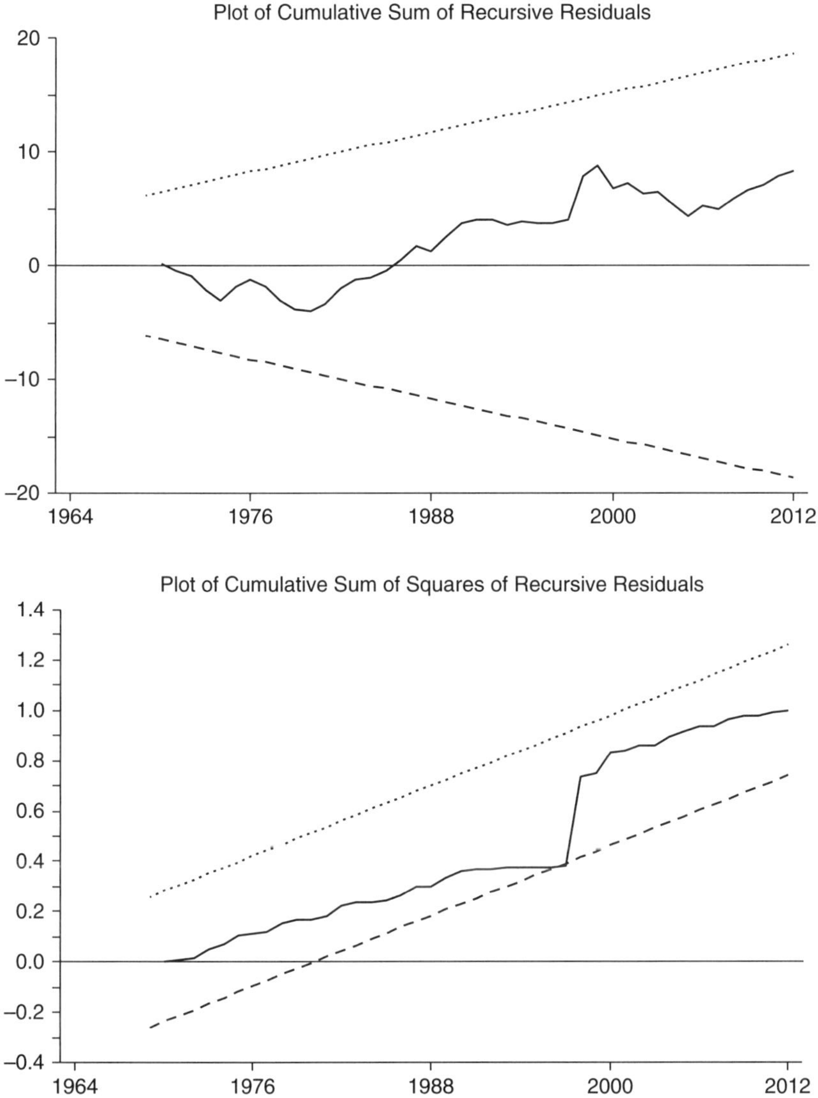

Note: The straight lines represent critical bounds at 5% significance level.

Figure 10.8 CUSUM and CUSUMSQ of residuals for real broad money-demand relationships in Singapore that the broad money-demand function remained stable over the study period.

Relationships Among Money, Output and Prices

Table 10.5 reports the cointegration test results among money, output and prices. The results obtained for a broad definition of money are found more robust than those obtained from the narrow money series. The Engle-Granger cointegration test results suggest a weak form of cointegral relationship among money, output and prices. The dynamic OLS (DOLS) estimates suggest that broad money is highly significant in the price level equation and that the coefficient value of broad money is significantly lower than one. As expected, real output bears a negative sign. The coefficient is, however, statistically significant only at the 15 per cent level.

Engle and Granger (1987) have suggested that one of the implications of a cointegral relation between two nonstationary variables is the presence of long-term causality between them running in at least one direction. Table 10.6 reports the bivariate Granger-causality test results among LCPI, LNM (LBM) and LRGDP. Test results are generated within a vector error-correction (VEC) modelling framework after selecting the optimal lag-length using the SBC. The test results suggest that for Singapore, there is causality running from narrow or broad money growth to inflation. Broad money growth is found to have some causal impact on output growth.

SUMMARY AND CONCLUSION

Since full political Independence in 1963, Singapore has maintained rapid economic growth, low inflation and a healthy balance-of-payments for most of the time. Sustained, rapid economic growth has been attributed to macroeconomic stability, openness to trade and capital flows, and flexible labour markets. These factors have attracted large-scale foreign investment and created an environment for export-led economic growth in a low-inflation environment. Singapore has promoted investment in some particular 'chosen' sectors, such as health and education, where it strives to gain and retain competitive advantage. These sectors have greater growth potential and strategic importance to Singapore's continued economic pre-eminence in the region.

In short, although Singapore's journey to developed country status was not uninterrupted, it is seen as a major economic success story and hence a model economy for other countries to emulate. Singapore's macroeconomic management, in particular, has been flexible and predictable to the

Table 10.5 *Cointegration test results among money, output and prices in Singapore*

Dependent variable = LCPI								
	Fully modified OLS				Dynamic OLS (lead = 1, lag = 1)			
With narrow money (NM)								
Regressor	coefficient	t-ratio	prob.		coefficient	t-ratio	prob.	
Intercept	1.55	2.05	0.05		0.68	1.00	0.32	
LNM	0.31	1.93	0.06		0.57	3.94	0.00	
LRGDP	−0.06	−0.28	0.78		−0.44	−2.23	0.03	
Sample period	1970–2012				1970–2011			
DW	0.22				0.5			
Adjusted R^2	0.91				0.95			
	tau-statistic	prob.	z-statistic	prob.	tau-statistic	prob.	z-statistic	prob.
The Engle-Granger cointegration tests	−2.37	0.56	−6.69	0.79	−2.37	0.56	−6.69	0.79
The Phillips-Ouliaris cointegration tests	−2.38	0.56	−6.96	0.77	−2.38	0.56	−6.96	0.77
With broad money (BM)								
Regressor	coefficient	t-ratio	prob.		coefficient	t-ratio	prob.	
Intercept	0.20	0.21	0.84		0.22	0.17	0.87	
LBM	0.59	2.89	0.01		0.63	2.35	0.03	
LRGDP	−0.64	−1.85	0.07		−0.71	−1.58	0.13	
Sample period	1970–2012				1970–2011			
DW	0.42				0.38			
Adjusted R^2	0.93				0.93			
	tau-statistic	prob.	z-statistic	prob.	tau-statistic	prob.	z-statistic	prob.
The Engle-Granger cointegration tests	−3.2	0.2	−11.36	0.46	−3.03	0.26	−9.23	0.61
The Phillips-Ouliaris cointegration tests	−3.2	0.2	−11.37	0.46	−3.04	0.26	−10.04	0.55

Note: Definitions of variables: LCPI = log of the consumer price index; LNM = log of narrow money stock; LBM = log of broad money stock; and LRGDP = log of real GDP.

Table 10.6 Granger-causality among money, output and prices in Singapore, 1963–2012

	Hypotheses No causality runs from:	Chi-square statistic (prob.)	Inference at 5% level
VEC specification	ΔLNM → ΔLCPI	13.92 (0.00)	Null hypothesis rejected
(With narrow money, NM)	ΔLNM, ΔLRGDP → ΔLCPI	14.99 (0.00)	Null hypothesis rejected
	ΔLCPI → ΔLNM	0.77 (0.68)	Null hypothesis not rejected
	ΔLRGDP → ΔLNM	0.64 (0.73)	Null hypothesis not rejected
	ΔLCPI → ΔLRGDP	3.10 (0.21)	Null hypothesis not rejected
	ΔLNM → ΔLRGDP	0.53 (0.77)	Null hypothesis not rejected
VEC specification	ΔLBM → ΔLCPI	5.14 (0.08)	Null hypothesis not rejected
(With broad money, BM)	ΔLBM, ΔLRGDP → ΔLCPI	8.39 (0.08)	Null hypothesis not rejected
	ΔLCPI → ΔLBM	1.63 (0.44)	Null hypothesis not rejected
	ΔLRGDP → ΔLBM	7.54 (0.02)	Null hypothesis rejected
	ΔLCPI → ΔLRGDP	1.51 (0.47)	Null hypothesis not rejected
	ΔLBM → ΔLRGDP	3.72 (0.16)	Null hypothesis not rejected

Note: Definitions of variables: LCPI = log of the consumer price index; LNM = log of narrow money stock; LBM = log of broad money stock; and LRGDP = log of real GDP. Optimal lag-length = 2 (selected based on the Schwarz Bayesian Criterion, SBC).

extent needed to avoid creating policy uncertainties. The *IMF Country Report 08/2008* (IMF, 2008) makes the following remarks to explain Singapore's impressive economic performance in an historical context:

> Singapore is an economic success story. Policies to fully exploit the opportunities by the world economy have laid the groundwork. Pragmatic macroeconomic management has underpinned resilience to external shocks; proactive structural reforms have allowed the economy to cope with rising regional competition and the challenges of globalization; and a business-friendly environment has been a pull-factor for foreign investment. As a result, Singapore's real GDP per-capita increased five-fold in a generation – from developing to advanced country level. [p. 4]

While Singapore has gained the status of an advanced economy, it remains vulnerable to external shocks. With its well-developed (broad and deep) capital markets, adoption of a flexible exchange rate system as a shock absorber is indicated. Presently, Singapore operates under an adjustable peg exchange rate system with an undisclosed basket of currencies and with perfect capital mobility. Singapore, therefore, has an exchange rate policy, but this deprives it of an autonomous, independent monetary policy for price stability. However, the aim of exchange rate policy is price stability, implying low inflation on average, but not the promotion of exports or output growth. This does not mean that exchange rate movement does not impact trade and capital flows. Consequently, the exchange rate is adjusted as required to maintain price stability but not to stabilize the economy. Under this arrangement, Singapore maintains low average inflation, while the volatility of inflation remains (perhaps too) high. This creates volatility in both the real interest rate and the real exchange rate, which in turn is transmitted both to real output and to its growth. This issue receives only low importance in the monetary policy literature in Singapore.

Singapore is expected to continue with the present exchange rate-based monetary policy, although there is scope for improvement of the monetary policy framework for price stability. To begin with, the transparency of the monetary policy framework can be improved substantially. For example, the MAS does not publish the weights that it applies to the trade-weighted exchange rate index and the precise limits of the band. The extent of MAS intervention in the foreign-exchange market is not disclosed. It is not clear whether the exchange rate is also adjusted to influence output over the business cycle.

The key research question is whether Singapore should gain independence of monetary policy under a flexible exchange rate system to maintain price stability, needed for economic stability. This chapter has investigated some monetary relations for Singapore. In order to examine whether Singapore should conduct monetary policy by adopting a more flexible exchange rate system, the money-demand behaviour in Singapore has been investigated. It is found that the broad money-demand function in Singapore has remained largely stable. There also exists a causal linkage between money supply growth and inflation. This is consistent with the view of McCallum and Nelson (2011) that the linkage between money supply growth and inflation could be robust irrespective of the exchange rate regime. In short, money remains important in the conduct of monetary policy irrespective of the strategy of monetary policy adopted to maintain price stability.

As the nominal exchange rate of Singapore is not fixed but adjustable, the question is whether the exchange rate would be more volatile if allowed to be determined by market forces. It is plausible that since Singapore maintains monetary and fiscal discipline and the financial system is developed, there is less possibility that the phenomenon of exchange rate overshooting might really occur in the markets. A floating exchange rate would generally absorb external shocks better if the institutional financial sector framework is well developed. This is an important issue for Singapore, as its economy is exposed to external shocks.

Provided that there is flexibility in the exchange rate, Singapore may even consider introducing inflation targeting. Low and stable inflation in Singapore is important for maintaining competitiveness of its exportable products. In its role as an international financial centre, it is debatable whether Singapore can or should introduce market-based capital controls to smooth capital flows while maintaining stability of the exchange rate. Under a floating exchange rate system, Singapore would acquire control over the interest rate. It can then use the interest rate or a monetary aggregate to stabilize prices. How effective would be the interest rate in managing demand is not known. The use of a monetary aggregate as an anchor to prices could be more stable than the exchange rate to keep inflation low and volatile. It is not always the level of inflation but the volatility of inflation that has a harmful effect on saving, investment and economic growth. The empirical analysis reported in this chapter suggests that real output in Singapore is highly sensitive to the movement of inflation. High volatility of inflation leads to high volatility, both of the real interest rate and the real exchange rate. They affect output and its growth.

NOTES

1. CIA World Factbook, available at https://www.cia.gov/library/publications/the-world-factbook/geos/sn.html.
2. For general information on Singapore and its financial system, see http://en.wikipedia.org/wiki/Singapore, Koh (1992) and McCallum (2005).
3. Abesinghe (2007, p. 1) has provided the following general description on the factors that played a role in the rapid economic transformation of Singapore: 'Singapore's founding leader, Lee Kuan Yew, is often asked the question by foreign observers "what was the secret of Singapore's success?" His answer to this question has been "there was no secret; we had no choice but to take a chance and sale into rough waters". Government's development ideology has been growth-driven, purely pragmatic and adaptable to changing circumstances. As a result a uniquely Singapore system has emerged that may not be easily emulated by others. On the one hand, Singapore is a tightly regulated planned economy and on the other hand it stands out as a beacon of the free market system. The pioneering economic architect, Goh Keng Swee, described Singapore as "a socialist economy that works". The present day Singapore may be described as a "market-driven guided economy".'
4. Information on this section is drawn from several publications available on the websites at the MAS and the IMF.
5. For early studies on money-demand behaviour in Singapore, see Daquila and Fatt (1993), Chaisrisawatsuk et al. (2004) and Abdullah et al. (2010).

REFERENCES

Abdullah, H., J. Ali and H. Matahir (2010), 'Re-examining the demand for money in ASEAN-5 countries', *Asian Social Science*, **6**(7), 146–55.

Abesinghe, T. (2007), 'Singapore: economy', Unpublished manuscript, Singapore National University.

Bercuson, K. (ed.) (1995), 'Singapore: a case study in rapid development', Occasional Paper No. 119, IMF, Washington, DC.

Chaisrisawatsuk, S., S. Sharma and A. Chowdhury (2004), 'Money demand stability under currency substitution: some evidence', *Applied Financial Economics*, **14**(1), 19–27.

Daquila, T.C. and A.P.K. Fatt (1993), 'Demand for money in Singapore revisited', *Asian Economic Journal*, **7**, 181–95.

Engle, R.F. and C.W.J. Granger (1987), 'Co-integration and error-correction: representation, estimation, and testing', *Econometrica*, **55**(2), 251–76.

IMF (International Monetary Fund) (various years), *International Financial Statistics*, Washington, DC: IMF.

IMF (International Monetary Fund) (various years), *World Economic Outlook*, Washington, DC: IMF.

IMF (2008), *Singapore: 2008 Article IV Consultation*, available at http://www.imf.org/external/pubs/ft/scr/2008/cr08280.pdf (accessed 20 March 2015).

Koh, A.T. (1992), 'Singapore: monetary and financial system', in P. Newman, M. Milgate and J. Eatwell (eds), *The New Palgrave Dictionary of Money and Finance*, Vol. 3, London: Macmillan, pp. 461–2.

McCallum, B.T. (2005), 'Is Singapore the model for China's new exchange rate policy?', Unpublished manuscript, Carnegie Mellon University.

McCallum, B.T. and E. Nelson (2011), 'Money and inflation: some critical issues', in B.M. Friedman and M. Woodford (eds), *Handbook of Monetary Economics*, Vol. 3A, Amsterdam: Elsevier Science, pp. 97–153.

MAS (Monetary Authority of Singapore) (1999), 'Monetary policy and the economy', *Economics Explorer 2*, MAS, Singapore.

MAS (Monetary Authority of Singapore) (2001), 'Singapore's exchange rate policy', MAS, Singapore.

Parrado, E. (2004), 'Singapore's unique monetary policy: how does it work?', IMF Working Paper WP/04/10, IMF, Washington, DC.

11. Sri Lanka

Sri Lanka is a multi-ethnic, multi-religious country. It is an island economy situated off the east coast of south India, almost a stone's throw across the Palk Strait from the Indian province of Tamil Nadu. Immigrants from Asia and Europe have settled this island dating back more than three thousand years. Sri Lanka's population numbers about 20 million, occupying a land mass of about 66 000 square kilometres. Population density is relatively low at around 323 persons per square kilometre. About 75 per cent of its people are Sinhalese-Buddhists. The remaining 25 per cent of the people is diversified across a range of ethnic-religious identities; the major groups being Tamils (mostly Hindus), Muslims and Burghers-Christians. As with Christianity in many Christian-majority countries and Islam in Muslim-majority countries, Buddhism in Sri Lanka receives special status in the legal system. The Sri Lankan constitution, for example, requires all Sri Lankans to commit 'to protect and foster the Buddha *sasana*'. The recent civil war that ravaged Sri Lanka for about three decades has long historical roots.[1]

Sri Lanka is strategic in South Asian politics because of its location as the westerly 'headland' of the Bay of Bengal, because of its deep harbours and because of its other geography. Given its strategic location along the sea route used for trade between Europe and East Southeast Asia, it was considered a prized European colonial possession from the sixteenth century. Sri Lanka's contemporary economic and political history can be said to have begun with its Independence from Britain in 1948. Sri Lanka has maintained good working relations with Britain, through such links as education, sport and other cultural activities. Since the end of Cold War politics in 1989, Sri Lanka has attracted strategic attention from a number of countries, including China, India, Pakistan and the United States. Sri Lanka maintains good relations with most countries in the East and Southeast Asia regions, especially Japan.

Sri Lanka's per capita income, at the time of writing about US$3000 in purchasing power parity terms, has defined it as a middle-income country since the mid 1990s. Unlike other countries in South Asia, the level of human development in Sri Lanka is high and improving rapidly. Poverty incidence has declined sharply since the 1990s. In particular,

Sri Lanka's pro-poor health care system has reduced the incidence of mortality and raised the level of human development. The three-decade civil war that began in the early 1980s was a major setback for Sri Lanka. The issue was resolved in the majority's favour in 2008. Improved management of Sri Lanka's relatively small minorities appears to have been the main lesson learned, with political and social normalcy having apparently returned to the country. In an historical context, the present state of Sri Lanka's economy exhibits major improvement. Political and religious tensions among the different communities are expected to continue diminishing.

At Independence in 1948, Sri Lanka was predominantly a plantation- and commodity export-oriented economy. It depended heavily on a few agricultural export commodities, namely tea, rubber and coconut products (Bruton, 1992; Snodgrass, 1966, 1988). Consequently, the economy was exposed to external terms-of-trade shocks affecting income and employment. Sri Lanka maintained an open trade policy during its first decade of Independence, then implemented the import-substituting industrialization strategy in the late 1950s. This move was initially triggered by sustained balance-of-payment difficulties. The government imposed high tariffs and other restrictions on the imports of even basic commodities to reorient economic activities. This was expected to establish a self-sufficient economy (Athukorala, 1998, 2004; Athukorala and Huyah, 1987). Consequently, as Athukorala (2007, p. 374) suggests, Sri Lanka's economy became heavily regulated by the mid 1970s:

> Following a hesitant and mild liberalisation attempt during 1968–1970, the period from 1970–1977 saw further Government intervention in the economy under the guise of creating a 'socialist society'. Significant and ever increasing segments of trade, industry, agriculture and banking were owned and managed by state-owned enterprises (SOEs). By the mid-1970s the Sri Lankan economy was one of the most inward-oriented and regulated economies outside the Communist block, characterised by stringent trade and exchange controls and pervasive state interventions in all areas of economic activity.

Under import-substituting industrialization, the Sri Lankan economy did not perform well (Hewavitharana, 1984). In response, the government undertook economic deregulation and reform measures in 1977. The reform process slowed in the early 1980s when civil war broke out between the minority Tamils and the majority Sinhalese. The reform process restarted in the early 1990s and has continued since then at a relatively slow and uneven pace. The process has nevertheless been sustained because a consensus has been built among the major political parties in Sri Lanka on the need for economic reforms to raise economic growth. Sri Lanka's economy is now highly open to trade and investment. Economic performance in Sri Lanka has been categorically superior, since the beginning of the economic reform period in the late 1970s, to its pre-reform performance from the 1950s (Athukorala and Huyah, 1987; Athukorala and Jayasuriya, 1994). It is significant that this step-up in Sri Lankan economic performance, both in the rapidity and the soundness of growth, took place in the midst of a three decade-long civil war.

Moderately high and steady economic growth since the early 1980s has brought major structural change to the Sri Lankan economy. The share of agriculture in output has declined steadily while the share of manufacturing has increased. The Sri Lankan economy is now more balanced and globally integrated than three decades ago. Sri Lanka has also made a successful transition from a civil war-torn economy to an orderly and rapidly growing open economy. The significant social and human development that has taken place in Sri Lanka since the 1950s is expected to continue playing a key role in the country's economic growth and development. Sri Lanka occupies a powerful position from which to sustain an acceleration in its economic growth, provided that the growth environment already created is retained through sustained monetary and fiscal policy discipline (Athukorala and Rajapatirana, 2000).

Economic growth in Sri Lanka has been moderately high since the early 1980s, and there is scope for improving macroeconomic management to promote and sustain accelerating growth. As a small, open economy, Sri Lanka is endemically exposed to external shocks. A more flexible exchange rate can absorb those shocks. The dual exchange rate system that operated in Sri Lanka from 1968 was abolished in 2001 in favour of a managed float. Under the managed float, however, the real exchange rate has exhibited high volatility contracted from Sri Lanka's high and volatile inflation. High inflation was partly due to the monetization of a sustained series of large budget deficits created by the long civil conflict. Because of the war-like situation, the government found itself unable to maintain monetary and fiscal discipline (Athukorala and Rajapatirana, 2000).

Recognizing the problems associated with high and volatile inflation, price stability has emerged as the primary objective of monetary policy in Sri Lanka. Presently, Sri Lanka operates under a soft form of monetary targeting. The average rate of inflation has not been very high, but inflation has remained volatile. The question remains whether with inflation now at sustainably low levels, Sri Lanka should switch its monetary policy strategy of choice from monetary targeting to inflation targeting. In investigating this issue, this chapter provides an historically contextualized overview of issues in central banking and monetary policy in Sri Lanka. It examines some key monetary relations, including the question of whether the money-demand function in Sri Lanka is stable or unstable and whether a causal linkage exists between the Sri Lankan rates of money supply growth and inflation.

THE CENTRAL BANK OF SRI LANKA: ORGANIZATION AND ACTIVITIES[2]

The Central Bank of Sri Lanka (CBSL) was established in 1950 under the Monetary Law Act (MLA) No. 58 of 1949, as amended. The main functions of the CBSL are to:

1. conduct monetary policy
2. conduct exchange rate policy
3. manage foreign-exchange reserves
4. issue and distribute currency notes
5. license, regulate and supervise commercial banks, finance companies and primary dealers in government securities
6. provide clearing and settlement facilities to financial institutions (commercial banks and primary dealers)
7. act as economic adviser, banker and fiscal agent of the government.

The monetary policy objectives of the CBSL have been streamlined by means of amendments made to the MLA in 2002. Presently, the CBSL has two objectives of monetary policy, stated at Section 5 of the MLA: (a) maintaining economic and price stability and (b) maintaining financial system stability.

Under the amendments, the CBSL has been delegated autonomy in achieving the monetary policy objective(s) with which it is tasked. Before the 2002 amendments, the CBSL was required to deploy monetary policy to multiple objectives, namely maintaining stability of the exchange rate; promoting production and employment; and developing productive resources. As these objectives were considered complementary, no overriding objective was set to deal with any cases that may potentially arise from tradeoff (conflict) between objectives.

The question remains as to whether the two objectives (a) and (b) reported above are simultaneously achievable. The concept of economic stability is rigorously defined in the literature; the Sri Lankan authorities are yet to publicly announce their working definition of economic stability in general and price stability in particular. Does it mean stabilizing economic fluctuations caused both by domestic and external shocks; or keeping inflation low and stable to promote economic growth? Does the establishment of financial stability involve controlling capital flows and intervening in the foreign-exchange market to stabilize the exchange rate?

The CBSL has been given autonomy to achieve the defined monetary policy objectives, within the requirement that it maintain liaison with the Ministry of Finance and coordinate its policy decisions with those of the fiscal authorities. The secretary of the Ministry of Finance is a member of the Monetary Board, the governing body of the CBSL. Subsection 8(2) of the MLA prescribes that the Monetary Board comprise five members: the governor of the CBSL; the secretary of the Ministry of Finance (*ex officio*); and three non-executive members.

The governor is the chairman of the Monetary Board and acts as the chief executive of the CBSL. The president of Sri Lanka, on the recommendation of the minister of finance, appoints the governor and the non-executive board members. The approval of the Constitutional Council is required for the appointment of non-executive board members.

The term of office of the governor and the non-executive board members is six years. The quorum for the Monetary Board meetings is three members. Except where the MLA requires a unanimous decision of the Monetary Board, the concurrence of three members is required for its decisions to remain valid. The MLA requires unanimous Board decisions in six specific circumstances:

Section 3(1) For currency stabilization purposes the full Board decides to recommend that the finance minister fix the exchange rate of the rupee (the Sri Lankan currency unit) to the Special Drawing Rights (SDR) of the International Monetary Fund (IMF).

Section 3(1) The full Board decides to recommend that the finance minister *not* fix to SDR, or that a previous decision to fix to SDR be reversed.

Section 3(2) In certain specified circumstances the full Board decides to recommend that the finance minister alter the exchange rate of the rupee.

Section 82(2) The full Board decides to make an exception to a previous Board decision to suspend CBSL credit to the banks in defence of Sri Lankan monetary stability.

Section 86(1) The full Board decides, in the face of an imminent financial panic or other emergency threatening monetary and banking stability, to grant and/or renew extraordinary loans to banks secured against bank assets.

Section 90(3) The full Board decides to make a public interest exception to a previous Board decision to suspend CBSL

> open market purchases of rupee securities in defence of Sri Lankan monetary stability.

The CBSL has a unique legal structure. It is not incorporated. In terms of the MLA, corporate status is conferred on the Monetary Board given that it is vested with all powers, functions and duties of the CBSL. As the governing body, the Monetary Board is responsible for making policy decisions and for the management, operation and administration of the Bank. When there is a difference of opinion on the stance of monetary policy between the minister of finance and the Monetary Board, the minister of finance may inform the Monetary Board that the government would accept responsibility for the Monetary Board, thereby directing the Monetary Board to adopt the government's policy. The government, therefore, has the final say on Sri Lankan monetary and financial matters. The presence of the secretary of the ministry of finance in the Monetary Board is a strong reminder of government influence on most, if not all, monetary policy decisions.

EVOLUTION OF MONETARY POLICY

Until financial reform began in the late 1970s, the Sri Lankan financial system was heavily repressed. Monetary policy was used to achieve multiple objectives by deploying various instruments, especially by controlling interest rates and directing credit to the predefined priority sectors. As indicated above, the amended objectives of monetary policy are still broad. They cover most objectives that were intended to be replaced by the 200 amendments. However, a narrow interpretation of the objectives of monetary policy indicates that the CBSL carries responsibility for the design and conduct of monetary policy to achieve economic and price stability, while simultaneously sustaining financial stability. As price stability is essential for financial and economic stability, it is plausible that the apparent multiple objectives set for monetary policy concertina into the single monetary policy objective of price stability.

Monetary policy operations influence the cost and availability of credit. The CBSL possesses a number of instruments to conduct monetary policy. The main instruments are open market operations; statutory reserve requirements; the bank rate (discount rate); foreign-exchange operations; quantitative restrictions on credits; interest rate ceilings; refinancing facilities; and moral suasion. Sri Lanka started financial liberalization in 1977. Since then it has moved away from deployment of conventional instruments for monetary management, such as the bank rate and the required reserve ratio, towards market-oriented instruments. In a deregulated financial system, open market operations have acquired primary importance for achieving monetary policy objectives.

Until June 2001 Sri Lanka operated under a fixed peg exchange rate system. Presently it operates under a managed float system, under which market forces play a role in determining the rupee exchange rate. The CBSL has the option to intervene in the foreign-exchange market to prevent excessive exchange rate volatility. It also maintains what it considers an adequate level of foreign-exchange reserves to keep the exchange rate at a level consistent with its estimation of Sri Lanka's economic fundamentals. Sri Lanka maintains some administrative controls over capital flows as an instrument of financial stability.

Under its soft form of monetary targeting, the CBSL prepares a monetary programme after taking into account fiscal and balance-of-payments developments, economic growth and forecasted inflation. The monetary programme sets out the desired path for monetary growth and determines those quarterly bank reserves money-volume 'sub-targets' that, if achieved, will yield the target money-growth rate. The CBSL conducts open market operations on a weekly cycle to achieve the reserve money target. The policy interest rate is reviewed and adjusted as and when necessary to maintain the target growth rate of reserve money.

Monetary Policy Transmission Mechanisms in Sri Lanka

The CBSL deploys two overnight interest rates as the policy rates for the conduct of monetary policy. They are the repurchase (repo) rate (the borrowing rate) and the reverse repurchase rate (the lending rate). Changes in these rates impact on interest rates in the interbank call money markets. Changes in the call money-market rates change short-term interest rates such as yields on Treasury bills and the deposit and lending rates of commercial banks. Changes in market interest rates alter aggregate demand that, subsequently, affects output and prices given aggregate supply. The transmission mechanisms of monetary policy suggested in Figure 11.1

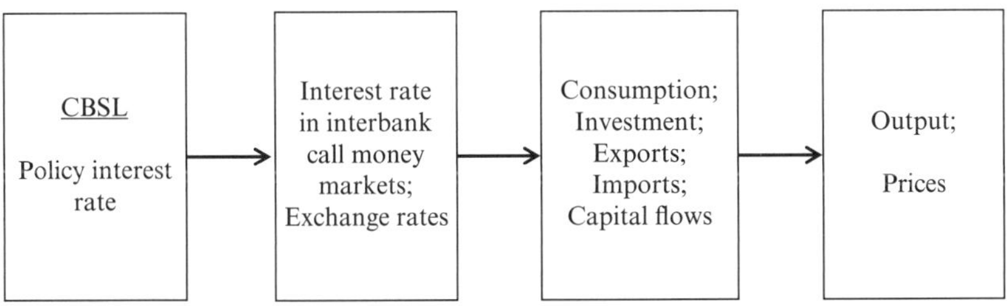

Figure 11.1 Monetary policy transmission mechanisms in Sri Lanka

rely on the assumption of short-run price and wage rigidities. If prices are unhedged, a change in the nominal interest rate represents a corresponding change in the real interest rate.[3]

MACROECONOMIC DEVELOPMENTS AND INFLATION PERFORMANCE

During the 1950s and 1960s Sri Lanka pursued an import-substituting strategy of development. Under this strategy, government provided a high degree of protection both to the traditional primary industries, including agriculture, and nascent secondary industries. Macroeconomic management in general relied heavily on regulatory mechanisms, together with controls over interest rates, exchange rates and capital flows. Emphasis was given to the promotion of large-scale enterprises covering industry, trade, transport, banking and insurance (Bruton, 1992: Kelegama and Wignaraja, 1991).

In a socialist policy framework, the government expanded social welfare policies, including free services in health and education and a free food-rationing scheme for the entire population. Government's pricing policies and subsidies on public utilities were designed to keep the prices of essential goods and services at low levels. Over time, given the competitive multi-party political system, the industrial and social welfare policies of the two major political parties converged. Consequently, government interventionism in economic activity grew. Not until the mid 1970s, when Sri Lanka experienced major economic crisis around its heavily negative and unstable current account of the balance-of-payments (Athukorala and Jayasuriya, 1994), could the idea of a smaller economic role of government be entertained.

Sri Lanka began experiencing serious macroeconomic imbalances in the late 1960s. They became more pronounced following the first OPEC oil price shock in 1973 and the consequent recession across the developed world. In Sri Lanka, economic growth slowed to less than 3 per cent and the unemployment rate climbed to about 20 per cent in the 1970s (discussion in this section uses the data provided in Table 11.1). The public sector became highly inefficient. The increasingly complex regulatory system stifled the growth of private enterprises. A comprehensive social welfare programme kept budget deficits relatively high. Budget deficits were largely monetized, fuelling high and volatile inflation. For political expediency, the social welfare programme became a permanent fixture and no political party was willing to reduce or withdraw social welfare services for fear of electoral defeat.

Table 11.1 Macroeconomic indicators, Sri Lanka, 1951–2012

Macroeconomic indicators	1951–55	1956–60	1961–65	1966–70	1971–75	1976–80	1981–85	1986–90	1991–95	1996–2000	2001–05	2006–10	2011	2012
Budget balance (% of GDP)	n.a.	n.a.	n.a.	n.a.	n.a.	n.a.	n.a.	−7.6	−7.9	−7.8	−8.0	−7.7	−6.9	−6.2
Money-growth rate (%)														
Narrow money growth	4.0	2.6	7.3	2.8	9.5	25.2	15.0	16.4	13.8	9.6	14.5	12.4	7.4	2.3
Broad money growth	5.2	5.2	8.6	6.3	8.9	35.0	19.0	12.6	23.5	13.3	16.2	15.5	19.1	17.5
Real GDP growth (%)	n.a.	n.a.	n.a.	5.4	2.6	5.5	5.2	3.4	5.4	5.0	4.0	6.4	8.2	6.4
GDP per capita, current prices, US dollar	n.a.	n.a.	n.a.	n.a.	n.a.	301	359	454	640	878	1012	1917	2880	2890
Unemployment rate (%)	n.a.	n.a.	n.a.	n.a.	n.a.	n.a.	n.a.	15.9	13.7	9.5	8.2	5.9	4.9	4.9
CPI inflation rate (%)	0.8	0.6	1.7	4.2	7.5	10.3	12.2	12.5	10.3	9.1	9.8	11.6	6.7	6.8
Current account balance (% of GDP)	n.a.	n.a.	n.a.	n.a.	n.a.	−19.3	−9.5	−7.5	−6.8	−4.5	−1.7	−4.4	−7.7	−5.4
Nominal interest rate (%)														
Treasury bill rate	n.a.	n.a.	n.a.	n.a.	n.a.	n.a.	13.3	12.1	15.2	14.3	11.0	13.6	7.6	12.1
Deposit rate of interest	n.a.	n.a.	n.a.	n.a.	n.a.	10.5	18.2	14.6	13.3	10.3	7.4	8.9	6.4	8.7
Real interest rate (%)[a]														
Treasury bill rate	n.a.	n.a.	n.a.	n.a.	n.a.	n.a.	1.3	−0.3	4.5	4.8	1.0	2.0	0.9	4.9
Deposit rate of interest	n.a.	n.a.	n.a.	n.a.	n.a.	−4.8	5.6	1.9	2.8	1.1	−2.2	−2.1	−0.3	1.7
Nominal exchange rate (Rp per US dollar)	4.8	4.8	4.8	5.5	6.4	13.0	23.2	33.1	46.8	65.3	96.7	110.2	110.6	127.6
Bilateral real exchange rate[b]	26.0	27.2	27.7	32.4	36.1	75.5	100.9	106.7	100.7	98.4	108.4	83.1	69.2	76.3

Notes:
n.a. = not available
a. Real interest rate is estimated as: 100(((1 + interest rate)/(1 + inflation rate))−1) where the interest rate and inflation rate are expressed in decimal.
b. Real exchange rate: data for the period 1951–70 represents the bilateral real exchange rate of the Sri Lankan rupee against the US dollar. A rise in the index value of the exchange rate represents appreciation.

Source: Author's computation based on IMF, *International Financial Statistics*; IMF, *World Economic Outlook*; and country-specific publications of the IMF website.

Sri Lanka came under pressure from some of its foreign aid donors to undertake policy reform that could reduce these macroeconomic imbalances. By the mid 1970s, the controlled economic system had become unsustainable. The volume of social welfare became an issue with the economy in the midst of a balance-of-payments crisis. This created an environment for a political change.

After the 1977 general elections, the new government under J.R. Jayawardene undertook comprehensive deregulation and liberalization measures aimed at removing state control and intervention in most economic activities. The dual exchange rate system, which had been in place since the early 1960s, was modified by a unified exchange rate system after implementing a major devaluation of the rupee. The system of exchange controls and import quotas was dismantled, controls over foreign-exchange transactions were relaxed and controls over interest rates were eased. Importantly, the government reduced the level of subsidies on essential items. Food subsidies were reduced and linked to family income under a food stamp scheme. The free rationing of rice was also restructured. The banking sector was opened up to competition by permitting entry both of domestic and foreign firms to the sector. Foreign banks were allowed to open branches and some new private sector banks were permitted to open. The rupee devaluation geared domestic production towards the tradable products sector. Domestic and foreign investment in export-oriented industries was encouraged. Reform initiatives did not, however, have any major impact on the economy. Deep structural reform in the economy was needed to promote sustained economic growth to reduce the incidence of poverty (Gunatilleke et al., 1994).

In 1987–90 several structural reform measures to improve macroeconomic management were undertaken. Budget deficits were lowered. Current account deficits were reduced by depreciating the real exchange rate. Inflation was brought under control through restrictive monetary policy. Efforts were made to raise economic growth and create jobs in the private sector. The private sector was encouraged to enter into such activities as insurance, banking, transport and communication. In the past, these activities were reserved for the public sector.

From the 1990s, and extending through to the mid 2000s, these policy measures were taken further. The government pursued an extensive privatization programme aimed at fiscal consolidation to reduce the level of budget deficits over the medium term. The proceeds of privatization of public enterprises were applied towards balancing budgets. In 1994 a complete liberalization of current account transactions took place, followed from 1997 onwards by selective liberalization of capital account transactions. The rupee was floated in 2001. In the meantime, the export-oriented industrialization policy was strengthened. Tax reforms and incentives were extended to the private sector to enhance investment in expanding the productive capacity of Sri Lankan export-oriented industries.

Since the long-awaited end of the civil war in 2008, Sri Lanka has made efforts to bring inflation under control through economic stabilization. These efforts were hampered almost immediately when economic growth fell sharply in 2009 as a consequence of the US-global financial crisis. The economy found itself unable to recover before 2010. Currently, Sri Lanka appears to be making efforts at developing its financial sector towards a point at which inflation targeting can be adopted for the purpose of institutionalizing monetary policy for price stability. Flexible exchange rate systems are well known to be able to absorb external shocks to a significant degree; however, flexible exchange rates are at risk of suffering from excessive volatility during periods of large-scale capital flows generated by economic shocks.[4]

Summing Up

Over the past three decades the Sri Lankan economy has been transformed from a highly regulated economy into an open, market-oriented economy without suffering serious adjustment costs. The sphere of private sector activity has expanded significantly while the scope of public sector activity has fallen somewhat. The political system has changed steadily from self-defeating social welfare-oriented politics to the politics of economic growth and stability while ensuring social equity and justice. Economic reform was, however, slow during the three decade-long civil war. Despite thoroughgoing restructuring that has accelerated during the past two decades, further deep economic and financial reforms are therefore needed to consolidate the gains that Sri Lanka has made since the early 1980s.

Inflation and Inflation Volatility

Figures 11.2a and 11.2b display inflation and inflation volatility in Sri Lanka across 1958q2–2012q4. Inflation in Sri Lanka has remained relatively high and volatile since the early 1970s. Despite something of an easing of the average inflation rate since the mid 1990s, inflation has remained highly volatile throughout. From the early 2000s inflation began trending upwards again, with large budget deficits having created growing inflationary pressure. With policy directed at development of Sri Lanka's capital market, the government appears to have embarked on a programme of preparations to adopt inflation targeting when the economy is in a position to sustain it.

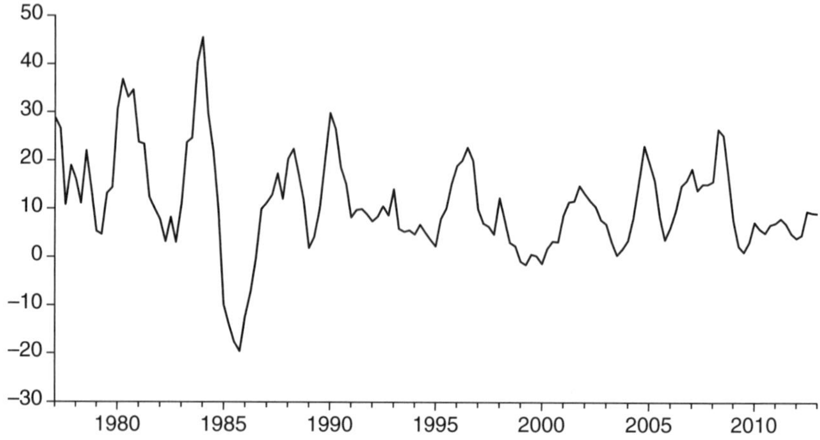

Figure 11.2a *Quarter-on-quarter CPI inflation in Sri Lanka, 1977q1–2012q4*

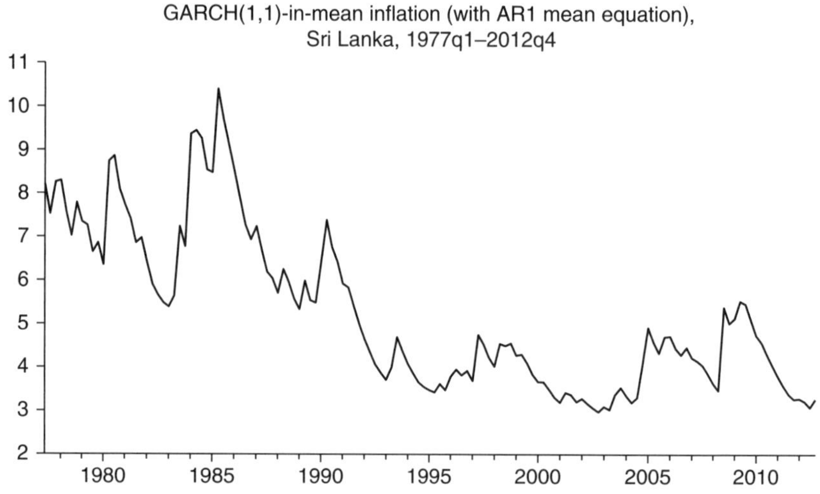

Figure 11.2b *Conditional standard deviation of CPI inflation in Sri Lanka, 1977q1–2012q4*

Inflation Persistence

Inflation in Sri Lanka exhibits a high degree of measured persistence across the study period. This is reflected in the high and stable coefficient value on the one-period lagged rate of inflation in an autoregressive model

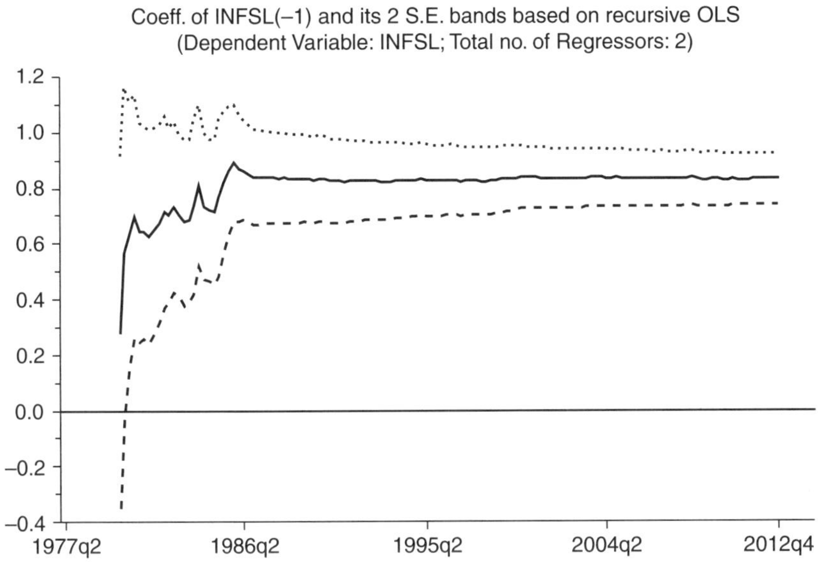

Note: INFSL = CPI inflation in Sri Lanka.

Figure 11.3a Recursive estimates of the coefficient on the one-period lagged rate of CPI inflation in Sri Lanka

AR(1), estimated by both the recursive and rolling regression techniques (Figures 11.3a and 11.3b). Rolling estimates of the coefficient on the one-period lagged rate of inflation suggest that the coefficient value has remained unchanged since the 1990s. High persistence of inflation is generally associated with low credibility of monetary policy. Given high and volatile inflation over decades, it is likely that high inflationary expectations are embedded in Sri Lankan economic activity, leaving monetary policy with little or no credibility in its efficacy to achieve and maintain low and stable inflation. A further factor embedding high inflation in the Sri Lankan system is the fact that the CBSL also does not have much autonomy in conducting monetary policy for price stability. The objectives of monetary policy, revised in 2002, have in practice remained broad and ambiguous despite the superficial appearance of having become narrower and more focused. Unless deep reforms are implemented, including statutory reform to reduce or remove the deeply installed fiscal influence on monetary policy formulation, it is highly unlikely that monetary policy can develop sufficient credibility of its own accord to enable it to achieve and maintain low and stable inflation for Sri Lanka. Table 11.2 reports the unit root test results for inflation over the period 1950–2012. The ADF and

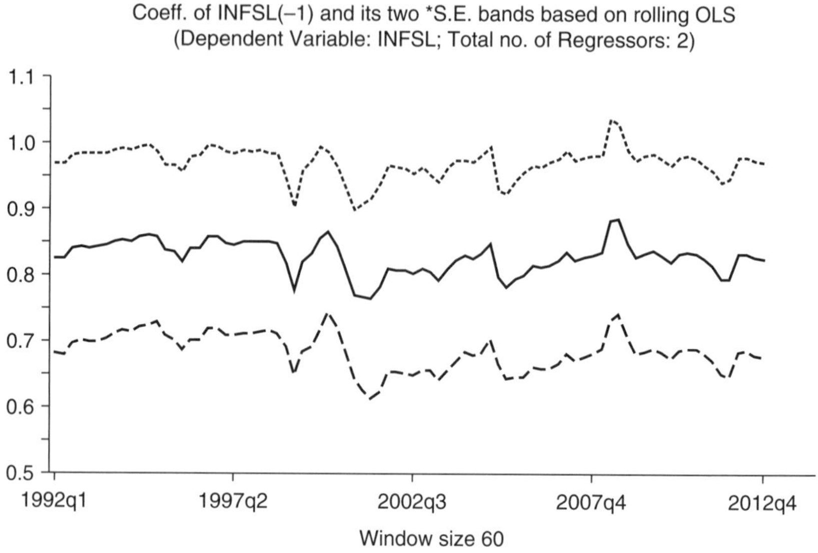

Figure 11.3b *Rolling sample estimates of the coefficient on the one-period lagged rate of CPI inflation in Sri Lanka*

KPSS tests reject the null hypothesis that inflation in Sri Lanka has a unit root. Sri Lankan inflation therefore has high persistence but no unit root.

Real Treasury Bill Rates

Sri Lanka has maintained a managed float exchange rate system since 2001. Figure 11.4a shows that, as expected under a pegged or managed float exchange rate system, there was a close association between the Treasury bill rate in Sri Lanka and the Federal funds rate in the United States. Figure 11.4b shows the real Treasury bill rate in Sri Lanka and the real Federal funds rate in the United States. The presence of real interest rate parity is thereby indicated, despite restricted capital flows.

Exchange Rates

Figure 11.5 plots the nominal and real effective exchange rates in Sri Lanka, displaying a steady depreciation in both rates since the mid 1980s. The real exchange rate is somewhat distinguished for its mild volatility. This suggests the question of whether Sri Lanka has at some time attempted a monetary policy strategy of real exchange rate targeting to enhance

Table 11.2 The unit root test results for CPI inflation in Sri Lanka

	Sample (adjusted)	Constant (C); Trend (T)	ADF test statistic (SBC-determined lag-length, l)	Inference at 5% level	The KPSS test statistic (Newey-West bandwidth)	Inference at 5% level	Sample (unadjusted)	Zivot-Andrews test statistic	Breakpoint	Inference at 5% level
LCPI	1951–2012	C and T	−2.64 (l = 1)	I(1)	0.238 (6)	I(1)	1949–2012	−3.74	1980	I(0)
LCPI	1951–2012	C	1.76(l = 1)	I(1)	0.982 (6)	I(1)	1949–2012	−3.97	1965	I(0)
Δ LCPI	1951–2012	C	−3.85 (l = 0)	I(0)	0.734 (5)	I(1)	1949–2012	−5.86	1978	I(0)

Note: LCPI = log of the consumer price index; ΔLCPI = first-order difference of LCPI; SBC = Schwarz Bayesian Criterion; ADF = augmented Dickey-Fuller; and KPSS = Kwiatkowski, Phillips, Schmidt and Shin.

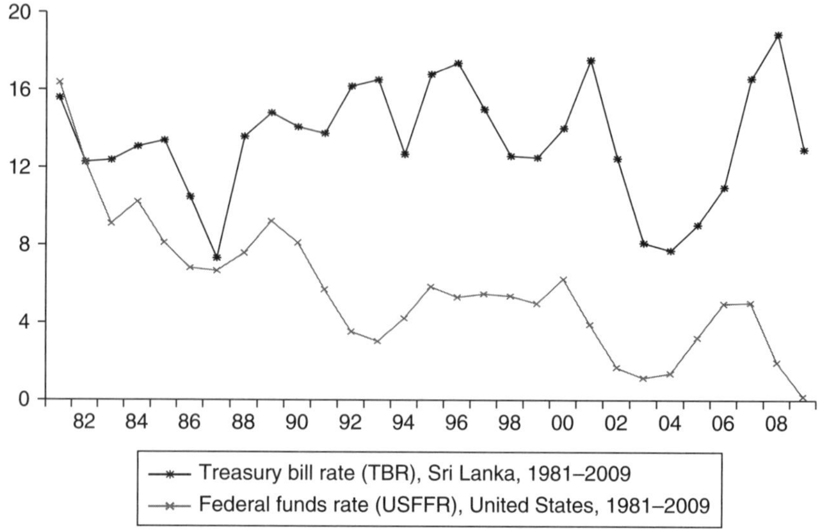

Figure 11.4a *The Treasury bill rate in Sri Lanka and the Federal funds rate in the United States, 1981–2009*

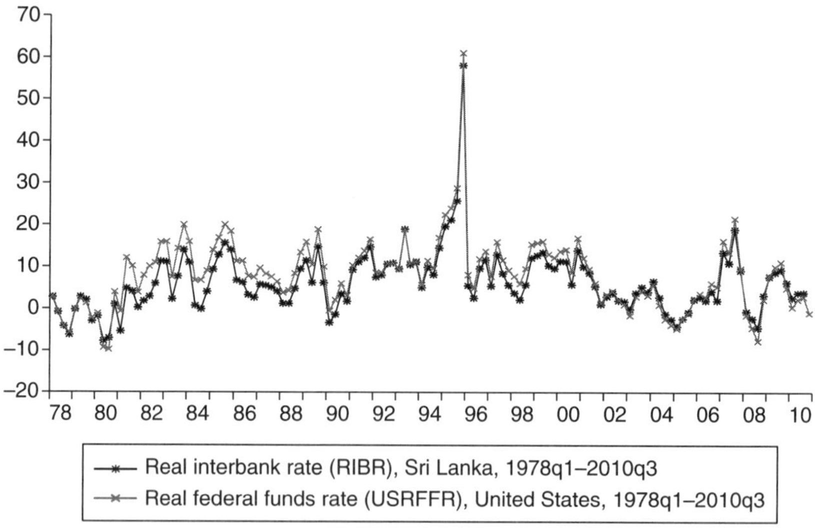

Figure 11.4b *The real interbank rate in Sri Lanka and the real Federal funds rate in the United States, 1978q1–2010q3*

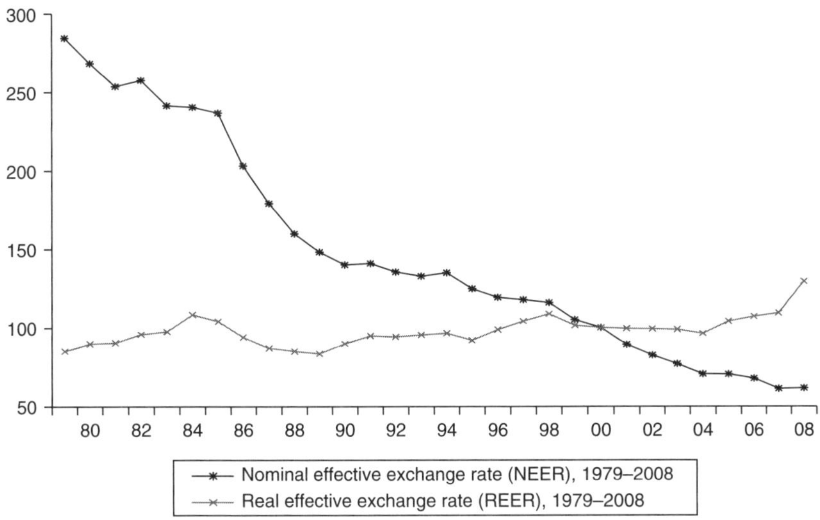

Figure 11.5 Nominal and real effective exchange rates in Sri Lanka, 1979–2008

exports. Symptoms of the long-run self-defeating strategy of real exchange rate targeting include high inflation or high real interest rates. Which of these is exhibited depends on the nature of the country's capital controls.

INFLATION, REAL INTEREST RATE, REAL EXCHANGE RATE AND REAL OUTPUT

One key problem for Sri Lankan monetary policy is that inflation persists both moderately high and highly volatile. Inflation volatility has decreased somewhat from the mid 1990s through the mid 2000s but remains relatively high, keeping the average rate unstable. Arguably, the relatively high volatility of moderately high average Sri Lankan inflation imposes an unacceptable level of opportunity cost on the economy. Because the nominal interest rate and the nominal exchange rate in Sri Lanka do not adjust fully to inflation differentials between Sri Lanka and its trading partners, high-inflation volatility in Sri Lanka leads to high volatility in both real interest rates and real exchange rates. The real interest rate and the real exchange rate have impacts on real output and its growth rate. Output growth in Sri Lanka remains highly volatile.

The Structural Vector Autoregressive (SVAR) Analysis

This subsection, using annual data, estimates a four-variable SVAR model for Sri Lanka to examine the interrelationships among inflation, the real interest rate, the real exchange rate and real output. The model is formulated on the assumption that inflation has a contemporaneous feedback relation with the real interest rate and the real exchange rate. All three variables impact real output. The order of variables in the model is arranged as follows: INFSL, RTBR, LREER and LRGDP where INFSL is the inflation rate in Sri Lanka, RTBR is the real Treasury bill rate, LREER is the log of the real effective exchange rate and LRGDP is the log of real GDP. The unit root test results suggest that while inflation, the real interest rate and the real exchange rate appear stationary, real output is nonstationary. Two versions of the model are then estimated and deployed to generate impulse responses and forecast error-variance decompositions. The first version of the model is defined as: INFSL, RTBR, LREER and LRGDP while the second version of the model is defined as: INFSL, RTBR, LREER and DLRGDP. In the second version of the model, all the variables are stationary; in the first version real output is nonstationary. The results generated from the second model are reported, as the respective outputs of both models are qualitatively similar. Figure 11.6 plots data deployed for estimation purposes.

The impulse responses in Figure 11.7 suggest the interrelations among the four variables in the SVAR model. The model does not include the ultimate source of inflation, monetary expansion. High and volatile inflation have monetary roots. When the rate of inflation is low, it is difficult to identify the key sources of inflation, since both demand and supply shocks overwhelm the impacts of core sources of inflation such as money growth. The relationship becomes more readily visible when inflation is high and sustained. The consensus view is that for developing countries, budget deficits constitute an important source of monetary growth and its frequent outcome: inflation. In such cases, the relationships among budget deficits, money growth and inflation are pronounced and readily detectable. There is causative feedback from inflation to budget deficits. For example, an increased rate of inflation reduces the real value of tax revenues. In consequence, budget deficits are raised to compensate for the loss of official revenues, causing faster money growth and hence a higher inflation rate.

The impulse response results should be taken as indicative, not conclusive. As suggested by the Fisher relation, a rise in inflation reduces the real rate of interest if the nominal interest rate does not adjust fully to the expected rise in inflation. The impulse response decomposition indicates that the nominal interest rate responds only slowly to a rise in inflation.

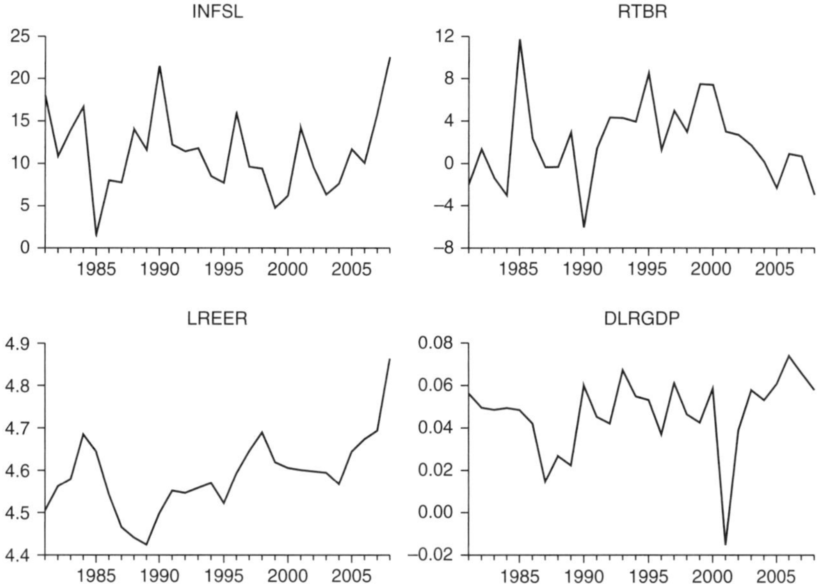

Note: Definitions of variables: INFSL = CPI inflation in Sri Lanka; RTBR = real Treasury bill rate; LREER = log of the real effective exchange rate of the rupee; and DLRGDP = first-order difference in the log of real GDP.

Figure 11.6 Data deployed for estimation of the SVAR model for Sri Lanka

A decrease in the real interest rate is generally expected to raise investment in theory, but this is an unlikely channel of influence in developing countries. A very low or negative real interest rate, caused by high inflation given unchanged nominal interest rates, creates financial repression. This reduces the levels of saving, investment and economic growth. High and volatile inflation creates other macroeconomic problems. A rise in inflation appreciates the real exchange rate, in turn simultaneously feeding back into the rate of inflation and feeding into economic growth. The real interest rate responds positively to an appreciation of the real exchange rate. This is because, following the open-economy real exchange rate parity condition, a grossly appreciated real exchange rate induces capital flight, thereby requiring the real interest rate to rise as an inducement to slow down or halt that capital flight. If stringent capital controls are in place in one country or more, there can be short-run deviation of real interest rates across countries. However, for many countries capital controls are not effective, irrespective of the range of official regulations and controls

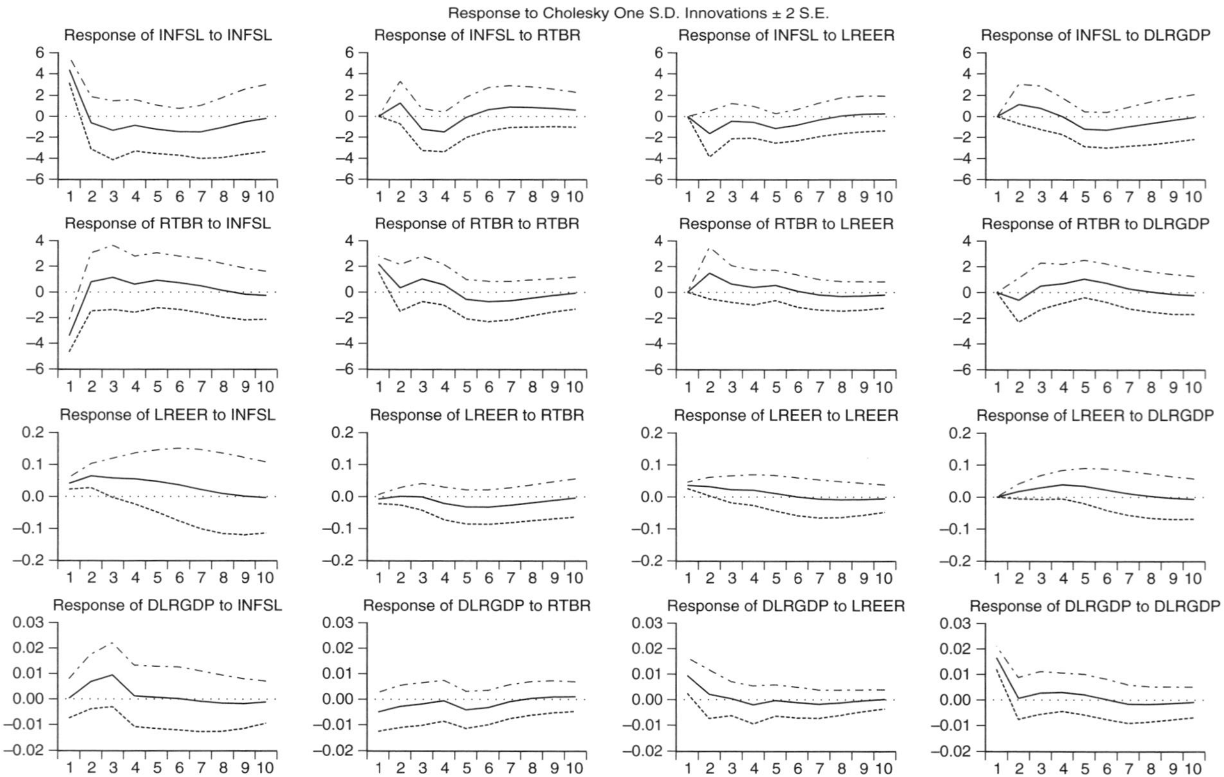

Note: Definitions of variables: INFSL = CPI inflation in Sri Lanka; RTBR = real Treasury bill rate; LREER = log of the real effective exchange rate of the rupee; and DLRGDP = first-order difference in the log of real GDP.

Figure 11.7 Impulse responses for variables in the SVAR model for Sri Lanka available to authorities. In general, an appreciation of the real exchange rate alters both trade and capital flows, while changes in the real interest rate alter the levels of saving and investment.

The overall results suggest significant interrelations among inflation, the real interest rate, the real exchange rate and output growth. While not investigated here, an expanded model is expected to show the impacts of the real interest and exchange rates on saving, investment and both trade and capital flows. The key message to emerge from the empirical results is that inflation and its volatility are not innocuous in relation to the rate and volatility of economic growth. The rate of inflation influences both the real interest rate and the real exchange rate and they, in turn, impact upon saving, investment and economic growth. This suggests the need for low, and stable, inflation as a platform from which the potential for a high, sustained and steady long-run rate of economic growth can be maximized.

Table 11.3 presents the forecast error-variance decompositions of INFSL, RTBR, LREER and DLRGDP. The numbers represent those percentages of forecast error variance of variables in the model that can be attributed to own innovations and those percentages of forecast error variance that originate in the innovations of other variables. The results show that for all four of the specified variables, the dominant source of the forecast error variance is own innovations. The extent of this influence across the full ten-year time horizon amounts to 59 per cent for inflation, 26 per cent for the real interest rate, 13 per cent for the real exchange rate and 49 per cent for real GDP growth. In the case of real output growth, innovations in the real interest rate and the real exchange rate jointly account for 27 per cent of real output growth's forecast error variance. The corresponding share of inflation is 24 per cent. The conclusion suggested is that Sri Lankan real output growth is highly sensitive to inflation and its volatility.

MONETARY AND EXCHANGE RATE POLICY ISSUES

One of the reasons for the abandonment of monetary targeting in many countries has been the alleged instability of the money-demand function. Until recently the prevailing view was that monetary targeting for price stability requires a stable money-demand function to establish causal linkage between money supply growth and inflation. The recent literature suggests that a causal relation between money supply growth and inflation exists irrespective both of the exchange rate regime and whether or not the money-demand function is stable (McCallum and Nelson,

Table 11.3 Forecast error-variance decomposition of variables in the SVAR model for Sri Lanka

Variance Decomposition of INFSL:					
Period	S.E.	INFSL	RTBR	LREER	DLRGDP
1	4.377	100.00	0.00	0.00	0.00
2	5.033	77.26	6.55	10.89	5.30
5	6.103	63.62	14.78	12.36	9.25
10	7.094	58.90	16.84	10.96	13.31
Variance Decomposition of RTBR:					
Period	S.E.	INFSL	RTBR	LREER	DLRGDP
1	4.055	71.11	28.89	0.00	0.00
2	4.444	62.26	24.60	11.30	1.84
5	5.148	55.73	24.63	11.59	8.04
10	5.436	52.89	26.32	11.26	9.53
Variance Decomposition of LREER:					
Period	S.E.	INFSL	RTBR	LREER	DLRGDP
1	0.056	55.22	2.03	42.75	0.00
2	0.094	68.15	0.75	27.35	3.75
5	0.154	62.04	6.57	14.80	16.59
10	0.171	57.73	13.38	12.79	16.09
Variance Decomposition of DLRGDP:					
Period	S.E.	INFSL	RTBR	LREER	DLRGDP
1	0.019	0.01	6.46	22.96	70.57
2	0.021	10.30	7.41	20.90	61.39
5	0.024	23.60	9.26	16.73	50.42
10	0.025	23.53	10.89	16.76	48.82
The Cholesky Ordering: INFSL RTBR LREER DLRGDP					

Note: Definitions of variables: INFSL = CPI inflation in Sri Lanka; RTBR = real Treasury bill rate; LREER = log of the real effective exchange rate of the rupee; and DLRGDP = first-order difference of the log of real GDP.

2011). Based on this view it is suggested that under a flexible exchange rate system, rule-based monetary policy may take the form of monetary targeting or inflation targeting. Nevertheless, this section tests for the presence of a stable money-demand function in Sri Lanka.[5] For estimation purposes, an open-economy money-demand function is specified as follows:

$$LRJM_t = \alpha_0 + \alpha_1 Ly_t + a_2 NIR_t + \alpha_3 FIR_t + \alpha_4 LRER_t + \alpha_5 \pi_t^v + u_t \quad (11.1)$$

where LRJM (J = N, B) is the log of real money balances (LRNM for narrowly defined money or LRBM for broadly defined money), Ly is the log of real income, NIR is a representative domestic interest rate, FIR is a representative foreign interest rate such as the US Treasury bill rate (USTBR), LRER is the log of a representative real exchange rate such as the real effective exchange rate (REER), π_t^v is a measure of inflation volatility and u_t is a random error term with zero mean and constant variance. In this specification, real income represents a scale variable and its coefficient is expected to bear a positive sign. The value of this coefficient is expected to be greater than one given the rapid structural change and monetization transforming the Sri Lankan economy. The coefficients on the domestic and foreign interest rates are expected to bear negative signs. However, as discussed in Appendix 5, the signs of the coefficients on the real exchange rate and inflation volatility remain a priori indeterminate.

The unit root test results suggest that each variable in the specified model has a unit root. Consequently, all the variables in the specified money-demand function are eligible for cointegration testing. Preliminary estimation results suggest that the deposit rate of interest in Sri Lanka and the US Federal funds rate (USFFR) become significant when one of them is used in the model. The model is then estimated using the USFFR as the opportunity cost variable. The USFFR is considered more appropriate as it has historically been largely market determined, while the Sri Lanka deposit interest rate was institutionally determined until the 2000s.

Table 11.4 reports both the autoregressive distributed lag (ARDL) and ordinary least squares (OLS) results for real narrow money-demand function. To conserve space, the results obtained by a broad definition of money are not reported. The results obtained by the ARDL model are found superior to those obtained by OLS/dynamic OLS (DOLS). The results suggest the presence of a strong form of long-run cointegral relationship among real narrow money balances, real income, the US Federal funds rate, the real exchange rate and inflation volatility. The estimated coefficient values are consistent with a priori predictions. The CUSUM and CUSUMSQ of residuals in Figure 11.8 suggest that the real narrow money-demand function remained stable for the study period.

As expected, real income remains the core determinant of narrow money-demand. The income elasticity of demand for real narrow money balances is below one. This is an unexpected finding for a developing country like Sri Lanka. The coefficient on LREER, as proxy for the real exchange rate, bears a positive sign and is statistically significant. Inflation instability bears a negative sign in the narrow money-demand function. It implies that as inflation instability rises, demand for the most highly liquid

Table 11.4 The ARDL and OLS regression results for real narrow money-demand relationships in Sri Lanka

F-statistic	9.88			
W-statistic	49.42			
Critical value bounds	F-test	W-test		
90%	(2.61, 3.75)	(13.03, 18.74)		
95%	(3.15, 4.38)	(15.76, 21.92)		
Sample period	1967–2012	1966–2012	1965–2012	1965–2012
	ARDL (1,0,1,1,0)	ARDL (1,0,1,1,0)	OLS	OLS
	(Selected based on SBC)	Long-run model	(Static model)	(Dynamic model)
Regressors	Coefficient (t-ratio) [prob.]	Coefficient (t-ratio) [prob.]	Coefficient (t-ratio) [prob.]	Coefficient (t-ratio) [prob.]
Intercept	4.66 (4.92) [0.00]	9.48 (57.08) [0.00]	9.48 (69.22) [0.00]	8.25 (11.30) [0.00]
LRNM(−1)	0.51 (5.09) [0.00]			0.14 (1.71) [0.94]
LRGDP	0.12 (2.08) [0.04]	0.25 (3.23) [0.00]	0.46 (8.57) [0.00]	0.38 (5.37) [0.00]
USFFR	−0.01 (−0.38) [0.70]	−0.04 (−3.66) [0.00]	−0.01 (−1.63) [0.11]	−0.01 (−1.73) [0.09]
USFER(−1)	−0.02 (−3.35) [0.00]			
LRER	−0.03 (−0.34) [0.74]	0.44 (4.86) [0.00]	0.18 (3.32) [0.00]	0.17 (3.22) [0.00]
LRER(−1)	0.24 (2.43) [0.02]			
INFVOL	−0.04 (−1.94) [0.06]	−0.08 (−1.85) [0.07]	−0.04 (−1.24) [0.22]	−0.05 (−1.52) [0.14]
Diagnostics				
Adjusted R^2	0.98		0.93	0.94

Lagrange multiplier test for serial correlation	F(1,37) = 1.63 [0.21]		F(1,42) = 32.29 [0.00]	F(1,45) = 3.74 [0.06]
Ramsey's RESET test of functional form mis-specification	F(1,37) = 1.11 [0.30]		F(1,42) = 0.08 [0.78]	F(1,41) = 2.18 [0.15]
Normality of residuals	$\chi^2_{(2)} = 0.39$ [0.82]		$\chi^2_{(2)} = 0.90$ [0.64]	$\chi^2_{(2)} = 0.39$ [0.82]
Heteroskedasticity	F(1,44) = 0.50 [0.48]		F(1,46) = 2.19 [0.15]	F(1,46) = 4.33 [0.04]
The Wald test:				
H_O: Coefficient on LRGDP = 0		$\chi^2_{(1)} = 10.42$ [0.00]	$\chi^2_{(1)} = 73.48$ [0.00]	
H_O: Coefficient on LRGDP = 1		$\chi^2_{(1)} = 90.95$ [0.00]	$\chi^2_{(1)} = 103.53$ [0.00]	
H_O: Coefficient on USFFR = 0		$\chi^2_{(1)} = 13.37$ [0.00]	$\chi^2_{(1)} = 2.64$ [0.10]	
H_O: Coefficient on LRER = 0		$\chi^2_{(1)} = 23.58$ [0.00]	$\chi^2_{(1)} = 11.02$ [0.00]	
H_O: Coefficient on INFVOL = 0		$\chi^2_{(1)} = 3.42$ [0.06]	$\chi^2_{(1)} = 1.53$ [0.22]	

Note: Definitions of variables: LRNM = log of real narrow money balances; LRGDP = log of real GDP; USFFR = US Federal funds rate; LRER = log of the real exchange rate; INFVOL = inflation volatility; ARDL = autoregressive distributed lag; and SBC = Schwarz Bayesian Criterion.

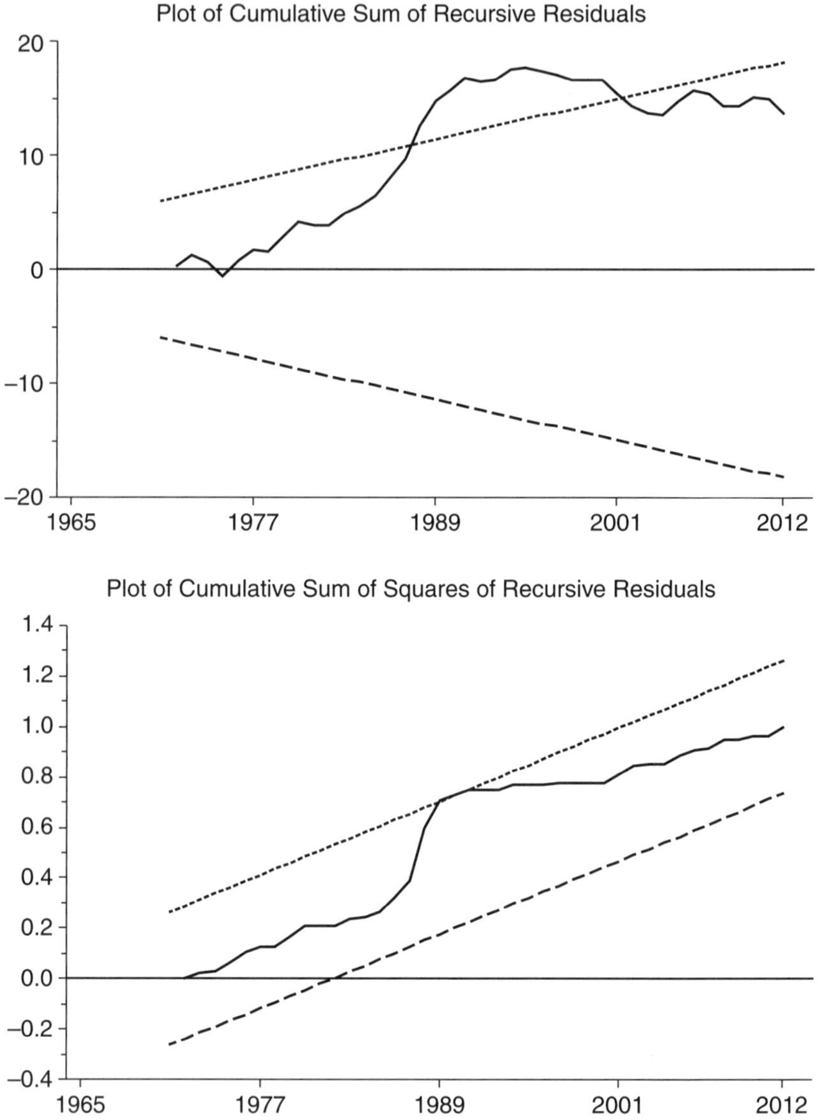

Note: The straight lines represent critical bounds at 5% significance level.

Figure 11.8 CUSUM and CUSUMSQ of residuals for real narrow money-demand relationships in Sri Lanka form of money falls. As expected, the US Federal funds rate bears a negative sign and is statistically highly significant.

Relationships Among Money, Output and Prices

Classical monetary theory suggests a causal linkage between money, output and prices. Table 11.5 reports the cointegration test results among money, output and prices. The Engle-Granger cointegration test results suggest a weak form of cointegral relationship among money, output and prices. The DOLS estimates suggest that either narrow or broad money is highly significant in the price level equation and that the coefficient value of broad money is significantly lower than one. Contrary to expectations, the real output coefficient bears a positive sign and is statistically highly significant.

Engle and Granger (1987) suggested that one of the implications of a cointegral relation between two nonstationary variables is the presence of long-term causality between them running in at least one direction. Table 11.6 reports the bivariate Granger-causality test results among LCPI, LNM (LBM) and LRGDP. Test results are generated within a vector error-correction (VEC) modelling framework after selecting the optimal lag-length using the Schwarz Bayesian Criterion (SBC). The test results suggest that for Sri Lanka, there is weak causality running from narrow or broad money growth to inflation. Either broad or narrow money growth is found to have a strong causal impact on output growth.

SUMMARY AND CONCLUSION

Sri Lanka is the fourth largest economy in South Asia. It has made significant economic and social progress since the 1950s, despite the damaging setbacks brought by long decades of civil war, and is well on the way to consolidating its position as a middle-income country. Since the 1950s through the 1970s Sri Lanka's economy performed at a moderately satisfactory level under the import-substituting strategy of industrialization. To promote import-substituting industries and to maintain a comprehensive social welfare system, the government created a highly regulated economy. Repression of the financial system can be singled out to have been a major influence stifling the growth of the private sector and retarding economic growth. Consequently, major imbalances emerged in Sri Lanka's economy in the late 1960s. These took a serious turn during the mid 1970s when the economy was hit by the OPEC's oil price shock. By that time a consensus had emerged among the political parties in Sri Lanka on the need to

Table 11.5 Cointegration test results among money, output and prices in Sri Lanka

Dependent variable = LCPI								
	Fully modified OLS				Dynamic OLS (lead = 1, lag = 1)			
With narrow money (NM)								
Regressor	coefficient	t-ratio	prob.		coefficient	t-ratio	prob.	
Intercept	−5.14	−33.99	0.00		−4.96	−45.84	0.00	
LNM	0.37	4.26	0.00		0.38	7.64	0.00	
LRGDP	1.12	4.43	0		1.12	7.58	0	
Sample period	1970–2012				1970–2011			
DW	0.54				1.38			
Adjusted R^2	0.99				0.99			
	tau-statistic	prob.	z-statistic	prob.	tau-statistic	prob.	z-statistic	prob.
The Engle-Granger cointegration tests	−3.42	0.14	−27.39	0.01	−3.42	0.14	−27.39	0.01
The Phillips-Ouliaris cointegration tests	−2.55	0.48	−12.83	0.37	−2.55	0.48	−12.83	0.37
With broad money (BM)								
Regressor	coefficient	t-ratio	prob.		coefficient	t-ratio	prob.	
Intercept	−4.61	−14.45	0.00		−4.55	−11.17	0.00	
LBM	0.32	3.03	0.00		0.34	2.87	0.01	
LRGDP	−1.03	2.68	0.01		1.01	2.29	0.03	
Sample period	1970–2012				1970–2011			
DW	0.41				0.53			
Adjusted R^2	0.99				0.99			
	tau-statistic	prob.	z-statistic	prob.	tau-statistic	prob.	z-statistic	prob.
The Engle-Granger cointegration tests	−1.82	0.81	−7.64	0.73	−1.82	0.81	−7.64	0.73
The Phillips-Ouliaris cointegration tests	−2.15	0.67	−10.42	0.53	−2.15	0.67	−10.42	0.53

Note: Definitions of variables: LCPI = log of the consumer price index; LNM = log of narrow money stock; LBM = log of broad money stock; and LRGDP = log of real GDP.

Table 11.6 Granger-causality among money, output and prices in Sri Lanka, 1965–2012

	Hypotheses No causality runs from:	Chi-square statistic (prob.)	Inference at 5% level
VEC specification	ΔLNM → ΔLCPI	1.10 (0.78)	Null hypothesis not rejected
(With narrow money, NM)	ΔLNM, ΔLRGDP → ΔLCPI	1.90 (0.93)	Null hypothesis not rejected
	ΔLCPI → ΔLNM	1.41 (0.70)	Null hypothesis not rejected
	ΔLRGDP → ΔLNM	5.57 (0.13)	Null hypothesis not rejected
	ΔLCPI → ΔLRGDP	2.36 (0.50)	Null hypothesis not rejected
	ΔLNM → ΔLRGDP	17.33 (0.00)	Null hypothesis rejected
VEC specification	ΔLBM → ΔLCPI	1.16 (0.76)	Null hypothesis not rejected
(With broad money, BM)	ΔLBM, ΔLRGDP → ΔLCPI	1.22 (0.75)	Null hypothesis not rejected
	ΔLCPI → ΔLBM	1.53 (0.68)	Null hypothesis not rejected
	ΔLRGDP → ΔLBM	4.79 (0.19)	Null hypothesis not rejected
	ΔLCPI → ΔLRGDP	2.83 (0.42)	Null hypothesis not rejected
	ΔLBM → ΔLRGDP	15.46 (0.00)	Null hypothesis rejected

Note: Definitions of variables: LCPI = log of the consumer price index; LNM = log of narrow money stock; LBM = log of broad money stock; and LRGDP = log of real GDP. Optimal lag-length = 2 (selected based on the Schwarz Bayesian Criterion, SBC).

undertake comprehensive economic reform, including financial deregulation and reform, to promote and sustain rapid economic growth.

Economic reforms began in 1977, but the reform process rapidly slowed down in the early 1980s with the outbreak of ethnic conflict between the minority Tamils and the majority Sinhalese, which quickly escalated to full-fledged civil war. The reform process restarted in the early 1990s, remarkably while the civil war continued to rage, but continued at only a slow and uneven pace. Nevertheless, Sri Lanka was able to maintain a moderately high rate of economic growth from the early 1980s through the early 2000s. This brought significant structural change in the economy and improved the balance of Sri Lanka's economic structure. This has served as a productive foundation upon which steady economic growth has been built and can continue in the future.

Since the late 2000s, Sri Lanka has effected major economic transition, from a civil war-torn economy to increasingly rapid economic growth. Economic fundamentals in Sri Lanka are strong, yielding great potential for rapid economic growth. The key issue remains improvement in the strategy of macroeconomic management to sustain rapid economic growth. Until the late 2000s, under conditions of war, the government was unable to maintain monetary and fiscal discipline to keep inflation low and stable. For sustained economic growth, both monetary and fiscal policies are important to maintain macroeconomic stability. As price stability is an important component of macroeconomic stability, monetary policy has gained importance in this respect.

As Sri Lanka's financial system is in transition, there is scope for improvement in monetary policy, to make price stability its sole or primary objective, both nominally and effectively. Sri Lanka's current monetary policy strategy of choice is a soft form of monetary targeting. The question remains whether Sri Lanka should continue with monetary targeting or move to inflation targeting when the economy, particularly the financial sector, becomes sufficiently developed to give effectiveness to inflation targeting. The advent of inflation targeting in Sri Lanka relies heavily on the flexibility of the exchange rate and the further development of the Sri Lankan money and capital markets. However, given that the foreign-exchange market in Sri Lanka remains thin and underdeveloped, it is plausible that a freely floating rupee would suffer from exchange rate volatility. To avoid financial instability, one policy option is to impose some market-based capital controls until the financial sector becomes sufficiently developed. Market-based capital controls may keep the exchange rate stable without adversely affecting the economy to any material degree, provided that the stance of monetary policy remains compatible with price stability and that no expansionist fiscal policy is undertaken, since this undermines the role of monetary policy in price stability. Fiscal dominance in monetary policy has diminished since the mid 1990s; however, it is still a factor to be considered for sustaining monetary and fiscal stability. Moreover, there is significant room to improve management of the banking sector through stronger prudential regulation and supervision. This is important under inflation targeting that requires the presence of a very flexible, preferably a floating, exchange rate system.

A major issue of relevance in the Sri Lankan monetary policy debate is whether the interest rate or a monetary aggregate should be used as the instrument of monetary policy. The basic proposition is that to maintain inflation low and stable, the money-growth rate should be low and stable on a sustained basis. This follows the monetary-neutrality proposition. Deployment of the interest rate as an instrument of monetary policy makes the money-growth rate unstable. This leads to unstable inflation, even though the inflation rate may remain low on average if the financial sector is sufficiently developed. The recent global experience of inflation targeting behaviour suggests that a short-term interest rate works best as an instrument of demand management in countries where the money and capital markets are developed. Problematically for the adoption of inflation targeting, the interest rate channel of monetary policy transmission remains relatively undeveloped in Sri Lanka. It is not known how changes in the nominal interest rate affect consumption and investment; however, there is evidence that the real exchange rate affects trade and capital flows. One plausible argument for deployment of the interest rate, however, remains that it may create some pressure on the Sri Lankan monetary authorities to undertake financial reform measures aimed at developing its money and capital markets.

A question that then arises is whether there exists scope for an alternative instrument of monetary policy demand management, such as a monetary aggregate. The deployment of a monetary aggregate under inflation targeting is broadly equivalent to monetary targeting with an inflation target. This chapter has examined some monetary relations, including the questions of whether the money-demand function remained stable in Sri Lanka over the study period and whether a causal linkage existed between money supply growth and inflation. The empirical results suggest that the narrow money-demand function in Sri Lanka remained stable over the study period. They also suggest the presence of a cointegration among money, output and prices. The short-run causal linkage between money supply growth and inflation is, however, weak. It is therefore not clear whether Sri Lanka should continue with monetary targeting for price stability or move to inflation targeting, under which a monetary aggregate can be used as an instrument of monetary policy. Whatever instrument of monetary policy is adopted, the ultimate objective of monetary policy should remain price stability for sustaining economic growth.

NOTES

1. Some general information on Sri Lanka is drawn from Sri Lanka, http://en.wikipedia.org/wiki/sri_Lanka.
2. Information on central banking and monetary policy in Sri Lanka is drawn from CBSL (1990).
3. For detailed discussion on monetary policy transmission mechanisms, see IMF (2004).
4. For discussion on recent developments in Sri Lanka, see the country-specific publications of the IMF, available at http://www.imf.org.
5. For early studies on money-demand behaviour in Sri Lanka, see Hossain and Rashid (1996), Weliwita and Ekanayake (1998), Rajapaksa (2004) and Narayan et al. (2009).

REFERENCES

Athukorala, P. (1998), *Trade Policy Issues in Asian Development*, London: Routledge.

Athukorala, P. (2004), 'Growth of manufactured exports and terms of trade, Sri Lanka: pessimism confounded', in S. Kelegama (ed.), *Economic Policy Issues and Debates in Sri Lanka: Essays in Honour of Gamini Corea*, New Delhi: Sage, pp. 37–53.

Athukorala, P.C. (2007), 'Outward-oriented policy reforms and industrialisation in Sri Lanka', *Economic Papers*, **26**(4), 372–91.

Athukorala, P. and F. Huyah (1987), *Export Instability and Growth*, London: Croom Helm.

Athukorala, P. and S. Jayasuriya (1994), *Macroeconomic Policies: Crises and Growth in Sri Lanka, 1969–1990*, Washington, DC: World Bank.

Athukorala, P. and S. Rajapatirana (2000), *Liberalisation and Industrial Transformation: Sri Lanka in International Perspective*, Oxford: Oxford University Press.

Bruton, H.J. (1992), *The Political Economy of Poverty, Equity and Growth: Sri Lanka and Malaysia*, New York: Oxford University Press.

CBSL (Central Bank of Sri Lanka) (1990), *40th Anniversary Commemorative Volume of the Central Bank of Sri Lanka, 1950–1990*, Colombo: Central Bank of Sri Lanka.

Engle, R.F. and C.W.J. Granger (1987), 'Co-integration and error-correction: representation, estimation, and testing', *Econometrica*, **55**(2), 251–76.

Gunatilleke, G., M. Perara, R, A.M.C. Wanigaratne et al. (1994), 'Sri Lanka', in M.G. Quibria (ed.), *Rural Poverty in Developing Asia*, Vol. 1, Hong Kong; Oxford University Press.

Hewavitharana, B. (1984), 'New patterns of developments for Sri Lanka', in P.K. Ghosh (ed.), *Developing South Asia: A Modernisation Perspective*, London: Westport, pp. 123–78.

Hossain, A. and S. Rashid (1996), *In Quest of Development: The Political Economy of South Asia*, Dhaka: University Press.
IMF (International Monetary Fund) (various years), *International Financial Statistics*, Washington, DC: IMF.
IMF (International Monetary Fund) (various years), *World Economic Outlook*, Washington, DC: IMF.
IMF (International Monetary Fund) (2004), 'The transmission mechanisms of monetary policy in Sri Lanka', in *Sri Lanka: Selected Issues and Statistical Appendix*, *IMF Country Report No. 04/69*, Washington, DC: IMF, pp. 3–13.
Kelegama, S. and G. Wignaraja (1991), 'Trade policy and industrial development in Sri Lanka', *Morga Quarterly Journal*, **2**(4), 27–53.
McCallum, B.T. and E. Nelson (2011), 'Money and inflation: some critical issues', in B.M. Friedman and M. Woodford (eds), *Handbook of Monetary Economics*, Vol. 3A, Amsterdam: Elsevier Science, pp. 97–153.
Narayan, P.K., V. Mishra and S. Narayan (2009), 'Estimating [money] demand function for South Asian countries', *Empirical Economics*, **36**(3), 685–96.
Rajapaksa, R.P.C.R. (2004), 'The money demand function for Sri Lanka for the period 1960–2002', *Social System Studies*, **8**, March, 51–73.
Snodgrass, D.R. (1966), *Ceylon: An Export Economy in Transition*, Homewood, IL: Richard D. Irwin.
Snodgrass, D.R. (1988), 'The economic development of Sri Lanka: a tale of missed opportunities', in R.I. Rotberg (ed.), *Creating Peace in Sri Lanka: Civil War and Reconciliation*, Washington, DC: Brookings Institution Press, pp. 89–107.
Weliwita, A. and E.M. Ekanayake (1998), 'Demand for money in Sri Lanka during the post 1977 period: a cointegration and error-correction analysis', *Applied Economics*, **30**, 1219–29.

12. Thailand

Thailand has one of the largest economies in Southeast Asia, second only to that of Indonesia. The Thai population numbers about 64 million. Thailand is the location of one of humanity's earliest civilizations. In the present day, it is a multi-ethnic society. About 75 per cent of Thai people are ethnically Thai, 14 per cent are Chinese, 3 per cent are Malay and the remainder have other ethnic origins. About 95 per cent of Thai people are Buddhist. Some southern states of Thailand are inhabited by Malay Muslims. The Thai culture has been influenced heavily both by Indian and Chinese culture and tradition.

Thailand is a constitutional monarchy. Absolute monarchy ended in 1932 following a bloodless revolution. A unique political feature of Thai history is that it is the only country in Southeast Asia that was not colonized by any European nation. Consequently, Thailand has inherited long-established political institutions compatible with its long history and associated culture and traditions. Nevertheless, Thailand has undergone a series of political upheavals since the 1940s. While other countries in the region have established democratic institutions, Thailand's democratic experimentation has so far failed to establish a durable political structure and culture to complement its steady economic progress and rising political clout in the region.

Thailand came under Japanese occupation during World War II. Since then political instability has been a recurrent phenomenon in this country. Military coup d'états were routine until the 1980s; a succession of military regimes replaced one another while, notably, leaving the monarchical system intact. From the 1980s the country was able to begin making some progress towards a democratic system. This lasted only until the military took over government once again in May 2014. In 1997 a revised constitution established a bicameral legislative system. Some other measures were imposed to strengthen the stability of democratically elected governments. There were some indications that democratic traditions were establishing tentative roots in Thailand in the midst of political instability. These were illusory, as the latest military takeover reveals. A democratically elected government is not expected to return until 2015. This negative development in the political arena has become a matter of concern given its economic, social and political implications.[1]

During the 1950s and 1960s Thailand's development strategy emphasized import-substituting industrialization. This was supported by repression of the financial system using controls over interest, bank credits and capital flows. Repression of the financial system created an inefficient economic structure. Macroeconomic performance was moderately satisfactory under financial repression in terms of economic growth. From the 1970s reorientation of strategy towards export promotion and development altered the macroeconomic performance landscape. This necessitated opening up of the economy to foreign investment through relaxation of capital controls. Both price stability and exchange rate stability are considered important components of the outward-oriented strategy of development. Accordingly these have been emergent in Thailand, though the birth is proving a difficult one (Kochhar and Associates, 1996; Robinson et al., 1991).

Taking the long view, the Thai monetary authorities have, testamentary to their extraordinary grasp of leading-edge macroeconomics and to their wisdom, generally avoided the temptation for expansionary fiscal and monetary policies to promote economic growth. Only in 1979 did the authorities adopt an expansionary fiscal policy in which sustained budget deficits were financed by external borrowing. The outcome was salutary: a rise in the trade deficit and an increase in the level of external debt. The response was definitive and permanent: the Thai authorities embarked on an IMF-supported structural adjustment programme in 1981. Following the restoration of macroeconomic stability under this programme, Thailand's ability to borrow in the international capital markets was restored in the late 1980s. By this time, the Latin American debt crisis was resolved. Southeast Asian countries then attracted large-scale foreign capital inflows from developed countries, including Japan, looking for high-return 'emerging market' investments. This led subsequently to the East-Southeast Asian financial crisis during 1997–98 (Fane and McLeod, 1999).

The Thai economy experienced a decade-long boom from 1986 that ended in 1995. Rapid growth of exports and large-scale foreign-capital inflows, mostly from Japan, Taiwan and Hong Kong SAR, created this boom (Alba et al., 1999; Jansen, 1997). The currency crisis that started in Thailand in July 1997 was triggered by a rapid appreciation of the real exchange rate of the baht (the Thai currency unit) during a period of economic boom under Thailand's pegged exchange rate system. By this time, monetary policy had lost its potency due to the combination of the pegged currency and the removal of most restrictions over capital flows. Consequently, large interest rate differentials in a rapidly expanding financial sector triggered capital inflows. In the absence of adequate regulation and supervision of the banking system, the rapidly expanding banking and non-banking financial institutions engaged in large-scale external borrowing without sufficient hedging for exchange rate risk. The newly expanded, yet underdeveloped, financial system could not cope with the resulting large-scale capital inflows. They comprehensively failed to intermediate these funds for investment in the tradable goods sector. As most investments were concentrated on real estate, office buildings and shopping malls, the prices of non-tradable goods rose sharply. This caused an appreciation of the baht real exchange rate that raised the levels both of the Thai current account deficit and its external debt balance (Disyatat and Vongsinsirikul, 2002; Jansen, 2001; Nakornthab, 2008).

Attempts by the Bank of Thailand (BOT, the Thai central bank) to control the monetary aggregates in the face of the large-scale capital inflows were unsuccessful. This ineffective sterilization of the capital flows left money-growth rates fluctuating widely. They raised the volatility of both output and prices. The rapidly appreciated real exchange rate and associated higher current account deficits undermined the pegged exchange rate system that, until then, had been considered credible and sustainable. Investors found themselves trapped in a one-way bet; that is, it was highly probable there would be a major devaluation of the baht. The outcome was a speculative attack on the Thai currency. The BOT initially tried to defend the baht by forward-selling foreign currencies at the prevailing exchange rates. In the process, the BOT depleted most of its foreign reserves. By 2 July 1997, no further foreign reserves were available to the BOT for defence of the currency. Left with no alternative, it allowed the baht to float in the foreign-exchange market; a decision that the Thai authorities have not to date rescinded. The outcome was a predicted rush to sell off baht, together with an essentially simultaneous sharp depreciation. This was the trigger that set off the East-Southeast Asian financial crisis. It took until the early 2000s for the impacted countries to fully work through the consequences. At the onset of the crisis, the IMF brought its weight to bear in Thailand's cause under a set of negotiated conditions, one of which was that Thailand adopt a comprehensive stabilization and structural adjustment programme. The IMF-supported stabilization measures were highly controversial, but turned out to be a blessing in disguise for the quality of Thailand's macroeconomic management, since they equipped the country to deal resiliently with the US-global financial crisis when it arrived in 2008. The IMF encouraged, perhaps even 'forced', the government to undertake much needed comprehensive economic and financial reforms to boost the resilience of the economy to absorb shocks, both domestic and external (Nakornthab, 2008; Nidhiprabha, 1998; Siregar and Rajaguru, 2005).

The Thai economy gradually recovered, with the authorities having implemented wide-ranging reforms, including significant deregulatory measures, to strengthen the financial system. With the floatation of the baht, Thailand acquired monetary policy independence, which was then available to target price stability. Until 1999, the BOT conducted monetary policy through a soft form of monetary targeting. This was part of the IMF stabilization and structural adjustment programme put in place immediately following the speculative attack on the currency. From 2000 the BOT began a policy of inflation targeting. Having applied stringent monetary control during the crisis, Thailand did not experience any major inflation spike in its wake; and the institutional reforms associated with the clampdown on monetary control eventually permitted inflation targeting to succeed monetary targeting. Thai inflation has remained under control ever since. Implementation of the inflation targeting strategy could reasonably have been expected to raise the credibility of the BOT in maintaining low and stable inflation; but the question of how effective inflation targeting has been remains a matter of contention (Pornpattanapaisankul, 2010).

The Thai economy was affected by the US-global financial crisis, but it has recovered since 2010. Following IMF policy prescription and the urgings of major economies such as the United States, part of Thailand's response to the crisis was to deploy some stimulatory fiscal-monetary measures to maintain steady economic growth. These measures have destabilized both the real interest rate and the real exchange rate. Thailand's success in keeping average inflation low has not reduced the instability of Thai inflation (Alp and Elekdag, 2012).

In summing up: sustained economic and financial reform in Thailand since the East-Southeast Asian financial crisis, including the improvement of prudential regulation and supervision, have strengthened the Thai financial system and enhanced the economy's resilience to shocks. Thailand has now emerged as a major industrializing economy with a level of per capita income of about US$10 000 in terms of purchasing power parity. Thailand's significantly improved economic fundamentals as a result of its experience of the last decade and a half are expected to stand it in good stead to make sustained economic progress in the coming decades.

The remainder of this chapter provides an overview of the evolution of central banking in Thailand and its conduct of monetary policy in an historical context. It also investigates some monetary relations, including the questions of whether there exists a stable money-demand function in Thailand and whether money growth and inflation are causally related. To bring the discussion into perspective, the next section provides a brief overview of the organization and activities of the BOT.

THE BANK OF THAILAND (BOT): ORGANIZATION AND ACTIVITIES[2]

The Thai National Banking Bureau, set up in 1939 with the status of a department of the Ministry of Finance, was the first organization to assume central banking activities for Thailand. The Bureau commenced operations on 24 June 1940. It was limited to issuing government bonds; to accepting deposits from and lending to the government, government agencies and commercial banks; and to transferring funds between the central region and other parts of the country. In 1941 the Bureau began executing control over foreign reserves. With the spread of World War II across Asia, the government formally recognized the role of the Bureau by promoting it to central bank. The BOT Act was promulgated in 1942. The Act decreed the BOT a juristic person and made it responsible for all central banking activities. The BOT commenced operations on 10 December 1942.

According to the BOT Act 1942, the minister of finance is empowered to oversee all affairs of the BOT. The general control and direction of the BOT is entrusted with a Court of Directors, comprising the governor, two deputy governors and at least five other members. The governor and the deputy governors are appointed by His Majesty the King as, respectively, chairman and vice chairman of the Court of Directors. The cabinet appoints other members of the court.

The roles and responsibilities of the BOT are to:

(a) promote monetary stability and formulate monetary policy
(b) promote and supervise financial institutions
(c) provide banking facilities and recommend economic policies to the government
(d) provide banking facilities to financial institutions
(e) manage foreign-exchange reserves
(f) print and issue banknotes
(g) undertake research on macro and monetary issues.

The Monetary Policy Committee (MPC) is one of the main committees of the BOT. The MPC comprises the governor, the deputy governor (monetary stability), the deputy governor (financial institutions stability) and four other persons. The main responsibility of the MPC is to determine the stance and direction of monetary policy. The MPC works closely with the relevant staff of the BOT to monitor the developments of domestic and foreign economies. The committee deploys research findings, statistics and other information, which are provided by BOT staff, to make policy decisions on monetary matters.

The main objective of monetary policy in Thailand is to achieve monetary and financial stability. The Thai authorities interpret this to comprise the following components: price stability; exchange rate stability; and a stable and efficient financial system. Economic growth is not formally acknowledged as an objective of monetary policy. Rather, monetary and financial stability are considered essential preconditions to achieving the most rapid possible sustained economic growth. Overall, price stability, interpreted as low average inflation, has emerged as the dominant objective of monetary policy under inflation targeting since 2000. Financial stability also remains a prominent consideration. Despite the absence of growth as a stated objective of monetary policy, there is reason to believe that the issue remains before the monetary authorities as to whether or not monetary policy should be used to stabilize the economy in the event of shocks or when the economy is in recession.

EVOLUTION OF MONETARY POLICY

Exchange Rate Arrangements

Monetary policy and exchange rate policy play important roles in Thai macroeconomic management. Thailand pegged the baht to one or more of the world's then major currencies from the early 1950s until the forced float in 1997. The monetary authorities in Thailand took this exchange rate arrangement seriously and exhibited conservatism in the conduct of monetary policy given some administrative controls over interest rates and capital flows. The pegged exchange rate acted as an anchor to domestic prices. As the authorities generally maintained disciplined fiscal and monetary policies, the pegged exchange rate system was credible in the market. The baht did not come under major pressure and the exchange rate at which the peg was fixed was adjusted only occasionally. Other than minor adjustments to the peg, there were two devaluations of Thai currency (baht) in 1981 and 1984. As discussed earlier, only on 2 July 1997 did the BOT abandon the pegged exchange rate system when the baht became grossly overvalued and thereby attracted speculative attack.

1947–97

Thailand came under Japanese occupation early in World War II as Japan swept down the Malay Peninsula to Singapore and on to Indonesia and ultimately New Guinea. One of Japan's first acts of occupation in Thailand was to impose the Exchange Control Act 1942. This prohibited capital outflows and forced Thailand into exclusive trade with Japan.

Post-World War II, Thailand experimented with a succession of exchange rate systems. Table 12.1 reports a summary of this series of exchange rate arrangements. After a sharp devaluation of the baht in 1947, it remained pegged to both the British pound sterling and the US dollar until 1955 and to the US dollar until 1978. In November 1978, the par value system of the baht with the US dollar was replaced by a basket of currencies system that remained until 30 June,1997. From the end of World War II, the system of pegging to a single currency or to multiple currencies remained in place until 1997, serving the country well with a largely stable exchange rate.

There were two major devaluations of the baht in the early 1980s. Both occurred during the 1981–86 period through which the Thai economy was applying IMF-World Bank-supported structural adjustment programmes as its management framework. The first devaluation was effected in July 1981 when the baht was devalued by 9.5 per cent from baht 21 to baht 23 per US dollar. This devaluation of baht occurred after three years during which rapid money supply growth had built up pressure on the balance-of-payments. The second devaluation of the baht occurred in November 1984. This time the baht was devalued by 17.4 per cent from baht 23 to baht 27 per US dollar. Again, there had been three years of rapid monetary expansion. Currency devaluation was the last resort, undertaken only after a series of monetary control measures implemented between December 1983 and March 1984 had failed to control the monetary expansion. In both cases, the major contributor to the rapid monetary expansion had been the high domestic interest rate. The consequently significant positive interest rate differential between domestic and foreign financial products had prompted Thai firms and financial institutions to borrow heavily from abroad. This led to rapid unsterilized growth of the net foreign assets of the BOT. The consequent large foreign-capital inflows necessarily translated into rapid money growth, fuelling high, volatile inflation.

After the baht devaluation in November 1984 the BOT made the exchange rate of the baht more flexible by implementing an adjustable peg to a basket of currencies. The composition and weightings of the component currencies were not disclosed. The perception was that the basket comprised roughly 50 per cent US dollar, with the remainder a mixture of the Japanese yen, the German deutschemark, the Singapore dollar, the Malaysian ringgit, the Hong King dollar and British sterling.

The adjustable peg was maintained until late 1985 when the baht came under speculative pressure due to the private sector's large-scale foreign borrowings. In December 1985, the baht was devalued by 2 per cent and the BOT revised the composition of a basket to contain about 90 per cent US dollar or US dollar-linked currencies. This regime persisted until 30 June 1997. Despite Thailand's abandonment of the US dollar peg in

Table 12.1 Exchange rate regimes in Thailand, 1947–97

Period	Exchange rate of Baht (Bt) per US$/pound sterling	Explanations
Before World War II	Bt 11 per pound sterling	Fixed exchange rate of the baht with the pound sterling. Minimal capital controls and restrictions.
During World War II		The Exchange Control Act 1942 was introduced under Japanese occupation and capital outflows were prohibited. Thailand was also forced to trade with Japan only.
1947	Bt 40 per pound sterling	A multiple exchange rate system was introduced, in which the exchange rates of the baht varied depending on the types of transactions. The market rates were generally much higher than the official rates.
1949	Bt 35 per pound sterling Bt 21.62 per US dollar	Thailand became an IMF member. The exchange rate of the baht was fixed with the US dollar (Bt 21.62 per US dollar). Thailand's reserve assets were re-evaluated with this official rate.
1955	Bt 56 per pound sterling Bt 21.64 per US dollar	An Exchange Equalization Fund (EEF) was established. Facing inflation and balance-of-payments problems, the multiple exchange rate system was abolished.
1955–63	Bt 21.02 per US dollar	This official rate was used to evaluate reserve assets. This rate was not, however, related to the market rate.
1 October 1963	Bt 20.80 per US dollar Gold 0.0427245 grams per Bt	The par value or the Bretton Woods system was introduced. The exchange rate of the baht was controlled within a band of 1 per cent of the par value; that is, between Bt 20.59 to Bt 21.00 per US dollar.

Table 12.1 (continued)

Period	Exchange rate of baht Baht (Bt) per US$/pound sterling	Explanations
1973–78	Bt 20 per US dollar	The exchange rate of the baht was revalued and re-fixed to Bt 20 per US dollar. The exchange rate movement was, however, allowed within a wider band of 2.25 per cent of the par value; that is, between Bt 19.55 to Bt 20.45 per US dollar.
1978–81	Bt 23 per US dollar	The exchange rate of the baht was fixed daily for commercial banks. From November 1978, the par value system was changed to a basket of currencies system.
1981–84		On 15 July, the baht was devalued by 8.7 per cent. The Exchange Equalization Fund abolished the daily-fixing system and became the sole agent determining the exchange rates.
2 November 1984	Bt 27 per US dollar	The exchange rate system was changed back to the basket of currencies system. The Exchange Equalization Fund announced daily the exchange rate of the baht against the US dollar and stood ready to purchase and sell the US dollar with commercial banks at the pre-announced rates from 8.30 am until noon.
5 November 1984		The baht was devalued by 15 per cent against the US dollar.
30 June 1997		The last day of the basket of currencies system.
2 July 1997	Bt 25.79 per US dollar Bt 27.383 per US dollar	A managed floating system is introduced, which remains in operation.

Source: Author's compilation/adaptation based on the Bank of Thailand (1998).

November 1984, intended to bring some flexibility to the exchange rate system, the baht returned to a quasi-US dollar standard after the period of experimentation with its adjustable peg against a basket of currencies (Bank of Thailand, 1998).

1997–2012

Since 2 July1997 Thailand has operated a managed float exchange rate system. Under this system the exchange rate of the baht is determined by market forces both on-shore and off-shore. The BOT allows the exchange rate of the baht to move in line with economic fundamentals, but it retains the option to intervene when necessary to smooth out high volatility of the exchange rate and to achieve any other economic policy objectives. Under this system, the exchange rate has shown a high degree of flexibility. This has improved the implementation of monetary policy under inflation targeting for price stability. As expected, the relatively flexible exchange rate system has raised the confidence of investors and improved the BOT's management of large-scale foreign-capital flows, especially during the US-global financial crisis.

Financial Deregulation and Reforms

Historically, the Thai financial system was heavily regulated and controlled. Dominated by a small number of banks with a high degree of ownership concentration, the domestic banking system was profitable, protected as it was from foreign competition. Banking operations were, however, subject to ceilings on both the deposit and lending rates of interest. There were portfolio and branching restrictions. Credit was government allocated and directed to designated priority sectors. Other indicators of this relatively light form of financial repression included the requirement that banks hold a policy-determined proportion of their deposit liabilities in the form of low-yielding government securities. The real interest rates paid on government securities were generally positive. Capital flows were generally restricted and regulated. Consequently, money and capital markets remained relatively underdeveloped. Informal credit markets existed to cater for the needs of small and medium-sized businesses. Overall, Thailand's financial system was mildly repressed and shallow. Saving, investment and economic growth were commensurately below potential.

Until the 1990s, financial reform was undertaken gradually. It began with the deregulation of interest rates after the second OPEC oil price shock in 1979. Section 654 of the Civil and Commercial Codes in Thailand restricted interest rates to a ceiling of 15 per cent from 1924. As foreign interest rates rose sharply in 1979–80, the promulgation of the Financial

Institutions Lending Rate Act BE2523 (190) helped to cushion the domestic financial system from the impact of volatile foreign interest rates. The Ministry of Finance raised the ceiling on the lending rate of interest above 15 per cent to a level that was deemed appropriate given financial conditions. In the first half of the 1980s a financial crisis erupted. It originated in the commercial failure of some banks and finance companies. Steps were taken to strengthen bank supervision and to deal decisively with those financial institutions that were weak and inefficient. Under a three-year financial reform plan, 1990–92, financial reform measures became comprehensive.

There were four major components of the financial reform plan. The first component of this plan included the deregulation of interest rates; financial institution portfolio management; and relaxation of exchange controls. The second component included the improvement of supervision and the examination procedure of banks; the monitoring and analytical procedure; adjustment of the capital-to-risk asset ratio to accord with BIS guidelines; the training of bank examiners; and development and management of information systems. The third component included promotion of financial innovations in both the primary and secondary markets. The fourth component of the financial reform plan included the improvement of the payments system and the establishment of second note-printing works. Thailand accepted the obligations under Article VIII of the IMF's Articles of Agreement in 1990. This liberalized the foreign-exchange regime to conform with the globalization of economic and financial systems that facilitate greater mobility of capital across the globe.

Strategies of Monetary Policy

Monetary targeting: July 1997–May 2000

Thailand received financial assistance from the IMF after implementation of its managed float exchange rate system on 2 July 1997. Initially, the monetary policy objective was to restore some of the confidence in the baht that had been lost with the collapse of the pegged exchange rate system and the forced float. An improvement of confidence in the baht was essential to re-establish macroeconomic stability. As the currency crisis evolved, Thailand put a limit on the growth rate of the monetary base with the twin aims of restoring monetary stability and keeping a lid on the rate of inflation. The BOT closed about 40 nearly insolvent financial firms and took steps to limit the creation of excess liquidity in the financial system. These measures in combination succeeded in their aims of returning stability to the financial system and preventing inflation from getting out of control.

As the IMF programmes came to an end in 1998, Thai authorities reassessed the appropriate strategy of monetary policy. The suggestion emerged that if the objective of policy was to achieve and maintain price stability, interpreted as low and stable inflation, then monetary targeting was a less effective strategy than inflation targeting. However, as monetary policy was allocated the (publicly unannounced) additional, conflicting objective of economic stabilization, the effectiveness of monetary policy on price stability was undermined by the very attempt to deploy a single macroeconomic management instrument, monetary policy, to target two conflicting objectives.

Inflation targeting: May 2000 to date

Thailand adopted inflation targeting with the stated objective of price stability in May 2000. Three years earlier when, under IMF-World Bank protection, the BOT adopted monetary targeting to address the currency crisis, the Thai economy had been in bad shape. By 2000 it had recovered significantly, regaining monetary stability due, not least, to the role played by tight monetary policy. Since it adopted inflation targeting in 2000, Thailand has maintained low average inflation. It has, however, remained volatile. Overall, the inflation targeting strategy is believed to have improved the conduct of monetary policy for Thailand. Grenville and Ito (2010, p. 2) provide an assessment of Thai inflation targeting:

> inflation targeting experience seems to have been a very positive and valuable one for Thailand. It was initiated at a time when the BoT's [Bank of Thailand] prestige and credibility was still reflecting the damage of the Asian crisis, and inflation targeting replaced a failed monetary policy anchor – the fixed exchange rate. Inflation targeting was put in place largely at the initiative of the BoT itself, but it not only provided an effective basis for monetary policy decisions and an anchor for inflation, but it also defined the nature of the relationship between BoT and the Government.

Monetary policy transmission mechanisms

Figure 12.1 exhibits a flowchart of the monetary policy transmission mechanisms in Thailand. The BOT uses a short-term interest rate as an instrument of monetary policy.[3] It affects market interest rates, asset prices and exchange rates. Changes in interest rates and exchange rates affect aggregate demand and hence both output and prices.[4] Overall, the monetary policy transmission mechanisms rely on the assumption of short-run price rigidity, both of goods and services. A second assumption is that monetary policy does not have any impact on real variables in the long run.

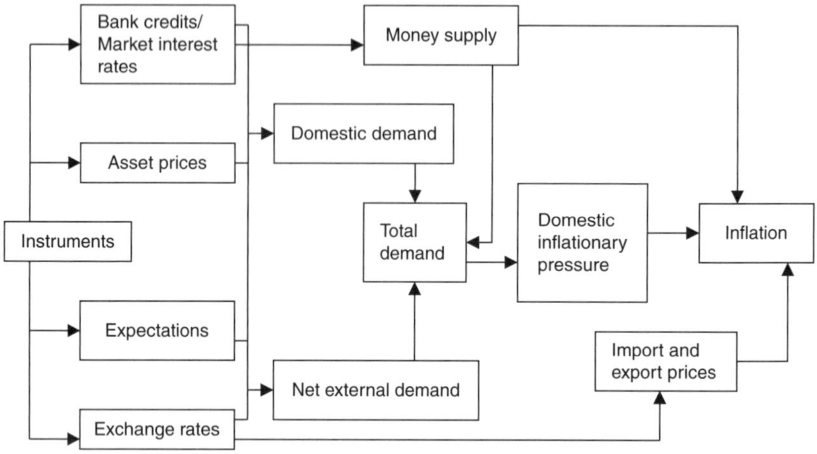

Source: Monetary Policy Department, Bank of Thailand.

Figure 12.1 Monetary policy transmission mechanisms in Thailand

MACROECONOMIC DEVELOPMENTS AND INFLATION PERFORMANCE

Table 12.2 reports summary data for Thailand's key economic indicators over 1950–2012. Thailand can be seen to have maintained low inflation until the 1970s. Inflation then went to about 10 per cent per annum during the 1970s. It then returned to around 5 per cent until the 1990s. Post-millennium inflation has fallen precipitously to just 1 per cent. Throughout these decades it has, however, remained unstable. A 'quiet achiever' until the mid 1990s, Thailand had maintained a rate of economic growth around 6 per cent per annum throughout the period from the early 1950s. For Thailand, substantial rates of economic growth and low average rates of inflation have reinforced each other. Low inflation has created an environment conducive to sustained, healthy, rapid economic growth; rapid economic growth, comprising effectively commensurate growth rates of demand and supply, in turn combined to conduce a relatively low average inflation rate. Under its pegged exchange rate systems, inflation however remained unstable throughout the 1950–2012 study period. Unstable inflation, in particular, affected real output and its growth.

Like other non-oil-producing countries of Asia, the Thai economy was affected by the OPEC-induced global oil price shocks of the 1970s. They imposed far-reaching effects on output, employment and prices.

Table 12.2 Macroeconomic indicators, Thailand, 1951–2012

Macroeconomic indicators	1951–55	1956–60	1961–65	1966–70	1971–75	1976–80	1981–85	1986–90	1991–95	1996–2000	2001–05	2006–10	2011	2012
Budget balance (% of GDP)	n.a.	n.a.	n.a.	n.a.	n.a.	n.a.	n.a.	n.a.	3.1	−3.2	−0.7	−0.3	−1.6	−3.1
General government gross debt (%)	n.a.	n.a.	n.a.	n.a.	n.a.	n.a.	n.a.	n.a.	n.a.	44.0	52.0	41.1	41.7	44.2
Money-growth rate (%)														
Narrow money growth	12.4	6.9	5.5	8.5	12.5	15.6	3.8	18.1	14.8	14.4	6.2	8.0	8.6	13.0
Broad money growth	12.9	9.2	11.0	15.0	19.9	19.6	18.8	20.9	16.7	9.5	4.4	8.3	15.1	10.4
Real GDP growth (%)	5.7	4.9	7.3	9.4	5.6	8.0	5.4	10.3	8.6	0.6	5.0	3.7	0.1	6.5
GDP per capita, current prices, US dollar	n.a.	n.a.	n.a.	n.a.	n.a.	696	773	1140	2188	2260	2313	4132	5395	5848
Unemployment rate (%)	n.a.	n.a.	n.a.	n.a.	n.a.	n.a.	n.a.	3.9	2.4	3.0	2.4	1.4	0.7	0.7
CPI inflation rate (%)	2.6	2.4	2.1	2.5	10.1	9.9	5.0	3.9	4.8	4.3	2.3	3.0	3.8	3.0
Current account balance (% of GDP)	n.a.	n.a.	n.a.	n.a.	n.a.	−6.4	−5.3	−2.9	−6.3	4.1	1.8	4.1	3.4	−0.2

Table 12.2 (continued)

Macroeconomic indicators	1951–55	1956–60	1961–65	1966–70	1971–75	1976–80	1981–85	1986–90	1991–95	1996–2000	2001–05	2006–10	2011	2012
Nominal interest rate (%)														
Treasury bill rate	n.a.	n.a.	n.a.	n.a.	n.a.	7.5	10.7	5.2	n.a.	n.a.	1.8	2.8	2.9	3.0
Loan rate of interest	n.a.	n.a.	n.a.	n.a.	n.a.	12.4	16.4	12.6	12.6	11.7	6.3	6.7	6.9	7.1
Real interest rate (%)[a]														
Treasury bill rate	n.a.	n.a.	n.a.	n.a.	n.a.	−3.3	5.6	2.4	n.a.	n.a.	−0.6	−0.1	−0.9	0.0
Loan rate of interest	n.a.	n.a.	n.a.	n.a.	n.a.	2.5	11.1	8.5	7.4	7.1	3.9	3.6	3.0	4.0
Nominal exchange rate (baht per US dollar)	20.3	21.0	20.9	20.8	20.6	20.4	23.7	25.7	25.3	35.2	41.9	34.3	30.5	31.1
Bilateral real exchange rate of baht against US dollar[b]	68.1	64.6	62.7	65.0	64.9	59.4	66.5	74.7	70.3	86.4	104.7	83.8	72.8	73.5

Notes:
n.a. = not available
a. Real interest rate is estimated as: 100(((1 + interest rate)/(1 + inflation rate))−1) where the interest rate and inflation rate are expressed in decimal.
b. An increase in the index value of the exchange rate represents depreciation.

Source: Author's computation based on IMF, *International Financial Statistics*; IMF, *World Economic Outlook*; and other country-specific publications on the IMF website.

The authorities restored price stability quickly and the economy exhibited some resilience, especially when it entered into its first IMF stabilization programme in the early 1980s. The 1997 currency crisis that destabilized the Thai economy, necessitating a second round of IMF-World Bank assistance, was a short-lived affair. Since then the Thai economy has moved to a higher growth path in a low-inflationary environment. The adoption of rule-based monetary policy as the crisis subsided has been the major contributor to the establishment of a stable economic system.

The early 1990s saw a major reorientation of national policy towards liberalization and internationalization of the Thai financial and economic system aimed at participating in the benefits flowing from the end of the Cold War and associated politics. In this respect, a full-fledged agenda was mapped out to promote Thailand as a regional centre for trade, investment and finance. Financial deregulation and liberalization reforms were undertaken to expand financial activities and deepen the financial system.

The 1997 financial crisis in Thailand originated in several interrelated factors, both external and domestic. The decade of high economic growth rates from the late 1980s, primarily driven by foreign investment inflows and increased exports, eventually overheated the economy. Under the pegged exchange rate system the real exchange rate appreciated. In turn, this created large current account deficits and raised the level of external debt.

Because the pegged exchange rate system was widely considered credible and sustainable, this very virtue meant that there were no systemic macroeconomic weaknesses to focus the attention of private sector decision-makers on the excessive risk that their excessive external borrowing entailed; rather, there were in place positive systemic incentives for the private sector to over-borrow externally, as discussed below. Thailand was accurately rated a low exchange rate risk. This, combined with the then prevailing steep positive slope of the yield curve for US dollar credits, encouraged short-term borrowing, which necessarily led to a rapid build-up of short-term external debt. When the economy ultimately came under pressure, both the financial and corporate sectors were left heavily exposed to exchange rate risk. In the precarious circumstances, all that was necessary to render Thailand's pegged exchange rate system untenable was the simple prediction that the baht would have to be devalued to rebalance the economy.

By the mid 1990s, investor sentiment about the sustainability of economic boom in Thailand shifted for many reasons, one of the foremost of which was a perceived inefficient use by Thailand of external resources. Foreign-capital inflows were mainly linked to borrowing by financial institutions for investment in non-tradable sector industries such as real estate, construction projects, office buildings, shopping malls and so on. This created a credit-led asset price bubble. Moral hazard problems, emergent from common knowledge that implicit loan guarantees by the Thai authorities were present in the system, together with weak supervision by those authorities of banks and financial institutions in the newly deregulated and rapidly expanding financial system, further facilitated poor investment decision-making. Many firms expanded their businesses without assessing the risks. Overall, investor risk management strategies were flawed and inadequate. Limited information on, and lack of transparency in, the borrowing and lending of foreign funds made it difficult for the BOT to undertake assessment of risks for the financial sector as a whole.

The liberal financial environment that was created in the early 1990s made it difficult for the monetary authorities to undertake appropriate measures to dampen an overheated economy. Given Thailand's 'credible' pegged exchange rate system and the lack of political will to tighten fiscal policy in the euphoria of the unprecedented economic 'dynamism' (overheating), declining domestic-investor sentiment about the sustainability of the country's economic imbalances began to spread worldwide. This put pressure on the BOT to raise the interest rate in defence of the currency. This high interest rate policy worked as intended, propping up the baht by attracting foreign-capital inflows into baht-denominated assets. This exacerbated the problems inherent in the already overheated economy.

Inflation and Inflation Volatility

Figure 12.2a plots quarter-on-quarter CPI inflation in Thailand between 1966 and 2012. As analysed above in discussion of Table 12.2, during the 1970s Thailand's inflation was about 10 per cent per annum. It then fell to around 5 per cent until the 1990s. In the last decade, inflation has reached just 1 per cent. Figure 12.2b displays inflation volatility, measured by the conditional standard deviation of inflation as obtained by a GARCH(1,1) model, for the period 1966q1–2012q4. It shows that Thailand's inflation was highly volatile during the 1970s, 1980s and 1990s. Since the mid 2000s inflation volatility has fallen to relatively low levels.

Inflation Persistence

Thai inflation has exhibited a high degree of persistence. This is reflected in the high and stable coefficient value on the one-period lagged rate of inflation in an autoregressive model AR(1), estimated by both the recursive and the rolling regression techniques (Figures 12.3a and 12.3b).

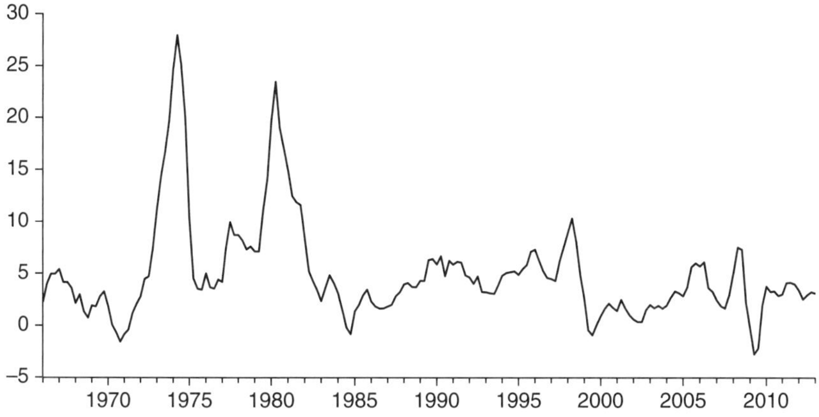

Figure 12.2a Quarter-on-quarter CPI inflation in Thailand, 1966q1–2012q4

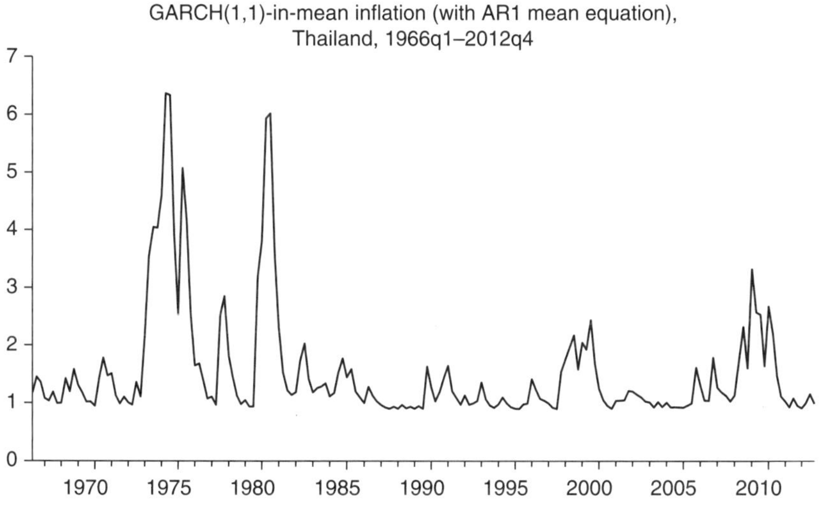

Figure 12.2b Conditional standard deviation of CPI inflation in Thailand, 1966q1–2012q4

Rolling estimates of the coefficient on the one-period lagged rate of inflation suggest that the coefficient value has shown only a mild declining trend since the late 2000s. High persistence of inflation is generally associated with low credibility of monetary policy. The BOT has gained some

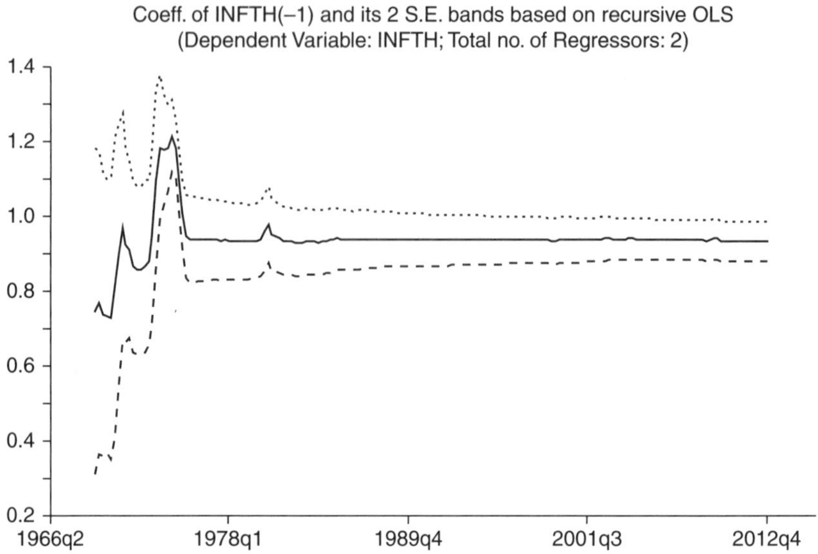

Note: INFTH = CPI inflation in Thailand.

Figure 12.3a Recursive estimates of the coefficient on the one-period lagged rate of CPI inflation in Thailand

autonomy in conducting monetary policy for price stability under inflation targeting. It has not, however, earned full credibility, in the sense of the level of public confidence in its determination to use this autonomy to wring inflation and volatility out of the system and embed both of these at sustainably low levels in the economy. Table 12.3 reports the unit root test results for inflation in Thailand over the period 1950–2010. The ADF and KPSS tests reject the null hypothesis that inflation in Thailand has a unit root. The overall results suggest that Thai inflation has high persistence but no unit root is present in the series.

Money-market Rate and the Federal Funds Rate

Figure 12.4a plots the money-market rate in Thailand and the US Federal funds rate. They show similar trends. Figure 12.4b shows that the real money-market rate and the real Federal funds rate also show similar trends. This suggests the presence of a real interest rate-parity relation despite restricted capital flows over the study period.

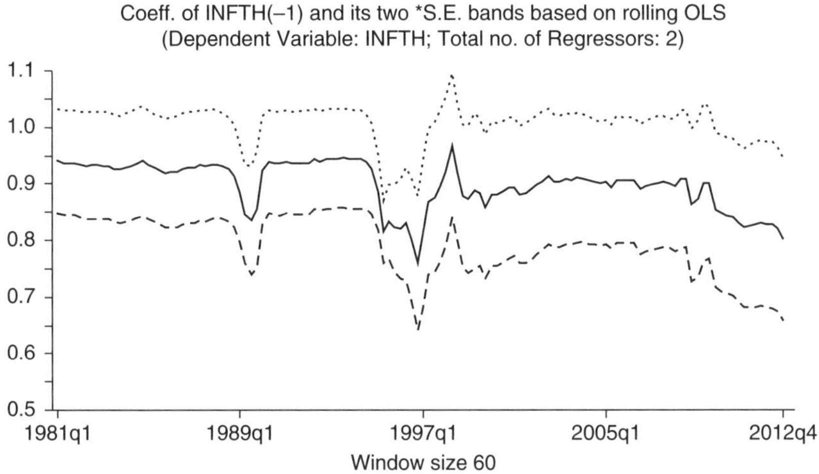

Note: INFTH = CPI inflation in Thailand.

Figure 12.3b Rolling sample estimates of the coefficient on the one-period lagged rate of inflation in Thailand

Exchange Rates

Figure 12.5 plots the nominal and real effective exchange rates in Thailand. It records a steady depreciation in both the nominal and the real effective exchange rates from the mid 1980s through the early 1990s. The trend then reversed, so that since the early 1990s both the nominal and real exchange rates have been appreciating.

INFLATION, REAL INTEREST RATE, REAL EXCHANGE RATE AND REAL OUTPUT

Thailand maintained moderately low, unstable inflation from the 1950s through the 1960s. Inflation rose to high levels and remained volatile through the 1970s. Inflation volatility fell during the 1980s, and remained low through the policy transition to inflation targeting and beyond. Thailand's interest rate and nominal exchange rate do not adjust fully to inflation differentials between Thailand and its trading partners, suggesting the inference that high-inflation volatility in Thailand transmitted to high volatility, both in real interest rates and exchange rates. This volatility in such key economic variables has adversely affected both Thai output and its growth.

Table 12.3 The unit root test results for CPI inflation in Thailand

	Sample (adjusted)	Constant (C); Trend (T)	ADF statistic (SBC-determined lag-length, l)	Inference at 5% level	The KPSS test statistic (Newey-West bandwidth)	Inference at 5% level	Sample (unadjusted)	Zivot-Andrews test statistic	Breakpoint	Inference at 5% level
LCPI	1955–2012	C and T	−1.79 (l = 1)	I(1)	0.118 (6)	I(0)	1953–2010	−3.47	1973	I(1)
LCPI	1955–2012	C	−0.69 (l = 1)	I(1)	0.947 (6)	I(1)	1953–2010	−3.71	1976	I(1)
ΔLCPI	1955–2012	C	−4.28 (l = 0)	I(0)	0.155 (3)	I(0)	1954–2010	−6.49	1972	I(0)

Note: Definitions of variables: LCPI = log of the consumer price index; Δ LCPI = first-order difference of LCPI; SBC = Schwarz Bayesian Criterion; ADF = augmented Dickey-Fuller; and KPSS = Kwiatkowski, Phillips, Schmidt and Shin.

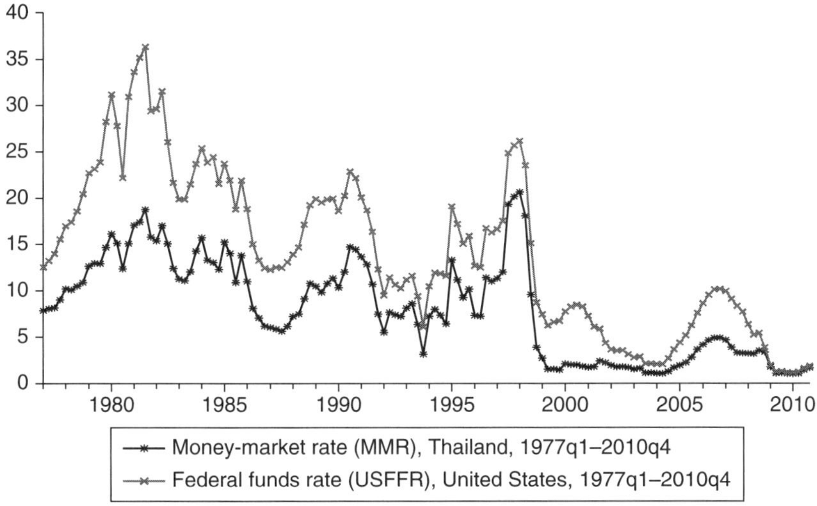

Figure 12.4a *The money-market rate in Thailand and the Federal funds rate in the United States, 1977q1–2010q4*

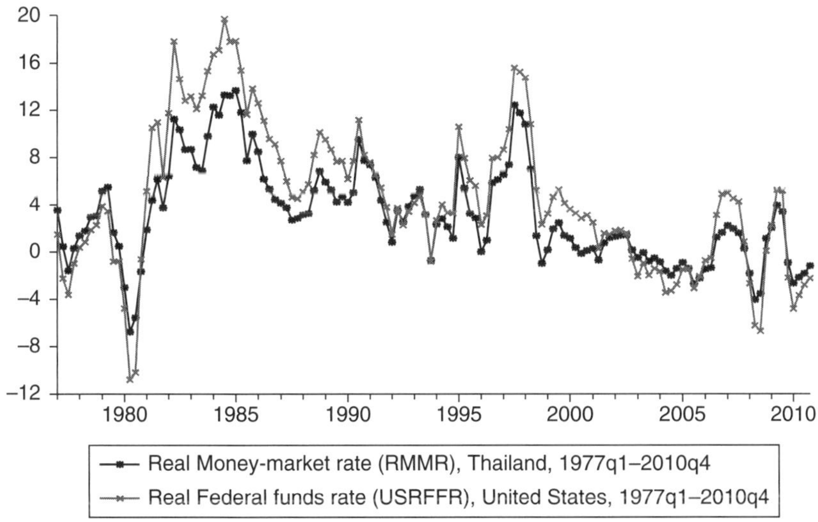

Figure 12.4b *The real money-market rate in Thailand and the real Federal funds rate in the United States, 1977q1–2010q4*

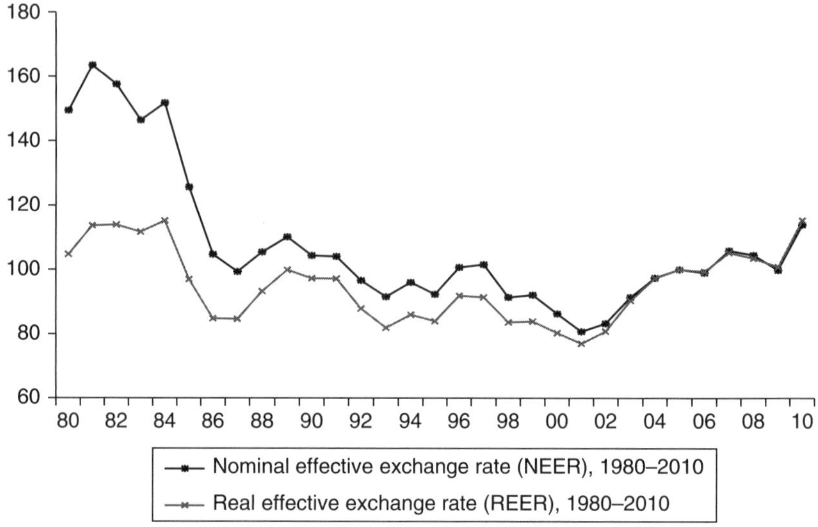

Figure 12.5 Nominal and real effective exchange rates in Thailand, 1980–2010

The Structural Vector Autoregressive (SVAR) Analysis

This subsection, using annual data, estimates a four-variable SVAR model to examine the interrelationships among inflation, the real interest rate, the real exchange rate and real output. The model is formulated on the assumption that inflation is largely determined externally, but has a contemporaneous feedback relation with the real interest rate and the real exchange rate. All these variables affect real output. The order of variables in the model is as follows: INFTH, RLRI, LREER and LRGDP, where INFTH is measured Thai inflation, RLRI is the real lending rate of interest, LREER is the log of the real effective exchange rate and LRGDP is the log of the real effective exchange rate.

The unit root test results suggest that inflation, the real interest rate and the real exchange rate are stationary, while real output is nonstationary. Two versions of the model are then estimated and deployed to generate impulse responses and the forecast error-variance decompositions. The first version of the model is defined as: INFTH, RLRI, LREER and LRGDP while the second version of the model is defined as: INFTH, RLRI, LREER and DLRGDP. In the second version of the model, all four variables are stationary while in the first version real output is nonstationary. The results obtained by the second model are reported,

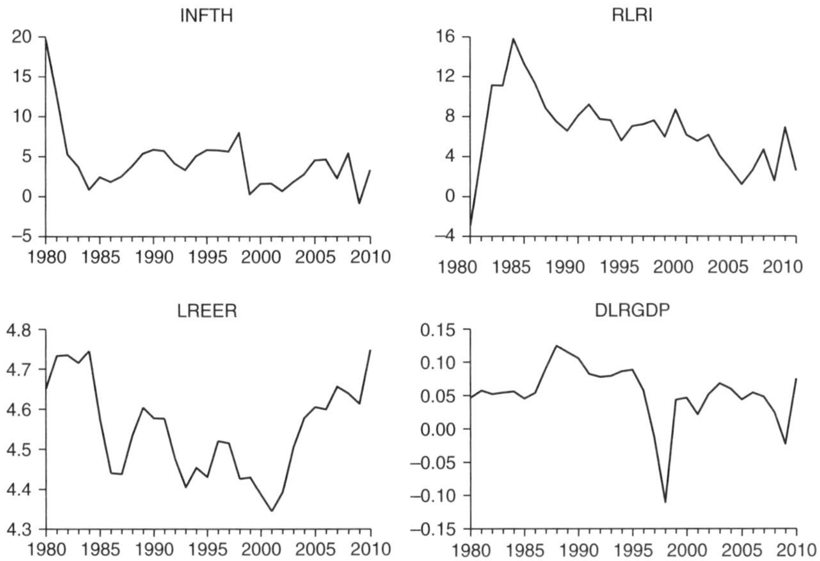

Note: Definitions of variables: INFTH = CPI inflation in Thailand; RLRI = real lending rate of interest; LREER = log of the real effective exchange rate of the baht; and DLRGDP = first-order difference in the log of real GDP.

Figure 12.6 Data deployed for estimation of the SVAR model for Thailand

as the results obtained by both the models are qualitatively similar. Figure 12.6 plots the data used for estimation purposes.

The impulse responses in Figure 12.7 reveal interrelations among all four variables in the SVAR model. The key source of inflation, monetary growth, is not incorporated in the model's specification. High and volatile inflation have monetary roots. When the rate of inflation is low, it is difficult to identify the main sources of inflation, since both demand and supply shocks overwhelm the impact of core sources of inflation such as money growth. The relationship becomes more readily visible when inflation is high and sustained. In developing countries, budget deficits become an important source of monetary growth and its frequent outcome: inflation. In such cases, the relationships among budget deficits, money growth and inflation are pronounced and detectable. There is feedback causation in the reverse direction. For example, a rise in inflation lowers the real value of tax revenues. Budget deficits are enlarged to make up the shortfall; this contributes to faster money growth, further fuelling inflation.

The impulse response results are indicative, not conclusive. As

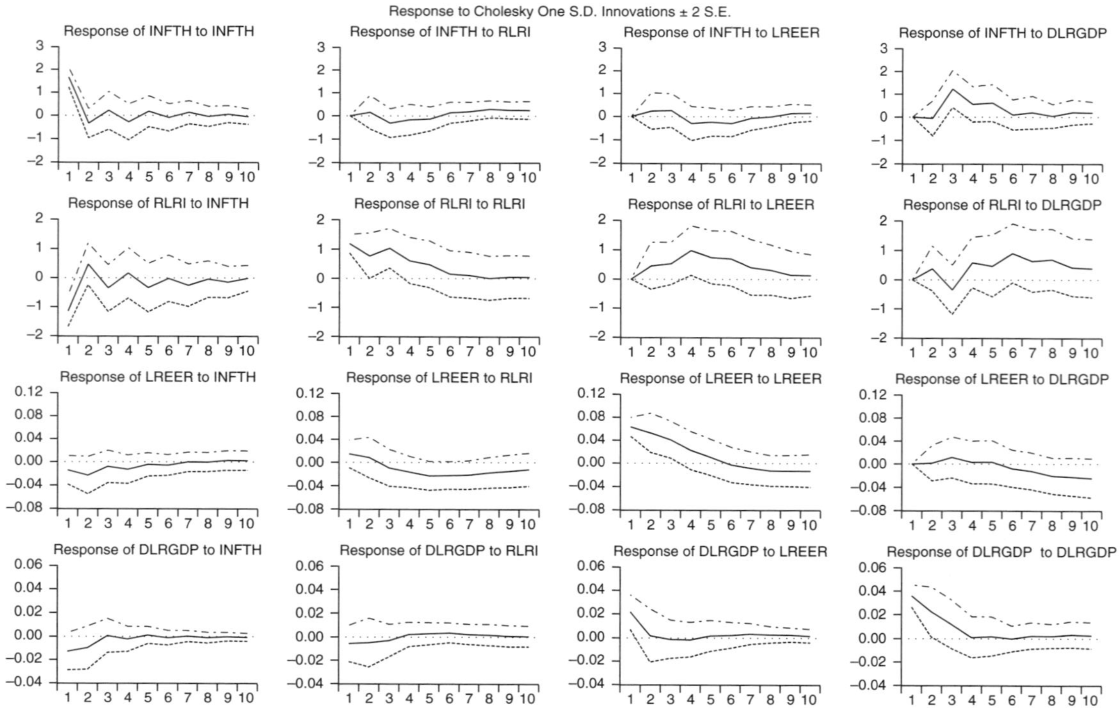

Note: Definitions of variables: INFTH = CPI inflation in Thailand; RLRI = real lending rate of interest; LREER = log of the real effective exchange rate of the baht; and DLRGDP = first-order difference in the log of real GDP.

Figure 12.7 Impulse responses for variables in the SVAR model for Thailand expected, a rise in inflation reduces the real rate of interest. The impulse response indicates that the nominal interest rate responds slowly to a rise in inflation. A decrease in the real interest rate is generally expected to raise investment in theory, but this is an unlikely channel of influence in developing countries. A very low or negative real interest rate, caused by high inflation given unchanged nominal interest rates, creates financial repression. This reduces the level of saving, investment and economic growth. High and volatile inflation creates other macroeconomic problems. A rise in inflation appreciates the real exchange rate, in turn affecting inflation and economic growth. The real interest rate responds positively to an appreciation of the real exchange rate. This is because, following the open-economy real exchange rate parity condition, a grossly appreciated real exchange rate induces capital flight, thereby requiring the real interest rate to rise as an inducement to slow down or halt that capital flight. When stringent capital controls are in place in one country or more, there can be short-run deviation of real interest rates across countries. However, for many countries capital controls are not effective, irrespective of the range of official regulations and controls exercised. In general an appreciation of the real exchange rate alters trade and capital flows, while changes in the real interest rate alter the levels of saving and investment.

The overall results suggest significant interrelations among inflation, the real interest rate, the real exchange rate and output growth. Not investigated here, an expanded model is expected to show the impacts of the real interest and exchange rates on saving, investment and both trade and capital flows. The key message to emerge from the empirical results is that inflation and its volatility are not innocuous in relation to the rate and volatility of economic growth. The rate of inflation influences both the real interest rate and the real exchange rate; and these then impact on saving, investment and economic growth. This suggests the need for low, stable inflation as a framework to maximize the potential for a high, sustained and steady long-run rate of economic growth.

Table 12.4 presents the forecast error-variance decompositions of INFTH, RLRI, LREER and DLRGDP. The numbers represent those percentages of forecast error variance of variables in the model that can be attributed to own innovations and those percentages of forecast error variance that originate from the innovations of other variables. The results show that for all four variables specified, the dominant source of the forecast error variance is own innovations. The extent of this influence across the full ten-year time horizon amounts to 49 per cent for inflation, 33 per cent for the real interest rate, 63 per cent for the real exchange rate and 69 per cent for real GDP growth. In the case of real output growth,

Table 12.4 Forecast error-variance decompositions of variables in the SVAR model for Thailand

Variance Decomposition of INFTH:					
Period	S.E.	INFTH	RLRI	LREER	DLRGDP
1	1.657	100.00	0.00	0.00	0.00
2	1.715	97.23	0.84	1.84	0.10
5	2.376	53.42	2.96	4.72	38.90
10	2.489	49.20	6.86	6.47	37.47
Variance Decomposition of RLRI:					
Period	S.E.	INFTH	RLRI	LREER	DLRGDP
1	1.654	48.39	51.6	0.00	0.00
2	1.977	39.64	51.36	5.30	3.70
5	2.885	21.83	44.17	24.10	9.90
10	3.355	16.92	33.02	24.85	25.20
Variance Decomposition of LREER:					
Period	S.E.	INFTH	RLRI	LREER	DLRGDP
1	0.066	4.47	4.89	90.64	0.00
2	0.088	9.34	3.67	86.96	0.03
5	0.107	8.57	10.26	79.81	1.36
10	0.124	6.63	18.23	62.86	12.29
Variance Decomposition of DLRGDP:					
Period	S.E.	INFTH	RLRI	LREER	DLRGDP
1	0.044	8.47	1.61	24.06	65.86
2	0.051	10.24	2.17	18.41	69.18
5	0.052	9.81	2.84	17.46	69.89
10	0.053	9.65	3.51	18.10	68.74
The Cholesky Ordering: INFTH RLRI LREER DLRGDP					

Note: Definitions of variables: INFTH = CPI inflation in Thailand; RLRI = real lending rate of interest; LREER = log of the real effective exchange rate of the baht; and DLRGDP = first-order difference in the log of real GDP.

innovations in the real interest rate and the real exchange rate jointly account for 22 per cent of real output growth's forecast error variance. The corresponding share of inflation is 10 per cent. The conclusion suggested is that real output growth is highly sensitive to inflation and its volatility. Inflation impacts the real interest rate and the real exchange rate. These, in turn, affect the rate and stability of real output growth.

MONETARY AND EXCHANGE RATE POLICY ISSUES

Thailand is likely to continue with its chosen monetary policy strategy of inflation targeting. The issue remains as to whether it can deploy a monetary aggregate as an instrument or an information variable. In the past, this issue has been debated in the context of the money-demand function.

Until recently the prevailing view was that monetary targeting for price stability requires a stable money-demand function to establish a causal linkage between money supply growth and inflation. The recent literature suggests that a causal relation exists between money supply growth and inflation irrespective of the exchange rate regime and irrespective of whether the money-demand function is relatively stable or unstable (McCallum and Nelson, 2011). This section examines whether there exists a stable money-demand function in Thailand.[5] For estimation purposes, an open-economy money-demand function is specified as follows:

$$LRJM_t = \alpha_0 + \alpha_1 Ly_t + \alpha_2 NIR_t + \alpha_3 FIR_t + \alpha_4 LRER_t + \alpha_5 \pi_t^v + u_t \quad (12.1)$$

where LRJM (J = N, B) is the log of real money balances (LRNM for narrowly defined money or LRBM for broadly defined money), Ly is the log of real income, NIR is a representative domestic interest rate, FIR is a representative foreign interest rate, LRER is the log of a real exchange rate such as the real effective exchange rate (REER), π_t^v is a measure of inflation volatility and u_t is a random error term. In this specification, real income represents a scale variable and its coefficient is expected to bear a positive sign and have a value not significantly different from one. The coefficients on both the domestic and foreign interest rate bear a negative sign. However, following the discussion in Appendix 5, the coefficients on the real exchange rate and inflation volatility remain indeterminate a priori.

The unit root test results suggest that all the variables in the specified model have a unit root. Consequently, they are eligible to form a cointegral money-demand relationship. Preliminary estimation results with a shorter period suggest that the deposit rate of interest in Thailand and the US Federal funds rate (USFFR) become significant when one of them is used in the model. The model is then estimated using the USFFR as the opportunity cost variable. The USFFR is considered more appropriate as it was largely market determined while in Thailand the deposit rate of interest was institutionally determined until the late 1990s.

Table 12.5 reports both the autoregressive distributed lag (ARDL) and ordinary least squares (OLS) results for real narrow money-demand function. To conserve space, the results obtained using the broad definition of

Table 12.5 The ARDL and OLS regression results of narrow money-demand relationship

F-statistic	6.41			
W-statistic	32.04			
Critical value bounds	F-test	W-test		
90%	(2.56, 3.73)	(12.80, 18.64)		
95%	(3.07, 4.33)	(15.37, 21.64)		
Sample period	1957–2012 ARDL (1,2,0,1,0) (Selected based on SBC)	1957–2012 ARDL (2,0,1) Long-run model	1955–2012 OLS (Static model)	1955–2012 OLS (Dynamic model)
Regressors	Coefficient (t-ratio) [prob.]	Coefficient (t-ratio) [prob.]	Coefficient (t-ratio) [prob.]	Coefficient (t-ratio) [prob.]
Intercept	0.57 (1.58) [0.12]	1.76 (1.52) [0.13]	0.82 (1.32) [0.19]	0.48 (1.25) [0.22]
LRNM(−1)	0.68 (10.29) [0.00]			0.70 (9.15) [0.00]
LRGDP	0.74 (2.55) [0.01]	0.82 (21.65) [0.00]	0.83 (37.98) [0.00]	0.25(3.98) [0.00]
LRGDP(−1)	−1.69 (−3.66) [0.00]			
LRGDP(−2)	1.21 (4.47) [0.00]			
USFFR	−0.01 (−3.23) [0.00]	−0.04 (−3.75) [0.00]	−0.04 (−6.91) [0.00]	−0.02 (−3.50) [0.00]
LRER	−0.30 (−1.81) [0.08]	0.34 (1.25) [0.22]	0.47 (3.14) [0.00]	0.10 (0.97) [0.34]
LRER(−1)	0.41 (2.36) [0.02]			
INFVOL	−0.004 (−0.04) [0.97]	−0.00 (0.04) [0.97]	0.05 (2.94) [0.01]	0.01 (0.79) [0.43]
Diagnostics				
Adjusted R^2	0.99		0.98	0.99

Lagrange multiplier test for serial correlation	F(1,46) = 0.02 [0.90]		F(1,52) = 24.93 [0.00]	F(1,51) = 0.64 [0.43]
Ramsey's RESET test of functional form mis-specification	F(1,46) = 1.11 [0.30]		F(1,52) = 42.94 [0.00]	F(1,51) = 0.73 [0.40]
Normality of residuals	$\chi^2_{(2)} = 7.18$ [0.03]		$\chi^2_{(2)} = 0.43$ [0.81]	$\chi^2_{(2)} = 582.27$ [0.00]
Heteroskedasticity	F(1,54) = 0.34 [0.56]		F(1,56) = 2.80 [0.10]	F(1,56) = 0.77 [0.38]
The Wald test:				
H_O: Coefficient on LRGDP = 0		$\chi^2_{(1)} = 468.82$ [0.00]	$\chi^2_{(1)} = 1442.4$ [0.00]	
H_O: Coefficient on LRGDP = 1		$\chi^2_{(1)} = 22.29$ [0.00]	$\chi^2_{(1)} = 63.12$ [0.00]	
H_O: Coefficient on USFFR = 0		$\chi^2_{(1)} = 14.05$ [0.06]	$\chi^2_{(1)} = 47.69$ [0.00]	
H_O: Coefficient on LRER = 0		$\chi^2_{(1)} = 1.57$ [0.21]	$\chi^2_{(1)} = 9.87$ [0.00]	
H_O: Coefficient on INFVOL = 0		$\chi^2_{(1)} = 0.01$ [0.97]	$\chi^2_{(1)} = 8.63$ [0.00]	

Note: Definitions of variables: LRNM = log of real narrow money balances; LRGDP = log of real GDP; USFFR = US Federal funds rate; LRER = log of the real exchange rate; and INFVOL = inflation volatility.

money are not reported. The results obtained by OLS are found superior to those obtained by ARDL. The ARDL results suggest the presence of a strong long-run cointegral relationship among real narrow money balances, real income and the US Federal funds rate. As expected, real income remains the core determinant of narrow money demand. The income elasticity of the demand for real narrow money balances is about one. The real exchange rate and inflation volatility are not significantly different from zero. The OLS-estimated results, however, suggest that the real exchange rate and inflation volatility have a significant impact on real narrow money balances. The CUSUM and CUSUMSQ tests results suggest that the narrow money-demand function remained stable over the study period (Figure 12.8).

Relationships Among Money, Output and Prices

Table 12.6 reports the cointegration test results among money, output and prices over 1970–2012. The results obtained for the broad money definition are found more robust than those obtained for the narrow definition. The Engle-Granger cointegration test results suggest a weak form of cointegral relationship among money, output and prices. The dynamic OLS (DOLS) estimates suggest that broad money is highly significant in the price level equation and that the coefficient value of broad money is significantly lower than one. As expected the real output coefficient bears a negative sign, but it is not statistically highly significant.

Engle and Granger (1987) suggest that one of the implications of a cointegral relation between two nonstationary variables is the presence of long-term causality between them running in at least one direction. Table 12.7 reports the bivariate Granger-causality test results among LCPI, LNM (LBM) and LRGDP. Test results are generated within a vector error-correction (VEC) modelling framework after selecting the optimal lag-length using the Schwarz Bayesian Criterion (SBC). The test results suggest that for Thailand, there is strong causality running from narrow or broad money growth to inflation. Money growth, either narrow or broad, is found to have a causal impact on output growth.

SUMMARY AND CONCLUSION

Thailand has emerged as one of the major industrializing economies in Southeast Asia. It has made substantive economic and social progress since the 1950s. After a decade-long economic boom from the mid 1980s through the mid 1990s, Thailand experienced a financial crisis in 1997.

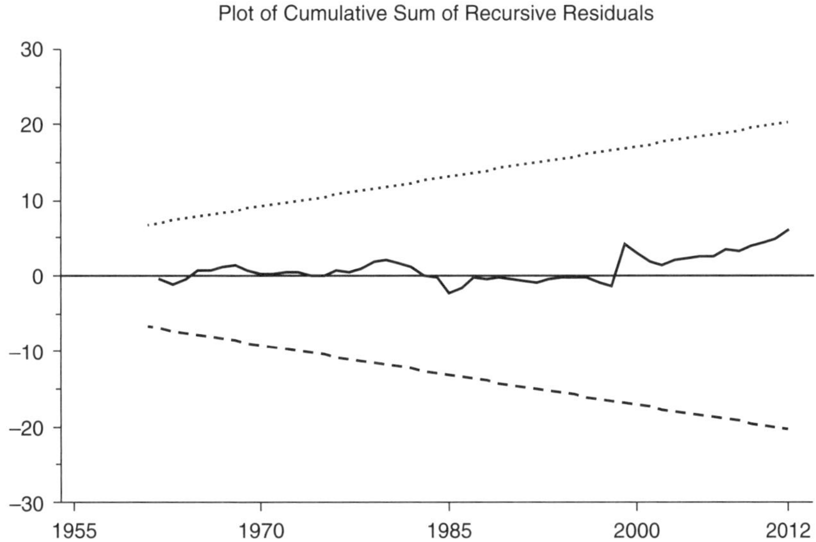

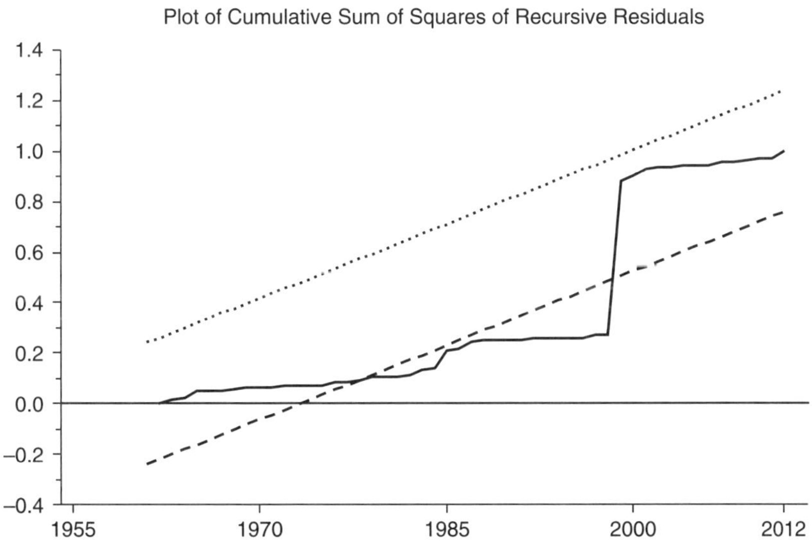

Note: The straight lines represent critical bounds at 5% significance level.

Figure 12.8 CUSUM and CUSUMSQ of residuals for real narrow money-demand relationships in Thailand

Table 12.6 Cointegration test results among money, output and prices in Thailand

Dependent variable = LCPI								
	Fully modified OLS				Dynamic OLS			
					(lead = 1, lag = 1)			
With narrow money (NM)								
Regressor	coefficient	t-ratio	prob.		coefficient	t-ratio	prob.	
Intercept	0.91	2.49	0.02		0.79	1.99	0.06	
LNM	0.06	0.30	0.77		−0.20	−0.71	0.48	
LRGDP	0.72	1.95	0.06		1.16	2.31	0.03	
Sample period	1970–2012				1970–2011			
DW	0.19				0.39			
Adjusted R^2	0.96				0.96			
	tau-statistic	prob.	z-statistic	prob.	tau-statistic	prob.	z-statistic	prob.
The Engle-Granger cointegration tests	−2.96	0.29	−12.52	0.38	−2.96	0.29	−12.52	0.38
The Phillips-Ouliaris cointegration tests	−2.23	0.63	−7.46	0.74	−2.23	0.63	−7.46	0.74
With broad money (BM)								
Regressor	coefficient	t-ratio	prob.		coefficient	t-ratio	prob.	
Intercept	1.98	6.45	0.00		1.93	4.15	0.00	
LBM	0.61	4.10	0.00		0.64	3.11	0.00	
LRGDP	−0.6	−1.72	0.09		−0.66	−1.35	0.19	
Sample period	1970–2012				1970–2011			
DW	0.26				0.3			
Adjusted R^2	0.98				0.98			
	tau-statistic	prob.	z-statistic	prob.	tau-statistic	prob.	z-statistic	prob.
The Engle-Granger cointegration tests	−3.02	0.26	−15.5	0.22	−3.02	0.26	−15.5	0.22
The Phillips-Ouliaris cointegration tests	−2.03	0.72	−7.64	0.73	−2.03	0.72	−7.64	0.72

Note: Definitions of variables: LCPI = log of the consumer price index; LNM = log of narrow money stock; LBM = log of broad money stock; and LRGDP = log of real GDP.

Table 12.7 Granger-causality among money, output and prices in Thailand, 1950–2012

	Hypotheses No causality runs from:	Chi-square statistic (prob.)	Inference at 5% level
VEC specification	ΔLNM → ΔLCPI	10.28 (0.01)	Null hypothesis rejected
(With Narrow Money, NM)	ΔLNM, ΔLRGDP → ΔLCPI	11.83 (0.02)	Null hypothesis rejected
	ΔLCPI → ΔLNM	2.53 (0.28)	Null hypothesis not rejected
	ΔLRGDP → ΔLNM	12.67 (0.00)	Null hypothesis rejected
	ΔLCPI → ΔLRGDP	0.68 (0.71)	Null hypothesis not rejected
	ΔLNM → ΔLRGDP	2.48 (0.29)	Null hypothesis not rejected
VEC specification	ΔLBM → ΔLCPI	7.33 (0.03)	Null hypothesis rejected
(With Broad Money, BM)	ΔLBM, ΔLRGDP → ΔLCPI	10.71 (0.03)	Null hypothesis rejected
	ΔLCPI → ΔLBM	3.68 (0.16)	Null hypothesis not rejected
	ΔLRGDP → ΔLBM	0.55 (0.76)	Null hypothesis not rejected
	ΔLCPI → ΔLRGDP	1.22 (0.54)	Null hypothesis not rejected
	ΔLBM → ΔLRGDP	3.72 (0.16)	Null hypothesis not rejected

Note: Definitions of variables; LCPI = log of the consumer price index; LNM = log of narrow money stock; LBM = log of broad money stock;. LRGDP = log of real GDP. Optimal lag length = 2 (selected based on the Schwarz Bayesian Criterion, SBC).

This affected the economy heavily, yet turned out to be a blessing in disguise in so far as the macroeconomic management of Thailand.

Thailand generally maintained conservative economic policy from the 1950s throughout the 1980s. Average inflation was relatively low, though unstable, under a succession of variations of the pegged exchange rate system deployed by the Thai authorities from the 1950s through the late 1990s. Thailand maintained some control over capital flows, leaving monetary policy with only limited potency to achieve and sustain the objective of price stability, until financial reform began in the early 1980s. The exchange rate was used as an anchor to prices; however, the pegged exchange rate system did not achieve price stability in the sense of sustaining low and stable inflation. The presence of a large non-tradables sector made inflation unstable as the economy was exposed to both domestic and external shocks. Moderately high and volatile inflation created high volatility of both the real interest rate and the real exchange rate in a mildly repressed financial system. This in turn affected real output and its growth.

The currency crisis of the late 1990s was the outcome of large-scale inflows of foreign capital in Thailand from the late 1980s through the mid 1990s. The authorities appreciated the real exchange rate in an overheated economy under a pegged exchange rate system. Consequently, foreign investors lost confidence in the monetary authority's ability to maintain a pegged exchange rate system in the face of a build-up in the level of external debt, mostly shorter term in nature. The ensued speculative currency attack on the baht forced the authorities to float the baht in the foreign currency markets in July 1997. Since then Thailand has limited the money-growth rate to control inflation. The 1997–98 IMF stabilization and structural adjustment programmes were influential in bringing about this policy stance. The BOT closed about 40 nearly insolvent financial firms and reduced excess liquidity in the financial market. After undertaking both economic and financial reforms that stabilized the economy, Thailand abandoned monetary targeting and moved to adopt inflation targeting in 2000.

The Thai economy has been progressing steadily since its recovery from the currency crisis. Following the adoption of inflation targeting, Thailand has maintained a rate of inflation of less than 2 per cent per annum. Inflation persistence has, however, remained high and inflation volatility has not diminished much. The low average rate of inflation in Thailand has been associated with economic growth of about 5 per cent per annum. This is significant as the relatively solid rate of growth has helped to dissipate economic pessimism in Thailand in the wake of the East-Southeast Asian financial crisis. Moreover, the Thai economy was exposed to three major shocks during 2008–12: (1) the US-global financial crisis during

2007–09; (2) the Japanese earthquake of 2010; and (3) the Thai floods of 2011. The Thai economy has shown an impressive resilience to these shocks under its managed float exchange rate system.

As Thailand's economic fundamentals have strengthened over the past decade, economic growth in the near future is expected to remain high, at about 5 per cent per annum. Thailand does face one major risk to its rate of economic development, however: political instability. A further risk for the economy originates in large-scale capital flows, which are often countercyclical and volatile. Facing volatile capital flows, the government remains committed to maintain fiscal discipline and to keep the level of public debt ratio under 50 per cent of GDP.

Under the managed float exchange rate system, Thailand's continuing use of inflation targeting remains an appropriate strategy of monetary policy. There is, however, scope for improvement in the implementation of monetary policy in Thailand. The issue is the choice of instrument by which the inflation target is achieved. The specific question is whether the policy interest rate should remain the preferred instrument, or whether the BOT should use a monetary aggregate instead.

One reason for the abandonment of monetary targeting was the alleged instability of the money-demand function and the breakdown of the linkages between money growth and inflation. The modern literature on monetary theory does not consider money-demand stability essential to establish a linkage between money growth and inflation. At the same time, money-demand stability does not lead to a linkage between money growth and inflation. This chapter has investigated some monetary relations for Thailand, especially the question of stability of the narrow money-demand function and the linkage between money growth and inflation. The narrow money-demand function in Thailand has been found more stable than the broad money-demand function. A strong causal relation is found to exist between money growth (narrow or broad) and inflation. The overall results indicate the need for deployment of money, whether as an instrument or as an information variable, to improve the conduct of monetary policy under inflation targeting. Money growth, especially, could be useful as a predictor of inflation, which is important in a forward-looking monetary policy.

Finally, in recent years large inflows of foreign capital from developed countries have created some problems for many developing countries. The question is whether governments should impose capital controls to stabilize exchange rates against such large-scale capital flows, especially in countries having only thin, underdeveloped money and capital markets. Market-based capital controls may be considered useful to maintain exchange rate stability. Given that Thailand maintains disciplined fiscal and monetary policies and has accumulated foreign reserves, the flexible exchange rate system would remain broadly stable while acting as a stabilizing factor in the event of large-scale capital flows. Market-based capital controls are unlikely to damage the economy or undermine the openness of the capital account of the balance-of-payments.

NOTES

1. Some general information on this chapter is drawn from a various country-specific publications, especially Thailand in http://en.wikipedia.org/wiki/Thailand, country information on the Bank of Thailand, http://www.bot.or.th/english/ and the IMF website, http://www.imf.org/external/country/THA/index.htm. For more detailed information on economic and political issues in Thailand, see Phongpaichit and Baker (2002).
2. Some information on this section is drawn from the Bank of Thailand, http://www.bot.or.th/english/.
3. For discussion on the conduct of monetary policy under inflation targeting, see Pornpattanapaisankul (2010).
4. For detailed discussion on the monetary policy transmission mechanisms in Thailand, see Bank of Thailand (2008), Baqir (2002), Charoenseang and Manakit (2007) and Nidhiprabha (1993).
5. For early studies on the money-demand function, see Chowdhury (1997), Hataiseree (1993) and Sumner (2009).

REFERENCES

Alba, P., L. Hernandez and D. Klingebiel (1999), 'Financial liberalization and the capital account: Thailand 1988–1997', World Bank Policy Research Paper No. 2188, Washington, DC.

Alp, H. and S. Elekdag (2012), 'Shock therapy! What role for Thai monetary policy', IMF Working Paper WP/12/269.

Bahmani-Oskooee, M. and A. Techaratanachai (2001), 'Currency substitution in Thailand', *Journal of Policy Modeling*, **23**, 141–5.

Bank of Thailand (various years), *Annual Report*, Bangkok: Bank of Thailand.

Bank of Thailand (1998), 'Focus on the Thai crisis', *Bank of Thailand Economic Focus*, **2**(2), April–June.

Bank of Thailand (2008), 'Changes in the monetary transmission mechanism in Thailand', Transmission Mechanisms for Monetary Policy in Emerging Market Economies, BIS Papers No. 35, Bank for International Settlements, Basel, 451–75.

Baqir, R. (2002), 'The channels of monetary policy transmission in Thailand', in *Thailand: Selected Issues and Statistical Appendix, Country Report No. 02/195*, Washington, DC: IMF, pp. 5–16.

Charoenseang, J. and P. Manakit (2007), 'Thai monetary policy transmission in an inflation targeting era', *Journal of Asian Economics*, **18**, 144–57.

Chowdhury, A.R. (1997), 'The financial structure and the demand for money in Thailand', *Applied Economics*, **29**, 401–9.

Disyatat, P. and P. Vongsinsirikul (2002), 'Monetary policy and the transmission mechanism in Thailand', *Journal of Asian Economics*, **14**, 398–418.

Engle, R.F. and C.W.J. Granger (1987), 'Co-integration and error-correction: representation, estimation, and testing', *Econometrica*, **55**(2), 251–76.
Fane, G. and R.H. McLeod (1999), 'Lessons for monetary and banking policies from the 1997–1998 economic crises in Indonesia and Thailand', *Journal of Asian Economics*, **10**, 395–413.
Grenville, S. and T. Ito (2010), 'An independent evaluation of the Bank of Thailand's monetary policy under the Inflation Targeting Framework, 2000–2010', available at https://www.bot.or.th/Thai/MonetaryPolicy/Documents/GrenvilleItoV10(Oct22).pdf (accessed 19 March 2015).
Hataiseree, R. (1993), 'The demand for money in Thailand: a cointegration and error-correction approach', *Singapore Economic Review*, **38**(2), 195–230.
IMF (International Monetary Fund) (various years), *International Financial Statistics*, Washington, DC: IMF.
IMF (International Monetary Fund) (various years), *World Economic Outlook*, Washington, DC: IMF.
Jansen, K. (1997), *External Finance in Thailand's Development: An Interpretation of Thailand's Growth Boom*, London: Macmillan.
Jansen, K. (2001), 'Thailand, financial crisis and monetary policy', *Journal of the Asia Pacific Economy*, **6**(1), 124–52.
Kochhar, K. and Associates (1996), 'Thailand: the road to sustained research', Occasional Paper 146, Washington, DC, IMF.
McCallum, B.T. and E. Nelson (2011), 'Money and inflation: some critical issues', in B.M. Friedman and M. Woodford (eds), *Handbook of Monetary Economics*, Vol. 3A, Amsterdam: Elsevier Science, pp. 97–153.
Nakornthab, D. (2008), 'Thailand's monetary policy since the 1997 crises', *Kobe University Economic Review*, **55**, 75–88.
Nidhiprabha, B. (1993), 'Monetary policy', in P.G. Warr (ed.), *The Thai Economy in Transition*, Cambridge: Cambridge University Press, pp. 172–98.
Nidhiprabha, B. (1998), 'Adverse consequences of capital inflows and Thailand's optimal policy mix', in C.H. Kwan, D. Vandenbrink and C.S. Yue (eds), *Coping with Capital Flows in East Asia*, Singapore: Institute of Southeast Asian Studies, pp. 192–219.
Phongpaichit, P. and C. Baker (2002), *Thailand: Economy and Politics*, Oxford: Oxford University Press.
Pornpattanapaisankul, K. (2010), 'Monetary policy rule under an inflation targeting framework: evidence from Thailand', *Thammasat Economic Journal*, **28**(3), 143–69.
Robinson, D., Y. Byeon and R. Teja (1991), 'Thailand: adjusting to success – current policy issues', Occasional Paper 85, Washington, DC, IMF.
Siregar, R. and G. Rajaguru (2005), 'Sources of variations between the inflation rates of Korea, Thailand and Indonesia during the post-1997 crisis', *Journal of Policy Modeling*, **27**, 867–84.
Sumner, M. (2009), 'Demand for money in Thailand', *Applied Economics*, **41**, 1269–76.

13. The United States

The United States of America is the third largest country by land area. The US population approximates 315 million. Its population density is about 34 persons per square kilometre. The United States is a multi-ethnic immigrant society, comprising diverse cultural and religious communities from across the globe. Until European colonization in the early seventeenth century, it was inhabited by the Paleo-Indians who migrated from Asia. About 70 per cent of the population is of European origin and 80 per cent are Christian of diverse denominations.

Politically, the United States is a constitutional republic and a federation of 50 constituent states with separate legislative and administrative bodies. The United States is a representative democracy, with well-developed constitutional checks and balances on political power and administration.[1]

The United States is the largest market-oriented economy in the world and outright the world's largest economy as measured by annual GDP, at US$16 trillion. While the United States has the third highest per capita income in the world, income inequality is among the highest of the developed countries. This has made the United States an inegalitarian society and stymied its social cohesion and progress.

The US economy is post-industrial, although it remains a dominant manufacturing country. Agriculture contributes only about 1 per cent of GDP despite the country being the largest producer of some agricultural commodities such as corn and soybeans. About 68 per cent of US GDP is generated by the services sector. As the United States produces about 20 per cent of global output in terms of purchasing power parity, the impact of US economic activity is felt across the globe. This is apparent whenever the United States encounters economic crisis: economists paraphrase this in the saying, 'if the US sneezes, the rest of the world catches cold'.

The US economy has become increasingly integrated with the global economy since the early 1970s when it opened its economy. Perhaps the most visible aspect of this process was the so-called détente process with China initiated by then US President Richard Nixon. Presently, the United States is the largest importer and the second largest exporter in the world. Its major trading partners are Canada, China, Mexico, Japan, Germany and Saudi Arabia. The United States is a resourceful country in terms of all four factors of production, and the third largest producer of oil while remaining a major importer of oil, mostly from the Gulf (Krugman et al., 2015).

As the largest economy in the world, the United States wields political and economic clout as a major trading partner with all other countries. New York is a major centre of international finance, while the US dollar is heavily used as a reserve currency across the globe. Consequently, US economic policies have a major impact on the economic performance of many countries. Large US budget deficits since the 1980s have led to accumulation of government debt to unprecedented levels, exceeding 100 per cent of GDP. China, Japan, South Korea, Singapore and Taiwan are among the largest foreign holders of US debt securities. Since the US-global financial crisis of 2007–09, US monetary, fiscal and exchange rate policies have generated heated debate because of their global impact on economic activity and performance. Moreover, there is the suggestion that the 1973 collapse of the Bretton Woods exchange rate system, which had delivered general financial stability from the late 1940s, was due largely to US expansionary monetary and fiscal policies implemented from the 1960s to finance the American war in Vietnam.

US monetary and fiscal policies remain highly relevant to other countries, especially those many countries that fix their currencies to the US dollar. The United States conducts monetary policy in a discretionary manner to achieve twin objectives: price stability and high employment. Consequently, the priority of policy objectives alters frequently, leaving monetary policy ambiguous and therefore diminished in its ability to maintain low and stable inflation. Elevated levels of volatility in both inflation and output growth, and consequently unnecessarily elevated levels of unemployment in the long run, are the main consequences.

US inflation was moderately high and volatile throughout the 1950s and 1960s. Inflation became particularly high and volatile during the 1970s. While it was already on an upward trend in the late 1960s, the OPEC oil price shocks of 1973–74 accelerated inflation. It was then sustained moderately high for about a decade. Attempting to bring it under control, the United States adopted monetary targeting in the late 1970s. The strategy was not strictly pursued, however, giving rise to the criticism that inflation remained high and volatile until the mid 1980s.

Since 1982 the Federal Reserve System (FRS), the central bank of the United States, also known as the ‘Fed’ (but referred to in this chapter as the FRS) has conducted monetary policy without explicitly designating a nominal anchor such as the monetary aggregate or an inflation target. It may have maintained a ‘rule-like’ monetary policy framework from 1985 to 2003, in which the Federal funds rate was used as the instrument of monetary policy to maintain low and stable inflation. Mishkin (2013) suggests that the FRS had a coherent strategy of monetary policy during the Greenspan era (1987–06), which Mishkin calls the 'just do it' policy. Following the principles of inflation targeting, the FRS monitored the key leading indicators of inflation. It used a wide range of information on macro variables and then took periodic pre-emptive action aimed at dissipating inflationary pressures before they could build. The FRS's success in maintaining low inflation under Greenspan's chairmanship was appreciated by most stakeholders in the economy, though monetary policy remained discretionary and non-transparent. A dark shadow has fallen on the Greenspan era as Taylor (2011, 2012a) argues strongly that US monetary policy, 2003–05, seeded the US-global financial crisis, 2007–09.

A serious concern is that US monetary policy has remained expansionary since the US-global financial crisis, creating monetary overhang and the potential for an acceleration of inflation in the near future. For monetary stability and steady economic growth, Taylor (2012b, p. 1024) suggests the introduction of rule-based monetary policy in the United States:

> Much economic theory supports the more straightforward explanation that rules-based policy caused the improved performance [in the United States during 1985–2003]. Economic models in which people are forward looking and take time to adjust their behavior imply that policy rules work better than discretion. Kydland and Prescott (1977) put forth the time-inconsistency argument in favor of rules and Lucas (1976) shows that rules are essential for conducting and evaluating policy. But there are many other reasons why rules-based policies work better. Rules reduce uncertainty about future policy. They help policymakers avoid pressures from special interest groups and instead take actions consistent with long-run goals. Policy rules facilitate communication and increase accountability.

This begs the key question of whether the FRS would be capable of maintaining low inflation, steady economic growth and financial stability simultaneously until it redirected monetary policy to the single goal of price stability. Its strategy of 'implicit' inflation targeting since 2013 is a move forward along these lines. Success, however, would depend on whether the FRS could exercise sufficient autonomy to achieve the redirection. There is the suggestion that in order to avoid creating time-inconsistency problems the FRS should discard its goal of achieving any real objectives external to its immediate concern.

THE FEDERAL RESERVE SYSTEM: ORGANIZATION AND ACTIVITIES[2]

Central banking in the United States began in 1913 with the establishment of the FRS. The aim was to ensure a safe form of commercial banking in the country. Bank failures were a common phenomenon in the United States during the eighteenth and early nineteenth centuries. A major reason for many pre-FRS bank failures was the absence of a central bank and the associated lender-of-last-resort (LLR) service.

Historically there had been opposition to the establishment of a central bank in the United States. A central banking institution was portrayed as a centralized power and a repository of 'moneyed interests'. Consequently, attempts to establish a central bank in the United States were unsuccessful. Through time, frequent bank failures led to the establishment in 1913 of a central bank with authority to act as LLR for commercial banks.

Since establishment in 1913 there has been an intermittently resurgent debate over whether the FRS has retained a level of independence from government sufficient for it to have performed its assigned role. One of the legacies of the FRS in the United States is its failure to prevent large numbers of bank failures during the Great Depression of the 1930s. Since 1933 the Federal Deposit Insurance System (FDIS) has been in place to prevent runs on commercial banks. Further, regulatory measures have been introduced to separate the commercial banking industry from the securities industry to restrain the deposit-issuing banks from engaging in risky behaviour. Over time, banking regulation has become highly complex under increasing layers of administrative jurisdiction. Since the US-global financial crisis of 2007–09 there has been pressure for national consolidation of, and administrative jurisdiction over, banking regulations. Financial stability has therefore gained importance as an issue in central banking in the United States (Mishkin, 2011, 2013).

The Federal Reserve Banks and the Federal Reserve System

The FRS is not a single entity operating at the centre of the financial system. It comprises 12 Federal Reserve Banks distributed across the country. Its founders designed this unusual decentralized structure under the Federal Reserve Act to decentralize monetary power along regional lines, between the private sector and the government and among bankers, businesspeople and the public. To establish a federated central banking system, the country has been divided into 12 Federal Reserve districts. Each of these districts has one main Federal Reserve Bank (FRB), with the provision of having branches in other cities within the district. The three largest Federal Reserve Banks are in New York, Chicago and San Francisco.

Unlike most central banks, the FRBs are quasi-public (part private, part government) institutions. They are owned by those private commercial banks that are members of the Federal Reserve System. Each FRB is governed by six directors elected by member banks in its district, plus three directors appointed by the Board of Governors of the FRS. These nine directors appoint the president of the Federal Reserve Bank in a district, subject to the approval of the Board of Governors of the FRS (Mishkin, 2013).

The Federal Reserve Banks have the following functions:

(a) clear cheques
(b) issue new currency notes
(c) withdraw damaged currency notes from circulation
(d) evaluate any proposed bank mergers and applications for expanding banks' activities
(e) administer and make discount loans to banks in their districts
(f) act as liaisons between the business community and the FRS
(g) examine bank-holding companies and state-chartered member banks
(h) collect data on regional economic and business conditions
(i) undertake research on issues in monetary theory and policy.

The FRS, headquartered in Washington, DC, is governed by a seven-member Board of Governors. Each governor is appointed by the president of the United States and confirmed by the US Senate. To limit presidential influence on the FRS and insulate it from political pressure, the governors serve a single, non-renewable 14-year term. One governor's term expires every other January. The governors are required to come from different Federal Reserve districts, leaving five of the twelve FRS districts contributing no governor to the Board. Nevertheless, the 'one-district-one-governor' provision mitigates overrepresentation of any one district on the Board. The US president chooses the chairman of the Board from the seven governors. It is a four-year appointment, renewable for one or more terms at the president's discretion. When a new chairman is chosen, the current incumbent resigns from the Board, even if his or her tenure as a governor remains unexhausted.

Since all seven governors sit on the Federal Open Market Committee (FOMC), the Board of Governors has significant input into US monetary policy decisions. The FOMC meets eight times a year and makes decisions on the stance and direction of monetary policy. It is commonly referred to as the 'Fed' in the press. The FOMC comprises, in addition to the seven members of the FRS Board of Governors, the president of the Federal Reserve Bank of New York and the presidents of four other Federal Reserve Banks. The chairman of the Board of Governors is the chairman of the FOMC and presides over meetings where monetary policy issues are debated and decisions are made. Even though only the presidents of five, out of twelve, of the FRBs are voting members of the FOMC, the presidents of all the FRBs attend FOMC meetings and participate in policy discussion. The chairman of the FOMC makes recommendations on the direction of monetary policy. These recommendations are voted on by the FOMC members for implementation. The appearance is of a democratic process of monetary policy decision-making, but there is criticism of its substance. It is claimed that the chairman's stance on monetary policy bears disproportionately high weighting and is ultimately adopted for implementation. This has personalized monetary decision-making and hence the governor of the FRS is widely quoted as the person who has the authority to change monetary policy in the United States.

Objectives and Strategy of Monetary Policy

The FRS conducts monetary policy under a dual mandate: achieving price stability and maximum employment (output stability).[3] The Federal Reserve Act does not specify any single objective of monetary policy to maintain monetary stability, and there is no penalty–reward framework to discipline the FRS. For example, the Amended Federal Reserve Act (Section 2A) states:

> Nothing in this Act shall be interpreted to require that the objectives and plans with respect to the ranges of growth or diminution of the monetary and credit aggregates disclosed in the reports submitted under this section be achieved.

The Federal Reserve Act therefore provides the FRS with discretion in choosing one or more objective(s) over others and in selection of the instruments to be deployed in pursuit of the chosen objective(s). Consequently, the priority order of the FRS's two objectives has oscillated over time depending on economic conditions and, moreover, depending on the personalities involved in decisions on US monetary policy. Disagreement remains on the issue of whether the twin objectives of monetary policy are compatible (Mishkin, 2007a). Economists generally consider economic growth and price stability complementary, provided inflation remains low and stable. Both theory and empirics suggest that price stability is necessary to create an environment for sustained and stable economic growth. There is, however, no consensus on whether price stability implies zero inflation and whether price stability overrides other objective(s). Further, the US-global financial crisis of 2007–09 has brought to the FRS the additional responsibility of maintaining financial stability. Labonte (2012, p. 2) has summarized this as follows:

> Thus, the Federal Reserve has a monetary policy function and a financial stability function. Its monetary policy function is one of aggregate demand management. The availability and cost of credit are used to manage aggregate demand in such a way as to promote a stable price level and through it maximum sustainable employment. Its financial stability function is as 'lender of last resort' to the nation's financial system.

Hence, the FRS remains in the mode of using monetary policy to achieve multiple objectives. The question of whether or not this is feasible is not apparently a pressing concern of the monetary authorities in general. Jordan (2014, pp. 215–16) points this out:

> As the FRS celebrates its centennial, politicians have come to view it as an activist instrument of economic policy making responsible for pursuing multiple objectives of financial stability, employment, output, low interest rates, and tolerable inflation – all with the single tool of the power to create fiat currency.

Independence of the FRS

Until recently the FRS was considered one of the most independent central banks in the world, with the ability to withstand pressure from the executive branch of the government. This view is no longer valid. While the FRS has instrument independence to pursue its monetary policy objectives handed down by the Federal Reserve Act, as amended, it lacks goal independence, since its goals are set out for it by the Act. The Congress and the president are known to put both overt and covert pressure on the FRS to influence monetary policy decisions. As Labonte (2012, p. 1) remarks, 'Congress has delegated responsibility for monetary policy to the FRS, but retains oversight responsibilities to ensure that the FRS is adhering to its statutory mandate of "maximum employment, stable prices, and moderate long-term interest rates".'

For example, the extraordinary monetary policy measures, known as quantitative easing, adopted in the United States since the US-global financial crisis to recover financial stability and to promote economic growth, are not consistent with best-practice monetary policy aimed at long-term price stability. The FRS justified its monetary stance under the statutory mandate. Whether despite this, or because of it, there is pressure to replace the current dual, and theoretically internally conflicting, mandate with the single mandate of price stability, as defined by a numerical inflation target. Debate continues on the merits and demerits of inflation targeting within the context of the rule versus discretion debate in monetary policy and its impact on the intensity of business cycles (Labonte, 2012).

EVOLUTION OF MONETARY POLICY

The FRS maintains the dual mandate of its Charter. It has varied its strategy of monetary policy over time with changing economic conditions. Here follows a brief discussion on the key features of monetary strategies adopted in the United States since the 1950s.

'Interest Rate Targeting' and 'Free Reserves Targeting': 1951–70

In the early 1950s the FRS maintained the view that monetary policy should be conducted taking into account money-market conditions as reflected in the nominal interest rate. In an operational sense in the FRS, it took the form of interest rate targeting. FRS interest targeting began in the early 1950s as an outcome of a conflict with the Treasury over ownership of monetary policy.

The origins of the conflict lie in FRS funding of Treasury spending during World War II, when the FRS pegged the interest rates on government bonds at their pre-war levels. This policy allowed the US Treasury, the issuer of government bonds, to finance large budget deficits cheaply as part of the war effort. However, the policy led to pro-cyclical money supply growth that created inflation volatility. Under the FRS Accord with the Treasury, the FRS was obligated to maintain control over the money supply. To do so, the FRS used both the 'free reserves' of the banking system (unloaned or excess bank reserves) and the short-term interest rate. The view of the FRS was that free reserves reflect slackness in the banking system. Accordingly, it sold securities (tightened monetary policy) when free reserves rose (that is, when real sector demand for them fell) and purchased securities (eased monetary policy) when free reserves fell (when demand was on the rise). Such action reduced the FRS's control over the money supply and made monetary policy pro-cyclical, boosting rises in demand and contributing force to downturns. Thus, in short, whether the FRS used 'interest rate targeting' or 'free reserves targeting', the outcome was pro-cyclical monetary policy that created high inflation and raised its volatility.

Monetary Targeting: 1970–79

In 1970, Arthur Burns became Chairman of FRS's Board of Governors. Monetarist economists in particular welcomed his appointment. Earlier, he had criticized the FRS's pro-cyclical monetary policy and its attendant high and volatile inflation during the 1950s and 1960s. Following Monetarist principles, Burns suggested that the FRS should deploy monetary aggregates as the intermediate target to control inflation. As it turned out, during his tenure in the 1970s, FRS monetary policy remained pro-cyclical, departing somewhat, as it did, from monetary targeting principles. Possibly FRS operating procedure was faulty. It continued with the Federal funds rate as an operating target. This made the money supply pro-cyclical. The rationale behind deploying the Federal funds rate as the operating target was the FRS's aim to maintain interest rate stability. Taylor (2012b) points out that the late 1960s and 1970s were the period when the FRS exercised little long-term thinking but a great deal of short-term fine-tuning. This led to a 'go-stop'-type money-growth cycle. The outcome was a series of boom-bust cycles and the ubiquitous high, volatile inflation. FRS behaviour became especially erratic when Burns abandoned monetary aggregates to maintain price stability and sought incomes policy (wage and price controls) to constrain inflation.

In July 1979, President Carter appointed Paul Volcker as Chairman of the FRS Board of Governors. Volcker committed to crush inflation and chose the monetary aggregates as the intermediate target. He replaced the Federal funds rate as the operating target with non-borrowed reserves where non-borrowed reserves were defined as total reserves minus those borrowed from the FRS discount window. This strategy created volatility in both the Federal funds rate and money supply growth (Friedman, 1983). Mishkin (2007b, p. 399) provides an explanation for this phenomenon:

> A more persuasive explanation for poor monetary control, however, is that controlling the money supply was never really the intent of Volcker's policy shift. Despite Volcker's statements about the need to target monetary aggregates, he was not committed to these targets. Rather, he was far more concerned with using interest-rate movements to wring inflation out of the economy. Volcker's primary reason for changing the FRS's operating procedure was to free his hand to manipulate interest rates and thereby fight inflation. It was necessary to abandon interest-rate targets if Volcker were to be able to raise interest rates sharply when a slowdown in the economy was required to dampen inflation. This view of Volcker's strategy suggests that the FRS's announced attachment to monetary aggregate targets may have been a smokescreen to keep the FRS from being blamed for the high interest rates that would result from the new interest-rate policy.

Back to Interest Rate Targeting After 1982

In October 1982, the FRS started to pay more attention to the Federal funds rate and reduced emphasis on monetary aggregates. This was effectively the abandonment in the United States of monetary targeting and the beginning of the conduct of monetary policy in a discretionary manner. Although there was no explicit nominal anchor to prices, the Federal funds rate was deployed to conduct monetary policy to achieve price stability while sustaining steady economic growth. In 1986, Alan Greenspan became Chairman of the FRS Board of Governors. He continued discretionary monetary policy and argued against rule-based monetary policy. During his regime (1986–2006), macroeconomic performance was highly satisfactory. US inflation remained low, while economic growth was about 3 per cent per annum. By the time Greenspan left the FRS, he had acquired 'icon' status. Since the US-global financial crisis, vigorous debate has been waged over the question of whether the FRS should have adopted a rule-based monetary policy, such as inflation targeting.

Ben Bernanke became Chairman of the FRS Board of Governors in 2006. As an academic economist, he advocated inflation targeting while Greenspan defended discretionary monetary policy. Greenspan argued that a greater emphasis should be placed upon employment generation because of the powerful short-term impact that monetary policy has upon the economy, and that greater focus on inflation under inflation targeting may create a volatile business cycle (Labonte, 2012). Fending off critics who suggested that US monetary policy was personalized and idiosyncratic, he maintained that the FRS should continue with discretionary monetary policy and not be constrained by policy rules or even by long-established traditions. According to Greenspan, the world economy is complex and policymakers should not assume that an economy behaves the way that standard economic models predict.

Bernanke's views on the discretion versus rule debate contrast against those of Greenspan. In a speech given at a conference at the FRB of St Louis in 2004, Bernanke outlined how the FRS should move towards inflation targeting. He suggested that the FRS should announce a numerical value for its long-run inflation goal that can be labelled as the optimal level of the inflation rate (OLIR). He emphasized that announcing the OLIR is consistent with the FRS's dual mandate of achieving price stability and maximum employment. He expected that the OLIR should be set above zero to avoid the danger of deflation that has harmful effects on employment. He expected no short-run inflation target because such targeting would require tighter control over inflation at the cost of employment fluctuation. Since becoming the FRS's Chairman, Bernanke maintained that any movement towards inflation targeting must result from consensus within the Federal Reserve System.

Over the past eight years monetary policy behaviour in the United States has remained discretionary, expansionary and erratic. Critics suggest that the US-global financial crisis was caused, propagated and sustained by misuse of monetary policy in the United States.[4] A brief discussion follows on this issue in a broad context.

US Monetary Policy and the Global Financial Crisis

The United States operates under a floating exchange rate system. Hence, it has monetary policy independence, in the sense that it gains control over interest rates or monetary aggregates that it can deploy to achieve a policy objective such as price stability. The FRS can conduct monetary policy either by applying policymaker discretion or under a policy rule, such as the Taylor rule for setting the Federal funds rate. As indicated, the FRS conducted discretionary monetary policy from the early 1980s. Nevertheless, as Taylor (2012a, 2012b) suggests, US interest rate movements mimicked the Taylor rule for the period 1985–2003, while ostensibly determined under a discretionary policy regime. Furthermore, although monetary policy probably took a Taylor rule-like form during the Volcker disinflation period, 1980–84, there is the suggestion that this strategy of monetary policy contributed to steady economic growth and low, stable inflation until the late 1990s. However, Taylor (2012a, 2012b) argues that the FRS kept the policy interest rate too low for too long a time during 2001–05 compared with any interest rate that could plausibly be argued to have prevailed had the FRS continued to operate under a Taylor rule.

The question remains as to why the FRS adopted an expansionary monetary policy during 2001–05. Taylor (2011, p. 59) suggests that '[deviation of the interest rate from its optimal level] was intended to ward off the perceived risk of deflation . . .'. This explanation is consistent with the proposition that the 2001 'mini-recession', followed closely by the technology dot-com bust in 2002, focused the attention of US policymakers acutely upon Japan's then decade-long deflation–stagnation malaise. They had developed a fear of the US economy sinking into comparable conditions. This explanation is consistent with the FRS Charter on the objectives of monetary policy. While long-term price stability remained the key objective of monetary policy in the United States throughout the period, Greenspan conducted discretionary monetary policy to achieve multiple objectives. One of these objectives was high employment generation. Inflation had been subdued in the 1980s, through both policy and conducive happenstance. Determined contractionary monetary policy had worked as well in the United States, in the same way as it had worked earlier when contractionary monetary policy was devised and implemented by the Bundesbank in Germany. The United States had also benefited from cheap imports from East Asian countries, especially from China, a region that had maintained a low-inflation environment. The consequence under the dual-objective policy regime was that the FRS's employment target acquired policy priority, together with the happily complementary policy goal of preventing a Japanese-style deflation. Bernanke (2010, pp. 3–4) confirmed this interpretation in his 2010 American Economic Association address, 'monetary policy and the housing bubble'. He writes:

> The aggressive monetary policy response in 2002 and 2003 was motivated by two principal factors. First, although the recession technically ended in late 2001, the recovery remained quite weak and 'jobless' into the latter part of 2003. Real gross domestic product (GDP), which normally grows above trend in the early stages of an economic expansion, rose at an average pace just above 2 percent in 2002 and the first half of 2003, a rate insufficient to halt continued increases in the unemployment rate, which peaked above 6 percent in the first half of 2003. Second, the FOMC's [Federal Open Market Committee] policy response also reflected concerns about a possible unwelcome decline in inflation. Taking note of the painful experience of Japan, policymakers worried that the United States might sink into deflation and that, as one consequence, the FOMC target interest rate might hit its zero lower bound, limiting the scope for further monetary accommodation. FOMC decisions during this period were informed by a strong consensus among researchers that, when faced with the risk of hitting the zero lower bound, policymakers should lower rates preemptively, thereby reducing the probability of ultimately being constrained by the lower bound on the policy interest rate.

Another politically inspired objective, one that played a key role in the housing bubble, was added to the list of monetary policy goals, partly as a consequence of the 2000–08 conservative Republican Presidency of George Bush. The objective was to use the Department of Housing and Urban Development to raise the proportion of US citizens able to own residential accommodation (raise the level of home ownership) 'through an intensive effort to reduce mortgage underwriting standards'. Consequently, expansionary monetary policy achieved and sustained the lowest possible mortgage interest rates, known as non-traditional mortgages (and including sub-prime mortgages). These rock-bottom mortgage prices boosted loan volumes to about 27 million mortgages in 2007. This objective disregarded the bluntness of monetary policy relative to other, more appropriate measures, as an instrument for achieving social policy objectives. Wallison (2011, p. 451) insists that the real reason behind the financial crisis was US government housing policy, which weakened the financial system:

> Although there were many contributing factors, the housing bubble of 1997–2007 would not have reached its dizzying heights or lasted as long, nor would the financial crisis of 2008 have ensued, but for the role played by the housing policies of the United States government over the course of two administrations. As a result of these policies, by the middle of 2007, there were approximately 27 million subprime and Alt-A mortgage in the US financial system – half of all mortgages outstanding – with an aggregate value of over $4.5 trillion . . . These were unprecedented numbers, far higher than any time

> in the past, and the losses associated with the delinquency and default of these mortgages fully account for the weakness and disruption of the financial system that has become known as the financial crisis.

The United States has continued with expansionary monetary policy since the US-global financial crisis. This has raised global concern as many developing countries in particular maintain an exchange rate peg with the US dollar and consequently import US monetary policy. US monetary policy has triggered large-scale capital flows, which have created opportunities and problems for many countries. Taylor (2012b), too, has been critical of US monetary policy since the early 2000s. He has consistently argued for rule-based monetary policy that sustains monetary and financial stability.[5]

MACROECONOMIC DEVELOPMENTS AND INFLATION PERFORMANCE

Table 13.1 reports the key macroeconomic indicators in the United States, 1950–2012. The United States maintained steady economic growth throughout the 1950s and 1960s, with economic growth averaging 4 per cent per annum. Growth then decelerated to 3 per cent per annum and remained there for three decades until the mid 2000s. US unemployment was 5 per cent throughout the 1950s and 1960s, rising to 7.5 per cent during the 1970s. From the early 1990s unemployment steadily improved to, and then remained around, 5 per cent until the US-global financial crisis of 2007–09. With the exception of the disrupted, and disruptive, oil price shock decade of the 1970s, inflation in the United States remained roughly about 3.5 per cent per annum. Since the early 2000s US annual inflation has remained around 2.5 per cent.

Unlike the turbulent 1970s, US macroeconomic performance was highly satisfactory over the next two and a half decades until the onslaught of the US-global financial crisis. The source of this good performance remains a matter of contention. There is some suggestion that, once inflation had been controlled in the early 1980s under the restrictive Volcker monetary policy, economic performance improved with respect to inflation, economic growth and employment. The strategy of monetary policy remained discretionary, but there is the suggestion that the FRS exercised the discretion to conduct implicitly what was effectively a form of flexible inflation targeting. There was no explicit numerical inflation target. Plausibly, however, the implicit target rate was both positive and sufficiently low such that it did not materially distort economic decision-making. An

Table 13.1 Macroeconomic indicators in the United States, 1951–2012

Macroeconomic indicators	1951–55	1956–60	1961–65	1966–70	1971–75	1976–80	1981–85	1986–90	1991–95	1996–2000	2001–05	2006–10	2011	2012
Budget balance (% of GDP)	n.a.	n.a.	n.a.	n.a.	n.a.	n.a.	n.a.	n.a.	n.a.	n.a.	−3.3	−7.2	−10.1	−8.7
General government gross debt (% of GDP)	n.a.	n.a.	n.a.	n.a.	n.a.	42.3	48.7	61.6	70.8	63.7	61.7	79.6	102.9	107.2
Money-growth rate (%)														
Narrow money growth	n.a.	0.6	3.6	5.0	6.1	7.3	8.6	6.0	6.6	−0.7	4.7	6.1	18.3	13.2
Broad money growth	n.a.	4.9	8.0	6.3	10.2	9.6	9.3	5.6	2.2	6.2	6.3	5.8	9.5	8.1
Real GDP growth (%)	4.5	2.5	5.0	3.4	2.7	3.7	3.3	3.2	2.5	4.3	2.4	0.7	1.8	2.2
GDP at current prices, US dollar	n.a.	n.a.	n.a.	n.a.	n.a.	12249	15406	20847	25742	32046	38874	46078	48328	49802
Unemployment rate (%)	n.a.	n.a.	n.a.	n.a.	n.a.	7.2	8.3	5.9	6.6	4.6	5.4	6.8	9.0	8.2
Output gap (% of potential GDP)	n.a.	n.a.	n.a.	n.a.	n.a.	−2.0	−2.3	0.9	−1.0	2.5	0.7	−1.6	−4.4	−4.1
CPI inflation rate (%)	2.2	2.0	1.3	4.3	6.8	8.9	5.5	4.0	3.1	2.5	2.6	2.2	3.2	2.1
Current account balance (% of GDP)	n.a.	n.a.	n.a.	n.a.	n.a.	0.1	−1.3	−2.4	−1.1	−2.6	−4.8	−4.3	−3.1	−3.1

Table 13.1 (continued)

Macroeconomic indicators	1951–55	1956–60	1961–65	1966–70	1971–75	1976–80	1981–85	1986–90	1991–95	1996–2000	2001–05	2006–10	2011	2012
Nominal interest rate (%)														
Treasury bill rate	1.6	2.8	3.2	5.5	5.8	7.8	10.1	6.8	4.3	5.1	2.1	2.2	0.1	0.1
Government bond yield	2.1	3.6	3.8	6.1	6.7	8.6	11.9	8.0	5.8	5.8	3.2	2.8	0.8	0.4
Real interest rate (%)[a]														
Treasury bill rate	−0.5	0.8	1.9	1.2	−0.9	−1.0	4.4	2.7	1.2	2.5	−0.4	−0.1	−3.0	−1.9
Government bond yield	0.0	1.6	2.5	1.7	0.0	−0.3	6.0	3.8	2.6	3.2	0.6	0.5	−2.3	−1.7
Nominal effective exchange rate[b]	n.a.	30.2	31.2	31.7	29.2	31.6	49.9	61.8	82.1	102.7	108.3	93.7	87.2	90.1
Real effective exchange rate[b]	n.a.	n.a.	n.a.	n.a.	108.9	101.7	123.4	102.2	93.4	102.0	107.0	94.3	86.9	89.6

Note:
n.a. = not available
a. Real interest rate is estimated as: 100(((1 + interest rate)/(1 + inflation rate))−1) where the interest rate and inflation rate are expressed as decimal.
b. A rise in the index value of the exchange rate represents appreciation.

Source: Author's computation based on IMF, *International Financial Statistics*; IMF, *World Economic Outlook*; and other country-specific publications on the IMF website.

implicit, rule-based monetary policy can therefore be viewed as the source of improved macroeconomic performance in the United States. Taylor (2012b, p. 1023) has provided a comparative assessment of US macroeconomic performance within the context of rule-based versus discretionary monetary policy:

> The overall economic performance during these two monetary eras is vastly different – a fact that is well known but too rarely attributed to the vastly different monetary policy environments. The more rules-based period from the mid-1980s until the early mid-2000s was a remarkably stable economic period, frequently called the Great Moderation. Inflation and interest rates and their volatilities fell compared to the 1970s. The volatility of real GDP was cut in half. Economic expansions became longer and stronger while recessions became shorter and shallower. The rate of unemployment declined. The discretionary period, in contrast, included a massive housing boom and bust with excessive risk taking, a financial crisis, and a Great Recession whose depth was much greater than any recession in the Great Moderation period. And the discretionary period also includes anaemic recovery with economic growth averaging only 2.4%, much lower than previous recoveries including the recovery from the severe early 1980s recession. Unemployment has been slow to come down and remains very high.

Inflation and Inflation Volatility

Figures 13.1a and 13.1b display inflation and inflation volatility in the United States over the period 1958q1–2012q4. They show that the US economy has operated in an environment of moderately high and volatile

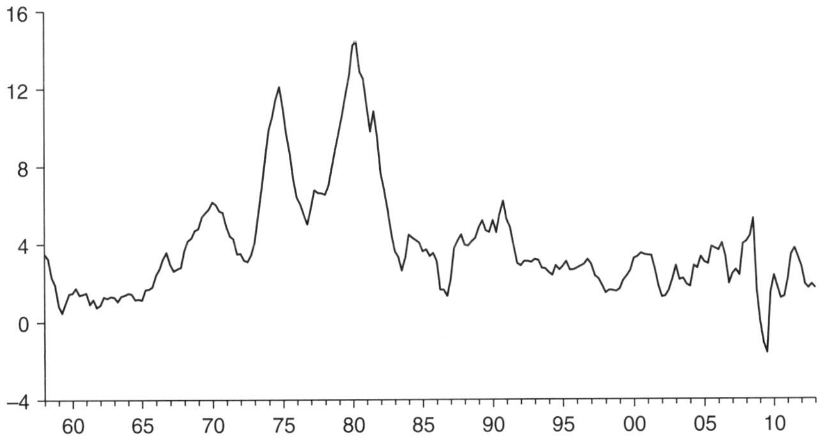

Figure 13.1a Quarter-on-quarter CPI inflation in the United States, 1958q1–2012q4

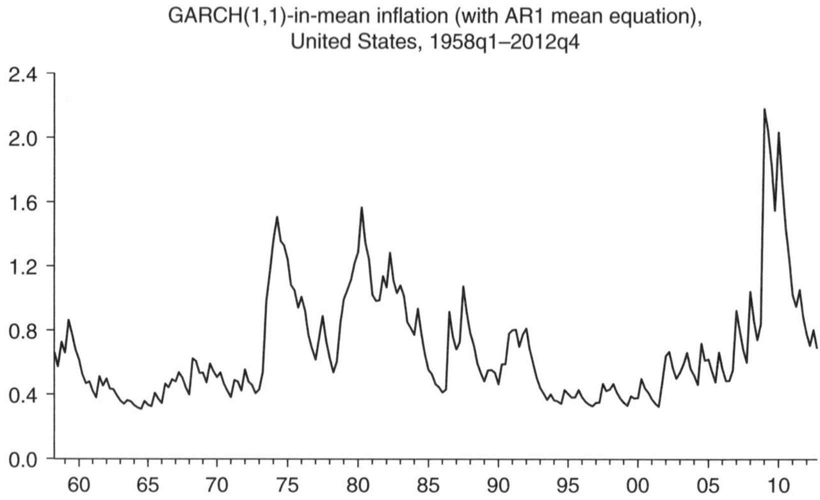

Figure 13.1b *Conditional standard deviation of CPI inflation in the United States, 1958q1–2012q4*

inflation for the past five decades. Inflation volatility peaked both in the 1970s and in the 2000s. Significantly, high volatility of inflation in the 2000s was associated with a relatively low average rate of inflation. This raises the fundamental issue of how high the benchmark for successful monetary policy should be set. The question is whether merely sustaining inflation at low average levels serves the citizens of a society sufficiently well. This is especially the case when monetary policy is conducted in a discretionary manner and there is controversy over the deployment of a short-term interest rate as the instrument of monetary policy when it approaches zero.

Inflation Persistence

The observation that inflation in the United States has been highly persistent is not hyperbolic. This is borne out by consideration of the coefficient on the one-period lagged rate of inflation in an autoregressive model AR(1), as obtained by the recursive and rolling regression techniques (Figures 13.2a and 13.2b). Figure 13.2a shows that there has been no change in the coefficient value of this one-period lagged inflation rate after its coefficient value stabilized in the mid 1980s. The rolling estimates of the coefficient in Figure 13.2b suggest instability in the coefficient value once the data for recent years, corresponding with the US-global financial crisis, are deployed for estimation purposes.

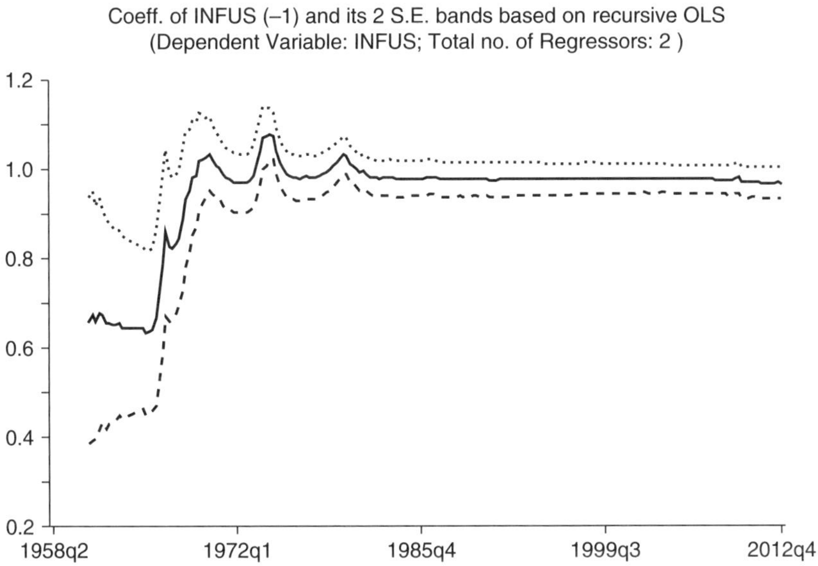

Note: INFUS = CPI inflation in the United States.

Figure 13.2a Recursive estimates of the coefficient on the one-period lagged rate of CPI inflation in the United States

The coefficient value appears to approximate unity, begging the question of whether or not inflation in the United States has a unit root. Table 13.2 reports the unit root test results for US inflation. The ADF test rejects the null hypothesis that inflation in the United States has a unit root. The KPSS test results in Table 13.2 also suggest that inflation is stationary. The Zivot-Andrews breakpoint test, however, does not reject the null hypothesis of a unit root in US inflation. The overall test results suggest that while inflation in the United States does have high persistence, it does not have a unit root. High persistence of inflation in the United States reflects low credibility of monetary policy, especially as monetary policy remains discretionary in nature and is used to achieve multiple, often conflicting, objectives.

Real Interest Rate and Real Exchange Rate

Figure 13.3 displays the real Federal funds rate in the United States for 1959q1–2012q4. This measure of the interest rate captures the monetary policy stance in this country in an historical context. It reveals that the

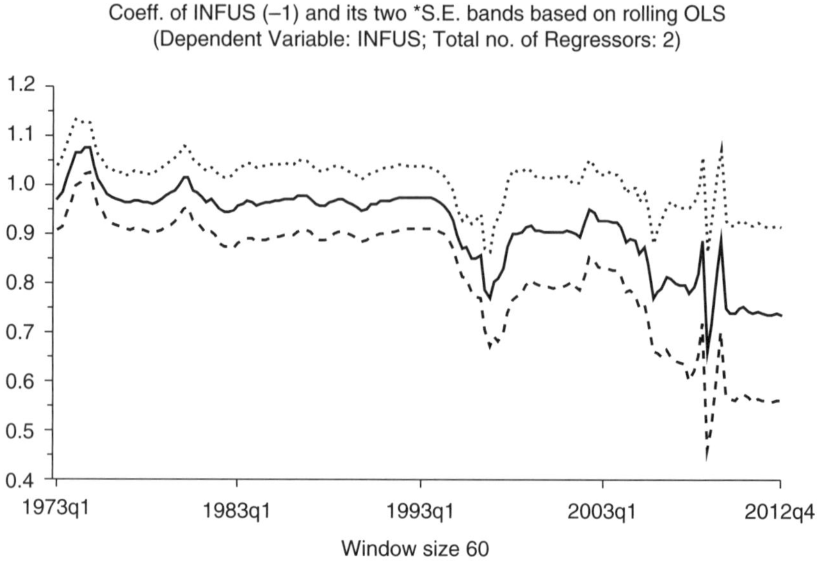

Note: INFUS = CPI inflation in the United States.

Figure 13.2b Rolling sample estimates of the coefficient on the one-period lagged rate of CPI inflation in the United States

real interest rate in the United States fluctuated widely over the past five decades. The real interest rate was highly negative (implying that inflation rates exceeded nominal interest rates) from the mid 1970s through the early 1980s, then became positive and exhibited unusually high levels until the late 1980s. The real interest rate again became positive and reached a peak level during the late 1990s. Since then the real interest rate returned to negative territory before rising steeply to very high levels, then became negative again during the late 2000s. This high volatility over the study period, moving from highly negative to highly positive, is a phenomenon damaging to investment, employment and growth.

Figure 13.4 displays the real effective exchange rate in the United States since the mid 1970s. Like the real interest rate, it is clear that the real effective exchange rate has been highly volatile for over three decades. The real exchange rate appreciated sharply during the mid 1980s and the early 2000s. During these periods, there were large current account deficits with associated accumulation of external debt. After the mid 2000s the real exchange rate depreciated steadily until 2011; thereafter, the real exchange rate has generally been appreciating.

Table 13.2 The unit root test results for CPI inflation in the United States

	Sample (adjusted)	Constant (C); Trend (T)	ADF test statistic (SBC-determined lag-length, l)	Inference at 5% level	The KPSS test statistic (Newey-West bandwidth)	Inference at 5% level	Zivot-Andrews test statistic	Breakpoint	Inference at 5% level
LCPI	1952–2012	C and T	−2.70 (l = 3)	I(1)	0.128 (6)	I(0)	−3.89	1973	I(0)
LCPI	1952–2012	C	−0.20 (l = 3)	I(1)	1.013 (6)	I(1)	−4.18	1987	I(0)
ΔLCPI	1952–2012	C	−2.25 (l = 2)	I(1)	0.203 (5)	I(0)	−3.02	1988	I(0)

Note: Definitions of variables: LCPI = log of the consumer price index; ΔLCPI = first-order difference of LCPI; SBC = Schwarz Bayesian Criterion; ADF = augmented Dickey-Fuller; and KPSS = Kwiatkowski, Phillips, Schmidt and Shin.

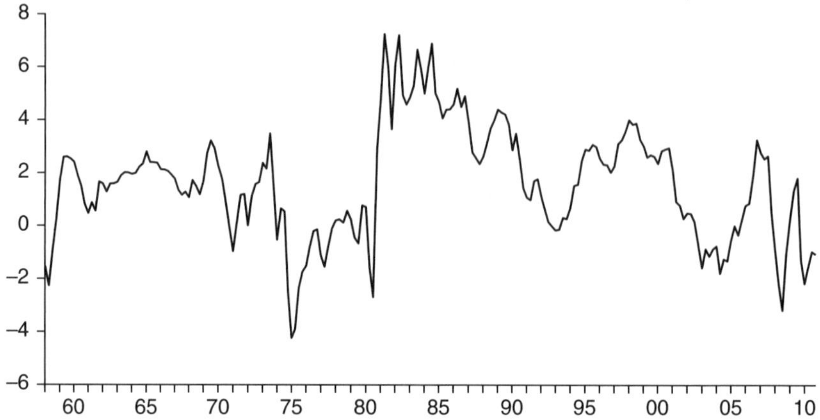

Figure 13.3 The real Federal funds rate in the United States, 1959q1–2012q4

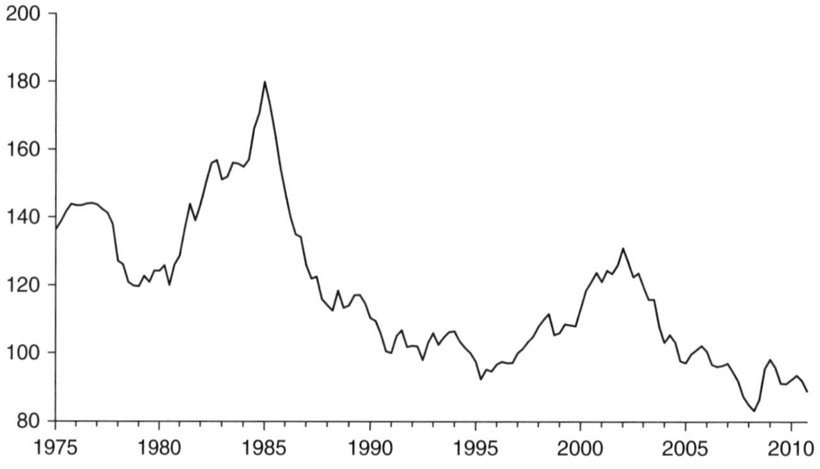

Figure 13.4 The real effective exchange rate in the United States, 1975q1–2010q4

There exists a positive short-run association between the real exchange rate and the real interest rate in the United States. The estimated correlation coefficient between them is 0.38, so the US currency value appreciates when the FRS funds rate is raised.

INFLATION, REAL INTEREST RATE, REAL EXCHANGE RATE AND REAL OUTPUT

One key problem for US monetary policy is high-inflation volatility even though the inflation rate on average remained relatively low over the past three decades. High volatility of inflation led to high volatility of both the real exchange rate and the real interest rate, which diminished economic growth – shorthand for subdued wealth creation comprised of an investment shortfall and more limited employment opportunities than were necessary had the monetary authorities achieved stability.

Structural Vector Autoregressive (SVAR) Analysis

This subsection, using quarterly data, estimates a four-variable SVAR model to examine the interrelationships among inflation, the real interest rate, the real exchange rate and real output. Figure 13.5 plots the data used for estimation purposes.

The model is formulated on the assumption that inflation has a contemporaneous feedback relation with the real interest rate and the real exchange rate. All these variables affect real output with a lag. The order of variables in the model is arranged as follows: INFUS, RFFR, LREER and LRGDP where INFUS is the inflation rate in the United States, RFFR is the real federal funds rate, LREER is the log of the real effective exchange rate and DLRGDP is the first-order logarithmic difference of real GDP.

The unit root test results suggest that while inflation, the real interest rate and the real exchange rate are stationary, real output is nonstationary (stochastic). Two versions of the model are then estimated and deployed to generate impulse responses and the forecast error variance decompositions of these variables. The first version of the model is defined as: INFUS, RFFR, LREER and LRGDP, with real output (LRGDP) nonstationary. The second version is defined as: INFUS, RFFR, LREER and DLRGDP, with all variables stationary, including DLRGDP. To conserve space, the results obtained with the second version of the model are reported, as the results obtained by both the models are qualitatively similar.

The impulse responses in Figure 13.6 suggest some expected results. A rise in inflation lowers the real interest rate and appreciates the real exchange rate. A decline in the real interest rate stimulates economic growth. Similarly a rise in the real interest rate lowers economic growth. An appreciated real exchange rate does not show any significant adverse impact on economic growth. However, as expected, an appreciated real exchange rate is found to lower inflation. An increase in inflation is found to have a positive impact on economic growth, which diminishes with the

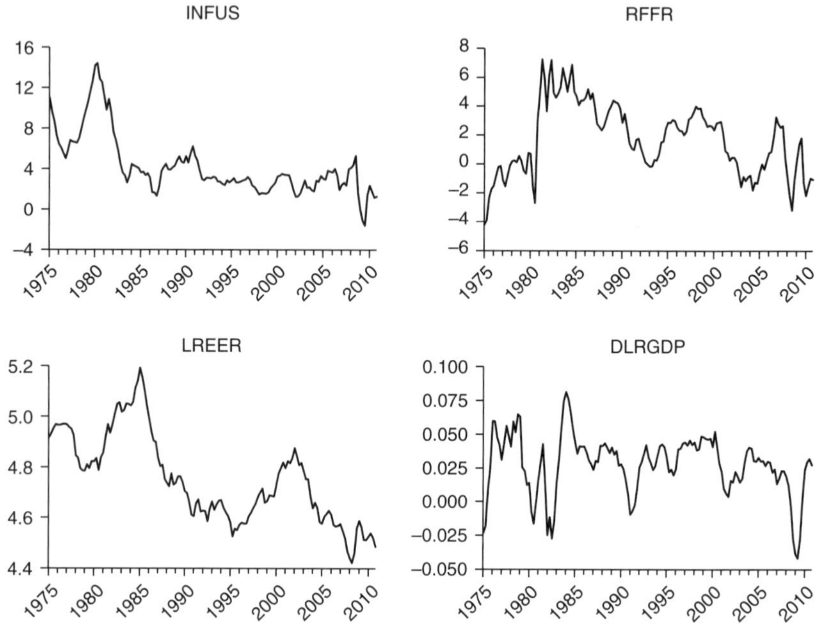

Note: Definitions of variables: INFUS = CPI inflation in the United States; RFFR = real Federal funds rate; LREER = log of the real effective exchange rate of the US dollar; and DLRGDP = first-order difference of the log of real GDP.

Figure 13.5 Data deployed for estimation of the SVAR model for the United States

passage of time. The overall results suggest interrelations among inflation, the real interest rate, the real exchange rate and output growth. Some relations are not pronounced but indicative.

Table 13.3 presents the forecast error-variance decompositions of variables INFUS, RFFR, LREER and DLRGDP. In the table, the numbers represent those percentages of forecast error variance of variables in the model that can be attributed to own innovations and those that originate from innovations of other variables. The results show that for all the variables, the dominant source of the forecast error variance is own innovations, to the extent of 83 per cent for inflation, 61 per cent for the real interest rate, 75 per cent for the real exchange rate and 70 per cent for real GDP growth over the ten-year time horizon. In the case of real output growth, innovations in the real interest rate and the real exchange rate jointly account for 23 per cent of its forecast error variance. The corresponding share of inflation is 8 per cent. This shows that real output growth is sensitive to inflation

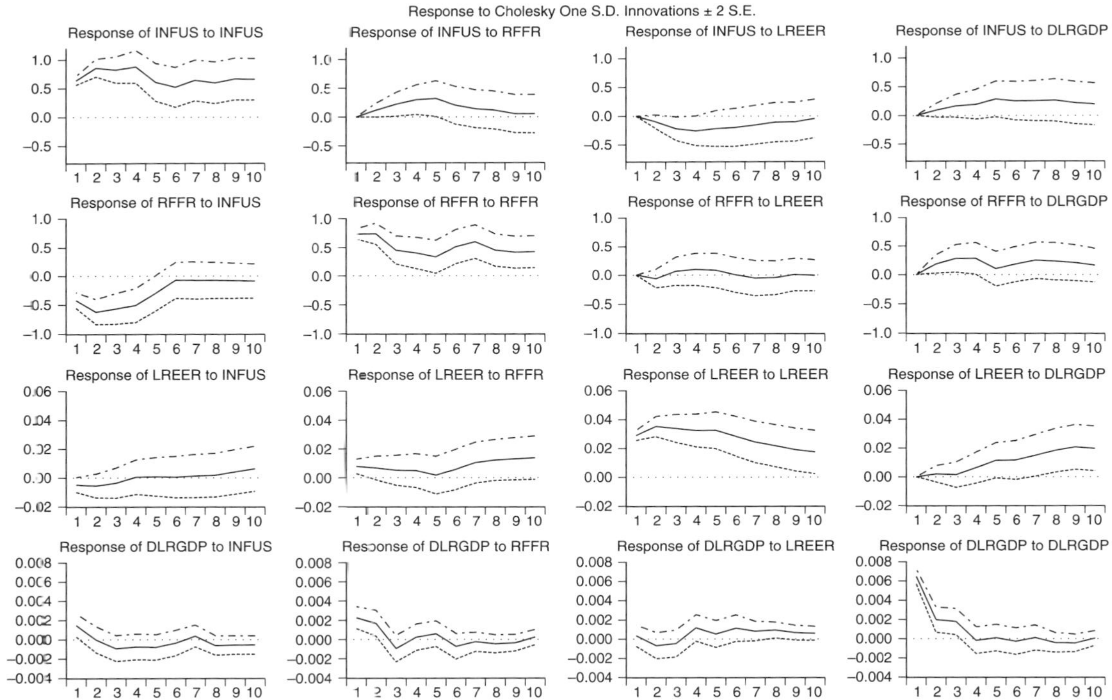

Note: Definitions of variables: INFUS = CPI inflation in the United States; RFFR = real Federal funds rate; LREER = log of the real effective exchange rate of the US dollar; and DLRGDP = first-order difference of the log of real GDP.

Figure 13.6 Impulse responses for variables in the SVAR model for the United States

Table 13.3 Forecast error-variance decomposition of variables in the SVAR model for the United States

Variance Decomposition of INFUS:					
Period	S.E.	INFUS	RFFR	LREER	DLRGDP
1	0.634	100.00	0.00	0.00	0.00
2	1.08	97.33	1.12	0.84	0.71
5	1.875	83.66	7.07	4.86	4.42
10	2.424	82.46	5.57	4.41	7.56
Variance Decomposition of RFFR:					
Period	S.E.	INFUS	RFFR	LREER	DLRGDP
1	0.849	25.09	74.91	0.00	0.00
2	1.299	33.71	64.07	0.23	1.99
5	1.738	41.06	51.47	0.82	6.64
10	2.105	28.71	61.29	0.68	9.32
Variance Decomposition of LREER:					
Period	S.E.	INFUS	RFFR	LREER	DLRGDP
1	0.030	2.62	6.60	90.77	0.00
2	0.047	2.49	4.69	92.64	0.18
5	0.076	1.23	2.75	92.97	3.05
10	0.102	1.25	7.73	75.09	15.92
Variance Decomposition of DLRGDP:					
Period	S.E.	INFUS	RFFR	LREER	DLRGDP
1	0.007	4.36	10.42	0.25	84.97
2	0.008	3.81	14.04	1.05	81.09
5	0.008	6.51	14.24	3.73	75.51
10	0.008	7.71	14.34	8.40	69.55
The Cholesky Ordering: INFUS RFFR LREER DLRGDP					

Note: Definitions of variables: INFUS = CPI inflation in the United States; RFFR = real Federal funds rate; REER = log of the real effective exchange rate of the US dollar; and DLRGDP = first-order difference of the log of real GDP.

and its volatility. Inflation affects both the real interest rate and the real exchange rate and therefore affects real output and its growth.

MONETARY AND EXCHANGE RATE POLICY ISSUES

The empirical results reported above suggest that the US economy is responsive to monetary policy actions. A rise in the real interest rate appreciates the real exchange rate and each reinforces the other's dampening impact on aggregate demand. Monetary policy remains discretionary and aims to stabilize the economy while attempting to maintain price stability. Price stability is defined for the purposes of US monetary policy as low and stable inflation.[6] Low inflation, however, is not necessarily also stable. Figure 13.3 reveals that the US real interest rate has remained highly volatile for three decades. This, along with the volatile real exchange rate, compromised wealth creation through muted investment, growth and unemployment.

One way of minimizing this problem is adoption of rule-based monetary policy for price stability under a flexible exchange rate. The question is which of two available rule-based strategies is appropriate for the United States to sustain price stability. It can adopt monetary targeting or inflation targeting. Under inflation targeting, a monetary aggregate can be used as an instrument of monetary policy instead of the interest rate, especially in a low-inflation environment. Presently the FRS uses the interest rate as the instrument of monetary policy without declaring an explicit target for inflation. This volatilizes money growth, keeping inflation volatile.

Until recently the prevailing view was that monetary targeting for price stability requires a stable money-demand function to establish a causal linkage between money supply growth and inflation. The recent literature suggests the presence of a cointegration among money, output and prices, which ensures a short-run causal linkage between money growth and inflation. The relationship between money supply growth and inflation exists irrespective of the exchange rate regime and whether or not the money-demand function is stable (McCallum and Nelson, 2011). This section examines whether the United States has a stable money-demand function.[7] For estimation purposes, an open-economy money-demand function is specified as follows:

$$LRJM_t = \alpha_0 + \alpha_1 Ly_t + \alpha_2 NIR_t + \alpha_3 LRER_t + \alpha_4 \pi_t^v + u_t \qquad (13.1)$$

where LRJM (J = N, B) is the log of real money balances (LRNM represents real narrow money balances or LRBM represents real broad money balances), Ly is the log of real income, NIR is a representative nominal interest rate such as the Federal funds rate, LRER is the log of a representative real exchange rate such as the real effective exchange rate (REER), π_t^v is a measure of inflation volatility and u_t is an error term. In this specification, real income represents a scale variable. The coefficient on real income is expected to bear a positive sign and have a value not significantly different from one. The coefficient on the nominal interest rate is expected to have a negative coefficient value. As discussed in Appendix 5, the coefficients on the real exchange rate and inflation volatility remain indeterminate.

The unit root test results suggest that all the variables in the model have a unit root. Consequently, they are eligible to form a cointegral money-demand relationship. Table 13.4 reports both the ARDL and OLS results for real narrow money-demand function. To conserve space, the results obtained by a broad definition of money are not reported. As the ARDL and OLS estimation techniques provide similar results, the results obtained by the ARDL technique are deployed for interpretation. The empirical findings suggest the presence of a weak form of long-run cointegral relationship among real narrow money balances, real income and the Federal funds rate. The coefficients on the real exchange rate and inflation volatility are not statistically significant. In the preferred equation, these variables are not included.

The income elasticity of demand for narrow money is less than one. The coefficient on the Federal funds rate bears a negative sign and is statistically highly significant. Several stability tests, including CUSUM and CUSUMSQ of residuals, suggest that the narrow money-demand function, with real income and the Federal funds rate, remained stable throughout the sample period (Figure 13.7).

Relationships Among Money, Output and Prices

Table 13.5 reports the cointegration test results among money, output and prices. The results obtained for a broad definition of money are found more robust than those obtained for a narrow definition of money. The Engle-Granger cointegration test results suggest a weak form of cointegral relationship among money, output and prices. The dynamic OLS (DOLS) estimates suggest that the broad money supply is highly significant in the price-level equation and that the coefficient value of the broad money stock is not significantly different from one. As expected, real output bears a negative sign although the coefficient is not statistically highly significant.

Engle and Granger (1987) have suggested that one of the implications of a cointegral relation between two nonstationary variables is the presence of long-term causality between them running in at least one direction. Table 13.6 reports the bivariate Granger-causality test results among LCPI, LNM (LBM) and LRGDP. The test results are generated within a vector error-correction (VEC) modelling framework after selecting the optimal lag-length using the SBC. The test results suggest that for the United States, there is strong causality running from money growth (narrow or broad) to inflation. A broad money growth is also found to have a strong short-run causal impact on output growth.

Table 13.4 The ARDL and OLS regression results for real narrow money-demand relationships in the United States

F-statistic	2.01			
W-statistic	6.02			
Critical value bounds	F-test	W-test		
90%	(3.33, 4.30)	(10.00, 12.89)		
95%	(4.06, 5.17)	(12.17,15.50)		
Sample period	1962–2012 ARDL (2,0,1) (Selected based on SBC)	1962–2012 ARDL (2,0,1) Long-run model	1959–2012 OLS (Static model)	1960–2012 OLS (Dynamic model)
Regressors	Coefficient (t-ratio) [prob.]	Coefficient (t-ratio) [prob.]	Coefficient (t-ratio) [prob.]	Coefficient (t-ratio) [prob.]
Intercept	0.88 (2.16) [0.04]	5.44 (17.14) [0.00]	5.42 (66.68) [0.00]	1.43 (3.42) [0.00]
LRNM(−1)	1.35 (10.81) [0.00]			0.74 (9.62) [0.00]
LRNM(−2)	−0.52 (−4.23) [0.00]			
LRGDP	0.07 (2.05) [0.05]	0.44 (6.13) [0.00]	0.42 (21.75) [0.00]	0.11 (3.18) [0.00]
USFFR	−0.01 (−4.62) [0.00]	−0.03 (−2.35) [0.02]	−0.02 (−6.22) [0.00]	−0.01 (−3.94) [0.00]
USFFR(−1)	0.01 (2.69) [0.01]			
Diagnostics				
Adjusted R^2	0.98		0.92	0.97

Table 13.4 (continued)

Lagrange multiplier test for serial correlation	$F(1,45) = 0.73$ [0.40]		$F(1,48) = 99.12$ [0.00]	$F(1,46) = 19.99$ [0.00]
Ramsey's RESET test of functional form mis-specification	$F(1,45) = 1.79$ [0.19]		$F(1,48) = 5.51$ [0.02]	$F(1,46) = 3.80$ [0.06]
Normality of residuals	$\chi^2_{(2)} = 1.75$ [0.42]		$\chi^2_{(2)} = 2.84$ [0.24]	$\chi^2_{(2)} = 5.85$ [0.05]
Heteroskedasticity	$F(1,50) = 12.99$ [0.01]		$F(1,50) = 4.55$ [0.04]	$F(1,49) = 3.89$ [0.05]
The Wald test:				
H_O: Coefficient on LRGDP = 0		$\chi^2_{(1)} = 37.57$ [0.00]	$\chi^2_{(1)} = 473.25$ [0.00]	
H_O: Coefficient on LRGDP = 1		$\chi^2_{(1)} = 58.63$ [0.00]	$\chi^2_{(1)} = 897.17$ [0.00]	
H_O: Coefficient on USFFR = 0		$\chi^2_{(1)} = 5.50$ [0.06]	$\chi^2_{(1)} = 38.65$ [0.00]	

Note: Definitions of variables: LRNM = log of real narrow money balances; LRGDP = log of real GDP; USFFR = US Federal funds rate; ARDL = autoregressive distributed lag; and SBC = Schwarz Bayesian Criterion.

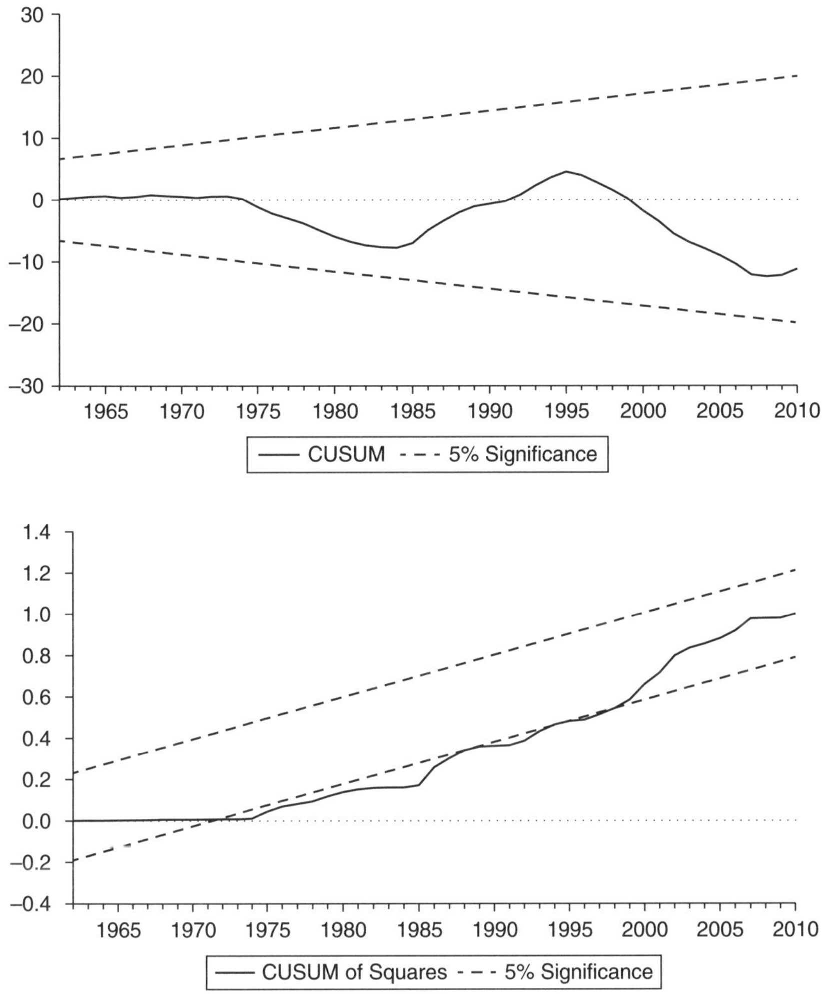

Figure 13.7 CUSUM and CUSUMSQ of residuals for long-run real narrow money-demand relationships in the United States

Figure 13.8 plots the growth rates of the money supply, both narrow and broad, and CPI inflation for the period 1962–2010. It shows a close relation between the growth rate of the broad money and inflation. The relationship between the growth rate of money, either narrow or broad, and inflation was close until the 1980s. Since then the relationship has weakened or broken down.

Table 13.5 *Cointegration test results among money, output and prices in the United States, 1970–2012*

	Fully modified OLS				Dynamic OLS			
					(lead = 1, lag = 1)			
With narrow money (NM)								
Regressor	coefficient	t-ratio	prob.		coefficient	t-ratio	prob.	
Intercept	−1.29	−4.36	0.00		−1.24	−3.14	0.00	
LNM	0.69	4.46	0.00		0.76	4.13	0.00	
LRGDP	0.19	0.68	0.5		0.07	0.2	0.84	
Sample period	1970–2012				1970–2011			
DW	0.22				0.18			
Adjusted R^2	0.97				0.97			
	tau-statistic	prob.	z-statistic	prob.	tau-statistic	prob.	z-statistic	prob.
The Engle-Granger cointegration tests	−2.4	0.55	−17.75	0.14	−2.4	0.55	−17.75	0.14
The Phillips-Ouliaris cointegration tests	−1.57	0.88	−6.59	0.8	−1.57	0.88	−6.59	0.8
With broad money (BM)								
Regressor	coefficient	t-ratio	prob.		coefficient	t-ratio	prob.	
Intercept	−1.14	−4.93	0.00		−1.00	−3.23	0.00	
LBM	0.82	5.85	0.00		0.87	5.72	0.00	
LRGDP	−0.32	−1.08	0.29		−0.44	−1.39	0.18	
Sample period	1970–2012				1970–2011			
DW	0.14				0.32			
Adjusted R^2	0.98				0.98			
	tau-statistic	prob.	z-statistic	prob.	tau-statistic	prob.	z-statistic	prob.
The Engle-Granger cointegration tests	−1.56	0.88	−8.3	0.68	−1.56	0.88	−8.3	0.68
The Phillips-Ouliaris cointegration tests	−0.83	0.98	−2.9	0.97	−0.83	0.98	−2.9	0.97

Note: Definitions of variables: LNM = log of narrow money stock; LBM = log of broad money stock; and LRGDP = log of real GDP.

Table 13.6 Granger-causality among money, output and prices in the United States, 1959–2012

	Hypotheses No causality runs from:	Chi-square statistic (prob.)	Inference at 5% level
VEC specification (With narrow money, NM)	ΔLNM → ΔLCPI	10.59 (0.01)	Null hypothesis rejected
	ΔLNM, ΔLRGDP → ΔLCPI	22.62 (0.00)	Null hypothesis rejected
	ΔLCPI → ΔLNM	0.75 (0.69)	Null hypothesis not rejected
	ΔLRGDP → ΔLNM	0.98 (0.61)	Null hypothesis not rejected
	ΔLCPI → ΔLRGDP	13.68 (0.00)	Null hypothesis rejected
	ΔLNM → ΔLRGDP	0.55 (0.76)	Null hypothesis not rejected
VEC specification (With broad money, BM)	ΔLBM → ΔLCPI	8.11 (0.02)	Null hypothesis rejected
	ΔLBM, ΔLRGDP → ΔLCPI	24.03 (0.00)	Null hypothesis rejected
	ΔLCPI → ΔLBM	5.18 (0.08)	Null hypothesis not rejected
	ΔLRGDP → ΔLBM	0.54 (0.76)	Null hypothesis not rejected
	ΔLCPI → ΔLRGDP	15.02 (0.00)	Null hypothesis rejected
	ΔLBM → ΔLRGDP	6.83 (0.03)	Null hypothesis rejected

Note: Definitions of variables: LCPI = log of the consumer price index; LNM = log of narrow money stock; LBM = log of broad money stock; and LRGDP = log of real GDP. Optimal lag-length = 2 (selected based on the Schwarz Bayesian Criterion).

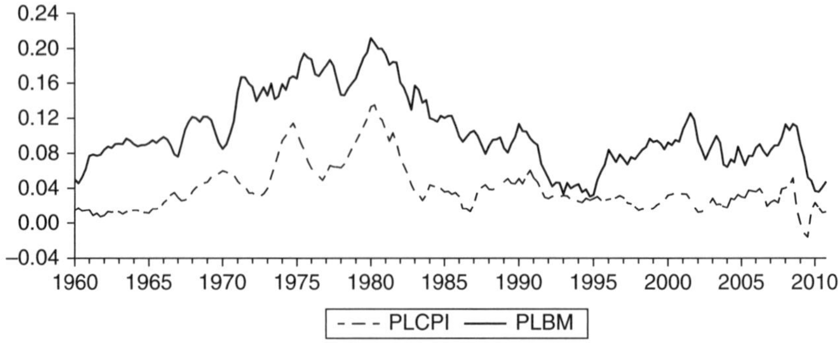

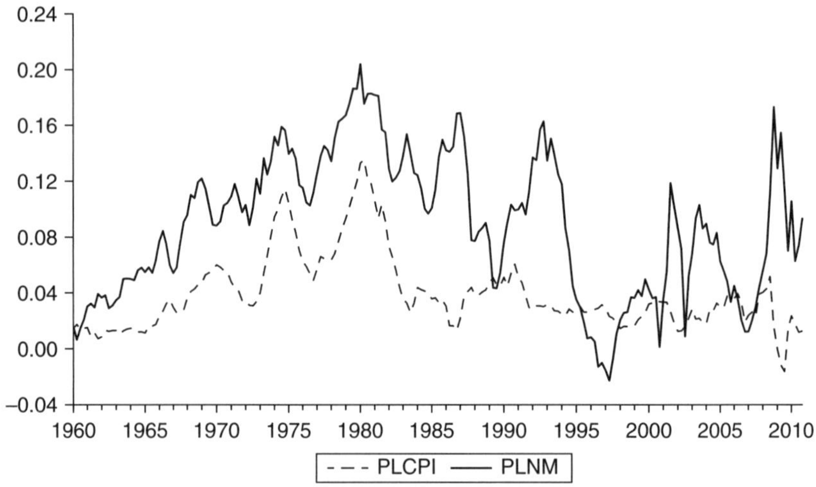

Note: Definitions of variables: PLCPI = first-order difference of the log of the consumer price index (CPI); PLNM = first-order difference of the log of narrow money (NM); and PLBM = first-order difference of the log of broad money (BM).

Figure 13.8 Money growth and inflation in the United States

SUMMARY AND CONCLUSION

This chapter has provided an overview of monetary policy in the United States since the 1950s. The United States has experienced moderately high and volatile inflation since the 1950s under a succession of monetary policy regimes. Until the early 1970s the United States was under the Bretton Woods exchange rate system where it operated under a gold standard system in the sense that the exchange rate of the US dollar for gold was fixed at the rate of US$35 per ounce of gold. Most currencies across the globe maintained either adjustable or fixed exchange rates with the US dollar. After the collapse of the Bretton Woods system in the early 1970s, the US dollar was floated against other currencies. There is the suggestion that excessive money growth from the late 1960s led to the demise of the Bretton Woods system.

During 1950–73 US inflation was moderately high but unstable. This was the period when the United States operated under the gold standard system. Inflation peaked during the 1970s mostly due to monetary accommodation of oil shocks. Therefore, except in maintaining nominal exchange rate stability, the Bretton Woods system did not achieve price stability. Volatile inflation in turn raised the volatility of the real interest rate, the real exchange rate and output growth. Although the FRS introduced monetary targeting in the late 1970s, it was not strict or sustained for long. Monetary targeting had been discontinued by 1982. The then newly appointed Chairman of the FRS, Paul Volcker, introduced a disinflation programme that kept the interest rate high during 1980–84 and succeeded in subduing inflation.

Since 1983 the FRS has conducted monetary policy under discretion without explicit nominal anchor. There is the suggestion that FRS monetary policy strategy was adopted with an implicit target for inflation. Accordingly, the FRS adopted a forward-looking monetary policy approach, which took the form of monitoring a wide range of information variables and periodic pre-emptive elimination of any inflation threat. However, as price stability was not the sole objective of monetary policy, there was ambiguity about policy stance and direction. Consequently, inflation remained low on average but unstable while output maximization gained apparent prominence. Any success of monetary policy in achieving both price and output stability depended on the personalities in the FRS rather than any institutional set-up to ensure transparency and accountability for the design and conduct of monetary policy.

Sustained expansionary monetary policy of the FRS since the US-global financial crisis has become a matter of concern across the globe. A body of literature on the US-global financial crisis has emerged since the late 2000s suggesting that expansionary monetary and fiscal stimulus did not move the US economy out of recession. It reinforces the case for primacy of rule-based monetary policy to prevent boom-bust cycles. Figure 13.9 reveals a positive relation between the rates of inflation and unemployment since the 1960s. This contrasts with Phillips curve theory, which argues for a negative relation between inflation and the rate of unemployment.

Since the US-global financial crisis, financial stability has emerged as

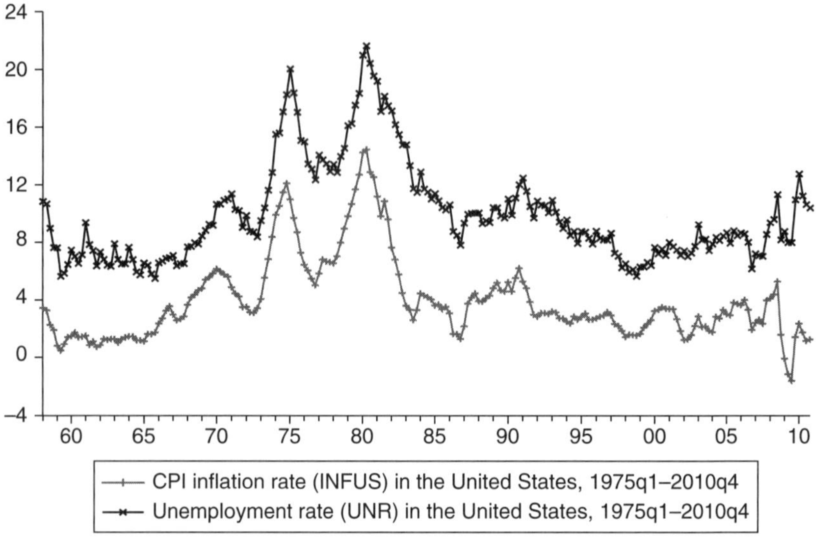

Figure 13.9 Relationship between the rates of inflation and unemployment in the United States, 1975q1–2010q4

one of the important goals of central banks. In so far as the FRS is concerned, the crisis has reinforced the importance of banking regulation and supervision along with policy coordination, policy compatibility and policy transparency of central banks. Considering wide-ranging implications, the FRS's recent decision to strengthen its financial regulatory and prudential supervision framework can be considered timely and consistent with the literature on central banking and monetary policy.

The experience of countries in Southeast and East Asia that underwent financial crisis in the late 1990s suggest that rule-based monetary and fiscal policies, together with improved financial regulation and supervision, are equally important to maintain price and financial stability in the midst of freely mobile capital. There is, however, no consensus as to whether regulatory measures should be undertaken by a central bank or by another regulatory body. Most central banks in the Asia-Pacific remain responsible for conducting monetary policy while ensuring financial stability through prudential regulation and supervision. Australia is an exception on this matter, having substantially transferred these functions from the central bank to other corporate-regulatory and prudential-supervisory specialist government agencies.

The view against a central bank having the responsibility for prudential supervision of banks and other financial institutions points to at least two concerns. Firstly, it has the potential to compromise the national independence and autonomy of the central bank's monetary policy decision-making. Secondly, central bank actions taken in the exercise of control may undermine financial stability. When a central bank has sole responsibility and authority to conduct monetary policy, free of potentially conflicting responsibilities, then its ability to establish unassailable credibility and effectiveness in controlling inflation through consistency of policy action is enhanced. Central bank independence is, however, not unlimited; rather, it is constrained in important ways. Central banks perform better in strong regulatory environments than environments comprising weak regulatory bodies for banks and financial institutions. Central banks perform better under strongly stated and enforced than under limited accountability provisions. Considering these facts and the available experience, both of the FRS and other central banks, the future course of US monetary policy practice needs to be rule-based, balanced and decisive while making strenuous efforts to improve the financial regulatory and supervisory structure given institutional constraints (Taylor, 2012a, 2012b). Orphanides (2014, p. 278) suggests that to avoid ambiguity and uncertainty in monetary policy, the FRS should declare price stability as the primary objective of monetary policy:

> A clearer mandate that properly acknowledges the primacy of price stability as the means for advancing maximum sustainable growth and employment over time would greatly reduce the likelihood of repeating past mistakes and would better ensure that the Federal Reserve will safeguard monetary stability going forward. The FRS needs a clearer mandate for its second hundred years. What is required is an Act of Congress to make price stability the primary objective of the Federal Reserve.

This view is shared by others, including Volcker (2013).

NOTES

1. Some general information on the USA is drawn from http://en.wikipedia.org/wiki/United_States.
2. Some general discussion on this topic is drawn from Mishkin (2013) and http://en.wikipedia.org/wiki/Federal_Reserve_System.
3. The mandate of the Federal Reserve System has been defined in the Federal Reserve Act, as amended, in 1977. The Act states that (Orphanides, 2014, p. 268): 'The Board of Governors of the Federal Reserve System and the Federal Open Market Committee shall maintain long run growth of the monetary and credit aggregates commensurate with the economy's long run potential to increase production, so as to promote effectively the goals of maximum employment, stable prices, and moderate long-term interest rates'

(Federal Reserve Act, Section 2A, 1977 amendment). According to Blanchard (2006, p. 546), the mandate of the FRS is to achieve not only low inflation in the medium and long run but also to stabilize economic activity in the short run.
4. For a detailed critical analysis of the US financial crisis, see FCIC (2011).
5. Taylor (2012b, p. 1027) writes: 'Whether or not one believes that these discretionary interventions worked, their consequences going forward are negative. First, they raise questions about central bank independence. The programs are not monetary policy as conventionally defined, but rather fiscal policy or credit allocation policy because they try to help some firms or sectors and not others and are financed through money creation rather than taxes or public borrowing. Unlike monetary policy, there is no established rationale that such policies should be run by an independent agency of government. By taking these extraordinary measures, the FRS has risked losing its independence over monetary policy . . .'.
6. For a critical overview of US economic policies, see Frankel (2006, 2009). For discussion on aspects of US monetary policy and financial crisis, see Greenspan (2004), Lothian (2009) and Taylor (2012a, 2012b).
7. For earlier studies on money-demand behaviour in the United States, see Friedman (1959, 1966), Goldfeld (1973, 1976), Allen (1982), Baba et al. (1992), Ball (2001), Blejer (1979), Bordo and Jonung (2003), Choudhry (1996) and Choi and Jung (2009).

REFERENCES

Allen, S.D. (1982), 'Klein's price variability terms in the U.S. demand for money', *Journal of Money, Credit and Banking*, **14**(4), November, 525–30.
Baba, Y., D.F. Hendry and R.M. Starr (1992), 'The demand for M1 in the USA, 1960–1988', *Review of Economic Studies*, **59**(1), 25–61.
Ball, L. (2001), 'Another look at long-run money demand', *Journal of Monetary Economics*, **47**, 31–44.
Bernanke, B. (2010), 'Monetary policy and the housing bubble', Paper presented at the Annual Meeting of the American Economic Association, Atlanta, Georgia, 3 January.
Blanchard, O.J. (2006), *Macroeconomics*, New York: Pearson-Prentice Hall.
Blejer, M.I. (1979), 'The demand for money and the variability of the rate of inflation: some empirical results', *International Economic Review*, June, 545–9.
Bordo, M.D. and L. Jonung (2003), *Demand for Money: An Analysis of the Long-run Behavior of the Velocity of Circulation*, New Brunswick, NJ and London: Transaction Publishers.
Choi, K. and C. Jung (2009), 'Structural changes and the US money demand function', *Applied Economics*, **41**, 1251–7.
Choudhry, T. (1996), 'Real stock prices and the long-run money demand function: evidence from Canada and the USA', *Journal of International Money and Finance*, **15**(1), 1–17.
Engle, R.F. and C.W.J. Granger (1987), 'Co-integration and error-correction: representation, estimation, and testing', *Econometrica*, **55**(2), 251–76.
FCIC (Financial Crisis Inquiry Commission) (2011), *The Financial Crisis Inquiry Report: Final Report of the National Commission on the Causes of the Financial and Economic Crisis in the United States*, Dissenting Statement, January, available at http://fcic.law.stanford.edu (accessed 12 July 2012).

Frankel, J. (2006), 'Could twin deficits jeopardize US hegemony?', *Journal of Policy Modeling*, **28**(6), 653–63.
Frankel, J. (2009), 'What's in and out in global money', *Finance and Development*, September, 13–17.
Friedman, M. (1959), 'The demand for money – some theoretical and empirical results', *Journal of Political Economy*, **67**, 327–51.
Friedman, M. (1966), 'Interest rates and the demand for money', *Journal of Law and Economics*, **9**, 71–85.
Friedman, M. (1983), 'Monetary variability: United States and Japan', *Journal of Money, Credit and Banking*, **15**, August, 339–43.
Goldfeld, S.M. (1973), 'The demand for money revisited', *Brookings Papers on Economic Activity*, **3**, 577–638.
Goldfeld, S. (1976), 'The case of the missing money', *Brookings Papers on Economic Activity*, **6**, 683–730.
Greenspan, A. (2004), 'Risk and uncertainty in monetary policy', *American Economic Review*, **94**(2), 33–40.
IMF (International Monetary Fund) (various years), *International Financial Statistics*, Washington, DC: IMF.
IMF (International Monetary Fund) (various years), *World Economic Outlook*, Washington, DC: IMF.
Jordan, J.L. (2014), 'A century of central banking: what have we learned?', *CATO Journal*, **34**(2), 213–27.
Krugman, P.R., M. Obstfeld and R. Melitz (2015), *International Economics: Theory and Policy*, New York: Pearson-Addison Wesley.
Kydland, F.E. and E.C. Prescott (1977), 'Rules rather than discretion: the inconsistency of optimal plans', *Journal of Political Economy*, **85**, 473–91.
Labonte, M. (2012), 'Monetary policy and the Federal Reserve: current policy and conditions', Congressional Research Service, 7–5700, available at http://www.crs.gov, RL30354 (accessed 12 July 2012).
Lothian, J.R. (2009), 'U.S. monetary policy and the financial crisis', *Journal of Economic Asymmetries*, **6**(2), 25–40.
Lucas, R.E., Jr (1976), 'Econometric policy evaluation: a critique', *Carnegie-Rochester Conference Series on Public Policy*, **1**, 19–46.
McCallum, B.T. and E. Nelson (2011), 'Money and inflation: some critical issues', in B.M. Friedman and M. Woodford (eds), *Handbook of Monetary Economics*, Vol. 3A, Amsterdam: Elsevier Science, pp. 97–153.
Mishkin, F.S. (2007a), 'Monetary policy and the dual mandate', Speech delivered at Bridgewater College, Bridgewater, Vancouver, 10 April.
Mishkin, F.S. (2007b), *Monetary Policy Strategy*, Cambridge, MA: MIT Press.
Mishkin, F.S. (2011), 'Over the cliff: from the subprime to the global financial crisis', *Journal of Economic Perspectives*, **25**(1), 49–70.
Mishkin, F.S. (2013), *The Economics of Money, Banking, and Financial Markets*, New York: Pearson Education.
Orphanides, A. (2014), 'The need for a price stability mandate', *Cato Journal*, **34**(2), 265–79.
Taylor, J.B. (2011), 'The cycle of rules and discretion in economic policy', *National Affairs*, Spring, 55–65.
Taylor, J.B. (2012a), 'Monetary policy during the past 30 years with lessons for the next 30 years', *Cato Journal*, **33**(3), 333–45.

Taylor, J.B. (2012b), 'Monetary policy rules work and discretion doesn't: a tale of two era', *Journal of Money, Credit and Banking*, **44**(6), 1017–31.
Volcker, P. (2013), 'Central banking at a crossroad', Remarks at the Economic Club of New York, 29 May.
Wallison, P.J. (2011), Financial Crisis Inquiry Commission, Dissenting Statement, January, available at http://fcic-static.law.stanford.edu/cdn_media/fcic-reports/fcic_final_report_wallison_dissent.pdf (accessed 12 July 2012).

APPENDIX A: MONETARY POLICY, CURRENT ACCOUNT BALANCES AND MACROECONOMIC ADJUSTMENT IN THE UNITED STATES

Two main factors have induced sustained current account deficits in the United States. They include the following. Firstly, there has been a long-standing policy bias to deploy expansionary fiscal and monetary policies to raise employment. This policy bias is informed by US cultural values. Secondly, from the early 1990s US policy authorities developed a phenomenon that has become known as 'fear of deflation'. This fed into the fear of unemployment element of US culture described above and reinforced the expansionary policy bias. Fear of deflation in the United States began with the Japanese long stagnation and was reinforced a decade later by the 2001 US mini-recession and the dot-com bust. Significant symptoms of US policy expansionism included an overvalued real exchange rate of the US dollar combined with a low real interest rate. This appendix illustrates the phenomenon with the help of the IS-LM-BP model.

Figure 13A.1 represents a stylistic IS-LM-BP model for the United States. This is a short-run Keynesian representation of an open economy with capital mobility. For simplicity, both wages and prices are assumed fixed. The vertical axis measures the real interest rate (r) and the horizontal axis measures real income (y). The LM curve is upward-sloping and derived for a real money stock (M) and a stable money-demand function. The IS curve is downward-sloping and shows a relationship between real income (y) and the real interest rate (r) when the goods market is in equilibrium. The position of the IS curve is determined by the real exchange rate under the assumption that both domestic and external prices are fixed. The real exchange rate is a determinant of aggregate demand, implying that any depreciation of the real exchange rate shifts the IS curve to the right and an appreciation of the real exchange rate shifts the IS curve to the left. The BP curve is assumed upward-sloping but flatter than the LM curve, implying imperfect capital mobility that brings equality between domestic and foreign real interest rates in the medium or long run. The BP curve is drawn at a given exchange rate (e). Point A, the intersection of $IS_0(e_0)$, $LM_0(M_0)$ and $BP_0(e_0)$, represents both internal and external equilibrium. The domestic interest rate is r_0 and income is y_0. At equilibrium A, r_0 equals the world interest rate r_w.

Assume that the world real interest rate (r_w) is determined in international capital markets by the interaction of world saving and investment. The real interest rate in the United States is assumed to converge to the world real interest rate in the long run. In the short run, the US real interest rate may deviate from the world real interest rate, but it would trigger capital flows. At equilibrium point A, there is no tendency for capital

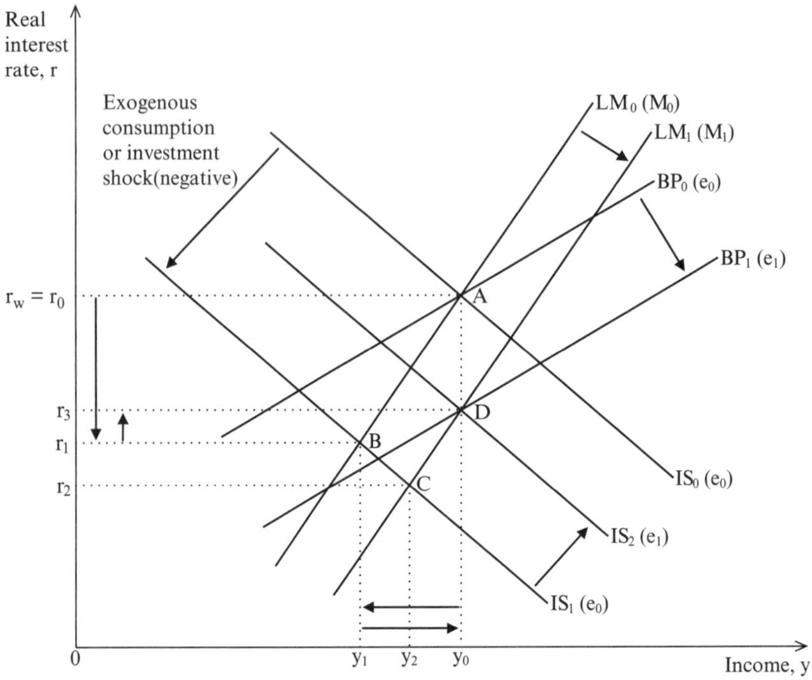

Notes:

1. At point A: $r_0 = r_w$ (x = 0), y = y_0 and the balance-of-payments (BP) are in equilibrium.
2. An exogenous shock to consumption (fear of deflation) or investment (dot-com bust) shifts the IS curve from IS_0 (e_0) to IS_1 (e_0). The real exchange rate e_0 is assumed to remain constant. IS_1 (e_0) cuts LM_0 at point B. This represents a lower real interest rate and lower output y_1. Since point B is below the BP curve, it represents current account deficits and an overvalued real exchange rate.
3. Since $y_1 < y_0$, the FRS adopts expansionary monetary policy. This shifts the LM_0 curve to LM_1. The new equilibrium is at point C. This shows a further decline in the real interest rate from r_1 to r_2 and an increase in income from y_1 to y_2.
4. Given that $r_2 < r_w$, it triggers capital outflows that lead to a depreciation of the real exchange rate, say from e_0 to e_1. The IS_1 (e_0) shifts to IS_2 (e_1) with the depreciated real exchange rate. The depreciated exchange rate also shifts the BP_0 curve to BP_1 (e_1). The new equilibrium is at point D. At point D, both internal and external equilibrium are restored over the medium term. The long-run equilibrium would be established at point A. This would represent a simultaneous increase in the real interest rate, a depreciated real exchange rate and an increase in output.

Source: Adapted from Corden (2009) and Salvatore (2006).

Figure 13A.1 The IS-LM-BP model and adjustment to shocks

inflows or outflows. The real exchange rate is at its equilibrium level (e_0). The real interest rate parity condition ensures that the rate of depreciation of the real exchange rate (x) at point A is zero: $r = r_w + x$ ($x = 0$ at equilibrium point A, such that $r_0 \approx r_w$).

This model can be applied to analyse the negative demand shocks received by the United States in the form of 'fear of deflation' and the dot-com boom-bust shock of the early 2000s. Two major consequences of these (or any) demand shocks included decreased consumption and increased saving. This is reflected in Figure 13A.1 by a shift of the IS curve from $IS_0(e_0)$ to $IS_1(e_0)$, which intersected the $LM_0(M_0)$ curve at point B. The outcome was a simultaneous decrease in the real interest rate, from r_0 to r_1, and income, from y_0 to y_1. This created 'Keynesian unemployment' due to lack of demand at the unchanged prevailing real wage rate. It follows that employment at y_1 was lower than the full employment level at y_0. At this time the short-term interest rate (for example, the Federal funds rate or the Treasury bill rate) was much lower than the long-term interest rate (long-term bond yield). There was the expectation that the economy would recover soon and the interest rate would rise in the near future. Consequently, the yield curve was expected to be upward-sloping.

However, as the recovery was slow, the Federal Reserve System, to maintain full employment following the shock, raised the money supply from M_0 to M_1. This, given a stable money-demand relationship, shifted the $LM_0(M_0)$ curve to $LM_1(M_1)$. At point C where the $IS_1(e_0)$ and $LM_1(M_1)$ intersected, the real interest rate was r_2 and income was y_2. This expansionary monetary policy was effective in the sense that it raised output from y_1 to y_2 given a much reduced real interest rate, r_2. Points B and C, however, represented a condition of current account deficit because the real exchange rate was overvalued at the original level (e_0). Under these circumstances, external balance could be restored if the BP curve were shifted to the right by a depreciation of the real exchange rate, say from e_0 to e_1. This would be realized by outflows of capital. A depreciated real exchange rate is shown to have shifted the $IS_1(e_0)$ curve to the right $IS_2(e_1)$. At point D, internal and external balances are both restored, but at a lower real interest rate, r_3, than the rate, r_0, that prevailed at the original equilibrium. Therefore point D represents medium-term equilibrium where the domestic interest rate remains lower than the global real interest rate r_w, assuming some capital market distortions, including taxes, home country preferences and so on. In the long run, the following effects can be expected: (1) a decrease in the price level due to a rise in income (given the money supply); (2) a further depreciation of the real exchange rate (given the foreign price level) due to capital outflows at low real interest rates; and (3) these processes then would restore the original internal and external balance at point A. However, if the money supply is increased, the increased money supply may exceed the money demand, so that the price level may rise rather than fall. The real exchange rate may then not depreciate and the current account may remain in deficit.

The above adjustment process can be reconciled with data reported in Table 13.1. Recall that 'fear of deflation', developed by the US policy authorities in response to the Japanese deflation throughout the 1990s and reinforced in them after the mini-recession and the dot-com bust of 2001–02, provoked the FRS to implement expansionary monetary policy. This decreased the real interest rate, which had earlier already fallen due to lower consumption or increased saving arising from the very fear of deflation at which the policy response was directed. At the twice-reduced real interest rate, the real exchange rate became overvalued, creating large current account deficits, which were financed by foreign-capital inflows. This suggests that capital inflows were passive and current account deficits, which represented an excess of spending over income, were caused by expansionary monetary and fiscal policies.

As the model shows, the rectification of this situation involved depreciation of the real exchange rate through capital outflows. This process began in 2007. Table 13.1 shows that the real effective exchange rate of the US dollar depreciated from 126.8 in 2002 to 86.9 in 2011. Consequently, US current account deficits decreased from 6 per cent of GDP over 2005–06 to 3.7 per cent of GDP over 2007–11. The United States has a long way to go before it brings its external sector into balance, which it last experienced around 1996. Such an adjustment process could be completed (1) through a depreciation of the US dollar; (2) through a fall in US inflation; (3) through a rise in global inflation; or (4) through a combination of these three. Unfortunately, the United States has implemented a monetary strategy since the start of the crisis that has created scope for rapid money supply growth and hence high US inflation in the near to medium term. US inflation in 2011 was 3 per cent, a significant rise from 1 per cent over the years 2009 and 2010. In the meantime, general government debt has increased from 67 per cent to 103 per cent of GDP. This reflects a massive rise in the fiscal deficit at the level of 10 per cent of GDP during 2009–11.

REFERENCES

Corden, W.M. (2009), 'The world credit crisis: understanding it, and what to do', *The World Economy*, 385–400.

Salvatore, D. (2006), 'Twin deficits in the G-7 countries and global structural imbalances', *Journal of Policy Modeling*, **28**, 701–12.

Appendices: overview

'Monetary macroeconomics' is a recent usage for the study of topics surrounding the effects of money on output, prices, interest rates and exchange rates. The topics included for analysis and discussion are problem-driven and policy-oriented. Controversies abound in monetary theory and policy; however, a broad consensus is emerging that the design and conduct of monetary policy needs to focus on long-run price stability. Since the floatation of many currencies in the 1970s, monetary policy has acquired increased significance in macroeconomic stability in general and price stability in particular. Sustained research on monetary theory and policy issues has narrowed differences in practitioners' views of monetary policy across the globe. Especially since the 1970s, the rapid progression of the literature towards developing the micro-foundations of monetary relations under the rational-expectations hypothesis has given rise to doubt about the scope of monetary policy in economic stabilization and growth.

This book as well as Hossain (2015) offer case studies covering a wide range of issues in monetary theory and policy, representing a wide range of stages of development. The countries studied operate under differing institutional arrangements and have experienced varied outcomes. The key issues under investigation are concerned with exchange rate regimes, capital movements, interaction between monetary and fiscal policy and the impacts of these variables upon inflation, interest rates and other macroeconomic variables.

Given the space constraint, only the key analytical and empirical issues in monetary theory and policy are addressed to develop arguments. The remaining space is then used to apply the arguments to interpret some empirical econometric results generated from historical data. The underlying monetary relations are wide ranging and intertwined with most macroeconomic relations that define the structure of the economy and its dynamic behaviour.

The appendices to the book provide brief discussion of selected topics in monetary economics and some of the econometric models and techniques deployed for empirical analysis in the case studies. The discussions are suggestive, not comprehensive in contents and analysis. They supplement the country-specific materials that are otherwise self-contained. For detailed discussion on issues reviewed in the text, interested readers should consult specialist books and journal articles on such topics as those listed below.

- Appendix 1: Money growth, output growth and inflation
- Appendix 2: Inflation persistence: a brief literature review
- Appendix 3: Non-linearity in inflation and the KSS test for unit root
- Appendix 4: The Taylor curve
- Appendix 5: Inflation volatility and money demand
- Appendix 6: Inflation, real interest rate, real exchange rate and real output
- Appendix 7: Controls over interest and exchange rates and inflation volatility
- Appendix 8: Money, output and prices
- Appendix 9: A SVAR model for money, output and prices
- Appendix 10: Money-growth rule and related issues.

REFERENCE

Hossain, A. (2015), *Central Banking and Monetary Policy in Muslim-Majority Countries*, Cheltenham, UK and Northampton, MA, USA: Edward Elgar.

Appendix 1: Money growth, output growth and inflation

This appendix provides a generalized macroeconomic framework for illustration of the role of monetary policy in demand management to stabilize output and prices.[1] It includes some macroeconomic relations used to interpret macroeconomic events and developments. From the interpretations, policy lessons and implications are drawn.

THE EQUATION OF EXCHANGE

The famous Equation of Exchange can be expressed as follows:

$$MV = Py \tag{A1.1}$$

where, for a given accounting period, M is the nominal money stock, V is the velocity of money (defined as the ratio of nominal output Py to the money stock M), P is the general price level and y is a scale variable simultaneously representing real output, real income and measuring both the level of economic activity and the volume of transactions.

The Equation of Exchange presumes that the velocity of money is determined by technological and institutional factors such that it can be assumed stable in a statistical sense. It is not, however, devoid of substance. Implicit in the velocity of money is a money-demand function that links real money balances with real income, the nominal interest rate and any other factors that may have a systematic impact on money demand. In this variable originates the continuing debate in macroeconomics over whether the money-demand function is sufficiently stable to make the velocity of money stable or predictable. In a Keynesian money-demand function, the interest rate is a key determinant of money demand, originating primarily through the speculative motive for holding money. As this may make the money-demand function unstable, the velocity of money is considered unstable enough to weaken the linkage between money and prices. Monetarists do not agree with this interpretation.

In the Keynesian literature, the interest rate is considered a monetary policy decision variable. Policy-induced changes in the interest rate trigger the process of adjustment of the economy, rather than the reverse direction of causation, in which oscillations and shifts in the structure of economic activity would determine the time value of money and thereby the interest rate. Unlike the Classical monetary proposition, money and monetary policy are considered non-neutral in Keynesian economics under general conditions (Lewis and Mizen, 2000). Monetarists hold a different view. They suggest that the inflation-adjusted interest rate is determined by real factors and that the real interest rate can be viewed as a relative price of current consumption vis-à-vis future consumption. Then the real interest rate is determined within an intertemporal model of borrowing and lending of investible funds. However, the nominal interest rate incorporates expected inflation, which is determined within the framework of a monetary model of inflation. Inclusion of interest rates and returns on diverse financial and real assets, representing the opportunity costs of holding money, does not make the money-demand function unstable.[2]

In a seminal essay, Friedman (1956) suggested that inclusion of the interest rate with other determinants in the money-demand function indicates that the velocity of money is not constant but a stable function of such variables as real income, the interest rate and economic uncertainty. Formally, the velocity of money is defined as: $V = \frac{y}{m^d(y^p, NIR)}$, where y is real income, NIR is the nominal interest rate and $m^d(y^p, NIR)$ is the level of demand for real balances in which y^p is the permanent component of real income, after the model provided by the Permanent Income Hypothesis (PIH). Define real income (y) as follows: $y = y^p + y^c$, where y^p is, as already defined, permanent real income and y^c is cyclical real income (known in the original PIH as transitory real income). This suggests that $E(y) = E(y^p) = y^p$, given that $E(y^c) = 0$ and $cov(y^p, y^c) = 0$. Based on such decomposition, V can be considered stable in a statistical sense, as it can be expressed as a function of real income and the nominal interest rate. The actual value of V can be pro-cyclical as measured income is higher during boom and lower during recessions, relative to the level of permanent income. V is stable because the cyclical (transitory) component of income is zero on average and the nominal interest rate has only a small and predictable impact on money demand.

Empirical studies in general suggest that the interest rate semi-elasticity of demand for real money balances remains within the range of −0.5 to −1.0 (Hossain, 2009). Moreover, an emerging consensus is that in a highly competitive, deregulated financial system, the interest rates and returns on all financial and real assets move closely and therefore the relative rates of return on financial and real assets do not change much over time. Consequently, the impact upon money demand of any change in the interest rate remains very low (Mishkin, 2013).

REAL MONEY GROWTH AND OUTPUT GROWTH

In growth terms, the relationship in equation (A.1) can be expressed as:

$$g^M = g^P + g^y \text{ (assuming that V is constant and hence } g^V = 0) \quad \text{(A1.2)}$$

Equation (A1.2) can be rearranged as:

$$g^M - g^P = g^y \quad \text{(A1.3)}$$

Equation (A1.3) then suggests inflation in the steady state as the difference between money supply growth and real GDP growth:

$$g^P = g^M - g^y \quad \text{(A1.4)}$$

This relation assumes that the long-run income elasticity of demand for money is unity and that the economy is in equilibrium. When these assumptions hold, then the rate of inflation is shown to be just the excess of the growth rate of the money supply over the growth rate of output. This is the Classical monetary theory of inflation, which establishes a casual relation between money supply growth and inflation. The money-growth rate is ultimately viewed as a policy variable of the monetary authorities. As the money-growth rate does not affect economic growth over the long run (super-neutrality of money), inflation is viewed as a monetary policy variable.

For further analysis, the relationship (A1.4) can be derived from the long-run equilibrium condition in the money market, such that $\frac{M}{P} = m^d(y, NIR)$. Define the growth rate of real money stock as $g^m = g^M - g^P$, such that equation (A1.3) can be rewritten as:

$$g^y = g^m \quad \text{(A1.5)}$$

This shows that in the long run the growth rate of the real economy (g^y) determines the optimal growth rate of real money balances (g^m). That is, in the steady state, $g^y = g^m$. In the short run, g^M can deviate from g^P and hence create a flow disequilibrium in the money market. If this happens, then g^y may change in the short run. Equation (A1.3) thus represents an aggregate-demand relation, which suggests a positively sloped relation between real money growth and output growth. That is, if the growth rate of the nominal money supply exceeds the rate of inflation, real-money growth becomes positive. This represents a positive demand shock (monetary stimulus) that raises output growth. Note, however, that this cannot be but an unsustainable short-run deviation from long-run values.

REAL OUTPUT GROWTH AND THE UNEMPLOYMENT RATE (OKUN'S LAW)

Okun's (1971) law suggests a relationship between the rates of economic growth (g^y) and the rate of unemployment (U), such that for a given period t,

$$U_t - U_n = -\beta(g_t^y - g_0^y) \tag{A1.6}$$

where g_0^y is the steady-state growth rate of output that depends on accumulation of the primary factors of production such as labour, capital and technological innovation, and U_n is the natural rate of unemployment as defined by Friedman (1968). Equation (A1.6) suggests that measured output growth in excess of the potential growth rate of output lowers the rate of unemployment (U) from its natural level (U_n). Equation (A1.6) can then be linked to the growth rate of real money stock, such that

$$\uparrow g^m \rightarrow \uparrow(g_t^y - g_0^y) \rightarrow \downarrow(U_t - U_n) \tag{A1.7}$$

THE PHILLIPS CURVE RELATIONSHIP

Within the Keynesian policy framework, a relation exists between changes in the rate of inflation and the deviation of unemployment from its natural rate at potential output. Under general conditions where the aggregate demand curve is upward sloping, an increase in the money-growth rate raises the growth rate of output and hence lowers the rate of unemployment. Changes in the unemployment rate in turn affect the rate of inflation. This is represented in the Phillips curve relationship, which suggests that a decline in the rate of unemployment below the natural rate raises the rate of inflation. This is expressed in the following form:

$$(g_t^P - g_{t-1}^P) = -\alpha(U_t - U_n) \tag{A1.8}$$

where g_{t-1}^P approximates the expected rate of inflation under an adaptive-expectations model of inflation.

Equation (A1.8) establishes a short-run bidirectional linkage between the rates of inflation and unemployment. It suggests that inflation accelerates when the unemployment rate falls below the natural rate of unemployment. Inflation in turn raises the rate of unemployment if it exceeds the growth rate of the money supply. The relations expressed in (A1.3), (A1.5), (A1.7) and (A1.8) thus constitute a dynamic system of interrelations among money growth, output growth, unemployment and inflation. However, since inflation and the unemployment rate are determined simultaneously within this system, the Phillips curve relation, as expressed in equation (A1.8), does not provide a consistent estimate of the effect on inflation of a change in the unemployment rate (Stock and Watson, 2012).

MECHANICS OF SHORT-RUN ADJUSTMENT OF THE ECONOMY

In this short-run model, the money-growth rate is a policy variable, set exogenously by the monetary authorities. Monetary policy 'surprises' bring output and employment benefits when prices and wages are rigid in the short run. Further, wages are considered more rigid than prices. Consequently, an expansion of the money supply raises the level of real money balances and hence output. With wages more rigid than prices, real wages fall when prices start to rise in response to an increase in the money supply. Then monetary policy is effective in raising output in the short run, because of the slow adjustment of prices and wages to monetary expansion.

Formally, this transmission mechanism of monetary policy is represented in the following wage-price model, as suggested by Tobin (1972) and illustrated by Blanchard (1990):

$$Ly_t = \delta(LMS - LP)_t \tag{A1.9}$$

$$LP_t = LW_t \tag{A1.10}$$

$$\Delta LW_t = \eta \Delta LP_{t-1} + \phi Ly_t \tag{A1.11}$$

where Ly is the log of real output, LMS is the log of money stock, LP is the log of the price level, LW is the log of the nominal wage rate and δ, η and ϕ are parameters.

In this model a monetary expansion leads to an increase in output, given the slow adjustment of prices and a slower pace of adjustment of wages to

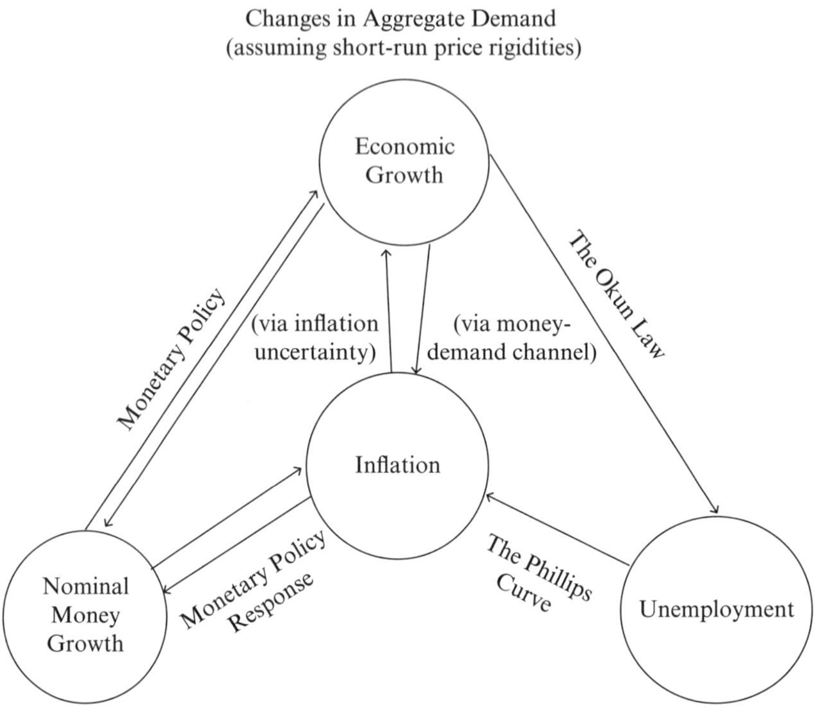

Figure A1.1 Money growth, output growth and inflation

prices. Although output returns to normal levels over time, the amount of time taken for the impact of a monetary expansion on output to dissipate depends on differential adjustment of both prices and wages to output changes.

The transmission mechanisms of money growth, output growth and inflation are illustrated in Figure A1.1. Assuming that prices and wages are rigid in the short run, a monetary expansion raises aggregate demand and hence output growth. Given the inverse relation between the rates of output growth and unemployment, an increase in demand lowers the rate of unemployment and raises the rate of inflation. Simultaneously, economic growth raises the growth of money demand and hence lowers the rate of inflation. Over a longer period, output growth returns to the potential growth rate, which is determined by accumulation of the real factors of production and technical innovation. The unemployment rate then returns to the natural level. In the long run, inflation rises proportionately to the growth rate of the money supply, implying no change in the growth of output. That is, in the long run monetary super-neutrality condition holds.

MONETARY POLICY

Assume that the exchange rate is flexible and that the nominal money stock (money base) is exogenously determined. Then the stock of money is equal to the money base multiplied by the money multiplier. The money multiplier depends on the currency-deposit ratio, the reserve-deposit ratio and the time-deposit to demand-deposit ratio (Mishkin, 2013). To the extent that these ratios remain stable or unchanged, the money multiplier can be considered stable. Assume that there is a short-run inverse relation, via the liquidity channel, between money supply growth and the nominal interest rate; then, over the long run, the relationship between money supply growth and the interest rate could be positive depending on the relative strengths of the liquidity, income and price expectations effects (Mishkin, 2013). As the monetary authorities have some control over the money stock or the interest rate but not both, an increase in the growth rate of the money supply is considered equivalent to a decrease in the nominal interest rate.

In the short run, an increase in the growth rate of the money supply represents an increase in the growth of real money balances (g^m), so that the impact of an increase in money growth is on aggregate demand and hence output. This relationship holds due to short-run wage and price rigidities, information imperfections and expectational errors. The stylized IS-LM model captures this phenomenon. Under the assumption that prices are rigid, an increase in the money supply shifts the LM curve to the right, which raises output given an unchanged IS curve. Over the ensuing medium term, prices and wages adjust to the monetary expansion. Subsequently, output returns to its natural level, making monetary expansion ineffective in raising output.

Although there is consensus over the short-run positive impact of monetary expansion on aggregate demand and hence output, the debate is whether monetary policy should be used to stabilize business cycles caused by both monetary and real shocks and other factors such as technological innovation. Keynesian economists in general argue for monetary activism to fight recession or stabilize output in the event of supply shocks. As Blanchard (2006, p. 151) remarks, 'The neutrality of money in the medium run does not mean that monetary policy cannot or should not be used to affect output. An expansionary monetary policy can, for example, help the economy move out of a recession and return faster to the natural level of output.' However, the money-neutrality proposition suggests that monetary policy cannot sustain output above its natural level indefinitely without accelerating inflation.

In developing countries, the linkage between money supply growth and inflation is strong and remains robust. Inflation, however, does not raise economic growth. Instead, high and volatile inflation raises economic uncertainty, reducing the rates of investment and economic growth down the track. The theoretical and empirical literature has established this theme conclusively (Hossain, 2009). To maintain low and stable inflation is therefore considered the key objective of monetary policy. This theme is indeed the key focus of this book of case studies of monetary policy in the Asia-Pacific as well as Hossain (2015). Emphasis is given to inflation volatility as it is costly to society, irrespective of whether the inflation rate on average is high or low.[3]

NOTES

1. The analysis is adapted based on Blanchard (2006).
2. In the context of time-series analysis, the velocity of money is stationary, or trend-stationary. The inflation rate and the interest rate are likely to be stationary variables, possibly exhibiting high persistence. This means that the velocity of money and the interest rate are likely to exhibit a short-term relation (Stewart, 2005). They do not establish a cointegral and causal relation such that it breaks the relationship between money supply growth and inflation. In contrast, the price level and money stock may have a common stochastic trend and hence may maintain a cointegral relation with real output. Real output is often found to be nonstationary with a dominant stochastic trend, capturing the impacts of supply shocks including technological innovation. This implies that even if the money-demand function becomes unstable, a cointegral relation may exist between the money supply and the general price level and then establish a dynamic relation between sustained money supply growth and inflation (defined as sustained growth of the price level). The relationship among money, output and prices is generally investigated within a cointegration and error-correction modelling framework (McCallum and Nelson, 2011). This book and Hossain (2015) contain some empirical results on these relationships. Given the limited scope of this study, the empirical results reported are suggestive, not conclusive, and hence require further investigation.
3. Sorensen and Whitta-Jacobsen (2005, pp. 606–7) have illustrated this problem as follows: 'Why do fluctuations in the rate of inflation imply a social welfare loss . . . in our AS-AD model a fluctuating rate of inflation means that people generally fail to anticipate the rate of inflation correctly. When households and firms underestimate or overestimate it, they end up with different real rates of return to their labour and capital than they expected. Due to these miscalculations, they will regret some of the economic decisions they made and will therefore suffer a welfare loss. Moreover, unanticipated inflation (an unexpectedly low real rate of interest) implies an arbitrary redistribution of wealth from creditors to debtors, while an unexpectedly low rate of inflation generates a similarly arbitrary redistribution in the opposite direction. Such unintended redistribution may threaten the stability of the society if it occurs on a large scale. This may be one reason why large fluctuations in inflation create a disproportionately greater welfare loss than small fluctuations . . .'.

REFERENCES

Blanchard, O.J. (1990), 'Why does money affect output? A survey', in B.M. Friedman and F.H. Hahn (eds), *Handbook of Monetary Economics*, Vol. II, Amsterdam: Elsevier Science, pp. 779–835.

Blanchard, O.J. (2006), *Macroeconomics*, New York: Pearson-Prentice Hall.

Friedman, M. (1956), 'The quantity theory of money: a restatement', in M. Friedman (ed.), *Studies in the Quantity Theory of Money*, Chicago, IL: University of Chicago Press, pp. 3–21.

Friedman, M. (1968), 'The role of monetary policy', *American Economic Review*, **58**(1), 1–17.

Hossain, A. (2009), *Central Banking and Monetary Policy in the Asia-Pacific*, Cheltenham, UK and Northampton, MA, USA: Edward Elgar.

Hossain, A. (2015), *Central Banking and Monetary Policy in Muslim-Majority Countries*, Cheltenham, UK and Northampton, MA, USA: Edward Elgar.

Lewis, M.K. and P.D. Mizen (2000), *Monetary Economics*, Oxford: Oxford University Press.

McCallum, B.T. and E. Nelson (2011), 'Money and inflation: some critical issues', in B.M. Friedman and M. Woodford (eds), *Handbook of Monetary Economics*, Vol. 3A, Amsterdam: Elsevier Science, pp. 97–153.

Mishkin, F.S. (2013), *The Economics of Money, Banking, and Financial Markets*, New York: Pearson Education.

Okun, A. (1971), 'The mirage of steady inflation', *Brookings Papers on Economic Activity*, **2**, 485–98.

Sorensen, P. and H.J. Whitta-Jacobsen (2005), *Introduction to Advanced Macroeconomics: Growth and Business Cycles*, New York: McGraw Hill.

Stewart, K.G. (2005), *Introduction to Applied Econometrics*, Belmont, CA: Thomson Brooks/Cole.

Stock, J.H. and M.W. Watson (2012), *Introduction to Econometrics*, New York: Pearson-Addison Wesley.

Tobin, J. (1972), 'Inflation and unemployment', *American Economic Review*, **62**, March, 1–18.

Appendix 2: Inflation persistence: a brief literature review

Price level stickiness and inflation persistence are the core issues in monetary policy. The extent to which monetary policy action has a short-term impact on real variables primarily depends on the extent to which prices are sticky in general and wages in particular.[1] When inflation persistence is high, restrictive monetary policy action takes a long time to lower inflation. This raises the costs of inflation control in terms of a lower rate of output growth and hence a higher rate of unemployment. Theoretically, there are multiple sources of inflation persistence. For example, inflation may have its own 'intrinsic persistence', or an 'inherited persistence' originating from some of the proximate determinants of inflation. Proximate determinants of inflation include the output gap and supply shifters, such as persistent rises in the relative prices of food and oil (Fuhrer, 2011). An understanding of these and other elements of the dynamic behaviour of inflation is integral to the formulation and implementation of monetary policy for monetary control and management. Within an open-economy macroeconomic management context, monetary control is key to price stability, which then provides the economy with a sound basis for sustained growth.

Some of the empirical research seeks to identify and document the two key characteristics of inflation: its origins and its dynamic behaviour. Economic theories are not, however, precise about the dynamic behaviour of inflation as embodied in the time-series properties of the price level and its growth. For example, in the sticky price models of Dornbusch (1976) and Taylor (1979), both the price level and inflation are stationary. In contrast, in the Phillips curve-type models of Calvo (1983) and Ball (1992), prices are nonstationary with a stochastic trend while inflation is stationary. In the empirical literature, one common finding is that in countries where inflation is low and steady and where monetary policy is conducted by rule, inflation acquires the mean-reverting characteristic. In contrast, in a country where inflation is high and volatile and where monetary policy is conducted by discretion rather than by rule, its measured inflation series may acquire the characteristic of a unit root or near-unit root. In the case of very high inflation or hyperinflation,[2] the inflation series may exhibit the characteristic of a stochastic trend and establish a cointegral relation with the (stochastic) real money balances series (Cagan, 1956). Hyperinflations, as rare occurrences emergent from extreme economic conditions and costly to bring under control, are excluded from general discussion on inflation and its dynamic behaviour (Hossain, 2009).

In a general context, Friedman's (1968) 'natural rate of unemployment' hypothesis postulates that in the steady state, inflation is stationary or trend-stationary. In the closely related accelerationist hypothesis, inflation may develop a unit root characteristic if the monetary authorities attempt to keep the unemployment rate below the natural level by tolerating ever-increasing inflation. An implication is that the rates of inflation and unemployment under such a regime are unlikely to have a common stochastic trend or, consequently, to establish a cointegral relation.[3] Friedman (1977) suggested that the natural rate of unemployment is stationary although it could be trend-stationary if there are significant structural changes in labour markets.

Structural factors that may shift the natural rate of unemployment include changes in labour productivity, real interest rates, real exchange rates, social security provisions and the costs of job search and other market and institutional imperfections. This implies that inflation, which generally yields a stationary series, does not necessarily form a cointegral relation with unemployment, in the sense of having an error-correction representation between the rates of inflation and unemployment. The possibility of a short-run relation is not precluded, but whether any such relationship, if present, would remain sufficiently stable for efficacious policymaking is an empirical issue. Under an extreme version of the rational expectations hypothesis, Lucas (1972) suggests that there is no monetary policy that can permanently keep output or employment away from their natural rate values, not even an ever-increasing or ever-decreasing rate of inflation. Any relation between the rates of inflation and unemployment is therefore likely to be episodic and unstable.

Presently many central banks conduct monetary policy within the New Keynesian paradigm,[4] which maintains optimality of price stability and suggests a short-run Phillips curve relationship while accepting no such relation in the long run. Due to wage and price rigidities, money is considered non-neutral in the short run but neutral in the long run. Non-neutrality of money is interpreted to provide some scope for the monetary authority to take a low-cost activist part in macroeconomic management. To make its participation more effective, New Keynesians suggest that the monetary and fiscal authorities somehow deploy monetary policy and fiscal policy complementarily to achieve output stabilization. Accepting wage and price rigidities as common phenomena, some central banks, of which the Reserve Bank of Australia is one, have adopted flexible inflation targeting in which a short-term interest rate is used as a policy instrument. Monetary operations change the value of the policy target as required. Given price rigidities, changes in the (real) interest rate influence aggregate demand to contain underlying inflation and stabilize output growth over the medium term, where the medium term is defined in relation to the business cycle.

Under flexible inflation targeting, the monetary policy reaction function includes the output gap[5] and the inflation gap[6] among the triggers for monetary operations to bring about changes in the policy interest rate. The time-series characteristics of the inflation rate depend on whether or not policymakers give priority to (relative) price stability over economic stabilization. Under strict inflation targeting (price stability), the monetary authorities attempt to keep the inflation rate close to the target level. The inflation rate then acquires the mean-reverting characteristic with the target rate acting as nominal anchor to inflationary expectations. Unless the authorities frequently alter the inflation target ('move the goalposts' on the community), sacrificing some credibility, inflation retains the characteristic of stationarity. The price level, however, becomes stochastic because past deviations of inflation from the target are usually not corrected. Such policy imparts the unit root characteristic to an accurately measured price level time series (Svensson, 2011).

Under flexible inflation targeting, price stability still receives policy priority, but secondarily the monetary authorities turn their attention to a subsidiary output or growth rate target whenever they expect the inflation rate to remain safely inside the target band. Under this policy regime, inflation may deviate from the target level for a considerable period of time and demonstrate the characteristic of a unit root or near-unit root. If the following two conditions are present, the inflation target could be altered frequently, imparting a stochastic trend to the inflation time series. Firstly, the initial target rate of inflation is not set at a relatively low level; and secondly, the central bank gives low priority to maintenance of its own policy credibility. Fuhrer (2011) suggests that in the case that a minor time variation in the inflation target adds a small unit root component to inflation, its contribution to inflation variance could be small. When, however, the inflation target is set relatively high and varies arbitrarily, and when a central bank has not achieved sufficient public confidence in its ability to keep inflation close to the target rate (policy credibility), inflation loses its anchor and can acquire the characteristic of a stochastic trend.

Kilian and Manganelli (2007, 2008) have developed a theoretical framework on the basis of risk management in monetary policy. They show that a central bank reacts to keep economic growth in line with inflation, depending on where the forecast distribution of inflation lies in relation to pre-set lower and upper limits. Their empirical results suggest that a central bank does not respond linearly to the conditional mean of inflation. Rather, it allows inflation to fluctuate within a band that remains unknown to the public, but differs from the officially announced target band. Aksoy et al. (2006, p. 1877) have stated this as follows: '[the] central bank controls inflation aggressively when inflation is far from its target, but concentrates more on output stabilisation when inflation is close to its target, allowing supply shocks and unforseen fluctuations in aggregate demand to move inflation within a certain band'. This lack of transparency in its policy actions raises inflation uncertainty, especially when a central bank does not have full policy credibility. The recent theoretical work on monetary policy shows that central banks operating under inflation targeting adjust their target inflation rates in a non-linear fashion (Martin and Miles, 2004; Orphanides and Wieland, 2000). In so doing, they stabilize output when the inflation outlook is close to the target level but pursue inflation aggressively when it deviates too far from that target.

Inflation persistence is a common phenomenon in most selected countries in this study. The presence of inflation persistence in a measured inflation series suggests a limited credibility of monetary policy in terms of its ability to achieve and maintain price stability. Central bank independence thus carries high importance in the design and conduct of monetary policy. Flexible inflation targeting suffers from the very time-inconsistency problem that rule-based monetary policy, in general, attempts to resolve. As Sorensen and Whitta-Jacobsen (2005, p. 610) explain:

> policy makers can only 'buy' credibility by announcing a fixed policy rule if they can convince the public that they are really bound by the rule. This will be easier if the rule is written into the law or into the mandate or statutes of the central bank, and if policy makers face the same kind of sanction if they break the rule. For example, the law regulating the central bank could specify that the central bank governor will be fired if he consistently misses the bank's inflation target. For a rule to be credible, it must also be reasonably simple so the public can easily understand the rule and check that policy makers actually stick to it.

NOTES

1. The debate remains whether inflation is highly persistent. In early studies, it was generally suggested that inflation is stubborn, has self-sustaining momentum and is not susceptible to cure by conventional monetary and fiscal measures. Following the rational expectations hypothesis, Sargent (1982) suggested no inherent momentum in the inflation process. Provided that a government makes comprehensive changes in fiscal and

monetary policies and that policy measures are credible, inflation can be eliminated with minimum costs.
2. Hyperinflation is understood technically, due to Cagan (1956), as a rate of inflation greater than 50 per cent per month or (by compounding) around 13 000 per cent per annum.
3. A cointegral relation between two stochastic variables implies a causal relationship between them running at least unidirectionally (Engle and Granger, 1987).
4. New Keynesian economics incorporates sticky prices into equilibrium models with optimizing consumers and firms. For detailed discussion, see Clarida et al. (1999), Williamson (2008) and Woodford (2011).
5. Defined as the difference between the actual and market-clearing output levels.
6. Defined as the difference between forecasted inflation and target inflation.

REFERENCES

Aksoy, Y., A. Orphanides, D. Small, V. Weiland and D. Wilcox (2006), 'A quantitative exploration of the opportunistic approach to disinflation', *Journal of Monetary Economics*, **53**, 1877–93.
Ball, L. (1992), 'Why does high inflation raise inflation uncertainty?', *Journal of Monetary Economics*, **29**(3), 371–88.
Cagan, P. (1956), 'The monetary dynamics of hyperinflation', in M. Friedman (ed.), *Studies in the Quantity Theory of Money*, Chicago, IL: University of Chicago Press, pp. 25–117.
Calvo, G. (1983), 'Staggered prices in a utility-maximizing framework', *Journal of Monetary Economics*, **12**, 383–98.
Clarida, R., J. Gali and M. Gertler (1999), 'The science of monetary policy: a new Keynesian perspective', *Journal of Economic Literature*, **37**, 1661–707.
Dornbusch, R. (1976), 'Expectations and exchange rate dynamics', *Journal of Political Economy*, **84**, 1161–76.
Engle, R.F. and C.W.J. Granger (1987), 'Cointegration and error correction: representation, estimation, and testing', *Econometrica*, **55**, 251–76.
Friedman, M. (1968), 'The role of monetary policy', *American Economic Review*, **78**, 1–17.
Friedman, M. (1977), 'Nobel lecture: inflation and unemployment', *Journal of Political Economy*, **85**, 451–72.
Fuhrer, J.C. (2011), 'Inflation persistence', in B.M. Friedman and M. Woodford (eds), *Handbook of Monetary Economics*, Vol. 3A, Amsterdam: Elsevier Science, pp. 423–86.
Hossain, A. (2009), *Central Banking and Monetary Policy in the Asia-Pacific*, Cheltenham, UK and Northampton, MA, USA: Edward Elgar.
Kilian, L. and S. Manganelli (2007), 'Quantifying the risk of deflation', *Journal of Money, Credit and Banking*, **39**, 561–90.
Kilian, L. and S. Manganelli (2008), 'The central banker as a risk manager: estimating the Federal Reserve's preferences under Greenspan', *Journal of Money, Credit and Banking*, **40**, 1103–29.
Lucas, R.E., Jr (1972), 'Econometric testing of the natural rate hypothesis', in O. Eckstein (ed.), *The Econometrics of Price Determination*, Washington, DC: Board of Governors of the Federal Reserve System, pp. 50–59.

Martin, C. and C. Miles (2004), 'Modelling monetary policy: inflation targets in practice', *Economica*, **71**, 209–21.
Orphanides, A. and V. Wieland (2000), 'Inflation zone targeting', *European Economic Review*, **44**(7), 1351–87.
Sargent, T.J. (1982), 'The end of four big inflations', in R.E. Hall (ed.), *Inflation*, Chicago, IL: University of Chicago Press, pp. 41–97.
Sorensen, P. and H.J. Whitta-Jacobsen (2005), *Introduction to Advanced Macroeconomics: Growth and Business Cycles*, New York: McGraw Hill.
Svensson, L.E.O. (2011), 'Inflation targeting', in B.M. Friedman and M. Woodford (eds), *Handbook of Monetary Economics*, Vol. 3B, Amsterdam: Elsevier Science, pp. 1237–302.
Taylor, J.B. (1979), 'Staggered wage setting in a macro model', *American Economic Review*, **69**(2), 108–13.
Williamson, S. (2008), 'New Keynesian economics: a monetary perspective', *Economic Quarterly*, Federal Reserve Bank of Richmond, **94**, 197–218.
Woodford, M. (2011), 'Optimal monetary stabilization', in B.M. Friedman and M. Woodford (eds), *Handbook of Monetary Economics*, Vol. 3B, Amsterdam: Elsevier Science, pp. 728–828.

Appendix 3: Non-linearity in inflation and the KSS test for unit root

The KSS (Kapetanios, Shin and Snell, 2003) test specification expands the standard ADF test by maintaining the null hypothesis of nonstationarity in the series against the alternative of a non-linear but globally stationarity process. The test is based on the following exponential, smooth-transition autoregressive specification:

$$y_t = y_{t-1} + \gamma y_{t-1}[1 - \exp(-\theta y_{t-1}^2)] + \varepsilon_t \,, t = 1,2,\ldots,T \quad \text{(A3.1)}$$

where y_t is the de-meaned or de-trended series of interest, ε_t is an independently and identically distributed (*i.i.d.*) error term with zero mean and constant variance

$$\varepsilon \sim i.i.d.(0,\sigma^2)$$

and $[1 - \exp(-\theta y_{t-1}^2)]$ is the exponential transition function that presents the non-linear adjustment. Equation (A3.1) can be rewritten as follows:

$$y_t = \{1 + \gamma[1 - \exp(-\theta y_{t-1}^2)]\} y_{t-1} + \varepsilon_t \quad \text{(A3.2)}$$

Following KSS (2003), equation (A3.2) can be further transformed as follows:

$$\Delta y_t = \gamma y_{t-1}[1 - \exp(-\theta y_{t-1}^2)] + \varepsilon_t \,, \theta \geq 0 \quad \text{(A3.3)}$$

The null hypothesis of a unit root in y_t (that is, $\Delta y_t = \varepsilon_t$) implies that $\theta = 0$, so that the term $[1 - \exp(-\theta y_{t-1}^2)]$ is zero. If θ is positive, it determines the speed of mean-reversion.

Hence, the KSS test directly focuses on the θ parameter by testing the null hypothesis of nonstationarity $H_o: \theta = 0$ against the alternative hypothesis of non-linear mean-reversion $H_A: \theta > 0$. Since θ in equation (A3.1) is not identified under the null, it is not feasible to directly test the null hypothesis. KSS (2003) have reparameterized equation (A3.3) by computing a first-order Taylor series approximation to obtain an auxiliary regression as specified in the form of equation (A3.4):

$$\Delta y_t = \delta y_{t-1}^3 + \text{error} \tag{A3.4}$$

When the errors in equation (A3.4) are serially correlated, the auxiliary regression can be expanded as follows:

$$\Delta y_t = \sum_{j=1}^{p} \rho \Delta y_{t-j} + \delta y_{t-1}^3 + \text{error} \tag{A3.5}$$

The null hypothesis for equation (A3.4) or (A3.5) is $H_o = \delta = 0$ and the alternative hypothesis is $H_A = \delta < 0$. Following the suggestion of KSS (2003, p. 365), the number of augmentations p is selected based on a significance testing procedure suggested by Ng and Perron (2001). It starts with a maximum lag, say, $p = 2$ chosen a priori for annual data and then estimates the ADF model with p lags. The decision rule or selection criterion for the optimal order of lags is as follows. If the coefficient on the last lag is significant at the 10 per cent level (critical value: 1.6), then the lag-length selected equals p. Otherwise, the order of lags p is reduced by one and the ADF model reiterated until the lag-length selection criterion is met. The critical values of the test are given in KSS (2003, p. 364). They show that the conventional t-values for testing non-linearity have non-standard asymptotic distributions under the unit root null and hence generated critical values through stochastic simulations.

The KSS test is conducted for CPI inflation only for a selected number of countries when the conventional ADF and KPSS tests are found inadequate to determine the time-series properties, especially confirming stationarity. Although this test can be conducted for other variables, it is not used given the limited scope of the empirical analysis in this book.

REFERENCES

KSS (Kapetanios, G., Y. Shin and A. Snell) (2003), 'Testing for a unit root in the nonlinear STAR framework', *Journal of Econometrics*, **112**, 359–79.

Ng, S. and P. Perron (2001), 'Lag length selection and the construction of unit root tests with good size and power', *Econometrica*, **69**, 1519–54.

Appendix 4: The Taylor curve

During the 1950s and 1960s monetary policy options were formulated in terms of a tradeoff between the rates of inflation and unemployment: the Phillips curve relationship. The empirical evidence of a negative relationship between the rates of inflation and unemployment required the development of various theories to interpret such a relation. Through time, however, theoretical and empirical developments have led macroeconomists in general, with the exception of some diehard Keynesians, to the by now well-established position that the evidence does not support any notion of a long-run policy tradeoff between the rates of inflation and unemployment.

The tide against the long-run Phillips curve relationship began to rise after Friedman (1968) and Phelps (1968, 1970) developed the 'natural rate theory of unemployment', which demonstrated that monetary policy cannot be deployed to lower the rate of unemployment below its natural level without accelerating inflation. At the very least, the Phillips curve relationship has been shown unfit for purpose as a policy menu, deployable in the public interest, to make any simultaneously target 'chosen' rates of inflation and unemployment.

Taylor (1979) suggests that while the Phillips curve relationship cannot be used as a policy menu, a tradeoff is present between the volatility of inflation and the volatility of output or unemployment, primarily via Okun's law (Okun, 1971). Taylor's suggestion is that besides opaque (and therefore probably erratic) conduct of monetary policy, there could be public developments, such as unduly optimistic or pessimistic views of consumers or investors (Keynes's 'animal spirits'), creating deviations of the unemployment rate from its natural level. Invoking this scenario of the environment, Taylor's variability-based tradeoff suggests that policymakers may decide the degree to which monetary policy can be deployed to buffer unemployment against non-fundamental disturbances. For instance, if consumers become unduly pessimistic about the future and the inflation rate turns out to be lower than the expected rate, the monetary authority can 'pre-emptively' expand the money supply to counteract the potential rise in the unemployment rate expected if the gathering disinflationary shock eventuates. Similarly, if consumers become unduly optimistic about the future and the actual inflation rate rises faster than the expected rate, the monetary authority can contract the money supply to counteract the threatened negative unemployment effect of any inflationary shock potentially generated by the undue optimism (Chatterjee, 2002).

Such central bank attempts to buffer the unemployment rate from its natural level is not considered inconsistent with the non-existence of a tradeoff between the rates of inflation and unemployment in the long run. This is based on the presumption that a central bank does not *ex ante* attempt to create unexpected 'inflation (or deflation) surprises'. Rather, it acts 'after the fact', or *ex post*, to offset any excess variability in the unemployment rate caused by the standard market failures that all too frequently deliver shocks serious enough to create discrepancies, and consequent excessive arbitrage opportunity, between actual and expected rates of inflation. The types of events that can cause actual inflation to depart from expected inflation are many and wide ranging in nature, leaving plenty of scope for beneficial monetary policy actions that remain consistent with the natural rate theory of unemployment.

Based on this premise, Taylor (1979) suggests the possibility of conducting monetary policy by taking into account a 'long-term' tradeoff between the variabilities in the rates of inflation and unemployment. While the traditional Phillips curve tradeoff between inflation and unemployment is short-lived, the tradeoff between their volatilities could be long-lasting. This suggested analytical framework is considered appropriate for assessing and comparing a country's macroeconomic performance under different monetary policy arrangements.

For illustrative purposes, the presence of a tradeoff between inflation volatility and output volatility, where output volatility proxies unemployment volatility, is represented by what is known as the Taylor curve. Graphically, the Taylor curve depicts a menu of the possible combinations of output volatility and inflation volatility from which policymakers can make a choice and design, preferably, a rule-based monetary policy. In sum, this strategy of monetary policy would entail targeting three outcomes simultaneously: an average (low) rate of inflation; and some preferred combination of inflation volatility and output (unemployment) volatility.

Figure A4.1 shows two Taylor curves: TC_1 and TC_2. Output volatility is measured on the vertical axis and inflation volatility is measured on the horizontal axis. The curve is downward sloping because it reflects the proposition that an optimizing policymaker is constrained to choose less of one type of volatility in the long run only by accepting more of the other. An implication is that monetary policy can achieve lower inflation volatility only by generating larger output volatility. The position and shape of the

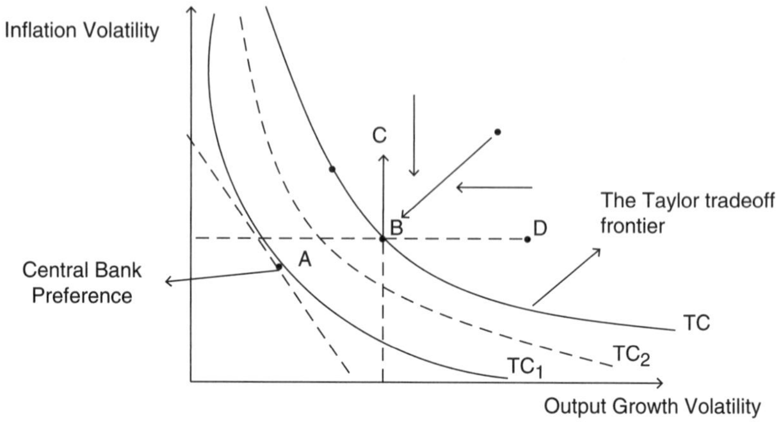

Figure A4.1 The volatility of both inflation and real output

Taylor curve depend on the underlying structure of the economy and the nature and magnitude of exogenous shocks to which the economy is vulnerable. Points lying either below or to the left of this tradeoff curve are infeasible given the structure of the economy. Points to the right and above are inefficient, in the sense that a better monetary policy option entailing less volatility in both variables is attainable by a shift back to the curve. An economy with less rigid wage and price setting has a tradeoff curve closer to the origin than an economy with more rigid wages and prices. An economy subject to relatively larger external shocks has a tradeoff curve further away from the origin than an economy experiencing smaller shocks (Chatterjee, 2002).

Having defined the tradeoff, the issue is the optimality of a tradeoff at any point other than in the Taylor curve. Bernanke (2004) suggests that shocks to aggregate supply constitute the ultimate source of the long-run Taylor curve tradeoff. Shocks to aggregate demand do not create the same tradeoff, since policy actions to offset an aggregate demand shock can stabilize both output and inflation. Improved monetary policy can make an important contribution by simultaneously reducing volatility in both inflation and output. The consequent improved macroeconomic stability can bring benefits to the economy:

> Lower volatility of inflation improves market functioning, makes economic planning easier, and reduces the resources devoted to hedging inflation risks. Lower volatility of output tends to imply more stable employment and a reduction in the extent of economic uncertainty confronting households and firms. (Bernanke, 2004, p. 1)

Taylor (2013) suggests that the recent deterioration in US output volatility (with inflation volatility remaining unchanged) was due to changes in the conduct of monetary policy. Although there was a rule-like monetary policy from the early 1980s until the end of the 1990s, monetary policy became much less rule-like, and more discretionary, from some time in the period 2003–05, when the policy interest rate was held far below levels that would have pertained in the 1980s and 1990s under similar conditions. In addition, there were: (1) intervention into particular markets, such as the mortgage-backed securities market; (2) an expansion of the Federal Reserve System's balance sheet; and (3) a commitment to hold the interest rate to zero at a time when correct application of the well-established rules of sound monetary policy called for higher interest rates.

The view that a central bank operates on the Taylor curve is not universally accepted. Friedman (2006) pointed out that the Taylor curve is an efficiency frontier yielding the tradeoff for optimal monetary policy; that is, the tradeoff between the volatility of inflation and the volatility of output is binding only if a central bank pursues an optimal monetary policy. As such, both volatilities can move in the same direction as the efficiency of monetary policy improves or worsens. He presented evidence showing that the correlation between US output variability and inflation variability is positive (0.81), not negative, over the period 1879–2005. To interpret this positive relation, he reported statistical data in support of the argument that money-growth variability raises output-growth variability, which in turn generates inflation volatility. The implication drawn is that steady money-growth rule can lower the volatility of both output and prices. According to Friedman, then, what was involved is not a tradeoff but direct cause-and-effect as the just described monetary targeting approach.

The main evidence that comes from this book (and also Hossain, 2015) is that most countries in the overall sample use monetary policy to keep inflation low on average but not necessarily stable. It indicates that in these countries, monetary policy is not required or intended to be implemented strictly. Even under an explicit policy rule, economic growth or higher employment is considered at least a secondary objective of monetary policy. The consequence of this strategy of monetary policy is to create inflation volatility as a major policy issue, and this book identifies the presence of this issue in most countries of the study. Low and stable inflation, not low but unstable inflation, is therefore flagged here as the key objective of monetary policy. This is a challenging task but central banks should strive to achieve it if their overarching goal is to avoid boom-bust cycles on behalf of their respective societies. One of the policy suggestions is therefore to adopt rule-based monetary policy in a strict form, such that it becomes credible and effective. This would keep inflation low and stable and also make the economy stable over the medium term.

REFERENCES

Bernanke, B.S. (2004), 'The great moderation', Remarks by Governor Ben S. Bernanke at the Eastern Economic Association, Washington, DC.

Chatterjee, S. (2002), 'The Taylor curve and the unemployment-inflation tradeoff', *Federal Reserve Bank of Philadelphia Business Review*, Third Quarter, 26–33.

Friedman, M. (1968), 'The role of monetary policy', *American Economic Review*, **58**(1), 1–17.

Friedman, M. (2006), 'Tradeoffs in monetary policy', Unpublished manuscript, Stanford University, available at http://web.stanford.edu/~johntayl/Friedman2006.pdf (accessed 19 March 2015).

Hossain, A. (2015), *Central Banking and Monetary Policy in Muslim-Majority Countries*, Cheltenham, UK and Northampton, MA, USA: Edward Elgar.

Okun, A. (1971), 'The mirage of steady inflation', *Brookings Papers on Economic Activity*, **2**, 485–98.

Phelps, E.S. (1968), 'Money-wage dynamics and labor-market equilibrium', *Journal of Political Economy*, **76**, August, 678–711.

Phelps, E.S. (1970), 'Introduction: the new microeconomics in employment and inflation theory', in E.S. Phelps (ed.), *Microeconomic Foundations of Employment and Inflation Theory*, New York: Norton, pp. 1–23.

Taylor, J.B. (1979), 'Staggered wage setting in a macro model', *American Economic Review*, **69**(2), 108–13.

Taylor, J.B. (2013), 'The effectiveness of central bank independence versus policy rules', Paper presented at Central Bank Independence: Reality or Myth, *American Economic Review* Annual Meeting, January, San Diego, California.

Appendix 5: Inflation volatility and money demand

There is emerging consensus that the ultimate objective of monetary policy is price stability, implying low and stable inflation. Although monetary policy generally aims at keeping inflation low on average over the business cycle, there is not much concern about money-growth volatility and associated inflation volatility making both the real interest rate and the real exchange rate volatile. The volatility of these is then transmitted to volatility in both real output and its growth.

Until the mid 1990s the prevailing view was that monetary targeting for price stability requires the presence of a stable money-demand function to establish a causal linkage between money supply growth and inflation. However, the recent literature suggests that a causal relation can exist between money supply growth and inflation irrespective of the exchange rate regime and whether the money-demand function is stable or not (McCallum and Nelson, 2011). This does not mean that the issue of stability of the money-demand function is not important for monetary analysis. Within the Friedmanite monetary framework, the money-demand function and the consumption function are each considered to be a stable function of real permanent income. Given that money is a temporary abode of purchasing power, the presence of a stable money-demand function allows the estimation of 'excess money supply' (monetary overhang) that may affect inflationary expectations and hence actual inflation. This issue has gained greater importance in recent years as the interest rate-based monetary policy strategy apparently bypasses money aggregates under the impression that money volume and growth volatility do not matter for monetary policy, leaving them unattended and unmodified by the monetary authorities. The resulting money-growth instability creates inflation instability, which in turn may affect money demand and hence inflation itself.

This appendix provides a brief discussion on the specification of a money-demand function in an open economy. The key issue is stability of the money-demand function, which remains a foundation in monetary economics. In the spirit of Friedman (1956, 1959), Judd and Scadding (1982) suggest that a stable money-demand function should include a small number of those arguments that can predict money demand with high precision. Real income and the nominal interest rate remain the two key arguments in the money-demand function. Their inclusion in the money-demand function is justified both by the asset theory and the transactions-based theory of money demand.

While the Keynesian money-demand function emphasizes the importance of the interest rate in the money-demand function via the speculative motive for holding money, the portfolio approach to the investigation of money-demand behaviour gives a lower weighting to the importance of the speculative demand for money. The reason is that narrowly defined money generates zero interest and hence becomes a dominated asset when highly liquid riskless assets, such as Treasury bills, yield positive interest. Asset demand for money combines the portfolio approach to holding money with the transactions costs approach (Goldfeld and Sichel, 1990).

A unique feature of the portfolio theory is its use of uncertainty in the rates of return on alternative assets. This uncertainty impacts demand for such assets. Friedman's (1956) restatement of the quantity theory of money parallels Tobin's portfolio approach in regarding the primary role of money as a form of wealth. Friedman (1956) dispenses with the separate motives for holding money posited by J.M. Keynes and treats money as an asset yielding a flow of services to money holders.

However, a basic money-demand function is found inadequate for explaining money-demand behaviour in an open economy where wealth-holders have the option to include a combination of domestic and foreign assets in their asset portfolios. Consequently, the foreign interest rate and the exchange rate of domestic currency are considered important in an expanded money-demand function that allows currency substitution (given the assumption of foreign currency-denominated asset holdings). Changes in the expected rates of return on domestic assets relative to those on foreign assets trigger portfolio adjustment by wealth-holders. Money demand therefore becomes sensitive to the movements of variables that bring about changes in the returns on money and other assets comprising the aggregate portfolio of wealth-holders.

Without undertaking a full review of the literature, an open-economy money-demand function of the following generic form can be used for estimation purposes:

$$LRJM_t = \alpha_0 + \alpha_1 Ly_t + \alpha_2 NIR_t + \alpha_3 FIR_t + \alpha_4 LER_t + u_t \quad (A5.1)$$

where LRJM (J = N,B) is the log of real narrow money balances or real broad money balances (so that LRNM denotes real narrow-money balances, while LRBM denotes real broad money balances), Ly is the log of real income that acts as a proxy for real permanent income, NIR is a representative nominal interest rate acting as a proxy for the opportunity cost of holding money relative to alternative financial assets, FIR is a representative foreign nominal interest rate (for example, the Treasury bill rate in the United States) acting as the opportunity cost of holding money in the form of domestic currency relative to foreign financial assets, LER is the log of a representative nominal or real exchange rate such as the nominal or real effective exchange rate and u is an error term, with zero mean and a constant variance, capturing random shocks to money demand.

This model is used for estimation purposes in this book, with minor variation for the sample countries depending on institutional arrangements. If the time series for every one of the specified variables has a unit root, the research question immediately becomes whether or not they are also cointegrated. Any instability in this money-demand function may originate from instability in the parameter values caused, for example, by financial deregulation and innovation. Most economists agree that financial reforms from the late 1970s created instability in the money-demand function in some countries through the 1980s and early 1990s. Some studies have found that the instability was due mainly to one-off shifts or break-points in money-demand functions, as would occur with changes in the functions' intercept parameters, rather than instability in the slope parameters. Laidler (1993) claims that instability in the money-demand function is evident only in the short-run money-demand specification, while the long-run money-demand function remains stable. Moreover, he argues for deployment of annual data for the estimation of money-demand functions, since high-frequency data are more volatile. Deployment of high-frequency data exhibits instability in the money-demand function when the model is estimated in dynamic form.

In the money-demand function (A5.1), real income is a proxy for permanent income (or wealth) and acts as the scale variable. The coefficient on real income (α_1) is expected to bear a positive sign and is to have a value equal to one. However, in developing countries, the income elasticity of demand for money is expected to exceed one. While the rapid pace of monetization is the standard interpretation, the more-than-unit income elasticity of demand for money could be due to mis-specification bias caused by the exclusion of wealth from the money-demand function. The nominal interest rate acts as the opportunity cost of holding money rather than alternative financial assets such as government-issued or corporate bonds. The estimated coefficient on the nominal interest rate (α_2) is expected to bear a negative sign, and the semi-interest elasticity of demand for money is usually less than one. In general, the nominal interest rate is not a major determinant of money demand in a controlled or repressed financial system in which regulatory restrictions on interest rates, exchange rates and capital flows are enforced. In countries where there is capital mobility, the foreign interest rate could be another determinant of money demand. Under fixed exchange rate arrangements with freely mobile capital, there is, however, no consensus on whether the coefficient on the foreign interest rate (α_3) bears a positive or negative sign. In general, the foreign interest rate bears a negative sign in a narrow money-demand function while its sign is indeterminate in a broad money-demand function.

In the literature, there is no consensus on whether a nominal or real exchange rate should be a determinant of money demand. Most studies deploy the nominal exchange rate for the purpose, but the real exchange rate could be deployed alternatively. This study experimentally alternates the nominal exchange rate and the real exchange rate in the money-demand specification, depending on data availability, and reports results that perform best on statistical grounds. An expectation about the sign of the coefficient on the exchange rate following estimation cannot be formed a priori.

In an open economy with freely mobile capital, the impact of the exchange rate on real narrow money balances is theoretically indeterminate because an appreciation of the exchange rate simultaneously exerts both upward and downward pressure on real balances. The net effect then depends on which of the two directions of impact dominates empirically. The mechanisms are as follows. In an open economy with freely mobile capital, wealth-holders have an option to hold both domestic and foreign assets in their portfolios. They adjust their portfolios in the event of changes in the expected rates of return on domestic and foreign assets. If they evaluate their portfolios in terms of domestic currency, an appreciation of the exchange rate can have a negative wealth effect on money demand. In contrast, an appreciation of the exchange rate can have a positive wealth effect on money demand when wealth-holders believe that the domestic currency is undervalued (despite recent appreciation) and may appreciate further. This may induce them to adjust their portfolios by shifting funds from foreign assets towards domestic assets, including domestic currency. Whether the wealth effect or currency substitution effect is dominant would determine the net effect of the exchange rate on money demand. Therefore, the net effect of currency appreciation on money demand is considered an empirical issue.

With other variables, the expected rate of inflation can be a potential determinant of money demand in developing countries. The nominal interest rate is institutionally determined in these countries, so does not have much impact on money demand. In high-inflation countries, the expected rate of inflation enters as an independent determinant of money demand. Whether the expected rate of inflation is a long-term determinant of money demand depends on the time-series properties of variables in the money-demand function. While real balances and real income are nonstationary with a common, dominant stochastic trend, the inflation rate is generally stationary and hence is not eligible for inclusion in the long-run money-demand function. However, the expected rate of inflation may be an important determinant of money demand in an error-correction model that is used to examine the dynamic behaviour of money demand.

With the above specified variables, inflation volatility (π^v) can be a determinant of money demand (Blejer, 1979; Klein, 1977). The level of demand for real money balances could vary with changing inflation volatility around a relatively stable average rate of inflation. Whether inflation volatility raises or lowers money demand is, however, ambiguous in theory. Inflation volatility is hypothesized to affect money demand in both positive and negative ways. When it generates economic uncertainty, then it can be expected to raise the precautionary demand for money. In contrast, when the aggregate asset portfolio requires adjustment due to changes in the risk structure of assets, inflation volatility may dampen money demand while raising the demand for inflation-hedging financial and real assets. Further, in developing countries, real balances in particular act as a complementary factor of production. As inflation volatility diminishes the productivity of real money balances in the production process, it lowers the demand for money balances (Deutsch and Zilberfarb, 1994). On balance, the net effect of inflation volatility on money demand is indeterminate a priori.

Both Blejer (1979) and Khan (1982) suggest that inflation volatility has a negative impact on money demand in countries where inflation is high and erratic, for example, in Latin America. In contrast, inflation volatility has an uncertain impact on money demand in countries with low but unstable inflation. Friedman (1986) argued that one way by which the financial system responds to a relatively volatile (mismanaged) fiat money is through induced financial innovation. Consequently, both money-demand instability and financial innovation could be viewed as the consequence of a third simultaneous cause: money-growth volatility. As money-growth volatility increases under the monetary policy strategy of flexible inflation targeting, inflation becomes volatile when the monetary aggregates are ignored by the policy authorities. As inflation has remained relatively low in most countries since the 1990s, inflation volatility has been generally ignored despite the costs it imposes upon investment and economic growth.

REFERENCES

Blejer, M.I. (1979), 'The demand for money and the variability of the rate of inflation: some empirical results', *International Economic Review*, June, 545–9.

Deutsch, J. and B.Z. Zilberfarb (1994), 'Inflation variability and money demand in developing countries', *International Review of Economics and Finance*, **3**(1), 57–72.

Friedman, M. (1956), 'The quantity theory of money: a restatement', in M. Friedman (ed.), *Studies in the Quantity Theory of Money*, Chicago, IL: University of Chicago Press, pp. 3–21.

Friedman, M. (1959), 'The demand for money – some theoretical and empirical results', *Journal of Political Economy*, **67**, 327–51.

Friedman, M. (1986), 'The resource cost of irredeemable paper money', *Journal of Political Economy*, **94**, June, 642–7.

Goldfeld, S.M. and D.E. Sichel (1990), 'The demand for money', in B.M. Friedman and F.H. Hahn (eds), *Handbook of Monetary Economics*, Vol. 1, Amsterdam: Elsevier Science, pp. 299–356.

Judd, J.P. and J.L. Scadding (1982), 'The search of a stable money demand function: a survey of the post-1973 literature', *Journal of Economic Literature*, **20**, 993–1023.

Khan, A.H. (1982), 'The demand for money and the variability of the rate of inflation: an empirical note', *Economics Letters*, **10**, 257–61.

Klein, B. (1977), 'The demand for quality adjusted cash balances: price uncertainty in the U.S. demand for money function', *Journal of Political Economy*, August, 691–715.

Laidler, D. (1993), *The Demand for Money: Theories, Evidence, and Problems*, New York: Harper Collins.

McCallum, B.T. and E. Nelson (2011), 'Money and inflation: some critical issues', in B.M. Friedman and M. Woodford (eds), *Handbook of Monetary Economics*, Vol. 3A, Amsterdam: Elsevier Science, pp. 97–153.

Appendix 6: Inflation, real interest rate, real exchange rate and real output

This appendix outlines a four-variable structural model, which provides a rationale explaining inclusion of the variables in a structural vector autoregressive (SVAR) model to examine their feedback relations in a dynamic context. The variables are defined in generic form: real output (y), real interest rate (RIR), real exchange rate (RER) and inflation (π). The model is adapted from Kamin (2001), Kamin and Rogers (2000) and Kamin and Klau (2003).

In an open-economy Keynesian model, output is linked to aggregate demand, which is determined by the real interest rate, the real exchange rate and other fiscal and monetary variables.

By definition, real output is expressed as:

$$y = A + NX \tag{A6.1}$$

where y is real output (or income), A is domestic absorption (consumption plus investment) and NX is net exports. Government spending is ignored in the specified model.

Domestic absorption is expressed as an increasing function of real income and a decreasing function of the real interest rate (RIR), while net exports are expressed as an increasing function of foreign income (y^f) and a decreasing function of the real exchange rate (RER) as a rise in the index value of the real exchange rate represents appreciation. For simplicity, y^f is assumed constant and normalized to unity.

$$A = A(y, RIR) \tag{A6.2}$$

$$NX = NX(RER) \tag{A6.3}$$

Using equations (A6.1) to (A6.3), real output is expressed as:

$$y = y(RIR, RER) \tag{A6.4}$$

Kamin (2001), Kamin and Rogers (2000) and Kamin and Klau (2003) suggest that in an open economy, inflation can be expressed as a decreasing function of both the real exchange rate and the nominal exchange rate. Kamin and Klau (2003, pp. 171–2) have provided the following rationale behind their inclusion of the real exchange rate in an inflation model:

> Intuitively, a depreciation of the real exchange rate relative to the level that clears the market for home goods, by raising foreign goods prices relative to home goods prices, shifts demand toward home goods while raising wages and home production costs – both of these factors lead to increase in home goods prices until the real exchange rate reverts to its original level.

They suggest that a series of policy actions attempting to keep the real exchange rate more depreciated than its market-clearing rate, for a given output gap, leads to ever-increasing inflation. Since money is not explicitly included in their model, they argue that there is a causality running from money to the nominal exchange rate and that the latter is linked to prices. The nominal exchange rate therefore acts as a predetermined policy variable, or a proxy intermediate variable, for the money stock (Hossain, 2010). Accordingly, the inflation rate is expressed as follows:

$$\pi = \pi\ (RER, y, NER) \tag{A6.5}$$

where NER is the nominal exchange rate. Real output (y) appears in this equation as a proxy for real money demand.

In the long run, the real exchange rate depends on real variables only. In the short run, the real exchange rate is affected by some nominal variables of both fiscal and monetary nature. The real exchange rate equation is expressed as an increasing function of real output, which captures the Balassa-Samuelson effect, and the rate of inflation. The inclusion of the inflation rate suggests that the monetary authorities do not instantaneously and fully adjust the nominal exchange rate to changes in the rate of inflation.

$$RER = RER(y, \pi) \tag{A6.6}$$

Following the Fisher equation, the real interest rate (RIR) can be expressed as:

$$RIR = NIR - \pi \tag{A6.7}$$

where NIR is the nominal interest rate. In developing countries, the responsiveness of the nominal interest rate to inflation is very low. The real interest rate therefore moves inversely with the rate of inflation. Therefore, the real interest rate can be expressed as: RIR = k − π, where k is a constant.

Substituting the equations the model can be simplified and specified as four reduced-form equations (A6.8) to (A6.11) for four endogenous variables y, RER, RIR and π:

$$y = y(RIR, RER) \tag{A6.8}$$

$$\pi = \pi(RER, y, NER) \tag{A6.9}$$

$$RER = RER(y, \pi) \tag{A6.10}$$

$$RIR = k - \pi \tag{A6.11}$$

In this model, the nominal exchange rate (NER) is the only policy variable. It is linked to the nominal interest rate or a monetary aggregate, depending on the strategy of monetary policy that a central bank adopts to maintain price stability.

In the model, equation (A6.11) can be ignored as it is approximated by the inflation rate. Equation (A6.11) suggests that the higher the rate of inflation, the lower the real rate of interest. The impact of the real interest rate on aggregate demand (and hence output) is ambiguous for financially repressed economies (Hossain, 2009).

Figure A6.1 provides an illustration of the interrelations among inflation, the real exchange rate and output. This illustration can be done under either fixed or flexible exchange rate arrangements. In most developing countries, the exchange rate is kept either fixed or pegged to a foreign stable currency such as the US dollar. Provided that the exchange rate is sufficiently flexible, the money stock becomes exogenous and therefore largely determinable by the monetary authority. Changes in the money supply are expected to bring about inverse changes in the interest rate in the short run. Given foreign interest rates, changes in the domestic interest rate may trigger capital flows, which in turn cause the exchange rate to adjust so that interest rate parity is maintained (that is, no pressure is placed on foreign interest rates to adjust). This interest rate parity condition holds that the domestic interest rate is equal to the foreign interest

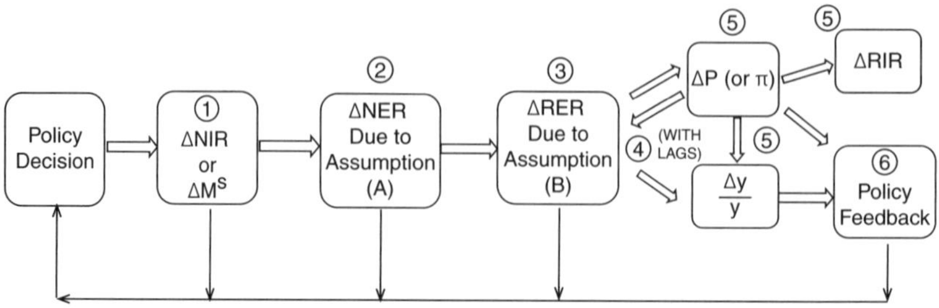

Note: Δ denotes a change in the adjacent variable; NIR is the nominal interest rate; M^s is the money supply; NER is the nominal exchange rate; RER is the real exchange rate; P is the general price level; π is the inflation rate; y is real output (real GDP); and RIR is the real interest rate.

Figure A6.1 Interrelations among inflation (ΔP or π), real interest rate (RIR), real exchange rate (RER) and real GDP growth ($\frac{\Delta y}{y}$)

rate with an additive adjustment for the expected appreciation or depreciation of the domestic currency over the investment period. Under a fixed exchange rate system, given freely mobile capital, the domestic interest rate follows the foreign interest rate.

In the short run, given price rigidities, changes in the nominal interest rate bring about changes in the real interest rate and in exchange rates. Both real interest rates and real exchange rates affect all components of real GDP. Policymakers dynamically adjust monetary policy in response to the best information they can obtain about changes in output and prices.

ASSUMPTIONS AND INTERPRETATION

Assumption (*A*): Relatively flexible forex market (for example, floating currency).
Assumption (*B*): Short-term price rigidities are present (prices/wages are 'sticky').

1. A monetary policy variable is chosen and altered: ΔNIR or ΔM^S.
2. Change in chosen policy variable leads to ΔNER if assumption (A) holds.
3. ΔNER causes ΔRER if assumption (B) holds.
4. With lags, ΔRER causes ΔP or π and y.

5. ΔP or π causes ΔRIR, Δy and 'feeds back' into ΔRER.
6. End-effects on all variables, especially the target variables y and π, feed back into future choices of instrument (ΔNIR or ΔM^S) and policy actions.

REFERENCES

Hossain, A (2009), *Central Banking and Monetary Policy in the Asia-Pacific*, Cheltenham, UK and Northampton, MA, USA: Edward Elgar.

Hossain, A. (2010), 'Monetary targeting for price stability in Bangladesh: how stable is its money demand function and the linkage between money supply growth and inflation?', *Journal of Asian Economics*, **21**, 564–78.

Kamin, S.B. (2001), 'Real exchange rates and inflation in exchange-rate based stabilizations: an empirical examination', *Journal of Development Economics*, **64**, 237–53.

Kamin, S.B. and M. Klau (2003), 'A multi-country comparison of the linkages between inflation and exchange rate competitiveness', *International Journal of Finance and Economics*, **8**, 167–84.

Kamin, S. and J. Rogers (2000), 'Output and the real exchange rate in developing countries: an application to Mexico', *Journal of Development Economics*, **61**, 85–109.

Appendix 7: Controls over interest and exchange rates and inflation volatility

Assume that a country operates under a fixed peg exchange rate system and conducts monetary policy under the monetary targeting strategy. If a country's national decision-making processes lead it to adopt the strategy of monetary targeting for price stability, then a key criterion for maximizing the effectiveness of this policy is the simultaneous implementation of a flexible exchange rate system, since this confers monetary policy independence upon the country's monetary authorities. While the monetary authorities gain control over the money supply under a flexible exchange rate system, both the exchange rate and the interest rate become market determined and hence may become more volatile, depending on the structural characteristics of the money-demand function and whether shocks to the economy are predominantly monetary or real in nature.

The manner in which monetary policy is generally conducted in developing countries predisposes them to inflation volatility. In general, under a repressed financial environment, the interest and exchange rates are controlled. The price level then remains the only variable that adjusts, in the event of real shocks to the economy, to re-equilibrate the money market. The price level volatility translates directly into inflation volatility, even if the inflation rate may converge over the medium term to the inflation rate of the anchor currency country. Most sample countries in the study experienced inflation volatility when they introduced monetary targeting in one form or other while retaining control over the interest rate and the exchange rate. This appendix develops a simple model to illustrate the phenomenon.

Assume that the money-demand function takes the following form:

$$m_t^d = \alpha_1 y_t - \alpha_2 NIR_t \tag{A7.1}$$

where m^d is real money balances, y is real income, NIR is the interest rate and the αs are structural parameters. Under perfect capital mobility, the uncovered interest rate parity condition establishes equilibrium in the foreign-exchange market:

$$NIR_t = FIR_t + \delta \qquad (A7.2)$$

where FIR is the foreign interest rate and δ is the expected rate of depreciation of the domestic currency against a representative foreign currency.

Define the money-market equilibrium condition as follows:

$$m^d(y, NIR) = (M/P) \qquad (A7.3)$$

where M is the nominal money stock and P is the price level. Substitution of (A7.1) and (A7.2) into (A7.3) yields:

$$\left(\frac{M}{P}\right)_t = \alpha_1 y_t - \alpha_2(FIR_t + \delta) \qquad (A7.4)$$

Equation (A7.4) can be rearranged as a price level equation, such that:

$$P_t = M_t - (\alpha_1 y_t - \alpha_2[FIR_t + \delta]) \qquad (A7.5)$$

This price level equation is specified in a line of Fisher's (1911) version of the *Quantity Theory of Money*. It assumes that the velocity of money is stable and determined by both institutional factors and the state of transactions technology.

Equation (A7.5) can be used to illustrate the emergence of inflation volatility under a fixed peg exchange rate system in the event of real shocks to the economy.

MONEY AND PRICES UNDER A FLEXIBLE EXCHANGE RATE SYSTEM

A second key criterion for maximum effectiveness of monetary targeting for price stability, beyond a flexible exchange rate system (because it renders the money stock (M) exogenous), is the use of a narrow definition of the money stock, such as the monetary base. Assuming that the money-demand function is stable, equation (A7.5) suggests a positive relation between P and M.[1] Implementation by the monetary authorities of an alteration to the policy variable, the money stock, is expected to cause an equi-proportional change in the target nominal variables, including the price level and the exchange rate. That is, an increase in the money supply, given money demand, raises the price level. Consequently, *ceteris paribus*, purchasing power parity suggests that the increased price level will depreciate the domestic currency. Any real sector shock to the economy affects real output and hence money demand. Unless there is a corresponding change in the money supply, this adjusts the exchange rate, and hence the interest rate, pushing the money market towards equilibrium. However, the impact of the supply shock on the price level is expected to be limited and only transitory in nature under a floating currency. In contrast, under a fixed peg exchange rate system, the impact of a supply shock on the price level is predicted to be much larger and more disruptive.

MONEY AND PRICES UNDER A FIXED PEG EXCHANGE RATE SYSTEM

Under a fixed peg exchange rate system, the exchange rate is set by means of continuous monetary authority interventions in the market for sustaining the peg against the anchor currency. This makes the domestic money stock endogenous, responsive to changes in money demand. That is, $M = M^d = \beta(Py)$, where β is the reciprocal of the velocity of money[2] and M^d is the level of nominal money demand that depends on the level of nominal income. This shows that the money stock responds to changes in income, the price level and any other factors that affect the velocity of money such as the nominal interest rate or expected inflation.

Under a monetary targeting strategy of monetary policy, the monetary authorities attempt to keep the growth rate of the money supply consistent with the targeted rate of inflation. This is feasible under a flexible exchange rate system that, by definition, confers upon the monetary authorities control over the money supply and its growth rate. However, as the monetary equilibrium condition shows, a negative relation exists between the price level and output under monetary targeting when the exchange rate remains fixed. Under a fixed peg system, money then becomes endogenous, with a link to the balance-of-payments. In general, inflation under a fixed peg system is more volatile than that in the anchor currency country if the domestic economy experiences asymmetric shocks vis-à-vis the anchor currency country and/or the domestic economy has a large non-tradable goods sector that remains exposed to shocks of both domestic and foreign origin, especially capital flows.

Supply Shocks and Inflation Volatility

Real output is determined in the real sector, which remains exposed to various supply shocks. As interest rates and exchange rates in developing countries are adjusted to inflation rises only occasionally, the price level and output move in opposite directions. Consequently, empirical evidence suggests an inverse relation between inflation and economic growth. This relation could be bidirectional when inflation remains high and volatile. An interpretation is that an increase in output raises money demand that, given the money supply, lowers prices.

The stability of the relationship between the price level (P) and real output (y) depends on the flexibility of interest rates and exchange rates. The monetary approach to balance-of-payments theory provides an interpretation of this relationship. Under a flexible exchange rate system, an increase in output raises money demand. This appreciates the exchange rate, simultaneously reducing the prices of tradables. If the money supply does not increase in response to an increase in income, the price level will fall. This potentially deflationary situation is eliminated over the medium term as the money stock changes to match the increased money demand through the balance-of-payments channel. Therefore, the extent of pressure on the price level arising from an increase in output depends on flexibility of the interest rate and the resilience of the economy to output shocks. The shorter the time required for dynamic adjustment to shocks, the more 'resilient' is the economy.

Assuming that prices are rigid in the short run, the real money stock remains unchanged under monetary targeting as both M and P are unchanged. However, if the interest rate is flexible, an increase in output raises money demand and hence the interest rate. This lowers money demand and re-establishes equilibrium in the money market. Therefore, an increase in output reduces the price level in the process of re-establishing equilibrium in the money market, in which the interest rate plays a role. That is, the interest rate bears some burden of adjustment to output shocks and plays a role in re-establishing equilibrium in the money market if prices are rigid in the short run. In the event that both prices and interest rates are flexible, an increase in output could be associated with a simultaneous decline in the price level and an increase in the interest rate.

Figure A7.1 illustrates this adjustment process. An increase in output from y_0 to y_1 is associated with a decline in the price level from P_0 to P_1. This represents a situation when the interest rate is fixed at NIR_0 and the money stock is fixed at M_0. In contrast, when the interest rate is flexible while the price level is fixed at P_0, an increase in output from y_0 to y_1 is associated with an increase in the interest rate from NIR_0 to NIR_1 (B*).

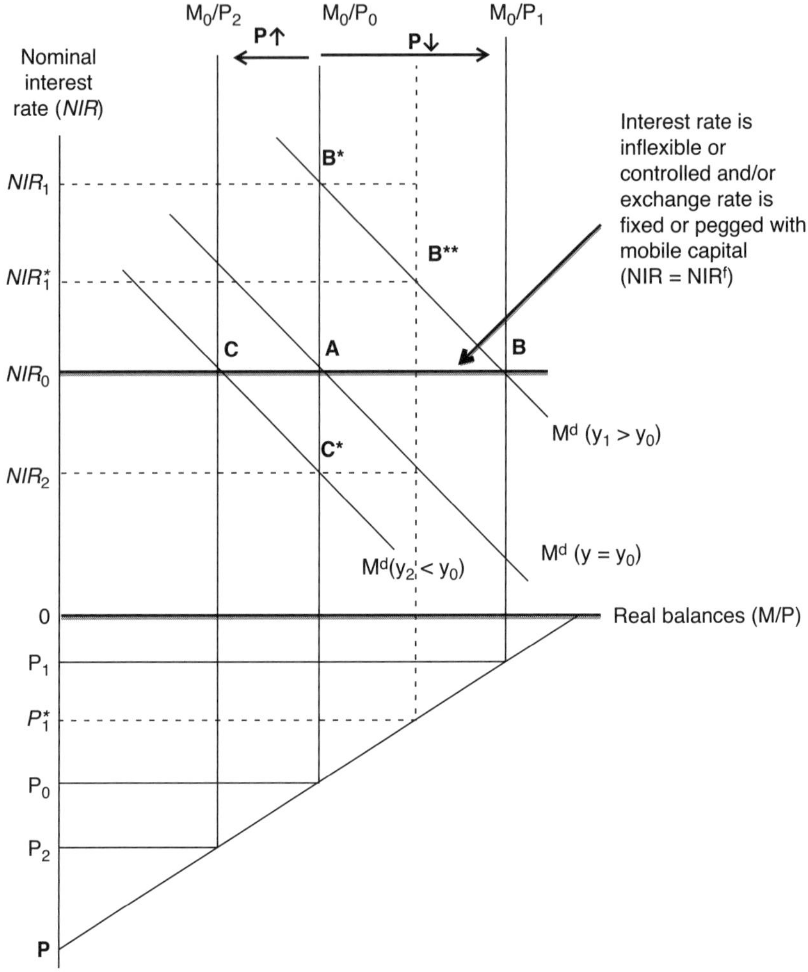

Figure A7.1 Inflation volatility and controls over interest rates and exchange rates

In the event that both prices and interest rates are flexible, an increase in output from y_0 to y_1 is associated with an increase in the interest rate from NIR_0 to NIR_1^* and a decrease in the price level from P_0 to $P_1^*(B^{**})$.

In summing up, the fixity of the interest rate under a fixed peg exchange rate system leads to excess inflation volatility in the event of supply shocks. A fixed exchange rate system also does not guarantee low and stable inflation even when the anchor currency country maintains low inflation on average.[3]

NOTES

1. Equation (A7.5) can be expressed in the following growth form (ignoring changes in the interest rate): $\pi = \mu - \eta_m^y g_y$, where π is the rate of inflation, μ is the growth rate of the money supply, g_y is the growth rate of the economy and η_m^y is the income elasticity of demand for money. As the growth rate of output is independent of the growth rate of the money supply, it gives a one-for-one relationship between the rates of money growth and inflation. Under a stable money-growth rate, the rate of change of the velocity of money becomes a stationary variable with constant mean and variance. The money-growth targeting thus becomes equivalent to stabilizing the inflation rate around a target level.
2. If the nominal interest rate remains under the control of monetary authority and money demand is unit income elastic and insensitive to the interest rate, β is considered constant. The velocity of money cannot, however, be considered constant in the long run as it depends on transactions technology and the pace of monetization of the economy. The income elasticity of demand for money is generally higher or lower than unity, depending on the economy's present stage of development.
3. This can be illustrated as follows. Define the following measure of the real exchange rate: $\Delta RER = \Delta NER + (\pi^f - \pi)$, where RER is the real exchange rate, NER is the nominal exchange rate, π^f is the foreign inflation rate and π is the domestic inflation rate. Under a fixed exchange rate system, $\Delta NER = 0$. As domestic inflation can then be expressed as $\pi = \pi^f + \Delta RER$, a low and stable inflation at home requires a low and stable inflation in the anchor currency country while the real exchange rate remains unchanged. The first component of this condition would be satisfied if the anchor currency country (usually the United States) follows a credible monetary policy that aims to maintain low and stable inflation. The second component of the condition requires that the real exchange rate remain stable (that is, $\Delta RER = 0$), which is unlikely unless the economies concerned experience symmetric shocks and follow similar stabilization policies (Sorensen and Whitta-Jacobsen, 2005).

REFERENCES

Fisher, I. (1911), *The Purchasing Power of Money*, New York: Macmillan.

Sorensen, P. and H.J. Whitta-Jacobsen (2005), *Introduction to Advanced Macroeconomics: Growth and Business Cycles*, New York: McGraw Hill.

Appendix 8: Money, output and prices

Both the Monetarist and the Keynesian frameworks suggest that monetary expansion has short-run impact on output. Monetarists hypothesize that money is neutral in the long run. Contrarily, Keynesians look for evidence that monetary expansions leading to lower interest rates can have a material long-run impact on output (Blanchard, 1990). If this can be shown unambiguously to be the case, then monetary policy can potentially be instrumental in stabilizing economies susceptible to frequent shocks, especially financial shocks, and whose market forces are not sufficiently developed to provide the needed strong and rapid adjustment in response to these shocks. At the least, to avoid lingering adverse impacts on output and employment, monetary policy can complement fiscal policy while fiscal policy remains the preferred policy instrument of Keynesian policymakers for economic stabilization. In an historical context, Keynes's (1936) explanation of the impact of money on output, as given in his *General Theory*, was based on two key assumptions. Firstly, he accepted the Classical principle that employment increases with a fall in real wages. He postulated that workers care about nominal wages and that, while nominal wages and prices both were slow to move, or 'sticky', particularly downwards, nominal wages are more rigid, or 'stickier' than prices. Consequently, he suggested that both prices and wages respond to the money supply after a lag. Prices first rise with an increase in the money supply, causing a corresponding fall in real wages, stimulating employment as firms seek to raise output.

In the present context, the debate is whether a monetary expansion can be brought about exogenously by a policy action, or whether there is a feedback impact of output change on the money supply. The monetary authority's control over the money supply is generally viewed as not absolute but adequate for policymaking in the medium term. Whether money is exogenous or endogenous does not matter much in so far as the dynamic relations among money, output and prices are concerned, since they maintain a feedback relation. The real business cycle models, in particular, do not incorporate an impact of monetary disturbances on output; instead, real shocks cause business cycles that then bring about changes in the money supply. Bidirectional causality therefore is a real possibility as an economy progresses under varied institutional and policy environments, while remaining exposed to monetary and real sector shocks. Real supply shocks may have a longer-term impact on the economy, while real demand shocks are transitory and hence dissipate quickly.

MONETARY SHOCKS AND PORTFOLIO ADJUSTMENT

Monetarists hypothesize that prices rise slowly following a monetary expansion, and that monetary expansion raises output in the short run. The Monetarist views on the transmission mechanism of monetary policy rely on the asset-theoretic demand for money, which emphasizes the store-of-value function of money while downplaying its function as a medium of exchange. In households' portfolio of assets, money appears with bonds, equities, human capital and consumer durables. The demand for money is determined simultaneously with the optimal holding quantities of all five asset classes, such that a portfolio balance is maintained. An implication is that the risk-adjusted rates of return on all assets remain equal over time. Within such a framework, the rates of return on assets are defined in such a way as to include both pecuniary (monetary) and non-pecuniary (non-monetary) returns. The return on real money balances then includes interest receipts, liquidity services and other attributes that monetary assets provide to money holders. Liquidity is a leading service or attribute here, since it is required to meet transaction needs, especially in emergencies.

The portfolio adjustment process in response to a monetary shock is generally represented in the monetary transmission mechanisms. Given an expansionary monetary shock, for example, households find their wealth portfolios out of balance. That is, they have excess real money balances, implying that the rate of return on money is lower relative to the returns on other assets in the portfolio. To lower the holding of real money balances, households then exchange money for other assets, both real and financial. Consequently, the prices of non-monetary assets, such as physical goods, rise and their rates of return fall. With the rise in prices, the quantity of real money balances falls. This raises the return on real money balances. This process continues until the rates of return on all assets in the portfolios are equalized (Marquis, 1996).

MONEY-GROWTH SHOCK AND THE DYNAMIC ADJUSTMENT OF THE ECONOMY

Monetarists suggest a well-defined adjustment process of the economy in the event of, say, a one-time increase in the growth rate of the nominal money supply. A rise in the growth rate of the money supply initially raises output above its long-run equilibrium level and subsequently output falls below its long-run equilibrium level, with attendant disruption to labour markets. Monetarists suggest that super-neutrality of money holds in the long run, that is, the steady-state growth rate of the economy remains independent of the money-growth rate. The initial response of the economy that shows a higher output growth is termed the nominal income effect and the latter response during the period of slower output growth is termed the price effect. These effects represent net additions (both positive and negative) to output growth in relation to what it would have been in the absence of a monetary expansion. The sequencing of such effects reflects the slow increase in prices initially and then they overshoot later such that the rate of inflation equals the money-growth rate over the adjustment period. Super-neutrality of money requires that after all of the dynamics are settled out, the cumulative change in nominal income equals the cumulative change in the price level. This ensures that real income growth remains unaffected by an increase in money growth over the long run (Marquis, 1996).

In the early literature on the relative importance of monetary and fiscal policies in output stabilization, Monetarists emphasized that monetary policy is more effective than fiscal policy. This was established in the St Louis model where output growth was regressed on money growth and government spending (or budget deficits) and the statistical significance of monetary and fiscal variables was compared to determine their relative effectiveness (Anderson and Jordan, 1968). The idea that money has a strong impact on output was the theme of the seminal study of Friedman and Schwartz (1963) on the US economy. Relying on the evidence from 1867–1960, and in particular on a study of turning points in money and output, they concluded that there was a strong and stable relation among money, nominal and real income, with causality running from money to economic activity. A second conclusion held that most of the movements in the money stock, especially the largest ones, rather than being responses to real sector developments, originated out of developments in the monetary sector. Thirdly, they showed that these monetary movements were 'exogenous' and followed by output movements in the same direction. Fourthly and finally, they concluded that, unless the money-output relationship in these episodes was an extraordinary fluke, it reflected causation running from money to output rather than in the opposite direction.

EMPIRICAL ANALYSIS

A reduced-form approach of the following form is usually used to examine the impact of money on output (Blanchard, 1990):

$$Ly_t = \alpha_0 + \sum_{i=1}^{n} \alpha_i Ly_{t-i} + \sum_{i=0}^{k} \beta_i LMS_{t-i} + \sum_{i=0}^{k} z_{t-i}\lambda_i + \varepsilon_t \quad \text{(A8.1)}$$

where Ly is the log of a measure of output, LMS is the log of money stock, z is a vector of other variables, including fiscal policy variables and exports, and ε is a random error term. The α_i, β_i and λ_i are reduced-form parameters whose significance can be examined by using the conventional F-test.

Equation (A8.1) is essentially a reduced-form equation. Then the key issue is the general theoretical problems associated with estimation of a reduced-form equation. Successful resolution of these will allow the estimation to determine the relative effectiveness of monetary versus fiscal impacts on real output (Anderson and Jordan, 1968). Critics suggest a range of problems with regressions where real output depends on the lagged growth of the money supply. Firstly, there is the suggestion that causation may run from output to money rather than from money to output. For example, when firms plan to increase production, they increase their money holdings, since money facilitates the process of acquiring raw materials and intermediate inputs. Similarly, households increase their money holdings when they plan to purchase goods and services. Based on such firm and household behaviour, it is suggested that an increase in money holding, prior to an increase in output, does not imply a causal relation running from money to output. The second problem with the St Louis model is related to the way in which monetary policy is conducted. Suppose a central bank adjusts the money stock to offset the impact on output of a change in one of the factors of production. If such monetary changes have real effects and the central bank's efforts to stabilize the economy are successful, then monetary changes may not lead to changes in output. This indicates that the absence of a relation between money and output does not imply the lack of impact of money on output; rather, the opposite is the case. The third difficulty with the St Louis model is that the relationship between money and output could be distorted due to financial deregulation and reform that affects the money-demand relationship (Blanchard, 1990).

POLICY INEFFECTIVENESS PROPOSITION

Lucas (1972) highlighted the issue of instability in the Phillips curve relationship as evidence that any anticipation of inflation by consumers would prevent the government from systematically lowering unemployment by exploiting the Phillips curve tradeoff between inflation and unemployment. In a series of papers, Barro (1976, 1977, 1978, 1979) examined the efficacy of monetary policy directly within a rational expectations framework. He reported evidence that unanticipated changes in the money supply bring about changes in output and unemployment but anticipated changes in money growth do not lead to changes in output. Rather, anticipated changes in the money supply are fully absorbed by inflation; whereas unanticipated changes are only partially absorbed by inflation, leaving some ability of the money supply change to effect changes in output and unemployment.

Barro's first task was to divide observed changes in the money supply into anticipated and unanticipated components. His strategy was to estimate the current rates of change in the money supply as a function of past variables that consumers would have already observed. He assumed that the fitted value of the growth rate of money-growth rate was the anticipated change in the money supply, and that the residual was the unanticipated change. In essence, he assumed consumer expectations comprised linear extrapolations of historical records. He then asked whether either anticipated or unanticipated changes in the money supply were relevant explanators in equations for output, employment and inflation.

Barro failed to reject the null hypothesis that anticipated money growth does not influence unemployment. In contrast, he rejected the null hypothesis that unanticipated money growth does not influence unemployment. Systematic, that is, predictable, monetary policy is found not to affect output or employment. His findings are consistent with the rational expectations models or policy-ineffectiveness hypothesis. Shortly after the publication of these results, however, Sargent (1979) established from theoretical first principles that this econometric approach could be misleading. His reasoning deployed the 'observational equivalence' argument. Using this argument, it can be shown that a model demonstrating that systematic monetary policy can affect output can be rearranged to show the contrary, with some plausible, reasonable, additional assumptions. That is, only unanticipated policy can affect output.

The problem for the econometric work is that while these models have different assumptions that set them apart in theory, they are observationally equivalent in practice because it is not possible to specify them in such a way that they can be separated on econometric grounds when estimated in reduced form.

In summing up: the key theme of the literature is that monetary expansion has an impact on output in the short run, but this does not last in the long run. The question is whether monetary policy should be deployed for economic stabilization. Monetarists do not see the need for stabilization to dampen business cycles. Over the course of a business cycle, as the economy moves away from full employment, the episodes are unlikely to be severe enough in magnitude and duration to justify attempts to dampen them out. Moreover, such attempts by the monetary authorities may exacerbate the severity of business cycle swings. Monetarists point to several problems associated with stabilization. Monetary policy actions have long and variable lags, and variable impact, due to the sluggish adjustment of prices and wages. A stimulatory policy first induces a 'nominal income effect', whereby output picks up with a lag of three to nine months. A 'price effect' follows during which inflation rises more rapidly than nominal income and real income therefore falls. This price effect persists a further nine to eighteen months. Therefore, a one-time increase in the monetary growth rate may introduce into the economy a set of dynamics that might then persist for as long as two years. The magnitude and timing of the income and price changes are unpredictable; therefore, frequent adjustment of the monetary growth rate induces instability in the economy as the dynamic effects accumulate in an unpredictable direction (Marquis, 1996).

The debate on the role of monetary policy in economic stabilization continues. Taylor (2009, 2011) has been highly critical of the deployment of monetary policy for economic stabilization since the US-global financial crisis. Most developing countries of the Asia-Pacific have been less than enthusiastic to adopt expansionary monetary policy to stabilize their economies despite the urge of the United States and international financial institutions such as the IMF.

REFERENCES

Anderson, L. and J. Jordan (1968), 'Monetary and fiscal actions: a test of their relative importance in economic stabilization', *Federal Reserve Bank of St. Louis Review*, November, 11–24.

Barro, R.J. (1976), 'Rational-expectations and the role of monetary policy', *Journal of Monetary Economics*, **2**(1), 1–32.

Barro, R.J. (1977), 'Unanticipated money growth and unemployment in the United States', *American Economic Review*, **67**(2), 101–15.

Barro, R.J. (1978), 'Unanticipated money growth, output and the price level in the United States', *Journal of Political Economy*, **86**, 549–80.

Barro, R.J. (1979), 'Money and the price level under the gold standard', *Economic Journal*, **89**, March, 13–33.

Blanchard, O.J. (1990), 'Why does money affect output? A survey', in B.M. Friedman and F.H. Hahn (eds), *Handbook of Monetary Economics*, Vol. II, Amsterdam: Elsevier Science, pp. 779–835.

Friedman, M. and A.J. Schwartz (1963), *A Monetary History of the United States, 1867–1960*, Princeton, NJ: Princeton University Press.

Keynes, J.M. (1936), *General Theory of Employment, Interest and Money*, London: Macmillan.

Lucas, R.E., Jr (1972), 'Expectations and the neutrality of money', *Journal of Economic Theory*, **4**, 103–24.

Marquis, M.H. (1996), *Monetary Theory and Policy*, New York: West Publishing Company.

Sargent, T. (1979), *Macroeconomic Theory*, New York: Academic Press.

Taylor, J.B. (2009), 'The lack of empirical rationale for a revival of discretionary fiscal policy', *American Economic Review* (*Papers and Proceedings*), **99**(2), 550–5.

Taylor, J.B. (2011), 'An empirical analysis of the revival of fiscal activism in the 2000s', *Journal of Economic Literature*, **49**, 686–702.

Appendix 9: A SVAR model for money, output and prices

A structural vector autoregressive (SVAR) model represents a multivariate dynamic system of endogenous variables that are contemporaneously and dynamically interdependent (Sims, 1992). In the present case, three variables, namely money ($m = \log M$), output ($y = \log RGDP$) and prices ($p = \log P$), are assumed to be contemporaneously and dynamically interdependent. According to Classical monetary theory, they establish a long-run equilibrium relationship with causality running from money to prices. The three variables under consideration can be represented in the following first-order autoregressive form, ignoring intercepts, where *t* is a time subscript and β_i and α_i are parameters to be estimated:

$$m_t + \beta_1 y_t + \beta_2 p_t = \alpha_1 m_{t-1} + \alpha_2 y_{t-1} + \alpha_3 p_{t-1} + \varepsilon_t^m \tag{A9.1}$$

$$\beta_3 m_t + y_t + \beta_4 p_t = \alpha_4 m_{t-1} + \alpha_5 y_{t-1} + \alpha_6 p_{t-1} + \varepsilon_t^y \tag{A9.2}$$

$$\beta_5 m_t + \beta_6 y_t + p_t = \alpha_7 m_{t-1} + \alpha_8 y_{t-1} + \alpha_9 p_{t-1} + \varepsilon_t^p \tag{A9.3}$$

Assume that the residuals ε_t^m, ε_t^y and ε_t^p are normally distributed with zero means and constant variances and are not serially correlated. In equations (A9.1) to (A9.3), the endogenous variables *m*, *y* and *p* may have contemporaneous feedback impacts that are captured by β_i. The structural form of this three-equation system is expressed in the following matrix:

$$\begin{pmatrix} 1 & \beta_1 & \beta_2 \\ \beta_3 & 1 & \beta_4 \\ \beta_5 & \beta_6 & 1 \end{pmatrix} \begin{bmatrix} m_t \\ y_t \\ p_t \end{bmatrix} = \begin{pmatrix} \alpha_1 & \alpha_2 & \alpha_3 \\ \alpha_4 & \alpha_5 & \alpha_6 \\ \alpha_7 & \alpha_8 & \alpha_9 \end{pmatrix} \begin{bmatrix} m_{t-1} \\ y_{t-1} \\ p_{t-1} \end{bmatrix} + \begin{bmatrix} \varepsilon_t^m \\ \varepsilon_t^y \\ \varepsilon_t^p \end{bmatrix} \tag{A9.4}$$

Equation (A9.4) can be abbreviated as:

$$\mathrm{B}Y_t = \mathrm{A}Y_{t-1} + \mathrm{E}_t \tag{A9.5}$$

$$\text{where B} = \begin{pmatrix} 1 & \beta_1 & \beta_2 \\ \beta_3 & 1 & \beta_4 \\ \beta_5 & \beta_6 & 1 \end{pmatrix},\ Y_t = \begin{bmatrix} m_t \\ y_t \\ p_t \end{bmatrix},$$

$$\mathrm{A} = \begin{pmatrix} \alpha_1 & \alpha_2 & \alpha_3 \\ \alpha_4 & \alpha_5 & \alpha_6 \\ \alpha_7 & \alpha_8 & \alpha_9 \end{pmatrix},\ Y_{t-1} = \begin{bmatrix} m_{t-1} \\ y_{t-1} \\ p_{t-1} \end{bmatrix} \text{ and } \mathrm{E}_t = \begin{bmatrix} \varepsilon_t^m \\ \varepsilon_t^y \\ \varepsilon_t^p \end{bmatrix}$$

Pre-multiply equation (A9.5) by the inverse of B, B^{-1} such that:

$$\mathrm{B}^{-1}\mathrm{B}Y_t = \mathrm{B}^{-1}\mathrm{A}Y_{t-1} + \mathrm{B}^{-1}\mathrm{E}_t \tag{A9.6}$$

Assume that B is non-singular so that $\mathrm{B}^{-1}\mathrm{B} = \mathrm{I}_{3\times3}$. Then equation (A9.6) simplifies to:

$$Y_t = \mathrm{B}^{-1}\mathrm{A}Y_{t-1} + \mathrm{B}^{-1}\mathrm{E}_t \tag{A9.7}$$

Expanding equation (A9.7) gives:

$$Y_t = \begin{pmatrix} 1 & \beta_1 & \beta_2 \\ \beta_3 & 1 & \beta_4 \\ \beta_5 & \beta_6 & 1 \end{pmatrix}^{-1} \begin{pmatrix} \alpha_1 & \alpha_2 & \alpha_3 \\ \alpha_4 & \alpha_5 & \alpha_6 \\ \alpha_7 & \alpha_8 & \alpha_9 \end{pmatrix} \begin{bmatrix} m_{t-1} \\ y_{t-1} \\ p_{t-1} \end{bmatrix} + \begin{pmatrix} 1 & \beta_1 & \beta_2 \\ \beta_3 & 1 & \beta_4 \\ \beta_5 & \beta_6 & 1 \end{pmatrix}^{-1} \begin{bmatrix} \varepsilon_t^m \\ \varepsilon_t^y \\ \varepsilon_t^p \end{bmatrix} \tag{A9.8}$$

The reduced-form matrix of equation (A9.8) gives the following simplified form:

$$\begin{pmatrix} m_t \\ y_t \\ p_t \end{pmatrix} = \begin{pmatrix} \delta_1 & \delta_2 & \delta_3 \\ \delta_4 & \delta_5 & \delta_6 \\ \delta_7 & \delta_8 & \delta_9 \end{pmatrix} \begin{pmatrix} m_{t-1} \\ y_{t-1} \\ p_{t-1} \end{pmatrix} + \begin{pmatrix} v_t^m \\ v_t^y \\ v_t^p \end{pmatrix} \tag{A9.9}$$

In matrix equation (A9.9) the δ_i are reduced-form parameters output by the operation $\mathrm{B}^{-1}\mathrm{A}$ and (v_t^m, v_t^y, v_t^p) are reduced-form errors output by the operation $\mathrm{B}^{-1}\mathrm{E}_t$. In this standard form of the VAR model, the reduced-form error terms (v_t^m, v_t^y, v_t^p) are composites of three pure shocks of the structural system: $(\varepsilon_t^m, \varepsilon_t^y, \varepsilon_t^p)$. Since these pure shocks are white noise, the reduced-form shocks (v_t^m, v_t^y, v_t^p) are assumed to have zero means and constant variances. However, the reduced-form shocks (v_t^m, v_t^y, v_t^p) could be correlated as the endogenous variables in the system (m, y, p) may have contemporaneous relations. Consequently, the variance-covariance matrix ($\sum_v$) of the reduced-form error terms can be written as:

$$\sum_v = \begin{pmatrix} \sigma_m^2 & \sigma_{my} & \sigma_{mp} \\ \sigma_{my} & \sigma_y^2 & \sigma_{yp} \\ \sigma_{mp} & \sigma_{yp} & \sigma_p^2 \end{pmatrix} \tag{A9.10}$$

Only when the endogenous variables (m, y, p) are not contemporaneously related will the reduced-form shocks (v_t^m, v_t^y, v_t^p) be uncorrelated. The variance-covariance matrix of the VAR shocks can then be represented in the following diagonal matrix form:

$$\sum_v = \begin{pmatrix} \sigma_m^2 & 0 & 0 \\ 0 & \sigma_y^2 & 0 \\ 0 & 0 & \sigma_p^2 \end{pmatrix} \tag{A9.11}$$

As the structural shocks in SVAR models can be provided a moving average representation, in empirical analysis, the impulse response estimates are computed to show the responses of all variables in the model to a standard deviation shock to structural innovations. This is done by normalizing the SVAR model by setting the variances of structural shocks to one, because the standard deviation shocks, with this normalization, correspond to unit innovations in ε_t^m, ε_t^y, ε_t^p, respectively. From this follows that the variance-covariance matrix of the structural innovations is assumed to have the form:

$$\sum_v = \begin{pmatrix} 1 & 0 & 0 \\ 0 & 1 & 0 \\ 0 & 0 & 1 \end{pmatrix} \text{ or in brief, } \sum_v = I \tag{A9.12}$$

As the normalization is about scaling, it does not make any substantive change in the system. In a mathematical sense, the structural innovations are linked to the reduced-form disturbances in the following form: E = BV where the variance-covariance matrix B is normalized so that $B\sum_\varepsilon B^{-1} = \sum_v = I$.

IDENTIFICATION AND ESTIMATION

The reduced-form equations expressed in matrix (A9.9) can be estimated by OLS to obtain estimates of the reduced-form parameters. These estimates can be given a meaningful economic interpretation if the structural system's parameters can be identified by imposing theory-consistent restrictions on contemporaneous relations in the system. There is, however, no consensus on the approach to follow to impose such restrictions. Sims (1972, 1980) has suggested the use of a recursive system to make the structural VAR model identified.[1] Care is taken to impose restrictions based on economic theory and institutional arrangements. Results obtained are therefore indicative, not conclusive.

The relationships under investigation in this study make the Cholesky decomposition technique appropriate. The Cholesky decomposition technique makes the β-matrix lower-triangular such that equation (A9.4) can be written as:[2]

$$\begin{pmatrix} 1 & 0 & 0 \\ \beta_3 & 1 & 0 \\ \beta_5 & \beta_6 & 1 \end{pmatrix} \begin{bmatrix} m_t \\ y_t \\ p_t \end{bmatrix} = \begin{pmatrix} \alpha_1 & \alpha_2 & \alpha_3 \\ \alpha_4 & \alpha_5 & \alpha_6 \\ \alpha_7 & \alpha_8 & \alpha_9 \end{pmatrix} \begin{bmatrix} m_{t-1} \\ y_{t-1} \\ p_{t-1} \end{bmatrix} + \begin{bmatrix} \varepsilon_t^m \\ \varepsilon_t^y \\ \varepsilon_t^p \end{bmatrix} \quad \text{(A9.13)}$$

The identification procedure adopted here follows Classical monetary theory, where prices in the steady state are determined by the money supply adjusted for potential output. In the specified model, money affects output contemporaneously but output may affect money after a lag. Likewise, both money and output affect prices contemporaneously while prices may affect both money and output after a lag. This follows the Classical monetary transmission mechanism, in which an increase in the money supply raises output initially and its impact on prices becomes stronger as time passes. In the long run money is neutral, so that it establishes a one-for-one relation with prices. Since prices rise slowly with an expansion of the money supply, output first rises and then falls, while prices rise steadily and may overshoot before establishing a one-for-one linkage with the money supply (Marquis, 1996).

In the present model, money supply shocks are treated as pure shocks. Accordingly, in the first row of the β-matrix, the off-diagonal elements are restricted to zero. In the second row of the β-matrix, the coefficient of money on output β_3 is non-zero: to be precise, it should be positive. This follows the rationale that monetary expansion raises aggregate demand and hence output. However, as prices do not have a contemporaneous impact on output, the off-diagonal element in the second row of the β-matrix is restricted to zero ($\beta_4 = 0$). Both money and output have contemporaneous impacts on prices. Consequently, in the third row of the β-matrix, the coefficients β_5 and β_6 are assumed non-zero.

Considering such a transmission mechanism of monetary expansion, the order of variables in the SVAR model is as follows: m, y and p. The relations between the pure shocks (ε_t^m, ε_t^y, ε_t^p) and reduced-form shocks (v_t^m,v_t^y,v_t^p) are then expressed in the following form:

$$\begin{bmatrix} \varepsilon_t^m \\ \varepsilon_t^y \\ \varepsilon_t^p \end{bmatrix} = \begin{pmatrix} 1 & 0 & 0 \\ \beta_3 & 1 & 0 \\ \beta_5 & \beta_6 & 1 \end{pmatrix} \begin{bmatrix} v_t^m \\ v_t^y \\ v_t^p \end{bmatrix} \tag{A9.14}$$

In equation form, the pure and structural residuals are presented as follows:

$$\varepsilon_t^m = v_t^m \tag{A9.15}$$

$$\varepsilon_t^y = \beta_3 v_t^m + v_t^y \tag{A9.16}$$

$$\varepsilon_t^p = \beta_5 v_t^m + \beta_6 v_t^y + v_t^p \tag{A9.17}$$

NOTES

1. For example, Enders (2010, p. 311) writes: 'the very idea of imposing a structure on a VAR system seems contrary to the spirit of Sim's argument against "incredible identifying restrictions". Unfortunately, there is no simple way to circumvent the problem; identification necessitates imposing some structure on the system. The Cholesky decomposition provides a minimal set of restrictions that can be used to identify the primitive model.'
2. The validity of the Cholesky decomposition can be investigated by estimating the correlation coefficients of the reduced-form residuals. The sensitivity of results obtained by the Cholesky decomposition technique can be evaluated by reversing the order of variables in the system. The importance of the ordering depends on the magnitudes of the correlation coefficients among the reduced-form residuals (Enders, 2010).

REFERENCES

Enders, W. (2010), *Applied Econometric Time Series*, New York: John Wiley and Sons.

Marquis, M.H. (1996), *Monetary Theory and Policy*, New York: West Publishing Company.

Sims, C.A. (1972), 'Money, income and causality', *American Economic Review*, **62**, 540–52.

Sims, C.A. (1980), 'Macroeconomics and reality', *Econometrica*, **48**(1), 1–48.

Sims, C.A. (1992), 'Interpreting the macroeconomic time series facts: the effects of monetary policy', *European Economic Review*, **36**(5), 975–1000.

Appendix 10: Money-growth rule and related issues

From the very birth of the economic sciences, economists have been interested in the design and implementation of monetary policy rules to maintain economic stability. In *Wealth of Nations* (1776), Adam Smith argued for the regulation of paper money to sustain economic stability or avoid a boom-bust cycle. Other prominent economists of the nineteenth century, namely Henry Thornton and David Ricardo, stressed the importance of rule-based monetary policy, following their observation of money-induced financial crises associated with the Napoleonic wars. In the early twentieth century, addressing the long period of widespread international recession and depression that marked the closing decades of the nineteenth century, Irving Fisher and Knut Wicksell proposed monetary policy rules to avoid high inflation or hyperinflation and depression (Taylor and Williams, 2011).

From the later part of the twentieth century, two interrelated monetary policy rules have become popular in the extant literature. Friedman (1960) proposed a constant money-growth rule in the 1950s to maintain price stability. Although it remains controversial, discussion of Friedman's rule dominated the literature until the 1990s. In the early 1990s, when the money-demand function apparently became unstable due to financial deregulation and innovation, Taylor (1993) proposed an interest rate rule as an alternative to the money-growth rule. Since then the Taylor rule has dominated the literature irrespective of whether the predominant shocks to an economy are real sector shocks or monetary shocks, or some combination of both. Both of these monetary policy rules have strong support and are well understood (Taylor and Williams, 2011). They are reviewed here to highlight the key features of a monetary policy rule and its usefulness in the conduct of monetary policy for price stability.

Monetarists in general make a case against stabilization policy. The argument is that activist policies are not needed, either because policy objectives are not defined (a common circumstance) or because they are unamenable to reasonable policy measures. To achieve desired policy objectives, policymakers require an in-depth knowledge of the operation of an economy. In general, policymakers are not in possession of detailed information on the operation of an economy or its dynamic behaviour in the event of shocks, whether activity-generated or even policy-induced. Therefore, Monetarists do not believe that short-run policy objectives are achievable, leaving aside the question of whether they are desirable. Instead, the Monetarist focus is on policy goals that are well defined and can be achieved over the medium or long term. For example, based on the idea of long-run neutrality of money, they suggest targeting price stability as the ultimate objective of a rule-based monetary policy. As the link between money and prices is well established, inflation can be kept low and stable provided that the growth rate of the money supply is kept low and stable under a flexible exchange rate system.

There is emerging consensus on the need for a rule-based monetary policy for price stability. There is no consensus, however, on the criteria by which the variant of monetary policy rule most appropriate for a particular country might be selected. The choice of monetary policy rule depends on the general institutional and structural characteristics of an economy. The following discussion compares the money-growth rule with the interest rate rule, which in recent decades has become increasingly popular among central bankers aiming at some form of price stability as the (primary) objective of monetary policy.

FRIEDMAN'S CONSTANT MONEY-GROWTH RULE

A rule-based monetary policy is a principle that prescribes the timing with which, and the quantum by which, the chosen instrument of monetary policy is adjusted to achieve or maintain the target of monetary policy set by the monetary authority. Under a money-growth rule, the growth rate of the monetary base is used as the operational or intermediate target. Achievement of this operational or intermediate target is expected to maintain price stability over the medium term. At an operational level, price stability is defined as low and stable inflation. Under a flexible exchange rate system, the money stock remains under the control of the monetary authority while the interest rate is determined by market forces. Following the Fisher proposition, the nominal interest rate includes both the expected rate of inflation and any risk premium, while the real interest rate is determined by real factors such as the productivity of capital and preferences for thriftiness. Consequently, when the inflation rate remains close to zero on average, the nominal and real interest rates move closely.

Under a money-growth rule, the central bank undertakes open market operations to change the money base to ensure that the growth rate of real money stock matches the growth rate of real money demand. For estimation purposes, the growth rate of real money demand is approximated by multiplying together the growth rate of the economy and the income elasticity of demand for money. The outcome of this simple calculation is modified, if needed, by taking into account any change in the demand for money due to any change in the interest rate over the estimation period. In general, the impact of the interest rate on long-run money demand is negligible in an economy where the financial system is competitive such that the returns on both real and financial assets move together and are equalized in equilibrium. When the interest rates are determined by market forces, the relative returns on money and other assets do not change much across the long term. Therefore, the demand for money is mainly determined by a measure of permanent income that remains broadly stable (Friedman, 1956).

On the supply side of the money market, the money multiplier is assumed constant such that the growth rate of the monetary base approximates the growth rate of some relatively broader definition of money. Under such general conditions, a growth rate of the money supply of about 4 to 5 per cent per annum is thought to generate a rate of inflation of about 1 to 2 per cent provided that the economy grows at a steady rate of about 2 to 3 per cent per annum due to the accumulation of capital, labour force growth and any technical innovation. In developing countries, the growth rate of the money supply, which is consistent with price stability, can be somewhat higher than for developed economies because of the expected higher rate of economic growth at the early stages of economic development. The income elasticity of demand for money is generally greater than one in developing economies, due to rapid monetization of such economies and the absence or scarcity of high-yielding financial assets in them.

Having established the money-growth rate as the key, if not the sole, determinant of inflation, Friedman (1960) argued that a constant money supply growth rate would provide the greatest degree of macroeconomic stability realistically achievable. A constant money-growth rate is expected to ensure a stable increase in nominal income given that real output is determined by real factors only. He developed the argument for rule-based monetary policy on the basis of a stable money-demand function in which the demand for money depends on a small number of arguments, mainly permanent income, and the relative rates of return on alternative assets. In his seminal article (Friedman, 1956), he developed a detailed hypothesis to predict that, and explain why, the interest elasticity of demand for money is either zero or very low. Establishment of this hypothesis removed interest elasticity of demand for money as a potential obstacle to implementation of a constant money-growth rule to ensure price stability.

The usefulness of a constant money-growth rule can then be illustrated using the relation: M = k(Py), where k is a constant, M is the money stock, P is the price level and y is real income. In this specification, the inverse of the velocity of money (k = 1/V) is constant and can be assumed equal to one for simplicity. Further, if the interest elasticity of demand for money is assumed zero and the income elasticity of demand for money is assumed unity, then the above equation predicts that the money supply growth rate (μ) equals the growth rate of real income (g^y) and the rate of inflation ($\mu = g^y + \pi$), with the inflation rate π defined as the growth rate of the price level. The policy implication is that if a central bank can secure a stable money-growth rate, an outcome will be stable growth of nominal income, which is equal to the sum of the rates of inflation and economic growth ($\pi + g^y$). Provided that the rate of economic growth is determined by real factors of production only, the growth rate of nominal income can be stable if the rate of inflation remains stable.

High and volatile inflation is a drag on economic growth. When policymakers attempt to accelerate economic growth through money-growth surprises, the long-run outcome is high and volatile inflation. The option is therefore clear to a central bank. Given the now largely accepted one-for-one link between money growth and inflation, inflation can be kept low and stable if the central bank keeps money growth low and stable. Under a flexible exchange rate system, the money-growth rate is controllable, bringing inflation within reach as a hittable policy target. Monetarists remain averse to 'monetary activism', which advocates sharp changes in the money-growth rate to create 'inflation surprises' in the economy to generate real gains. The gains are short run only; they dissipate in the long run; hence their benefits in terms of enhanced profitability and lower unemployment fall far short of their costs in terms of unstable inflation and the associated investment, output and employment uncertainty and consequences.

INTEREST RATE ADJUSTMENT UNDER A MONEY-GROWTH RULE

Defending a constant money-growth rule, Friedman (1960) argued that activist monetary policy leads to economic instability because of the imprecise and lag effects of monetary policy. Frequent policy changes to fine-tune an economy create an erratic dynamic response of output. Over time, this requires increasingly erratic policy with even more increasingly erratic response. Consequently, activist monetary policy becomes self-defeating or counterproductive (Marquis, 1996). When wages and prices remain flexible, the discipline of the market should be strong enough to ensure that real output and employment remain close to their natural levels for most of the time and minimize the duration of any major deviations for the remaining time. In the absence of policy shocks, both output and employment are determined by real factors, namely labour, capital and technology. These tend to remain stable and grow steadily. In the absence of monetary shocks from the supply side, monetary shocks are random as the money-demand function is generally measured stable unless economic uncertainty affects the money-demand behaviour of households, firms and other economic agents. The main area of concern remains the volatility of the interest rate under the constant money-growth rule.

A money-growth rule implies that the interest rate adjusts to disequilibrium in the money market. Changes in the interest rate then can be linked to both the inflation gap and output gap in the form of an interest rate response function. Following Sorensen and Whitta-Jacobsen (2005), this can be illustrated as follows. Assume that the money-market equilibrium condition takes the following form:

$$\frac{M}{P} = m^d(y, NIR) = ky^{\eta}e^{-\beta NIR} \qquad (A10.1)$$

where M is the money stock, P is the price level, NIR is the nominal interest rate, y is real income, k is a constant and η and β are structural parameters in the money-demand function. Sorensen and Whitta-Jacobsen (2005) have shown that when the economy is not far from its long-run trend and a number of conditions hold such that: $M = (1 + \mu)M_{-1}$; $P = (1 + \pi)P_{-1}$; and $NIR = \bar{r} + \pi = \bar{r} + \mu$, then the constant money supply growth rule yields a short-run interest rate response function of the following form:

$$NIR = \bar{r} + \pi + \left(\frac{1 - \beta}{\beta}\right)(\pi - \mu) + \left(\frac{\eta}{\beta}\right)(y - \bar{y}) \qquad (A10.2)$$

where $\bar{r}$ is the real interest rate, $y - \bar{y}$ is the output gap, π is the rate of inflation, μ is the constant growth rate of the money supply and η and β are, respectively, the income elasticity of demand for money and the interest rate semi-elasticity of demand for money.

In this specification, η and β are expected positive-valued, reflecting the a priori hypothesis that the interest rate moves positively with the output gap. Assuming that the semi-interest elasticity of demand for money is less than one, the nominal interest rate increases more than one-for-one with the rise in inflation, implying an increase in the real interest rate. In the long run, $\pi - \mu$ is expected zero, that is, the inflation rate equals the (constant) growth rate of the money supply while output is expected to return to its potential level yielding $y - \bar{y} = 0$. The model is thereby specified in the expectation that the Fisher equation holds; that is, the nominal interest rate is the outcome of some combination of the real interest rate and the expected rate of inflation.

Under a money-growth rule, the constant money-growth rate can therefore be interpreted as the central bank's target rate of inflation. Under a flexible exchange rate system, the central bank sets the target money-growth rate given its inflation preference or the way it defines price stability. The rate of long-run inflation then becomes a monetary policy variable. The nominal interest rate then rises proportionately to the rise in inflation.

Equation (A10.2) suggests that if the nominal interest rate is controlled by the monetary authority, changes in the inflation gap or the output gap, or in both of these, would cause a change in the real interest rate. This flows through the system to changes in the levels of saving, investment and economic growth. In an open economy, changes in the real interest rate also affect capital flows and bring about changes in the exchange rate.

TAYLOR'S INTEREST RATE RULE

The Taylor rule is a monetary policy rule calculating the timing and level at which a central bank should set its policy interest rate to maintain price stability, given (1) the monetary policy target and (2) the observed state of the economy for a given accounting period. Unlike Friedman's money-growth rule, the Taylor rule is active as the central bank reacts by adjusting the policy rate to changes in inflation and the output gap. Taylor's interest rate rule can then be specified as follows:

$$\text{NIR} = \bar{r} + \pi + \omega_\pi(\pi - \pi_T) + \omega_y(y - \bar{y}) \qquad \text{(A10.3)}$$

where ω_π and ω_y are weights assigned by a central bank for the purpose of deciding which combination of the inflation gap and the output gap should influence its monetary policy decisions. For the sake of comparing this rule with the interest rate response under a money-growth rule, equation (A10.3) can be specified as

$$\text{NIR} = \bar{r} + \pi + \omega_\pi(\pi - \mu) + \omega_y(y - \bar{y}) \qquad \text{(A10.4)}$$

where $\pi_T = \mu$.

The key difference between (A10.2) and (A10.3), the two specifications of interest rate responses, is that under the constant money-growth rule, the coefficients on the inflation gap and the output gap are related to the parameters of the money-demand function. If money demand is stable, the interest rate response becomes predictable unless interest rate and exchange rate movements are regulated or otherwise restricted. In the Taylor rule, the parameters in the interest rate response function are chosen by policymakers depending on their relative aversions to inflation variability and to output variability from the respective inflation rate and growth rate target levels. Transparency and policy credibility then become important to make the interest rate response predictable. If the central bank does not behave consistently, interest rate changes may become unpredictable, creating policy ambiguity and thereby reducing the credibility and effectiveness of monetary policy.

However, adoption of a monetary targeting approach to monetary policy does not mean that a central bank commits to maintain low and stable inflation by following a steady-money-growth rule. Monetary policy can still be activist in nature or accommodative to economic shocks when central banks have multiple objectives of monetary policy. This is commonly the case in countries where central banks, following their charters, have obligations to achieve multiple objectives.

Whether the monetary policy stance of a central bank is active or passive can be assessed by observation of interest rate behaviour under monetary targeting. Under passive monetary targeting, the interest rate is determined endogenously; that is, it is not set as a policy target but instead responds to economic and monetary conditions. Under active monetary targeting, the nominal interest rate is controlled and then adjusted by a central bank with or without consideration of real sector or money-market conditions. Consequently, inflation, the real interest rate and real exchange rate all exhibit high volatility. The lesson is that when monetary targeting is not enforced strongly and the interest rate is controlled, the money-growth rate will become volatile even under money-growth targeting. Then inflation remains high and volatile, and the volatility is transmitted to the real interest rate, the real exchange rate and output growth. Money-growth targeting therefore does not necessarily lead to price and output stability unless there is firm commitment by the central bank, necessarily supported by the government, (1) to follow the policy rule with minimal discretionary departures from it, and only those that are absolutely necessary and (2) to allow the interest and exchange rates to move with market forces.

The main criticism of the constant money-growth rule is that it may not bring stability of the nominal income growth if the parameters of the money-demand function become unstable. This is the reason why the perceived instability of the money-demand function led to the abandonment of monetary targeting in most developed countries in the 1990s or earlier.

Inflation, however, remains volatile in both developed and developing countries irrespective of the widespread adoption in the 1990s and 2000s of monetary policy strategies targeting price stability.

A prominent feature of the world economy is the frequent occurrence of supply shocks to developing economies. Choice of an appropriate strategy of monetary policy is therefore critical to approach the best available output and price stability for these economies. In general, the usefulness of publicly announced rule-based monetary policy, such as a constant money-growth rule, resides in the rule's potential to enable the monetary authority to withstand the periods of intense political pressure for expansionary monetary policy following each supply shock. Simultaneously, an overt monetary policy rule provides a criterion for judging the performance of the central bank and supplies a high degree of economic policy certainty for private agents, both direct and implied. Implied, because a public monetary policy rule simultaneously directs prudential pressure towards the fiscal authorities. Friedman's argument for a constant growth rate rule is often interpreted as pragmatic. His argument for a constant money-growth rule, rather than an active feedback rule, is that there are long, variable and unpredictable lags, and variable and unpredictable magnitudes of impact, of the effects of monetary policy on output and prices. Then any active policy that responds to current events may have its effects only at an inappropriate (pro-cyclical) time. Uncertainty about the lag effects of monetary policy means that the active use of monetary policy adds variability to both output and prices. Active monetary policy strategy may also produce instrument instability, requiring ever-larger changes in the money stock to offset any lagged effects of previous policy changes to the money supply.

Nevertheless, the strongest argument against a constant money-growth rule is that the velocity of money may vary substantially and unpredictably (Fischer, 1990). This is unlikely to be the case unless the velocity of money is affected by unpredictable monetary policy. Technical progress in the payments system is generally gradual; hence, does not generally destabilize the money-demand function. Money-demand shocks are random so that unless money supply shocks are able to create economic uncertainty, the random nature of monetary shocks is unlikely to cause instability in the velocity of money. Monetarists maintain the view that the velocity of money is not constant per se but predictable in a statistical sense, since it is expressable as a stable function of a small number of variables, such as income and the interest rate.

THE McCALLUM RULE

The discussion so far suggests that the usefulness of a constant money-growth rule relies on the predictability of the velocity of money and stability in the money-demand function. In response to the perennial criticism that the velocity of money may be volatile, McCallum (1989) devised a money-growth rule that accommodates (the predictable) changes in the velocity of money. The McCallum rule defines the instrument of monetary policy in terms of the growth rate of the money base (M_0). This is essentially an expanded feedback rule and can be written as follows:

$$\mu_t^0 = \kappa_{t-1} + v_{t-1} + \alpha(z^* - z)_{t-1} \tag{A10.5}$$

where μ_t^0 is the growth rate of the monetary base M_0, κ_{t-1} is the target rate of money growth, v_{t-1} is the lagged moving average of the growth rate of the velocity of money, $(z^* - z)$ is the deviation of the growth rate of nominal income from its targeted level and α is the weight given by the monetary authority to the nominal output growth gap. When the economy remains at the target growth rate for output and the level of money demand equals its desired level (or the velocity of money is constant), then the growth rate of the monetary base equals the growth rate of the monetary target. McCallum's rule approximates to Friedman's money-growth rule when κ_{t-1} is the growth rate of the economy, assuming that the income elasticity of demand for money is unity. Depending on the average growth rate of the velocity of money, the money-growth rate is modified in a way that brings about equality between the money-growth rate and the growth of money demand.

In an operational sense, this rule can be specified in the following money-growth response function or a feedback rule, such that

$$\mu_t^0 = \kappa_{t-1} + v_{t-1} + \alpha_1(\pi^* - \pi)_{t-1} + \alpha_2(g^{y*} - g^y)_{t-1} \tag{A10.6}$$

In this expanded specification, $(z^* - z)$ is decomposed into the deviation of inflation from its target and the deviation of real output growth from the potential growth rate of the economy such that $z^* - z = \alpha_1(\pi^* - \pi)_{t-1} + \alpha_2(g^{y*} - g^y)_{t-1}$. This shows that the McCallum rule approximates the Taylor rule where the growth rate of the money base, rather than the interest rate, is deployed as the monetary policy instrument.

This explains why Taylor (2000) has suggested substituting an appropriate monetary aggregate to replace the interest rate as an instrument of monetary policy in periods when the interest rate is rendered ineffective for the purposes of demand management. Even when the interest rate continues to be deployed for demand management under inflation targeting, the McCallum rule can be used as a monitoring device to determine whether there exists a monetary overhang that may undermine price stability over the medium term given the robust link between money supply growth and inflation. As McCallum and Nelson (2011) have argued, there exists a link between money growth and inflation irrespective of (1) the exchange rate regime in place; *and* (2) whether or not the money-demand function is stable; *and* (3) whether money is exogenous or endogenous. Even under inflation targeting, the money-growth rate cannot be ignored even though the relation between money growth and inflation may not be strong in the short run. In essence, the McCallum rule can be thought productively of as a 'velocity-adjusted money supply growth rule' that considers price stability the ultimate objective of monetary policy. Implicit in the McCallum rule is Friedman's view that inflation is ultimately a monetary phenomenon. This is an important consideration in developing country choice of monetary policy strategy, since the interest rate remains an important instrument of monetary policy for demand management.

SUMMING UP

There is a growing literature on the various types of policy rules deployable by central banks to bring about changes in policy instruments for demand management. Most rules have well-known weaknesses, both theoretical and empirical. Nevertheless, both the money-growth rule and the Taylor rule have gained popularity among practitioners of monetary policy across the globe. In developing countries, money-growth targeting is widely used in one form or another. The Taylor rule is also used in some countries that have adopted inflation targeting. When monetary policy is conducted in discretionary form, the interest rate is adjusted for demand management. The question of whether changes in the interest rate can generate economic flows of sufficient volume or power to keep inflation low and stable is another matter entirely. At a deeper level, the issue is whether the central bank's policy interest rate can even be considered rigorously exogenous; since an argument can be made that the central bank, in reality, sets the interest rate endogenously under flexible inflation targeting.

The fact that the nominal interest rate is set by a central bank under the Taylor rule does not necessarily make it an exogenous policy variable. The relationship between the nominal interest rate and inflation is bidirectional and hence a causal linkage between them can be established only within a simultaneous equation system. Stock and Watson (2012, p. 662) have explained this as follows:

> Although the short [term interest] rate is determined by the central bank, it is not set by the central bankers at random (as it would be in an ideal randomized experiment) but rather is set endogenously: The central bank determines the short rate based on an assessment of the current and future rates of inflation. The rate of inflation in turn depends on the interest rate (higher interest rates reduce aggregate demand), but the interest rate depends on the rate of inflation, its past value, and its (expected) future value. Thus the short rate is endogenous, and the causal dynamic effect of a change in the short rate on future inflation cannot be consistently estimated by an OLS regression of the rate of inflation on current and past interest rates.

When the interest rate is targeted or pegged, the money stock becomes endogenous. The money supply and the price level then are determined endogenously and they maintain a cointegral relation while the link between the interest rate and inflation could be tenuous.

In the present context, the debate is less about the usefulness of a monetary aggregate relative to the interest rate as the preferred instrument of monetary policy. The heart of the debate remains the issue of whether rule-based monetary policy is preferable to monetary discretion; that is, policy activism. Although there are strong reservations about the money-growth rule, Hall (1982, p. 4) has made the following remarks in support of such a rule:

> What is key is not the constancy of the growth rate or the particular number for the rate or the precise definition of the monetary aggregate, but rather the commitment to and hence anchor on some future nominal values.

The main argument for rule-based monetary policy is that it allows the central bank to conduct monetary policy in a way that the broader public can understand and in which it can take a larger (political) interest. Rule-based monetary policy becomes credible to the markets and the broader public if conducted in a transparent and consistent manner and there is demonstrated commitment for low and stable inflation. As policy credibility can only be earned over time, central banks are required to keep the rule simple and transparent and to maintain regular communication with the public about the goals of monetary policy.[1] Central banks also need to explain why and how changes in the policy instrument are expected to impact output and prices, while recognizing the considerable time lags, following monetary policy changes, before those impacts are realized. Further, a rule-based monetary policy becomes credible only when binding on the monetary authorities and when monetary policy is able consistently and effectively to avoid falling into the time-inconsistency trap. The only protection from this so far proposed for central banks is exclusion from their objective functions of the kinds of goals that make them susceptible to the trap, together with the setting of a single objective of monetary policy. Multiple objectives of monetary policy generally lead to the time-inconsistency problem. Time inconsistency refers to the phenomenon of optimal policy chosen at one point in time optimal at the time of its implementation.

A body of literature has emerged since the 1970s on a range of related knotty issues, such as (in no particular order): (1) whether rule-based monetary policy is optimal; (2) whether central banks have incentive to break the policy rule; (3) how to create incentives for central banks to follow rule-based monetary policy to achieve the most effective policy possible and simultaneously to promote policy credibility. While the frontier research is exploring ideas for making rule-based monetary policy optimal and credible, the emphasis in practice remains on the established approaches to achieving these desirable properties of monetary policy: the conservative and predictable conduct of monetary policy to achieve price stability. The 'conservative' approach reflects the spirit of Milton Friedman, who was concerned that monetary activism all too often leads to boom-bust because of the long and variable lags in the transmission mechanisms of monetary policy. The financial crises in different parts of the world since the 1990s have yielded evidence against monetary activism (Taylor, 2012).

This book and Hossain (2015) review the evolution of monetary policy strategies in selected countries and their plausible effects on macroeconomic outcomes, especially inflation and the volatility of inflation. The monetary policy strategies reviewed include exchange rate pegging, monetary targeting and inflation targeting. Although each of these strategies has the ability to keep inflation low, each can easily lead to inflation volatility unless the authorities conduct national monetary policy in a predictable, transparent manner. Choice of exchange rate regime is an essential complementary consideration. For either monetary targeting or inflation targeting to operate properly, the interest rate and the exchange rate must each be determined by the respective market forces. Controls over either market generally lead to inflation volatility when, as is common for developing countries, the economy experiences frequent shocks. Inflation volatility makes the real interest rate and the real exchange rate volatile. This feeds directly into reduced rates of national saving, investment and economic growth – in short, the rate of economic development is compromised.

NOTE

1. Taylor and Williams (2011, p. 855) draw the following conclusion: 'Over the past two decades, research on policy rules has shown that simple rules have important robustness advantages over fully optimal or more complex rules in that they work well in a variety of models. Experience has shown that simple rules also have worked well in the real world. Progress has also been made in understanding how to adjust simple rules to deal with measurement error, expectations, learning, and the lower bound on interest rates.'

REFERENCES

Fischer, S. (1990), 'Rules versus discretion in monetary policy', in B.M. Friedman and F. Hahn (eds), *Handbook of Monetary Economics*, Vol. II, Amsterdam: Elsevier Science, pp. 1155–84.

Friedman, M. (1956), 'The quantity theory of money: a restatement', in M. Friedman (ed.), *Studies in the Quantity Theory of Money*, Chicago, IL: University of Chicago Press, pp. 3–17.

Friedman, M. (1960), *A Program for Monetary Stability*, New York: Fordham University Press.

Hall, R.E. (1982), 'Introduction', *Inflation: Causes and Effects*, Chicago, IL: University of Chicago Press.

Hossain, A. (2015), *Central Banking and Monetary Policy in Muslim-Majority Countries*, Cheltenham, UK and Northampton, MA, USA: Edward Elgar.

McCallum, B. (1989), *Monetary Economics: Theory and Policy*, New York: Macmillan.

McCallum, B.T. and E. Nelson (2011), 'Money and inflation: some critical issues', in B.M. Friedman and M. Woodford (eds), *Handbook of Monetary Economics*, Vol. 3A, Amsterdam: Elsevier Science, pp. 97–153.

Marquis, M.H. (1996), *Monetary Theory and Policy*, New York: West Publishing Company.

Smith, A. (1776), *An Enquiry into the Nature and Causes of the Wealth of Nations*, London: W. Strahan and T. Cadell.

Sorensen, P. and H. J. Whitta-Jacobsen (2005), *Introduction to Advanced Macroeconomics: Growth and Business Cycles*, New York: McGraw Hill.

Stock, J.H. and M.W. Watson (2012), *Introduction to Econometrics*, New York: Pearson-Addison Wesley.

Taylor, J.B. (1993), 'Discretion versus policy rules in practice', *Carnegie-Rochester Conference Series on Public Policy*, **39**(1), 195–214.

Taylor, J.B. (2000), 'Using monetary policy rules in emerging market economies', Paper presented at the 75th Anniversary Conference Stabilization and Monetary Policy: The International Experience, Bank of Mexico, 14–15 November.

Taylor, J.B. (2012), 'Monetary policy rules work and discretion doesn't: a tale of two era', *Journal of Money, Credit and Banking*, **44**(6), 1017–31.

Taylor, J.B. and J.C. Williams (2011), 'Simple and robust rules for monetary policy', in B.M. Friedman and M. Woodford (eds), *Handbook of Monetary Economics*, Amsterdam: Elsevier Science, pp. 829–59.

Index